SEX / MACHINE

THE INDIANA SERIES IN THE PHILOSOPHY OF TECHNOLOGY

Don Ihde, general editor

SEX/MACHINE

Readings in Culture, Gender, and Technology

EDITED BY PATRICK D. HOPKINS

Indiana University Press / Bloomington & Indianapolis

This book is a publication of

Indiana University Press
601 North Morton Street
Bloomington, Indiana 47404-3797 USA

www.indiana.edu/~iupress

Telephone orders   800-842-6796
Fax orders   812-855-7931
Orders by e-mail   iuporder@indiana.edu

© 1998 by Indiana University Press

Library of Congress Cataloging-in-Publication Data

Sex/machine : readings in culture, gender, and technology / edited by
Patrick D. Hopkins.
    p.   cm. — (Indiana series in the philosophy of technology)
Includes index.
    ISBN 0-253-33441-1 (cl : alk. paper). — ISBN 0-253-21230-8 (pa :
alk. paper)
    1. Sex role.   2. Technology—Social aspects.   3. Technology—
Sociological aspects.   I. Hopkins, Patrick D.   II. Series
HQ1075.S475   1998   98-48337

2   3   4   06   05   04

CONTENTS

Part I: Inventing Histories
Gender and Technological Development

Part II: (Mis?)Conceptions
Morality and Gender Politics in Reproductive Technology

Part III: (Re)Locating Fetuses
Technology and New Body Politics

Part IV: Body Building
The (Re)Construction of Sex and Sexuality

Part V: (Virtual?) Gender
From Computer Culture to Cyberspace

Part VI: Our Machines/Our Selves
Gender and Cyborg Subjects

ACKNOWLEDGMENTS

This book could not have been produced without substantial institutional support. My most extensive thanks, then, go to the Department of Philosophy at Bowling Green State University, whose Postdoctoral Fellowship in Applied Philosophy and generous financial and office support gave me the time and resources needed to put this book together. Special thanks for their support and assistance are due to Marvin Belzer, Patricia Bressler, Margy Deluca, and Diane Petteys.

Thanks also go to the Program in Women's Studies and the Department of Philosophy at Washington University in St. Louis, for whom I first created and taught a course on gender, feminism, and technology. My gratitude also goes to the Departments of Women's Studies and of Philosophy at Webster University in St. Louis, for whom I also taught and revised the course. This book is the result of extensive research and syllabus preparation required for those classes. I am indebted to the students who participated in the courses for their insights into the issues discussed, assessments of the value of various readings, and loathing of the nonexistence of a single bound textbook. They contributed mightily to the compilation of *Sex/Machine*.

Additional thanks go to friends who took the time to read and comment on organization, text selection, and my own writing—especially Robert Hood and Jennifer McCrickerd; to my editor at Indiana University Press—Dee Mortensen—who fielded countless questions about the labyrinthine complexities of copyright law and reprint permissions; and to those authors who generously forewent a portion of their permission fee to make reprinting their articles possible.

Grateful acknowledgment is also made to the following sources for permission to reprint material in this anthology:

"Surrogate Motherhood: The Challenge for Feminists," by Lori B. Andrews, from *Law, Medicine & Health Care* 16(1–2). © 1988 by the American Society of Law and Medicine, Inc. Reprinted by the kind permission of the American Society of Law, Medicine & Ethics.

phy 6(3). © 1991 by Kathryn Pauly Morgan. Reprinted by the kind permission of the author.

"Artificial Insemination: Who's Responsible?" by Ronald Munson. Earlier versions published in *Intervention and Reflection: Basic Issues in Medical Ethics* (Belmont, CA: Wadsworth, 1997). © by Ronald Munson. Reprinted by the kind permission of the author.

"Is Pregnancy Necessary? Feminist Concerns about Ectogenesis," by Julien S. Murphy, from *Hypatia: A Journal of Feminist Philosophy* 4(3). © 1989 by Julien S. Murphy. Reprinted by the kind permission of the author.

"Reproductive Controls and Sexual Destiny," by Timothy F. Murphy, from *Bioethics* 4 (1990): 121–42. © by Blackwell Publishers, Ltd. Reprinted by the kind permission of the author and publisher.

"Does Technology Work for Women Too?" by Lilia Oblepias-Ramos, from *The Role of Women in the Development of Science and Technology in the Third World*, ed. A. M. Faruqui, M. H. A. Hassan, and G. Sandri, pp. 161–65. © 1991 by World Scientific Publishing Co. Pte. Ltd: River Edge, NJ. Reprinted by the kind permission of the publisher and author.

"New Reproductive Technology: Some Implications for the Abortion Issue," by Christine Overall, from *Journal of Value Inquiry* 19 (1985): 272–92. Reprinted by the kind permission of Kluwer Academic Publishers.

"Excluding Women from the Technologies of the Future? A Case Study of the Culture of Computer Science," by Bente Rasmussen and Tove Håpnes, from *Futures* (December). © 1991 by Butterworth-Heinemann, Ltd. Reprinted by the kind permission of Elsevier Science LTD.

"Sappho by Surgery: The Transsexually Constructed Lesbian-Feminist," by Janice G. Raymond, from *The Transsexual Empire: The Making of the She-Male* (New York: Teachers College Press, 1979, 1994). © by Janice G. Raymond. Reprinted by the kind permission of the author.

"Femininity and the Electric Car," by Virginia Scharff, from *Taking the Wheel: Women and the Coming of the Motor Age* (New York: The Free Press). © 1991 by Virginia Scharff. Reprinted by the kind permission of The Free Press, A Division of Simon & Schuster.

"The Pleasure of the Interface," by Claudia Springer, from *Screen* 32 (3): 303–23. © 1991 John Logie Baird Centre. Reprinted by the kind permission of Oxford University Press.

"Women Hold Up Two-Thirds of the Sky: Notes for a Revised History of Technology," by Autumn Stanley, from *Machina Ex Dea: Feminist Perspectives on Tech-*

nology, ed. J. Rothschild (New York: Teachers College Press), pp. 5–22. © 1983 by Joan Rothschild. All rights reserved.

"*In Novel Conditions:* The Cross-Dressing Psychiatrist," by Allucquère Rosanne Stone, from *The War of Desire and Technology at the End of the Mechanical Age* (Cambridge: MIT Press). © 1995 by Allucquère Rosanne Stone. Reprinted by kind permission of the MIT Press.

"The *Empire* Strikes Back: A Posttranssexual Manifesto," by Sandy Stone, from *Body Guards: The Cultural Politics of Gender Ambiguity,* ed. Julia Epstein and Kristina Straub (New York: Routledge). © 1991 by Routledge, Chapman, and Hall, Inc. Reprinted by the kind permission of the author and the publisher.

"Male Pregnancy," by Dick Teresi and Kathleen McAuliffe, from *OMNI* 8. © 1985 Omni Publications International, Ltd. Reprinted by the kind permission of OMNI.

"Computational Reticence: Why Women Fear the Intimate Machine," by Sherry Turkle, from *Technology and Women's Voices: Keeping in Touch,* ed. Cheris Kramarae, pp. 41–61. © 1988 by Routledge. Reprinted by the kind permission of the author and publisher.

"Tinysex and Gender Trouble," by Sherry Turkle, from *Life on the Screen: Identity in the Age of the Internet* (New York: The Free Press). © 1995 by Sherry Turkle. Reprinted by the kind permission of The Free Press, A Division of Simon & Schuster.

"The Ethics of Sex Preselection," by Mary Anne Warren, from *Biomedical Ethics Reviews-1985,* ed. James M. Humber and Robert F. Almeder (Totowa, NJ: The Humana Press, 1985), pp. 73–89. Reprinted by the kind permission of the publisher.

SEX/MACHINE

INTRODUCTION
THE INTERSECTION OF CULTURE, GENDER, AND TECHNOLOGY

PATRICK D. HOPKINS

- In a small Tennessee city, a divorcing couple argues about abortion. One claims that their embryos are unborn children with a right to life; the other argues they are just lumps of disposable tissue. Standard legal reasoning about abortion, privacy, and the right to control one's body doesn't help much in the argument, however—because the embryos arc not inside any-one's body. They never have been. They sit frozen in a small cylinder on the other side of town. The abortion debate is raging and no one is even pregnant.
- In Sri Lanka, well-meaning innovators import water pumps to ease the drudgery of women's long, hot walks to wells—but they only teach men how to repair the devices. When the pumps break, the actual users, women, don't know how to fix them. So the pumps sit there unused while women lug water back and forth.
- Medical technologists figure out a way to choose the sex of a baby—and make it available to a culture which prefers their firstborn children to be male. Could an entire generation of firstborn male children make a differ-ence?
- Women try to take advantage of a new invention, the automobile—but they find out that only electric cars are considered appropriate for women. Gaso-line cars are for men.
- The entire abortion controversy might be put to rest, some feminists argue—if only we could find a way to get machines pregnant, rather than women.
- Healthy babies are born all the time that are neither male nor female, or that are perhaps both—but they don't get out of the hospital that way. Someone chooses what sex they will be.
- A lesbian feminist is called an "intruder" and an "oppressor" by other lesbian feminists—because she used to be a man.
- A researcher suggests using amniocentesis to test fetuses for homosexual-ity—and then "curing" them with androgen injections.
- On the Internet, you can fall in love with a clever, articulate, beautiful young woman—and then find out that her personality was generated by a

dull, laconic, unattractive, middle-aged man. Have you been lied to? Or does your version of reality serve you poorly?

- Scientists come up with a way to get men pregnant—and are swamped with requests.
- A theorist looks toward science fiction novels for inspiration—and argues that the best way to be a feminist is to become a cyborg.

These situations only hint at the degree to which issues of gender and technology are complex, far-reaching, and fascinating. As powerful interacting social and physical forces, gender and technology shape our experiences, cultures, and identities—sometimes in such comfortable and subtle ways that it takes effort to appreciate them; sometimes in such conspicuous and explosive ways that everyone recognizes their importance. Delving into these issues is an opportunity to discover how technology promises or threatens to rewrite our ideas about sex, sexuality, and gender identity. It is an opportunity to debate ethical and legal issues at the very core of human experiences—procreation, labor, sex, our bodies. It is the chance to find out how sex role restrictions prevent each of us from using certain technologies, or require us to use others.

Examining these topics can be both illuminating and unsettling, particularly because we discover how our own lives are and will be affected by shifts in ideas of gender and by changes in technology. In my classes on these issues, students often remark that they never realized how much their daily lives, their career choices, their thoughts on ethical and social issues, and even their self-concepts have been affected by assumptions about technology, sex, and gender. What seemed like little things before (so little they were ignored)—why a student's husband automatically gets into the driver's side of their car, or why she tends to think of hunting as a technological activity, but not cooking—take on larger significance. Topics that previously attracted little attention or seemed like science fiction—sex selection, ectogenesis, cloning, or concepts of personal identity on the Internet—now have the potential to produce culture shock.

The issues in this book, then, are both global and personal. Like race, age, religion, science, culture, and politics, gender and technology form and transform society and individuals. Questions about these forces and their interactions get at the multiple hearts of major philosophical and social problems—questions of ethics, social justice, epistemic constraints, personal and social identity, economics and labor, realism and irrealism, and ideas of human nature. Since these sorts of questions have generated such exciting, interdisciplinary work, it is time to create a single text large enough to give readers a taste of the issues and methods that exist at the intersection of gender studies and technology studies. This book attempts to meet that goal, showcasing the variety of perspectives that inform this diverse field of study. Although approaches and topics are varied, there is enough information here for me to generate a useful classification for considering the ways in which technology and gender interact.

I begin with the givenness of both technology and gender. Humans (like many other animals) are a technology-using and technology-producing species. Technology is always present in variegated forms, both subdued and obvious, and is always fundamental to the basic structure and activity of society. Similarly, humans are always already embedded in some sex/gender system, some ideological framework that varies in significant detail from culture to culture and time to time, but which layers vast cultural meaning on the evolved sexual dimorphism of the human organism, setting different roles, expectations, assessments, and values for members of different sexes.

Neither technology nor gender is static, of course. They are both dynamic, though material technology has a way of building upon itself so that its kind of dynamism is often seen as "progressive," not necessarily in the sense of getting continually better (even cancer can be diagnosed as "progressive"), but in the sense of developing finer, greater, and different kinds of manipulability without losing earlier effectiveness. Typically then (though not always), technology increases, and does not merely change into other forms. As such, there is a strong tendency (at least in historical spurts) for technology to "arrive," for technology to be "new" (whether or not "improved"). This important, ever-present association of newness with technology has itself grown stronger. While technology has always been around, it has increased in power and capability exponentially in the nineteenth and twentieth centuries. In the late twentieth century, at least in "high"-tech areas of the world, people have come to expect newer and newer technologies, faster and faster. Much of the debate over technology in general, and technology's effects on gender roles and identity in particular, is generated by the fear that new technologies are moving too fast, or too far, or in the wrong direction from traditional, or at least temporarily established, gender norms.

Gender, on the other hand, though certainly dynamic and in some ways capable of being developed into new and improved forms by inventive experts, does not have the material quality that most technologies do. Changes in gender, even if parallel to changes in technology in many substantial ways, are typically not subject to the kinds of economic distribution or production that technologies are. Changes in gender (as an ideological system) are less likely to be available through a catalog, or at a local factory, or at a trade show. They are less likely to be instantly upgradable or purchasable. The upshot of this is that new technologies are at least somewhat more likely to arrive in existing gender systems than new gender ideologies are to arrive in existing technology systems (though the latter can and does happen). For my purposes here, this means that a significant part of the study of technology and gender is the study of how new technologies are evaluated through the lens of an existing gender system and how new technologies alter existing concepts and practices of that system for better or worse. There are at least four ways in which these sorts of evaluations and alterations can occur—either separately or in various combinations—all of which are examined in this volume.

TECHNOLOGY'S ASSOCIATION WITH GENDER

The very concept of technology, as well as its practices, may be more or less strongly embedded in a gender framework itself. Since most gender arrangements are dichotomous, with fairly fixed categories of masculine and feminine, it is not surprising that various other concepts and phenomena get associated with one or the other of these poles. In Western culture men have historically been associated with technology, while women are more typically associated with "nature," perceived (incorrectly, I would argue) as the opposite of technology. Layering these dichotomies on top of one another—man/woman, nature/technology, nature/culture—tends to influence assessments of technology and gender in particular and often contrary ways.

For instance, if men are associated with technology and masculine psychology is considered technology-oriented, then technological development may be interpreted as predominantly a masculine act, the outcome of a masculine drive. This is rather weighty when cashed out in historical, anthropological, and moral terms. As a matter of historical appraisal, when advances in technology such as spears, knives, hammers, and other hunting and building devices are understood as innovations of male hunters, then major leaps forward in human cultural evolution are attributed to men. Male psychology itself is seen as pushing culture ahead. Women, on the other hand, are often assumed to be absent from technological history and cultural evolution, stuck in their primeval homes giving birth, raising children, and gathering food while males roam the countryside, building, warring, changing, and disrupting human society.

As a matter of moral discourse, these associations can lead to conflicting and influential judgments. While some may valorize men's purported technological drive as a positive force, indispensable to intellectual and cultural progress, others may vilify it, claiming that male technophilia is dangerous, and is responsible for environmental destruction, war, the nuclear threat, and alienation from "nature." Some feminists have argued, for example, that men's obsession with technology is a form of "womb envy," a degraded and inferior attempt to imitate women's more purely "natural" creativity. Women, closer to "nature" and more concerned with healthy, authentic lives, may be idealized as moral exemplars in this view, which counters the androcentric dichotomies of *male/technology/cultural/progress* and *female/procreation/cultural/ stasis* with the gynocentric dichotomies of *male/technology/bad* and *female/ nature/good.*

Whatever the consequences of these long-standing associations, they need to be deeply and critically examined. In fact, the very definition of technology needs to be scrutinized because cultural ideas about gender and technology may detrimentally constrain and bias historical and moral assessments on all sides. The technological character of traditionally "feminine" activities may be ignored—as with technologies of gathering, cooking, and sewing. Female inventors may be disregarded or their inventions attributed to men, gestures that further the idea that women are not technologists. Potentially beneficial technologies created by men (such as some reproductive technologies) may be reflexively rejected because of the assumption that the technology is tainted by male worldviews or the drive to conquer "nature." Technologies that blur the distinctions between the sexes may be automatically interpreted as "threatening" because of their blurring effects.

TECHNOLOGY REINFORCING GENDER SYSTEMS

New technologies that arrive in existing gender systems (which are almost always hierarchical and typically male-dominated) may be used to shore up those in power, entrench current standards, or extend the ideals of the system. This can happen in several ways, sometimes consciously, sometimes reflexively. Most explicitly and crudely, technology may be used simply to enforce gender roles and restrictions. A chastity belt is a simple device for controlling women's sexual activity and extending the property status of wives. Cosmetic surgeries may be aggressively marketed to magnify sexual differences and ideals—breast implants for increasing women's sexual attractiveness to heterosexual men, or pectoral and bicep implants for increasing men's apparent physical strength. Sex-specific toys encourage children to model particular sex roles—family and dating for girls, war for boys. In more extreme forms, technologies may be used to ensure other cultural gender ideals, such as identifying and eradicating homosexuality through genetic testing or guaranteeing firstborn male children through sex selection techniques.

Another kind of reinforcement occurs when one's gendered social position limits access to technology (new or old). This is likely to happen when there is a strong sexual division of labor or when cultural roles are sharply divided along gender lines. For example, if women are not permitted to work outside the home, particularly in management positions, and a technology like the telephone or computer is marketed primarily as a business machine, then their access to these technologies will be limited. If cooking and sewing are seen as feminine tasks, then microwave ovens and computerized sewing machines may be seen as frivolous expenses by male heads-of-household, or if such devices are purchased, men may be so reluctant to learn how to use them that they are unable to perform the simple tasks of stitching up a seam or baking a potato. If women's social spheres are limited to church and home, they may be refused access to the "family" automobile because it is thought they simply have no reason to drive.

Unequal access is also sometimes the result of beliefs about the "natural" abilities of the sexes. Some technologies are seen as psychologically or physically inappropriate for members of a particular sex—something they could not operate or could not understand. For example, if women are perceived as passive, physically weak, and technically inept, it may be seen as inappropriate for them to use guns, and thus their experience with guns will be limited, despite the fact that lightweight materials and automatic innovations have made guns easy to use or that women might have the need for guns in the first place (e.g., for defending themselves against dangerous men). If men are seen as clumsy, hotheaded, and useful mainly for brute-force manual labor, particularly in cheap export labor markets, they may be excluded from high-tech electronics manufacturing jobs which are thought to need the "delicate" fingers, patience, and task precision of women.

Restricted access also occurs when particular technologies retain their gender connections in the form of cultural prohibitions, even after formal obstacles have been dropped or previous rationales for restrictions (such as physical strength) have been surmounted. The "masculine" or "feminine" aura may still linger, making it more difficult for someone to approach a technology. For instance, cars are still often seen as men's machines and responsibility, even though the computerization of cars has left many formerly "mechanically-minded" men as ignorant of how to fix them as supposedly "non-mechanically-minded" women. A woman who knows how to fix her sewing machine may not be lauded as "technically-minded" even though contemporary sewing machines are complex, computerized devices. Men, on the other hand, can be praised for their technical know-how for replacing the blade on a power mower, a task that requires minimal technical knowledge. Female fighter pilots are still a rarity, even though the old military concerns about upper-body strength and hand-to-hand combat are hardly relevant.

TECHNOLOGY SUBVERTING GENDER SYSTEMS

While technology can be used to reinforce particular gender roles, it can also be used to subvert them. Technologies can open up options for challenging sex-based restrictions, allowing people to "break out" of proscribed roles and limited spheres of action. This can occur when technology permits people to enter labor markets and professions from which they had previously been excluded because of an actual or perceived sex-based lack of ability. For example, in the military and police, on assembly lines and farms, in construction and landscaping, and in other professions, brute strength was often a (sometimes specious) requirement excluding women from participation. When machines begin to perform most of the hard labor, or in the case of the military, when they vastly decrease hand-to-hand combat in favor of machine-to-machine or machine-to-soldier combat, then the job of the humans involved is to assist, manage, program, or take care of the machines rather than to labor directly themselves. This allows women either to enter professions that no longer require (if they ever really did) assumed male-specific strength, or to extend their previous roles—today's female technician "nurses" fighting machines as the female nurse of yesteryear "repaired" fighting men.

Another kind of alteration occurs when technology changes or eliminates a profession outright, including sex-segregated ones. Sometimes mechanization or other technological shifts eradicate specialized positions, such as typists, gas station attendants, and blacksmiths. If not eradicated, sometimes jobs are changed in ways that eliminate their masculine and feminine associations. For example, the difficult and time-consuming procedure of carrying water from a well often gets cast as a woman's job, because much of the water's use is for domestic chores. However, when indoor plumbing arrives on the scene, the task of water collection is simply abolished and most of its gender connotations along with it. Femininity does not make it through the transition. Turning on a faucet is not considered woman's work, though the water-using domestic chores are still likely to be hers.

Technology can also subvert gender roles by permitting activities which cross restrictive cultural, social, ethical, and interpersonal boundaries, expanding one's movements, social scope, and access to information. For example, women might use automobiles to get out of their house and see a bit of the world. Women might use guns to protect themselves while traveling (the "great equalizer"), lessening their sense of vulnerability. And while television can reinforce gender roles by bringing Donna Reeds and Carol Bradys into the household, it can also open up new possibilities by bringing Mary Tyler Moores, Cagneys and Laceys, and Captain Janeways into the household.

More extensive technologies can shake our assumptions about gender in other ways by opening up the very biological correlates of sex to alteration. Women and men can be turned into each other, at least on a certain anatomical and hormonal level, which generates the very important concept that sex and gender can be divided into kinds or levels, such as anatomical, genetic, hormonal, social, psychological, and sartorial. Women can modify their experiences of childbirth, and the various cultural values that go along with the act, by using anesthesia (considered a sinful technology early on) when giving birth, using reproductive technology to overcome infertility, scheduling C-sections for particular days to work around their calendars, or using treatments which can allow a sixty three-year-old, post-menopausal woman to have a healthy baby.

As a matter of politics and morality, these gender-subverting uses of technologies are particularly interesting because they are both resisted and demanded. Depending on which ideals of gender are dominant, these technologies can take on an aura of perversion for allowing men and women to step out of their "natural," traditional, and socially legitimated roles, or they can take on a salvific role, offering release from toil, drudgery, and the limitations of social and biological sex.

TECHNOLOGY ALTERING THE VERY NATURE OF GENDER AND SEX

These last examples begin to get at issues which go beyond merely challenging gender roles and restrictions. They point toward the possibility of a more radical challenge to gender by the technological transformation of sex and of the human body itself.

For some time now, gender studies and feminist theory have been involved in a debate over the meaning of gender and sex, over the very character of gender and sex. Divided roughly into camps of "essentialists" versus "social constructionists," the debate parallels older realist and idealist battles. The essentialist position may be oversimplified this way: some core, objective property (typically understood as biological or biopsychological) defines what it means to be a woman or a man, and the categories of male and female are thus culture-independent and mind-independent "natural" kinds. The social constructionist position may be oversimplified this way: the categories of male, female, man, and woman are not "natural" kinds but are rather culturally constructed ideals, irreducible to biological or psychological properties, which change demonstrably in meaning and practice over time and across cultures.

The political outcome of these positions is that essentialists tend to view gender differences as innate and immutable, closed at some fundamental level to modification by education, parenting, or ideological movements, with some basic differences in gender roles pragmatically and objectively justified. Social constructionists tend to view gender differences as created, learned, and alterable, with gender role divisions always historically relative, contingent, and ultimately unwarranted by appeal to an objective reality outside human culture. While both sides of this debate can marshal compelling evidence for their general claims, neither is unassailable. The dominant criticism of essentialism is that it does not account for actual observed variability in these "natural" categories and ignores a tremendous amount of conceptual fuzziness and empirical counterexample in its biologistic definitions. The dominant criticism of social constructionism is that it simply seems to rule out any influences of the physical body on behavior, social categories, and self-concepts, treating human beings as if they were only pure minds, exempt from the biological and evolutionary forces that constrain all other organisms.

Irrespective of the theoretical merits of these two positions, technology threatens or promises to circumvent the political heart of the debate by altering the connection between the premises and conclusions of both sides. Essentialists move from the belief that sex and gender differences are hardwired, largely immutable, and socially valuable to the conclusion that attempts to ignore or eradicate them are futile, harmful, and sexually confusing. Social constructionists move from the belief that sex and gender differences are culturally produced and often socially detrimental to the conclusion that they can be radically altered for the better through education, legal reform, and improved theoretical understanding.

While both sides depend for these moves on the assumption that "biological" equals "immutable," technology increasingly erodes that assumption. Taking seriously the essentialist idea that gender identity, behavior, or cognitive and personality traits may be sex-linked physical characteristics of the body does not mean that they are fixed. "Genetic," "biological," and "bodily" do not imply "unchangeable." Even if we doubt the simplified social constructionist claims that sex and gender are categories unconstrained by objective, empirical bodily facts, we have to grant that technology can nonetheless allow us to alter the body in such ways that gender's "naturalness" or "reality" no longer has any permanent sway. Categories of gender and sex, regardless of their possible "essentialist" foundations, are as open to change and difference as the categories of social constructionism.

At proximal technological levels, the "natural" or "biological" constraints of sex are already being modified as reproductive technology permits procreation without sexual intercourse, removes menopause as a barrier to pregnancy, and allows gender-disorienting or gender-ignoring personal interaction through Internet technologies and virtual reality. At slightly more distal levels, technologies such as cloning and *in vitro* gestation allow reproduction without either sexual dimorphism or pregnancy. At more speculative levels, radical bodily changes produced by genetic engineering, cybernetic implants, nanotechnological reconstruction, and artificial intelligence uploading open the possibility of a completely postgendered cyborgism and perhaps even a posthuman subjectivity altogether.

As with the use of technology to more mildly subvert existing gender systems, these potential effects on gender identity and sexual being are both resisted and invited. However, these radically disruptive effects on sexual biology and gender identity seem to be more anxiety-producing and politically explosive than mere gender-role shifting technologies because altering the very physicality of sex appears to get at the heart of some cherished and previously unalterable correlates of human social and personal identity. This can be received as a great liberating step forward, or rejected as a great and dangerous loss. It is in response to these sorts of radical technological changes that familiar social and political alliances realign in odd ways. Religious conservatives and radical feminists can find themselves on the same side responding to reproductive technologies, or gender-bending virtual technologies, while gruff old male science fiction writers can find themselves being theorized as postmodern feminists.

This classification system may not exhaust the possibilities for studying technology and gender, but it does get at the core of many debates, evaluations, hopes, and anxieties. This book attempts to demonstrate the complexity of these four interactions and to inform the reader of the breadth and content of important issues. To that end, the book is divided into six sections.

Part I introduces historical and cultural issues, with conceptual pieces about the very definition of technology and the historical association of technology with men; historical pieces about the gendered impact of specific new technologies such as the automobile, telephone, and washing machine; and policy pieces on the problems of introducing new technologies to Third World women.

Part II begins the discussion about one of the obvious areas where technology meets issues of sex and gender—reproductive technology. Covering technologies that are already widely available and entrenched but which have provoked considerable ethical debate, this section includes feminist debates over sex-preselection and gestational surrogacy; analyses of how technology permits the separation of social, gestational, and genetic motherhood; questions of the moral significance of genetic relationships; and issues related to sperm donation and the moral obligations of biological fathers.

Part III furthers the discussion of reproductive technologies, moving past changes in conception and genetic relationships to situations where the fetus itself is located somewhere outside a woman's body. Pointing to the enormous moral and legal impact this could have on abortion, parenting, and legal custody, these articles address the possibility of male pregnancy, the question of which parent should get custody of frozen embryos in a contentious divorce, concerns about gestating fetuses entirely inside incubators, and the implications for abortion rights of the technological ability to remove live, healthy fetuses from uteruses.

Part IV speaks to the use of technology to alter our bodies themselves. Cosmetic surgery is an issue feminists have debated for some time, asking whether the choice of surgical changes can really be free in a society that trains women to obsess about their appearance. But other significant body-altering technologies go further, revealing the tenuous nature of biological sex: physicians' decisions to surgically and hormonally assign a sex to healthy hermaphroditic infants; transsexualism, sex reassignment surgery, and the debate over what it means to be a "real" woman or man; and the possible use of technology to determine the sexual orientation of infants.

Part V draws out the complexities of gender in a world shaped by computers and computer-generated environments, with articles examining the social and psychological differences between men's and women's computer use, the gendered cultural divides in computer education and the dearth of female hackers, the practice of gender-swapping in MUDS and virtual realities, and basic issues of truth about your "real" sex in a world where you exist only though text and manipulable images.

Part VI concludes the book with a look into the politics, dreams, and realities of cyborgs—bodies so entwined and enmeshed with technology that old identities based on sex and gender lose their relevance. The selections discuss the meaning and value of cyborgs, the relationship between feminism and cyborgism, the shift from a radical feminist rejection of technology to a postmodern feminist identification with technology, and the ways in which hopeful feminist visions of cyborg futures are countered by dystopian and hypermasculine images of cyborgs in novel and films.

Ideally, this book can be a springboard for introducing, analyzing, and discussing an entire set of issues that often doesn't get the time and space it deserves. But time and space for consideration is exactly what the issues of technology, culture, and ideas of gender need. As never before, we stand on the threshold of opportunity for transforming ourselves and our understanding of ourselves in the most direct ways imaginable. As never before, we have the responsibility for determining who and what we become and for challenging ourselves and each other to question our ideas of sex, sexuality, and gender. Should our cultural ideas of gender forbid us from taking control of our bodies and identities? Should we produce communities where gender is fragmented, shifting, or absent? Is biological sex a moral obligation, a constraint on what we should pursue with our technology, a limit beyond which we should not pass even when we are able? Or is technology sitting before us like a revelation, opening up paths for us to explore and providing the means to recreate ourselves outside the genetic, bodily, and social constraints we were born with? Whatever the case, there is no better time than now to think, to debate, and to ask.

PART I: INVENTING HISTORIES

Gender and Technological Development

It is a highly interactive picture. Existing sex roles and ideas of gender affect how technologies are used, which ones come to dominate in a particular context, and even what things are defined as technology. However, the technologies themselves often change sex roles and even notions of gender. They reorganize social systems; they permit us to step outside gendered social spheres whose boundaries are braced by technological limits on communication, labor, and mobility; they let us extend and alter "our place" in the world. The selections in this section discuss these complex interactions, focusing on historical and conceptual issues and the extraordinary impact of several specific technologies.

Asking some fundamental questions about the basic historical understanding of gender and technology, Autumn Stanley challenges the received view that there have been almost no women inventors and that men alone have been responsible for important technological changes. She argues that this view is factually incorrect, not only due to historical mistakes and unfairness in the actual attribution of who invented what, but also due to conceptual mistakes about what counts as technology and what counts as significant technology. Stanley proposes to remedy the historical errors of erasing women's contributions to technology by reassessing some major issues. What is technology? Why do people tend to think of spears and knives as technologies but not cradles or food preservatives? What makes a technology historically significant? Are weapons and hunting devices more important than horticulture and cooking? Why are "domestic" tools and techniques usually considered simple and unimpressive? Might they not be early forms of mechanization, medicine, and chemistry? Are the unnamed wives, companions, sisters, and employees of inventors really just insignificant helpers? Or are they major and uncredited contributors in their own right? Stanley's answers to these questions upset the conventional connection between technology and men—a connection accepted not only by nonfeminists but by many feminist critics of science and technology as well.

Ruth Schwartz Cowan's concern with the perceived significance and impact of technology draws our attention away from the historically conspicuous machinery of railroads, computers, and industrial production to the quieter technological changes in our own homes. While we tend to think of locomotives and factories as radically transforming society, we lose sight of the "industrial revolution in the home," where electric washing machines and ovens, canned foods, internal plumbing, and refrigerators have changed family activities and women's daily lives and social positions in powerful ways. Even when we do think of the effects of these domestic inventions, we may get it wrong. The idea that mechanizing housework made women's lives easier and reduced their workload doesn't take into account that new "scientific" standards of cleanliness, health, efficiency, and childraising were introduced into homes right along with new appliances. Cowan shows that, with women losing hired help and facing newly introduced fears of "invisible germs," technology doesn't simply reduce work, but changes it.

Michèle Martin describes the social development and gendered practices of one of the most influential technologies ever invented—the telephone. Today, most of us tend to think of the telephone as a basic life appliance, but in its early days it was considered primarily a business machine and mostly limited to male users. As the office was partially extended into the home, however, women gained access to the new technology and began to transform its use. Martin shows how women turned telephones into social technologies even as the assumptions of male control and male usage lingered. She also demonstrates that while the telephone became an instrument for relationships and community as well as commerce, it eroded previous technologies used for building relationships, such as letter writing. [Bibliographic references to this chapter have not been reprinted in this collection but may be found in the author's book.]

Virginia Scharff examines another tremendously important modern invention and demonstrates how ideologies of gender shape the use of particular technologies from the start. Looking at the marketing and manufacturing of early automobiles, she notes that Victorian ideas about the separate spheres of men and women linked gasoline-powered cars to men and electric cars to women. Women were considered "too weak, timid, and fastidious" to drive gas-powered vehicles, while men's presumed interest in "power, range, economy, and thrift" made the distance limitations of electrics unattractive for their needs. These notions not only limited women's access to automobiles and the power they offered, of course; they also affected the very development of the electric car, for its feminine qualities meant men were less likely to buy one for themselves. In a fascinating historical turn of events, then, women's demand for freedom and equality ended up contributing to the decline of the electric car. Scharff's paper draws out the question of how other technologies, including those newly introduced, are marketed toward one sex or the other and how this affects both the technology's development and the fortunes of those who get and do not get to use it.

Taking these sorts of gender-linked cultural limitations on technology use very seriously, Lilia Oblepias-Ramos introduces the important concept of "appropriate technology." Looking specifically at technological development in and technology transfer to the Third World, Ramos points out that many times technology intended to help women is introduced with little or no understanding of the particular cultural values of an area, or of the differences in women's and men's labor and social roles. This leads well-meaning people who want to improve the backbreaking labor conditions in many locations to import useless technologies, to train the wrong people to use and fix the technologies, to introduce technologies that local custom forbids women to use, or inadvertently to eliminate women's income by mechanizing their jobs. Ramos presents a framework for analyzing the appropriateness of certain technologies before introducing them into a particular cultural setting. Giving examples of both successes and failure, she shows how technology can be used to improve women's lot—but only if one takes into account the specific gender and cultural context into which technology will be placed.

CHAPTER 1
WOMEN HOLD UP TWO-THIRDS
OF THE SKY

Notes for a Revised History of Technology

AUTUMN STANLEY

(1 9 8 3)

Over two centuries ago, Voltaire declared, "There have been very learned women as there have been women lawyers, but there have never been women inventors" (1764, *s.v.* "Femmes"). Just three decades ago, Edmund Fuller wrote, "For whatever reason, there are few women inventors, even in the realm of household arts. . . . I cannot find a really conspicuous exception to cite" (1955, p. 301). Although Voltaire and Fuller were both mistaken, their view permeates most available accounts of human technological development. A revised account of that development, fairly and fully evaluating women's contributions through the ages, is long overdue.

What would such a revised history of technology look like? In the first place, the very *definition of technology would change,* from what men do to what *people* do. We would no longer find anthropological reports using the active voice to describe male activities (the men *choose* the wood for their bows with care) and the passive voice to describe women's activities (cooking *is done* in watertight baskets: But by whom? And how did the baskets get to be watertight?) Nor would any anthropologist say, as George Murdock did in 1973, "The statistics reveal no technological activities which are strictly feminine. One can, of course, name activities that are strictly feminine, e.g., nursing and infant care, but they fall outside the range of technological pursuits" (Murdock and Provost 1973, p. 210). The ethnologist doing a book on cradles (Mason 1889) would no longer be an oddity; and the inventions of the digging stick, child- and food-carriers, methods of food-processing, detoxification, cooking, and preserving, menstrual absorbers and other aspects of menstrual technology, infant formulas, trail foods, herbal preparations to ease (or prevent) childbirth would receive their proper share of attention and be discussed as technology (see, for example, Cowan 1979).

In the second place, *the definition of significant technology would change.* In prehistory, for example, the main focus would shift from hunting and its weapons to gathering and its tools (Tanner 1981)—gathering provided 60 to 80 percent by weight, and the only reliable part, of foraging peoples' diet

(Lee and DeVore 1968, p. 7)—and eventually to horticulture and its tools and processes. In later times, the focus would shift from war and its weapons, industry and its machines, to healing and its remedies, fertility and antifertility technology, advances in food production and preservation, child care, and inventions to preserve and keep us in tune with our environment. Again, the change would be from what men do to what people do, with the added dimension of a shift in priorities.

To the degree that these major changes were slow in coming, two further or interim changes would take place. First, the *classification of many women's inventions would change*. For example, the digging stick would be classed as a simple machine, the first lever; the spindle whorl, the rotary quern, and the potter's wheel would be credited with the radical breakthrough of introducing continuous rotary motion to human technology; and women's querns (hand-operated grain mills) would be better known as bearing the world's first cranks. Herbal and other remedies would no longer be classified as "domestic inventions" when invented by women and as medicines or drugs when invented by men. Cosmetics would be classed as the chemical inventions they are, and built-in, multipurpose furniture, moveable storage walls or room dividers, and the like would no longer be classed as architectural when invented by a man and as domestic when invented by a woman. The nineteenth century's inventions inspired by the Dress Reform Movement could be classed not as wearing apparel but as health and medicinal inventions; and food-processing in all its aspects, including cooking, would fall under agriculture.

Second, *women's creation of or contributions to many inventions significant by either or both definitions would be acknowledged*. In prehistory, women's early achievements in horticulture and agriculture, such as the hoe, the scratch plow, grafting, hand pollination, and early irrigation, would be pointed out. Architecture would grow out of weaving, chemistry out of cooking and perfumery, and metallurgy out of pottery. In more modern times, Julia Hall's collaboration with her brother in his process for extracting aluminum from its ore (Trescott 1979), Emily Davenport's collaboration with her husband on the small electric motor (Davenport 1929), Bertha Lammé's contribution to early Westinghouse generators and other great machines (Matthews n.d.), and Annie C-Y. Chang's contribution to genetic engineering (Patent 1981) would all be recognized.

As a result, we would almost certainly see females as primary technologists in proto- and early human societies, especially in any groups whose division of labor resembled that of the Kurnai ("Man's work is to hunt and fish and then sit down; women's work is all else," Reed 1975, p. 106); as at least equal technologists in such societies as those of the North American Indians and the African !Kung; and as highly important technologists in much of the so-called developing world today. Even in recent Western culture, when women's technological areas regain their true status and significance, and "Anonymous" is no longer so often a woman, women's contributions to technology emerge as much greater than previously imagined. In short, if we consider

both history and prehistory, women hold up at least two-thirds of the technological sky.

To see how such a new view of technology might work out in practice,
let us look at three areas of human technological endeavor—two that have
traditionally been considered significant, but male, preserves; and one originally female preserve that began to be considered significant (i.e., worth including in histories of technology) only when males began to dominate it.

SIGNIFICANT, ASSUMED MALE, TECHNOLOGIES: FIRE AND MACHINES

The taming of fire is one of the most important technological advances of
prehistory. Coming as it did (in Europe) in the midst of an ice age, between
75,000 and 50,000 years ago, it enabled Neanderthals to compete with large
animals for cave dwellings, and in those dwellings to survive the ice-age win-
ters. It also transformed early human technology. Food could for the first time
be cooked, softening it for toothless elders and allowing them to survive
longer to transmit more of their culture. Foods could be created out of toxic
or otherwise inedible plants, opening up entire new food supplies, and so on.
Although this revolutionary advance is usually ascribed to men, Elise Boulding suggests "it seems far more likely that the women, the keepers of home
base and the protectors of the young from wild animals, would be the ones
whose need for [fire] would overcome the fear of it" (1976, p. 80).

Mythological evidence connects women strongly with the taming of fire.
The deities and guardians of the hearth and of fire are often female, from Isis
and Hestia, Unči Ahči (Ainu), Chalchinchinatl, and Manuiki (Marquesas) to
the Vestal Virgins and the keepers of Brigit's sacred flame in Ireland (Corson
1894, pp. 714–15; Frazer 1930, p. 83; Graves 1955, I, pp. 43, 75; Ohnuki-
Tierney 1973, p. 15). The ancient aniconic image of the Great Goddess herself was a mound of charcoal covered with white ash, forming the center of
the clan gatherings. A hymn to Artemis tells how she cut her first pine torch
on Mysian Olympus and lit it at the cinders of a lightning-struck tree (Graves
1955, I, pp. 75, 84). In Yahi (American Indian) myth, an old woman stole a
few coals of fire from the Fire People and brought them home hidden in her
ear (Kroeber 1964, p. 79). In Congo myth, a woman named Favorite brought
fire from Cloud Land to Earth (Feldman 1963, pp. 102–03).

Several myths show women, particularly old women, as the first possessors
of fire, and men stealing fire not from the gods but from women. Examples
come from Australia, the Torres Straits, mainland New Guinea, Papua, Dobu
Island, the Admiralty Islands, the Trobriand Islands, from the Maori, the Fa-
kaofo or Bowditch Islands north of Samoa, Yap, and Northern Siberia. In a
Wagifa myth (Melanesia) the woman, Kukuya, gives fire willingly to the people
(Frazer 1930, pp. 5, 15, 18, 23–28, 40, 43–45, 48–49, 50, 55–57, 74, 90–91,
104).

Other myths connect women directly with the making of fire, of course coming later than the taming of existing fire. A rather confusing and probably transitional Guiana Indian explanatory tale begins with an old woman who could vomit fire. At her death, "the fire which used to be within her passed into the surrounding fagots. These fagots happened to be hima-heru wood, and whenever we rub together two sticks of this same timber we can get fire" (Roth 1908–09, p. 133). From the Taulipang of northern Brazil comes a very similar myth representing perhaps a more nearly complete transition: An old woman named Pelenosamo had fire in her body and baked her manioc cakes with it, whereas other people had to bake their cakes in the sun. When she refused to share fire with the people, they seized and tied her, collected fuel, than set Pelenosamo against it and squeezed her body till the fire spurted out. "But the fire changed into the stones called *wato*, which, on being struck, give forth fire" (Frazer 1930, p. 131).

Among the Sea Dyaks of Borneo, a lone woman survived a Great Flood. Finding a creeper whose root felt warm, she took two pieces of this wood, rubbed them together, and thus kindled fire. "Such was the origin of the fire-drill" (apparatus for making fire by friction). Biliku, ancestress of the Andaman Islanders and a creator figure, made fire by striking together a red stone and a pearl shell. In this case, a dove stole fire for the people. Among the Nagas of Assam, two women invented the fire-thong (another fire-making device where the friction comes from pulling) by watching a tiger (or an ape) pull a thong under its claw. The ape, having lost fire, is all hairy, whereas people, having fire to keep them warm, have lost their hairy covering. In the New Hebrides, a woman discovered how to make fire while amusing her little boy by rubbing a stick on a piece of dry wood. When the stick smoked and smoldered and finally burst into flame, she laid the food on the fire and found it tasted better because of it. From that time on, all her people began to use fire (Frazer 1930, pp. 51, 94–95, 99, 105–06).

In the Torres Straits, the very operation of fire-making is called "Mother gives fire," the board from which the fire is extracted by the turning of the stick or drill upon it seen as "mother," and the drill as "child" (Frazer 1930, pp. 26–27). More common is a sexual analogy. Commenting on some of these myths, Frazer (1930) says:

> The same analogy may possibly also explain why in the myths women are sometimes represented as in possession of fire before men. For the fire which is extracted from the board by the revolution of the drill is naturally interpreted by the savage as existing in the board before its extraction . . . or, in mythical language, as inherent in the female before it is drawn out by the male. . . . (pp. 220–21)

This of course would not explain myths ascribing fire first to women in cultures using other fire-making methods.

Whatever the origins of fire in various cultures, women put fire to more uses in their work than men did: protecting infants from animals, warming their living area, fire-hardening the point of their digging sticks, cooking, detoxifying and preserving food, hollowing out wooden bowls and other vessels, making pottery, burning vegetation for gardens. Our familiar Prometheus myth may need a footnote.[1]

When Prometheus was on Olympus stealing fire from Hephaestus, he also stole "mechanical skill." Significantly enough, he stole it from a goddess, Athena, who shared a workshop with Hephaestus (Frazer 1930, p. 194). This seldom-cited Platonic version of the myth takes on new meaning when we reflect that women almost certainly invented the first lever, the digging stick (Stanley 1981, pp. 291–92; Tanner and Zihlman 1976, p. 599), that the crank may have appeared first in the West on women's querns (Lynn White 1978, p. 18; Mason 1894, p. 23), and that at least one historian of technology rates the crank second only to the wheel in importance (Lynn White 1978, p. 17). Women also invented a cassava-processing device called *mapiti* or *tipiti*, combining the principles of press, screw, and sieve (Mason 1902, pp. 60–61; Sokolov 1978, pp. 34, 38).

In the development of many mechanical processes, the first stages imitated human limb action in using reciprocal (back-and-forth) motion, as for instance in an ordinary handsaw. Real advances came with continuous or rotary motion, as in the wheel and the circular saw (Singer et al. 1954, ch. 9; Smith 1978, p. 6).[2] Women seem to have introduced rotary motion to human technology; at least three important early examples of rotary motion pertain unmistakably to women's work: the spindle whorl, the rotary quern, and the potter's wheel. In the spindle whorl, women invented the flywheel (Mason 1894, pp. 57–58, 279–80; Lynn White 1978, p. 18n). These early examples of axial rotary motion would certainly have influenced the invention of the vehicular wheel—which may have been women's doing in some cultures. In Meso-America (Mexico and Central America) wheeled vehicles appeared only as miniatures that may be either children's toys or religious objects (Doster et al. 1978, p. 55; Halsbury 1971, p. 13). If toys, they could easily have been made by women.

As we move into the industrial era, we find further evidence refuting stereotypes about women and machines. Women invented or contributed to the invention of such crucial machines as the cotton gin, the sewing machine, the small electric motor, the McCormick reaper, the printing press, and the Jacquard loom. Catherine Greene's much-debated contribution to the cotton gin may never be proven conclusively; but note that Whitney did arrange to pay her royalties and, according to a Shaker writer, once publicly admitted her help (*Shaker Manifesto* 1890; Stanley 1984). In his most famous lecture, "Acres of Diamonds," nineteenth- and early twentieth-century journalist and lecturer Russell H. Conwell has Mrs. Elias Howe completing in two hours the sewing machine her husband had struggled with for fourteen years. Conwell's source was impressive—Elias Howe himself (Conwell 1968, p. 46; Boulding 1976, p. 686). It was also a woman, Helen Augusta Blanchard (1839–1922) of Portland, Maine, who invented zigzag sewing and the machine to do it (Willard and Livermore 1893, p. 97). The nineteenth century patent records show literally dozens of sewing machine improvements by women.

Emily Goss Davenport's role in the invention of the small electric motor usually ascribed to her husband Thomas—her continuous collaboration with him and her crucial suggestion that he use mercury as a conductor—is best described by Walter Davenport (1929, pp. 47, 55, 62). Other sources merely sentimentally praise her for sacrificing her silk wedding dress to wind the coils of Thomas' first homemade electromagnet.

In the case of the reaper, Conwell (1968) cites "a recently published interview with Mr. McCormick," in which the inventor admitted that after he and his father had tried and failed, "a West Virginia woman . . . took a lot of shears and nailed them together on the edge of a board. Then she wired them so that when she pulled the wire one way it closed them, and . . . the other way it opened them. And there she had the principle of the mowing machine" (pp. 45–46). Another American woman, Ann Harned Manning of Plainfield, New Jersey, invented a mower-reaper in 1817–18. This was apparently a joint invention with her husband William, who patented and is usually credited with inventing it. Ann and William also invented (and he patented) a clover-cleaner (U.S. Patents of Nov. 24, 1830 and May 3, 1831; Hanaford 1883, p. 623; Mozans 1913, p. 362; Rayne 1893, pp. 116–17). The Manning Reaper, predating McCormick's by several years, was important enough to be mentioned in several histories of farm machinery.

Russell Conwell (1968) and Jessie Hayden Conwell (1962) state baldly that farm women invented the printing press and that Mme. Jacquard invented the loom usually credited to her husband.

SIGNIFICANT TECHNOLOGY WHEN TAKEN OVER BY MALES: MEDICINE

As keepers of home base and then of the home, as preeminent gatherers and then propagators of plants, and as caretakers of children until puberty, women traditionally cared for the sick, creating the earliest form of medicine—herbal medicine. The original deities of healing were probably female. Many such deities and reports of their attributes survive, from Neith, Isis, and Gula in the Middle East to Panacea in Greece and Brigit in Ireland. Minerva Medica parallels Athena Hygeia—Great Goddesses worshipped in their healing aspect (Graves 1955, I, pp. 80–81; Hurd-Mead 1938, pp. 11, 32–33; Jayne 1925, pp. 64–68, 71–72, 121, 513; Rohrlich 1980, pp. 88–89).

Except for contraceptives, abortifacients, preparations to ease labor, and other elements of women's or children's medicine, it is difficult to state unequivocally that women invented or discovered any specific remedy or procedure. However, in general, the more ancient any given remedy, the likelier it is to be a woman's invention; and, of course, if a remedy occurs in a group where the healers are women, the presumption is strong.

Many plants are both foods and medicines: asparagus, whose species name *officinalis* means that it once stood on apothecary shelves; clover, a styptic (Weiner 1972, p. 144) and heart stimulant and also a food; rhubarb, both a stewed dessert and an effective laxative. Plants may be both foods and contraceptives: wild yams, Queensland matchbox bean (Himes 1970, pp. 28–29;

cf. Goodale 1971, pp. 180–81). Or they may serve as food, medicine, and contraceptive, depending on method of preparation, dosage, and concomitant regimen. An example of this triple usage is the Indian turnip or jack-in-the-pulpit, *Arisaema triphyllum*. The root or corm of this North American wildflower contains needlelike crystals of calcium oxalate (oxalate of lime). After proper preparation, however—drying and cooking or pounding the roots to a pulp with water and allowing the mass to dry for several weeks—the Iroquois and other Indians used it as food. The Pawnee also powdered the root and applied it to the head and temples to cure headache, and the Hopi used it to induce temporary or permanent sterility, depending on the dosage (Jack-in-the-pulpit 1958, p. 851; Weiner 1972, pp. 41, 64–65).

The most ancient medical document yet discovered, a Sumerian stone tablet, dates from the late third millennium BC, when Gula was Goddess of healing and medicine, and most healers were probably still women. The tablet's several prescriptions call for plants and other natural curatives, mentioning not a single deity or demon, and giving no spells or incantations. A tablet from the time of Hammurabi (around 1750 BC) by contrast—when medicine had become a male profession serving mainly elites—blames diseases on demons and suggests incantations as cures. But women healers still ministered to the lower classes, probably continuing to use herbal remedies (Kramer 1963, pp. 93–98; Rohrlich 1980, pp. 88–89).

Precisely parallel developments occurred centuries later in Greece (see, e.g., Graves 1955, I, pp. 174ff.) and still later in Northern Europe, where male doctors trained mostly in theology in Church-run universities wrested control of medicine from their herbally trained female counterparts, some of whom still practiced the old religion. These male usurpers were aided, intentionally or unintentionally, by the Christian Church, which threatened the wise women they called witches with both hell- and earthly fire. Innumerable precious medical secrets no doubt burned with these women at the stake.[3]

To get some idea of what may have been lost in that medieval holocaust, we need only reflect that European peasant women bound moldy bread over wounds centuries before Alexander Fleming "discovered" that a *Penicillium* mold killed bacteria; that medieval wise women had ergot for labor pains and belladonna to prevent miscarriage; and that an English witch discovered the uses of digitalis for heart ailments (Ehrenreich and English 1973, p. 14; Raper 1952, p. 1). Ergot derivatives are the main drugs used today to hasten labor and recovery from childbirth; belladonna is still used as an antispasmodic, and digitalis is still important in treating heart patients (Ehrenreich and English 1973, p. 14). Medieval wise women knew all this at a time when male practitioners knew little to prescribe except bleeding and incantations. Edward II's physician, for example, boasting a bachelor's degree in theology and a doctorate in medicine from Oxford, recommended writing on a toothache patient's jaw "In the name of the Father, the Son, and the Holy Ghost, Amen," or touching a needle first to a caterpillar and then to the tooth (Ehrenreich and English 1973, p. 17). Ladies of medieval epic poetry, repeatedly called upon to treat the ghastly wounds of errant knights, worked their miraculous-seeming cures not through prayer but through deep herbal knowledge and careful nursing (Hughes 1943).

Indeed, these women were the repositories of medical knowledge coming to them in a line of women healers from the days when Hecate the Moon Goddess invented aconite teas for teething and children's fevers, when Rhea invented liniments for the pains of children, when the Egyptian Polydamna gave her pupil Helen the secret of Nepenthe, and when Artemisia of Caria—famed for knowing every herb used in medicine—discovered the uses of artemisia to cause (or in other combinations to prevent) abortion and to expel a retained placenta, the value of wormwood, and the delights of absinthe (Hurd-Mead 1938, pp. 32, 37n, 40; Jayne 1925, p. 345). Thus, we should not be surprised to hear that in the sixteenth century Paracelsus burnt his text on pharmaceuticals because everything in it he had learned from "the Sorceress," i.e., from a wise woman or women he had known (Ehrenreich and English 1973, p. 17).

Although women are connected most intimately with herbal medicine, ancient women healers had accomplishments in other areas. The only surgery mentioned in the Bible is gynecological or obstetrical surgery—or circumcisions—done by women with their flint knives (Hurd-Mead 1938, p. 19). Flint in pre-Hellenic Greek myth was the gift of the Goddess (Spretnak 1978, p. 42). Ancient Scandinavian women's graves contain surgical instruments not found in men's graves. And California Indian medicine women used a technique only now being rediscovered, and still controversial in modern medicine—visualization, for focusing the body's own mental and physical powers of healing on the illness, tumor, or pain (Hurd-Mead 1938, pp. 6, 14).

In late medieval and early modern Europe, women healers continued to work unofficially. The most outstanding of them, such as Trotula, Jacoba or Jacobina, Felicie, and Marie Colinet, sometimes were given more or less recognition by the male medical profession or protected by wealthy patients. Marie Colinet learned surgery from her husband, the renowned surgeon Fabricius of Hilden, but by his own admission she excelled him. For shattered ribs she opened the chest and wired together the fragments of bone—this in the seventeenth century. Her complex herbal plasters prevented infection and promoted healing. She also regulated the postoperative diet and used padded splints. Marie Colinet was first to use a magnet to remove fragments of iron or steel from the eye. Though most sources credit Fabricius with this invention, he credits her (Boulding 1976, pp. 472–75; Hurd-Mead 1938, pp. 361, 433).

During the American colonial period, it is thought that more women practiced medicine than did men (Hymowitz and Weissman 1978, p. 7). Even in the nineteenth century, women healers still ministered to a great many American families, especially in rural areas. Some operated as informally as the Misses Roxy and Ruey Toothacre portrayed in Harriet Beecher Stowe's *Pearl of Orr's Island* (1862, pp. 17–18), and some more formally or professionally. But they relied on time-tested herbal knowledge brought from the Old World and enriched by contact with Indian women healers, while male practitioners relied heavily on bleeding and the poisonous calomel (containing mercury). Moreover, like Lady Aashild in *Kristin Lavransdatter*, like the medieval ladies in the epics, like the German Mother Seigel (b. ca. 1793), and like Sister Kenny in the Australian Outback in the twentieth century, they not merely made house calls, but stayed with their seriously ill patients for weeks at a time, personally conducting or supervising their care, medication, and diet (Kenny 1943, e.g., pp. 21–29, 71–72; Stage 1979, ch. 2, pp. 45–63; Anna J. White 1866). Women who observed their patients day and night, watching every symptom and the effect of every remedy, quite naturally gained more practical knowledge than the doctor who spent just a few moments with a patient.

Although the twentieth century finds male practitioners firmly in control of formal Western medicine, women doctors and healers still have important inventions and innovations to their credit.

For example, although three men received the Nobel Prize for penicillin, women participated significantly in the team effort that brought the drug to medical usefulness. Women had discovered the mold's usefulness centuries or perhaps millennia earlier (Halsbury 1971, p. 19; Raper 1952, p. 1), and one nineteenth-century Wisconsin woman, Elizabeth Stone, an early antibiotic therapist, specialized in treating lumberjacks' wounds with poultices of moldy bread in warm milk or water: she never lost an injury patient (Stellman 1977, p. 87). In the twentieth-century development of the drug, it was a woman bacteriologist, Dr. Elizabeth McCoy of the University of Wisconsin, who created the ultraviolet-mutant strain of *Penicillium* used for all further production, since it yielded *nine hundred times as much penicillin* as Fleming's strain (Bickel 1972, p. 185; O'Neill 1979, p. 219).[4] And as Howard Florey, leader of the British penicillin team, was quick to point out, it was Dr. Ethel Florey's precise clinical trials that transformed penicillin from a crude sometime miracle worker into a reliable drug. It was also a woman, Nobel laureate and X-ray crystallographer Dr. Dorothy Crowfoot Hodgkin, who finally determined the precise structure of the elusive penicillin molecule (Bickel 1972, p. 216; Opfell 1978, pp. 211, 219).

Women were also involved in developing the sulfa drugs that preceded penicillin. For instance, it was a married pair of chemists, Prof. and Mme. Tréfouël, and their colleagues at the Pasteur Institute in Paris who split red azo dye to create sulfanilamide (Bickel 1972, p. 50).

At least two women have invented new antibiotics for which they receive sole credit. Dr. Odette Shotwell of Denver, Colorado, came up with two new antibiotics—duramycin and azacolutin—during her first assignment as a research chemist at the Agriculture Department laboratories in Peoria, Illinois. She has also invented new methods for separating antibiotics from fermentation by-products, and in doing so has played an important role in the development of two other antibiotics: cinnamycin and hydroxystreptomycin. Dr. Marina Glinkina of the USSR directed the laboratory effort that produced a new antigangrene antibiotic during World War II. Her postwar work as a senior scientist has been theoretical (Dodge 1966, p. 226; O'Neill 1979, p. 32; Ribando 1980).

Follies-girl-turned-scientist Justine Johnstone Wanger (1895–) was the laboratory part of the team that developed the slow-intravenous-drip method of administering drugs and other substances to the human body. She then joined a different medical team in applying this new method to the treatment of early syphilis, in an advance that was called the "greatest step since Ehrlich" (Hobson 1941, p. 298).

The DPT vaccine that protects virtually all infants in the developed world against three of their former mass killers (diphtheria; pertussis, or whooping cough; and typhus) was invented by Dr. Pearl Kendrick (1890–1980) and Dr. Grace Eldering (1900–) in the early 1940s. In 1939 they had invented a whooping cough vaccine. Unlike Drs. Salk and Sabin, they refused to allow their vaccines to be named for them. In the 1920s, Dr. Gladys Henry Dick (1881–1963) and her husband conquered another great childhood killer, scarlet fever. They not only isolated the streptococcus causing the disease, but created the toxin and the antitoxin that prevent and cure it, respectively. They then went on to develop the Dick test, a skin test showing susceptibility to the disease. They were recommended for the Nobel Prize in 1925, but no prize was given in medicine for that year. They did, however, receive the Mickle Prize of the University of Toronto, the Cameron Prize of the University of Edinburgh, and several honorary degrees (Dr. Kendrick 1980–81, p. 12; Kendrick 1942; O'Neill 1979, p. 217; *Notable American Women* 1980, pp. 191–92; *Time* 1980, p. 105).

Although two male doctors are credited with developing the vaccines that conquered polio in the developed world, it was a woman, Sister Elizabeth Kenny (1886–1952) of Australia, who invented the only treatment useful once the disease had struck. Whereas the doctors of her day were splinting the affected limbs to prevent spasm—but also causing the damaged muscles to waste away and become useless for life—Sister Kenny used moist hot packs, massage, and daily gentle exercise, plus muscle reeducation. About 87 percent of her patients escaped paralysis, while about 85 percent of the doctors' patients were paralyzed for life. In spite of these results, the established medical profession long rejected her treatment. It was in the United States that she finally found acceptance. By the early 1940s, the National Infantile Paralysis Foundation had officially endorsed her treatment, and she saw the opening of the Elizabeth Kenny Institute in Minneapolis. Awarding her an honorary Doctor of Science degree, the President of the University of Rochester said, "In the dark world of suffering you have lit a candle that will never be put out" (Kenny 1943, passim and p. 267; Marlow 1979, pp. 259–65).

In still more recent times, women have contributed significant inventions or innovations in the battle against cancer, on many fronts. Outstanding examples are Drs. Charlotte Friend and Ariel Hollinshead. While working as a virologist at the Sloan-Kettering Institute for Cancer Research in the 1950s, Dr. Friend (1921–) not only demonstrated the viral origins of leukemia (the Friend mouse-leukemia virus), but developed the first successful anticancer vaccine for mammals. She won a *Mademoiselle* magazine achievement award for her work in 1957, and has since then won many other honors, including the Alfred P. Sloan Award (1954, 1957, and 1962), the American Cancer Society Award (1962), and the Virus-Cancer Progress Award from the National Institutes of Health (1974). In 1966, she became director of the Center for Experimental Cell Biology at New York's Mt. Sinai School of Medicine, where her work continues at this writing (Achievement awards 1958, p. 68; *American Men and Women of Science* 1979, p. 1602; O'Neill 1979, p. 224).

Dr. Hollinshead (1929–   ) is Professor of Medicine at George Washington Medical Center in Washington, DC, and director of its Laboratory for Virus and Cancer Research. Doing both basic and clinical research on cancer, she has helped develop immunotherapy for breast, lung, and gastric cancers as well as melanomas. But she may be best remembered for her lung-cancer vaccines. In the process of inventing these vaccines, which are made from antigens in cancer-cell membranes and are specific for their cancer of origin, she also invented a method of getting antigens out of membranes without destroying their structure, using low-frequency sound. Completed clinical tests show an 80 percent survival rate among those receiving the antigens as opposed to a 49 percent survival rate among the controls. Dr. Hollinshead's work, which opens possibilities for preventing as well as treating cancer, has been called brilliant, "the most advanced and exciting in the world" (*American Men and Women of Science* 1979, p. 2238; Arehart-Treichel 1980; Cancer vaccines 1979, p. 248).

Severely neglected by medical research is the field of menstrual disorders. Although this health condition affects 35 million people in the United States alone, and not just once but every month, in 1974 only eight articles on menstrual pain appeared in the entire world medical literature. Quipped Thomas Clayton, Vice-President for Medical Affairs at Tampax in 1979, "If men had cramps, we'd have had a National Institute of Dysmenorrhea for years" (Thorpe 1980, p. 36; Twin 1979, p. 8).

Dr. Penny Wise Budoff, a family practitioner and medical school professor at the State University of New York (Stony Brook), undertook some dysmenorrhea research. Beginning in the 1970s with new findings on antiprostaglandins (drugs resembling aspirin but much stronger), she experimented first on herself. Most effective was mefenamic acid, and she next recommended mefenamic acid to a few women in her practice. When these patients also reported some relief, Dr. Budoff set up further experiments. By 1980 the U.S. Food and Drug Administration had approved mefenamic acid for treating menstrual pain. Eighty-five percent of the women tested so far have reported significant relief not only from pain but from nausea, vomiting, dizziness, and weakness. Dr. Budoff has also studied premenstrual tension, and recommends a simple dietary change that may give relief without drugs (Budoff 1980; Thorpe 1980, p. 36).

It seems fitting to climax and close this brief review of women inventors and innovators in health and medicine with Nobel laureate Dr. Rosalyn Sussman Yalow. Born in the Bronx in 1921, a brilliant and strong-willed child, she took Marie Curie for a role model at age seventeen, and seems to have moved with unswerving purpose ever since. She graduated from Hunter College with a physics major at age nineteen. If she was discouraged at being refused a graduate assistantship at Purdue because she was a New Yorker, Jewish, and a woman—or at being told at Columbia that she must start as secretary to a medical school professor—she did not reveal it. She received her Ph.D. in physics from the University of Illinois in 1945.

After working briefly as an electrical engineer, and teaching physics at Hunter College, she became interested in nuclear medicine and took a research position at the Bronx Veteran's Administration Hospital. Thus began the collaboration with Solomon Berson, M.D., that lasted until Berson's death and produced one of the most powerful research techniques, and one of the most powerful diagnostic tools, of the twentieth century: radioimmunoassay (RIA). RIA is a measurement technique so sensitive that it could detect a teaspoon of sugar in a lake 62 miles long, 62 miles wide, and 30 feet deep. In more practical terms, it has allowed doctors for the first time to measure the circulating insulin in a diabetic's blood.

Physicians and researchers continually find new and exciting uses for RIA. Pediatricians can prevent one kind of mental retardation by detecting and treating an infant thyroid deficiency. The RIA test uses only a single drop of the baby's blood, and costs only about a dollar. Thousands of blood banks now screen their blood with RIA to prevent transfusion hepatitis (the test can detect Hepatitis-B virus). RIA can also detect deficiencies or surpluses in human growth hormone in children so that they can be treated to prevent certain kinds of dwarfism and gigantism; can help explain high blood pressure and infertility; can detect hormone-secreting cancers and other endocrine-related disorders. It can detect heroin, methadone, and LSD in the bloodstream; it can gauge circulating vitamins and enzymes to shed light on human nutrition. It can make antibiotic treatment more precise and even help catch murderers, by revealing minute traces of poison in their victims' bodies. RIA was recently used to diagnose Legionnaires' Disease at an early stage, by detecting *Legionella* antigen in the urine.

Had Yalow and Berson decided to patent RIA, they could have been millionaires. Laboratories selling RIA kits do some $30 million in business each year. Thinking like scientists, however, instead of like entrepreneurs, the two freely published their work.

In awarding Rosalyn Yalow the Nobel Prize for Physiology and Medicine in 1977, the Prize Committee specifically recognized RIA as "the most valuable advance in basic research directly applicable to clinical medicine made in the past two decades" (Levin 1980, p. 135). In her acceptance speech she said:

> We still live in a world in which a significant fraction of people, including women, believe that a woman belongs and wants to belong exclusively in the home; that a woman should not aspire to achieve more than her male counterparts, and particularly not more than her husband. . . . But if women are to start moving toward [our] goal, we must believe in ourselves, or no one else will believe in us; we must match our aspirations with the competence, courage, and determination to succeed, and we must feel a personal responsibility to ease the path for those who come afterward. (Stone 1978, p. 34)

Rosalyn Yalow has come a long way from the South Bronx to the chair of Distinguished Professor of Medicine at Mt. Sinai School of Medicine in New York City, where her outstanding work continues (Levin 1980, pp. 133–37; Opfell 1978; Rapid diagnosis 1981, p. 358; Stone 1978, pp. 29–34ff; Yalow 1979).

Through examples from the taming and making of fire to the development of machines and medicine, we have glimpsed the history and prehistory of technology as they would be if women's contributions were included.[5] Most historians of technology to date, looking backward through the distorted glass of a prevailing cultural stereotype that women do not invent, have found, not surprisingly, that women never did invent. If, instead, we examine the evidence—from mythology, anthropology, and history—we find that, as H. J. Mozans wrote nearly seventy years ago:

> More conclusive information respecting woman as an inventor is . . . afforded by a systematic study of the various races of mankind which are still in a state of savagery [*sic*]. Such a study discloses the interesting fact that woman has . . .—*pace* Voltaire—been the inventor of all the peaceful arts of life, and the inventor, too, of the earliest forms of nearly all the mechanical devices now in use in the world of industry. (1913, p. 338)

Our task now is to carry that systematic study of woman's achievement through to the present so that we can, once again, let her own works praise her in the gates.[6]

NOTES

1. Or indeed, a full-scale companion myth. The Prometheus myth is late and literary. The name Prometheus apparently comes from the Sanskrit word for the fire-making drill, or for the process of making fire by friction. Thus it may be saying only that by inventing fire-making devices, humans stole fire from the realm of the gods and brought it down to the realm of the human (Corson 1894, p. 714).

2. In a striking nineteenth-century recapitulation of this ancient breakthrough, Sister Tabitha Babbitt (d. 1858) of the Harvard, Massachusetts, Shakers independently invented the circular saw about 1810. After watching the brothers sawing, she concluded that their back-and-forth motion wasted half their effort, and mounted a notched metal disk on her spinning wheel to demonstrate her proposed improvement (Deming and Andrews 1974, pp. 153, 156, 157; Anna J. White and Taylor 1904, p. 312). Joseph and Frances Gies reveal that Sister Tabitha intended the blade to be turned by water power (1976, pp. 255–56).

3. Mary Daly (1978) presents the most radical view of this tragic event in human history, accepting the highest reported figure for the almost entirely female deaths: 9,000,000. More conservative scholars have estimated as high as 3,000,000; and calmly rational Elise Boulding (1976) says:

> One could argue that there never was any overt decision to "get the women out," that it all happened by default. On the other hand, given the number of instances in which the church combined with various economic groups from

doctors to lawyers to merchant guilds, not only to make pronouncements about the incapacities of women, but often to accomplish the physical liquidation of women through witchcraft and heresy trials, one can hardly say that it all happened without anyone intending it. The exclusion of women was a result of impersonal and intentional forces. (p. 505)

4. Had she done this today, she could have patented the organism (*Diamond v. Chakrabarty* 1980).

5. For further discussion, see Stanley (1984).

6. "Give her of the fruit of her hands, and let her own works praise her in the gates" (Proverbs 31:31).

WORKS CITED

Achievement awards, Dr. Charlotte Friend. 1958. *Mademoiselle,* January, p. 68.

American Men and Women of Science. 1979. Ed. Jacques Cattell Press. 14th ed. New York: Bowker.

Arehart-Treichel, Joan. 1980. Tumor-associated antigens: Attacking lung cancer. *Science News* 118 (July 12): 26–28.

Bickel, Lennard. 1972. *Rise up to Life: A Biography of W. H. Florey.* New York: Scribner's.

Boulding, Elise. 1976. *The Underside of History: A View of Women through Time.* Boulder, CO: Westview Press.

Budoff, Penny Wise. 1980. *No More Menstrual Cramps and Other Good News.* New York: Putnam.

Cancer vaccines in the works. 1979. *Science News* 117 (April 14): 248.

Conwell, Jessie Hayden. 1926 (c. 1865). Inaugural editorial, Ladies' Department, *Minneapolis Daily Chronicle,* weekly ed., *Conwell's Star of the North. Russell H. Conwell and his work.* Ed. Agnes Rush Burr. Philadelphia: J. C. Winston. Pp. 141–44.

Conwell, Russell H. 1968 (1877). *Acres of Diamonds.* Kansas City, MO: Hallmark.

Corson, Juliet. 1894. The evolution of home. *Congress of Women,* Ed. Mary K. Eagle. Chicago: Conkey. Vol. 2: 714–18.

Cowan, Ruth Schwartz. 1979. From Virginia Dare to Virginia Slims: Women and technology in American life. *Technology and Culture* 20, 1 (January): 51–63.

Daly, Mary. 1978. *Gyn/ecology: The Metaethics of Radical Feminism.* Boston: Beacon Press.

Davenport, Walter Rice. 1929. *Biography of Thomas Davenport, the "Brandon Blacksmith," Inventor of the Electric Motor.* Montpelier, VT: The Vermont Historical Society.

Deming, Edward, and Faith Andrews. 1974. *Work and Worship: The Economic Order of the Shakers.* Greenwich, CT: New York Graphic Society.

Diamond v. Chakrabarty. 100 US 2204 (1980).

Dr. Kendrick dies. 1980–81. *National NOW Times* (Dec./Jan.): 12.

Dodge, Norton T. 1966. *Women in the Soviet Economy: Their Role in Economic, Scientific, and Technical Development.* Baltimore: Johns Hopkins.

Doster, Alexis III, Joe Goodwin and Jane M. Ross. 1978. *The Smithsonian Book of Invention.* Washington, DC: Smithsonian Exposition Books.

Ehrenreich, Barbara, and Deirdre English. 1973. *Witches, Midwives, and Nurses: A History of Women Healers.* Old Westbury, NY: Feminist Press.

Feldmann, Susan, ed. 1963. *African Myths and Tales.* New York: Dell.

Frazer, Sir James George. 1930. *Myths on the Origin of Fire.* London: Macmillan.

Fuller, Edmund. 1955. *Tinkers and Genius.* New York: Hastings House.

Gies, Joseph, and Frances Gies. 1976. *The Ingenious Yankees.* New York: Crowell.

Goodale, Jane C. 1971. *Tiwi Wives: A Study of the Women of Melville Island, North Australia.* Seattle: University of Washington Press.

Graves, Robert. 1955. *The Greek Myths.* 2 vols. Baltimore: Penguin.
Halsbury, Earl of. 1971.Invention and technological progress (fourth annual Spooner Lecture). *The Inventor* (London), June, pp. 10–34.
Hanaford, Phebe A. 1883. *Daughters of America.* Augusta, ME: True and Company.
Himes, Norman E. 1970 (1936). *Medical History of Contraception.* New York: Schocken.
Hobson, Laura Z. 1941. Follies girl to scientist. *Independent Woman* 20 (October): 297–98ff.
Hughes, Muriel Joy. 1943. *Women Healers in Medieval Life and Literature.* New York: King's Crown Press.
Hurd-Mead, Kate Campbell. 1938. *A History of Women in Medicine.* Haddam, CT: Haddam Press. [1973. Boston: Milford House.]
Hymowitz, Carol, and Michaele Weissman. 1978. *A History of Women in America.* New York: Bantam.
Jack-in-the-pulpit. 1958. *Encyclopedia Britannica* 12.
Jayne, Walter Addison. 1925. *The Healing Gods of Ancient Civilizations.* New Haven, CT: Yale University Press.
Kendrick, Pearl L. 1942. Use of alum-treated pertussis vaccine, and of alum-precipitated combined pertussis vaccine and diphtheria toxoid for active immunization. *American Journal of Public Health* 32 (June): 615–26.
Kenny, Elizabeth. 1943. *And They Shall Walk.* New York: Dodd Mead.
Kramer, Samuel N. 1963. *The Sumerians: Their History, Culture, and Character.* Chicago: University of Chicago Press.
Kroeber, Theodora. 1964. *Ishi, Last of His Tribe.* Berkeley: Parnassus.
Lee, Richard B., and Irven De Vore, eds. 1968. *Man the Hunter.* Chicago: Aldine.
Levin, Beatrice S. 1980. *Women and Medicine.* Metuchen, NJ: Scarecrow.
Marlow, Joan. 1979. *The Great Women.* New York: A & W Publishers.
Mason, Otis T. 1889. *Cradles of the North American Indians.* Seattle: Shorey.
Mason, Otis T. 1894. *Woman's Share in Primitive Culture.* New York: D. Appleton.
Mason, Otis T. 1902 (1895). *Origin of Inventions.* London: Scott.
Matthews, Alva. N.d. Some Pioneers, unpub. speech delivered to the Society of Women Engineers, n.p.
Mozans, H. J. 1913. *Woman in Science.* New York: D. Appleton.
Murdock, George P., and Caterina Provost. 1973. Factors in the division of labor by sex. *Ethnology* 12 (April): 203–25.
Notable American Women: the Modern Period. 1980. Ed. Barbara Sicherman and Carol Hurd Green. Cambridge: Harvard University Press.
Ohnuki-Tierney, Emiko. 1973. The shamanism of the Ainu. *Ethnology* 12 (March): 15 ff.
O'Neill, Lois Decker, ed. 1979. *The Women's Book of World Records and Achievements.* Garden City, NY: Doubleday/Anchor.
Opfell, Olga S. 1978. *The Lady Laureates; Women Who Have Won the Nobel Prize.* Metuchen, NJ: Scarecrow Press.
Patent for gene-splicing, cloning, awarded Stanford. 1981. *Stanford Observer* (January): 1f.
Raper, Kenneth B. 1952. A decade of antibiotics in America. *Mycologia* 45 (Jan./Feb.): 1–59.
Rapid diagnosis of legionellosis. 1981. *Science News* 6 (June): 358.
Rayne, Martha Louise. 1893. *What Can a Woman Do: Or, Her Position in the Business and Literary World.* Petersburgh, NY: Eagle.
Reed, Evelyn. 1975. *Woman's Evolution: from Matriarchal Clan to Patriarchal Family.* New York: Pathfinder.
Ribando, Curtis P. 1980. Personal communication, March 26; Patent Advisor, United States Department of Agriculture Northern Regional Research Center, Peoria, Illinois.
Rohrlich, Ruby. 1980. State formation in Sumer and the subjugation of women. *Feminist Studies* 6 (Spring): 76–102.

Roth, Walter E. 1908–09. An inquiry into the animism and folk-lore of the Guiana Indians. 30th Annual Report, Bureau of American Ethnology, Washington, DC.

Shaker Manifesto. 1980. American women receiving patents. Vol. 2, no. 7, July, n.p.

Singer, Charles, E. J. Holmyard, and A. R. Hall. 1954. *A History of Technology.* Oxford: Oxford University Press.

Smith, Denis. 1978. Lessons from the history of invention. *The Inventor* (London), January, p. 6ff.

Sokolov, Raymond. 1978. A root awakening. *Natural History* 87 (November): 34 ff.

Spretnak, Charlene. 1978. *Lost Goddesses of Ancient Greece: A Collection of Pre-Hellenic Mythology.* Berkeley: Moon Books.

Stage, Sarah. 1979. *Female Complaints: Lydia Pinkham and the Business of Women's Medicine.* New York: W. W. Norton.

Stanley, Autumn. 1981. Daughters of Isis, daughters of Demeter: When women sowed and reaped. *Women's Studies International Quarterly* 4(3): 289–304.

Stanley, Autumn. 1984. *Mothers of Invention: Women Inventors and Innovators through the Ages.* Metuchen, NJ: Scarecrow.

Stellman, Jeanne M. 1977. *Women's Work, Women's Health: Myths and Realities.* New York: Pantheon.

Stone, Elizabeth. 1978. A Madame Curie from the Bronx. *The New York Times Magazine,* April 9, pp. 29–34ff.

Stowe, Harriet Beecher. 1862. *The Pearl of Orr's Island.* Boston: Houghton Mifflin.

Tanner, Nancy M. 1981. *On Becoming Human: A Model of the Transition from Ape to Human and the Reconstruction of Early Human Social Life.* Cambridge: Cambridge University Press.

Tanner, Nancy, and Adrienne Zihlman. 1976. Women in evolution. Part I: Innovation and selection in human origins. *Signs* 1 (Spring): 585–608.

Thorpe, Susan. 1980. The cure for cramps: It took a woman doctor. *Ms.,* November, p. 36.

Time. 1980. Kendrick obit. October 20, p. 105.

Trescott, Martha Moore. 1979. Julia B. Hall and aluminum. *Dynamos and Virgins Revisited.* Ed. M. M. Trescott. Pp. 149–79.

Trescott, Martha Moore, ed. 1979. *Dynamos and Virgins Revisited: Women and Technological Change in History.* Metuchen, NJ: Scarecrow Press.

Twin, Stephanie L., ed. 1979. *Out of the Bleachers: Writings on Women and Sport.* Old Westbury, NY: Feminist Press.

Voltaire. 1764. *Dictionnaire Philosophique.* Paris: Garnier.

Weiner, Michael A. 1972. *Earth Medicine—Earth Foods: Plant Remedies, Drugs, and Natural Foods of the North American Indians.* London: Collier Macmillan.

White, Anna J. 1866. The mystery explained. *Shaker Almanac,* p. 6ff.

White, Anna J., and Leila S. Taylor. 1904. *Shakerism, its Meaning and Message.* Columbus, OH: Fred J. Heer.

White, Lynn, Jr. 1978. *Medieval Religion and Technology.* Berkeley: University of California Press.

Willard, Frances E., and Mary A. Livermore, eds. 1893. *A Woman of the Century.* Buffalo: Moulton.

Yalow, Rosalyn. 1979. Speech delivered to the American Physical Society Convention, January, New York City.

CHAPTER 2
THE "INDUSTRIAL REVOLUTION" IN THE HOME

Household Technology and Social Change in the Twentieth Century

RUTH SCHWARTZ COWAN

(1976)

When we think about the interaction between technology and society, we tend to think in fairly grandiose terms: massive computers invading the workplace, railroad tracks cutting through vast wildernesses, armies of women and children toiling in the mills. These grand visions have blinded us to an important and rather peculiar technological revolution which has been going on right under our noses: the technological revolution in the home. This revolution has transformed the conduct of our daily lives, but in somewhat unexpected ways. The industrialization of the home was a process very different from the industrialization of other means of production, and the impact of that process was neither what we have been led to believe it was nor what students of the other industrial revolutions would have been led to predict.

Some years ago sociologists of the functionalist school formulated an explanation of the impact of industrial technology on the modern family. Although that explanation was not empirically verified, it has become almost universally accepted.[1] Despite some differences in emphasis, the basic tenets of the traditional interpretation can be roughly summarized as follows:

Before industrialization the family was the basic social unit. Most families were rural, large, and self-sustaining; they produced and processed almost everything that was needed for their own support and for trading in the marketplace, while at the same time performing a host of other functions ranging from mutual protection to entertainment. In these preindustrial families women (adult women, that is) had a lot to do, and their time was almost entirely absorbed by household tasks. Under industrialization the family is much less important. The household is no longer the focus of production; production for the marketplace and production for sustenance have been removed to other locations. Families are smaller and they are urban rather than rural. The number of social functions they perform is much reduced, until almost all that remains is consumption, socialization of small children, and tension management. As their functions diminished, families became atomized; the social bonds that had held them together were loosened. In these postindustrial families women have very little to do, and the tasks with which they fill their time have lost the social utility that they once possessed. Modern women are in trouble, the analysis goes, because modern families are in trouble; and modern families are in trouble because industrial technology has either eliminated or eased almost all their former functions, but modern ideologies have not kept pace with the change. The results of this time lag are several: some women suffer from role anxiety, others land in the divorce courts, some enter the labor market, and others take to burning their brassieres and demanding liberation.

This sociological analysis is a cultural artifact of vast importance. Many Americans believe that it is true and act upon that belief in various ways: some hope to reestablish family solidarity by relearning lost productive crafts—baking bread, tending a vegetable garden—others dismiss the women's liberation movement as "simply a bunch of affluent housewives who have nothing better to do with their time." As disparate as they may seem, these reactions have a common ideological source—the standard sociological analysis of the impact of technological change on family life.

As a theory this functionalist approach has much to recommend it, but at present we have very little evidence to back it up. Family history is an infant discipline, and what evidence it has produced in recent years does not lend credence to the standard view.[2] Philippe Ariès has shown, for example, that in France the ideal of the small nuclear family predates industrialization by more than a century.[3] Historical demographers working on data from English and French families have been surprised to find that most families were quite small and that several generations did not ordinarily reside together; the extended family, which is supposed to have been the rule in preindustrial societies, did not occur in colonial New England either.[4] Rural English families routinely employed domestic servants, and even very small English villages had their butchers and bakers and candlestick makers; all these persons must have eased some of the chores that would otherwise have been the housewife's burden.[5] Preindustrial housewives no doubt had much with which to occupy their time, but we may have reason to wonder whether there was quite as much pressure on them as sociological orthodoxy has led us to suppose. The large rural family that was sufficient unto itself back there on the prairies may have been limited to the prairies—or it may never have existed at all (except, that is, in the reveries of sociologists).

Even if all the empirical evidence were to mesh with the functionalist theory, the theory would still have problems, because its logical structure is rather weak. Comparing the average farm family in 1750 (assuming that you knew what that family was like) with the average urban family in 1950 in order to discover the significant social changes that had occurred is an exercise rather like comparing apples with oranges; the differences between the fruits may have nothing to do with the differences in their evolution. Transferring the analogy to the case at hand, what we really need to know is the difference, say, between an urban laboring family of 1750 and an urban laboring family one hundred and then two hundred years later, or the difference between the rural nonfarm middle classes in all three centuries, or the difference between the urban rich yesterday and today. Surely in each of these cases the analyses will look very different from what we have been led to expect. As a guess we might find that for the urban laboring families the changes have been precisely the opposite of what the model predicted; that is, that their family structure is much firmer today than it was in centuries past. Similarly, for the rural nonfarm middle class the results might be equally surprising; we might find that married women of that class rarely did any housework at all in 1890 because they had farm girls as servants, whereas in 1950 they bore the full brunt of the work themselves. I could go on, but the point is, I hope, clear: in order to verify or falsify the functionalist theory, it will be necessary to know more than we presently do about the impact of industrialization on families of similar classes and geographical locations.

With this problem in mind I have, for the purposes of this initial study, deliberately limited myself to one kind of technological change affecting one aspect of family life in only one of the many social classes of families that might have been considered. What happened, I asked, to middle-class American women when the implements with which they did their everyday household work changed? Did the technological change in household appliances have any effect upon the structure of American households, or upon the ideologies that governed the behavior of American women, or upon the functions that families needed to perform? Middle-class American women were defined as actual or potential readers of the better-quality women's magazines, such as the *Ladies' Home Journal, American Home, Parents' Magazine, Good Housekeeping,* and *McCall's.*[6] Nonfictional material (articles and advertisements) in those magazines was used as a partial indicator of some of the technological and social changes that were occurring.

The *Ladies' Home Journal* has been in continuous publication since 1886. A casual survey of the nonfiction in the *Journal* yields the immediate impression that that decade between the end of World War I and the beginning of the depression witnessed the most drastic changes in patterns of household work. Statistical data bear out this impression. Before 1918, for example, illustrations of homes lit by gaslight could still be found in the *Journal;* by 1928 gaslight had disappeared. In 1917 only one-quarter (24.3 percent) of the dwellings in the United States had been electrified, but by 1920 this figure had doubled (47.4 percent—for rural nonfarm and urban dwellings), and by 1930 it had risen to four-fifths percent).[7] If electrification had meant simply the change from gas or oil lamps to electric lights, the changes in the housewife's routines might not have been very great (except for eliminating the chore of cleaning and filling oil lamps); but changes in lighting were the least of the changes that electrification implied. Small electric appliances followed quickly on the heels of the electric light, and some of those augured much more profound changes in the housewife's routine.

Ironing, for example, had traditionally been one of the most dreadful household chores, especially in warm weather when the kitchen stove had to be kept hot for the better part of the day; irons were heavy and they had to be returned to the stove frequently to be reheated. Electric irons eased a good part of this burden.[8] They were relatively inexpensive and very quickly replaced their predecessors; advertisements for electric irons first began to appear in the ladies' magazines after the war, and by the end of the decade the old flatiron had disappeared; by 1929 a survey of one hundred Ford employees revealed that ninety-eight of them had the new electric irons in their homes.[9]

Data on the diffusion of electric washing machines are somewhat harder to come by; but it is clear from the advertisements in the magazines, particularly advertisements for laundry soap, that by the middle of the 1920s those machines could be found in a significant number of homes. The washing machine is depicted just about as frequently as the laundry tub by the middle of the 1920s; in 1929, forty-nine out of those one hundred Ford workers had the machines in their homes. The washing machines did not drastically reduce the time that had to be spent on household laundry, as they did not go through their cycles automatically and did not spin dry; the housewife had to stand guard, stopping and starting the machine at appropriate times, adding soap, sometimes attaching the drain pipes, and putting the clothes through the wringer manually. The machines did, however, reduce a good part of the drudgery that once had been associated with washday, and this was a matter of no small consequence.[10] Soap powders appeared on the market in the early 1920s, thus eliminating the need to scrape and boil bars of laundry soap.[11] By the end of the 1920s Blue Monday must have been considerably less blue for some housewives—and probably considerably less "Monday," for with an electric iron, a washing machine, and a hot water heater, there was no reason to limit the washing to just one day of the week.

Like the routines of washing the laundry, the routines of personal hygiene must have been transformed for many households during the 1920s—the years of the bathroom mania.[12] More and more bathrooms were built in older homes, and new homes began to include them as a matter of course. Before the war most bathroom fixtures (tubs, sinks, and toilets) were made out of porcelain by hand; each bathroom was custom-made for the house in which it was installed. After the war industrialization descended upon the bathroom industry; cast-iron enamelware went into mass production and fittings were standardized. In 1921 the dollar value of the production of enameled sanitary fixtures was $2.4 million, the same as it had been in 1915. By 1923, just two years later, that figure had doubled to $4.8 million; it rose again, to $5.1 million, in 1925.[13] The first recessed, double-shell cast-iron enameled bathtub was put on the market in the early 1920s. A decade later the standard American bathroom had achieved its standard American form: the recessed tub, plus tiled floors and walls, brass plumbing, a single-unit toilet, an enameled sink, and a medicine chest, all set into a small room which was very often five feet square.[14] The bathroom evolved more quickly than any other room of the house; its standardized form was accomplished in just over a decade.

Along with bathrooms came modernized systems for heating hot water: sixty-one percent of the homes in Zanesville, Ohio, had indoor plumbing with centrally heated water by 1926, and eighty-three percent of the homes valued over $2,000 in Muncie, Indiana, had hot and cold running water by 1935.[15] These figures may not be typical of small American cities (or even large American cities) at those times, but they do jibe with the impression that one gets from the magazines: after 1918 references to hot water heated on the kitchen range, either for laundering or for bathing, become increasingly difficult to find.

Similarly, during the 1920s many homes were outfitted with central heating; in Muncie most of the homes of the business class had basement heating in 1924; by 1935 Federal Emergency Relief Administration data for the city indicated that only 22.4 percent of the dwellings valued over $2,000 were still heated by a kitchen stove.[16] What all these changes meant in terms of new habits for the average housewife is somewhat hard to calculate; changes there must have been, but it is difficult to know whether those changes produced an overall saving of labor and/or time. Some chores were eliminated—hauling water, heating water on the stove, maintaining the kitchen fire—but other chores were added—most notably the chore of keeping yet another room scrupulously clean.

It is not, however, difficult to be certain about the changing habits that were associated with the new American kitchen—a kitchen from which the coal stove had disappeared. In Muncie in 1924, cooking with gas was done in two out of three homes; in 1935 only five percent of the homes valued over $2,000 still had coal or wood stoves for cooking.[17] After 1918 advertisements for coal and wood stoves disappeared from the *Ladies' Home Journal;* stove manufacturers purveyed only their gas, oil, or electric models. Articles giving advice to homemakers on how to deal with the trials and tribulations of starting, stoking, and maintaining a coal or a wood fire also disappeared. Thus it seems a safe assumption that most middle-class homes had switched to the new method of cooking by the time the depression began. The change in routine that was predicated on the change from coal or wood to gas or oil was profound; aside from the elimination of such chores as loading the fuel and removing the ashes, the new stoves were much easier to light, maintain, and regulate (even when they did not have thermostats, as the earliest models did not).[18] Kitchens were, in addition, much easier to clean when they did not have coal dust regularly tracked through them; one writer in the *Ladies' Home Journal* estimated that kitchen cleaning was reduced by one-half when coal stoves were eliminated.[19]

Along with new stoves came new foodstuffs and new dietary habits. Canned foods had been on the market since the middle of the nineteenth century, but they did not become an appreciable part of the standard middle-class diet until the 1920s—if the recipes given in cookbooks and in women's magazines are a reliable guide. By 1918 the variety of foods available in cans had been considerably expanded from the peas, corn, and succotash of the nineteenth century; an American housewife with sufficient means could have purchased almost any fruit or vegetable and quite a surprising array of ready-made meals in a can—from Heinz's spaghetti in meat sauce to Purity Cross's lobster à la Newburg. By the middle of the 1920s home canning was becoming a lost art. Canning recipes were relegated to the back pages of the women's magazines; the business-class wives of Muncie reported that, while their mothers had once spent the better part of the summer and fall canning, they themselves rarely put up anything, except an occasional jelly or batch of tomatoes.[20] In part this was also due to changes in the technology of marketing food; increased use of refrigerated railroad cars during this period meant that fresh fruits and vegetables were in the markets all year round at reasonable prices.[21] By the early 1920s convenience foods were also appearing on American tables: cold breakfast cereals, pancake mixes, bouillon cubes, and packaged desserts could be found. Wartime shortages accustomed Americans to eating much lighter meals than they had previously been wont to do; and as fewer family members were taking all their meals at home (businessmen started to eat lunch in restaurants downtown, and factories and schools began installing cafeterias), there was simply less cooking to be done, and what there was of it was easier to do.[22]

Many of the changes just described—from hand power to electric power, from coal and wood to gas and oil as fuels for cooking, from one-room heating to central heating, from pumping water to running water—are enormous technological changes. Changes of a similar dimension, either in the fundamental technology of an industry, in the diffusion of that technology, or in the routines of workers, would have long since been labeled an "industrial revolution." The change from the laundry tub to the washing machine is no less profound than the change from the hand loom to the power loom; the change from pumping water to turning on a water faucet is no less destructive of traditional habits than the change from manual to electric calculating. It seems odd to speak of an "industrial revolution" connected with housework, odd because we are talking about the technology of such homely things, and odd because we are not accustomed to thinking of housewives as a labor force or of housework as an economic commodity—but despite this oddity, I think the term is altogether appropriate.

In this case other questions come immediately to mind, questions that we do not hesitate to ask, say, about textile workers in Britain in the early nineteenth century, but we have never thought to ask about housewives in America in the twentieth century. What happened to this particular workforce when the technology of its work was revolutionized? Did structural changes occur? Were new jobs created for which new skills were required? Can we discern new ideologies that influenced the behavior of the workers?

The answer to all of these questions, surprisingly enough, seems to be yes. There were marked structural changes in the workforce, changes that increased the work load and the job description of the workers that remained. New jobs were created for which new skills were required; these jobs were not physically burdensome, but they may have taken up as much time as the jobs they had replaced. New ideologies were also created, ideologies which reinforced new behavioral patterns, patterns that we might not have been led to expect if we had followed the sociologists' model to the letter. Middle-class housewives, the women who must have first felt the impact of the new household technology, were not flocking into the divorce courts or the labor market or the forums of political protest in the years immediately after the revolution in their work. What they were doing was sterilizing baby bottles, shepherding their children to dancing classes and music lessons, planning nutritious meals, shopping for new clothes, studying child psychology, and hand stitching color-coordinated curtains—all of which chores (and others like them) the standard sociological model has apparently not provided for.

The significant change in the structure of the household labor force was the disappearance of paid and unpaid servants (unmarried daughters, maiden aunts, and grandparents fall in the latter category) as household workers—and the imposition of the entire job on the housewife herself. Leaving aside for a moment the question of which was cause and which effect (did the disappearance of the servant create a demand for the new technology, or did the new technology make the servant obsolete?), the phenomenon itself is relatively easy to document. Before World War I, when illustrators in the women's magazines depicted women doing housework, the women were very often servants. When the lady of the house was drawn, she was often the person being served, or she was supervising the serving, or she was adding an elegant finishing touch to the work. Nursemaids diapered babies, seamstresses pinned up hems, waitresses served meals, laundresses did the wash, and cooks did the cooking. By the end of the 1920s the servants had disappeared from those illustrations; all those jobs were being done by housewives—elegantly manicured and coiffed, to be sure, but housewives nonetheless.

If we are tempted to suppose that illustrations in advertisements are not a reliable indicator of structural changes of this sort, we can corroborate the changes in other ways. Apparently, the illustrators really did know whereof they drew. Statistically the number of persons throughout the country employed in household service dropped from 1,851,000 in 1910 to 1,411,000 in 1920, while the number of households enumerated in the census rose from 20.3 million to 24.4 million.[23] In Indiana the ratio of households to servants increased from 13.5/1 in 1890 to 30.5/1 in 1920, and in the country as a whole the number of paid domestic servants per 1,000 population dropped from 98.9 in 1900 to 58.0 in 1920.[24] The business-class housewives of Muncie reported that they employed approximately one-half as many woman-hours of domestic service as their mothers had done.[25]

In case we are tempted to doubt these statistics (and indeed statistics about household labor are particularly unreliable, as the labor is often transient, part-time, or simply unreported), we can turn to articles on the servant problem, the disappearance of unpaid family workers, the design of kitchens, or to architectural drawings for houses. All of this evidence reiterates the same point: qualified servants were difficult to find; their wages had risen and their numbers fallen; houses were being designed without maid's rooms; daughters and unmarried aunts were finding jobs downtown; kitchens were being designed for housewives, not for servants.[26] The first home with a kitchen that was not an entirely separate room was designed by Frank Lloyd Wright in 1934.[27] In 1937 Emily Post invented a new character for her etiquette books: Mrs. Three-in-One, the woman who is her own cook, waitress, and hostess.[28] There must have been many new Mrs. Three-in-Ones abroad in the land during the 1920s.

As the number of household assistants declined, the number of household tasks increased. The middle-class housewife was expected to demonstrate competence at several tasks that previously had not been in her purview or had not existed at all. Child care is the most obvious example. The average housewife had fewer children than her mother had had, but she was expected to do things for her children that her mother would never have dreamed of doing: to prepare their special infant formulas, sterilize their bottles, weigh them every day, see to it that they ate nutritionally balanced meals, keep them isolated and confined when they had even the slightest illness, consult with their teachers frequently, and chauffeur them to dancing lessons, music lessons, and evening parties.[29] There was very little Freudianism in this new attitude toward child care: mothers were not spending more time and effort on their children because they feared the psychological trauma of separation, but because competent nursemaids could not be found, and the new theories of child care required constant attention from well-informed persons— persons who were willing and able to read about the latest discoveries in nutrition, in the control of contagious diseases, or in the techniques of behavioral psychology. These persons simply had to be their mothers.

Consumption of economic goods provides another example of the housewife's expanded job description; like child care, the new tasks associated with consumption were not necessarily physically burdensome, but they were time consuming, and they required the acquisition of new skills.[30] Home economists and the editors of women's magazines tried to teach housewives to spend their money wisely. The present generation of housewives, it was argued, had been reared by mothers who did not ordinarily shop for things like clothing, bed linens, or towels; consequently modern housewives did not know how to shop and would have to be taught. Furthermore, their mothers had not been accustomed to the wide variety of goods that were now available in the modern marketplace; the new housewives had to be taught not just to be consumers, but to be informed consumers.[31] Several contemporary observers believed that shopping and shopping wisely were occupying increasing amounts of housewives' time.[32]

Several of these contemporary observers also believed that standards of household care changed during the decade of the 1920s.[33] The discovery of the "household germ" led to almost fetishistic concern about the cleanliness of the home. The amount and frequency of laundering probably increased, as bed linen and underwear were changed more often, children's clothes were made increasingly out of washable fabrics, and men's shirts no longer had replaceable collars and cuffs.[34] Unfortunately all these changes in standards are difficult to document, being changes in the things that people regard as so insignificant as to be unworthy of comment; the improvement in standards seems a likely possibility, but not something that can be proved.

In any event we do have various time studies which demonstrate somewhat surprisingly that housewives with conveniences were spending just as much time on household duties as were housewives without them—or, to put it another way, housework, like so many other types of work, expands to fill the time available.[35] A study comparing the time spent per week in housework by 288 farm families and 154 town families in Oregon in 1928 revealed 61 hours spent by farm wives and 63.4 hours by town wives; in 1929 a U.S. Department of Agriculture study of families in various states produced almost identical results.[36] Surely if the standard sociological model were valid, housewives in towns, where presumably the benefits of specialization and electrification were most likely to be available, should have been spending far less time at their work than their rural sisters. However, just after World War II economists at Bryn Mawr College reported the same phenomenon: 60.55 hours spent by farm housewives, 78.35 hours by women in small cities, 80.57 hours by women in large ones—precisely the reverse of the results that were expected.[37] A recent survey of time studies conducted between 1920 and 1970 concludes that the time spent on housework by nonemployed housewives has remained remarkably constant throughout the period.[38] All these results point in the same direction: mechanization of the household meant that time expended on some jobs decreased, but also that new jobs were substituted, and in some cases— notably laundering—time expenditures for old jobs increased because of higher standards. The advantages of mechanization may be somewhat more dubious than they seem at first glance.

As the job of the housewife changed, the connected ideologies also changed; there was a clearly perceptible difference in the attitudes that women brought to housework before and after World War I.[39] Before the war the trials of doing housework in a servantless home were discussed and they were regarded as just that—trials, necessary chores that had to be got through until a qualified servant could be found. After the war, housework changed: it was no longer a trial and a chore, but something quite different—an emotional "trip." Laundering was not just laundering, but an expression of love; the housewife who truly loved her family would protect them from the embarrassment of tattletale gray. Feeding the family was not just feeding the family, but a way to express the housewife's artistic inclinations and a way to encourage feelings of family loyalty and affection. Diapering the baby was not just diapering, but a time to build the baby's sense of security and love for the mother. Cleaning the bathroom sink was not just cleaning, but an exercise of protective maternal instincts, providing a way for the housewife to keep her family safe from disease. Tasks of this emotional magnitude could not possibly be delegated to servants, even assuming that qualified servants could be found.

Women who failed at these new household tasks were bound to feel guilt about their failure. If I had to choose one word to characterize the temper of the women's magazines during the 1920s, it would be "guilt." Readers of the better-quality women's magazines are portrayed as feeling guilty a good lot of the time, and when they are not guilty they are embarrassed: guilty if their infants have not gained enough weight, embarrassed if their drains are clogged, guilty if their children go to school in soiled clothes, guilty if all the germs behind the bathroom sink are not eradicated, guilty if they fail to notice the first signs of an oncoming cold, embarrassed if accused of having body odor, guilty if their sons go to school without good breakfasts, guilty if their daughters are unpopular because of old-fashioned, or unironed, or— heaven forbid—dirty dresses. In earlier times women were made to feel guilty if they abandoned their children or were too free with their affections. In the years after World War I, American women were made to feel guilty about sending their children to school in scuffed shoes. Between the two kinds of guilt there is a world of difference.

Let us return for a moment to the sociological model with which this essay began. The model predicts that changing patterns of household work will be correlated with at least two striking indicators of social change: the divorce rate and the rate of married women's labor force participation. That correlation may indeed exist, but it certainly is not reflected in the women's magazines of the 1920s and 1930s: divorce and full-time paid employment were not part of the lifestyle or the life pattern of the middle-class housewife as she was idealized in her magazines.

There were social changes attendant upon the introduction of modern technology into the home, but they were not the changes that the traditional functionalist model predicts; on this point a close analysis of the statistical data corroborates the impression conveyed in the magazines. The divorce rate was indeed rising during the years between the wars, but it was not rising nearly so fast for the middle and upper classes (who had, presumably, easier access to the new technology) as it was for the lower classes. By almost every gauge of socioeconomic status—income, prestige of husband's work, education—the divorce rate is higher for persons lower on the socioeconomic scale—and this is a phenomenon that has been constant over time.[40]

The supposed connection between improved household technology and married women's labor force participation seems just as dubious, and on the same grounds. The single socioeconomic factor which correlates most strongly (in cross-sectional studies) with married women's employment is husband's income, and the correlation is strongly negative; the higher his income, the less likely it will be that she is working.[41] Women's labor force participation increased during the 1920s but this increase was due to the influx of single women into the force. Married women's participation increased slightly during those years, but that increase was largely in factory labor—precisely the kind of work that middle-class women (who were, again, much more likely to have labor-saving devices at home) were least likely to do.[42] If there were a necessary connection between the improvement of household technology and either of these two social indicators, we would expect the data to be precisely the reverse of what in fact has occurred: women in the higher social classes should have fewer functions at home and should therefore be more (rather than less) likely to seek paid employment or divorce.

Thus for middle-class American housewives between the wars, the social changes that we can document are not the social changes that the functionalist model predicts; rather than changes in divorce or patterns of paid employment, we find changes in the structure of the workforce, in its skills, and in its ideology. These social changes were concomitant with a series of technological changes in the equipment that was used to do the work. What is the relationship between these two series of phenomena? Is it possible to demonstrate causality or the direction of that causality? Was the decline in the number of households employing servants a cause or an effect of the mechanization of those households? Both are, after all, equally possible. The declining supply of household servants, as well as their rising wages, may have stimulated a demand for new appliances at the same time that the acquisition of new appliances may have made householders less inclined to employ the laborers who were on the market. Are there any techniques available to the historian to help us answer these questions?

In order to establish causality, we need to find a connecting link between the two sets of phenomena, a mechanism that, in real life, could have made the causality work. In this case a connecting link, an intervening agent between the social and the technological changes, comes immediately to mind: the advertiser—by which term I mean a combination of the manufacturer of the new goods, the advertising agent who promoted the goods, and the periodical that published the promotion. All the new devices and new foodstuffs that were being offered to American households were being manufactured and marketed by large companies which had considerable amounts of capital invested in their production: General Electric, Procter & Gamble, General Foods, Lever Brothers, Frigidaire, Campbell's, Del Monte, American Can, Atlantic & Pacific Tea—these were all well-established firms by the time the household revolution began, and they were all in a position to pay for national advertising campaigns to promote their new products and services. And pay they did; one reason for the expanding size and number of women's magazines in the 1920s was, no doubt, the expansion in revenues from available advertisers.[43]

Those national advertising campaigns were likely to have been powerful stimulators of the social changes that occurred in the household labor force; the advertisers probably did not initiate the changes, but they certainly encouraged them. Most of the advertising campaigns manifestly worked, so they must have touched upon areas of real concern for American housewives. Appliance ads specifically suggested that the acquisition of one gadget or another would make it possible to fire the maid, spend more time with the children, or have the afternoon free for shopping.[44] Similarly, many advertisements played upon the embarrassment and guilt which were now associated with household work. Ralston, Cream of Wheat, and Ovaltine were not themselves responsible for the compulsive practice of weighing infants and children repeatedly (after every meal for newborns, every day in infancy, every week later on), but the manufacturers certainly did not stint on capitalizing upon the guilt that women apparently felt if their offspring did not gain the required amounts of weight.[45] And yet again, many of the earliest attempts to spread "wise" consumer practices were undertaken by large corporations and the magazines that desired their advertising: mail-order shopping guides, "product-testing" services, pseudoinformative pamphlets, and other such promotional devices were all techniques for urging the housewife to buy new things under the guise of training her in her role as skilled consumer.[46]

Thus the advertisers could well be called the "ideologues" of the 1920s, encouraging certain very specific social changes—as ideologues are wont to do. Not surprisingly, the changes that occurred were precisely the ones that would gladden the hearts and fatten the purses of the advertisers; fewer household servants meant a greater demand for labor and timesaving devices; more household tasks for women meant more and more specialized products that they would need to buy; more guilt and embarrassment about their failure to succeed at their work meant a greater likelihood that they would buy the products that were intended to minimize that failure. Happy, full-time housewives in intact families spend a lot of money to maintain their households; divorced women and working women do not. The advertisers may not have created the image of the ideal American housewife that dominated the 1920s—the woman who cheerfully and skillfully set about making everyone in her family perfectly happy and perfectly healthy—but they certainly helped to perpetuate it.

The role of the advertiser as connecting link between social change and technological change is at this juncture simply a hypothesis, with nothing much more to recommend it than an argument from plausibility. Further research may serve to test the hypothesis, but testing it may not settle the question of which was cause and which effect—if that question can ever be settled definitively in historical work. What seems most likely in this case, as in so many others, is that cause and effect are not separable, that there is a dynamic interaction between the social changes that married women were experiencing and the technological changes that were occurring in their homes. Viewed this way, the disappearance of competent servants becomes one of the factors that stimulated the mechanization of homes, and this mechanization of homes becomes a factor (though by no means the only one) in the disappearance of servants. Similarly, the emotionalization of housework becomes both cause and effect of the mechanization of that work; and the expansion of time spent on new tasks becomes both cause and effect of the introduction of timesaving devices. For example the social pressure to spend more time in child care may have led to a decision to purchase the devices;

once purchased, the devices could indeed have been used to save time—although often they were not.

If one holds the question of causality in abeyance, the example of household work still has some useful lessons to teach about the general problem of technology and social change. The standard sociological model for the impact of modern technology on family life clearly needs some revision: at least for middle-class nonrural American families in the twentieth century, the social changes were not the ones that the standard model predicts. In these families the functions of at least one member, the housewife, have increased rather than decreased; and the dissolution of family life has not in fact occurred.

Our standard notions about what happens to a workforce under the pressure of technological change may also need revision. When industries become mechanized and rationalized, we expect certain general changes in the workforce to occur: its structure becomes more highly differentiated, individual workers become more specialized, managerial functions increase, and the emotional context of the work disappears. On all four counts our expectations are reversed with regard to household work. The workforce became less rather than more differentiated as domestic servants, unmarried daughters, maiden aunts, and grandparents left the household and as chores which had once been performed by commercial agencies (laundries, delivery services, milkmen) were delegated to the housewife. The individual workers also became less specialized; the new housewife was now responsible for every aspect of life in her household, from scrubbing the bathroom floor to keeping abreast of the latest literature in child psychology.

The housewife is just about the only unspecialized worker left in America—a veritable jane-of-all-trades at a time when the jacks-of-all-trades have disappeared. As her work became generalized the housewife was also proletarianized: formerly she was ideally the manager of several other subordinate workers; now she was idealized as the manager and the worker combined. Her managerial functions have not entirely disappeared, but they have certainly diminished and have been replaced by simple manual labor; the middle-class, fairly well educated housewife ceased to be a personnel manager and became, instead, a chauffeur, charwoman, and short-order cook. The implications of this phenomenon, the proletarianization of a workforce that had previously seen itself as predominantly managerial, deserve to be explored at greater length than is possible here, because I suspect that they will explain certain aspects of the women's liberation movement of the 1960s and 1970s which have previously eluded explanation: why, for example, the movement's greatest strength lies in social and economic groups who seem, on the surface at least, to need it least—women who are white, well-educated, and middle-class.

Finally, instead of desensitizing the emotions that were connected with household work, the industrial revolution in the home seems to have heightened the emotional context of the work, until a woman's sense of self-worth became a function of her success at arranging bits of fruit to form a clown's face in a gelatin salad. That pervasive social illness, which Betty Friedan characterized as "the problem that has no name," arose not among workers who found that their labor brought no emotional satisfaction, but among workers who found that their work was invested with emotional weight far out of proportion to its own inherent value: "How long," a friend of mine is fond of asking, "can we continue to believe that we will have orgasms while waxing the kitchen floor?"

NOTES

1. For some classic statements of the standard view, see W. F. Ogburn and M. F. Nimkoff, *Technology and the Changing Family* (Cambridge, MA, 1955); Robert F. Winch, *The Modern Family* (New York, 1952); and William J. Goode, *The Family* (Englewood Cliffs, NJ, 1964).

2. This point is made by Peter Laslett in "The Comparative History of Household and Family," in *The American Family in Social Historical Perspective,* ed. Michael Gordon (New York, 1973), pp. 28–29.

3. Philippe Aries, *Centuries of Childhood: A Social History of Family Life* (New York, 1960).

4. See Laslett, pp. 20–24; and Philip J. Greven, "Family Structure in Seventeenth Century Andover, Massachusetts," *William and Mary Quarterly* 23 (1966): 234–56.

5. Peter Laslett, *The World We Have Lost* (New York, 1965), passim.

6. For purposes of historical inquiry, this definition of middle-class status corresponds to a sociological reality, although it is not, admittedly, very rigorous. Our contemporary experience confirms that there are class differences reflected in magazines, and this situation seems to have existed in the past as well. On this issue see Robert S. Lynd and Helen M. Lynd, *Middletown: A Study in Contemporary American Culture* (New York, 1929), pp. 240–44, where the marked difference in magazines subscribed to by the business-class wives as opposed to the working-class wives is discussed; Salme Steinberg, "Reformer in the Marketplace: E. W. Bok and *The Ladies Home Journal*" (Ph.D. diss., Johns Hopkins University, 1973), where the conscious attempt of the publisher to attract a middle-class audience is discussed; and Lee Rainwater et al., *Workingman's Wife* (New York, 1959), which was commissioned by the publisher of working-class women's magazines in an attempt to understand the attitudinal differences between working-class and middle-class women.

7. *Historical Statistics of the United States, Colonial Times to 1957* (Washington, DC, 1960), p. 510.

8. The gas iron, which was available to women whose homes were supplied with natural gas, was an earlier improvement on the old-fashioned flatiron, but this kind of iron is so rarely mentioned in the sources that I used for this survey that I am unable to determine the extent of its diffusion.

9. Hazel Kyrk, *Economic Problems of the Family* (New York, 1933), p. 368, reporting a study in *Monthly Labor Review* 30 (1930): 1209–52.

10. Although this point seems intuitively obvious, there is some evidence that it may not be true. Studies of energy expenditure during housework have indicated that by far the greatest effort is expended in hauling and lifting the wet wash, tasks which were not eliminated by the introduction of washing machines. In addition, if the introduction of the machines served to increase the total amount of wash that was done by

the housewife, this would tend to cancel the energy-saving effects of the machines themselves.

11. Rinso was the first granulated soap; it came on the market in 1918. Lux Flakes had been available since 1906; however it was not intended to be a general laundry product but rather one for laundering delicate fabrics. "Lever Brothers," *Fortune 26* (November 1940): 95.

12. I take this account, and the term, from Lynd and Lynd, p. 97. Obviously, there were many American homes that had bathrooms before the 1920s, particularly urban row houses, and I have found no way of determining whether the increases of the 1920s were more marked than in previous decades. The rural situation was quite different from the urban; the President's Conference on Home Building and Home Ownership reported that in the late 1920s, seventy-one percent of the urban families surveyed had bathrooms, but only thirty-three percent of the rural families did (John M. Cries and James Ford, eds., *Homemaking, Home Furnishing and Information Services*, President's Conference on Home Building and Home Ownership, vol. 10 [Washington, DC, 1932], p. 13).

13. These data come from Siegfried Giedion, *Mechanization Takes Command* (New York, 1948), pp. 685–703.

14. For a description of the standard bathroom see Helen Sprackling, "The Modern Bathroom," *Parents' Magazine* 8 (February 1933): 25.

15. *Zanesville, Ohio and Thirty-six Other American Cities* (New York, 1927), p. 65. Also see Robert S. Lynd and Helen M. Lynd, *Middletown in Transition* (New York, 1936), p. 537. Middletown is Muncie, Indiana.

16. Lynd and Lynd, *Middletown*, p. 96, and *Middletown in Transition*, p. 539.

17. Lynd and Lynd, *Middletown*, p. 98, and *Middletown in Transition*, p. 562.

18. On the advantages of the new stoves, see *Boston Cooking School Cookbook* (Boston, 1916), pp. 15–20; and Russell Lynes, *The Domesticated Americans* (New York, 1957), pp. 119–20.

19. "How to Save Coal While Cooking," *Ladies' Home Journal* 25 (January 1908): 44.

20. Lynd and Lynd, *Middletown*, p. 156.

21. Ibid.; see also "Safeway Stores," *Fortune* 26 (October 1940): 60.

22. Lynd and Lynd, *Middletown*, pp. 134–35, 153–54.

23. *Historical Statistics*, pp. 16, 77.

24. For Indiana data, see Lynd and Lynd, *Middletown*, p. 169. For national data, see D. L. Kaplan and M. Claire Casey, *Occupational Trends in the United States, 1900–1950*, U.S. Bureau of the Census Working Paper no. 5 (Washington, DC, 1958), table 6. The extreme drop in numbers of servants between 1910 and 1920 also lends credence to the notion that this demographic factor stimulated the industrial revolution in housework.

25. Lynd and Lynd, *Middletown*, p. 169.

26. On the disappearance of maiden aunts, unmarried daughters, and grandparents, see Lynd and Lynd, *Middletown*, pp. 25, 99, 110; Edward Bok, Editorial, *American Home* 1 (October 1928): 15; "How to Buy Life Insurance," *Ladies' Home Journal* 45 (March 1928): 35. The house plans appeared every month in *American Home*, which began publication in 1928. On kitchen design, see Giedion, pp. 603–21; Editorial, *Ladies' Home Journal* 45 (April 1928): 36; advertisement for Hoosier kitchen cabinets, *Ladies' Home Journal* 45 (April 1928): 117. Articles on servant problems include "The Vanishing Servant Girl," *Ladies' Home Journal* 35 (May 1918): 48; "Housework, Then and Now," *American Home* 8 (June 1932): 128; "The Servant Problem," *Fortune* 24 (March 1938): 80–84; and *Report of the YWCA Commission on Domestic Service* (Los Angeles, 1915).

27. Giedion, p. 619. Wright's new kitchen was installed in the Malcolm Willey House, Minneapolis.

28. Emily Post, *Etiquette: The Blue Book of Social Usage*, 5th ed., rev. (New York, 1937), p. 823.

29. This analysis is based upon various child-care articles that appeared during the period in the *Ladies' Home Journal, American Home,* and *Parents' Magazine.* See also Lynd and Lynd, *Middletown,* ch. 11.

30. John Kenneth Galbraith has remarked upon the advent of woman as consumer in *Economics and the Public Purpose* (Boston, 1973), pp. 29–37.

31. There was a sharp reduction in the number of patterns for home sewing offered by the women's magazines during the 1920s; the patterns were replaced by articles on "what is available in the shops this season." On consumer education see, for example, "How to Buy Towels," *Ladies' Home Journal* 45 (February 1928): 134; "Buying Table Linen," *Ladies' Home Journal* 45 (March 1928): 43; and "When the Bride Goes Shopping," *American Home* 1 (January 1928): 370.

32. See, for example, Lynd and Lynd, *Middletown,* pp. 176, 196; and Margaret G. Reid, *Economics of Household Production* (New York, 1934), ch. 13.

33. See Reid, pp. 64–68; and Kyrk, p. 98.

34. See advertisement for Cleanliness Institute—"Self-respect thrives on soap and water," *Ladies' Home Journal* 45 (February 1928): 107. On changing bed linen, see "When the Bride Goes Shopping," *American Home* 1 (January 1928): 370. On laundering children's clothes, see, "Making a Layette," *Ladies' Home Journal* 45 (January 1928): 20; and Josephine Baker, "The Youngest Generation," *Ladies' Home Journal* 45 (March 1928): 185.

35. This point is also discussed at length in my unpublished paper "What Did Labor-saving Devices Really Save?"

36. As reported in Kyrk, p. 51.

37. Bryn Mawr College Department of Social Economy, *Women During the War and After* (Philadelphia, 1945); and Ethel Goldwater, "Woman's Place," *Commentary* 4 (December 1947): 578–85.

38. JoAnn Vanek, "Keeping Busy: Time Spent in Housework, United States, 1920–1970" (Ph.D. diss., University of Michigan, 1973). Vanek reports an average of fifty-three hours per week over the whole period. This figure is significantly lower than the figures reported in the text, because each time study of housework has been done on a different basis, including different activities under the aegis of housework, and using different methods of reporting time expenditures; the Bryn Mawr and Oregon studies are useful for the comparative figures that they report internally, but they cannot easily be compared with each other.

39. This analysis is based upon my reading of the middle-class women's magazines between 1918 and 1930. For detailed documentation see my paper, "Two Washes in the Morning and a Bridge Party at Night: The American Housewife Between the Wars," *Women's Studies* (in press). It is quite possible that the appearance of guilt as a strong element in advertising is more the result of new techniques developed by the advertising industry than the result of attitudinal changes in the audience—a possibility that I had not considered when doing the initial research for this paper. See A. Michael McMahon, "An American Courtship: Psychologists and Advertising Theory in the Progressive Era," *American Studies* 13 (1972): 5–18.

40. For a summary of the literature on differential divorce rates, see Winch, p. 706; and William J. Goode, *After Divorce* (New York, 1956), p. 44. The earliest papers demonstrating this differential rate appeared in 1927, 1935, and 1939.

41. For a summary of the literature on married women's labor force participation, see Juanita Kreps, *Sex in the Marketplace: American Women at Work* (Baltimore, 1971), pp. 19–24.

42. Valerie Kincaid Oppenheimer, *The Female Labor Force in the United States,* Population Monograph Series, no. 5 (Berkeley, 1970), pp. 1–15; and Lynd and Lynd, *Middletown,* pp. 124–27.

43. On the expanding size, number, and influence of women's magazines during the 1920s, see Lynd and Lynd, *Middletown,* pp. 150, 240–44.

44. See, for example, the advertising campaigns of General Electric and Hotpoint

from 1918 through the rest of the decade of the 1920s; both campaigns stressed the likelihood that electric appliances would become a thrifty replacement for domestic servants.

45. The practice of carefully observing children's weight was initiated by medical authorities, national and local governments, and social welfare agencies, as part of the campaign to improve child health which began about the time of World War I.

46. These practices were ubiquitous. *American Home,* for example, which was published by Doubleday, assisted its advertisers by publishing a list of informative pamphlets that readers could obtain; devoting half a page to an index of its advertisers; specifically naming manufacturer's and list prices in articles about products and services; allotting almost one-quarter of the magazine to a mail-order shopping guide which was not (at least ostensibly) paid advertisement; and as part of its editorial policy, urging its readers to buy new goods.

CHAPTER 3
THE CULTURE OF THE TELEPHONE

MICHÈLE MARTIN

(1991)

In the 1890s, women in the wealthy classes were using a telephone system built and shaped by the economic incentives of the telephone industry and by political and ideological forces. Women's activities were not seen as being of prime importance in the business world of the telephone entrepreneurs. Nor did these entrepreneurs see the utility of this new technology for working-class housewives, or for rural populations. As Marvin pointed out, telephone-company managers thought that "women's use of men's technology would come to no good end" (1988, p. 23). Capitalists considered the telephone only to be a means of facilitating business activity or to link the businessman to his office when he chose to stay at home. Its initial impact on other social groups was slight.

This began to change when the telephone network expanded to residential areas. This expansion resulted from a developmental dynamic involving several components. No general consensus among women forced telephone companies to extend the telephone system for their use. At first, women's access to the telephone on a personal basis was very much subject to their husbands' trust in the technology. Businessmen who used the telephone system generally had their offices connected to their homes. Consequently, women gained access to the telephone, at first for practices recommended by the companies, but soon for activities of their own. The early structure of telephonic networks shows that they were used primarily within friendship circles, which later expanded as new exchanges were opened. Thus, for some subscribers, the opening of an exchange was the equivalent of the "pedestrianization" of their elite telephone network. It was from within closed and approved circles that the domestic use of the telephone grew, accompanied, much later, by telephone companies' advertising of the utility of the telephone for women's practices. Only when women started to use the telephone extensively for their own activities could a (female) telephone culture emerge. Women's contribution to changing the social practices of telephone use was important, although we must be critical of contemporary male accounts of it.

OBTAINING THE USE OF A TELEPHONE

Means of communication are not determined simply by technology. Siegelaub says that a form of communication represents "a bond between real people taking place in real time and real space" (1979, p. 12). As a link between people, it is bound to take different forms when applied to different classes, cultures, and epochs. In effect, to situate the practices related to a new form of communication is to associate the terms "communication" and "culture." This "world of reference" varies according to the structure of social classes, and according to the nature of social organization and the degree of people's solidarity in daily life. This results in the development of divergent networks which make possible other uses of the means of communication (Mattelart 1983). This differentiation in the world of reference is also gender-related. M. Mattelart (1985b) asserts that women have different communicational activities from men, and that a means of communication adapted to male practices will not necessarily be suitable to female activities. Hence, women may use a means of communication in ways unexpected by men.

The telephone developed in different ways according to the period and the areas in which the systems expanded. Indeed, technological development of telephone systems changed dramatically over the period studied, and these modifications influenced the production of telephone calls as well as the use of the telephone. It is to be expected, then, that these technological developments had also some impact on the reproduction of social activities. Nevertheless, the period during which expansion took place was not the only factor affecting telephone systems; the areas in which expansion took place were also influential. For instance, an examination of telephone systems reveals that more sophisticated technology was used on more important routes. Use of the system was influenced accordingly, with the result that telephone activities took different forms in relation to the areas in which the system expanded, and the social practices that it helped to reproduce were differentiated by class and gender. In practical terms, the spatial distribution of telephone systems influenced the kinds of uses people made of them.

Since Bell Telephone Co. monopolized development of telephone systems in profitable areas, its policy was to supply the best technological apparatuses where it was economically and politically advantageous, and cheaper material in less promising locations. The areas to which Bell refused to extend its system were taken over by independent telephone companies, mostly in rural areas, where they thrived from the early 1890s. In 1885, part of Bell's patent was declared void. Although this affected only a part in the receiver and not the most important element of the technology, it left some room for independent companies to expand. When the American patent expired, in 1893, independent companies could buy their equipment from American manufacturers that were not related to Bell. Between 1892 and 1905, eighty-three independent telephone companies were created in Ontario alone (Babe 1988, p. 17). After the telephone inquiry in 1905, the Railway Act of 1906 brought state regulation to development of telephone systems, obliging Bell Telephone Co. to connect independent companies' networks to their long-distance lines. Six hundred and seventy-six mainly rural independent telephone companies were established in Ontario between 1906 and 1915 (Babe 1988, p. 18).[1] These were small firms, often developed spontaneously by people living in the area, which charged very low rates for the service. From this uneven expansion emerged diversified systems. Various types of telephone systems installed in different places reproduced divergent communicational forms. In rural areas, the relationship between the development of a specific telephone network and the form of communication it engendered was particularly distinctive. Several rural telephone companies were cooperatives whose structure was determined by the users themselves. This contrasted with the more rigid system established by Bell in urban areas.

PRIVACY IS LIBERTY

Very early, specific telephone practices influenced people's daily activities. At the same time, a controversial issue was raised by this new set of telephone practices: the capacity of the telephone to reproduce the degree of privacy already extant in the social practices of the ruling classes. The accommodation of telephone systems to private communication, in order to satisfy these classes, certainly affected the types of interaction between users, and differentiated them from those occurring on party lines. Thus, the different kinds of telephone lines provided to subscribers influenced the form of long-distance interactive communication in a community, creating various telephonic practices, some of them unexpected, which led to a "culture of the telephone."

The ruling classes in late-Victorian society had a highly developed sense of privacy. To many members of these classes, the idea of having a conversation overheard by eavesdroppers was in itself a limitation to "freedom of speech." Since the telephone was financially available only to the wealthy classes, especially in urban areas which were mostly controlled by Bell, the nature of its service and the form of communication it created were determined by the social requirements of these classes, notwithstanding the needs of other social groups. Privacy in bourgeois and petit-bourgeois telephone practices was preserved at two levels: secrecy in telephonic communication, and protection of the household from intrusive telephone calls.

During the early period of telephone development, privacy was not particularly problematic, since telephone networks took the form of several "domestic lines" linking small groups of households and businesses, and constituted a supplementary link within an already entrenched social group. They were formed despite the fact that Bell Telephone Co. did not advise "the use of more than two [stations] on the same line where privacy [was] required" (BCA, sf.ind 1877). However, since exchanges were not yet in use, and telephonic communications were possible only between people connected on the same line, private lines were not practical because they limited the possibility of contacts to two places. A telephone system without a public aspect did not have a significant use value. As a result, groups of two or more businessmen connected their offices and households onto one line, which was primarily used for business transactions. Women were not expected to use the precious technology for more than a few minutes a day, to order supplies or organize social engagements. Those who monopolized the line for a chat with a friend or a relative at times when it was required for business were likely to be disciplined. For example, a man who had tried for about ten minutes to get his telephone line without success because his wife was talking to a friend gave her a lecture when he finally reached her, and subsequently had his residential telephone removed (BCA, qa 1919, p. 112). Another businessman, from Burford, Ontario, also had his home telephone "removed at once" after his wife had called him at work to ask to borrow five dollars! (BCA, d 12113, 1878).

Privacy became more problematic when all of these domestic lines were finally connected through a central exchange which indiscriminately linked different groups of subscribers on party lines. Not only could people no longer choose those with whom they shared their line, but the bad quality of the wires produced cross talk which allowed subscribers to hear conversations on other lines as well as on their own. As one writer pointed out, these "outside interferences" with private conversations were "annoying" (BCA, d 12016, 1884a, p. 1). The press began to emphasize "the danger [that] the telephone" would put "an immediate end to all privacy" (BCA, d 12015, 1877c, p. 12). In fact, some of the complaints were justified, as the "remedies" suggested by telephone companies to counter abuses on party lines were usually not followed. "Listening on the line" was generally practiced. The result was that the telephone was seen as an "indiscreet instrument" (BCA, d 12016, 1880d, p. 25). The solution to the problem of privacy appeared to be found exclusively in private lines, since secrecy devices attached to telephones were not promoted by the companies.[2]

Indeed, some subscribers were requesting private lines. Despite their expense, "the majority of our customers in Montreal are demanding separate lines on our exchange," wrote McFarlane to Swinyard (BCA, d 1173, 1880). High rates did not deter wealthy subscribers; for them, privacy was worth the money. However, a different problem plagued the promoters and consumers of private lines: the mediation of operators. Operators were accused, rightly or wrongly, of all the evils of indiscretion. As one irate subscriber claimed,

> Whatever is said in the secrecy of the piazza by youthful students of the satellites of Mars will be proclaimed by the way of the housetop to the eavesdropping telephone operator. No matter to what extent a man will shut his doors and windows, and hermetically seal his key-holes and furnace-registers with towels and blankets, whatever he may say, either to himself or a companion, will be overheard. Absolute silence will be our only safety, conversation will be carried on exclusively in writing, and courtship will be conducted by the use of a system of ingenious symbols. An invention which thus mentally makes silence the sole condition of safety cannot be too severely denounced, and while violence, even in self-defence, is always to be deprecated, there can be but little doubt that the death of the inventors and manufacturers of the telephone would do much toward creating that feeling of confidence which financiers tell us must precede any revival of business. (BCA, d 12015, 1877c)

These attitudes had both a class and a gender context. Most subscribers from the ruling classes considered working-class operators to be "devoted servants of indulgent male overseers . . . [and] intruders of dubious ability and fragile reputation" (Marvin 1988, p. 26). Because these women needed work, they were considered untrustworthy. Moreover, women in general were thought of as being afflicted with a compulsion for listening on the lines which they could not control. These opinions persisted in spite of the denials of telephone companies. Bell Telephone Co. invited journalists to visit the exchanges in order to show them that "the operators . . . [had] too much to do to pay attention to the conversations that [were] passing, and thus the people [had] the whole thing entirely to themselves" (BCA, 12016, 1884b). The operators' consistently bad reputation in relation to privacy was detrimental to the company's expansion, as it deterred some people from subscribing.

Just as eavesdropping was eliminated by private lines, the remedy for operators' listening to check the lines was found in automatic telephony. In the early 1880s, a newspaper predicted that the problem for "every man who desires secrecy for his communications" would be solved only when he "will be his own operator" (BCA, d 6453, n.d.). In 1905, when the first automatic telephones were marketed in Canada,[3] newspapers claimed that the "modern marvel of telephoning" gave a "delightful sense of privacy" (BCA, ncm 1880–1905). Its major advantage was that "it guarantee[d] an absolute secret transmission of all conversation" (BCA, nca 1911a), "as closely guarded as though two persons spoke together in a brick walled room" (BCA, ty 9 (5) 1905, p. 390).

It did not take long, however, to discover that even automatic telephony could not ensure *perfect* privacy, and that the practice of eavesdropping could not be attributed solely to operators. With private lines and automatic telephones, eavesdropping gave place to wiretapping by various parties, including telephone companies. Indeed, during the 1907 Ontario Select Committee, Mr. Maw of Bell Telephone Co. did not deny the existence of a "listening board" in the company, and said that "no girls refused to do *listening duty* except for the long hours such work entailed" (BCA, ncm 1907b, my emphasis).[4] The *Globe* asserted that "the company ha[d] the machinery for a system of espionage more than Russian in its perfection" (BCA, ncm 1907a). Police forces also revealed that "the telephone service [was] invaluable" in social control, and that they were "entitled to every aid," including wiretapping, "in frustrating the plot of crooks and confidence men" (BCA, nct 1916e). Given such violations of the "right of a man to privacy," provincial governments decided to act. In 1917 in Ontario, and in 1918 in Quebec, bills were passed to regulate eavesdropping and wiretapping on the telephone, imposing severe penalties—one hundred dollars or three months' imprisonment in Quebec, twenty-five dollars or thirty days' imprisonment in Ontario—for offenders.[5] (These regulations, however, did not explicitly cover wiretapping by the police.[6]) This led to a process of legalization of the right to privacy in telephone calls. What started as a *domestic* issue became a provincial—and later a federal—*legal* question. Legislation was passed to regulate what was heretofore ruled by *etiquette,* and *disciplining subscribers changed to controlling users*. Privacy, then, an issue of overriding importance to the ruling classes, became institutionalized as a general feature of the telephone system applying to all classes, notwithstanding their different social practices and cultures.

Although the issue of secrecy over the wires was considered the major problem, there were other forms of violation of privacy attached to telephone use. In the early days, weak transmission obliged people to shout into the instrument in order to be heard at the other end. Public telephones in drugstores provided no possibility of privacy for the working classes who used them. Some businessmen and professionals refrained from using the telephone because it did not allow for quiet conversation—"A telephone caller had to shout as if he were speaking to another person 80 feet away" (BCA, bb 1951).

The development of the telephone also created encroachments on privacy at another level. People thought that the telephone was a terrible invader of domestic intimacy. Once they were connected with an exchange, the question was "how far each householder [would] be *at liberty to reject the temporary union*" (Bedford 1879, p. 413, my emphasis). Housekeepers and their families "complain[ed] that when they [were] busy they [were] continually being rung up about trivial matters" (Hastie 1898, p. 894). As one writer pointed out, "The doors may be barred and a rejected suitor kept out, but how is the telephone to be guarded?" (BCA, ty 10 (3) 1905, p. 221)[7]

The fact was that late-Victorian women were caught off-guard. The barriers that their society had built in order to preserve privacy did not work with the telephone, and there was no time to construct new ones. Yet, in spite of this inconvenience, women continued to use the telephone, and the system developed rapidly, especially from the early 1900s onward.

CREATING "STANDARD" TELEPHONE PRACTICES

Telephone practices related to recreational uses were introduced slowly as the telephone developed, springing from the form of communication created by telephone systems shaped by men from the ruling classes. These men prescribed women's early recreational uses of the telephone. As Marvin says, "Male control of female communication was justified by women's ignorance and should have guaranteed it as well" (1988, p. 25). The recreational telephone uses specified by male managers were to be *rational* activities— "appropriate" uses governed by an ensemble of rules and procedures. Female consumers did not necessarily agree.

Daytime telephone service appeared in cities and towns toward the end of the 1890s, with the extended use of copper wires, and night and Sunday service was provided to all exchanges with more than one hundred subscribers (BCA, bb 1950). Although night service raised relatively few objections, Sunday service caused much controversy in Toronto. The president of the Toronto Ministerial Association wrote to "the president and directors of the Bell Telephone Co." in 1881 to urge management to keep the exchanges closed on the Lord's Day, arguing that "very much of it [the Sunday telephone business] is not justified by any requirement either of necessity or mercy," and therefore "the Association desires very respectfully to urge your board to cease keeping the office open for business on the Lord's Day" (BCA, d 9498, 1881). The Association was supported by the Toronto *Globe,* which deplored Bell's encroachment on the day of rest. According to the newspaper, there was "no sufficient reason for depriving the young women employed in the office of their weekly rest." Since all places of business were closed, the *Globe* found there was "small occasion" to use the telephone on that day; its most common use was for hiring a cab, which, according to the *Globe,* could be done the day before (BCA, nct 1881). In spite of such public opposition, however, the telephone was very much used on Sundays as well as on weekdays; at the same time as operators' working hours were extended to Sundays, an intensive advertising campaign suggesting other uses for the telephone began.

Very specific telephone uses were prescribed by the companies: shopping, making appointments, protection, and personal conversations. Each recommended telephone activity was confined to a particular period of the day. During the daytime, when the lines were "indispensable" for business, housekeepers were requested to restrict the use of their telephones to shopping and to short calls to arrange social engagements. In the evenings, when business traffic was so low that telephone companies offered special rates to encourage consumption, women were permitted to call friends "for a chat." Finally, the threats and mysteries of the night could be kept at bay by the use of the telephone to summon the police, the doctor, the fire department, or other services (BCA, nca 1911b). "The night calls," said a writer in 1914, "are laden with portent" (Husband 1914, p. 331).

A great number of advertisements were related to the use of the telephone for shopping. This speaks to Strasser's notion that the companies "linked the activities of the consumer housewife to their own through advertising" (1982, p. 251). Telephone advertisements were oriented to increasing mass production and consumption, if not of the telephone, at least of other products, in order to gain new subscribers. Strasser also observes that, as early as 1891, some advertisers had already decided that "women made the purchasing decisions," and that advertising was to be directed toward them (Strasser 1982, p. 244). Bell certainly did not share this opinion. Indeed, its early advertising, which was aimed at males, explained that the advantage of shopping on the telephone was that it "save[d] car fare, shoe leather, your wife's patience" (BCA, sf.ad 1900). This implied that the savings gained in the use of other commodities—including the wife's labor—covered the cost of the telephone. A few years later, the advertisements took a different tack, appealing directly to the housewives: "WOMAN SLAVES! Enough about household duties and cares without being obliged to run down almost daily for supplies. A telephone would save her time and energies and costs but a few cents a day" (BCA, nca 1903–13). Although the first part of the message harangued women directly, when the price of the product was mentioned the husband was addressed once again, and the wife was referred to in the third person.

The capitalists who were developing the telephone systems did not consider women to be their direct clients.

These invitations to shop over the telephone were complemented by department-store advertisements encouraging the use of the phone. In effect, for these businesses, telephone shopping represented an increase of sales coupled with a reduction of labor in the form of messengers. Although the stores had to hire telephone operators for their private switchboards, it can be safely assumed that their number was smaller than that of the messengers, since they could take many more orders during an average day.

The telephone directory also provided facilities for shopping over the telephone. Some people called it "the buying guide" (Lyon 1924, p. 175); its "first function . . . was largely one of publicity" (Lyon 1923, p. 187). Advertising had a concrete effect on the telephone business. The telephone bill of Eaton's department store amounted to over one thousand dollars per annum in 1899, in contrast to the regular business rate of thirty-five dollars. Sise wrote that Eaton's was not to be affected by the general increase in business rates because the firm was "a large subscriber." Moreover, "there [were] about fifty firms like Eaton, who [were] large users, and [were] not to be disturbed" (BCA, slo.14 (1899): 71). Clearly, by 1899, housekeepers were extensively shopping over the telephone. This activity was so popular that, in the middle of the next decade, some department stores started a service for "all-night orders received by telephone" (BCA, ty 10 (3) 1905, p. 221b).

The second use of the telephone suggested by Bell Telephone Co. was as a "nightly protection" against unforeseeble situations such as illness, fires, thieves, and so on: "A telephone in your house is always useful, always reliable, and a great comfort. Every housekeeper should have one" (BCA, sf.a 1902); and it should be "on duty day and night" (BCA, sf.a 1904). As early as 1912, the telephone was considered "a necessary part of the doctor's equipment" (*Literary Digest*, 1912, p. 1037). Even earlier, the police were equipped with "a police patrol system of huts or kiosks with signalling and telephone equipment connected to the police stations" (BCA, hit 1877–1909; tg 2 (2) 1910, p. 9). The police could make arrests with the aid of a telephone call (BCA, qa 1881a, p. 48). It was said that the police department saw the telephone as "a very important part of the city's police system" (BCA, ty 10 (4) 1905, p. 294). In fact, one of the first expected uses of the telephone was as an adjunct to law-enforcement agencies responsible for social control. Only the fire department was not adequately provided with telephones (BCA, nct 1914c); people continued to use firebox alarms until the 1940s.

An interesting feature of Bell Telephone Co.'s advertising policy was that some telephone practices that had been considered unnecessary, and even unjustifiable, in early periods were later legitimized. Lengthy chats on the telephone, for instance, were strongly condemned prior to 1890, and disapproved of before 1900. Advertising suggesting use of the telephone for a chat began with the expansion of private lines. Although Bell never explicitly stated that chatting over the telephone was limited to private lines, the rules for "etiquette for party lines" recommended that the latter be used only for indispensable, short calls so that the lines would be available for more serious purposes. The fact was that what was called "gossip" by male journalists and company managers—but what really consisted of conversation between friends—was still "a subject of jesting and scorn." Nonetheless, the alternative, the "numbing solitude of hours of loneliness," was not considered "elevating and edifying" either (BCA, ncm 1906c). In any case, advertisements promoting the use of the telephone for a chat were rare. The first one appeared in 1911, followed, in 1912, by another one presenting the telephone as "a very comforting thing to call friends and relatives . . . and have a fine chat." The accompanying illustration portrayed an evening scene (BCA, nca 1912, p. 85).[8]

Later inspired by women's recurrent use of the telephone for sociability, the telephone companies modified the discourse in their advertising, and presented the telephone as a psychological support against loneliness, stress, and fatigue. An extension phone, for example, saved labor, time, and thus, nervous strain (BCA, nca 1911a, p. 47). Ads presenting the telephone as a psychological aid suggest that telephonic communication had become a "way of living." No longer was the telephone a mere accessory to daily physical domestic chores; it was becoming an integral part of the housewife's life, transcending it, and regulating her psychological activities, her unconscious. In M. Mattelart's words, it rendered "her exile more gentle." Since the advertising was addressed primarily to the husband, he became the conscience of the household, purchasing a telephone to give his wife more rest and his family more happiness. The telephone had become a "living thing with creative and transformative powers." This perfectly fit a McLuhanite scenario in which the medium was the message: the technology unilaterally transformed society. The role of the ruling classes in determining the pattern of distribution of telephone systems and in controlling the production of telephone calls was completely hidden by the implication that the technology itself exclusively had that power.

These advertised practices were generally approved by the social groups in which they developed. The prescription of *standard* uses in advertising implied that other ways of employing the telephone were not acceptable to those who controlled the systems. However, the restrictions were not always respected, and some subscribers used their telephones for "unreasonable" activities. A large number of these users were women who did not accept the telephone company's prescriptions. In fact, these "delinquent" telephone activities created by women were largely responsible for the change in the company's advertising policies over the years.

By the early 1900s, women from the bourgeois and petit-bourgeois classes were using the telephone extensively, not only for shopping or other indispensable activities, but also for social purposes. A detailed agenda of telephone uses by women during that period[9] shows that women's use of the telephone for a chat was extended over the entire day (BCA, ncm 1907e). This type of use became part of women's social practices, and had some influence on the development of the telephone, not only in terms of the code of telephone practices but also in terms of the pattern of distribution of the systems. Indeed, while early development was planned exclusively for business areas in cities and towns, women's use of the telephone soon obliged Bell to revise its plan and to take domestic development into account. Urban sectors that hitherto had been overlooked began to look attractive to the company. Later, houses were equipped with extensions or supplementary lines in order to allow for the husband's business calls as well as the wife's social calls. Most of these changes were due to unexpected practices.

UNEXPECTED TELEPHONE PRACTICES

Among the new social activities developed by the telephone and practised by women, phoning friends and relatives was certainly one of the most popular. Conversing over the telephone was seen as "taking the place of visiting" (Spofford 1909). It was faster and more convenient than having to harness the horses and, sometimes, convincing the husband to make the journey. Although it is impossible to determine the percentage of residential calls made just to chat, complaints published in newspapers and magazines about women's habit of talking on the phone for "futile motives" (BCA, ncm 1919g) suggest that the telephone was regularly used for that purpose.[10] Motives for making calls included chatting, courting, discussing, gossiping, and so on. This activity came to be so popular that some newspapermen called the telephone "our tap of communication" ("Back to the Land" 1906, p. 530). Since, in spite of telephone-company advertising, these calls were made at any time of the day, they multiplied contacts with friends or relatives, the more so since they did not require any preliminary preparation such as change of clothes. "Telephone service enables morning gossiping . . . afternoon visits to be paid without the necessity of dressing up or of driving on a dusty road in the hot glare of the summer's sun, or in the biting winds of a wintry day; evening visits to be returned while reclining in one's own comfortable rocking chair" (BCA, ty 9 (3) 1905, p. 257).

This was a significant improvement for women of the 1890s, since getting dressed was an elaborate and time-consuming process for them. According to Haller and Haller, "it was the duty of every [middle-class] woman to look as beautiful as she possibly could" (1974, p. 141). For the Victorian middle-class woman, "cleanliness was next to Godliness," and she was "continually advised to keep herself spotless" (Haller and Haller 1974, p. 145). As a consequence, she "redressed several times during the day," each time tightly bound in corset, bustle, petticoat, and extravagant dresses, in order to receive visitors, to go out to visit, or simply to "await [her] husband['s] return" (Haller and Haller 1974, p. 161). Telephone visiting diminished the number of "visual" contacts necessitating a change of clothes. At the same time, it permitted these women to remain in "talking" contact with each other.

The possibility of several telephonic contacts per day was said to put women "on the tenterhooks of expectation and desire": the expectation of being "called up" by someone, and the desire to call someone else up. "Thus may life be made miserable by the very attempts to make it easy and happy," said a male writer in *Chambers's Journal* ("The Telephone" 1899, p. 313). Use of the telephone, like that of the bicycle, was seen as a moral issue necessitating a specific set of rules. Indeed, both technologies became popular with women in the 1890s. The bicycle was considered a "curse" because, like the telephone, it provided women with "evil associations and opportunities" for contacts with strangers without the presence of a chaperon. The use of both technologies by Victorian women, then, had to be controlled by "correct etiquette" elaborated by men, who considered that, "in their weakness," women were "best protected in the privacy of the home."[11] The etiquette was intended to prevent women from using these technologies for "undesirable" and "dangerous" practices.

The "social" aspect of telephone technology had not been foreseen by the early capitalist developers of the telephone system. It is legitimate to assert that the popularity of the telephone with women was partly due to several technological characteristics specific to this means of communication. For instance, the sense of privacy created by conversations transmitted from ear to ear and involving the whole person, to borrow McLuhan's words (1964, p. 240), endowed telephonic communication with a kind of intimacy which women had not previously experienced. Since, in addition, telephone service was developing into a private-line system in large cities, a conversation on these lines took the form of sharing a secret. However, on party lines, which were the majority in small towns and villages and still numerous in cities, women had quite different telephonic experiences, and were attracted by other features of the means of communication.

In rural areas, the independent telephone companies that developed party lines applied much looser rules to the use of their telephones and charged much lower rates, so that in many areas almost everyone could afford a telephone. Moreover, rural communities were more closely knit socially than urban ones, although they were more sparsely distributed geographically. A letter from K. J. Dunstan, local manager in Toronto, discussing the possibility of opening an exchange in the Beaches area (which was still a rural district at the time), asserted that there was "considerable local intercourse" between the inhabitants (BCA, sb 84141b, 3146–3, 1902).[12]

All of these elements helped generate different types of telephone activities. What was considered rude and "unethical" in the set of rules specifying approved uses of the telephone became helpful behavior within the code of unexpected practices. These represented a complete reversal of the standard uses—so much so that big-company managers were scandalized by the practices allowed on rural party lines, saying that "no company which ha[d] the best interests of itself and its subscribers at heart, [would] operate them," because they did "not embrace the highest ideals of telephony." On the other hand, some small-company managers thought that "the party line was a necessity and ha[d] come to stay" (BCA, ty 7 (6) 1904, p. 453). Some users eavesdropped and participated in other subscribers' conversations. The operator of the exchange of the small telephone company owned by Dr. Beatty recounted that he "liked to listen in on the conversations . . . and would often feel moved to break in and give his views on the topic under discussion. This would have disconcerted town or city folks, but the doctor's subscribers . . . knew his ways and took this in their stride" (BCA, d 29909, 1967).

Actually, in the code of rural party-line activities, listening to others' conversations was not seen as eavesdropping by subscribers, but rather as participation in community life: "Every country user did [it] . . . it was the way they got the news" (BCA, d 29909, 1967). Often, in small communities, a listener entered a conversation with information which the two original callers did not have. For instance, *Telephony* reported that when a woman cut her finger while cooking dinner and phoned a friend to ask for advice, "before the friend could answer someone else piped up, 'Bind it up in salt pork.' Still another voice advised court plaster and someone else had another remedy to offer" (BCA, ty 8 (3) 1904, p. 211). Most of the time, though, listeners tried to go unnoticed, just as they would if they were eavesdropping on a conversation in a public place. When a man called a friend to announce his visit, he added at the end of the call, " 'The rest of you on the line—Martha, Grace, Mary, Rachel—tell the men I'll buzz wood tomorrow afternoon.' The men all appeared and there was no explanation asked or offered about how they knew when to come" (BCA, qa 1936). Although this example implies a sexist tendency by presuming that women, and not men, were the listeners, it shows how party lines were used in rural communities. As one observer pointed out, "The strange part about a party line in the country is the fact that everybody listens but very, very few ever admit that they do" (BCA, qa 1936, p. 51). People knew that they were often overheard, but most of them did not mind. They knew that, in time, *they* would be the listeners. It was part of rural life.

One of the most important characteristics of party lines, especially in rural areas, was that they were regularly used for "meeting on the lines." For instance, when eavesdroppers decided to enter a conversation initiated by two other parties, the telephone call generated a group discussion: "It is . . . evident . . . that if one person calls up another in the far end of the town many receivers between these two points come down and sometimes more than two persons join in the conversation," the manager of an American independent company remarked (BCA, ty 8 (3) 1904, p. 211). Sometimes, the technological features of the telephone network were responsible for these meetings. Indeed, some small companies did not have a discriminating ringing system— the same ring applied to every house—so that when the telephone rang, all subscribers had to answer to check if the call was for them. Often, several users stayed on the line to participate in the conversation (BCA, qa 1918, p. 120; d. 29909, 1967; d 29912, 1961). At other times, the operator was asked to connect a subscriber with several others, instigating a meeting. One operator recalled that she "would connect two or three lines and hold them open so the women could talk back and forth and arrange church meetings or other projects" (BCA, d 29909, 1967). Sometimes, a woman would keep the telephone receiver to her ear while she was working: "There sat his wife in the rocking chair. She was sewing and tied to the back of the chair was the receiver of the telephone, so adjusted that she could place her ear to it without changing her position . . . it enabled her to hear the gossip of her neighbors at the other end" (BCA, ty 6 (6) 1903, p. 480). Finally, party lines were also used to comfort the sick. The telephone receiver was placed on the ill person's pillow so that he or she could listen to conversations on the line and keep in contact with what was going on in the vicinity (Spofford 1909). These examples show some women's initiatives to decrease the loneliness they felt in their isolated homes. For them, the telephone was a means of staying in touch with the rest of the community. They did not need to participate directly in all activities occurring over the phone. In fact, before the advent of the radio, the telephone was the only way for these women to hear other people's voices without having to leave their homes. Most men, however, ridiculed, or altogether dismissed, these ways of using the telephone to improve women's lives.

The unexpected uses of the telephone practiced by women influenced the companies' notion of its value. This technology, which had been conceived exclusively for business, seemed to have alternative uses that were worth considering. However, among these uses, only those approved by management were retained. For instance, collective calls, regularly practised by women on party lines, were gradually replaced by private lines and telephone calls between two parties.[13] However, of the practices retained by the companies, some had been created by women. One of them was the use of the telephone for sociability.

This suggests that if women had restricted their use of the telephone to that promoted by the companies, today it probably would not be so inconspicuous a technology in the household. Indeed, at the domestic level, it would still be a form of communication to be used on special occasions only. Yet, although the telephone system was adjusted to take into account some activities practiced by women, it was not planned primarily for them, as their social and cultural practices were not directly taken into consideration in its expansion. Here, it is useful to use Cockburn's concept of "male tenure" over technology to explain the participation of women in the structuring of the telephone system. In her article entitled "The Relations to Technology" (1986), Cockburn suggests that men have what she calls a "tenure" over the technological sphere, which means that they "appropriate and sequester" each new area of development at the expense of women. This appropriation by men is manifested not only in development and ownership of technology but also in its uses and values, which are, according to Cockburn, mostly determined by men. She argues that "technological competence correlates strongly with masculinity and incompetence with femininity" (1986, p. 78). In the telephone values developed by dominant-class males, women's specific uses of a telephone system developed by and for men were clearly deemed incompetent. Women's persistence in using the system their way, and the lure of profit that these unexpected female practices represented to the telephone business, finally resulted in the development of a service that was better adapted to women. Thus, as users, women had only an indirect impact in the pattern of development of the telephone. However, their contribution was an *active* one, since some of their telephone practices forced the companies to modify their development strategy. In addition, the various uses made of the telephone engendered some social change, and a culture of the telephone was slowly developing.

THE TELEPHONE CULTURE

The elaborate system of telegraphy that existed before the advent of the telephone served those who later became telephone users. The telegraph, which constituted an important improvement in terms of speed over letter-writing, had been used extensively for almost fifty years. When the telephone began to be marketed, however, the telegraph came to be seen as a slow means of communication. Transactions which took days to be made by post, and hours by telegraph, could be completed instantaneously by telephone. Telephone companies' advertisements stressed the speed of the telephone in comparison to other means of communication. "The mail is quick, the telegraph is quicker, but the long-distance telephone is instantaneous and you dont [sic] have to wait for an answer," said one (BCA, d 1544, 1898). These particularities of the telephone influenced social practices. Although, as some claimed, the telephone had not "revolutionized the modes of correspondence" (BCA, d 12016, 1879b, p. 10), it did modify several cultural practices.

The telephone did not supplant existing means of communication. As a writer pointed out, "A letter was different from a conversation . . . In a letter, you could get down on paper exactly what you wanted to say in the best possible language, and leave out whatever didn't fit it. It was like addressing a jury without the presence of opposing counsel, in some courtroom where you had a free hand with the judge." (Langton 1987, p. 82). Whether for this reason or because it was less expensive, written correspondence was still extensively used. In 1905, for example, while the telephone had superseded the telegraph for short-distance communications (e.g., communications within a city), the latter was still generally used for long-distance transactions (BCA, ncm 1905a). The postal service was also regularly utilized. The rush that Bell Telephone Co. experienced in 1918, during a postal strike (BCA, nct 1918b), was evidence of massive use of the mail system at the time. Yet use of the telephone was growing rapidly all over the world (see Figures 1 and 2).[14] It had evolved from being seen as a "nuisance" and an "indignity" to being a "sign of civilization." "Failure to adopt the use of telephones," said a writer in 1905, "indicates, in general way, a backward condition, a lack of enterprise, in any modern city" (BCA, ty 7 (6) 1904, p. 456).

Extensive utilization of the telephone by the wealthy classes was bound to create some specific habits. Actually, use of the phone was affected by the time of the day and the weather: "The more inclement the weather, the more of people resort to their telephones. There are appointments to be cancelled or deferred and taxicabs to be summoned" (Rhodes 1929, p. 21). Some women would rather phone their friends than go out in the rain or the snow

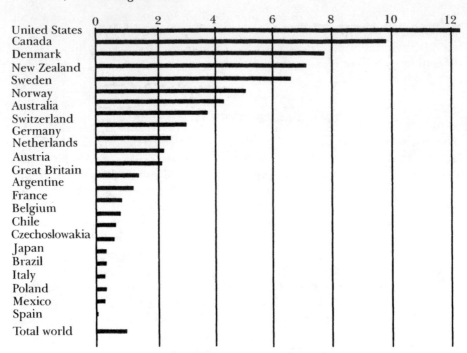

FIGURE 1: Telephones per 100 Persons in Selected Countries, January 1921.
(*Bell Telephone Quarterly* 1922, 1(3): p. 49)

to visit: "We can tell what kind of weather it is from the College Exchange," said one operator, referring to residential calls (BCA, nct 1914b).[15] An observant operator divided the daily activities of "leisure class" women over the telephone as follows.

> At seven o'clock, there are scattered calls . . . for doctors. . . . At eight o'clock, the nice, early-morning women come on the market with patient, affable butchers. . . .
>
> At ten, interminable communications between women . . . with infinite details as the clothes. . . . I've known them to keep it up for three quarters of an hour.
>
> At eleven to half past . . . nippy ladies calling up employment agencies, or stupid servant girls replying. At eleven thirty till twelve thirty there's a wild rush, everybody trying to catch everybody else for lunch.
>
> From then till three or so there are characteristic calls of all sorts: peevish, hurried females who use the nickel 'phones in downtown drug stores . . . silly school girls mischievously calling men they don't know. . . .
>
> From three to four . . . a flurry of women trying to call up stores before they close, or in the catch of the last deliveries.
>
> At five, wives begin to call up to know if husbands are coming home . . . 'Be sure to bring home a steak or a lobster.'

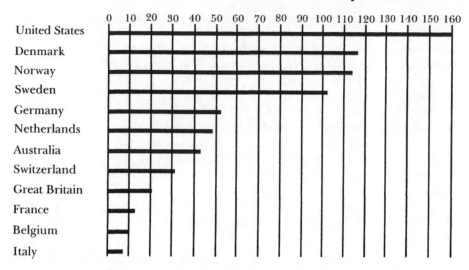

FIGURE 2: Telephone Conversations per Capita in Selected Countries, December 1920. (*Bell Telephone Quarterly* 1922, 1(3): p. 50)

> From six to seven everybody seems to be busy to call up . . . a club . . . a garage . . . towards eight, comes the nervous maiden[16] calling up her men. . . .
> After ten thirty come the carriage calls, garage orders, and the hotel private exchanges begin to get busy. (BCA, ncm 1907e)

Women used the telephone for various purposes. It was said that a woman "no more need[ed] to make appointments by letter with the dressmaker, or to drive to the box-office of the theater to take tickets, or to be kept waiting for forty-eight hours before she knows whether Mrs Blank can meet her or come for tea" ("Back to the Land" 1906, p. 530). It was faster to use the telephone, and get what she wanted without leaving her home. The fact that women were using the telephone in this manner meant that they no longer expected to meet a regular group at such locations as the market. The telephone was taking the place of the daily shopping trip, at least for some women, especially on inclement days. Housekeepers were slowly changing their daily habits, thereby modifying the characteristics of the places they used to patronize.

Technological features of telephone systems also contributed to the development of certain cultural practices. The fact that the phone allowed oral communication without visual contact created a kind of intimacy which people previously had not experienced (Barrett 1940, p. 129). However, these features had some drawbacks as well. Having a conversation ear to ear did not always create the desired intimacy. It was reported in some scientific journals that this mode of communication sometimes generated insecurity, especially when the person calling was unknown ("Action at a Distance" 1914, p. 39).

Indeed, it seemed that the anonymity provided by the telephone had evil effects on the personality of some callers, so much so that the telephone was seen as having "a brutalising influence": "The sensitive-minded man who would shrink from saying a disagreeable thing in ordinary conversation, when talking through the telephone, will speak his mind . . . bluntly and argue . . . roughly . . ." (BCA, ncm 1906d). Thus, the telephone was said to encourage the use of foul language (BCA, nct 1916d) and "trespassing" by telephone. Some men importuned women over the telephone in such a persistent manner that judges deemed the offense a "breach of the peace" (BCA, ty 10 (3) 1905, p. 221). This contradictory effect created by the telephone of feeling nearby and far away at the same time seemed to embolden some people, leading to new breaches of the law to which the legal system had to adjust.

In fact, the problem of aggressiveness and "foul language" on the telephone became so serious that an amendment to the Telephone Act was passed in 1915 naming the use of "abusive language on the telephone as an offence punishable with a fine of $25 or imprisonment for 30 days" (BCA, nct 1915a).[17] Whether the telephone was entirely responsible for such behavior is debatable. Industrialization of society was causing rapid changes in some social practices and encouraging more liberal and emancipated social behaviors. Since the instantaneous characteristic of the telephone constituted "a means of projecting personality," as stated in an advertisement (BCA, nca 1925), without the necessity of identifying oneself, it permitted some hidden features of a personality to surface. "The use of the telephone gives little room for reflection," stated a writer in the *Chambers's Journal* in 1899. "It does not improve the temper, and it engenders a feverishness in the ordinary concerns of life which does not make for domestic happiness and comfort." The telephone, by making life "so easy," represented an "immanent danger of relapsing into barbarism" ("The Telephone" 1899, p. 313). This notion imparted to the telephone a responsibility which should have been attributed to the social conditions created by industrial capitalism as a whole. The *only* contribution of the telephone was to *facilitate*, through the anonymity it afforded, the emergence of unpleasant characteristics which already existed.

Such evils led to the necessity to develop *telephone etiquette*. Telephone etiquette was elaborated from the standard uses prescribed by the telephone companies. People were told to use good manners on the telephone, to employ such general courteous phrases as "Please" and "Thank you," to apologize for making callers wait, to utilize "correct" language instead of familiar expressions or abridged sentences (BCA, ty 8 (2), 1904, p. 130). Users were also advised to answer their telephone themselves to avoid making the other party wait for them (BCA, ty 8 (4) 1904, p. 311), and to identify themselves when answering or calling (BCA, ty 8 (2) 1904, p. 130). Failure to follow telephone etiquette was seen as a matter of gender, as women were presented as the main offenders in terms of telephone manners. Operators reported that women callers "have an exasperating way of asking, 'Who is this?' when some one answers their call whose voice they do not recognize." "Girls" were accused of unduly using their employers' telephones during business hours

(BCA, ncm 1915a). The ultimate abuse, however, was attributed to women who did not have a telephone at home and who used telephones in drug-stores. These women were seen as the "chief patrons" in "carry[ing] on all the conversation you wish" of "the most trivial nature." They went to the nearest store and, with a "May I use a telephone, please?" they used the store-keeper's telephone and "for 20 minutes or half an hour they will carry on the most milk-and-water conversation" (BCA, d 30114, 1965). The ultimate of-fense was that they left the store "without spending a cent."

Still, even when "good manners were observed," telephone calls were con-sidered "hopelessly vulgar" for "ladies of the high society." In her book *Eti-quette for Americans* (BCA, qa 1906), a "Lady of Fashion" claimed that the telephone call, due to its instantaneous character, was a "blessing in adjusting details" for a reception. However, it "should be used sparingly." Informal "invitations to bicycle or play golf [could] be transmitted in this way . . . but for most social matters, the use of the telephone [was] questionable." More-over, there was "no excuse for telephoning an invitation when time [was] not an object, or when the person invited [was] not an intimate friend" (BCA, qa, 1906, p. 37). This book was written exactly thirty years after the telephone was first marketed. Old cultural practices die hard.

The only concessions made by the "Lady of Fashion" to telephone use were for intimate relationships and casual encounters. In spite of her recom-mendations, though, the telephone was sometimes used at first for invitations. In such cases, other means of communication were usually employed to con-firm the telephone call. In Wharton's *The House of Mirth* (1905), the petit-bourgeois heroine, Miss Lily Bart, used three different means of communica-tion for a single invitation. She first made the invitation over the telephone, the call being answered by a maid. A note written by Miss Bart and delivered by a servant was then used to confirm the telephone call. Finally, she sent a telegram to finalize the whole process. In rural areas, however, etiquette was not as binding, and telephone advertisements suggested the use of the instru-ment to send invitations for an "impromptu party." Instead of spending an afternoon driving from house to house to invite people, "in less than half an hour, you could ring up your friends, living miles away, and invite them to come, without trouble or fatigue" (BCA, d 21203–2, 1908). There were clear differences in accepted telephone practices between rural and urban areas.

The telephone had other cultural effects, especially in relation to letter-writing. Although people recognized the importance of letter-writing for seri-ous matters,[18] as early as 1906 "the idea of writing a series of letters with a pen and ink, directing, sealing, and stamping the envelopes, and then waiting till the day after to-morrow for an answer simply paralyse[d]" many people ("Back to the Land" 1906, p. 530–1). Some writers (e.g., Lang 1906) were alarmed by the decreasing popularity of letter-writing. It "seems to be in decay," said Lang, "and no wonder, for few people have time to read a long letter. . . . Indeed, talk is mainly done through the telephone . . . the art of spelling, even, may come to be lost" (1906, p. 508). Even the government replaced some written documents by use of the telephone. "Government by telephone!" exclaimed Casson. "This is the new idea . . . arrived at in the more efficient departments of the Federal" (1911, p. 899). Lang lamented that it was the end of "the excitement of reading for material in the archives." Since people telephoned instead of writing letters, it would become impossible to trace the development of political, economic, and social organizations, he said. An ex-Chancellor of the English Exchequer confessed that, during his entire career, he had not kept more than twelve letters, most of his business having been done by telephone. Lang exclaimed, "Let us rejoice that the thing was not discovered sooner! If Horace Walpole could have chatted with Horace Mason, in Florence, by telephone; or Madame de Sévigny with her daughter; or Thackeray with Mrs Brookfield; or Mr Stevenson, from Samoa, with Mr Gosse and others, our literature would be poorer" (1906, pp. 507–8).

Undeniably, the telephone has enlarged the field of oral culture. The diary disappeared from most women's lives long ago, and communications between friends occur mostly through the telephone, at least for short-distance interactions. As a result, writing a biography of a person whose life extends past invention of the telephone with the aid of written records only is almost impossible. While the telephone is a technology of rapid and easy contact, it is also a source of transient evidence. For example, it is impossible to know exactly the number and the context of the "visits" paid by telephone during a period of its development. The only sources of information are indirect ones, such as newspaper reports, journal articles, and operators' stories, which may be biased. This means that telephone technology has hampered feminist researchers, for instance, in retracing long-distance friendships between women, which was relatively easy during the time of letter-writing. It is also impossible to trace telephone practices related to working classes. I mentioned earlier that some low-wage women working as maids used, furtively it seems, their employers' telephones. It is almost unthinkable that other members of the working classes did not use public telephones at all, in spite of their poverty. The proliferation of public telephones supports this assumption. However, since they did not have phones in their households, it is difficult to know the volume of use. The extension of oral culture due to the telephone certainly represents an inconvenience for researchers. In fact, Lang suggested that each telephone be attached to a recorder so that future generations could keep track of their ancestors! The records, he said, could be likened to letters.

Nonetheless, if there has been a loss of literature with the use of the telephone, there has also been some gain. Very early in its development, the technology was a source of stimulation for artists, and of entertainment for people. Novels were written in which the plot was based on the use of the telephone (e.g., Sayers 1921). The telephone inspired poets,[19] cartoonists (BCA, nct 1918a), and playwrights. In 1880, for example, George Bernard Shaw wrote a sketch on telephone conversation which suggested that the phone "was a tool for female's gossip" (Brooks 1977, p. 210).[20] In 1923, literary works on the telephone presented its use as an "expression of female desperation" (Brooks 1977, p. 218). The constant was that women were rarely presented in a positive light in works about the telephone.

Other effects of the telephone on popular culture were related to its physical features. Indeed, people talked about "the telephone voice" and "the telephone ear." The telephone voice was said to be revealing of "whether gentility [was] a thin veneer or a solid substance," the "thin veneer" being proved when an unpleasant answering voice changed suddenly into "amazing mellowness" upon learning who was calling. Using the right voice over the telephone was considered a "difficult art," because the instrument deprived the voice of its nuances. As a result, only two categories of users could be identified on the basis of their voice: those who rarely used the telephone and whose timidity regarding the technology was translated into a "solemnity of the performance"; and regular users, who were relaxed and talked as if they were having an intimate conversation (BCA, tg 3 (1) 1911, p. 5). Several people thought that the telephone developed "a soft voice," a well-modulated, "lady-like voice" (BCA, tg 1 (8) 1909, p. 10; ty 10 (5) 1905, p. 360). In any case, the voice was regarded as a key element in use of the telephone, and there was general agreement among specialists that the voice itself was influenced by the new technology. The ear was also said to be affected by the telephone. The fact that the cord of the apparatus was on the left side encouraged users to hold it in the left hand and to put the receiver to their left ear. According to some researchers, this caused telephone users to become "left-eared" (BCA, ty 8 (1), 1904, p. 74). They discovered that those who frequently used the phone had more sensitive left ears. Left-eared and soft-voiced people were thus deemed to be a product of telephone technology.

The telephone was also said to affect physical and mental health. It was seen as a "germ collector," and doctors "urge[d] that the health department compel the telephone companies to equip their instruments with antiseptic devices which would destroy all germs as they entered the transmitter" (BCA, ncm 1906f). The number of articles written on this issue[21] shows that it was seen as a serious problem starting around 1905. Public telephones were considered unsafe because it was thought that they were packed with diphtheria, influenza, and consumption germs (BCA, ncm 1908d). It was suggested that hygienic devices be installed to lessen the risk of infection. This perception vanished as suddenly as it had appeared, without any apparent change in the telephone apparatus.

The telephone was also considered a "nerve-racking" technology because of its capacity to intrude on one's privacy at any time of the day. As one woman attested, "I have been called to the telephone three times this morning by some of my friends who just wanted to visit. Twice the bell woke the baby up and once my blackberry jam burned while I was trying to make an excuse to get away" (BCA, ty 10 (6) 1905, p. 429). Anxiety was increased by the fact that subscribers were instructed by the companies to answer the phone promptly.[22] Night calls were particularly aggravating, to the point that some physicians refused to have a telephone at their bedside (BCA, d 1009, 1934). It was a fact that the telephone was altering a society previously ruled by rigid, well-determined social practices.

The changes in popular practices brought about by the technology were instrumental in the creation of a telephone culture. The new form of communication created by telephone systems reproduced some social activities and modified others. One characteristic of the telephone system planned by and for the ruling classes was its speed. Casson said that the telephone had made life "more tense, alert, vivid" (1910a, p. 231). *Booklovers' Magazine* claimed that the telephone had "doubled pressure, condensed the world, [made] us all next-door neighbours" ("Behind the Scene at 'Central'" 1903, p. 390). The effect was multidimensional. The telephone was developed in response to capitalist society's requirement for faster means of communication, and it had indeed accelerated the speed of transactions. Moreover, its capacity for long-distance contact gave people the illusion that it had strengthened the nation's solidarity (Carty 1922b, p. 9), and eliminated class differentiation (Carty 1926a, p. 2). In reality, it only permitted entrenched social groups to communicate more often and more rapidly. Telephone contacts between members of the working classes and those of the ruling classes always occurred through an already existing rigid etiquette. Moreover, wealthy women on party lines often complained of the bad manners of low-wage women, and pressed the telephone companies to give them private lines. But what was the deeper impact of the telephone on women?

EMANCIPATING WOMEN?

The telephone had contradictory effects on women: it had some emancipatory influence, yet it often contributed to reproduction, and even reinforcement, of sexist attitudes. Often presented as a liberator for women, it was said that "its power to aid in accomplishment serve[d] to stimulate the wife, the mother, into achievements that [made] life worth living" (BCA, ty 8 (3) 1904, p. 232). The fantastic capacities of the telephone were to liberate "slave women" from domestic chores, and allow them to be more rested, more sociable, and happier (BCA, nca 1903–1913). Still, when women began to use the instrument for sociability, in order to break out of their isolation in the household, men started to object to this frivolous use of the telephone, and to ridicule them in newspapers by accusing them of having a "gossiping instinct" (BCA, ncm 1906g); in journal articles by calling their practices "irrational use[s]" (BCA, ncm 1907a, ty 10 (3) 1905, p. 211); and even in books (BCA, sf.ind 1895). The clergy also joined the chauvinist movement. In New York, for instance, the Reverend Parks publicly denounced "women of the leisure class who waste their time in unprofitable chatter over the telephone." They were spending valuable time "in idle talk and in gossip . . . in calls that were of no value to any one," instead of busying themselves in cleaning their houses and raising their children (BCA, ncm 1908a). However, Ryan (1983) points out that a significant group of these "women of elite status were involved in voluntary associations, performing such activities as care of the poor, self-improvement of young men," and so on. It is therefore reasonable to assume that some, if not most, of their telephone conversations were to discuss issues related to these pursuits. However, telephone use by women produced the same sexist reaction as that toward women's gatherings. For men, who "wanted control of all communication conducted through the technology that belonged to them" (Marvin 1988, p. 24), women did not meet for important reasons, but merely to gossip. The telephone, which was a technology developed exclusively for business purposes, was losing its seriousness with women's practices.

Yet, at the same time as the telephone helped to reinforce male chauvinism, it also contributed to women's emancipation. An observer in the 1890s asserted that "the telephone permitted girls to be bolder in their approach then [sic] it had to be made face to face" (BCA, sf.ind, n.d.). The new technology was seen as playing a part "in changing the prudish attitudes" of nineteenth-century women. An elderly woman was "appall[ed] . . . to see how they use the telephone nowadays." She was referring to her niece and her male friend talking on the phone while her niece was only partially dressed: "The two of them stood talking to one another just as if they were entirely dressed and had stopped for a little chat on the street!" (BCA, qa 1903, p. 343) Men, and some women, felt uneasy about this new "breeze of liberation." A male writer reported that "the telephone has been instrumental in bringing the young woman of today to a point where her grandmother wouldn't recognize her; that it is in no little degree responsible for her increasing loose manners and looser habits, any mother who takes the time to realize the situation will doubtless agree" (BCA, sf.ind 1921). Sometimes, this boldness amounted to no more than young women calling male telephone operators during the evening for "flirtatious purposes." Although this is not a serious instance, women did become more outspoken over the years when they talked on the telephone. "The telephone gives the flapper courage—and more it permits a girl to lie in her bed and to talk with a man lying in his bed; it permits her half-clothed, to talk with him a moment after its ring had made him hop nude out of his bathtub. Its delicate suggestiveness is not lost in these instances. The most modest girl in America, the girl who blushes even at a man's allusion to his chillblains, once she gets her nose in a telephone mouthpiece acquires a sudden and surprising self-assurance and aptitude at wheeze" (BCA, sf.ind 1921).

Was it the contradictory feelings of closeness and remoteness, creating a sense of intimacy and safety at the same time, that encouraged women to be more intrepid on the telephone? This "impersonal instrument of personal communication," which enabled women to talk without being seen, was undoubtedly disturbing for some men in this period of female sexual repression, when the "vision" of sexuality was thought most crude, and where its expressions were limited to suggestive gestures (Haller and Haller 1974). It seems that the "delicate suggestiveness" created by the technological particularities of the telephone was well adapted to the prudishness of late-Victorian women, since writers reported that they were not embarrassed by sexual connotations when talking to the other sex over the phone. This "audacity"—which perhaps amounted only to an absence of a nonverbal expression of embarrassment which, of course, could not be seen at the other end of the line[23]— appeared to be due to the telephone, since, at social gatherings, women were said to recover their attitude of submissiveness and prudery. In fact, their audacity was very limited. Some researchers (e.g., Maddox 1977) found that women tended to be passive on the telephone, reproducing their behavior in society. In other words, they called male friends, but did not initiate a new relationship with a man by telephone, preferring to wait for a call.

Thus, telephone development had a mixed impact on women. On the one hand, it granted them some liberation by decreasing domestic chores and freeing them from some social restrictions in mixed relationships. It also permitted them to "visit" by telephone without having to rely on anyone to harness the horses or drive them. On the other hand, access to the telephone may have reduced the number of visits they made to friends and outings to concerts, which were transmitted over the telephone.

In short, a study of the development of the telephone system in relation to women's social and cultural practices points to a contradiction between the privatization and the socialization of women's communication. The public aspect of the telephone enlarged women's opportunities for socialization by allowing them to have instantaneous contact with a much larger number of people. However, these contacts occurred in the privacy of their home, which may have reduced women's opportunities for socializing outside the household.

In any case, women's contributions to the forms of telephone practices, unforeseen by the male inventors and owners, forced telephone companies to rethink their expansion plans. They definitely influenced use of the telephone, shifting it from a strictly business-oriented one to one oriented toward socialization. In addition, women's use *en masse* of the telephone stimulated expansion of the system, not only in business areas of cities and big towns, but in residential sectors and in rural areas.

NOTES

1. Fischer (1988a) situates the rapid growth of rural telephony by independent companies in United States at around 1893, after Bell's patents expired. For more information on American rural telephone-system development, see Fischer 1988a.
2. No secrecy switch of any kind was promoted by Bell Telephone Co., or by any other company for that matter, whereas private lines were strongly recommended, in the very first advertisement, as something which could be built "on reasonable terms" (BCA, d 12016, 1885b).
3. Automatic telephones had been marketed earlier in Paris and New York.
4. He did not say, however, what pressure was put on the operator if she refused to do it.

5. For more information on this issue, see BCA, ncm, 1918a.

6. There was another lengthy debate on the right of police forces to tap telephone wires in the late 1960s, when John Turner was justice minister, and a more specific bill was enacted by Ottawa to limit police activities.

7. For additional reports on invasion of the home by telephone, see BCA, ty 1904, 7 (4), p. 309; ty 1905, 10 (6), p. 433.

8. Fischer situates the beginning of the American telephone companies' advertisement of the telephone for sociability at the end of the 1920s. For more information on American development, see Fischer 1988b.

9. The agenda was drawn up by an operator.

10. See BCA, ty 1905, 10 (3), p. 211; ncm, 1908a; 1919a. Marvin also makes the point that men in the telephone business thought that "women failed to understand electrical messages the way their male protectors did, as scarce and expensive commodities," and that "their [women's] conversation [was] trivial and uninformative, and could [have been] easily managed face-to-face." Marvin 1988, pp. 22–32.

11. The home, however, was itself becoming less private with the advent of the telephone. For more information on the danger of the bicycle for Victorian women, see Haller and Haller 1974, pp. 174–87.

12. On the other hand, Fischer argues that in the United States rural residents were independent and had very little intercourse with their neighbors. See Fischer 1988b.

13. It is interesting to note that, a few years after Bell Telephone Co. had, with great effort, eliminated party lines in cities and built its system on the basis of private lines only, with the hope that one day it would be preeminent even in rural areas, it reintroduced, for an extra fee, a service with the advantages of the party line. The "telephone conference service," started in the early 1930s, was available for business and for "social use" (Banning 1936, p. 146). One difference between these services lay in the distance they covered. Party-line service was limited to local calls, whereas conference service was available for long-distance communication. Still, it was possible to adapt party-line service to long-distance service. Another important difference was that "meetings" on party lines did not involve as exclusive a group of callers as did "conference calls," since any subscriber connected to the party line could listen to or participate in conversations, whereas conference-call participants were predetermined.

14. Statistics on telephone conversations for Canada are not available. However, as Figure 1 shows, Canada was only slightly behind the United States in terms of telephones per capita—ten percent of the population in Canada in comparison to twelve percent for the United States—and Canadians had a reputation for being heavy telephone users. Consequently, the figures for telephone conversations for the United States give a good idea of what was happening here. Development of the telephone in the United States was generally comparable to that in Canada, as one might expect, since many factors were similar: the same company, with management in continual contact, same types of population, and so on. There were, however, some variations, as Fischer (1988b) points out.

15. See also Rhodes 1927.

16. She was probably afraid of being caught by her employer. Domestics usually were not allowed to use their employers' telephone for personal calls.

17. Application of the law began early in 1916. See: BCA, nct 1916d; 1916e.

18. As late as 1905, Bell managers were still writing to each other, instead of telephoning, for business matters. See: BCA, sle 1905a, b. Although they complained about the poor postal service, they continued to do business via correspondence, even to locations within telephone reach. Was the telephone too indiscreet for them—or perhaps, too expensive?

19. See BCA, d 12016, 1880e; qa 1880e, 1880d, 1914.

20. Shaw worked for a British telephone company for some years at the beginning of his writing career.

21. Here are some samples: "Telephone and Germs," *Montreal Star,* September 11, 1905; "New Way to Telephone," *Montreal Gazette,* January 24, 1907; "The Telephone and Microbes," *Montreal Star,* July 30, 1908; "Germs in the Telephone," *Telegram,* January 13, 1916; "Germ Proof Phone," *Herald,* February 17, 1916.

22. The operator was instructed to ring a subscriber no more than twice.

23. Blushing, which was Victorian women's general expression of embarrassment, was, of course, not discernible over the telephone. Embarrassment was thus expressed in vocal nuances, which were imperfectly transmitted over the telephone.

CHAPTER 4
FEMININITY AND THE
ELECTRIC CAR

VIRGINIA SCHARFF

(1991)

While American women chafed at their social, spatial, and political limitations, some carmakers began to fashion new wheels to preserve the dainty domain of Victorian decorum. Colonel Albert A. Pope, president of the Pope Manufacturing Company of Hartford, Connecticut, believed that "you can't get people to sit over an explosion." As he moved his company out of bicycle manufacturing and into the automobile business, he determined to concentrate not on noisy, smelly gasoline-powered cars, but instead, on clean, quiet electric vehicles. By 1897, the Pope Manufacturing Company had produced some five hundred electric cars.[1]

While Pope pursued this entrepreneurial strategy, thousands of Americans proved him a bad prophet and purchased gasoline motorcars. In response to demand, Pope began to produce some gasoline cars, but the company remained committed to the idea that there was a natural market for slower, cleaner electrics. As Pope suggested in a 1903 advertisement for the Pope-Waverly electric model, "electrics . . . will appeal to any one interested in an absolutely noiseless, odorless, clean and stylish rig that is always ready and that, mile for mile, can be operated at less cost than any other type of motor car." Lest this message escape those it was intended to attract, the text accompanied a picture of a delighted woman driver piloting a smiling female passenger.[2]

Pitching electric cars to women represented a strategy that was at once expansive and limiting, both for automakers' opportunities, and for women who wanted to be motorists. After all, in the infancy of the automobile industry, men like Pope had to unravel mysteries of design and production—what kinds of devices might make a carriage move without benefit of a horse? Would gasoline, steam, or electricity prove to be the most practical source of power? Might not all three have their disparate uses? How should such devices be manufactured? What materials should they be made of? How might they be distributed? Neither omniscient nor omnipotent, auto manufacturers generally produced individual vehicles on order and groped only haltingly toward perceiving a wider market.

The French and German automakers who pioneered the business in the late nineteenth century had produced luxury motorcars for the sporting rich, and at first, American manufacturers followed the European example in catering to the domestic carriage trade. As early as 1900, American socialites, male and female, vied with one another in devising ways of using the auto for entertainment. Wealthy men held races and rallies at various posh watering holes; women attended, and sometimes participated.[3] Prominent women also developed their own automotive spectacles. They besieged Newport in flower-decked car convoys, held drive-in dinner parties where they demanded curb service at fashionable Boston restaurants, or simply stepped from their elegant conveyances at the opera house door, dripping diamonds and pearls. In keeping with the tastes of their owners, expensive motorcars featured such "refinements" as cut-glass bud vases and built-in vanity cases.[4]

These male and female motoring larks differed more in terms of style than substance; wealthy men and women shared a taste for luxury and leisure, as well as bracing adventure, in their motoring. Nevertheless, manufacturers tended to associate the qualities of comfort, convenience, and aesthetic appeal with women, while linking power, range, economy, and thrift with men. Women were presumed to be too weak, timid, and fastidious to want to drive noisy, smelly gasoline-powered cars. Thus at first, manufacturers, influenced by Victorian notions of masculinity and femininity, devised a kind of "separate spheres" ideology about automobiles: gas cars were for men, electric cars were for women.

The electric automobile had been around since the birth of the motor age, and its identification with women took hold early and tenaciously. Genevera Delphine Mudge of New York City, identified by one source as the first woman motorist in the United States, drove an electric in 1898, and one Miss Daisy Post also drove an electric vehicle as early as 1898.[5] In 1900, the City Engineer of Chicago complained that many women drivers were not bothering to get licenses, and *Horseless Age* magazine, conflating all women drivers with those who drove electrics, noted that "so far only eight women have secured permits to operate electric vehicles, but . . . there are twenty-five to fifty women regularly running the machines through the city."[6]

Certainly some women who wanted the increased mobility that came with driving a car believed that gasoline vehicles, being powerful, complicated, fast, dirty, and capable of long-distance runs, belonged to men, while electric cars, being simple, comfortable, clean, and quiet, though somewhat short on power and restricted in range, better suited women. Electrics tended to be smaller and slower than gasoline-powered cars, and often were designed as enclosed vehicles.[7] If electrics offered less automobility than gas cars, they offered greater mobility than horses, and more independence and flexibility than trolleys. Understandably, some women—most of them well-to-do—thus chose to drive electrics. In April of 1904, *Motor* magazine's society columnist noted:

Mrs. James G. Blaine has been spending the last few weeks with her parents at Washington, and has been seen almost daily riding about in an electric runabout. The latter appears to be the most popular form of automobile for women, at any rate in the National Capital. . . . Indeed, judging from the number of motors that one sees driven by women on a fine afternoon, one would imagine that nearly every belle in Washington owned a machine.[8]

Like Pope, other electric car manufacturers were quick to see women as a potential gold mine. In the years before World War I, articles on electric vehicles, or on women drivers, and advertisements for electrics in such publications as *Motor* and *Country Life in America* featured photographs of women driving, charging, and otherwise maintaining electrics, reflecting both a specific marketing strategy and a more diffuse cultural tendency to divide the world between masculine and feminine.[9] Electric vehicle manufacturers including the Anderson, Woods, Baker, Borland, and Milburn companies featured women in their advertisements. Touting such virtues as luxury, beauty, ease of operation, and economy, manufacturers attempted to appeal to an affluent female clientele without alienating men who might wish to purchase an electric for their wives or daughters, or even for themselves. The Argo company advertised its 1912 model, a sporty low-slung electric vehicle, as "a woman's car that any man is proud to drive."[10] The Anderson Electric Car Company invited men to purchase its Detroit model "for your bride-to-be—or your bride of many Junes ago. . . . No other bridal present means so much— expresses so perfectly all that you want to say. . . . the most *considerate choice* for her permanent happiness, comfort, luxury, safety."[11] The Detroit electric was said to be not only "the last word in luxury and beauty, as well as efficiency," but also a boon to feminine comeliness:

> To the well-bred woman—the Detroit Electric has a particular appeal. In it she can preserve her toilet immaculate, her coiffure intact.
> She can drive it with all desired privacy, yet safely—in constant touch with traffic conditions all about her.[12]

However much manufacturers trumpeted the appealing qualities of electrics, automobiles powered by electric batteries had serious disadvantages compared to gas-powered vehicles. They were generally more expensive to manufacture, had limited range (averaging twenty to fifty miles per charge), and were too heavy to climb hills or run at high speeds.[13] Inventor Thomas Edison promised that he would develop a long-distance electric storage battery, but his efforts in this regard proved fruitless.[14] By 1908, even some of those who applauded the use of electrics admitted their limitations. Writer Herbert H. Rice noted that despite improvements in charging technology and vehicle design, "there are not apparent any great opportunities for extraordinary changes unless in the battery."[15] Rice advised the motoring public to give up hoping for a battery that would go one hundred miles on a single charge (a hope which, he admitted, had caused electric sales to suffer) since "not one in one hundred users requires a service extending beyond thirty-five miles, while in the majority of cases the odometer would record less than fifteen miles for the day's errands."[16]

This acknowledgment of the electric auto's problems suggests that its association with women was at once a symptom of, and an attempted cure for, its competitive disadvantages. The electric's circumscribed mobility seemed adequate to those who assumed that "the electric is the vehicle of the home," adequate, that is, for homemakers who did not expect to take long trips, or frequent trips, or to get stuck in traffic jams.[17] Playing on the domestic theme, the General Electric Company asserted, "any woman can charge her own electric with a G-E Rectifier," advertising with a photograph of a woman charging her car, using a machine that occupied most of one wall of the family garage. Declaring that "there are no tiresome trips to a public garage, no waiting— the car is always at home, ready when you are," General Electric implied that using the rectifier would relieve the woman motorist of such inconveniences as often accompanied having to leave home.[18]

At times the electric car and its purportedly female clientele seemed entwined, as the electric's advocates used a Victorian language of gender to talk about cars. *Country Life in America* writer Phil M. Riley combated the criticism that "electric power is weak," by asserting, "It is important with an electric not to waste power needlessly, that is all." Riley assured his readers that "the proper sphere of the electric vehicle is not in competition with the gasolene [sic] touring car."[19] Just as conservative commentators admonished women to forego high-powered business and political activity and conserve their energy for domestic tasks, so, Riley said, the electric vehicle might fulfill its mission as "an ever-ready runabout for daily use," leaving extended travel and fast driving to men in gas-powered cars. Moreover, both Rice and Riley chose to refer to the electric vehicle's venue of operation as a "sphere." Victorian Americans commonly represented women's and men's respective social roles as "separate spheres." This simple visual image often served as a shorthand description of complex relations not only between individuals of different biological sexes, but between feminine and masculine attributes (including passivity and activity), private and public life, household and workplace, homemaking and paid work, culture and politics.[20] The automobile might be novel, but it could not escape entanglement in a web of meaning spun with the threads of masculinity and femininity.

That many people subsumed a variety of ideological, economic, familial, political, and spatial relations under the heading of "separate spheres" testified to Americans' tenacity in using gender to order experience. But however powerfully evocative, this image vastly oversimplified both human relations and social forces.[21] Sometimes people act in accordance with gender prescriptions; sometimes they do not. Men, supposedly rugged, seek shelter from the rain. Women, supposedly soft-spoken, yell at their children. Men and women continually revised both their actions and their expectations, more often by the minute adjustments of private negotiation than by legal fiat or national proclamation. Through the small changes of personal life, leading to larger transformations on a social scale, activities and entities assigned to one sphere or the other, considered appropriate for either women or men, sometimes lost or recast their gendered meanings. When women refused to conform to expectations, when new technologies unsettled traditional assumptions, when entrepreneurs defied common wisdom in search of profits, change accelerated.[22]

All three forces—female nonconformity, technological innovation, and economic competition—were very much in play in the first third of the century, and the future of the car culture was far from clear. Consumers, engineers, and businessmen would interact in ways no one could predict precisely. In the years before 1920, Americans used all kinds of transportation: their own legs, mules and horses, trains and trolleys, and electric, gas, and steam automobiles. Each method had benefits and drawbacks. Supporters of electric motorcars were at least as inclined to point out the electric's advantages over the horse and buggy as they were to compare electric and gas vehicles. C. H. Claudy, an early and staunch advocate of electric vehicles (he would later become the automotive columnist for the *Woman's Home Companion*), had written in 1907 that the electric car "now does more work, in certain lines, than horses ever did."[23] Claudy claimed the electric would be a boon to all women, asking whether there had "ever been an invention of more solid comfort to the feminine half of humanity than the electric carriage?" He observed that the woman who drove an electric "finds it very convenient to call up the garage, have her runabout sent around instantly and not have to wait for a complicated hitching or a currying and combing of horses."[24]

Although Claudy staunchly supported women's driving, he was slow to recommend gasoline cars for women. Describing the electric as "the car which has a circumscribed radius," he joined the ranks of those who envisioned the electric in terms of woman's special, yet limited, sphere. Women, he believed, might use electrics to accomplish the social and domestic tasks that were part of the middle-class homemaker's vocation, without overstepping the bounds of feminine propriety. "What a delight it is," he wrote, "to have a machine which she can run herself, with no loss of dignity, for making calls, for shopping, for a pleasurable ride, for the paying back of some small social debt."[25] The electric might even be just the thing to reconcile motoring and motherhood. Pointing out that "in no way can a child get so much air in so little time as by the use of the automobile" Claudy declared that "it would not be amiss to call the electric the modern baby carriage. . . . It is the light electric runabout which deserves the title of scientific perambulator."[26] Thus he painted a rather odd, infantile picture of the woman driver, tucked in alongside her baby in a "scientific perambulator."

While promoters of electrics tried to forge a positive link between the woman driver and the battery-powered motorcar, an occasional critic suggested that women's purported deficiencies in driving ought to disqualify them from operating anything more powerful than rather tame electrics. In an article on reckless drivers published in *The Outlook*, writer Montgomery Rollins drew on the notion that femaleness unfitted some people for the adult responsibility of driving a powerful gasoline automobile. Rollins argued, "It's no child's play to run a motor car. No license should be granted to anyone under eighteen . . . and never to a woman, unless, possibly, for a car driven by electric power."[27]

Against such disparagement of both electrics and women, electric vehicle manufacturers and their supporters worked to protect whatever claim they might have to women motorists, while also struggling to get a foothold in the male market so clearly dominated by gasoline cars. C. H. Claudy believed that electrics would be useful to an elite group of men who might value comfort, cleanliness, and everyday utility over extended range and sportiness. Like others, Claudy assumed that a few fastidious men, such as doctors and some businessmen, would be willing to forego speed and range for the advantages of simple mechanical construction, reliability on short errands, quietness, cleanliness, and simplicity of operation.[28] The implicit corollary of such assumptions was that most men had little desire for the kinds of comforts and conveniences electrics offered, preferring a more rugged and vigorous, less restrictive form of motoring. The Detroit company tried in 1910 to counteract the electric's fussy feminine image by introducing one of its electric models as a "new car for 'him' . . . a brand-new extra-low and rakish Detroit Electric model for *men* is our Gentlemen's Underslung Roadster."[29] Yet men continued to spurn the electric, quite simply because it did not go far enough or fast enough.[30]

As men registered their indifference to the electric, women were demonstrating their own unwillingness to leave long-distance touring and high-speed driving to men. As a consequence, the application of separate spheres ideology to motive power in automobiles had lost force by 1912, when C. H. Claudy announced that "the time has gone by when motor cars had sex—when the gasolene [sic] car was preeminently for the man, and the electric, because of its simplicity, for the women." Beliefs, however, die hard, and even this exponent of technological progress remained unable to abandon completely the idea that "motor cars had sex." Once again invoking a female disposition toward convenience, Claudy predicted that "of all the types of self propelled vehicles, the electric is now, and seems likely to remain, the simplest to handle on the road and to care for at home, whereby it still is, and seems likely to continue to be, the ladies' favorite."[31]

Like Colonel Pope before him, Claudy very quickly proved a poor prognosticator. Relating the story of a bride who told her young husband, "I don't want an electric. I want a car that can go a long distance. I want a car that can go fast, and an electric can't go either far or fast," Claudy commented incredulously. "The lady was right in one thing—she did not want an electric. What she wanted was a six-cylinder touring car!"[32] Instead of acknowledging women's similarity to men in this matter of automotive taste, he set about trying to reconcile female drivers to the more womanly form of motoring. Rather than demanding the speed, range, and hill-climbing power of gasoline vehicles, he advised female motorists to accept the electric's limitations. Claudy admitted, "A practical electric vehicle cannot be built so that it can go fast *and* far *and* climb hills. *Speed* you can have, or great *radius* you can have—but not both at once and still keep down weight and cost."[33] Women, he maintained, had no need for speed:

It can be roundly stated without fear of contradiction that the times a woman wants to run an electric 30 miles an hour, are few and far between. . . . It is an unnecessarily fast speed for pleasure driving. . . . If the car you select has a maximum speed of 25 miles on the level, it goes quite fast enough.[34]

In much the same manner that he had dismissed women's claim to velocity, he would also disparage women's desire to cover distance. Claudy explained that "a radius of 60 to 80 miles is ample for any electric car," stretching the capabilities of the average electric vehicle, and suggesting that women had no need to go further. For women to accept such circumscribed mobility ruled out cross-country travel, or even extended day trips, in an era when gas stations were beginning to dot the countryside, but electric charging stations had not spread beyond major cities. In addition, electric batteries needed servicing so often that they would have forced cross-country travelers to stop more frequently, and for much longer periods of time, than most Americans cared to do, particularly in an era when poor road quality forced more than enough stops for the average traveler.[35] Ignoring such restrictions, Claudy reminded readers of the electric's advantages for women, given their bulky clothing, innate preference for luxury, and inability to learn to shift gears:

Practically all the modern electric cars are arranged with special reference to their ease of control by women—that is, the controlling and reverse levers are (or should be) simple in operation and few in number, they work easily, and are so placed and arranged as not to catch and tear the dress. Besides these points, women naturally choose those cars the interior appointments of which please them the most.[36]

Despite their narrow view of women's talents and desires, we need not blame the electric's advocates too much for finding virtue in electric automobiles. After all, motorists of any era and either sex might find the qualities of simplicity, convenience, and aesthetic appeal worth having in a motor vehicle. However, when automotive designers and promoters, acting in part under the influence of cultural imperatives regarding gender, coupled these desirable attributes with the electric's limited power and circumscribed range, they misread their audience. No law of nature dictated that automobiles could not be designed to be comfortable, reliable, handsome, and powerful, qualities that might appeal to men and women alike. And even if automakers continued to insist that males and females had different automotive preferences, a sex-specific promotional strategy made very little business sense in an economy where consumers, male or female, had some choice, and where families buying only one vehicle were likely to have to accommodate male drivers who were presumed to want to go farther and faster than their female counterparts.

Perhaps most damaging, the electric was too cumbersome to manage bad roads. At the turn of the century, few localities in the United States could claim many miles of improved highways. Thus the electric car had limited appeal for motorists of either sex in places where distances were great and paved roads were few. In Tucson, Arizona, for example, twenty-three women owned autos in 1914. Twenty-one of those owned gasoline-powered vehicles, and none of the 402 male car owners listed in the *Tucson Automobile Directory* owned electrics. Only one vehicle listed could be definitely identified as an electric, and one other may have been an electric.[37] The Houston, Texas automobile directory of 1915 revealed that only 30 out of 425 women auto owners had electrics, and most of those appeared to have registered their vehicles in the very earliest years of the car culture. Thus in Houston, by 1915, only one woman car owner in fourteen, or seven percent of the total, had an electric. Even during the electric's pre-Model T heyday, four out of five women auto owners in Houston had gasoline cars.[38] The economic folly of Claudy's advice was compounded by the fact that, particularly after Henry Ford's introduction of the Model T in 1908, numerous gasoline cars were available for prices under $1,500, while electric autos appear to have remained more expensive than gas cars[39] (see Table 1).

The rapidly growing number of women driving gasoline cars did as much to disrupt the link between women and electrics as any force of nature or engineering. By 1913, C. H. Claudy, who had put so much effort into promoting electric vehicles to female drivers, had changed his mind. He had come to believe that many women had both the ability and the determination to drive gas-powered automobiles. Moreover, he recognized that male prejudice, more than female preference, stood in the way of women who wished to drive gas cars. In a piece on "The Woman and Her Car," Claudy imagined the feelings of a young woman who aspired to the driver's seat: "Oh, I'd love to have a car, but father doesn't think I could drive it. He wants me to have an electric, and they don't go either fast or far enough."[40] The columnist noted: "Father frequently does think his daughter hasn't the strength, skill, or natural ability to acquire it, necessary to drive a gasolene car successfully. Many husbands think the same about their wives." By this time, however, he no longer shared such views, and argued that "there is no reason at all why . . . you [women] cannot drive with pleasure to your friends, as skilfully [sic], as gracefully, and with as obedient a car as anyone, even father, can wish."[41] Thereafter, in articles for the *Woman's Home Companion,* Claudy encouraged women to drive gasoline vehicles, providing sensible advice on motoring and introducing women to the intricacies of auto maintenance.[42] Having placed the gas-powered motorcar within the compass of woman's sphere, Claudy also had stretched his definition of the feminine. By 1920, he would assert, "The number of women who drive motor cars with skill and enjoyment is sufficient proof that there is nothing in the modern Pegasus which femininity cannot master."[43] In an effort to keep up with consumers' changing demands, producers would at once modify their notions of gender and the machines they made.

A few gasoline auto manufacturers had long since recognized that there was a female market for their products. They realized that the automobile was unlikely to supersede the horse as a popular mode of transportation until it became a family vehicle, offering power as well as simplicity, range as well as convenience. The Winton Company, promoting its Model C in 1905, declared that "Women Praise the Winton," a vehicle "ideal for women's use" because it was "as easily controlled as the best mannered horse," but "safer, because it cannot scare." The company also noted that the Model C went "as far, and as fast or as slow, as the lady at the wheel desires."[44] To prove its point, Winton included testimonials from two women drivers. One had written, "I much prefer my new WINTON to the electric I formerly owned, and its control is fully as perfect. It is a comfort to know that one has the power to go fast or slow as desired."[45] Another satisfied female motorist belied the image of women drivers as too feminine to tackle gear-shifting, cranking, and simple mechanical work. The ad quoted her to the effect that

> every day since [the Winton] came into our possession it has had no small mileage, and at no time has the engine "missed" an explosion. Neither has there been occasion to make a single adjustment, beyond once retightening the clutch. I have not the slightest difficulty in handling the car—motor has not yet failed to start with a single throw of the crank. I like the magneto. The WINTON system of individual clutch is pleasingly effective, and the control is so delightfully simple that to drive the car—even through congested city thoroughfares, is the easiest thing imaginable.[46]

In 1909, the Maxwell-Briscoe company also made an effort to market gas-powered cars to families that included women drivers, sending Alice Huyler Ramsey and three women passengers on a highly publicized cross-country drive and mounting an advertising campaign based on the notion of the inexpensive family car.[47] In praise of its Model AA, a "reliable business runabout" priced at $600 to compete with the Ford Model T, the company asserted: "Everyone should own this car, because it fills the universal need. As easy to drive as an electric. Your wife, daughter, or son can run this MAXWELL and care for it—a chauffeur is unnecessary."[48] The Maxwell, advertising copywriters insisted, was much more than a pleasure car for buffs or thrill seekers. "For errands, shopping, calls, meeting trains, taking the children to school, for business or pleasure, this automobile is the gateway to outdoors and health. Picture yourself in it—how would you use it?"[49]

By 1910, the White Motor Company had joined Winton and Maxwell-Briscoe in the effort to attract women drivers to gasoline cars. The company promoted its White coupe as "a woman's town car," explaining that "most women have felt compelled to drive electric cars—especially in the Winter—because no gasoline car was designed for a woman to drive." White, however, claimed to have solved this design problem with the "inside drive coupe," a closed car very much resembling the boxy electric coupes of the day, featuring doors on both sides wide enough to accommodate cumbersome skirts and a driver's seat that folded up "to make entrance easy from either side."[50] Calling attention to the car's "upholstery, electric lights, and the little accessories . . . all of the finest imported materials," the company insisted that "nothing has been overlooked that could contribute to a woman's satisfaction in a car

TABLE 1
Some Prices of Electric Automobiles, 1903–1919

Manufacturer	Price range (Dollars)	Year
Pope-Waverly	850–900	1903
Woods	2100–2700	1909
Bailey	2400–2600	1910
Hupp-Yeats	1750	1910
Waverly	2250	1912
Standard	1850	1912
Argo	2500–3100	1913
Detroit	2550–3000	1913
Milburn*	1285–1685	1916
Milburn*	1885	1917
Milburn*	1885	1918
Milburn*	2385	1919

Source: *Motor* magazine, advertisements for electric vehicles including price information, 1903–1920.
*Prices given are for the "Milburn Light Electric," a model that apparently became more expensive between 1916 and 1919.

which is so particularly designed for her personal use."[51] While upholding most of the sex-stereotyped ideas about women's automotive abilities and preferences, such advertisements undermined the exclusive identification of gasoline power with male drivers, thus gently challenging the consignment of women to the realm of the electric-powered vehicle.

As these pre-World War I reworkings of the notion of separate automotive spheres indicate, many observers recognized that women were driving in increasing numbers, and were not confining themselves to electrics. The most ambitious automotive capitalist might imagine a potential female market numbering into the millions; if such consumers could not be manipulated, they had to be heeded. In 1913, the high-toned *Vanity Fair* ran a "Casual Cutouts" column on "motoring for the very rich," highlighting technical information on various vehicles and illustrated with photographs of women drivers.[52] In 1915, a writer for the *Illustrated World* announced: "Starting a few years go with a little timid venturing on the boulevards in their electrics, women have gradually conquered the motorcar. . . . Their fear of gasoline and monkey wrenches has vanished."[53] Moreover, middle-class women's magazines like the *Ladies' Home Journal,* sensitive to women's consumer power in both the magazine and automotive marketplaces, began to include features on driving and maintaining cars.[54] Such publications had also begun to attract auto advertisements.

Notions about femininity and women's growing demand for automobility had collided in the automotive marketplace, and the chief casualty was the electric car. The surprising thing, however, is not that electrics faded so early, but that they lasted so long, given their manifestly lower power, frequently higher prices, and smaller range than gas cars. Even in their heyday, electrics

TABLE 2
The Number of Electrics in Use, 1908
(Selected Cities)

City	Approximate Number
Toledo, Ohio	400
Cleveland, Ohio	650
Atlanta, Georgia	175
Columbus, Ohio	140
Denver, Colorado	450
Detroit, Michigan	250
Washington, D.C.	300
Chicago, Illinois	900
Buffalo, New York	300
Rochester, New York	350
Indianapolis, Indiana	125
Hartford, Connecticut	100
Rockford, Illinois	75
Binghamton, New York	75
TOTAL	4290

Source: Wilhelm Nassau, *Motor* magazine, July 1908.

never comprised more than a tiny share of the market for cars. As early as 1908, according to a survey of fourteen major cities in which electrics were relatively widely used, in no city were more than 900 electrics in operation, and there were fewer than 4,300 electric vehicles in use all together (see Table 2). Furthermore, these figures do not reflect purely private use of electric vehicles, since the Electric Vehicle Company (popularly known as the "Lead Cab Trust") had operated a fleet of some two thousand electric cabs in a number of these cities between 1899 and 1907.[55] While this survey did not include figures from a number of major cities (New York, Boston, and Philadelphia are among those omitted), the cities included represented centers of electric vehicle manufacturing, where electrics were likely to have been in proportionally more widespread use than anywhere else. That same year, a total of 194,400 automobiles were registered in the United States.[56] In 1915, *Motor* magazine estimated that there were some 50,000 electric motor vehicles in service in the United States, representing approximately two percent of the total of 2,490,900 motor vehicles of all types registered in the country that year.[57] Electric models continued to be produced on order until 1938, but passenger cars powered by electric batteries had largely disappeared by the mid-twenties.[58]

The electric car, marketed primarily as a woman's vehicle, provides a striking example of the influence of gender ideology on automotive production. Paradoxically, the electric's failure also illustrates the impossibility of maintaining rigid gender distinctions in motorcar technology at a time when a declining proportion of customers could afford the luxury of his-and-hers automobiles, and where in any case consumers shared certain preferences regardless of sex. Still, we should be wary of declaring a victory for technology over culture, for the power of the automobile over the stubbornness of gender ideology. The electric vehicle would slip off the automotive stage, reappearing occasionally at the behest of environmental visionaries and (more often) golfers. Culture, however, continued to influence technology. Since people, regardless of sex, insisted on sitting over an explosion, contested notions about masculinity and femininity entered the domain of the gasoline car. As the century moved into its second decade, the auto industry's towering figures engraved differing ideas about gender into the early car culture's epic machines.

NOTES

1. John B. Rae, *The American Automobile* (Chicago: University of Chicago Press, 1965), pp. 11–13; and Theodore F. MacManus and Norman Beasley, *Men, Money, and Motors: The Drama of the Automobile* (New York: Harper and Brothers, 1930), p. 6.

2. *Motor,* December 1903.

3. On early women racing and rally drivers, see Scharff, *Taking the Wheel: Women and the Coming of the Motor Age* (New York: The Free Press, 1991), ch. 5.

4. Frank Donovan, *Wheels for a Nation* (New York: Thomas Y. Crowell, 1965), pp. 1–12; S. E. Lasher, "Society and the Motor Car," *Motor,* December 1910, p. 67.

5. The first electric vehicle to run on American city streets was built by William Morrison of Des Moines, Iowa in 1891. Bonnie Remsberg, "Women Behind the Wheel," *Redbook,* September 1973, reprinted in the Motor Vehicle Manufacturers' Association, *News Review,* September 12, 1973, p. 1; Allan Nevins and F. E. Hill, *Ford: The Times, the Man, the Company, 1865–1915,* vol. 1 (New York: Scribner's, 1954), pp. 197–98.

6. "Chicago Warns Women Automobilists," *Horseless Age,* September 12, 1900, p. 24.

7. Electric car manufacturers adopted closed vehicle design earlier and with more frequency than did makers of most gasoline cars. One magazine writer reported that "gasoline cars set the style, in open cars, although they have borrowed many of the closed car ideas from the electric town car." See "Trend in Electric Car Construction," *Motor,* December 1910, p. 101.

8. "Motoring in Society," *Motor,* April 1904, pp. 22–23.

9. Joseph B. Baker, "The Care of the Electric Vehicle," *Motor,* May 1910, pp. 79–80; C. H. Claudy, "The Electric as a Convenience and a Necessity," *Motor,* April 1907, pp. 47–48; also C. H. Claudy, "The Lady and the Electric," *Country Life in America,* July 15, 1912, pp. 36, 44, 46, 48; C. H. Claudy, "The Woman and Her Car," *Country Life in America,* January 1913, pp. 41–42; "Establishing the Electric," *Motor,* October 1915, pp. 58–59, 132; Wilhelm Nassau, "The Number of Electrics in Use," *Motor,* July 1908, p. 54; Phil M. Riley, "What an Electric Car Can Do," *Country Life in America,* January 1913, pp. 23–36, 70–76. I have also surveyed advertising in all issues of *Motor,* from 1903 through 1929.

10. *Motor,* June 1912, p. xxiii.

11. *Motor,* June 1911.

12. *Motor,* December 1910.

13. James J. Flink, *America Adopts the Automobile* (Cambridge: MIT Press, 1970), p. 45.

14. See articles on Edison's scheme to develop such a battery, *New York Times,* July 29, 1905; August 4, 1905; October 21, 1906; October 23, 1906.

15. Herbert H. Rice, "The Electric of Today," *Motor,* July 1908, p. 49.

16. Ibid., p. 50.

17. Ibid., p. 49.

18. *Motor,* June 1914, p. 186.

19. Riley, pp. 23–36, 70–76.

20. Historians have identified "woman's sphere" as both a source of female subordination and a force in the creation of an autonomous women's culture. Assessing the costs, benefits, and significance of separate spheres for women and men has been a central task of women's history. See Barbara Welter, "The Cult of True Womanhood," *American Quarterly* 18 (1966): 151–74; Kathryn Kish Sklar, *Catharine Beecher: A Study in American Domesticity* (New Haven: Yale University Press, 1973); Carroll Smith-Rosenberg, "The Female World of Love and Ritual: Relations Between Women in Nineteenth-Century America," *SIGNS: Journal of Women in Culture and Society* 1 (1975): 1–30; Nancy F. Cott, *The Bonds of Womanhood: "Woman's Sphere" in New England, 1780–1835* (New Haven: Yale University Press, 1977); Estelle Freedman, "Separatism as Strategy: Female Institution Building and American Feminism, 1870–1930," *Feminist Studies* 5, 3 (Fall 1979): 512–29. Victoria Brown has richly documented the use of similar language to describe woman's nature and prescribe sex role socialization in the United States in the Progressive Era. See Victoria Brown, "Golden Girls: Female Socialization in Los Angeles, 1880–1910" (Ph.D. diss. University of California at San Diego, 1985), especially pp. 93–153.

21. Linda K. Kerber, "Separate Spheres, Female Worlds, Woman's Place: The Rhetoric of Women's History," *Journal of American History* 75, 1 (June 1988): 9–39. Historian Nancy Woloch's description of woman's sphere as "not merely a place or even a vocation, but a values system," reflects the ways in which this term has been used to locate women spatially, occupationally, and morally, conflating social factors that should be kept separate in order to see their interactions. Nancy Woloch, *Women and the American Experience* (New York: Alfred A. Knopf, 1984), p. 101.

22. For analyses of such revisions in American women's history see Myra H. Strober and Audri Gordon Lanford, "The Feminization of Public School Teaching: Cross-Sectional Analysis, 1850–1880," *SIGNS: Journal of Women in Culture and Society* 11 (Winter 1986): 212–95; Virginia Drachman, *Hospital with a Heart: Women Doctors and the Paradox of Separatism at the New England Hospital, 1862–1969* (Ithaca, NY: Cornell University Press, 1984). On the process of social change, see Anthony Giddens, *A Contemporary Critique of Historical Materialism* (New York: Macmillan, 1981).

23. Claudy, "The Electric as a Convenience and a Necessity," p. 47.

24. Ibid., p. 48.

25. Ibid., pp. 47–48.

26. Ibid.

27. Montgomery Rollins, "Sane Motoring—Or Insane?" *The Outlook,* May 29, 1909, p. 279.

28. Rice, p. 50; C. H. Claudy, "The Electric as a Convenience and a Necessity," pp. 47–48. An advertisement for the Argo electric in *Motor,* June 1912, pointed out that the car was "easily handled by a lady, yet any man who motors feels 'right at home' with it." See also ads for the Detroit (*Motor,* December 1910), the Argo (*Motor,* June 1913), and the "Exide" Electric Storage Battery (*Country Life in America,* n.d.).

29. *Motor,* December 1910.

30. By 1922, electric vehicle promoters had even given up on doctors, though they continued to press women to buy electrics. See Dingman Lewis, "The Modern Electric," *Motor,* September 1922, pp. 31, 96.

31. Claudy, "The Lady and the Electric," p. 36.

32. Ibid.

33. Ibid.

34. Ibid., pp. 36, 44.

35. As of 1915, *Motor* magazine reported that there were some six thousand charging stations in the nation, and that other schemes for expanding the electric's range, such as battery exchanges, were being tried. See "Establishing the Electric," p. 59.

36. Claudy, "The Lady and the Electric," p. 44.

37. *Tucson Automobile Directory* (Tucson: J. A. Scott, 1914), Arizona Historical Society, Tucson, Arizona.

38. The 7,732 auto owners listed in the *Houston Automobile Directory, 1915* (Houston: C. L. and Theo Bering, Jr., 1915) appear to have been assigned numbers in chronological order of vehicle registration, judging from the makes of cars listed for each owner. As the numbers got higher, more and more people (women included) were listed as owning Fords. Twenty-six out of the thirty women listed as owning electrics had numbers under 2,500. In this same numerical subset, 102 women were listed as owners of gas-powered vehicles.

39. Rae, pp. 65–67.

40. Claudy, "The Woman and Her Car," p. 41.

41. Ibid., pp. 41–42.

42. C. H. Claudy, "Some Points on Good Driving for the Woman Motorist," *Woman's Home Companion*, February 1917, p. 33; "Putting the Car in Order," *Woman's Home Companion*, March 1917, p. 33.

43. C. H. Claudy, "The Nervous Driver and How She May Acquire Confidence," *Woman's Home Companion*, February 1920, pp. 130–31.

44. *Motor*, June 1905, back cover.

45. Ibid.

46. Ibid.

47. See Alice Huyler Ramsey, *Veil, Duster, and Tire Iron* (Covina, CA: Castle Press, 1961), p. 1.

48. *Motor*, December 1909, p. 11. James S. Couzens, business manager at Ford, calculated that auto manufacturers could reach a mass market by selling a car for $600, but at the time the Ford Motor Company had not managed to achieve that objective. A 1909 Model T touring car sold for $950. By 1912, because of innovations in production technique anticipating the revolutionary moving assembly line, the same car would be available at the target price of $600. See Rae, pp. 60–61.

49. *Motor*, December 1911, p. 11.

50. *Motor*, December 1910.

51. Ibid.

52. "Casual Cutouts," *Vanity Fair*, September 1913, p. 54.

53. F. G. Moorhead, "Women Drive to Fortune," *Illustrated World*, November 1915, p. 334.

54. See, for example, B. McManus, "The Woman Who Drives Her Own Car," *Harper's Bazaar*, July 1912, p. 354; Mrs. A. Sherman Hitchcock, "Woman at the Motor Wheel," *American Home* 10 (April 1913): sup. 6; Ann Murdock, "The Girl Who Drives a Car," *Ladies' Home Journal*, July 1915, p. 11; "Little Things About a Car That Every Woman Who Means to Drive One Ought to Know," *Ladies' Home Journal*, March 1917, p. 32.

55. James J. Flink, *The Car Culture* (Cambridge: MIT Press, 1975), p. 46; Rae, pp. 35–38.

56. *Historical Statistics of the United States, Colonial Times to 1970* (Washington, DC: U.S. Bureau of the Census, 1976), p. 716.

57. "Establishing the Electric," p. 58; *Historical Statistics of the United States*, p. 716.

58. G. Marshall Naul, ed., *The Specification Book for U.S. Cars, 1920–1929; A Complete Guide to the Passenger Automobiles of the Decade* (Osceoloa, WI: Motorbooks International, 1978), p. 92. Rae, p. 106, notes that the 1924 National Automobile Show in New York featured gasoline cars exclusively. Auto shows, then as now, were intended to present state-of-the-art design in motorcars, as well as to publicize new models.

CHAPTER 5
DOES TECHNOLOGY WORK FOR WOMEN TOO?

LILIA OBLEPIAS-RAMOS

(1991)

There is a movement going on in the Third World today towards understanding the whys and hows of technology. Not to be left behind are the millions of women in this part of the world whose needs for technology are only now being felt. According to a report from the Mid-Decade Conference held in Copenhagen on the United Nations Decade for Women (1975 to 1985), "little or no positive improvements had taken place since the beginning of the Decade. Although more assistance has been directed towards women, it is predominantly of a type inappropriate to their needs and circumstances." At the end of the said Decade, a positive relationship between women and technology was still nowhere to be found. To many of the women, especially in the Third World, it is still an uphill climb.

We are all aware of the fact that, in many societies, roles have been "assigned" to genders. I say this in quotes because, surely, this kind of "occupational segregation" most often is merely a result of tradition—transmitted as it is from generation to generation.

Because of this, we see in the Third World numerous technologies which fail to reduce women's burdens and responsibilities in culturally meaningful ways. In many cases, the nature of these technologies seems to prevent, deliberately or inadvertently, women's access to and control over forces—whether social, economic, or political—that affect their lives.

For women in the Third World, life is unceasing toil. In the countries of Asia, Africa, and Latin America, reports INSTRAW, the International Research and Training Institute for the Advancement of Women, women bear the brunt of forty to eighty percent of all agricultural production and are totally responsible for the support of nearly thirty percent of all rural families. The report estimates that on average, in developing countries, a woman works sixteen hours to each man's hour.

In the field of technology, there has, furthermore, been a failure to seriously take women into account. For example, a bicycle pump technology may appear to be the most innocuous of technologies. But what happens when it is introduced in a society where it is considered improper for women to sit on a bicycle? The women of that society are automatically deprived access to what might have been a worthwhile innovation.

In some regions where the majority of subsistence farming is carried out by women, the introduction of commercial cropping has displaced them, without offering alternative sources of income or food. Drinking water schemes are designed and installed to suit the capacities of men—mostly in rural areas—where it is largely the women's job to collect and transport water.

In Sri Lanka's dry zone, women walk under the searing heat to fetch water for their families. Although there have been instances where water pumps have been installed in villages, the technology was transferred without regard for the needs of the end users, namely the women. Once a pump broke down, it stayed that way. No woman knew how to repair them; and the men were nowhere to be found. Very little consideration was given to the idea of training the women themselves to repair and maintain the pumps.

In Indonesia, the introduction of mechanized rice hullers has completely destroyed women's opportunity to earn income through hand-pounding rice. And in India's Gujarat state, a modern dairy complex was introduced with not a single woman trained in the use of the new technology—a technology that took over her traditional tasks of making butter and cheese. These and many other examples show that, far from being eased by the introduction of technology, women's lot is actually deteriorating.

Thus, there is a challenge before the women scientists and technologists of the world to explore the possibilities of designing and implementing appropriate technology projects for women which will fit local conditions and which will take into account the traditional habits, values, perceptions, and the needs of the women who will use the technologies. Not only must the tools be provided at the right time, the right place, and the right cost; they must also involve minimal violence to the physical and sociocultural environment where they will be used, as well as maximum participation of the women who will use them.

In the main, your work as technology innovators must proceed with a thorough awareness of the impact which a certain kind of technological innovation will have on women's lives. Without this awareness, women's concerns will not be taken seriously, and the innovations will not ease women's lot in any meaningful way.

There are important questions to be addressed in a forum of eminent women scientists such as this: Are your inventions not only acceptable, but also appropriate to women; that is, does your technology accept a human and also a female "face"? Are the women informed of the choices they can make on which technologies will serve or harm them? Can they, in fact, choose what they feel is appropriate for them, or are they obliged to fit themselves to the technologies they need to use?

I am suggesting here a framework for developing technology for women which should take several aspects into consideration:

1) *Technology control.* Women must be given the chance to exercise control over technology. Quite often, when a certain innovation is introduced to im-

prove a certain technology, that technology, although it may have been traditionally performed by women, is soon taken over by the men. The potter's
wheel may be cited as an example. Before the potter's wheel was invented,
pottery was a tedious chore assigned to the women of the village. Then, with
the coming of the potter's wheel, the craft was made more efficient and more
profitable. But the potter's wheel needed to be handled with more strength
and more agility. Soon after, the men took over from the women.

2) *Access to technology resource support systems.* The actual control over a technological innovation calls for the necessary access to those resources which
make it possible for women to use the technology and benefit from it. These
resources include training in attitudes, knowledge, and skills as well as access
to capital, and extension assistance, among others. Indeed, technology control would not be possible without these resources, and gender biases built
into these systems ultimately means that the women will not be able to benefit
from certain potentially useful technologies.

In many cases, the biases result from oversight or from a superficial understanding of the reality of the female condition. The Food and Agriculture
Organization (FAO) believes, for instance, that Third World women (especially those living in rural areas) are severely handicapped, not only by their
multiple roles, but also by such other factors as illiteracy, poor health, and
frequent pregnancies—factors that limit their other capabilities or talents
from showing. A technology that does not adequately take these factors into
account cannot be meaningfully transferred.

3) *Access to technology decisions.* Besides control of technology and access to
resource support systems, the vital factor of the women themselves acting as
prime movers of the available technologies is a much needed component of
the framework. The urgent need is for women to become involved in the
mainstream of technology development, planning, transfer, and application.
"The search for change," says Dr. Dunja Pastizzi-Ferencic, INSTRAW Director, "should concentrate not only on problems facing women, but should
also recognize them as equal participants and as tremendous assets." Indeed,
women must take it upon themselves to have impact on the changes which
technology is bringing to their workplaces.

4) *Gender-specific appropriate technology development.* The framework should
develop systems of technology transfers for women which include know-how
and technique, and which promote woman's own ability to become, herself,
a technologist. The framework should develop the capacity of women for indigenous innovation. Partly, this is realizable if women are able to develop
a certain degree of familiarity with existing technologies. To quote Mary B.
Anderson in her seminar paper on women and technology development:

> Technological familiarity does several things. It instills the idea that things can
> be done better, with less effort, with more favourable results, or with less cost.
> It also teaches that a person can make this occur by control over a technique.
> It teaches various mechanical, chemical, and biological processes which form
> the basis for new discoveries, inventions, and adaptations. It gives people the
> ability and power to solve their own problems of production.

THE MOVEMENT TOWARD APPROPRIATE
TECHNOLOGY FOR WOMEN

As a consortium of nongovernment organizations involved in human development activities in Asia, the Asian Alliance of Appropriate Technology Practitioners (APPROTECH ASIA), to which I belong, is especially aware of its advocacy role in promoting the cause of womanhood within the context of appropriate technology. The alliance is vigorously exploring avenues for increased women's access to and participation in appropriate technology development and dissemination.

APPROTECH ASIA has coordinated the training of women inventors in the commercialization of their products, for example. It has organized and participated in dialogues meant to improve the status of women in Asia and the Pacific. The APPROTECH ASIA members who come from India, Bangladesh, Sri Lanka, Indonesia, Pakistan, Singapore, Malaysia, Thailand, and the Philippines have each, in their own way, geared their programs of action to be more responsive to the particular needs of their women constituents, thus giving women a forum where their struggle for recognition as users and inventors of technologies can be recognized and attended to.

South-South exchanges among women with the purpose of exposing their talents, ideas, and capabilities not only to one another but also to future markets have also been sponsored by APPROTECH ASIA. Besides these, South-South exchanges have been found to be particularly useful in making appropriate technology work for Asian women.

Concrete examples form a bulk of APPROTECH ASIA's experiences in making technologists aware of the special needs and difficulties of women in Asia. In Sri Lanka, the Sarvodaya Shramadana Movement—a member of APPROTECH ASIA—is operating a program to train village women in hand-pump technology, including the manufacture, installation, repair, and maintenance of the units. The pump they are learning to make is based on a design by Canada's International Development and Research Centre (IDRC). "Our aim," according to Sarvodaya, "is to bring this technology to the village. Since women are the primary users, we have decided that the technology should be transferred to them."

The technology which the women are learning in Sarvodaya's training center is entirely new to the women in Sri Lanka, but the women take their lessons seriously, willingly, and enthusiastically. And small wonder; water gathering in many parts of rural Sri Lanka is a laborious female task. Twenty-year-old Tamara Dharmasiri, for example, decided to learn the water pump technology because, "sometimes water had to be brought by government bowser (tank) from 50 miles away, just for drinking. Often we have to do without baths or manage with bathing in a muddy pool."

The Centre for Science and Environment in India is another example of a member organization of APPROTECH ASIA which consistently prepares and publishes studies on the discriminated status of women in many areas of Indian national life. The Manila Community Services, Inc. of the Philippines, makes credit and finance available to large numbers of women micro-entre-preneurs who would otherwise have no access to this resource. India's Work-ing Women's Forum is an organization which works for the proper treatment of poverty-stricken women entrepreneurs in rural and urban India. Yayasa Dian Desa of Indonesia designs water systems and cooking stoves meant to ease the household work of rural Indonesian women.

Women and appropriate technology is one of the program priorities of APPROTECH ASIA which is founded on the very firm belief that it cannot be morally tenable for the other half of humanity to have to struggle to deal with basic existence.

WOMEN INVENTORS BANDING TOGETHER

In the Philippines, a group of women from various backgrounds have banded together to form the Women Inventors' Association of the Philippines. Most members of the group are housewives who, on their own, have come up with several highly useful inventions that directly address the needs of women. I will mention two.

One is called the "Siroca Cooking Fuel," a nonliquid fuel made of pure alcohol, turned into a wax-like substance that is packed into a can. It is smoke-less and odorless when burnt. It does not produce fly ash to pollute the kitchen, and thus is no health hazard to anyone there. The other is called the "Nellcor Ice Shaver." It is a manually operated food processor that not only produces chips from ice but also from bananas, potatoes, and other vegeta-bles—all this with considerably less effort. This last invention has been partic-ularly useful to many women food vendors in my country.

TOWARDS A TECHNOLOGY WITH A HUMAN (AND FEMALE) FACE

As I end this paper, let me repeat my appeal that for technology to be of genuine benefit to women, it must be developed within a conscious female framework. Appropriate technology is "technology with a human face." wrote Dr. E. F. Schumacher. At the risk of oversimplifying, it may be said that tech-nologies become appropriate when they carry a deliberate bias for a specific underprivileged sector of a community, as well as an appreciation of that sec-tor's overall physical and cultural environment. Putting it another way, tech-nology becomes appropriate when it results in tools, techniques, knowledge, skills, and attitudes that contribute to the compassionate raising of the quality of human life.

Liberating human development is the goal, technology the means, not the other way around. Rather than trying to change human beings to fit the technology, it is technology that should be studied within the context of human needs and sensibilities. And in Asia, these human needs and sensibilit-ies must include those of the female gender who are inextricably involved in using them.

In the final reckoning, the efficacy and value of our technology efforts for women will, to borrow the words of one Asian woman, be assessed by "how much more speedily it hastens a world where women—and in effect, the poor—are no longer invisible but are, in fact, partners with equal say in the building of a more just and humane society."

WORKS CITED

Anderson, M. B."Technology transfer: implications for women." *Gender Roles in Development Projects*. Kumarian Press Case Study Series, 1975.

———. "A. T. in the eighties: in search of a philosophy." *A. T. '80* 1, 1 (May 1982) (Agency for Community Education Services, Quezon City, Philippines).

Ceniza, S. C. "Casting away the cloak of invisibility." *A. T. '80* 2, 4 (December 1983) (Agency for Community Extension Services, Quezon City, Philippines).

"Countdown Nairobi: the decade ends." *Approtechnews,* 2nd quarter, 1984. (Asian Alliance of Appropriate Technology Practitioners, Manila, Philippines).

Devadas, D. "Work, technology, and environment." *One World* 144 (April 1986) (World Council of Churches, Geneva, Switzerland).

"I want my inventions to be useful to my country—Ma. Carlita Rex Doran." *A Collage: Women and Appropriate Technology*. Asian Alliance of Appropriate Technology Practitioners, July 1985.

Lang, K. "Monitoring the progress of the world's women." *Development Forum* 11, 8 (United Nations Division for Economic and Social Information/DPI and the United Nations University).

Lechte, R. "Women and Technology." *Approtechnews,* 3rd and 4th quarter, 1983 (Asian Alliance of Appropriate Technology Practitioners, Manila, Philippines).

Ramos, L. O. "Making Appropriate Technology Work for Women." Paper presented to the Sub Regional Workshop on Appropriate Technology and Training for Women in South Asia, Oct. 26–Nov. 1, 1986, Islamabad, Pakistan.

Sisters of Innovation. The World YWCA, 1983.

Soedjarwo, A. "Diffusion of rural technology: obstacle or resource?" *Technology in the Hands of the People—Asian Experience.* Asian Alliance of Appropriate Technology Practitioners, Manila, 1984.

Women Taking Hold of Technology. International Women's Tribune Center, September 1984.

"Technology and small business: women's perspectives." *The Tribune (Women and Development Quarterly)*, Newsletter 27. (International Women's Tribune Center, 1984).

Wanigasundara, M. "Women of the pump." *The IDRC Reports* 3 and 4 (October 1985) (International Development and Research Centre, Ottawa, Canada).

World Development Report 1984. The World Bank.

PART II: (MIS?)CONCEPTIONS
Morality and Gender Politics in Reproductive Technology

The intersection of technology, sex roles, and ideas about gender is perhaps most readily apparent in reproductive technologies. Certainly, no other set of technologies has produced more debate. The essays in this section address some of the major moral and social issues that have developed around our more conventional abilities to manipulate reproduction, and showcase the conflicting intuitions that arise in topics involving parenthood, rights, and autonomy.

If technology can separate intercourse from procreation, what does that do to one's responsibility for children produced using one's biological material? Daniel Callahan takes on this moral issue as it plays out in anonymous sperm donation and in sperm banks. He argues that the connection between moral responsibility and biological fatherhood is direct and nondispensable. That is, the man who provides sperm for procreation is the true father of the resulting child and is permanently morally responsible for him or her, regardless of anonymity, legal regulations, permission forms, contracts between the parties, social standards, or the wishes of the mother. Consequently, anonymous sperm donation is immoral because it involves abandoning children. The low-level technology of the sperm bank, then, highlights the question of how much significance we should place on a purely genetic relationship.

Ronald Munson occupies a decidedly different position on this question, arguing that mere biological fatherhood is not enough to make someone a moral father. It is possible to supply a causal condition (sperm) for a pregnancy without being the actual causal agent of the pregnancy—and we are not morally responsible for things we do not cause. Ultimately, Munson argues, the sperm donor is no more morally responsible for what is done with his sperm than a blood donor is morally responsible for what is done with her blood or a merchant for what is done with his merchandise once it's sold. Adding to the concerns about genetic relationships in this mini-debate, Munson's article challenges us to figure out where we have to be in a chain of events to be morally responsible for the outcome.

If the entire sperm donation phenomenon is motivated by a desire to have a baby, what about the desire to have a specific kind of baby? Parents get to choose their children's religion, their children's school, their children's medical treatment. Should they also be allowed to choose their children's sex? Helen Bequaert Holmes looks at this thorny problem. Setting the debate in the context of a moderate to extreme preference for firstborn male children in various cultures (which often leads to selective abortion), she looks not only at the sheer moral worry about sex selection, but also at its practical effects. Potential problems such as sexist motivations, increases in male violence and crime, an increase in men with firstborn psychologies, and the glorification of masculinity lead Holmes to a sharp moral criticism of sex selection. But even if it is immoral, whether the state should outlaw it is another question.

Mary Anne Warren criticizes Holmes' moral conclusions about sex preselection. She argues that while sex preselection may sometimes be motivated by sexism, it is not always so. Within a patriarchal society women may choose to have male children in order to benefit their family, to increase economic gains, or simply to spare a potential daughter the danger and ignominy of living in a patriarchal society. Similarly, in a somewhat different culture, parents may choose to have a daughter because sons are much more likely to turn out violent and commit crimes. None of these motivations are necessarily sexist and do not involve being unjust to anyone because no distinct individual yet exists. Warren is also skeptical of the supposed practical dangers of sex selection, remaining unconvinced that it would result in such terrible consequences, and, essentially, leaving the question: what actual harm would result from permitting sex selection?

With sex selection, as with many issues of reproductive technology, there is no simple division between feminist and antifeminist positions. The basic principle of permitting one to control one's own body often conflicts with other principles. Nowhere is this better exemplified than in the debate over surrogate motherhood. Lori B. Andrews discusses the range of feminist responses to surrogacy, in which conflicting commitments have sometimes pitted feminist interests in women's autonomy and reproductive freedom against feminist concerns about women's exploitation in a sexist society. In analyzing the major feminist objections to surrogacy, however, Andrews argues that they threaten rather than protect women by dangerously recapitulating old arguments used to outlaw abortion and reduce women to vulnerable mothers in need of government oversight. The issues in this debate are fundamentally political: when should the government regulate a woman's body for her own good?

CHAPTER 6
BIOETHICS AND FATHERHOOD

DANIEL CALLAHAN

(1992)

For most of the rest of our culture, the twin issues of the meaning of masculinity (or maleness, depending on your tastes), and the significance of fatherhood are well-developed topics of public discussion. Whether as a response to feminism, on the one hand, or to independent uncertainties about what it means to be a male, on the other, the question of masculinity attracts considerable attention. While fatherhood was not exactly a neglected topic in years past, there seems little doubt that the nasty phenomena of more and more single-parent families, mainly headed by females, and a growing number of absent and neglectful fathers, has given the issue a fresh urgency. What does it mean to be a father? What is the importance of the father for the nurturing of children? What can be done to encourage and assist more responsible fatherhood? What is the relationship between fatherhood and masculinity?

These are interesting and important questions, and timely as well. One would, however, never guess that from reading the literature of bioethics. For whatever reason, that literature, when it focuses on gender at all, is almost exclusively interested in women. And when it focuses on parenthood, it almost exclusively focuses on motherhood. While the general topics of reproductive choices and artificial means of reproduction have had a central place in bioethics, the literature and debate have usually centered on women's choices or women's role in such things as surrogate motherhood and *in vitro* fertilization. Fathers and fatherhood are just absent from the discussion altogether.

The absence of fatherhood in the debate is puzzling, especially since the topic of artificial means of reproduction is a central one in the field. My surmise is that, because those means of reproduction depend so heavily upon anonymous male sperm donations, and since such donations are rarely questioned for their moral propriety, there has been no need or place to talk about fathers. They just don't really count in that brave new world of reproduction. I will return later to that topic. Of more general importance is whether fatherhood can be given a fresh look and a reinvigorated role in bioethics.

At the heart of the problem and future of parenthood, and thus of the most basic and indispensable kind of human nurturing, is a *relationship,* of men, women, and children bound together. Professionals seem to have lost a sense of and feel for that relationship—of the way men, women, and children need and best flourish in the company of the other. Instead, professionals have done conceptually what society has been doing legally and socially— treating men, women, and children as separate and distinguishable, with their own needs and rights. Thus we now speak easily of women's rights, and children's rights, and (hardly surprising, even if amusing) we have seen the growth of a men's rights movement. Doubtless there are some good reasons for this fragmenting development, the most important being the way earlier generations were prone to stack the family relationship, and its ground rules, too heavily in favor of men; or, where children were concerned, to treat them too much as the property of their parents, not as persons in their own rights.

But it is time for some reintegration. The fragmentation is, unless corrected in the long run, going to be harmful for men, women, and children, both individually and in their relationship. A revived and reinvigorated place for fathers and the institution of fatherhood is as good a place as any to begin. I want to develop three points: 1) biological fatherhood carries with it permanent and nondispensable duties; 2) the rapid and widespread acceptance of artificial insemination donors was much too thoughtless and casual, but for just that reason symbolic of the devaluation of fatherhood; and 3) feminism as a movement has hurt both men and children, but also women, by its tendency to substantively displace fathers from a central role in the making of procreation decisions.

THE DUTIES OF FATHERHOOD

I begin here with the most simple and primitive of moral axioms, rarely articulated as such but as undeniable as anything can possibly be in ethics. The axiom is this: Human beings bear a moral responsibility for those voluntary acts that have an impact on the lives of others; they are morally accountable for such acts. I will not discuss the many nuances and problems that this axiom raises: what counts as "voluntary," how great must be the impact upon others, and which effects of actions on others are morally more or less important.

In the case of biological fatherhood those nuances will not ordinarily be of great importance. From this moral axiom I will argue that given the obvious importance of procreation in bringing human life into existence, fathers have a significant moral responsibility for the children they voluntarily procreate. What human action could be more important than that which creates new life, the burden of which the newly born person must live with for the rest of his or her life? What causal connection could be more direct than biological procreation, without which human existence would not be possible? A father can hardly be held wholly responsible for *what* a child becomes—much will depend upon circumstances—but a father can be held responsible with the mother for the fact the child comes to be at all.

One philosopher has advanced the notion that our only serious moral obligations are those we voluntarily impose upon ourselves, as in specific contracts.[1] There cannot be, she says, involuntary obligations. This is not the place to debate the full implications of such a theory—which must systematically close its eyes to what it means to live in a community with other people—but it is pertinent to make a single point. Unless a male is utterly naive about the facts of procreation, to engage in voluntary sexual intercourse is to be responsible for what happens as a result. To enter into a contract with another is, at the least, to undertake a voluntary activity with a known likely outcome. Sexual intercourse for an informed male is fairly close to that, so even on a contract theory of moral obligation, intercourse shares many critical features with a contract. Society, curiously, seems to have been faster in establishing the moral and causal links between drinking and driving than between sexual activity and pregnancy. But that may be because society prefers to think that accidental, unwanted pregnancies come more from contraceptive ignorance and failure than from the sexual activities that require them; the former is a more comforting thought to sustain the sexual revolution.

From my moral axiom, therefore, and from what we know about the biology of human procreation, I believe there is no serious way of denying the moral seriousness of biological fatherhood and the existence of moral duties that follow from it. The most important moral statement might be this: Once a father, always a father. Because the relationship is biological rather than contractual, the natural bond cannot be abrogated or put aside. I conclude, that just as society cannot put aside the biological bond, so neither ought it put aside the moral bond, the set of obligations that go with that biological bond. If there are to be moral duties at all, then the biological bond is as fundamental and unavoidable as any that can be imagined.[2] Does this mean that each and every father has a full set of moral obligations toward the children he procreates? My answer is yes—unless he is mentally or financially incompetent to discharge those duties. To treat the matter otherwise is to assume that fatherhood *is* some kind of contractual relationship, one that can be set aside by some choice on the part of the father, or the mother and father together, or on the part of the state. This position does not preclude allowing one person to adopt the child of another, to play the role of father with a legal sanction to do so. This arrangement, however, is legitimate only when there are serious obstacles standing in the way of the biological father playing that role himself. Even then, however, he remains the biological father, and should the alternative arrangements for the child fail, he is once again responsible, and responsible whether he likes it or not, accepts it or not. The obligation stems from his original, irreversible act of procreation; so too is his moral obligation irreversible.

Imagine the following scenario. A father has, through the assorted legal ways society allows fathers to turn over their parental authority to another, legally ceased to act as a father and someone else is caring for the child. But imagine that the other person fails to adequately act as a father; fails, that is, to properly care for and nurture the child. The child then returns to the father and says: "You are still my father biologically; because of you I exist in this world. I need your help and you are obliged to give it to me." I have

never been able to imagine even *one* moral reason why a father in that circumstance could disclaim responsibility, and disclaim it if, even in principle, there
was someone else available who could take care of the child. A father is a
father is a father.

FATHERHOOD AND ARTIFICIAL INSEMINATION

I find it remarkable that, with hardly any public debate at all, the practice—
indeed, institution—of artificial insemination by an anonymous male donor
so easily slipped in. What could society have been thinking about? In this
section I will argue that it is fundamentally wrong and should have no place
in a civilized, much less a supposedly liberal society. It is wrong for just the
reasons I have sketched about the moral obligations that go with fatherhood.
A sperm donor whose sperm is successfully used to fertilize an ovum, which
ovum proceeds through the usual phases of gestation, is a *father*. Nothing
more, nothing less. He is as much a father biologically as the known sperm
inseminator in a standard heterosexual relationship and sexual intercourse.

If he is thereby a biological father, he has all the duties of any other biological father. It is morally irrelevant that 1) the donor does not want to act as a
father, 2) those who collect his sperm as medical brokers do not want him to
act as a father, 3) the woman whose ovum he is fertilizing does not want him
to act as a father, and 4) society is prepared to excuse him from the obligations of acting as a father. Fatherhood, because it is a biological condition,
cannot be abrogated by personal desires or legal decisions. Nor can the moral
obligations be abrogated either, unless there are reasons why they *cannot* be
discharged, not simply that no one wants them to be discharged. Just as a
"surrogate mother" is not a "surrogate" at all but a perfectly real and conventional biological mother, so also is a sperm donor whose sperm results in a
child a perfectly real and conventional biological father.

Why was it decided to set all that aside? Why was it deemed acceptable for
males to become fathers by becoming sperm donors but then to relieve them
totally of all responsibility of being fathers, leaving this new father ignorant of
who his child is and the child ignorant of who the father is? I was not present
at that great cultural moment, but two reasons seem to have been paramount.

First, it was introduced under medical auspices and given a medical legitimation. Artificial Insemination by a Donor ("AID"), one author wrote, is
"medically indicated in instances of the man's sterility, possible hereditary
disease, rhesus incompatibility, or in most cases of oligospermia."[3] "Medically
indicated?" But it does not cure anyone's disease—not some other would-be
father who is sterile, or the woman who receives the sperm who is perfectly
capable of motherhood without donated sperm. What is cured, so to speak, is
a couple's desire to have a child; but medicine does not ordinarily treat relational problems (save in psychotherapy), so there is no reason to call the
matter medical at all. Moreover, of course, since artificial insemination only
requires a single syringe, inserted in a well-known place, there is nothing
"medical" even about the procedure.

As Daniel Wikler has nicely pointed out, the professional dominance of doctors in the history of AID is a perfect case of the medicalization of a non-medical act, and the establishment of a medical monopoly and legitimization as a result.[4] Just how far this medicalization has gone can be seen by the very language used to describe the procedure: "[Artificial Insemination] is of two basic types: homologous, when the semen is obtained from the husband (AIH); and heterologous, when the semen is acquired from a donor (AID)."[5] I wonder how many males, working pleasurably to produce some sperm, understood themselves to be engaged in a heterologous activity? There is very little that medical science cannot dress up with a technical term.

The second reason for ready acceptance was probably that, in the name of helping someone to have a child, society seems to be willing to set aside any existing moral restraints and conventions. Perhaps in an underpopulated world, whose very existence is threatened by low birth rates, a case for artificial procreation might be made.

But it is hard to see why, in our world, where the problem of feckless and irresponsible male procreators is far more of a social crisis, society lets that one pass. One can well understand the urge, often desperate, to have a child. But it is less easy to understand an acceptance of the systematic downgrading of fatherhood brought about by the introduction of anonymous sperm donors. Or perhaps it was the case that fatherhood had already sunken to such a low state, and male irresponsibility was already so accepted, that no one saw a problem. It is as if everyone argued: Look, males have always been fathering children anonymously and irresponsibly; why not put this otherwise noxious trait to good use?

As a symbol of male irresponsibility—and a socially sanctioned symbol at that—one could hardly ask for anything better than artificial insemination with the sperm of anonymous donors. It raises male irresponsibility to the high level of a praised social institution, and it succeeds in getting males off the hook of fatherhood and parenthood in a strikingly effective and decisive way. The anonymity is an especially nice touch; no one will know who did what, and thus there can never be any moral accountability. That is the kind of world all of us have wished we could live in from time to time, especially in its sexual subdivision. From the perspective of the sperm donor, if the child's life turns out poorly, the donor will neither know about that nor inconveniently be called upon to provide help, fatherly help. Home free!

FEMINISM AND FATHERHOOD

As a movement, feminism has long had a dilemma on its hands. If women are to be free of the undue coercion and domination of males, they must establish their own independent sphere of activities and the necessary social and legal rights to protect that sphere. Women cannot and should not leave their fate in the hands of males, much less their reproductive fates. Meanwhile, feminists have also deplored feckless, irresponsible males who leave women in the lurch. Yet if males are to be encouraged to act more responsibly, to take seriously their duties to women and children, then they must be allowed to share the right to make decisions in those domains that bear on their activities and responsibilities. Males, moreover, have rights corresponding to their duties; they should be empowered to do that which their moral duties require of them.

For the most part, this dilemma has been resolved by the feminist movement in favor of stressing the independence of females from male control. This is evident in two important respects. First, in the abortion debate there has been a firm rejection of the claim that males should be either informed that a woman is considering an abortion or that the male should have a right to override her decision. The male should, in short, have neither a right to information nor choice about what happens to the conception.

Second, in its acceptance of single-parent procreation and motherhood, for both heterosexual and lesbian women, some branches of feminism have in effect declared fathers biologically irrelevant and socially unnecessary. Since this kind of motherhood requires, as a necessary condition, some male sperm (provided *in vitro* or *in vivo*), it has not been possible to dispense altogether with males. No such luck. But it has been possible to hold those males who assist such reproduction free of all responsibility for their action in providing the sperm. The only difference between the male who impregnates a woman in the course of sexual liaison and then disappears, and the man who is asked to disappear voluntarily after providing sperm, is that the latter kind of irresponsibility is, so to speak, licensed and legitimated. Indeed, it is treated as a kindly, beneficent action. The effect on the child is of course absolutely identical—an unknown, absent father.

Both of these moves seem understandable in the short run, but profoundly unhelpful to women in the long run. It is understandable why women would not want their abortion decision to depend upon male permission. They are the ones who will have to carry the child to term and nurture, as mothers, the child thereafter. It is no less understandable why some women want children without fathers. Some cannot find a male to marry but do not want to give up motherhood altogether; they view this as a course of necessity, a kind of lesser evil. Other women, for reasons of profound skepticism about males, or hostility toward them, simply want children apart from males altogether.

Please note that I said these motives are "understandable." I did not say they are justifiable. What is shortsighted about either of these choices is that, by their nullification of the moral obligations that ought to go with biological fatherhood, they contribute to the further infantilization of males, a phenomenon already well advanced in our society, and itself a long-standing source of harm for women.

If the obligations of males to take responsibility for the children they have procreated is sharply limited due to women deciding whether to grant males any rights, then males quickly get the message. That message is that the ordinary moral obligations that go with procreation are contingent and dispensable, not nearly as weighty as those of women. For even the most advanced feminists do not lightly allow women who have knowingly chosen to become mothers to jettison that obligation. Mothers are understood to be mothers forever, unlike fathers, who are understood to be fathers as long as no one has declared them free of responsibility. If you are a sperm donor, of course, that declaration can readily be had.

What social conditions are necessary to have the responsibilities of fatherhood taken seriously? The most obvious, it would seem, is a clear, powerful, and consistent social message to fathers: You are responsible for the lives of the children you procreate; you are always the father regardless of legal dispensations; only the gravest emergencies can relieve you of that obligation; you will be held liable if you fail in your duties; and, you will be given the necessary rights and prerogatives required to properly discharge your duties. Only recently has there been a concerted effort, long overdue, to require fathers to make good on child-support agreements. And only recently, and interestingly, has the importance of biological parenthood been sufficiently recognized to lower some of the barriers erected to keep adopted children from discovering the identity of their biological parents, including fathers.

Those feminists who believe that fathers should have no role in abortion decisions should reconsider that position or at least add some nuance. There are probably good reasons to not legally require that fathers be informed that the mother is considering an abortion; the possibilities of coercion and continuing stress thereafter are real and serious. But that is no reason to dispense with a *moral* requirement that the fathers be informed and their opinion requested if there are no overpowering reasons not to. The fetus that would be aborted is as much the father's doing as the mother's, and the loss to the father can obviously be considerable. Acting as if the only serious consequences are for the woman is still another way of minimizing the importance of fatherhood.

Far too much is made of the fact that the woman actually carries the fetus. That does not make the child more hers than his, and in the lifetime span of procreation, childbearing, and childrearing, the nine-month period of gestation is a minute portion. Only very young parents who have not experienced the troubles of teenage children or an adult child's marital breakup could think of the woman's pregnancy as an especially significant or difficult time compared with other phases of parenthood.

Fathers, in short, have a moral right to know that they are fathers and to have a voice in decisions about the outcome of pregnancy. To deny males such a right is also to reject the very concept of paternal responsibility for one's procreative actions. The right to be a father cannot rest upon someone else's decision to grant such a right; that is no right at all. If the right to be a father is that poorly based, then there will be no better basis for upholding the moral obligation of fathers, or holding them accountable for their actions. I see no possibility of having it both ways. Society often asserts as a general principle that rights entail obligations. In this case, I am arguing the converse: If society wants obligations taken seriously, rights must be recognized.

The argument for a father's moral right to knowledge and choice does not entail a corresponding legal right to force a woman to bear a child against her will. There are a number of prudential and practical reasons not to require legal notification that a woman plans to have an abortion or to require the father's permission. Such a requirement, I suspect, would be both unworkable and probably destructive of many marital relationships. But as a moral norm, this requirement is perfectly appropriate. It puts moral pressure on women to see the need to inform fathers they are fathers, and to withhold such knowledge only when there are serious moral reasons to do so.

Women should, in general, want to do everything possible to encourage fathers to take their role and duties seriously. Women, and the children they bear, only lose if men are allowed to remain infantile and irresponsible. The attempt to encourage more responsible fatherhood and the sharing of childbearing duties while simultaneously promoting the total independence of women in their childbearing decisions only sends a mixed message: Fathers should consider themselves responsible, but not too much; and they should share the choices and burdens of parenthood, but more the latter than the former; and all parents are created equal, but some are more equal than others.

I have mainly laid the emphasis so far on abortion decisions. But the same considerations apply when women, heterosexual or lesbian, make use of donated sperm deliberately to have a single-parent child. Women have been hurt throughout history by males who abandon their parental duties, leaving to women the task of raising the children. A sperm donor is doing exactly the same thing. The fact that he does it with social sanction does not change the outcome; one more male has been allowed to be a father without taking up the duties of fatherhood. Indeed, there is something symbolically destructive about using anonymous sperm donors to help women have children apart from a permanent marital relationship with the father.

For what action could more decisively declare the relevance of fatherhood than a specific effort to keep everyone ignorant? A male who would be a party to such an arrangement might well consider himself some kind of altruistic figure, helping women to get what they want. He would in reality be part of that grand old male tradition of fatherhood without tears, that wonderful fatherhood that permits all of the pleasures of procreation but none of its obligations. Women who use males in this way, allowing them to play once again that ancient role in a new guise, cannot fail to do harm both to women and parenthood.

PARENTHOOD, FAMILIES, AND RELATIONSHIP

A great deal of fun is made these days of those old-fashioned families of the 1950s, especially the television versions, where the emphasis was placed on the family as a unit. They are spoofed in part because they failed to account for all of the families in those days that were simply not like that. Fair enough. They are derided as well because they often treated the women as empty-headed creatures good for nothing other than cleaning up after the kids and keeping father happy. And sometimes they are attacked because they did not present those fathers as strong leaders and role models for children. Rather, they portrayed fathers as weak and childish, capable of manipulation by wives and children.

But what the old-fashioned families saw clearly enough is that parenthood is a set of relationships, a complex web of rights, privileges, and duties as well as the more subtle interplay of morality in intimate relationships. Feminists have been prone to pose the problem of procreative rights as principally a female problem. Traditionalists have been wont to view fatherhood as a role of patriarchical hegemony. Both are wrong, however, because they fail to see the complexity of the relationship or to place the emphasis in the right place. Both mothers and fathers, as individual moral beings, have important roles as well as the rights and duties that go with those roles.

Those roles, most importantly, are conditioned by, and set in a context of, their mutuality. Each needs and is enriched by the role of the other. The obligations of the one are of benefit to the other; indeed, the mutuality of their obligations amplifies all of them. A mother can better be a mother if she has the active help of a father who takes his duties seriously. Likewise, the father will be a better father with the help of an equally serious mother. The child will, in turn, gain something from both of them, both individually and as a pair. It is important, therefore, that society return fatherhood to center stage not only for the sake of fathers, who will be forced to grow up, but also for mothers, who will benefit from a more mature notion of what fatherhood and parenthood are.

NOTES

1. Judith J. Thompson, *A Defense of Abortion,* 1 Phil. & Pub. Aff. 47, 65 (1971).

2. James L. Nelson, *Parental Obligations and the Ethics of Surrogacy: A Causal Perspective,* 5 Pub. Aff. Q. 49 (1991).

3. Mark S. Frankel, *Reproductive Technologies: Artificial Insemination,* 4 Encyclopedia of Bioethics 1439, 1444 (Warren T. Reich ed., 1978).

4. Daniel Wikler and Norma J. Wikler, *Turkey-baster Babies: The Demedicalization of Artificial Insemination,* 69 Milbank Q. 5, 8 (1991).

5. See Frankel, supra note 3, at 1444.

CHAPTER 7

ARTIFICIAL INSEMINATION

Who's Responsible?

RONALD MUNSON

(1997)

When Onan cast his seed on the ground, according to the Biblical account, that was the end of the possibility his sperm might generate offspring. Modern biomedical technology has substantially altered the situation. Sperm cast into a sterile plastic container may immediately be used in an attempt to fertilize an ovum of a woman who has requested the procedure. Or the sperm might be frozen and later used toward the same end.

Onan may have had responsibilities to his God, but neither he nor anyone else had any particular moral responsibilities concerning the use of his cast-off sperm. By contrast, artificial insemination (AI) presents a great variety of moral, legal, and social issues. Some of the questions concern individual rights and responsibilities: Can a child born from AI legitimately demand to know the name of her biological father? Should any woman be permitted to be inseminated "on demand"? Should self-described lesbians be acknowledged as having the same right to have children by AI as other women? Should a woman be allowed to order sperm donated by a man who approximates her ideal (ethnic group, hair and eye color, height, body type, intelligence, physical attractiveness, sexual orientation)?

Other questions concern the proper role and responsibilities of sperm banks as social institutions: How thoroughly must sperm donors be screened for genetic and infectious diseases? Given the possibility of HIV infection, should intravenous drug users or others in high-risk groups be accepted as sperm donors? Because some think homosexuality may have a genetic basis, should acknowledged homosexuals be permitted to be donors? (If so, should informed consent be secured from potential AI recipients?) What physical, education, or general social traits (if any) should individuals possess to qualify as donors? Should national records be maintained and shared to prevent the marriage or mating of individuals born from AI with the same biological father (that is, the same anonymous donor)?

My concern here cannot be with all issues raised by AI. I wish to limit consideration to a single, although central, one: Are there special moral difficulties associated with the donation of sperm for use in AI? In particular, does the sperm donor have any special responsibilities or rights? If the sperm donor is exactly similar to the blood donor or organ donor, then there will be no special moral difficulties associated with the role. The responsibilities of each sort of donor will be the same. Yet if there are morally relevant features that distinguish donating sperm from donating blood, it is possible the sperm donor may have rights or responsibilities not shared by the blood donor.

Before addressing the question, it is worth considering the issues involved in two court cases concerning AI. The legal issues show that the moral ones are not purely speculative.

TWO COURT CASES

Since the turn of the century, a variety of legal questions have been discussed in connection with AI. Most have concerned inheritance and legitimacy, but two relatively recent court decisions raise issues that bear more directly on moral rights and responsibilities. One is the 1968 California Supreme Court decision in the case of *People v. Sorenson.*[1] The Sorensons, a married couple, agreed that Mrs. Sorenson would be artificially inseminated by a physician employing the sperm of an anonymous donor. The procedure was carried out, Mrs. Sorenson became pregnant, and a child was born. Four years afterwards, the couple separated, and Mrs. Sorenson took custody of the child. She requested child-support payments, but Mr. Sorenson refused to pay on the grounds that he was not the father of the child.

The court rejected Mr. Sorenson's argument and held that he was liable for child support. According to the court, "the word 'father' is construed to include a husband who, unable to accomplish his objective of creating a child by using his own semen, purchases semen from a donor and uses it to inseminate his wife to achieve his purpose."[2] Furthermore, the court held that the donor could not be regarded as the father, for "he is no more responsible for the use made of his sperm than is the donor of blood or a kidney."[3] For the court, then, the "natural father" of the child was the husband who consented to his wife's being inseminated with donor sperm. The sperm donor was explicitly held to be no different from a blood donor or an organ donor.

A more unusual court case also focused on the question of identifying the "natural father" of a child conceived by AI. The case of *CM v. CC* in the New Jersey Juvenile and Domestic Relations Court involved a situation considered to be without legal precedent.[4] The woman in the case, CC, wished to have a child, but she neither wished to marry at the time nor to have intercourse before marriage. Her male friend, CM, whom she was dating exclusively, offered to provide the sperm to be used in AI. The physician at the sperm bank to which CC applied for assistance refused to perform the procedure, but CC acquired sufficient information to inseminate herself. This she did, with the cooperation of CM. However, three months before the birth of the child, CC and CM severed their relationship.

After the child was born, CC refused to allow CM to visit, and CM turned to the court to claim visitation rights. The issue, as the court saw it, was whether CM should be recognized as the natural father of the child, given that his sperm had been "transferred to CC by other than natural conventional means." If so, then CM would have visitation rights, for courts have repeatedly held that the natural fathers of illegitimate children have such a right.

In making its decision, the court reasoned that if a child is conceived by intercourse between two unmarried people, the fact that they are unmarried does not alter the fact that the man is the father. Similarly, if a child is conceived between two unmarried people by employing the sperm of the man, the fact that the sperm was delivered by artificial means does not alter the fact that the man is the father. CM was a willing participant in CC's becoming pregnant, and in the circumstances, the manner in which the sperm was "delivered" was irrelevant. The court accordingly granted CM visitation rights, but it also enjoined him with the parental obligation of providing "support and maintenance of the child and payment of any expenses incurred in his birth."[5]

DONORS AS SUPPLYING A PRODUCT TO BE USED BY OTHERS

In the Sorenson case, the court held that the sperm donor was no more responsible for the use made of his sperm than a blood donor is for the use made of his blood. In either case, the donor is only supplying a product to be used by others. Presumably, then, if there are relevant moral differences between blood transfusions and AI, the differences are ones connected with the actions. Consequently, only the agents who perform the actions or consent to them are the proper subjects of moral evaluation.

The court was concerned primarily with the question of legal paternity, and it would be wrong to read the decision as implying that just as blood donors have no moral responsibilities, so neither do sperm donors. This view of the moral situation is too simple.

A person who knowingly sells a quantity of rat poison to a reputed bluebeard is not guilty of any ensuing act of poisoning by his customer, but he surely is guilty of something—an insufficient concern for human life at the least. Similarly, someone who donates blood knowing it is going to be used to lengthen the life of someone who is being tortured to death bears some degree of blame for contributing to the victim's suffering. Likewise, a sperm donor who sells sperm he suspects is going to be used to impregnate a woman against her will is surely blameworthy in some way and to some extent.

Such cases make it plain that a person who knowingly supplies the material conditions necessary for an immoral act does not escape all responsibility for the act merely because he does not perform it himself. Under appropriate conditions, supplying materials is one way of acquiring responsibility. In this respect, there is no morally relevant difference between being a blood donor and being a sperm donor. In either case, the donor has some responsibility for the use to which his contributed product is put. This also means he has some responsibility for finding out how it will be used before he contributes (or sells) it.

Some have contended that AI is inherently immoral, for it requires masturbation, which violates the "natural end" of sex.[6] On this view, the very fact of donating sperm would be wrong. However, if AI is not in itself wrong and masturbation is not in itself wrong (views I accept but will not argue for), then whatever responsibilities a sperm donor may have, they do not stem from contributing to or performing an invariably wrong act.

DONORS AS RESPONSIBLE FOR THE QUALITY OF THE PRODUCT

So far in discussing blood and sperm donors we have focused on the material supplied for use in an action performed by another. Thus, potential wrongfulness in both instances is acquired only at second hand, because it depends on the actions of those who make use of the materials. However, there is a way in which wrongfulness may attach directly to the action of a donor.

Suppose a donor falsifies his genetic history or lies about being the carrier of a heritable genetic defect (such as Tay-Sachs disease). In such an instance, he is directly responsible for the birth of a child with the associated relevant genetic defect. The physician who performs the insemination has not acted wrongly. Rather, the blame attaches to the donor. The donor has knowingly provided a defective and potentially deadly product.

Here again there is no disanalogy between sperm donation and blood donation. Before the procedure for testing blood for the presence of AIDS antibodies was introduced, someone diagnosed as having AIDS could have concealed that fact and knowingly put others at risk of dying from the disease communicated via his blood. Now that a test is available, we would think a physician or sperm bank was also blameworthy in a case in which a donor lied about his HIV-positive status and was not tested for the virus.

So far as blameworthiness is concerned, there seems to be no real difference between donating blood and donating sperm. In both instances, wrongfulness may be attributed directly to the action of a donor.

SPERM DONATION AND SEXUAL INTERCOURSE

The comparison between donating blood and donating sperm has produced results that support the view that there are no special moral problems or responsibilities connected with sperm donation. But perhaps by focusing on the fact that both are donations of a product, we have been led to overlook significant disanalogies between the two sorts of acts.

Certainly there are important differences between donating blood and "donating" sperm through intercourse. The most significant difference is connected with the potential outcome of the acts. While donating blood is at most a contribution toward someone's interest (health, well-being, treatment, etc.), "donating" sperm may lead to the conception and birth of another human being—a dependent child. The biological difference between blood and sperm makes the acts of giving quite different. Thus, in considering AI, it may be more reasonable to compare the results of sperm donation to the results of sexual intercourse, rather than to the results of blood donation.

The responsibility for a child normally falls to the biological parents. Exceptions to this are made in law only in special circumstances. For example, a child conceived by a woman as a result of an adulterous relationship may be considered the legal progeny of the woman's husband for certain purposes. Except in such cases, responsibility is typically assigned to both biological parents, and whether or not they are married to one another is irrelevant. Thus, if we take seriously the fact that AI and intercourse may lead to the same outcome, should we not say that the sperm donor is responsible for the child conceived from his sperm?

This view seems both counterintuitive and simplistic. But why should this be? Are there really morally relevant differences between delivering sperm by intercourse and delivering it by AI? The question is one that merits an answer if we are to avoid an uncritical dogmatism that assumes that the answer is obvious and needs no argument to support it.

At least two differences between the two sorts of cases stand out, and prima facie they may seem to explain why we are unwilling to count the sperm donor as the (so to speak) moral father of a child, even though he may be the biological father. First, it might be argued that the sperm donor has no intention of impregnating the woman who might receive his sperm. She is, most likely, a total stranger, someone he has never met and probably never will meet. Thus, it is ridiculous to suggest he could have the intention of making her pregnant or becoming a father. Most likely, the donor has only the intention of making money by being paid a fee for donating his sperm. Or, at best, the sperm donor, like the blood donor, has the intention of providing a material that may be of assistance to someone who has a specific need that he is in a position to satisfy.

The flaw in this argument is that men who "deliver" sperm by having sex do not always have the intention of impregnating their partners either. The news has been out for some time that men (as well as women) engage in intercourse for a variety of reasons, and conceiving a child is not invariably one of them. Consequently, the man who delivers sperm through intercourse may be just as lacking in intention as the sperm donor may be imagined to be. In neither case need pregnancy have anything to do with the aim of the action, and intention cannot be the grounds for holding that the man who engages in intercourse is the biological father who must accept attendant responsibilities, while the man who donates his sperm is the biological father who has no such responsibilities.

Second, it might be held that the likelihood of producing a pregnancy marks the difference between intercourse-and-responsibility and sperm donation-and-no-responsibility. After all, if a man has sex with a woman capable of becoming pregnant, there is a probability she will conceive. The probability might be lowered by birth-control procedures, including vasectomy, but some degree of probability always remains. If we assume the male knows there is at least some risk, no matter how small, of pregnancy resulting from intercourse, then it is reasonable to hold him responsible if it occurs. By contrast, a sperm donor has no way of knowing exactly what is going to be done with his sperm. It might be used for research purposes, discarded after its "shelf-life" has passed, mixed with a husband's for insemination, or used as merely one of a series of inseminations in which the sperm of other men is also employed.

Once again, however, such a contrast is more apparent than real. Ordinarily, the sperm donor can be assumed to know there is some degree of probability his sperm will be used in AI. In this respect, then, he is in exactly the same position as the man who engages in intercourse, and there is no morally relevant difference (based on likelihood of pregnancy) between the cases.

However, let us assume that the sperm donor is completely ignorant of the likelihood his sperm will be used to produce a pregnancy. This ignorance does not alter the fact that there is a certain degree of probability someone will become pregnant by means of his sperm. Notice, though, it is also possible for a male engaging in intercourse to be ignorant of the fact there is a probability his partner will become pregnant. (He may simply be ignorant of the realities of sex or hold certain false beliefs. For example, he may think it is impossible for a nursing mother to become pregnant or believe his vasectomy guarantees he is incapable of insemination.)

It is difficult to imagine a situation in which we would hold that ignorance on the part of the male who engages in intercourse excuses him from the responsibilities that attach to being the biological father of a resulting child. But if in the intercourse case ignorance is not a reason for setting aside the responsibilities of the biological father, then there seems to be no reason it should be in the sperm-donation case.

Are we thus forced to accept the counterintuitive conclusion that since the sperm donor is the biological father, he must also be the moral father? We are not, if we can show that being the biological father is not a sufficient condition for being the moral father.

Under ordinary conditions, we are inclined to identify the biological father with the moral father. The reason for this lies in the general principle that someone who causes something to happen is responsible for its happening. Indeed, when we ask "Who is responsible for this?" about the occurrence of an event, it is a request for the identity of the person or persons who are candidates for praise or blame. We expect and require that people (as we say) accept the consequences of their actions. If a woman becomes pregnant as a result of having sex with A, we hold A responsible (partially) for the child, because A is the cause of the pregnancy. It is irrelevant that the woman also had sex with B and C. They might have been responsible for the pregnancy, but as a matter of fact they were not. A is responsible, we hold, not because he has genetic characteristics that are different from B and C or anything of the kind, but because he is causally responsible, because the pregnancy resulted from his actions. We then expect and require him to accept the conse-quences of his actions. We thus identify him as both the biological and the moral father of the child.

In contrast to the actions of A in our example, the sperm donor does nothing to impregnate the recipient of his sperm. He is not responsible for her becoming pregnant, even though it is his sperm that makes her pregnant. He is the biological father, just as is A, but he is not the moral father, for unlike A, he is not the causal agent. Not being the causal agent, the sperm donor is not appropriately placed to "accept the consequences of his ac-tions," when this means accepting responsibility for the child produced by the use of his sperm. The donor's actions consist only in donating (selling) his sperm; as we discussed earlier, some responsibilities attach to such actions, but the responsibility of being a moral father is not among them.

In saying that the donor is not the causal agent of the pregnancy, I do not mean to deny he is part of the causal complex. If "the cause" of an event is the set of conditions sufficient for the occurrence of the event, then the donor provides what is usually called a contributory condition. In this respect, his role is no different from that of the person who supplied the pigments Michelangelo used to paint the Sistine Chapel ceiling. Just as it would be absurd to identify the paint supplier as responsible for the paintings, it would be absurd to identify the sperm donor as responsible for the child. (It is tempting to say the donor's sperm is a necessary condition for the occurrence of the pregnancy, but that is not correct. Sperm is a necessary condition, but not his sperm. At most, he supplies a necessary condition relative to that particular set of conditions that is jointly sufficient.)

It is in causal agency that we can locate the relevant moral difference be-tween being a sperm donor whose sperm is used in AI and someone who impregnates a woman through intercourse. However, this seems to require us to conclude that the physician who uses the sperm to perform AI is the moral father of the child. Because the physician causes the pregnancy, it would seem to follow that he or she is responsible for it.

This particular counterintuitive outcome indicates that the AI situation is more complicated than we have allowed for so far. We have assumed that an action that causes an outcome entails a responsibility for the outcome. This is true so far as causal responsibility is concerned; however, causal responsibility is, at most, a necessary condition for moral responsibility. If a terrorist has filled a hospital ward with methane gas, and by turning on the light I unsus-pectingly cause the gas to explode, I am causally responsible for the explo-sion. That is, I performed the action that completed the causal chain. However, moral responsibility lies with the terrorist who filled the room with explosive gas.

The physician who performs AI is causally responsible for a woman's be-coming pregnant. It is his act that makes her pregnant. However, she does not become pregnant because, to use an apt phrase from the last century, he "has his way with her." She becomes pregnant because the physician is not merely acting with her consent, but acting as her agent. She is as morally responsible for her own pregnancy as the terrorist is morally responsible for the explosion.

It is true that the physician must agree to act as the agent and, in doing so, accepts certain responsibilities. The physician must be assured that the woman is in a state of health compatible with being pregnant, that she genuinely wants to be pregnant, that she is not having a baby merely to sell for profit, and so on. Additional responsibilities attach to how the physician performs the task—has a serious effort been made to choose a sperm donor free of genetic disease, is the procedure performed in accordance with professional standards, and has meaningful consent been secured? However, in acting as the woman's agent, the physician is in no way responsible for the child conceived. The real causal agent is the woman herself.

What about the circumstance in which a male agrees to the AI of his female partner, with her consent, by the use of donor sperm? Does the male then have no responsibilities, since he has not acted as a causal agent? The reasoning of the court in Sorenson seems quite correct in such a case. The male, as one of the parties to the initial agreement, explicitly assumes responsibility for the child. He acknowledges himself to be the moral father. If he later changes his mind, he is still responsible because of his original commitment. His partner becomes pregnant with his consent, and he can no more cease to be the moral father than he could if he were also the biological father. If the partner acts as a result of the agreement with the male, then he too is causally responsible to some degree for the birth of the child.

It is now easy to see why the courts in *Sorenson* and in *CM v. CC* adopted different views toward the sperm donors. In *Sorenson*, the husband was a causal agent in the sense described above, for his wife became pregnant with his consent. Accordingly, the anonymous sperm donor played no role at all as a causal agent. By contrast, in *CM v. CC*, CM cooperated with CC in her conception, and each played the same sort of causal role they would have played had actual intercourse taken place. CM was a sperm "donor" only in an unusual sense.

A general result that follows from the position argued for is the recognition that being a biological father is not sufficient condition for being a moral or social father. We must now acknowledge that the special circumstances of AI make the role of biological father irrelevant to assigning responsibilities for the care of a child after it is born. The biological father in AI also has no rights as moral or social father. Since he played no role as a causal agent in the conception of the child, he can make no claim on the child, nor can the child or the child's representatives make any claim on him.

The exception to this concerns the area in which the sperm donor does have responsibilities. If he has in ignorance or through deception been responsible for the birth of a child with a genetic disorder or a communicable disease, then he is liable to be held at least morally accountable for his action of contributing sperm. If he acted in ignorance, the only claim on him might be to provide medical information that might be of help to the child. If he acted with the intent to deceive, then he might be liable for more than our moral condemnation. We might argue, for example, that he should be forced to pay an indemnity.

CONCLUSION

The question we began with was whether a sperm donor has any special responsibilities or rights. In particular, we asked, are there any morally relevant differences between the sperm donor and the blood donor? Prima facie it seemed that there might be, for donating blood does not lead to the same potential outcome that donating sperm does, for sperm may result in the birth of a dependent child.

What we have found is that there is no reason to hold that a sperm donor is the moral father of the child conceived by his sperm. I argued that being the biological father is not sufficient condition for being the moral father. The sperm donor is not a causal agent in the conception of the child and so is not responsible for the child. Further, although the physician who inseminates plays a causal role, he or she is not responsible for the child either. Causal responsibility is only a necessary condition for moral responsibility, and the physician is acting as the agent of the woman who has requested AI. A male who agrees that his partner will have a child by AI is also acting as a causal agent, and in his agreement he has committed himself to becoming the moral father of the child. His partner has become pregnant by his consent, rather than by his sperm.

There are differences between the sperm donor and the blood donor, but the differences are not morally relevant ones. Both have responsibilities, but they are responsibilities that come from providing a product. The fact that sperm can be used to produce a child, but blood cannot be, is not morally significant.

NOTES

1. *The People v. Falmer J. Sorenson.* Supreme Court of California, Cr. 11708 (Feb. 26, 1968). 437 P. 2d 495.
2. Op. cit., 500.
3. Op. cit., 498.
4. *C. M. v. C. C.* Juvenile and Domestic Relations Court, Cumberland County, NJ, 152 Super. 160 (July 19, 1977). 377A. 2d 821.
5. Op. cit., 825.
6. See Congregation for the Doctrine of the Faith, "Instruction on Respect for Human Life in its Origin and on the Dignity of Procreation: Replies to Certain Questions of the Day," in Ronald Munson, *Intervention and Reflection: Basic Issues in Medical Ethics,* 5th ed. (Belmont, CA: Wadsworth Publishing Company, 1996), p. 520.

CHAPTER 8
SEX PRESELECTION

Eugenics for Everyone?

HELEN BEQUAERT HOLMES
(1985)

Genetic birth defects are relatively infrequent, but *every* baby has a genetic sex. If one sex were unwanted, then it could be argued that every fetus is at 50% risk for a "defect." Therefore, should sex predetermination technologies become cheap and widely used, each and every family might be making a eugenic decision for each and every pregnancy.

In this paper I shall survey briefly the mid-1980s state of the art of sex determination and sex detection technologies. Thereafter, I shall a) comment on the literature on sex preferences, b) look at several speculations about the effects of sex ratio imbalances, and c) consider in some detail three strong, morally based arguments for rapid development and use of such technologies. The paper ends with a discussion of the progression of John Fletcher's ethical reasoning on this topic and a composite argument *against* the selection of the sex of children.[1]

SEX SELECTION: THE STATE OF THE ART, MID-1980S

In humans, sex is determined at the moment of conception, when the sperm merges with the egg, usually as the egg passes down one of the fallopian tubes. Each human egg contains 23 chromosomes, one of these being the X-chromosome. Each human sperm also contains 23 chromosomes, but one of these is either an X *or* a Y. At fertilization the chromosome count is brought to 46, and either a female (XX) or a male (XY) progeny results.

Inventing methods to interfere with or manipulate this step seems a logical maneuver. But such manipulations have been surprisingly unsuccessful. Of the three types of approaches proposed to select or favor X- or Y-sperm before fertilization, two involve technology and the third prescribes specific behaviors during coitus.

Chemical or Physical Barriers

The first suggestion is to create a barrier (chemical, such as a selective spermicide; or physical, such as a diaphragm or filter) that would allow only one type of sperm to pass the cervix for the subsequent journey through the uterus and up the fallopian tube. The publicized wish for a "manchild pill" is a plea to invent a systemic method for chemical destruction of X-sperm.[8,9] However, there has been little or no progress toward the development of either chemical or physical barriers, probably because of the very slight difference in properties between X- and Y-sperm.

In-Vitro Sperm Separation

Researchers have put considerable effort—with some slight success—into a second approach: the separation of sperm in semen samples (for subsequent artificial insemination). Because one sex of a domestic animal has more commercial value than the other, research veterinarians have done most of the exploratory work in sperm separation. Two international conferences recently considered the accomplishments: In 1970 the American Society of Animal Science sponsored "Sex Ratio at Birth—Prospects for Control"; in 1982 the Warwick Land Company of Rhode Island funded "Prospects for Sexing Mammalian Sperm." Proceedings of each of these conferences have been published.[10,11]

The results reported in these two books are discouraging. One difficulty is that there is no simple way to test the accuracy of a sperm separation technology. For one test, separated sperm are killed and stained with the fluorescent dye quinacrine: the human Y-chromosome usually, but not always, contains a fluorescent "F-body." Veterinarians at such centers as the Lawrence Livermore Laboratory in California are perfecting a fluorescence-activated cell sorter, which can count and separate 1,000 cells per second, for this purpose.[12]

Checking the sex ratio of progeny after artificial insemination with separated sperm is the logical and ultimately definitive method, but it is expensive. To date, progeny counts from separated bull sperm have been disappointing.[13] The claims for human sperm are more positive but are reported only by those with a vested interest in their own techniques (as one example, see note 14).

Ericsson and Glass recently summarized the literature on the speculated differences between X- and Y-sperm.[15] Purported differences in size, in shape, or in migration patterns to negative or positive electrodes have not been verified. Experiments reporting reactions to antisera have not been repeated successfully. As yet, there is no good experimental evidence for differential survival of the two kinds of sperm in fluids of low or high pH, although pH of a vaginal douche is a key factor in the Rorvik and Shettles method of sex preselection.[16,17] However, one fully confirmed difference exists: the X-chromosome is considerably larger than the Y, and therefore the total DNA from the chromosomes in an X-sperm weighs about 2.7% more than the DNA in a Y-sperm. From this fact, researchers hypothesize that X-sperm may be heavier and that Y-sperm may swim faster.

The Y-sperm's alleged "differential progressive mobility" is the basis of the "Ericsson technique," which ranch owner Ericsson first attempted as a method to separate bull sperm, and then applied to human sperm. To use this technique, clinicians place semen samples into an albumin column; the Y-sperm allegedly swim faster through the viscous liquid, and are collected to use for artificial insemination.[14,15,18–20] Ericsson holds U.S. Patents 4,007,087, 4,009,260, and 4,339,434 on this process. According to the latest brochure from his firm Gametrics Limited, ten clinics in various U.S.A. cities and four in southeast Asia use "our semen technology to isolate sperm for sex selection (male) and/or male infertility."

But does it work? Of the first 91 children delivered at these clinics, 68 (75%) were male.[14] Except for staff members at some of the clinics, most workers in fertility are skeptical.[21] Each client does sign a detailed informed consent form that states clearly that the technique merely *increases the probability* for conceiving a boy; clients are not accepted if interviewers believe that an unwanted girl baby will be abused or aborted.

The sex selection clinic in Philadelphia is pioneering another technique, one that allegedly enriches for X-sperm.[24] Invented in 1975 by Steeno et al.,[25] improved later by Quinlivan et al.,[26] this method requires the pipeting of semen into a glass column filled with tiny beads of a gel (Sephadex gel). Fractions 5, 6, and 7 collected from the column have X-sperm enriched to 62–84% (checked by quinacrine staining). Apparently more Y-sperm than X-sperm adhere to the beads of gel and do not pass through. This procedure is so new, and so few patients have requested girl babies, that no meaningful data on results are available yet.

Coital Behavior

Many formulae for coital behavior to conceive a boy or a girl have been handed down in folklore.[27] Although one or another aspect of some of these formulae may indeed be true, no biological basis has been unequivocally demonstrated. Yet some of these methods appear in the medical literature, and twentieth-century gynecologists sometimes suggest them to their patients. In America, authors apparently find it worthwhile financially to continue to write magazine articles and books on the subject.[16,17,32,33]

Bits of evidence and feasible biological hypotheses have kept some do-it-yourself methods alive in clinical circles, although skeptics greatly outnumber proponents. One theory has led to the "preconception gender diet." Several French and Canadian physicians claim to have evidence that minerals in the mother's diet can influence which sperm fertilizes her egg.[32,34–36] Biological hypotheses invented to explain clinical results obtained by the proponent physicians suggest that a woman's internal mineral balance may affect the cervical mucus through which sperm must travel, the internal surface of the fallopian tube up which sperm must swim, or the "zona pellucida" around her egg's membrane.[37]

A second theory is that a high sperm count in the female tract increases the chance that a Y-sperm fertilizes an egg. High sperm counts are found in healthy, well-nourished males who wear loose clothes around the testicles, whose mothers did not take DES during pregnancy, and who have abstained from intercourse for 2–3 days before producing the sperm sample. Several ejaculations within the same day into the same vagina apparently build up sperm count.[38]

The third theory has the most support from papers in recognized medical journals: the theory that timing of intercourse in relation to ovulation can favor X- or Y-sperm in the race to the egg.[16,17,33,40–46] However, even here experimental results from different sources produce different hypotheses; Shettles' popular books recommend timing procedures contrary to those in Whelan's book and in some of the medical articles; furthermore, some authors reverse their timing schemes for artificial insemination. If peristalsis and secretions in the female vagina affect Y-sperm mobility, then different results from artificial insemination without sexual arousal would be plausible.[47]

In their papers in the Bennet anthology,[3] James and Williamson summed up well the current status of home methods for sex selection.[45,48] James, who has probably written more papers than anyone else on the connection between timing of intercourse and sex of progeny, asserted:

> Preconceptual control of sex of infants in a topic that has attracted the attention of hoaxers, incompetents, madmen, and cranks, as well as scientists. . . . I shall call them all *sex hypothesizers*. . . . In sex hypotheses [there is] a great potential for confusion [because] the time interval between conception and delivery is so long that false predictions made at conception may be forgotten or revised at parturition. (p. 73)[45]

And Williamson stated, "Sex selection techniques have been widely publicized before being tested and even those of known ineffectiveness have been touted" (p. 129).[48]

The fact that home methods of sex determination sell books and occupy space in popular magazines and medical journals without any real supporting evidence is instructive to bioethicists. The desire to determine the sex of one's child is widespread and every child is "at risk" for this trait. In advance of the discovery of cheap and accurate methods that are likely to be popular, bioethicists ought to prepare by serious consideration of the ethical issues.

SEX DETECTION: THE STATE OF THE ART

Medicine's prying into nature's secrets about the sex of the unborn child has been much more successful. Where Western medicine is practiced, most women have come to accept many manipulations to their bodies as part of standard medical "management" during pregnancy. From prenatal medicine have come a variety of sex detection techniques, which I classify as: a) speculative methods, b) marginal methods (those with equivocal results or accurate only in the third trimester when the fetus is viable), or c) essentially 100% accurate methods.

Speculative Methods

In the first scenario, a clinician removes a few cells from an in-vitro-fertilized (IVF) embryo (a "test-tube" baby), checks the sex (by staining for X- and Y-chromosomes, or by using a recombinant DNA "probe"), then implants the remaining cells only when they are of the wanted sex. (In mammals, a whole animal can usually be formed even if a few of the early divided cells are taken away.) Indeed, in rabbits, Gardner and Edwards used cells from a later stage (the blastocyst) to predict sex correctly; subsequently they succeeded in implanting and bringing to term 20% of these sexed blastocysts.[49] And in humans, a pregnancy was established (and carried for five and one-half months) from a frozen embryo with only five of its eight cells intact after freezing and thawing.[50] Deliberate removal of a healthy cell from an early human embryo for sex detection has—to my knowledge—not yet been reported.

A second scenario, again for use with IVF babies, is to determine whether the embryo will react to an antibody against a product of the Y-chromosome, either the HY- or the SDM-antigen. This method would select for females: A male embryo would clump with the antibody and could not be implanted; a female one would not clump and thus could be implanted. Although Epstein et al. claimed successful use of the technique with mice at the eight-cell stage,[51] Chapman reported that the Epstein method was unreliable.[52]

Sex selection by one or the other of these methods is sometimes proposed as a spin-of "benefit" of IVF research. If and when the rabbit and mouse results improve, and when IVF spreads to more countries, teaching hospitals, and private clinics, certainly some researchers and clinicians will surreptitiously (or openly) attempt "test-tube" sex detection.

Marginal Methods

SEX HORMONE LEVEL

Attempts have been made to detect androgens (male steroids such as testosterone) in women carrying male fetuses. Fetal steroid hormones cross the placenta and add to the hormones in the mother's blood and in her saliva. However, the mother also produces androgens; in both fetus and mother hormone production is cyclic. To date, methods of measuring androgen levels in blood in the first trimester,[53] and in saliva later in pregnancy,[54,55] have given results essentially as predictive as guessing. The popular press in Austria, Switzerland, and Germany reported prematurely the "spit test" (Speicheltest) research in those countries. In still other attempts to detect hormones produced by male fetuses, investigators have analyzed amniotic fluid, obtaining the fluid by an amniotic tap (amniocentesis). In the fluid from 60 amniocenteses, Méan et al. of Switzerland found a wide range of testosterone levels, with a statistically significant difference between the *averages* from fluid surrounding male and female fetuses.[56] However, they found so much overlap in hormone level that in 30% of the cases, no sex prediction could be made. Nevertheless, work continues with these three fluids as clinicians attempt to find new methods to predict sex reliably.

FETAL CELLS IN MATERNAL BLOOD

Cells from the fetus can cross the placenta; thus, clinicians have checked maternal blood samples for F-bodies (from a male fetus) with fluorescence-activated cell sorters. Reports on such attempts come from Finland, Belgium, and the U.S.[57,58] The original excitement about this method seems to have faded, apparently because results differed when experiments were repeated.

ULTRASONIC VISUALIZATION

Competent ultrasonographers can detect the penis or vulva in the third trimester of pregnancy except when poor images are obtained because of interference by fetal bones, breech presentation, scanty amniotic fluid, or maternal fat or bowel gas.[59,60] In one report from Australia, the genitalia were "seen" in 66% of 137 fetuses scanned at 24–40 weeks, with only a 2% error.[61] In Sweden, diagnoses were made in 74% of 101 fetuses at 32 weeks, with a 3% error.[62] Over the past five years, various medical journals have presented data from three continents that show 50–86% successful recognition of sex during the third trimester. In pregnancy management in many parts of the United States and Europe, where ultrasonograpy is routine in the third trimester to assess gestational age and fetal position, mothers are usually told the sex of their fetus when the body parts are clear. According to Hobbins,[63] "knowing the sex of a fetus in the third trimester is of dubious clinical value, but may be of psychological benefit to some patients."

However, knowing the sex during the *second* trimester would be of value in decision-making about therapeutic abortion. Therefore, clinicians around the world have also attempted to use ultrasonic visualization of genitalia during that part of pregnancy. Success rates have been low; for example, Plattner et al. predicted sex in 61% of 194 fetuses at 16–24 weeks gestational age, with a 14% error,[60] and Birnholz determined sex in 41% of 367 fetuses of that age.[59] But the technology of ultrasonic scanners and the techniques of using them are constantly being improved. In a rather startling report, Stephens and Sherman of the University of California at San Francisco describe "100% accuracy of fetal anatomic-sex determination by linear-array real-time ultrasound in 100 consecutive cases of fetuses whose gestational ages ranged from 16 to 18 weeks."[64] Stephens scanned in two planes of orientation; sometimes it took as long as 10 minutes to assign sex. Should other clinicians succeed in obtaining similar results, ultrasonography may come to fall in the category below.

Essentially 100% Accurate Methods

FETAL CELLS OBTAINED THROUGH THE CERVIX

During the second month of gestation, some cells from the embryo's portion of the placenta slough off and can be found in the lower, endocervical part of the uterus. These can be obtained with a syringe in a relatively noninvasive way through the mother's cervix. Clinicians from Anshan, China, in 1975 stained such cells for F-bodies. They reported 93% accuracy in 100 pregnancies.[65]

In a recent refinement of this procedure, a tiny piece from the chorion of the embryonic placenta is aspirated through a catheter inserted via the cervix under ultrasound guidance. Recently, recombinant DNA biotechnologies have led to elegant applications of this "chorionic biopsy" technique (also called chorionic villus sampling, CVS).[66,67] A manufactured radioactive "probe" for Y-chromosome DNA can be mixed with the DNA extracted from chorionic cells. If the fetus is male, the probe will bind in two to three days in a complementary fashion to Y-chromosome DNA, a test much more accurate than the F-body stain.[68] Using this method on 13 cases in Scotland, Gosden et al. reported 100% correct sex prediction.[69] Pregnancy loss—possibly 3-4%—caused by the CVS technique itself is currently under investigation in international controlled studies.[70] However, physicians are very excited about the early diagnosis potential of this technique for use with families at risk for sex-linked disorders.

AMNIOCENTESIS

From clinical use starting in 1969, this test has now become commonplace in Western obstetrics. Invented originally to detect chromosome abnormalities, amniocentesis followed by cell culture easily identifies sex chromosomes. During the second trimester of pregnancy, a small sample of amniotic fluid is removed via a hollow needle guided through the mother's abdomen into the amniotic sac. The few fetal cells present in the fluid are coaxed into growth in tissue culture medium. When enough cells are present, sometimes after four weeks, chromosomes from dividing cells are stained and identified. Golbus et al. reported a 99.93% accuracy rate in 1979.[71] Now, in medical centers with sophisticated molecular medicine, the new recombinant-DNA probes have revolutionized this procedure also: With the DNA from a few fetal cells, and no lengthy culture procedure, the probes can identify sex in a few days. A pregnant woman and/or her physician can make an abortion decision before the woman has begun to feel the fetus move.

PREFERENCES FOR SEX OF OFFSPRING

Preferences in the United States

Since 1930, the social science literature has reported more than 30 attitudinal studies or fertility behavior analyses that purport to reveal Americans' preferences for sex of offspring.[72] College students are a favorite captive experimental group for sociologists and psychologists; somewhat fewer studies have been done with pregnant women, married women, or married couples.

Despite different research designs and approaches, the results of the attitudinal studies are quite similar. As summarized by Williamson (p. 131) essentially all studies show a slight but persistent preference for boy children, combined with a wish for balance. "Americans rarely want only (or mostly) daughters. . . . The most popular combinations are: just one boy and one girl, at least one of each sex, and more boys than girls (including a single boy if only one child)"[48] Pregnant women have been less willing to express sex preference than other women,[76–78] couples who already had children tended to rationalize their existing sex composition,[76] although men were less likely than women to rationalize having daughters.[79] After their recent study in Texas, Pharis and Manosevitz concluded that, although the status of women may have improved during the past decade, there is little evidence of a reduction in the preference for male babies.[77]

A strong preference that the *firstborn* be male also continues. Norman believed that he had detected a change in the preferences of students when he compared data from his research in 1974 with that done by Dinitz et al. in 1954.[81] The earlier data, obtained from about equal numbers of male and female university students, showed that 60.3% wished their first child to be male, and 34.5% had no preference.[81] Norman's data showed 48.3% wanted a firstborn male, with 45.1% showing no preference.[80] However, in 1983, among the students tested then by Pharis and Manosevitz, 62% wanting a firstborn son; 32% responded "either OK."[77] Clearly over this recorded span of 30 years, Americans have maintained their explicit, albeit moderate, preference that their firstborns be male.[82]

Powledge (p. 194) strongly criticized all studies on preference for sex of offspring as "worthless because a) they tell us that people prefer boys, which we already knew; b) they cannot answer the question of whether the sex ratio will change, or how much: and c) . . . they cannot help us assess the likely consequences of sex choice."[83] However, in contrast to Powledge, McClellan (p. 43) has stated, "in coming to grips with the magnitudes of the potential effects of sex-selection techniques on fertility," data yielded by surveys based on the questionnaire method are better than none.[75]

Some demographers have argued that analyses of actual reproductive behaviors, in terms of the total children in families of certain sex configurations, reveal real sex preferences. Couples whose first several children were of the same sex or predominantly female tended to have another child sooner or to have larger completed families than did other couples.[73,85 87] Such data, therefore, seem to confirm the son preference/family balance conclusions drawn from simple preference studies. However, McClelland has pointed out several problems in drawing conclusions from the configuration of sexes in families of certain sizes.[84] Subjective probabilities affect whether the family accepts the "risk" of another pregnancy. For example, a family with two girls may believe that they are now more likely to have a boy, a belief known as the *gambler's fallacy;* or another such family may believe that they are "girl producers," a belief that may have some biological basis, but is more likely to be the *trend fallacy.*[75]

Acceptance of Sex Selection Technologies in the United States

A few researchers have used "behavioral intention" measures by asking whether, if sex selection techniques were available, the interviewee would use them. In 1968, of 283 students at three Florida colleges, 26% said that they would like to choose the sex of their future children.[74] In their 1970 national fertility study, Westoff and Rindfuss found that 38.8% of 5,805 currently married women responded positively to the question, "How would you feel about being able to choose the sex of a child?"[88] In 1977, Hartley and Pietraczyk analyzed 2,138 responses from a random sample of students (53% of them male) in classes at five different northern California colleges.[89] They found more acceptance of the idea than the earlier workers: A majority of their respondents (65.9%) "agreed" that the technology of sex predetermination should be available to all parents; and 44.6% would want to use such procedures themselves. One could conclude that during the 1970s, a period in which medical technologies were burgeoning and copiously reported in the popular press, people became readier to accept such technologies, whereas preferences about sex of offspring did not change.

Preferences in "Non-Western" Countries

Son preference in the United States seems trivial compared to that in most of the "developing" nations, as anthropological data clearly demonstrate. China, Korea, Taiwan, Hong Kong, Singapore, and India provide the most extreme examples; only certain ethnic groups in Thailand and the Phillipines seem to prefer family balance.[31,48] Reports on strong son preference come also from Africa.[90] Until this century, male and female infanticide was widely practiced for population control and other reasons.[39,91] However, "systematic infanticide, wherever . . . practiced [was and] is directed primarily toward females.[92] Now that explicit infanticide is prohibited by the laws of most nations, neglect or abuse causes deaths of female infants and young children.[92–94]

An illustration of this situation can be seen in India and China. In the state of Punjab in North India, a girl is a burden to a family because of the few employment opportunities for women and the large dowry that must be given when she marries. In a study of the condition of women, Horowitz and Kishwar conducted interviews in a rural village in Punjab.[95] Women often said that personally they would like to have daughters for emotional support and for help with chores. But they dread having daughters: Their life is more miserable when they produce daughters, whereas their status and treatment improve when sons are born; they suffer so much as women that they do not want to subject their own children to such misery. And the family as an economic unit will have trouble providing the dowry.[93,95]

Despite the rhetoric of equal rights for women, including many excellent laws in Indian legislation, modernization has actually exacerbated the problems of Indian women. When more male peasants were made landowners through land reform measures, the value that women once had had as equal agricultural laborers almost vanished. With mechanized threshers and grinders run by men, the hard hand labor that women used to do was no longer marketable. Son-preference became more intense and spread into other parts of India. After infanticide was outlawed in 1890 and punished by fines to the village as well as to the family, son-preference was expressed by the slow death of little girls through inadequate feeding or failure to provide medical treatment, especially for infant diarrhea. Sex ratios of 970 women for every 1,000 men in 1901 fell to 930 per 1,000 in 1981.[93,94,96]

Now, into this scenario came amniocentesis! Indian physicians learned the technology in the West and brought it to India. Because Indian women may legally terminate a pregnancy, it is not possible to prohibit abortions done after the results of amniocentesis are reported. Thus, this technology has come to provide a more modern and unpunishable "solution" to the daughter problem than infanticide or neglect. It has come into widespread use in India as word is spread by enthusiasts and by not-so-subtle advertising on billboards, such as "Boy or Girl? Know the sex of your unborn child . . . with the aid of . . . sophisticated scientific techniques."[94,97] The editors of the Indian feminist magazine *Manushi* decided NOT to publish a report on the extent of usage of amniocentesis for sex selection because they felt that such an exposé would boomerang by attracting more customers for the procedure![98]

For data from China, newspaper accounts are essentially the only source. The one-child policy, which started in 1979, has made parents desperate that the one child be male. The official census of 1981 recorded among some two million births that year 921 girls to 1,000 boys. For children born in 1983, unofficial figures from Chinese demographers give 901 girls to 1,000 boys. Apparently most little girls are eliminated by "accidents" during delivery.[99] Both chorionic biopsy and amniocentesis are available in areas with advanced medical facilities. Officially used to detect birth defects, each of these procedures is done "blind" because of the general lack of ultrasound facilities.[70]

EFFECTS OF SEX RATIO IMBALANCES

Those who have speculated about the social consequences of sex choice have expected that boys would be preferentially selected. In 1968, Etzioni's predictions in *Science* included: an increase in crime, "some of the rougher features of a frontier town," reduced support for the arts, and the demise of religion and moral education.[100] Since in those pre-Reagan days more women than men voted Republican, Etzioni also predicted the end of the two-party system because the proportion of Republican voters would decrease. Later, Postgate, who strongly advocated sex choice to control population, also expected unpleasant consequences (to be tolerated for the greater good of society):

> It is probable that a form of *purdah* would become necessary. Women's right to work, even to travel alone freely, would probably be forgotten transiently. Polyandry might well become accepted in some societies; some might treat their women as queen ants, others as rewards for the most outstanding (or most determined) males. (p. 16)[9]

For data on what actually happens when sex ratios are imbalanced, Guttentag and Secord present in the book *Too Many Women? The Sex Ratio Question* their studies of several actual modern and historical populations with imbalances.[39] They observed that societies with a preponderance of males may treat women as possessions to be bought and sold; such societies usually place emphasis on female virginity, proscribe adultery, and have a low divorce rate. Women may be forced to marry, sometimes as child brides. Also:

Women [often are] regarded as inferior to men . . . [in] reasoned judgment, scholarship and political affairs. [They may be] excluded from any but the most elementary education. (p. 79)[39]

Paradoxically, in India where women are the minority, the gender is so devalued that the scarcity of females continues to be augmented by female infanticide, girl-child neglect, bride murders, and suttee (the self-cremation of Hindu widows on the funeral pyre of their husbands).

What sort of scenario did Guttentag and Secord find in populations with a preponderance of women?

[Men] can negotiate exchanges that are most favorable to them. . . . Men are more reluctant to make a commitment to any one woman, and if they make it, it is a weaker one, and is more apt to be broken. . . . Women are apt to feel exploited, because even when they meet a male partner's demands, he may break off the relationship . . . This feeling of being exploited generates attempts by women to redefine male and female roles in a relationship, to reject a male partner, and/or to reduce their dependency by becoming more independent. (p. 190)[39]

To explain their observation that women get short shrift whether or not they are the majority sex, Guttentag and Secord formulated a social exchange theory, to which they gave major emphasis in their book. They described two forms of power in society: dyadic power and structural power. Dyadic power belongs to the sex in short supply; it determines who can "call the shots" in making dyads. However, the other form of power, structural power, is always in the hands of men and is usually the determining power. Currently in most countries women outnumber men, and men have both dyadic and structural powers. They can exploit women and always find a woman when they want one. On the other hand, in places where women are scarce, women theoretically should be determining relationships. In a very few such societies, such as the early medieval period in Europe, women did exercise some of this sort of power (p. 57). However, it is more usual for men to take tight control over women when they are a scarce resource. Daughters and wives may be kept in purdah, and/or exchanged and sold as a market commodity. When there is a hierarchy of wealth or prestige, the wealthy man may show his power by collecting more than one wife (p. 49).[39]

However, the correlation of certain social behaviors found in a variety of times and places with specific sex ratio imbalances does not necessarily indicate that the skewed sex ratios have caused those behaviors. There could be no cause-and-effect relationship. Or, particular social customs may themselves lead to, or exacerbate, unusual sex ratios, rather than the other way around. Data showing that imbalanced sex ratios tend to perpetuate themselves provide evidence that prevailing customs maintain existing sex ratios.[39]

Some of those who have speculated about bad effects of skewed sex ratios claimed that imbalances would be trivial and only temporary. Westoff and

Rindfuss believed that any slight variations in sex ratio would correct themselves naturally:

> If effective sex control technologies were rapidly and widely adopted in the
> United States, the current sex preferences of married women indicate that the
> *temporary effect* would be a surplus of male births in the first couple of years.
> This would be followed by a *wave of female births* to achieve balance, and the
> oscillations would eventually damp out (p. 636, emphasis mine.)[88]

Similarly, Keyfitz stated: "The shortage of girls in the population would begin
to be felt within much less than 50 years, and this would act back on the
preferences of parents."[101] Such thinking assumes that parents would be motivated to bring about 50–50 sex ratios in society. The evidence from Laila
Williamson's study of infanticide[91] and the data of Guttentag and Secord on
the perpetuation of skewed sex ratios[39] refute such hypotheses. To change a
low proportion of females in any population, the underlying low regard for
females and the economic advantage of males must be changed.

However, the current preference for firstborn sons means that an even
lower regard and lower economic status for women might result should
Americans be able to select children's sex easily and cheaply. Currently husbands are, on the average, 2.5 years older than their wives (p. 175).[39] With
sex selection this gap might widen, augmenting the current power imbalance
between men and women.

The many studies on firstborn characteristics concur that firstborns tend
to become more distinguished and have more managerial positions than laterborns. Firstborns are likely to be "more ambitious, creative, achievement-
oriented, self-controlled, serious and adult-oriented . . . more likely to attend
college and to achieve eminence" (p. 93).[102] Altus found that firstborn men
and women were overrepresented in elite undergraduate colleges in the
United States.[103] (see also, Breland, Forer, and Williamson.)[73,104,105] As Pogrebin put it, "At present, at least some firstborn girls have a crack at these
special advantages. But, with sex control, boys will monopolize the eldest-child
bonuses in addition to other male privileges."[29]

MORAL ARGUMENTS FOR CHOOSING CHILDREN'S SEX

Several authors have taken strong positions in the medical, philosophical and
popular literature that urge the development of effective sex selection technologies. Three views that deserve serious consideration are the arguments
that sex choice will improve family planning, that it will reduce suffering from
sex-linked disease, and that it will control the population explosion. Let us
look at each of these.[106]

A Bonanza for Families?

The first argument might go this way: "Every child a wanted child" is a well-
known goal of family planning. Some parents may believe that they cannot

properly rear a child of one particular sex. A child of wanted sex may be less likely to suffer abuse or emotional or nutritional neglect. Grandparents will be more pleased. If parents get what they consider to be the ideal family constellation—that is, sexes of children in a particular order—they will be happier than with some other constellation. All children in a family will benefit from this parental satisfaction. In Bangladesh, for example, girls born into families with more boys than girls have a higher survival rate than those born into families with more girls than boys.[48] Furthermore, if parents do succeed in getting a wanted son or daughter, they may stop childbearing sooner, and the smaller family provides better economic advantages to all their children.

During the *Hard Choices* TV program "Boy or Girl? Should the Choice Be Ours?" Bill Allen, prospective father who used the Ericsson technique, said, "You know, it's simply a more sophisticated form of family planning. And why shouldn't we have the right, if the opportunity is available to us, to do that sort of planning?"[114]

The fact that parental expectations of whatever sort are often frustrated is the first rebuttal to these arguments. If the "wanted" boy or girl is a disappointment and does not behave as imagined, and if trouble and expense went into his/her predetermination, then he or she is at greater risk of abuse than the child of randomly determined sex.[120] And how do we decide the happy family constellation when parents disagree? If one child creates problems in the resulting family, the parent whose plan was not followed can keep the wound open. The problems in raising a family are unpredictable; the satisfactions and joys, likewise; neither of these can be spelled out in advance nor determined by sex choice.

Because sperm separation and chorionic biopsy (to be followed by selective abortion) are the two methods of sex selection most likely to be improved for use in Western nations, such sophisticated techniques would probably be available only to "a small elite of higher-income, urban, and well-informed couples" (p. 140).[48] Then these methods might become yet further examples of medical technologies unfairly distributed. Furthermore, if those who select firstborn males are already members of dominant groups, then those groups' advantages would become more firmly entrenched. Therefore, sex selection for family planning, like so many technological advancements, has the potential for increasing injustice.

Selection of children's sex starts us on a slippery slope. What traits would we like to be able to specify in our children? Hair color? IQ? The physique for our favorite sport? For many parents such traits in their children are more important than sex; children can be neglected or abused for failing to meet a variety of expectations. If we are going to custom-design our children, for which traits is there moral justification? There are no such traits. Any specification means that we are not genuinely interested in adding a unique person to our home. Positive eugenics—that is, the deliberate selection of genetic traits for human beings coming into this world—is morally wrong. After all, we humans are not really wise enough to know what traits will be best for the good of humankind through all eternity. Besides, we would harm the individual person we design: she or he would lose considerable freedom with the physical and mental characteristics prescribed by the humans with the power of conception. Moreover, the Nazi eugenics program clearly demonstrated the potential diabolical nature of eugenics policies. I believe with Powledge that we are blind if we think that eugenic ideas can be imposed only by governments:

> We simply do not see attempts by individual couples to achieve particular kinds of children are no different, except that the one is imposed by state power and the other appears voluntary. . . . It is not the hypothetical actions of governments that should fill [us] with trepidation, but those of the people themselves. (p. 211)[116]

Preventing Sex-Linked Disease

But suppose that we wish to alleviate the suffering of children from fatal genetic diseases that can be detected by amniocentesis. Is it justifiable to eliminate all children with such diseases? This sort of eugenics (negative eugenics) may under some circumstances be morally acceptable.[121] Abortion of a fetus that has been shown with certainty to have a serious genetic or developmental defect is often in the best interests of its parents and society. The suffering of a child, such as one with Nieman-Picks disease, who wastes away in pain over five to ten years, may be eliminated. Indeed, the use of scarce resources for the palliative care of such fatal disorders as Tay-Sachs disease and microcephaly may be unjustifiable.

Evaluation of the argument for using sex selection technologies in families at risk for sex-linked diseases requires an understanding of what is meant by sex-linkage. The more correct terminology is "X-linkage." Such a disease is caused by a defective protein that is coded for by a gene located on the X-chromosome.

Females are much less likely to suffer sex-linked diseases than males for the following reason: Genes for serious defects are rare in human populations. Let us consider a hypothetical case of a certain deleterious gene that is found on 0.2% of all human X-chromosomes. Two of every thousand males would have the disease. And 0.2% females would carry the defective gene on one X-chromosome, and would *not* be sick, because they would carry a gene for a good protein on the other X-chromosome. The probability that a female would be sick with this hypothetical sex-linked disease would be 2/1000 times 2/1000, or 4/1,000,000; that is four out of every million women. With this particular gene frequency, a male is 500 times more likely to be afflicted with the disease.

An affected male always passes his defective gene to all his daughters, making all of them carriers, but never to his sons, for he gives only a Y-chromosome to each son. A family with such a father is not considered to be at risk because neither sons nor daughters will actually get the disease. But the healthy mother who carries the sex-linked gene will on the average pass that gene to half of her sons. Therefore the family with the carrier mother is defined as the one at risk for the disease.

Currently there are no prenatal tests for the more common, serious sex-linked diseases, such as hemophilia, Lesch-Nyhan disease, and Duchenne muscular dystrophy. Therefore, in a family at risk, one would test a fetus for sex and abort any male because he has a 50% chance of being diseased. The female, with a 50% chance of being completely free of the gene and a 50% change of being a carrier, would be allowed to come to term.

This form of negative eugenics, i.e., abortion of males who have a 50% chance of being affected, is considered to be medically (and morally?) justified by most prenatal diagnosticians. They often urge the rapid developments of sex detection technologies for this purpose.[26,63] Although I support the personal reproductive rights of parents to choose *not* to bear and raise a defective child, I cannot wholeheartedly support the use of sex detection and selective abortion for sex-linked disease. First, half the abortions are of nondefective males; second, half the survivors are girl carriers who will then face the same problem as their mothers.

Some proponents of sex selection who are not geneticists have used a "benefit to future generations" argument to advocate sex selection in families at risk for sex-linked disease.[17] They believe erroneously that if every such family produced only daughters, the population would be rid of the disease. However, relatively few people have access to sophisticated genetic counseling; the defective gene can arise anew in the population by random mutation; and, most importantly, the many surviving carrier females may give birth to a son with the disease at any time. Indeed, the gene for a lethal sex-linked disease may actually increase in frequency when families produce daughters to compensate for the loss of sons.

However, ethical discussion about sex choice for sex-linked disease may be unnecessary in the future. Recombinant-DNA technologies are snowballing. Soon there may be radioactive DNA probes for all of the common and many of the rare genetic diseases. Such a probe would bind to the defective gene in the DNA isolated from fetal cells obtained by amniocentesis or chorionic biopsy. When the *gene itself* can be detected, only a son who *actually has* the genetic disease need be aborted. Such developments in sophisticated Western medicine would convert ethical questions about the morality of choosing sex to avoid disease into those about prenatal diagnosis in general.

Population Control

Sex selection has been proposed as a means to control the population explosion, for example by Paul Ehrlich in *The Population Bomb* in 1968. John Postgate, a British microbiologist, writing in 1973, said:

> [T]he only really important problem facing humanity to-day is over-population
> . . . [M]ultiplication in under-developed unenlightened communities is favoured, and these are the ones most prone to perpetuate the population explosion in ignorance . . . [M]y . . . panacea, one which would take advantage of

such ignorance and short-sightedness . . . is a pill, or other readily administered
treatment which, taken at coitus, would ensure (with . . . greater than 90%
certainty) that the offspring would be male. . . . Countless millions of people
would leap at the opportunity to breed male: no compulsion or even propaganda would be needed to encourage its use. (pp. 12, 14)[9]

Also advocating the manchild pill, Clare Booth Luce stated:

The determining factor in the growth of all animal populations is . . . the birth
rate of female offspring. Only women have babies. And only girl babies grow
up to be women . . . In the overpopulated countries, the preference for males
amounts to an obsession. . . . [A] pill . . . which . . . would assure the birth of a
son would come as man-ah! from Heaven. (p. C-1)[8]

Luce and Postgate believed that overpopulation was the most serious problem
facing our planet and that drastic methods must be used to stop mass starva-
tion. According to them the invention of a "manchild pill" would save humankind. Indeed, their logic is excellent. No compulsion to take this pill
would be needed. People in countries such as India and China would gladly
choose to breed boys. Once they had enough sons to establish family security
and the mother's status, they might well stop reproducing. Moreover, according to Ehrlich, Luce, Postgate, and others, the real population reduction
breakthrough would occur in the following generation. Since the number of
babies produced depends on the number of available uteruses, one generation after widespread sex selection very few babies *could* be produced.

Postgate's article inspired some spirited negative letters to the editor of
New Scientist, with arguments that fall into three categories. The first objection,
a Kantian one, is that Postgate's plan is morally wrong because the end (solving the "only important" problem facing humanity) is being used to justify
the means. "[T]he kind of standpoint . . . embodied in his thesis [is that] . . .
the species *homo sapiens* must be kept going, whatever kind of creature he
(she!) turns into."[122] According to Masson, most of those in power over the
centuries have believed that the end justifies the means, and that terrorism,
torture, and a myriad other "human-inflicted" wrongs are defended by this
creed. Sex selection as a means would corrupt the end, resulting in female
slavery in one or another guise.[122] And another letter stated, "Although mankind is the peak of God's creation, his perpetual preservation on this planet
is not something I would sacrifice all else for."[123]

The second argument is that Postgate's plan is racist and classist (as well
as sexist). Postgate used the terms "unenlightened," "ignorance," "short-
sightedness" to describe underdeveloped countries. In his letter, Ibbett
pointed out Postgate's failure to mention "the main problem to be faced: that
of the lack of any will from the rich minority of the world to sacrifice much
of their affluence for the benefit of the poor majority."[124] Prosperous citizens
of the richer countries of the world have always blamed the poorer countries
for threatening their opulence by breeding too many people.

The third argument from these letters is that a "manchild pill" might have results far worse than the intended ones. Some argued that entrepreneurs might breed daughters for financial gain, resulting in an excess of women and an acceleration of population growth.[125] And Johnston wrote, "the women would have to be locked up under state control."[123] The state would reward "its panting male population . . . with . . . sex for those who serve well the party machine." According to Masson "male frustration and aggression . . . would stand a good chance of destroying the species . . . , not so much in wars as in riots, raids, and drug-addiction on a vast scale."[122] Overpopulation may not be as great a threat to the world as the policies and behaviors that are associated with masculinity and maleness.

Therefore, sex selection as a means to cure overpopulation is likely to be pernicious. Proposing such a method is particularly ironic when existing evidence has already demonstrated that population growth slows with improvement in social welfare and extension of the roles of women beyond that of childbearing. Family-planing programs are generally unsuccessful when there is no improvement in providing the necessities of life. Birth rates are lowered with increases in income levels, health care, employment opportunities, education, and the status of women. "The countries in which [birth rates have dropped sharply] . . . are those in which the broadest spectrum of the population has shared in the economic and social benefits of significant national progress."[126] "The more education women have, the fewer children they bear."[127]

FLETCHER'S ETHICAL ANALYSES

John Fletcher has written on this topic more extensively than any other contemporary bioethicist. In 1979 in the *New England Journal of Medicine,* he argued that it was inconsistent in a society that (through Supreme Court decisions) permits abortion before 24 weeks for any reason, for physicians to refuse access to amniocentesis for sex choice.[128] The press distorted his view to be an "advocacy" of sex choice. Then several competent bioethics scholars criticized his moral arguments through letters to the *New England Journal* and responses published in the February 1980 issue of *The Hastings Center Report.* Childress and Steinfels pointed out that Fletcher had misinterpreted the Supreme Court's rulings: according to the Court, a woman has a negative right of noninterference, but not a positive right to assistance.[129,130] Childress further objected that Fletcher was appealing "to a formal principle, consistency, rather than to a substantive principle, such as fairness, which counts for more in ethical argument."[129]

In 1981, Fletcher reconsidered his position in a lengthy essay for the Bennett book *Sex Selection of Children,* published late in 1983.[132] In this essay, Fletcher applied what he considers to be the dominant ethical stance of contemporary Americans toward values issues in reproduction, namely, "freedom with fairness":

> The limits of freedom begin when harm is inflicted upon all by its unlimited expression. . . . There are two risks to society and its institutions by disseminat-

ing the technology to make sex choice decisions. First, the unharmful desire to plan or balance children in a family could result in harm to the ideal of equality between males and females if there are significant increases in first-born males. . . . A second risk is a precedent for a reintroduction of some of the ideas of positive eugenics . . . that reflect the inordinate desire of one generation to instill its concepts of ethics and virtue in succeeding generations. (pp. 222, 247, 248)[132]

Despite acknowledging these risks to society, Fletcher concluded that policy makers should not restrict sex choice technologies. He felt that if any harms were later demonstrated, "the mills of a democratic society, strongly propelled by concepts of freedom and fairness, are probably sufficient to grind and resolve the problem" (p. 248).[132]

Two years later, however, Fletcher,[131] reconsidered this conclusion and took a very strong stance against sex selection (except to avoid sex-linked disorders). He claimed that selection of a child's sex is unfair and sexist and that any reasons given by parents for preferring one sex can also hold for the other sex.[131] He further asserted that harmful consequences from the practice of sex selection would "far outweigh the few fleeting beneficial consequences" (see also, notes 133, 134).

CONCLUSION

I concur with Fletcher's most recent position, and here extend the position, first to societies in which son-preference is extreme, and then to societies like the United States.

In countries like India, China, and Korea, any available technological method for sex selection would be eagerly sought. (Since they would interfere too much with established social customs, nontechnological methods like diet and timing of intercourse would probably be less acceptable.) Because these overpopulated nations do have population-control programs, a cheap and effective method of son selection, such as a manchild pill or shot, could well be officially welcomed; methods involving selective abortion might be unapproved but condoned, as apparently is the case now in China and India.[93,94] As shown earlier, devaluation of women is often self-reinforcing; therefore, if amniocentesis should become more widely used, or if simpler technologies were available, the situation in India and China might become unbearable for women.

Under these circumstances, however, it is important not to lay blame on parents for selecting sons. Women make correct moral choices, using flawless utilitarian reasoning, when they maximize their own and their family's happiness and minimize the suffering of little girls. Before a decision to have a daughter has utility, societal practices must change so that women acquire value as persons. Women should be provided with education, meaningful employment, and the right to own land.

In Western nations, where preferences are less extreme—for firstborn sons, for "balance," for a child to fill a certain role—methods involving late abortions would probably be only marginally acceptable. However, if a cheap preconception sex-choice method really worked, or if chorionic biopsy became easily available to permit selective early abortions, couples might well act on their preferences. Probable outcomes would include increased inequality between the sexes, a curtailment of women's freedom, more glorification of stereotypically masculine traits, and a variety of negative social effects from the higher proportion of firstborn males.

But will a simple method become available soon? In 1968, Etzioni reported scientists' estimates that routine sex control of humans would be available in seven to 15 years.[100] Now more than 15 years have passed and no such methods have been invented. There is good reason to think that simple sex control is unattainable in principle for these reasons: In animals and plants various methods of sex determination have evolved. Through natural selection, mechanisms for maintaining a highly advantageous sex ratio have also evolved for each species. Therefore, only clever and involved technological mechanisms will succeed in interfering in this sex determination process. There are complicated technical difficulties in developing a shot or pill that would kill all the X-bearing sperm in a male without otherwise harming him and/or the Y-sperm, or in developing a vaginal suppository that would kill one kind of sperm in an ejaculate. And in the laboratory, scientists still cannot cleanly separate the two kinds of sperm from each other.[22]

The most feasible foolproof method for wide adoption in Western nations (and probably eagerly snatched by other nations) is the chorionic biopsy. As yet, however, its safety and quality controls have not been worked out, although much research attention is focused here.[70] Though this procedure seems simple, it qualifies as high technology because of the sophisticated cell culture and/or recombinant-DNA biotechnologies needed to make it useful. It may be expensive and perhaps not permitted for sex selection in some places.

It might here be asked: if no methods are feasible, is this paper a case of tilting at windmills? No. It is important for bioethicists to stay aware of current progress in the various technologies and to examine the arguments that have been used to urge rapid development of sex selection. I have shown here that reasons for promoting sex selection may be unethical. Problems that sex selection allegedly can solve may instead be solved in morally acceptable ways, and, in fact, might be aggravated if sex selection, or even the mindset necessary for sex selection, were prevalent.

Finally, I wish to reemphasize two great dangers intrinsic in the pro-sex-control mindset. Each danger jeopardizes the survival of humankind. First, if people increase masculinity and glorify it and the values associated with it, they exacerbate the traits that lead to world instability. Second, if individuals design particular characteristics into their children, they practice eugenics: No human is wise enough to choose the kinds of people who ought to perpetuate our species. There may be some things that we *can* do, but that we *ought not* to do: Perhaps sex selection is one of them.

ACKNOWLEDGMENTS

I am grateful to Robert Almeder, Diana Axelsen, Francis Holmes, and Jodi Simpson for their thoughtful suggestions and criticisms of an earlier version of this chapter, and especially to Betty B. Hoskins for the benefit of our extensive previous collaboration. However, any errors and all opinions remain my responsibility.

NOTES AND REFERENCES

1. Two recent collections of essays have dealt with interdisciplinary issues raised by sex preselection. For the first, which emerged from the 1979 workshop, "Ethical Issues in Human Reproduction Technology: Analysis by Women," Janice Raymond and Emily Culpepper have coordinated three papers by feminist scholars, followed by three responses and a lively audience discussion.[2] In the more recent anthology,[3] twelve authors from six disciplines have provided bibliographic information through 1981 and have discussed the issues competently from a variety of perspectives. Recommended earlier interdisciplinary reviews are those by Largey, Rinehart, and Williamson.[4-7]

2. Janice Raymond, section ed. (1981) Sex Preselection, in *The Custom-Made Child? Women-Centered Perspectives*, ed. Helen B. Holmes, Betty B. Hoskins, and M. Gross (Clifton, N.J.: Humana), pp. 177–224.

3. Neil G. Bennett, ed. (1983) *Sex Selection of Children.* (New York: Academic Press).

4. Gale Largey (1972) Sex control, sex preferences, and the future of the family, *Social Biolgoy* 19: 379–92.

5. Gale Largey (1973) Sex control and society: A critical assessment of sociological speculations, *Social Problems* 20(3): 310–18.

6. Ward Rinehart (1974) Sex preselection—not yet practical, *Population Report*, series I, no. 2 (The George Washington University Medical Center, Washington, DC), pp. I-21-I-32.

7. Nancy E. Williamson (1976) *Sons or Daughters: A Cross-Cultural Survey of Parental Preferences* (Beverly Hills: Sage).

8. Clare Boothe Luce (1978) Next: Pills to make most babies male, *Washington Star*, July 9, C1–4.

9. John Postgate (1973) Bat's chance in hell, *New Scientist* 58(841): 12–16.

10. C. A. Kiddy and H. D. Hafs, eds. (1971) *Sex Ratio at Birth—Prospects for Control* Champaign, IL: (American Society of Animal Science).

11. Rupert P. Anmann and George E. Seidel, Jr., eds. (1982) *Prospects for Sexing Mammalian Sperm* Boulder, CO: Colorado Associated University Press).

12. Barton L. Gledhill, Daniel Pinkel, Duane L. Garner, and Marvin A. Van Dilla (1982) Identifying X- and Y-Chromosome-Bearing Sperm by DNA Content: Retrospective Perspectives and Prospective Opinions, in Anmann and Seidel,[11] pp. 177–91.

13. Robert H. Foote (1982) Functional Differences Between Sperm Bearing the X- or Y-Chromosome, in Anmann and Seidel,[11] pp. 212–18.

14. F. J. Beernink and R. J. Ericsson (1982) Male sex preselection through sperm isolation, *Fertility and Sterility* 38(4): 493–95.

15. Ronald J. Ericsson and Robert H. Glass (1982) Functional Differences Between Sperm Bearing the X- or Y-chromosome, in Anmann and Seidel,[11] pp. 201–11.

16. David Rorvik and Landrum B. Shettles (1970) *Your Baby's Sex: Now You Can Choose* (Toronto: Dodd, Mead).

17. Landrum B. Shettles and David Rorvik (1984) *How to Choose the Sex of Your Baby* (New York: Doubleday).

18. A. Adimoelja, R. Hariadi, I. G. B. Amitaba, P. Adisetya, and Soeharno (1977) The separation of X- and Y-spermatozoa with regard to the possible clinical application by means of artificial insemination, *andrologia* 9(3): 289–92.

19. W. Paul Dmowski, Liliana Gaynor, Ramaa Rao, Mary Lawrence, and Antonio Scommegna (1979) Use of albumin gradients for X and Y sperm separation and clinical experience with male sex preselection, *Fertility and Sterility* 31(1): 52–57.

20. Ronald J. Ericsson (1977) Isolation and storage of progressively motile human sperm, *andrologia* 9(1): 111–14.

21. See the conference discussion on page 219 of Anmann and Seidel[11] and the remarks by Foote.[13,22] Furthermore, recently staff at Michael Reese Hospital in the clinic licensed by Gametrics Limited has seemed less than enthusiastic.[23] Also Ericsson and Glass themselves were skeptical about all other sperm separation techniques except their own.[15]

22. Robert H. Foote (1982) Prospects for Sexing: Present Status, Future Prospects and Overall Conclusions, in Anmann and Seidel,[11] pp. 285–88.

23. Ramaa, Rao, Mary Lawrence, and Antonio Scommegna (1983) Use of albumin columns in sperm separation for sex preselection (Abstract), *Fertility and Sterility* 40(3): 409.

24. Stephen L. Corson, Frances R. Batzer, and Sheldon Schlaff (1983) Preconceptual female gender selection, *Fertility and Sterility* 40(3): 384–85.

25. O. Steeno, A. Adimoelja, and J. Steeno (1975) Separation of X- and Y-bearing human spermatozoa with the Sephadex gel-filtration method, *andrologia* 7: 95–97.

26. W. Leslie G. Quinlivan, Kathleen Preciado, Toni Lorraine Long, and Herlinda Sullivan (1982) Separation of human X and Y spermatozoa by albumin gradients and Sephadex chromatography, *Fertility and Sterility* 37(1): 104–07.

27. For entertaining accounts, see Guttmacher and Hechinger; Pogrebin; Rorvik and Shettles; Sangari; and Williamson.[16,17,28–31]

28. A. F. Guttmacher and G. Hechinger (1961) Old wives' tales about having a baby, *Parents Magazine*, October, p. 184.

29. Letty Cottin Pogrebin (1981) Bias Before Birth, in *Growing Up Free: Raising Your Child in the 80's* (New York: Bantam Books), pp. 81–101.

30. Kumkum Sangari (1984) If You Would Be the Mother of a Son, in *Test-Tube Women: What Future for Motherhood?* ed. Rita Arditti, Renate Duelli Klein, and Shelley Minden (London: Routledge), pp. 256–65.

31. Nancy E. Williamson (1978) *Boys or Girls? Parents' Preferences and Sex Control*, Population Bulletin (Washington, DC: Population Reference Bureau).

32. Sally Langendoen and William Proctor (1982) *The Preconception Gender Diet* (New York: M. Evans).

33. Elizabeth Whelan (1977) *Boy or Girl?* (Indianapolis: Bobbs-Merrill).

34. J. Lorrain and R. Gagnon (1975) Sélection préconceptionnelle du sexe, *L'Union Médicale du Canada* 104: 800–03.

35. J. Stolkowski and J. Choukroun (1981) Preconception selection of sex in man, *Israel Journal of Medical Sciences* 17: 1061–66.

36. J. Stolkowski and M. Duc (1977) Rapports ioniques: ($K^+/Ca^{2+} + Mg^{2+}$) et ($K^+ + Na^+ /Ca^{2+} + Mg^{2+}$) dans l'alimentation de femmes n'ayant que des enfants du même sexe, Enquête rétrospective, *L'Union Médicale du Canada* 106: 1351-55.

37. Charles H. Debrovner (1982) Foreword to Langendoen and Proctor 32, pp. 5–8.

38. "The Talmud says that if a man wants all of his children to be sons, he should cohabit twice in succession."[39] On pages 100–11, Guttentag and Secord have cited sources and evaluated several biological theories.

39. Marcia Guttentag and Paul F. Secord (1983) *Too Many Women? The Sex Ratio Question* (Beverly Hills: Sage Publications).

40. Rodrigo Guerrero (1974) Association of the type and time of insemination within the menstrual cycle with the human sex ratio at birth, *N. Eng. J. Med.* 291(20): 1056–59.

41. Rodrigo Guerrero (1975) Type and time of insemination within the menstrual cycle and the human sex ratio at birth, *Studies in Family Planning* 6:367–71.

42. Susan Harlap (1979) Gender of infants conceived on different days of the menstrual cycle, *N. Eng. J. Med.* 300(26): 1445–48.

43. William H. James (1971) Cycle day of insemination, coital rate, and sex ratio, *Lancet* i: 112–14.

44. William H. James (1976) Timing of fertilization and sex ratio of offspring—A review, *Ann. Hum. Biol.* 3(6): 549–56.

45. William H. James (1983) Timing of Fertilization and the Sex Ratio of Offspring, in Bennett,[3] pp. 73–99.

46. Sophia J. Kleegman (1954) Therapeutic donor insemination, *Fertility and Sterility* 5(1): 7–31.

47. Guttentag and Secord have listed flaws in published studies, and have attempted to explain away discrepancies in reports about the timing of intercourse, citing most of the pertinent literature.[39] Also, Shettles and Rorvik (pp. 70–79)[17] and James (pp. 73–80)[45] evaluated theories that confirm or compete with theirs.

48. Nancy E. Williamson (1983) Parental Sex Preferences and Sex Selection, in Bennet,[3] pp. 129–45.

49. R.L. Gardner and R. G. Edwards (1968) Control of the sex ratio at full term in the rabbit by transferring sexed blastocysts, *Nature* 218: 346–48.

50. Alan Trounson and Linda Mohr (1983) Human pregnancy following cryopreservation, thawing and transfer of an eight-cell embryo, *Nature* 305: 707–09.

51. C. J. Epstein, S. Smith, and B. Travis (1980) Expression of H-Y antigen in preimplantation mouse embryos, *Tissue Antigens* 15: 63–67.

52. Verne M. Chapman (1982) Gene Products of Sex Chromosomes, in Anmann and Seidel,[11] pp. 115–17.

53. Allan R. Glass and Thomas Klein (1981) Changes in maternal serum total and free androgen levels in early pregnancy: Lack of correlation with fetal sex, *Am. J. Ob. Gyn.* 144: 656–60.

54. K. R. Held, U. Burck, and Th. Koske Westphal (1981) Pränatale geschlectsbestimmung durch den GBN-speicheltest. Ein vergleich mit den Ergebnissen der pränatalen chromosomendiagnostik, *Geburtshilfe und Frauenheilkunde* 41: 619–21.

55. von K. Loewit, H. G. Kraft, and W. Brabec (1982) Zur geschlechtsbestimmung des fetus aus dem speichel der mutter, *Wiener klinische Wochenschrift* 94: 223–26.

56. M. Méan, G. Pescia, D. Vajda, J. B. Pelber, and G. Magrini (1981) Amniotic fluid testosterone in prenatal sex determination, *Journal de Génétique humaine* 29(4): 441–47.

57. L. A. Herzenberg, D. W. Bianchi, J. Schröder, H. M. Conn, and G. M. Iverson (1979) Fetal cells in the blood of pregnant women: detection and enrichment by fluorescence-activated cell sorting, *Proc. Natl. Aca. Sci. (U.S.)* 76: 1453–55.

58. M. Kirsch-Volders, E. Lissens-Van Assche, and C. Susanne (1980) Increase in the amount of fetal lymphocytes in maternal blood during pregnancy, *J. Med. Gen.* 17: 267–72.

59. Jason C. Birnholz (1983) Determination of fetal sex, *N. Eng. J. Med.* 309: 942–44.

60. Gunther Plattner, Wilhelm Renner, John Went, Laura Beaudette, and Gilles Viau (1983) Fetal sex determination by ultrasound scan in the second and third trimesters, *Ob. Gyn.* 61: 454–58.

61. Lachlan Ch. deCrespigny and Hugh P. Robinson (1981) Determination of fetal sex with ultrasound, *Med. J. Aust.* 2: 98–100.

62. E-M. Weldner (1981) Accuracy of fetal sex determination by ultrasound, *Acta Ob. Gyn. Scand.* 60: 333–34.

63. John C. Hobbins (1983) Determination of fetal sex in early pregnancy. *N. Eng. J. Med.* 309: 979–80.

64. John D. Stephens and Sanford Sherman (1983) Determination of fetal sex by ultrasound, *N. Eng. J. Med.* 309: 984.

65. Tietung Hospital (1975) Fetal sex prediction by sex chromatin of chorionic villi cells during early pregnancy, *Chin. Med. J. 1: 117.*

66. Virginia Cowart (1983) First-trimester prenatal diagnostic method becoming available in U.S., *J. Am. Med. Assoc.* 250(10): 1249–50.

67. Michel Goossens, Yves Dumez, Liliana Kaplan, Mieke Lupker, Claude Chabret, Roger Henrion, and Jean Rosa (1983) Prenatal diagnosis of sickle-cell anemia in the first trimester of pregnancy, *N. Eng. J. Med.* 309(14): 831–33.

68. J. R. Gosden, C. M. Gosden, S. Christie, H. J. Cooke, J. M. Morsman, and C. H. Rodeck (1984) The use of cloned Y chromosome-specific DNA probes for fetal sex determination in first trimester prenantal diagnosis, *Hum. Gen.* 66: 347–51.

69. J. R. Gosden, A. R. Mitchell, C. M. Gosden, C. H. Rodeck, and J. M. Morsman (1982) Direct vision chorion biopsy and chromosome-specific DNA probes for determination of fetal sex in first-trimester prenatal diagnosis, Lancet ii: 1416–19.

70. Bernadette Modell (1985) Chorionic villus sampling: Evaluating safety and efficacy, *Lancet* i: 737–40.

71. Mitchell S. Golbus, William D. Loughman, Charles J. Epstein, Giesela Halbasch, John D. Stephens, and Bryan D. Hall (1979) Prenatal genetic diagnosis in 3,000 amniocenteses, *N. Eng. J. Med.* 300(4): 157–63.

72. In 1976, Williamson thoroughly reveiwed the sex preference studies and then summarized her review in later papers.[7,48,73] Largey, Markle and Nam, and especially Rinehart presented fairly complete bibliographies of the early preference studies.[4,6,74] McClelland has given a recent critical analysis of types of studies and what can be gained from them.[75]

73. Nancy E. Williamson (1976) Sex preferences, sex control, and the status of women, *Signs: Journal of Women in Culture and Society* 1: 847–62.

74. Gerald E. Markel and C. B. Nam (1971) Sex predetermination: Its impact on fertility, *Soc. Bio.* 18: 73–82.

75. Gary H. McClelland (1983) Measuring Sex Preferences and Their Effects on Fertility, in Bennett,[3] pp. 13–45.

76. E. Eckard (1978) Sex Preference for Children and its Relationship to Current Family Composition, Intent to Have More Children, and Important Demographic Characteristics: Provisional Results From the National Survey of Family Growth, Cycle II, paper presented at the Annual Meeting of the Southern Regional Demographic Group, San Antonio, Texas.

77. Mary E. Pharis and Martin Manosevitz (1984) Sexual stereotyping of infants: Implications for social work practice, Social Work Research and Abstracts 20: 7–12.

78. Roberta Steinbacher (1984) Sex Choice: Survival and Sisterhood, paper presented at the Second International Interdisciplinary Congress on Women, Groningen, the Netherlands. Also in (1987) *Man-Made Woman*, ed. Genoveffa Corca, Renate Duelli Klein, Jalna Hanmer, Helen B. Holmes, Betty B. Hoskins, Madhu Kishwar, Janice Raymond, Robyn Rowland, and Roberta Steinbacher (Bloomington: Indiana University Press).

79. Gerald E. Markle (1974) Sex ratio at birth: Values, variance, and some determinants, *Demography* 11: 131–42.

80. Ralph D. Norman (1974) Sex differences in preferences for sex of children: A replication after 20 years, *J. Psych.* 88: 229–39.

81. S. Dinitz, R. R. Dynes, and A. C. Clarke (1954) Preference scales for number and sex of children, *Population Studies* 29: 273–98.

82. For anecdotal information on firstborn son preference in jokes and from transcripts during childbirth, see Pogrebin (pp. 84, 87–88).[29]

83. Tabitha Powledge (1981) Unnatural Selection: On Choosing Children's Sex, in *The Custom-Made Child?*[2] pp. 193–99.

84. For example, some studies combined the effect of number preference with that of sex preference, and some surveys were based on spot decisions given to an interviewer, without a chance for spouses to confer. Furthermore, responses may have reflected what the interviewee thinks the interviewer ought to hear (impressions management), as Steinbacher believed after her study with Faith Gilroy in which 59% of women pregnant for the first time expressed "no preference" for the sex of that child.[78] For more detailed descriptions of faulty experimental methods, see McClelland and Powledge.[75,83]

85. D. S. Freedman, R. Freedman, and P. K. Whelpton (1960) Size of family and preferences for children of each sex, *Am. J. Soc.* 66: 141–46.

86. Elmer Gray and N. Marlene Morrison (1974) Influence of sex of first two children on family size, *J. Heredity* 65: 91–92.

87. Charles F. Westoff, R. B. Potter, Jr., and P. C. Sagi (1963) *The Third Child: A Study in the Prediction of Fertility* (Princeton: Princeton University Press).

88. Charles F. Westoff and Ronald R. Rindfuss (1974) Sex preselection in the United States: Some implications, *Science* 184: 633–36.

89. Shirley Foster Hartley and Linda M. Pietraczyk (1979) Preselecting the sex of offspring: Technologies, attitudes, and implications, *Soc. Bio.* 26(2): 232–46.

90. Elmer Gray, Valina K. Hurt, and S. O. Oyewole (1983) Desired family size and sex of children in Nigeria, *J. Heredity* 74: 204–06.

91. Laila Williamson (1978) Infanticide: An Anthropological Analysis, in *Infanticide and the Value of Life*, ed. Marvin Kohl (Buffalo, NY: Prometheus).

92. Barbara D. Miller (1981) *The Endangered Sex: Neglect of Female Children in Rural North India* (Ithaca: Cornell University Press) pp. 44–48.

93. Madhu Kishwar (1984) Amniocentesis for Female Feticide in India in the Context of a Growing Deficit of Women, paper presented at the Second International Interdisciplinary Congress on Women, Groningen, the Netherlands. Also in *Man-Made Woman*.[78]

94. Viola Roggencamp (1984) Abortion of a Special Kind: Male Sex Selection in India, in *Test-Tube Women*,[30] pp. 266–77.

95. Bernard Horowitz and Madhu Kishwar (1982) Family life—the unequal deal, *Manushi* 11: 2–18.

96. I was unable to examine directly the Indian census data. There is a slight discrepancy between the figures reported by Kishwar and by Roggencamp. However, demographers consider even the ratio found in 1901 extreme. Indeed, since World War II, in essentially all countries except India, China, and Korea, women have outnumbered men. For example, in the United States in 1975 there were 1,024 women for every 1,000 men (p.15).[39]

97. Arun Chacko (1982) Too many daughters? India's drastic cure, *World Paper*, November, pp. 8–9.

98. Madhu Kishwar (1984) Personal communication with the author.

99. Michael Weisskopf (1985) China's crusade against children, *The Washington Post National Weekly Edition*, January 28, pp. 6–9.

100. Amitai Etzioni (1968) Sex control, science, and society, *Science* 161: 1107–12.

101. Nathan Keyfitz (1983) Foreword to Bennett,[3] pp. xi–xiii.

102. N. Lauersen and S. Whitney (1977) *It's Your Body: A Woman's Guide to Gynecology* (New York: Grosset & Dunlap).

103. William D. Altus (1965) Birth order and academic primogeniture, *J. Personality and Social Psychology* 2(6): 872–76.

104. H. M. Breland (1973) Birth order effects: A reply to Schooler, *Psychological Bull* 10(3): 86–92.

105. L. Forer (1977) *The Birth Order Factor* (New York: Pocket Books).

106. Bioethical analyses on this topic are less common than those on other issues in reproductive medicine. Gale Largey provided the entry for the *Encyclopedia of Bioethics*.[107] Holly Goldman analyzed specifically amniocentesis as a method of sex selec-

tion.[108] Janice Raymond raised some issues from a feminist perspective in her contribution to the interdisciplinary collection she compiled.[109] Roberta Steinbacher, a psychologist, raised questions and took some firm feminist positions in a series of papers.[110-112] The subject was one of those considered by the Genetics Research Group of The Hastings Center, codirected by Tabitha Powledge and John Fletcher[113] and discussed briefly in five short articles in the February 1980 issue of *The Hastings Center Report*. Sex selection was chosen as one of six topics for the NOVA TV series *Hard Choices*.[114] In his book *Reproductive Ethics*, Michael Bayles devoted 4 1/2 pages to the subject depending heavily on the arguments presented in the Raymond collection.[2,115] The most extensive work is that of John Fletcher, Tabitha Powledge, Helen Holmes, and Betty Hoskins. Fletcher's evolution of ethical reasoning is described later in this chapter. Powledge, calling sex preselection "the original sexist sin," presented well-reasoned utilitarian and deontological arguments.[83,116] Hoskins and Holmes in several papers contributed "feminist values analyses."[117-119]

107. Gale Largey (1978) Reproductive technologies: Sex selection, *Encyclopedia of Bioethics* (New York: Macmillan), pp. 1439-44.

108. Holly S. Goldman (1980) Amniocentesis for sex selection, *Ethics, Humanism, and Medicine* (New York: Liss), pp. 81-93.

109. Janice Raymond (1981) Sex Preselection: A Response, in *The Custom-Made Child?*[2] pp. 209-12.

110. Roberta Steinbacher (1980) Preselection of sex: The social consequences of choice, *The Sciences*, 20: 6-9, 28.

111. Roberta Steinbacher (1981) Futuristic Implications of Sex Preselection, in *The Custom-Made Child?*[2] pp. 187-91.

112. Roberta Steinbacher (1984) Sex Preselection: From Here to Fraternity in *Beyond Domination: New Perspectives on Women and Philosophy*, ed. Carol Gould (Totowa, NJ: Rowman and Allanheld), pp. 274-82.

113. Tabitha Powledge and John Fletcher (1979) Guidelines for the ethical, social, and legal issues in prenatal diagnosis, N. Eng. J. Med. 300: 168-72.

114. PBS (1981) Boy or girl? Should the choice be ours? *Hard Choices*, TV series. Transcript available from PTV Publications, P.O. Box 701, Kent, OH 44240.

115. Michael D. Bayles (1984) *Reproductive Ethics* (New Jersey: Prentice-Hall).

116. Tabitha Powledge (1983) Toward a Moral Policy for Sex Choice, in Bennett,[3] pp. 201-12.

117. Helen B. Holmes (1976) Sex Preselection: A Feminist Perspective, paper presented at "Assembly on the Future," Rochester, NY.

118. Helen B. Holmes and Betty B. Hoskins (1984) Preconception and Prenatal Sex Choice Technologies: A Path to Femicide? paper presented at the International Interdisciplinary Congress on Women, Groningen, the Netherlands. Also in *Man-Made Woman*.[78]

119. Betty B. Hoskins and Helen B. Holmes (1984) Technology and Prenatal Femicide, in *Test-Tube Women*,[30] pp. 237-55.

120. An expectation of any sort lays a heavy burden on a child. Sons may be driven to succeed in materialistic ways. Once a perceptive student told me that, although she was constantly reminded through her childhood that her parents had really wanted her to be a boy, she felt that in her family the burden on a wanted boy would have been unbearable. According to Steinbacher, for a daughter, "the psychological ramifications subsequent to the discovery that one was chosen-to-be-second are unmeasurable but predictably negative."[112]

121. One problem with negative eugenics is, of course, how to define "defect." Should we define one sex as a defect to be eliminated because it would suffer under current social conditions?

122. David I. Masson (1973) Letter to the editor, *New Scientist* 58(841): 121.

123. Jos. Johnston (1973) Letter to the editor, *New Scientist* 58(844): 305.

124. Peter Ibbett (1973) Letter to the editor, *New Scientist* 58(841): 121.

125. G. S. Cardona (1973) Letter to the editor, *New Scientist* 58(841): 121.

126. Wiliam Rich (1973) *Smaller Families Through Economic and Social Progress,* monograph no. 7 (Washington, DC: Overseas Development Council).

127. Kathleen Newland (1979) *The Sisterhood of Man* (New York: Norton).

128. John C. Fletcher (1979) Ethics and amniocentesis for fetal sex identification, *N. Eng. J. Med.* 301: 550–53. Also in *The Hastings Center Report* 10(1): 15–17.

129. James C. Childress (1980) Prenatal diagnosis for sex choice—Negative and positive rights, *The Hastings Center Report* 10(1): 18–19.

130. Margaret O'Brien Steinfels (1980) Prenatal diagnosis for sex choice: The Supreme Court and sex choice, *The Hastings Center Report* 10(1): 19–20.

131. John C. Fletcher (1983) Is sex selection ethical? in *Research Ethics* (New York: Liss), pp. 333–48.

132. John C. Fletcher (1983) Ethics and Public Policy: Should Sex Choice Be Discouraged? in Bennett,[3] pp. 213–52.

133. See Warren's paper in *Biomedical Ethics Reviews-1985* for a clear exposition of and criticism of the argument presented by Fletcher[131] and Bayles[115] that sex preference is irrational because any reasons for preferring one sex can hold for the other sex.

134. Dr. McIntyre of Case Western Reserve University reluctantly decided to perform amniocentesis for sex detection for a family with two daughters that would come into a million dollar inheritance if they had a son to carry on the family name.[114] The sexism in the will is obvious. Was Dr. McIntyre's decision right? It was probably not possible for him to examine the will. Could the money have gone to one of the daughters if she kept her maiden name and passed that name to her children? And what would be the disposition of the money otherwise? If it would go to a well-managed charitable or educational institution, perhaps that would be more just than to have it go to one family.

1997 ADDENDUM TO "SEX PRESELECTION: EUGENICS FOR EVERYONE?"

Technology with embryos and fetuses has developed rapidly in the past 12 years. Removing a cell from an early IVF embryo to test for sex and for certain deleterious genes has become a standard practice in the more sophisticated clinics around the world. Tests are reasonably accurate, but the success rate for an implanted embryo becoming a full-term infant remains below 25 percent. Sex detection is ostensibly used only for embryos at risk of sex-linked disease. Although this test is expensive and requires several skilled professionals, the technique has nevertheless moved out of the "speculative" and into the "marginal" category.

Ultrasonic visualization is now "essentially one hundred percent accurate." Both the instrumentation and the skill at reading images have improved immensely. Ultrasound has become a routine part of prenatal medicine wherever Western medicine is practiced, and mothers are told the sex of their fetuses, whether or not they wish to know. In India, where amniocentesis has become illegal for sex detection, ultrasonography is now used for this purpose.

Lastly, John Fletcher has made further contributions to the ethical debate, essentially espousing the views in his piece in *Research Ethics* (note 131). Dorothy C. Wertz and he have written (1992) Sex selection through prenatal diagnosis: A feminist critique, in *Feminist Perspectives in Medical Ethics,* ed. Helen Bequaert Holmes and Laura M. Purdy (Bloomington: Indiana University Press), pp. 240–53; and (1989) Fatal knowledge? Prenatal diagnosis and sex selection, *Hastings Center Report* 19(3): 21–27.

CHAPTER 9
THE ETHICS OF SEX PRESELECTION

MARY ANNE WARREN

(1985)

In the previous chapter in this volume, "Sex Preselection: Eugenics for Everyone?" Dr. Helen B. Holmes argues that it is morally wrong to preselect the sex of one's children, or even to wish to do so. (She does not, however, believe that it ought to be legally banned.) In the first part of the article, Holmes provides a comprehensive overview of the current state of the art of sex preselection. She then summarizes the rather depressing facts about the prevalence of son-preference throughout the world: In almost every culture, the majority of prospective parents, women as well as men, would rather have a male firstborn child (or only child, if they plan to have just one) and/or more males than females. Finally, she presents a number of moral arguments against the development and use of either pre- or postconceptive methods of sex preselection. Since Holmes has done an excellent job of presenting the factual background. I will confine my comments to the moral arguments.

Holmes' view is that sex preselection is a sexist act, although it is sometimes inappropriate to blame individual parents for their desire to preselect their children's sex. Moreover, she argues that if the use of new medical technologies for preselecting sex were to become widespread, the consequences for women would probably be harmful. I will argue that, on the contrary, sex preselection is not necessarily a sexist act, though it may be so in many instances. Furthermore, I doubt that it is possible to know in advance what the long-term social consequences of sex preselection will be, or that these consequences will be, on balance, detrimental to women or society as a whole. That there is a risk of harmful consequences is enough to justify continued research and monitoring of the social and psychological effects of sex preselection; but it does not justify a wholesale condemnation of the practice.

IS SEX PRESELECTION SEXIST?

Sexism is usually defined as wrongful discrimination on the basis of sex. Discrimination based on sex may be wrong either because it is based on false and invidious beliefs about persons of one sex or the other, or because it unjustly harms those discriminated against. For now, let us concentrate upon the claim that sex preselection is sexist because it is invariably motivated by sexist beliefs.

Tabitha Powledge presents the argument for this claim in its simplest form. In her view, sex preselection is "the original sexist sin," because it makes "the most basic judgment about the worth of a human being rest first and foremost on its sex" (p. 197).[1] In this form, her argument is unsound; it is false that all persons who would like to preselect the sex of their children believe that members of one sex are inherently more valuable. Some people, for instance, would like to have a son because they already have one or more daughters (or vice versa), and they would like to have at least one child of each sex. Others may believe that, because of their own personal background or circumstances, they would be better parents to a child of one sex than the other. On the surface, at least, such persons need not be motivated by any invidious sexist beliefs. They may well believe that women and men are equally intelligent, capable, and valuable; they may even be feminists, dedicated to the elimination of restrictive sex roles and sexist discrimination of all sorts.

It may, however, be argued that the desire to preselect sex is always based on covertly sexist beliefs. Michael Bayles notes that the desire for a child of a particular sex is often instrumental to the fulfillment of other desires, such as the desire that the family name be carried on. Such instrumental reasons for sex preference, he argues, are always ultimately based upon irrational and sexist beliefs. For instance, in many jurisdictions it is no longer true that only a man can pass his family name to his children; hence, he says, it would be irrational (in those jurisdictions) to prefer a son for this particular reason. Even the desire to have a child of each sex is, according to Bayles, irrational, because there are no valid reasons for supposing that this would be better than having several children of the same sex. He considers the case of a man who already has two daughters and would like to have a son as well, "so that he could have certain pleasures in child-rearing—such as fishing and playing ball with him" (p. 35).[2] This man would be making a sexist assumption, since he could perfectly well enjoy such activities with his daughters.

John Fletcher also argues that the desire to preselect a child's sex (except for certain medical reasons) can only be based on irrational and sexist beliefs. Holmes apparently agrees with Fletcher's conclusion:

> *Prima facie* examination of any argument for sex selection cannot overcome the unfair and sexist bias of a choice to select the sex of a child. The desire to control the sex of a child is not rational, since any claim that is made for the parents' preference for one sex can be demonstrated to be provided also by the other sex. (p. 347)[3]

Fletcher is not opposed to sex preselection when it is done in order to avoid the birth of a child with a sex-linked disease, such as hemophilia. Women who are genetic carriers of a sex-linked disease often choose to abort male fetuses because males, unlike females, will have about fifty percent chance of suffering from the disease. This is not a sexist reason for preselecting sex, although, as Holmes points out, even this use of sex preselection has some morally troubling aspects. (For one thing, it requires the abortion of some perfectly normal male fetuses; for another it entails the birth of some female children who are themselves carriers of the genetic disease.) The question is whether there are any other nonsexist reasons for sex preselection.

Holmes speaks of the situation of women in the rural parts of northern India. The society is a harshly patriarchal one, in which the birth of a male child is celebrated, but the birth of a female is regarded as a severe misfortune. Son-preference is traditionally so strong that, up to about the end of the last century, the members of some tribes killed virtually all of their female infants.[4] Although infanticide is no longer openly practiced, female children still have a higher death rate than males, because they are more often neglected, underfed, or denied essential medical care.[5] Women in this society sometimes say that they are reluctant to bring a female child into a world in which she will be abused and devalued, as they themselves have been. Holmes notes that their preference for sons would seem to be morally correct on utilitarian grounds. I would add that their son preference is not necessarily a sign of sexism on their part. To accuse such women of sexism because they act upon their understanding of the intense sexism of their society would be a case of blaming the victim. Their motivations are at least partly altruistic, and do not appear to be in any way irrational. Thus, although the use by such women of selective abortion or other methods of sex selection to produce sons must be seen as a symptom of sexist institutions and ideology, there is not necessarily anything in its motivation that would justify calling it a sexist action—even one for which the women in question are personally blameless.

Another highly pragmatic reason for son-preference in northern India (and many other parts of the world) is that a son is an economic asset, whereas a daughter usually is not. Because of sexist discrimination in the job market, a daughter will almost certainly earn far less than a son. If the family is well-to-do, she is apt not to enter the job market at all. Thus, she will not be able to contribute as much to her family's economic support. Furthermore, the cost of providing her with a dowry is likely to be extremely high. Without a large dowry she will probably be unable to marry, and thus will be apt to remain dependent upon her family indefinitely. If she does marry without a dowry that is considered suitably large (or, indeed, even with such a dowry), she may be tormented or murdered by her husband or in-laws. Under these conditions, it would be difficult to show that the desire to have sons rather than daughters is irrational. It would surely be wrong to condemn the decision of a couple not to have children because they judge that they cannot afford to raise them. Why, then, should we condemn their decision not to have daughters, for the same reason?

If son-preference is rational in rural Punjab, and not necessarily a sexist action, then it will be difficult to argue that this is not also true in much of the rest of the world. Wherever son-preference is especially pronounced, it is because, in large part, of powerful economic motivations. Even in societies that provide some social support for the aged, sons are often an important part of old-age security—more so than daughters, whose earning capacity is generally far less. For this reason, son-preference is often (though not always) stronger among the poorer class. Giurovich, for instance, found that son-pref-erence is stronger among lower-class Italian couples, primarily because sons are seen as more conducive to the family's upward economic mobility.[6] Even among (some groups of) Americans, son-preference has been found to corre-late negatively with socioeconomic class, suggesting that here, too, economic factors may be among the motivations for it (p. 131).[7]

It will not do to argue, as Fletcher does, that such economic motivations for son-preference are irrational because, "Few jobs exist that women cannot perform as well or better than men when performance is the criterion for evaluation" (p. 343).[3] Although this is certainly true, the fact remains that women's average earning capacity is far from commensurate with the true value of their work. As everyone knows, the average full-time employed woman in America earns just fifty-nine percent of what the average man earns, and the average woman with a college degree still earns less than the average man with only a high school education. Poor women, especially if they have children, have few opportunities of escaping poverty. The morally appro-priate social response to this situation would be to remove the economic in-centives for son-preference through such measures as the elimination of unjust discrimination against women in education, hiring, and promotion, the provision of more adequate unemployment, old-age, and disability sup-port for all persons, and the reduction of economic differentials through a more just distribution of wealth. But until such social changes occur, it is not necessarily irrational for poor people to seek to better their economic status through the preselection of sons.

Is it nevertheless immoral for them to do so? It might be argued that in opting for sons for economic reasons, parents are, in effect, seeking to exploit the sexism of their society for their own economic gain. Yet we cannot con-demn their actions for this reason alone, unless we are also prepared to con-demn the actions of women who earn a living through (for instance) modeling in bikinis for soft drink commercials. Such women may profit from sexist attitudes and institutions, but they are more often victims than victimiz-ers; and they often have very few economically comparable options. If their actions, or those of parents who preselect sons for economic reasons, are immoral, it can only be because of their unintended social consequences.

Before turning to the consequentialist arguments against sex preselection, I would like to consider some other apparently nonsexist reasons for sex-preference. Even in the industrialized nations, prospective parents may have sound reasons to prefer that their children, for their own sake, be male. Women are still far from enjoying the full range of freedoms and opportuni-ties available to men. On the average, they not only earn much less, but also work longer hours, because regardless of whether they have jobs, they are still expected in most cases to shoulder heavier domestic responsibilities. Male violence and the threat of male violence still turn the lesser size and lesser upper-body strength of females into a serious liability. The threat of rape still curtails women's freedom of movement. As long as these many forms of sexist oppression persist, I think that it is wrong to suggest that women are performing a sexist action if they seek to have male children in order that the latter may enjoy the freedoms that women are still denied.

I am not, of course, suggesting that most women reason in this way; still less that most women ought to. Many prospective mothers would be equally content with a child of either sex; and many others would prefer to have a daughter. Of these, some are planning to raise a child without a male partner and believe that under the present conditions they would have more in common with a child of their own sex, and thus, (they hope) a better relationship with her. A son could share most of their particular interests or activities, but he could not share the basic experience of being female in a society that still values males more highly. However much he may sympathize with the plight of women, he will still be a member of the more privileged sex. Although such expectations may prove mistaken in particular cases, I see no ground for condemning them as either sexist or irrational.

Other women may prefer to have daughters because they fear that, in Sally Gearhart's words,

> . . . if they have sons, no amount of love and care and nonsexist training will save those sons from a culture where male violence is institutionalized and revered. These women are saying, "No more sons. We will not spend twenty years of our lives raising a potential rapist, a potential batterer, a potential Big Man." (p. 282)[8]

Men, as a group, are far more apt to resort to serious violence against other persons (and, for that matter, against nonhuman animals) than are females. We need not speak of war, into which men are often conscripted against their will; it is enough to glance at the statistics on individual acts of violence. In the United States, for instance, males commit five times as many murders as females.[9] Rape and child molesting are primarily (though not exclusively) male crimes, and most battered spouses are female victims of male violence. The question is whether it is morally wrong to take account of such proven statistical differences between the sexes in deciding whether and how to make use of the new methods of sex preselection.

Most feminists would agree that it is usually unjust to discriminate against individuals of either sex on the basis of merely statistical differences between the sexes. Individuals have the right to be judged on their own merits, not condemned by association with some group to which they happen to belong. But choosing to have a daughter rather than a son, on the grounds that females tend to be less violent, is not a case of injustice against an individual person. The son one might have had instead might or might not have turned out to be violent, but since he does not exist, there is no way to evaluate him as an individual. Furthermore, since he does not exist he cannot have been treated unjustly; he will not suffer from his nonexistence. This is most clearly true when preconceptive methods of sex selection are used. But even sex-selective abortion cannot be regarded as an injustice against an individual person, because, as I have argued elsewhere, fetuses are not yet persons and do not yet have a right to continued existence.[10,11]

CONSEQUENTIALIST OBJECTIONS

Numerous speculations have been made about the long-term consequences, should an effective means of sex preselection become widely available. Some writers have welcomed sex preselection as a voluntary means of reducing the birth rate and the number of unwanted children born in the attempt to get one of the "right" sex. Others, including Holmes and Fletcher, argue that the results are likely to be primarily detrimental. They fear that females may be psychologically harmed by the implementation of son-preference. Equally disturbing are the possible social consequences of sex ratio increases, i.e., increases in the relative number of males. An undersupply of women might result in their being increasingly confined to subordinate "female" roles and/or subjected to increased male violence. Let us look first at these possible negative results of sex preselection.

Birth-Order Effects

Throughout most of the world, a majority of prospective parents would prefer a male firstborn child. And firstborns, it has often been claimed, enjoy certain social and psychological advantages, perhaps because they have, for a time, a monopoly on their parents' attention. There have been hundreds of studies purporting to prove or disprove linkages between birth order and such personal traits as initiative, creativity, anxiety, affiliation, dependence, conservatism, rebelliousness, authoritarianism, mental illness, criminality, and alcoholism. The results are enormously complex and frequently contradictory. However, among the most consistent findings are that firstborns tend to achieve more in terms of formal education and career, and to be more dependent and affiliative (p. 411).[12] Alfred Adler argued that each birth-order position carries with it characteristic advantages and disadvantages. In his view, firstborns tend to be more responsible, conservative, and achievement-oriented, but may also suffer from anxiety and other mental problems because of the traumatic experience of "dethronement" by the birth of a younger sibling.[13,14,15] Robert Zajonc has argued that first born children tend to be more intelligent than laterborns because of the progressive degradation of the family's "intellectual environment" supposedly produced by the birth of each additional child.[16,17]

If either of these theories about the psychological effects of birth order were empirically well supported, there might be good reason to fear that increases in the relative number of male firstborns will have a detrimental effect upon women. However, the evidence for these theories is, at best, highly ambiguous. The isolation of birth-order effects from the effects of socioeconomic status, ethnicity, religion, family size, urban versus rural background, and other social variables represents an extremely difficult methodological problem, and one that has not been resolved in most of the studies that have been done. In many of the early studies that found firstborns to be superior in intelligence, motivation, and achievement, there were no controls for family size. Obviously, firstborns are more apt to come from small families than laterborns. In most of the industrialized nations, parents of large families tend to have less money and education and to score lower on standard tests of intelligence than parents of smaller families. Thus, where family size is not held constant, comparisons between first- and laterborn children are biased. The latter have, on the average, less privileged socioeconomic backgrounds, and any psychological differences found are as likely to be a result of this factor as of birth order itself. Where sample groups of first- and laterborns are matched for family size and socioeconomic status, most (though not quite all) of the apparent superiorities of the firstborn disappear (p. 45).[18]

The birth-order debate continues, with some psychologists presenting new evidence of the influence of birth order upon personality and others debunking the idea. But at present, the weight of the evidence seems to support a sceptical view. In 1983 two Swiss psychologists, Cecile Ernst and Jules Angst, published an exhaustive review of the birth-order research of the past four decades. Their conclusion is that nearly all of the reports of significant birth-order effects are a result of errors in the design of studies and the statistical analysis of the data (p. 13).[18] They believe that there are some general differences in the socialization process undergone by firstborns and laterborns, i.e., firstborns tend to be better cared for in infancy and to be more advanced in linguistic development. But they conclude that these differences "do not seem to leave indelible traces that can be predicted" (p. 187). They do not deny that being a first, middle, last, or only child may have great importance for the personal development of some individuals, but only that it has any general and lasting significance. Birth-order theories, they argue, ignore the fact that each child has a unique genetic constitution that influences his or her intelligence and personality, and that consequently, "each child in a sibship will interact in a novel way with the environment, and, from the first day on, will mold it and be molded by it in a highly individualistic way" (p. 242).

Other Psychological Harms

What about the fact that many females will know that their parents chose to have sons first? Roberta Steinbacher asks, "What are the implications of being second born, and knowing at some early age that you were planned-to-be-second?" (p. 187).[19] It might seem self-evident that girls will suffer a loss of self-esteem from the knowledge that their parents chose to have a son first. And Fletcher argues that even a firstborn girl is apt to be damaged if she learns that, whereas she was not sex-selected, her younger brother was. Addressing the parent who already has a daughter and is considering a sex-selected son, Fletcher says,

> . . . put yourself in your daughter's place. How will she respond to your reasons why you went to the fertility clinic to start a pregnancy with baby brother, when you did not do the same with the conception of her? What reasons will you give her? . . . You would not let her continue believing that only boys can be police, firefighters, or surgeons, would you? . . . You conclude that if you would not neglect her need to aspire equally to almost any job that a man might do, you will sabotage that parental duty by preselecting sex. (p. 343)[3]

This argument rests upon the assumption that there can be no nonsexist reasons for preselecting sex—or none that a female child can be expected to understand. But surely one need not believe that only boys can grow up to be police or firefighters to want a son as well as a daughter. One might, for instance, believe that children are apt to develop a better understanding of persons of the opposite sex if they have an opposite-sex sibling. Or one might believe that the best way to raise a nonsexist child is to raise her in the company of an opposite-sex sibling whom one does not treat any differently. Even if these beliefs are false, they are not obvious instances of sexism. Nor is it obvious that a girl would be apt to suffer psychological harm as a result of learning that her parents preselected a son because of such beliefs.

But what of the girl who learns that her brother was sex-selected for reasons that are sexist, e.g., because her father wants a male heir? No doubt she may be hurt by this knowledge. Yet, if her parents are sexist in their current behavior, if they treat her as worth less than her brother because of her sex, then the discovery that his sex was preselected can only come as one more confirmation of what she must already know. On the other hand, if her parents are not biased in their current treatment of her brother and her, then this particular discovery need not shake her conviction that she is equally valued—although, of course, it might. Every female must eventually come to terms with the sexist biases of her society. It would be difficult to prove that the implementation of son-preference through sex preselection will do much extra damage to female psyches.

Sex Ratios and the Status of Women

Very few studies have been made of the relationship between sex ratios and sex roles. The only well-developed theory in this area is that presented by Marcia Guttentag and Paul Secord.[20] Guttentag and Secord argue that women tend to be disadvantaged in both high and low sex ratio societies—although not necessarily any more so than in societies with a 50:50 sex ratio. On their theory, high sex ratio societies tend to impose rigid restrictions upon the sexual behavior of women and to confine them to the domestic role. Low sex ratios, on the other hand, tend to contribute to male misogyny and the devaluation of both women and marriage. This is because when there is an "oversupply" of women, men become reluctant to commit themselves to long-term relationships with a single woman. In such circumstances, women are apt to become dissatisfied with the terms of marriage, and to seek other means of achieving economic security; hence, feminist movements may appear. According to Guttentag and Secord, whichever sex is in short supply is likely to gain an advantage in "dyadic power," i.e., power within two-person heterosexual relationships. Yet men are usually able to limit women's freedom even when sex ratios are low, because they have the advantage in "structural power," i.e., control of the economic, legal, and other key social institutions.

On this theory, high sex ratios may be either good or bad for women, depending upon the structural power that women already have. If women are economically dependent and lack basic legal rights and protections, they cannot make use of whatever dyadic power they might otherwise gain as a result of their scarcity value. But if they have a degree of economic independence and legal autonomy, then they may be able to take advantage of this dyadic power to drive a better bargain in relationships with men. This benefit applies primarily to heterosexual women. Guttentag and Secord say very little about nonheterosexual women, except that lesbianism is apt to be more severely discouraged in a high sex ratio society. Insofar as compulsory heterosexuality is a basic part of the oppression of women, this must be seen as an additional danger of sex ratio increases.

However, as Holmes points out, we cannot assume that the differences between typical high and low sex ratio societies are actually caused by sex ratios. It may be that the causal relationship tends to run in the opposite direction. Rather than high sex ratios causing women's confinement to the domestic role, societies that confine women to the domestic role may tend to have high sex ratios because many parents conclude that raising females is less worthwhile than raising males, and therefore practice sex selection through female infanticide or the neglect of female children. The high sex ratios may be relatively harmless in themselves. They might, conceivably, even be beneficial to women, in the context of a society that allows them very few opportunities to lead a decent life outside of the wife-and-mother role.

Even if it is true that in the past high and low sex ratios have tended to have the social consequences that Guttentag and Secord describe, it would be a mistake to assume that in the future the results will be the same. One may speculate that women in the more severely patriarchal societies will be apt to suffer a further loss of freedom should sex preselection lead to a significant increase in sex ratios; without substantial structural power, women cannot benefit from their own increased "value." Yet nothing in this scenario is inevitably predetermined. Improved education and movements toward socialism and democracy tend to facilitate the loosening of traditional constraints upon women, and might tip the balance in favor of sexual egalitarianism even in the face of declining sex ratios. The power of women's liberation movements throughout the world is another unpredictable factor. I suspect, however, that the growth of mass communication will make it increasingly difficult for women to be kept ignorant of their own oppression and the need to struggle against it.

Women in the more industrialized and/or less severely patriarchal nations probably have somewhat less need to fear increased oppression as a result of sex ratio increases. Not only is the relative increase in the number of males apt to be smaller, but because women often have greater (though still inadequate) opportunities for economic independence and political influence, they may be able to successfully defend those rights already won, while continuing to improve their legal and economic status. This is not predetermined either; the forces of reaction are strong, and the gains that women have already made may be lost, with or without sex ratio increases. Nevertheless, sweeping predictions of a loss of freedom for women should sex ratios increase are unjustified.

Are We on a Slippery Slope?

Another consequentialist objection to sex preselection is that it may lead to the predesigning of children in other respects than sex. Holmes notes that some parents may be more concerned about a child's hair color or IQ than a about its sex. She asks, "if we are going to custom design our children, for which traits is there moral justification?" Her reply is that, "There are no such traits. Any specification means that we are not genuinely interested in adding a unique person to our home." There are two strands of argument here. One is a version of the slippery slope argument: We should reject sex preselection because it will lead to other forms of positive eugenics, which are objectionable. The other is that we should reject all forms of positive eugenics, because any attempt to predesign a child indicates a refusal to treat that child as a unique individual. Both arguments are questionable.

All slippery slope arguments presuppose that people cannot (learn to) make certain distinctions that the arguer considers vital; if the relevant distinctions can be made, then there is no reason to suppose that acceptance of the one form of behavior will lead to acceptance of the other. Such arguments fail if either (1) people can make such distinctions, or (2) these distinctions do not have the significance that the arguer takes them to have. In this case, both conditions apply. Many people who do not object to sex preselection would object to the preselection of hair color or IQ, because they perceive that these cases involve quite different considerations. Most of the arguments for and against sex preselection would not normally apply to the preselection of hair color, which usually has much less social significance than sex. Preselecting for intelligence would raise much more serious moral questions, because intellectual ability has a much more direct effect upon a person's life prospects than hair color normally does. These questions can and must be treated separately.

I am puzzled by the suggestion that all forms of positive eugenics are indicative of an unwillingness to perceive a child as a unique individual. Positive eugenics includes all attempts to select for certain traits that are positively desired, as opposed to selecting against certain undesirable traits, such as hemophilia or Down's Syndrome. Positive eugenics tends to evoke the image of dictatorial governments predesigning people to serve their own nefarious ends, or of parents predesigning children to fit their own entirely selfish preferences. It is easy to forget that some forms of positive eugenics might serve children's own interests. Suppose, for instance, that there was a perfectly safe preconceptive or prenatal procedure that would endow a child with excellent vision or an increased life expectancy. I can see no *a priori* reason to deny that such a procedure might provide a real benefit to future persons. Why should we assume that parents who wish to provide their children with such benefits are uninterested in adding a unique individual to their home? As in the case of sex preselection, their reasons might be selfish or irrational, but they might also be altruistic and well reasoned.

Positive eugenics may be feared for a number of reasons: It might be abused for immoral purposes; it might prove to have unforeseen side effects; it might divert medical resources from more important purposes; and, above all, the advocacy of eugenics has been historically associated with vicious racist doctrines. These are sound reasons for proceeding cautiously, with full public disclosure and extensive public discussion of each new or proposed procedure—just as should be done in every other area of medical technology. They are not, however, reasons for a blanket rejection of all such procedures. Many possible eugenic procedures will prove too expensive or too dangerous to be worth pursuing. But each must be evaluated on its own merits. If we refuse to make the essential distinctions, insisting that all forms of positive eugenics must be accepted or rejected as part of a single package, then we may inadvertently contribute to the very sorts of abuses that we fear.

Will More Women Be Born Poor?

Some observers have predicted that if sex preselection becomes readily available, the poorer classes will become increasingly male, since son-preference is often strongest among the most economically deprived (p. 1109).[21] On the other hand, if the new methods of sex preselection continue to be expensive, or if governments, fearing their social consequences, seek to ban their use, sex preselection may become a prerogative of the relatively wealthy. In that case, it will probably be the upper classes that experience the greatest increase in sex ratios. As Steinbacher points out, this would mean "that increasing numbers of women in the future are locked into poverty while men continue to grow in numbers in positions of control and influence" (p. 188).[19]

This is perhaps the most damning of all the consequentialist objections to sex preselection. The detrimental effects of a further "masculinization of wealth" would be difficult to overestimate. Increased wealth and power in the hands of men could only result in the aggravation of the entire range of injustices against women. Yet we cannot move directly from this fact to the conclusion that the development and use of sex preselection is morally objectionable. What is morally objectionable is that it should be made available only to the wealthy. If we want to avoid some of the worst social consequences of sex selection, we must either suppress it completely (which is probably impossible), or seek to make it equally available to all social classes. It is much too early to predict that the latter goal will prove impossible.

THE POSSIBLE BENEFITS

The possible benefits of sex preselection are just as difficult to predict as are the possible harms. I agree with Holmes that sex preselection should not be lauded as a means of reducing the birth rate. We cannot be sure that fewer children will be born if parents are able to preselect sex; some parents may have more children if they can be assured that they will be of the preferred sex. Nor do we know that decreases in the relative number of women will have the effect of reducing birth rates. In those cases in which pronatalism remain strong, high sex ratios may only result in each women being expected to have

more children. If a shortage of women were to result in polyandrous marriages, women who received support from several men might find it possible—and perhaps necessary—to have more children than would be feasible
in a monogamous marriage. Fertility drugs might even be used to increase
the number of multiple births.

A more realistic possibility is that governments would take steps to prevent
sex selection from resulting in a severe shortage of women. Whereas any absolute prohibition would probably be unpopular and ineffective, a variety of less
severe measures might be employed. Couples might be forbidden to use sex
preselection to produce sons until they have already produced at least one
daughter; or tax penalties or other disincentives might be used to reduce
the attractiveness of all-male families. Ways might even be found to reduce
economic discrimination against women, thus reducing son-preference.
Thus, the long-term effect of sex selection upon birth rates is quite unpredictable.

Moreover, as Holmes points out, there are better ways of promoting voluntary reductions in the birth rate than by encouraging the use of sex selection
to produce sons. Free universal access to contraception and abortion is essential (and nonexistent in much of the world), but will be insufficient unless
combined with more far-reaching social reforms. Improved economic security, education, and health care, and expanded opportunities for women outside of the maternal role have consistently proven effective in lowering birth
rates. These measures are desirable on independent moral grounds, and
should be supported even by those who doubt that overpopulation is a real
problem.

I also agree with Holmes that we cannot be certain that parents will be
happier if they are able to choose the sex of their children. No doubt some
will be happier and others will only be disappointed when their sex-selected
children fail to live up to their expectations. Getting what one wants is never
a guarantee of happiness—although it is usually more conducive to happiness
than not getting what one wants.

There are, however, two predictable benefits of sex preselection that do
much to counterbalance its possible ill effects. The most important is that
fewer children will be doomed to abuse or neglect because they are of the
"wrong" sex—in most cases, because they are female. It is true that even a
wanted girl or boy may suffer from unrealistic parental expectations. But
wanted children are less likely to be deliberately deprived of food, affection,
and necessary medical care; and fewer wanted children die from such neglect.
We will never know how many short and miserable lives will be avoided
through sex preselection, but the data on differential mortality rates for female children in northern India and many other parts of the world suggest
that the number will be quite significant. In my mind, this potential benefit is
at least as weighty as any of the potential harms that Holmes describes. I doubt
that any of the possible benefits to be gained through discouraging the development and use of new methods of sex preselection is worth condemning
even a few children to rejection and neglect.

Sex preselection will also provide at least some women with a new means of resistance to patriarchy. It is part of the oppression of women that they have generally had little choice but to bear and raise sons, thereby perpetuating the ruling sex/class. Women may soon have the option of refusing to do this, without avoiding motherhood altogether or abandoning their male children, as the legendary Amazons were said to do. Other women, less optimistic about the prospects for change, may resist patriarchy by refusing to add to the female underclass. The freedom to preselect the sex of one's children is far less vital to women's interests than the freedom to decide whether to bear a child or not; yet having the former option will still be important to some women. Granted, some women may be forced by their husbands or families to have sons when they would prefer daughters, just as some are forced to complete pregnancies they would prefer to abort, or to abort those they would prefer to complete. But the option of sex choice will still have value for those women with the desire and the opportunity to use it.

CONCLUSION

I have not argued that the net effects of sex preselection are bound to be beneficial. They may well prove to be detrimental, just as Holmes fears. My primary point is rather that we cannot possibly know in advance what the effects of sex preselection will be, and that we ought not to condemn it on the basis of what can be little more than speculation. Were it possible to prove that sex preselection is, in every instance, a sexist act, then it could be condemned without proof of a high probability of serious harm. But if, as I have argued, there are many nonsexist reasons for son-preference or daughter-preference, then sex preselection can be morally condemned only if the consequentialist arguments against it are very strong. Because these arguments are not particularly strong, because there are probable compensatory benefits as well as possible ill effects, and because the possibility of net losses does not justify categorical condemnation, the presumption must be in favor of moral, as well as legal, toleration. Should the feared detrimental effects of preselection begin to materialize at some future time, then will be the time to reassess this moral stance.[22]

NOTES AND REFERENCES

1. Tabitha Powledge (1981) Unnatural selection: On choosing children's sex, in *The Custom-Made Child? Women-Centered Perspectives*, ed. Helen B. Holmes, Betty B. Hoskins, and Michael Gross (Clifton, NJ: Humana).

2. Michael B. Bayles (1984) *Reproductive Ethics* (New Jersey: Prentice-Hall).

3. John C. Fletcher (1983) Is sex selection ethical? in *Research Ethics* (New York: Alan R. Liss).

4. Kanti B. Pakrasai (1970) *Female Infanticide in India* (Calcutta: Editions India).

5. Barbara D. Miller (1981) *The Endangered Sex: Neglect of Female Children in Rural North India* (Ithaca: Cornell University Press).

6. G. Giurovich (1956) Sul desiderio dei coniungi di avere figle e di avere figle di un data sesso [On the wish of married couples to have children and to have children of a specified sex.] (Rome: *Atti Della 16 Ruinoine Scientifica della Societa Italiana de Statistica*).

7. Lee Rainwater (1965) *Family Design* (Chicago: Aldine).

8. Sally Gearhart (1982) The future—if there is one—is female, in *Reweaving the Web of Life: Feminism and Nonviolence*, ed. Pam McAllister (Philadelphia: New Society).

9. National Commission on the Causes and Prevention of Violence (1969) *Violent Crime* (New York: George Brazillen).

10. Mary Anne Warren (1973) On the moral and legal status of abortion, *The Monist* 57(1):43–61.

11. Mary Anne Warren (1977) Do potential people have moral rights? *Can. J. Phil.* 7(2).

12. Bert N. Adams (1972) Birth order: A critical review, *Sociometry* 35(3): 411–39.

13. Alfred Adler (1927) *Understanding Human Nature* (New York: Greenberg).

14. Alfred Adler (1928) Characteristics of the first, second, and third child, *Children* 3 (14).

15. Alfred Adler (1931) *What Life Should Mean to You* (Boston: Little Brown).

16. Robert B. Zajonc (1975) Dumber by the Dozen, *Psychol. Today*, January, pp., 37–43.

17. Robert B. Zajonc, Hazel Markus, and Gregory B. Markus (1979) The birth order puzzle, *J. Pers. Soc. Psychol.* 37(8): 1325–41.

18. Cecile Ernst and Jules Angst (1983) *Birth Order: Its Influences on Personality* (Berlin, Heidelberg, and New York: Springer-Verlag).

19. Roberta Steinbacher (1981) Futuristic implications of sex preselection in *The Custom-Made Child?*

20. Marcia Guttentag and Paul F. Secord (1983) *Too Many Women? The Sex Ratio Question* (Beverly Hills: Sage).

21. Amitai Etzioni (1968) Sex control, science, and society, *Science* 161: 1107–12.

22. The arguments in this article are further developed in the author's 1985 book *Gendercide: The Implications of Sex Selection* (New Jersey: Rowman and Allanheld).

CHAPTER 10
SURROGATE MOTHERHOOD
The Challenge for Feminists

LORI B. ANDREWS

(1988)

Surrogate motherhood presents an enormous challenge for feminists. During the course of the *Baby M* trial, the New Jersey chapter of the National Organization of Women met and could not reach consensus on the issue. "The feelings ranged the gamut," the head of the chapter, Linda Bowker, told the *New York Times.* "We did feel that it should not be made illegal, because we don't want to turn women into criminals. But other than that, what you may feel about the *Baby M* case may not be what you feel about another." "We do believe that women ought to control their own bodies, and we don't want to play big brother or big sister and tell them what to do," Ms. Bowker continued. "But on the other hand, we don't want to see the day when women are turned into breeding machines."[1]

Other feminist groups have likewise been split on the issue, but a vocal group of feminists came to the support of Mary Beth Whitehead with demonstrations[2] and an amicus brief[3]; they are now seeking laws that would ban surrogate motherhood altogether. However, the rationales that they and others are using to justify this governmental intrusion into reproductive choice may come back to haunt feminists in other areas of procreative policy and family law.

As science fiction has taught us, the types of technologies available shape the nature of a society. Equally important as the technologies—and having much farther-reaching implications—are the policies that a society devises and implements to deal with technology. In Margaret Atwood's *The Handmaid's Tale*, a book often cited as showing the dangers of the technology of surrogacy, it was actually policy changes—the criminalization of abortion and the banning of women from the paid labor force—that created the preconditions for a dehumanizing and harmful version of surrogacy.

In the past two decades, feminist policy arguments have refashioned legal policies on reproduction and the family. A cornerstone of this development has been the idea that women have a right to reproductive choice—to be able to contracept, abort, or get pregnant. They have the right to control their bodies during pregnancy, such as by refusing Cesarean sections. They have a right to create nontraditional family structures such as lesbian households or single-parent families facilitated by artificial insemination by donor. According to feminist arguments, these rights should not be overridden by possible symbolic harms or speculative risks to potential children.

Another hallmark of feminism has been that biology should not be destiny. The equal treatment of the sexes requires that decisions about men and women be made on other than biological grounds. Women police officers can be as good as men, despite their lesser strength on average. Women's larger role in bearing children does not mean they should have the larger responsibility in rearing children. And biological fathers, as well as nonbiological mothers or fathers, can be as good parents as biological mothers.

The legal doctrine upon which feminists have pinned much of their policy has been the constitutional protection of autonomy in decisions to bear and rear one's biological children.[4] Once this protection of the biologically related family was acknowledged, feminists and others could argue for the protection of nontraditional, nonbiological families on the grounds that they provide many of the same emotional, physical, and financial benefits that biological families do.[5]

In many ways, the very existence of surrogacy is a predictable outgrowth of the feminist movement. Feminist gains allowed women to pursue educational and career opportunities once reserved for men, such as Betsy Stern's position as a doctor and medical school professor. But this also meant that more women were postponing childbearing and suffering the natural decline in fertility that occurs with age. Women who exercised their right to contraception, such as by using the Dalkon Shield, sometimes found that their fertility was permanently compromised. Some women found that the chance for a child had slipped by them entirely and decided to turn to a surrogate mother.

Feminism also made it more likely for other women to feel comfortable being surrogates. Feminism taught that not all women relate to all pregnancies in the same way. A woman could choose not to be a rearing mother at all. She could choose to lead a child-free life by not getting pregnant. If she got pregnant, she could choose to abort. Reproduction was a condition of her body over which she, and no one else, should have control. For some women, those developments added up to the freedom to be a surrogate.

In the surrogacy context, feminist principles have provided the basis for a broadly held position that contracts and legislation should not restrict the surrogate's control over her body during pregnancy (such as by a requirement that the surrogate undergo amniocentesis or abort a fetus with a genetic defect). The argument against enforcing such contractual provisions resounds with the notion of gender equality, since it is in keeping with common law principles that protect the bodily integrity of both men and women, as well as with basic contract principles rejecting specific performance of personal services provisions.[6] It is also in keeping with constitutional principles giving the pregnant woman, rather than the male progenitor, the right to make abortion decisions. In this area, feminist lobbying tactics have met with considerable success. Although early bills on surrogacy contained provisions that would have constrained surrogates' behavior during pregnancy, most bills regulating surrogacy that have been proposed in recent years specifically state that the surrogate shall have control over medical decisions during the pregnancy.[7] Even the trial court decision in the *Baby M* case, which enforced the surrogacy contract's termination of parental rights, voided the section that took from the surrogate the right to abort.[8]

Now a growing feminist contingent is moving beyond the issue of bodily control during pregnancy and is seeking to ban surrogacy altogether. But the rationales for such a ban are often the very rationales that feminists have fought against in the contexts of abortion, contraception, nontraditional families, and employment. The adoption of these rationales as the reason to regulate surrogacy could severely undercut the gains previously made in these other areas. These rationales fall into three general categories: the symbolic harm to society of allowing paid surrogacy, the potential risks to the woman of allowing paid surrogacy, and the potential risks to the potential child of allowing paid surrogacy.

THE SYMBOLIC HARM TO SOCIETY

For some feminists, the argument against surrogacy is a simple one: to sell babies demeans us as a society. And put that way, the argument is persuasive, at least on its face. But as a justification for policy, the argument is reminiscent of the argument that feminists roundly reject in the abortion context: that to kill babies demeans us as a society.

Both arguments, equally heartfelt, need closer scrutiny if they are to serve as a basis for policy. In the abortion context, pro-choice people criticize the terms, saying we are not talking about "babies" when the abortion is done on an embryo or fetus still within the woman's womb. In the surrogacy context, a similar assault can be made on the term "sale." The baby is not being transferred for money to a stranger who can then treat the child like a commodity, doing anything he or she wants with the child. The money is being paid to enable a man to procreate his biological child; this hardly seems to fit the characterization of a sale. Am I buying a child when I pay a physician to be my surrogate fallopian tubes through *in vitro* fertilization (when, without her aid, I would remain childless)? Am I buying a child when I pay a physician to perform a needed Cesarean section, without which my child would never be born alive?

At most, in the surrogacy context, I am buying not a child but the preconception termination of the mother's parental rights. For decades, the preconception sale of a father's parental rights has been allowed with artificial insemination by donor. This practice, currently facilitated by statutes in at least thirty states, has received strong feminist support. In fact, when, on occasion, such sperm donors have later felt a bond to the child and wanted to be considered legal fathers, feminist groups have litigated to hold them to their pre-conception contract.[9]

Rather than focusing on the symbolic aspects of a sale, the policy discussion should instead analyze the advisability of pre-conception terminations for both women and men. For example, biological parenting may be so important to both the parent and the child that either parent should be able to assert these rights after birth (or even later in the child's life). This would provide sperm donors in artificial insemination with a chance to have a relationship with the child.

Symbolic arguments and pejorative language seem to make up the bulk of the policy arguments and media commentary against surrogacy. Surrogate motherhood has been described by its opponents not only as the buying and selling of children but as reproductive prostitution,[10] reproductive slavery,[11] the renting of a womb,[12] incubatory servitude,[13] the factory method of child-bearing,[14] and cutting up women into genitalia.[15] The women who are surrogates are labeled paid breeders,[16] biological entrepreneurs,[17] breeder women,[18] reproductive meat,[19] interchangeable parts in the birth machinery,[20] manufacturing plants,[21] human incubators,[22] incubators for men's sperm,[23] a commodity in the reproductive marketplace,[24] and prostitutes.[25] Their husbands are seen, alternatively, as pimps[26] or cuckolds.[27] The children conceived pursuant to a surrogacy agreement have been called chattel[28] or merchandise to be expected in perfect condition.[29]

Feminists opposing surrogacy have also relied heavily on a visual element in the debate over Baby M. They have been understandably upset at the vision of a baby being wrenched from its nursing mother or being slipped out a back window in a flight from governmental authorities. But relying on the visceral and visual, a long-standing tactic of the right-to-life groups, is not the way to make policy. Conceding the value of symbolic arguments for the procreative choice of surrogacy makes it hard to reject them for other procreative choices.

One of the greatest feminist contributions to policy debates on reproduction and the family has been the rejection of arguments relying on tradition and symbolism and an insistence on an understanding of the nature and effects of an actual practice in determining how it should be regulated. For example, the idea that it is necessary for children to grow up in two-parent, heterosexual families has been contested by empirical evidence that such traditional structures are not necessary for children to flourish.[30] This type of analysis should not be overlooked in favor of symbolism in discussions of surrogacy.

THE POTENTIAL HARM TO WOMEN

A second line of argument opposes surrogacy because of the potential psychological and physical risks that it presents for women. Many aspects of this argument, however, seem ill founded and potentially demeaning to women. They focus on protecting women against their own decisions because those decisions might later cause them regret, be unduly influenced by others, or be forced by financial motivations.

Reproductive choices are tough choices, and any decision about reproduction—such as abortion, sterilization, sperm donation, or surrogacy—might later be regretted. The potential for later regrets, however, is usually not thought to be a valid reason to ban the right to choose the procedure in the first place.

With surrogacy, the potential for regret is thought by some to be enormously high. This is because it is argued (in biology-is-destiny terms) that it is unnatural for a mother to give up a child. It is assumed that because birth mothers in traditional adoption situations often regret relinquishing their children, surrogate mothers will feel the same way. But surrogate mothers are making their decisions about relinquishment under much different circumstances. The biological mother in the traditional adoption situation is already pregnant as part of a personal relationship of her own. In many, many instances, she would like to keep the child but cannot because the relationship is not supportive or she cannot afford to raise the child. She generally feels that the relinquishment was forced upon her (for example, by her parents, a counselor, or her lover).[31]

The biological mother in the surrogacy situation seeks out the opportunity to carry a child that would not exist were it not for the couple's desire to create a child as a part of their relationship. She makes her decision in advance of pregnancy for internal, not externally enforced reasons. While seventy-five percent of the biological mothers who give up for adoption later change their minds,[32] only around one percent of the surrogates have similar changes of heart.

Entering into a surrogacy arrangement does present potential psychological risks to women. But arguing for a ban on surrogacy seems to concede that the *government*, rather than the individual woman, should determine what risks a woman should be allowed to face. This conflicts with the general legal policy allowing competent individuals to engage in potentially risky behavior so long as they have given their voluntary, informed consent.

Perhaps recognizing the dangers of giving the government widespread powers to "protect" women, some feminists do acknowledge the validity of a general consent to assume risks. They argue, however, that the consent model is not appropriate to surrogacy since the surrogate's consent is neither informed nor voluntary.

It strikes me as odd to assume that the surrogate's consent is not informed. The surrogacy contracts contain lengthy riders detailing the myriad risks of pregnancy, so potential surrogates are much better informed on that topic than are most women who get pregnant in a more traditional fashion. In addition, with volumes of publicity given to the plight of Mary Beth Whitehead, all potential surrogates are now aware of the possibility that they may later regret their decisions. So, at that level, the decision is informed. Yet a strong element of the feminist argument against surrogacy is that women cannot give an informed consent until they have had the experience of giving birth. Robert Arenstein, an attorney for Mary Beth Whitehead, argued in congressional testimony that a "pre-birth or at-birth termination, is a termination without informed consent. I use the words informed consent to mean full understanding of the personal psychological consequences at the time of surrender of the child."[33] The feminist amicus brief in *Baby M* made a similar argument.[34]

The New Jersey Supreme Court picked up this characterization of informed consent, writing that "quite clearly any decision prior to the baby's birth is, in the most important sense, uninformed."[35] But such an approach is at odds with the legal doctrine of informed consent. Nowhere is it expected that one must have the experience first before one can make an informed judgment about whether to agree to the experience. Such a requirement would preclude people from ever giving informed consent to sterilizations, abortions, sex-change operations, heart surgery, and so forth. The legal doctrine of informed consent presupposes that people will predict in advance of the experience whether a particular course will be beneficial to them.

A variation of the informed consent argument is that while most competent adults can make such predictions, hormonal changes during pregnancy may cause a woman to change her mind. Virtually a whole amicus brief in the *Baby M* appeal was devoted to arguing that a woman's hormonal changes during pregnancy make it impossible for her to predict in advance the consequences of her relinquishment.[36] Along those lines, adoption worker Elaine Rosenfeld argues that

> [t]he consent that the birth mother gives prior to conception is not the consent of . . . a woman who has gone through the chemical, biological, endocrinological changes that have taken place during pregnancy and birth, and no matter how well prepared or well intentioned she is in her decision prior to conception, it is impossible for her to predict how she will feel after she gives birth.[37]

In contrast, psychologist Joan Einwohner, who works with a surrogate mother program, points out that

> women are fully capable of entering into agreements in this area and of fulfilling the obligations of a contract. Women's hormonal changes have been utilized too frequently over the centuries to enable male dominated society to make decisions for them. The Victorian era allowed women no legal rights to enter into contracts. The Victorian era relegated them to the status of dependent children. Victorian ideas are given renewed life in the conviction of some people that women are so overwhelmed by their feelings at the time of birth that they must be protected from themselves.[38]

Surrogate Carol Pavek is similarly uncomfortable with hormonal arguments. She posits that if she is allowed the excuse of hormones to change her mind (thus harming the expectant couple and subjecting the child to the trauma of litigation), what's to stop men from using their hormones as an excuse for rape or other harms? In any case, feminists should be wary of a hormone-based argument, just as they have been wary of the hormone-related criminal defense of premenstrual syndrome.

The consent given by surrogates is also challenged as not being voluntary.

Feminist Gena Corea, for example, in writing about another reproduction arrangement, *in vitro* fertilization, asks, "What is the real meaning of a woman's 'consent' . . . in a society in which men as a social group control not just the choices open to women but also women's *motivation* to choose?"[39]

Such an argument is a dangerous one for feminists to make. It would seem to be a step backward for women to argue that they are incapable of making decisions. That, after all, was the rationale for so many legal principles oppressing women for so long, such as the rationale behind the laws not allowing women to hold property. Clearly, any person's choices are motivated by a range of influences—economic, social, religious.

At a recent conference of law professors, it was suggested that surrogacy was wrong because women's boyfriends might talk them into being surrogates and because women might be surrogates for financial reasons. But women's boyfriends might talk them into having abortions or women might have abortions for financial reasons; nevertheless, feminists do not consider those to be adequate reasons to ban abortions. The fact that a woman's decision could be influenced by the individual men in her life or by male-dominated society does not by itself provide an adequate reason to ban surrogacy.

Various feminists have made the argument that the financial inducement to a surrogate vitiates the voluntariness of her consent. Many feminists have said that women are exploited by surrogacy.[40] They point out that in our society's social and economic conditions, some women—such as those on welfare or in dire financial need—will turn to surrogacy out of necessity rather than true choice. In my view, this is a harsh reality that must be guarded against by vigilant efforts to assure that women have equal access to the labor market and that there are sufficient social services so that poor women with children do not feel they must enter into a surrogacy arrangement in order to obtain money to provide care for their existing children.

However, the vast majority of women who have been surrogates do not allege that they have been tricked into surrogacy, or that they have done it because they needed to obtain a basic of life such as food or health care. Mary Beth Whitehead wanted to pay for her children's education. Kim Cotton wanted money to redecorate her house.[41] Another surrogate wanted money to buy a car. These do not seem to be cases of economic exploitation; there is no consensus, for example, that private education, interior decoration, and an automobile are basic needs, nor that society has an obligation to provide those items. Moreover, some surrogate-mother programs specifically reject women who are below a certain income level to avoid the possibility of exploitation.

There is a sexist undertone to an argument that Mary Beth Whitehead was exploited by the paid surrogacy agreement into which she entered to get money for her children's education. If Mary Beth's husband, Rick, had taken a second job to pay for the children's education (or even to pay for their mortgage), he would not have been viewed as exploited. He would have been lauded as a responsible parent.

It undercuts the legitimacy of women's role in the workforce to assume that they are being exploited if they plan to use their money for serious purchases. It seems to harken back to a notion that women work (and should work) only for pin money (a stereotype that is the basis for justifying the firing of women in times of economic crisis). It is also disturbing that in most instances, when society suggests that a certain activity should be done for altruism, rather than money, it is generally a woman's activity.

Some people suggest that since there is a ban on payment for organs, there should be a ban on payment to a surrogate.[42] But the payment for organs is different from the payment to a surrogate, when viewed from either the side of the couple or the side of the surrogate. As the New Jersey Supreme Court has stated, surrogacy (unlike organ donation) implicates a fundamental constitutional right—the right to privacy in making procreative decisions.[43] The court erroneously assumed that the constitutional right did not extend to commercial applications. This is in conflict with the holdings of other right-to-privacy cases regarding reproductive decisions. In *Carey v. Population Services*, for example, it was acknowledged that constitutional protection of the use of contraceptives extended to their commercial availability.[44] The Court noted that "in practice, a prohibition against all sales, since more easily and less offensively enforced, might have an even more devastating effect on the freedom to choose contraception" than a ban on their use.[45]

Certainly, feminists would feel their right to an abortion was vitiated if a law were passed prohibiting payment to doctors performing abortions: such a law would erect a major barrier to access to the procedure. Similarly, a ban on payment to surrogates would inhibit the exercise of the right to produce a child with a surrogate. For such reasons, it could easily be argued that the couple's right to pay a surrogate is constitutionally protected (unlike the right to pay a kidney donor).

From the surrogate's standpoint, the situation is different as well. An organ is not meant to be removed from the body; it endangers the life of the donor to live without the organ. In contrast, babies are conceived to leave the body and the life of the surrogate is not endangered by living without the child.[46]

At various legislative hearings, women's groups have virtually begged that women be protected against themselves, against their own decisions. Adria Hillman testified against a New York surrogacy bill on behalf of the New York State Coalition on Women's Legislative Issues. One would think that a women's group would criticize the bill as unduly intruding into women's decisions—it requires a double check by a court on a contract made by a woman (the surrogate mother) to assure that she gave voluntary, informed consent, and does not require oversight of contracts made by men. But the testimony was just the opposite. The bill was criticized as empowering the court to assess whether a surrogacy agreement protects the health and welfare of the potential child, without specifying that the judge should look into the agreement's potential effect on the natural mother.[47] What next? Will women have to go before a court when they are considering having an affair—to have a judge discern whether they will be psychologically harmed by, or later regret, the relationship?

Washington Post writer Jane Leavy has written:

> I have read volumes in defense of Mary Beth, her courage in taking on a lonely battle against the upper classes, the exploited wife of a sanitation man versus the wife of a biochemist, a woman with a 9th grade education versus a pediatrician. It all strikes me as a bit patronizing. Since when do we assume that a 29-year-old mother is incapable of making an adult decision and accepting the consequences of it?[48]

Surrogate mother Donna Regan similarly testified in New York that her will was not overborne in the surrogacy context: "No one came to ask me to be a surrogate mother. I went to them and asked them to allow me to be a surrogate mother."[49] "I find it extremely insulting that there are people saying that, as a woman, I cannot make an informed choice about a pregnancy that I carry," she continued, pointing out that she, like everyone, "makes other difficult choices in her life."[50]

THE POTENTIAL HARM TO POTENTIAL CHILDREN

The third line of argument opposes surrogacy because of the potential harm it represents to potential children. Feminists have had a long-standing concern for the welfare of children. But much feminist policy in the area has been based on the idea that mothers (and family) are more appropriate decision-makers about the best interests of children than the government. Feminists have also fought against using traditions, stereotypes, and societal tolerance or intolerance as a driving force for determining what is in a child's best interest. In that respect, it is understandable that feminists rallied to the aid of Mary Beth Whitehead in order to expose and oppose the faulty grounds on which custody was being determined.[51]

However, the opposition to stereotypes being used to determine custody in a best-interests analysis is not a valid argument against surrogacy itself (which is premised not on stereotypes about the child's best interests being used to determine custody, but on a pre-conception agreement being used to determine custody). And when the larger issue of the advisability of surrogacy itself comes up, feminists risk falling into the trap of using arguments about potential harm to the child that have as faulty a basis as those they oppose in other areas of family law.

For example, one line of argument against surrogacy is that it is like adoption and adoption harms children. However, such an argument is not sufficiently borne out in fact. There is evidence that adopted children do as well as non-adopted children in terms of adjustment and achievement.[52] A family of two biological parents is not necessary to assure the child's well-being.

Surrogacy has also been analogized to baby-selling. Baby-selling is prohibited in our society, in part because children need a secure family life and should not have to worry that they will be sold and wrenched from their existing family. Surrogacy is distinguishable from baby-selling since the resulting child is never in a state of insecurity. From the moment of birth, he or she is under the care of the biological father and his wife, who cannot sell the child. There is thus no psychological stress to that child or to *any other existing child* that he or she may someday be sold. Moreover, no matter how much money is paid through the surrogacy arrangement, the child, upon birth, cannot be treated like a commodity—a car or a television set. Laws against child abuse and neglect come into play.

Paying a biological mother to give her child up for traditional adoption is criticized since the child may go to an "undeserving" stranger, whose mere ability to pay does not signify sufficient merit for rearing a child. In paid surrogacy, by contrast, the child is turned over to the biological father. This biological bond has traditionally been considered to be a sufficient indicator of parental merit.

Another argument about potential harm to the resulting children is that parents will expect more of a surrogate child because of the $10,000 they have spent on her creation. But many couples spend more than that on infertility treatments without evidence that they expect more of the child. A Cesarean section costs twice as much as natural childbirth, yet the parents don't expect twice as much of the children. Certainly, the $10,000 is a modest amount compared to what parents will spend on their child over her life span.

Surrogacy has also been proposed because of its potential effect on the surrogate's other children. Traditionally, except in cases of clear abuse, parents have been held to be the best decision-makers about their children's best interests. Applying this to surrogacy, the surrogate (and not society) would be the best judge of whether or not her participation in a surrogacy program will harm her children. Not only are parents thought best able to judge their child's needs, but parents can also profoundly influence the effects of surrogacy on the child. Children take their cues about things from the people around them. There is no reason to believe that the other children of the surrogate will necessarily feel threatened by their mother's contractual pregnancy. If the children are told from the beginning that this is the contracting couple's child—not a part of their own family—they will realize that they themselves are not in danger of being relinquished.

Surrogate Donna Regan told her child that "the reason we did this was because they [the contracting couple] wanted a child to love as much as we love him." Regan contrasted her case to the Whitehead case: "In the Mary Beth Whitehead case, the child did not see this as something her mother was doing for someone else, so, of course, the attitude that she got from that was that something was being taken away rather than something being given."[53]

It seems ironic for feminists to embrace the argument that certain activities might inherently lead their children to fear abandonment, and that consequently such activities should be banned. Feminists have fought hard to gain access for women to amniocentesis and late-stage abortions of fetuses with a genetic defect[54]—even in light of similarly anecdotal evidence that when the woman aborts, her *other* children will feel that, they too, might be "sent to heaven" by their mother.[55] Indeed, it could be argued that therapeutic abortion is more devastating to the remaining children than is surrogacy. After all, the brother or sister who is aborted was intended to be part of the family; moreover, he or she is dead, not just living with other people. I personally do not feel that the potential effect of either therapeutic abortion or surrogacy on the pregnant woman's other children is a sufficient reason to ban the procedures, particularly in light of the fact that parents can mediate how their children perceive and handle the experiences.

The reactions of outsiders to surrogacy may, however, be beyond the control of parents and may upset the children. But is this a sufficient reason to ban surrogacy? William Pierce seems to think so. He says that the children of surrogates "are being made fun of. Their lives are going to be ruined."[56] It would seem odd to let societal intolerance guide what relationships are permissible. Along those lines, a judge in a lesbian custody case replied to the argument that children could be harmed by stigma by stating:

> It is just as reasonable to expect that they will emerge better equipped to search out their own standards of right and wrong, better able to perceive that the majority is not always correct in its moral judgments, and better able to understand the importance of conforming their beliefs to the requirements of reasons and tested knowledge, not the constraints of currently popular sentiment or prejudice.[57]

FEMINISM REVISITED

Feminists are taking great pride that they have mobilized public debate against surrogacy. But the precedent they are setting in their alliance with politicians like Henry Hyde and groups like the Catholic church is one whose policy is "protect women, even against their own decisions" and "protect children at all costs" (presumably, in latter applications, even against the needs and desires of women). This is certainly the thrust of the New Jersey Supreme Court decision against surrogacy, which cites as support for its holding the notorious *In re A. C.* case. In that case a woman's decision to refuse a Cesarean section was overridden based on an unsubstantiated possibility of benefit to her future child.[58]

In fact, the tenor of the New Jersey Supreme Court decision is reminiscent of earlier decisions "protecting" women that have been roundly criticized by feminists. The U.S. Supreme Court in 1872 felt it was necessary to prevent Myra Bradwell and all other women from practicing law—in order to protect women and their children. And when courts upheld sexist employment laws that kept women out of employment that men were allowed to take, they used language that might have come right out of the New Jersey Supreme Court's decision in the *Baby M* case. A woman's

> physical structure and a proper discharge of her maternal functions—having in view not merely her health, but the well-being of the race—justify legislation

to protect her from the greed as well as the passion of man. The limitations which this statute place upon her contractual powers, upon her right to agree with her employer as to the time she shall labor, are not imposed solely for her benefit, but also largely for the benefit of all.[59]

The New Jersey Supreme Court rightly pointed out that not everything should be for sale in our society. But the examples given by the court, such as occupational safety and health laws prohibiting workers from voluntarily accepting money to work in an unsafe job, apply to both men and women. In addition, an unsafe job presents risks that we would not want people to undertake, whether or not they received pay. In contrast, a policy against paid surrogacy prevents women from taking risks (pregnancy and relinquishment) that they are allowed to take for free. It applies disparately—men are still allowed to relinquish their parental rights in advance of conception and to receive money for their role in providing the missing male factor for procreation.

Some feminists are comfortable with advocating disparate treatment on the grounds that gestation is such a unique experience that it has no male counterpart at law and so deserves a unique legal status.[60] The special nature of gestation, according to this argument, gives rise to special rights—such as the right for the surrogate to change her mind and assert her legal parenthood after the child is born.

The other side of the gestational coin, which has not been sufficiently addressed by these feminists, is that with special rights come special responsibilities. If gestation can be viewed as unique in surrogacy, then it can be viewed as unique in other areas. Pregnant women could be held to have responsibilities that other members of society do not have—such as the responsibility to have a Cesarean section against their wishes in order to protect the health of a child (since only pregnant women are in the unique position of being able to influence the health of the child).

Some feminists have criticized surrogacy as turning participating women, albeit with their consent, into reproductive vessels. I see the danger of the antisurrogacy arguments as potentially turning *all* women into reproductive vessels, without their consent, by providing government oversight for women's decisions and creating a disparate legal category for gestation. Moreover, by breathing life into arguments that feminists have put to rest in other contexts, the current rationales opposing surrogacy could undermine a larger feminist agenda.

NOTES

1. Iver Peterson, "Baby M Custody Trial Splits Ranks of Feminists over Issue of Exploitation," New York Times, February 24, 1987 (quoting Linda Bowker).
2. Bob Port, "Feminists Come to the Aid of Whitehead's Case," St. Petersburg Times, February 23, 1987, 1A.
3. Brief filed on behalf of Amici Curiae, the Foundation on Economic Trends, et

al., In the matter of Baby M, New Jersey Supreme Court, Docket No. FM-25314-86E (hereafter cited as "Brief"). The feminists joining in the brief included Betty Friedan, Gloria Steinem, Gena Corea, Barbara Katz Rothman, Lois Gould, Michelle Harrison, Kathleen Lahey, Phyllis Chesler, and Letty Cottin Pogrebin.

4. See, e.g., *Roe v. Wade,* 410 U.S. 113 (1973); *Griswold v. Connecticut,* 381 U.S. 49 (1965); *Meyer v. Nebraska,* 262 U.S. 390 (1923); *Pierce v. Society of Sisters,* 268 U.S. 510 (1928).

5. See, e.g., Karst, "The Freedom of Intimate Association," Yale Law Journal 89 (1980): 624.

6. Prior to conception and during pregnancy, the surrogate mother contract is a personal-service contract. However, after the child's birth, no further services on the part of the surrogate are needed. Thus, enforcing a provision providing for the father's custody of the child is not the enforcement of a personal services contract. It is like the enforcement of a court order on custody or the application of a paternity statute.

7. Lori Andrews, "The Aftermath of Baby M: Proposed State Laws on Surrogate Motherhood," Hastings Center Report 17 (Oct./Nov. 1987): 31–40, at 37.

8. In re Baby M, 217 N.J. Super. 313, 525 A.2d 1128, 1159 (1987).

9. *Jhordan C. v. Mary K.,* 179 Cal. App. 3d 386, 224 Cal. Rptr. 530 (1986).

10. *Surrogate Parenthood and New Reproductive Technologies, A Joint Public Hearing, before the N.Y. State Assembly, N.Y. State Senate, Judiciary Committees* (October 16, 1986) (statement of Bob Arenstein at 103–04, 125); *In The Matter of a Hearing on Surrogate Parenting before the N.Y. Standing Committee on Child Care* (May 8, 1987) (statement of Adria Hillman at 174, statement of Mary Ann Dibari at 212 ["the prostitution of motherhood"]).

11. *Surrogacy Arrangements Act of 1987: Hearing on H.R. 2433, before the Subcomm. on Transportation, Tourism, and Hazardous Materials,* 100th Cong., 1st Sess. (October 15, 1987) (statement of Gena Corea at 3, 5); Robert Gould, N.Y. Testimony (May 8, 1987), supra note 10, 233 (slavery).

12. Arthur Morrell, U.S. Testimony (October 15, 1987), supra note 11, at 1.

13. William Pierce, U.S. Testimony (October 15, 1987), supra note 11, at 2, citing Harvard Law Professor Lawrence Tribe.

14. Brief, supra note 3, at 19.

15. Port, supra note 2, at 7A, quoting Phyllis Chesler.

16. Gena Corea, U.S. Testimony (October 15, 1987), supra note 11, at 3; Hillman, N.Y. Testimony (May 8, 1987), supra note 10, at 174.

17. Ellen Goodman, "Checking the Baby M Contract," Boston Globe, March 24, 1987, p. 15.

18. Gena Corea, U.S. Testimony (October 15, 1987), supra note 11, at 5; Hillman, N.Y. Testimony (May 8, 1987), supra note 10, at 174.

19. Gena Corea, U.S. Testimony (October 15, 1987), supra note 11, at 5.

20. Id.

21. Id.: 2.

22. Elizabeth Kane, U.S. Testimony (October 15, 1987), supra note 11, at 1.

23. Kay Longcope, "Standing up for Mary Beth," Boston Globe, March 5, 1987, pp. 81, 83 (quoting Janice Raymond).

24. Brief, supra note 3, at 14.

25. Robert Gould, N.Y. Testimony (May 8, 1987), supra note 10, at 232.

26. Judianne Densen-Gerber, N.Y. Testimony (May 8, 1987), supra note 10, at 253; Robert Gould, N.Y. Testimony (May 8, 1987), supra note 10, at 232.

27. Robert Gould, N.Y. Testimony (May 8, 1987), supra note 10, at 232.

28. Henry Hyde, U.S. Testimony (October 15, 1987), supra note 11, at 1 ("Commercial surrogacy arrangements, by rendering children into chattel, are in my opinion, immoral."); DiBari, N.Y. Testimony (May 8, 1987), supra note 10, at 212.

29. John Ray, U.S. Testimony (October 15, 1987), supra note 11, at 7.

30. See, e.g., Maureen McGuire and Nancy J. Alexander, "Artificial Insemination of Single Women," *Fertility and Sterility* 43 (February 1985): 182–84; Raschke and Raschke, "Family Conflict and Children's Self-Concept: A Comparison of Intact and Single Parent Families," *Journal of Marriage and the Family* 41 (1979): 367; Weiss, "Growing up a Little Faster," *Journal of Social Issues* 35 (1979): 97.

31. See, e.g., Rynearson, "Relinquishment and Its Maternal Complications: A Preliminary Study," *American Journal of Psychiatry* 139 (1982): 338; Deykin, Campbell, Patti, "The Postadoption Experience of Surrendering Parents," *American Journal of Orthopsychiatry* 54 (1984): 271.

32. Betsy Aigen, N.Y. Testimony (May 8, 1987), supra note 10, at 18.

33. Robert Arenstein, U.S. Testimony (October 15, 1987), supra note 11, at 9.

34. Brief, supra note 3, at 30–31.

35. In re Baby M, 109 N.J. 396; 537 A.2d 1227, 1248 (1988).

36. See Brief filed on behalf of Amicus Curiae the Gruter Institute, In the Matter of Baby M, New Jersey Supreme Court, Docket No. FM-25314-86E.

37. Hearing in re Surrogate Parenting: Hearing on S.B. 1429, before Senators Goodhue, Dunne, Misters Balboni, Abramson, and Amgott (April 10, 1987) (statement of Elaine Rosenfeld at 187). A similar argument made by Adria Hillman, N.Y. Testimony (May 8, 1987), supra note 10, at 175.

38. Joan Einwohner, N.Y. Testimony (April 10, 1987), supra note 37, at 110–11.

39. Gena Corea, *The Mother Machine* (New York: Harper & Row, 1985), p. 3.

40. Brief, supra note 3, at 10, 13; Judy Breidbart, N.Y. Testimony (May 8, 1987), supra note 10, at 168.

41. K. Cotton and D. Winn, *Baby Cotton: For Love and Money* (1985).

42. Karen Peters, N.Y. Testimony (May 8, 1987), supra note 10, at 121.

43. In re Baby M, 109 N.J. 396; 537 A.2d 1227, 1253 (1988).

44. *Carey v. Population Services Int'l.*, 431 U.S. 678 (1977).

45. *Carey v. Population Services Int'l.*, 431 U.S. 678, 688 (1976) (citation omitted).

46. Betsy Aigen, N.Y. Testimony (May 8, 1987), supra note 10, at 11–12.

47. Adria Hillman, N.Y. Testimony (May 8, 1987), supra notes 10, at 177–78.

48. Jane Leavy, "It Doesn't Take Labor Pains to Make a Real Mom," Washington Post, April 4, 1987.

49. Donna Regan, N.Y. Testimony (May 8, 1987), supra note 10, at 157.

50. Id.

51. Michelle Harrison, "Social Construction of Mary Beth Whitehead," *Gender and Society* 1 (September 1987): 300–311.

52. Teasdale and Owens, "Influence of Paternal Social Class on Intelligence Level in Male Adoptees and Non-Adoptees," *British Journal of Educations Psychology* 56 (1986): 3.

53. Donna Regan, N.Y. Testimony (May 8, 1987), supra note 10, at 156.

54. See, e.g., the briefs filed by feminist organizations in Thornburgh v. American College of Obstetricians, 476 U.S. 747 (1986).

55. See, e.g., J. Fletcher, Coping with Genetic Disorders: A Guide for Counseling (San Francisco: Harper & Row, 1982).

56. William Pierce, N.Y. Testimony (May 8, 1987), supra note 10, at 86. It should be pointed out that kids hassle other kids for a wide range of reasons. A child might equally be made fun of for being the recipient of a kidney transplant or being the child of a garbage man.

57. *M.P. v. S.P.*, 169 N.J. Super. 425, 438, 404 A.2d 1256, 1263 (Super. Ct. App. Div. 1979).

58. In re Baby M, 109 N.J. 396; 537 A.2d 1227, 1254 n. 13 (1988), citing In re A.C., 533 A.2d 611 (D.C. App. 1987).

59. *Muller v. Oregon*, 208 U.S. 412, 422 (1907).

60. See Brief, supra note 3, at 11.

PART III: (RE)LOCATING FETUSES

Technology and New Body Politics

While the last essays dealt mostly with technologies that alter methods and circumstances of conception, the selections here deal with technologies that alter methods and circumstances of gestation. In particular, they are concerned with the ways in which technology lets us locate fetuses in places other than a woman's uterus. Though gestational technology is already commonly employed in the form of incubators for younger and younger premature infants, it is likely that varieties of gestational technology will develop to the point that normally developing fetuses may be located in any number of places. An important physical implication of this, of course, is that fetuses may mature and babies may be born without necessarily involving any pregnant women. The social and moral implications of these facts are only beginning to be debated.

Do you think you need a womb to have a baby? Dick Teresi and Kathleen McAuliffe point out that, actually, you don't. Women have become pregnant after having a hysterectomy, male baboons have been pregnant, and male mice have also carried babies. Eventually, a human male might become pregnant, the biology of gestation being quite adaptable. As Teresi and McAuliffe explain, embryos produce a placenta, a versatile organ able to attach to any blood-rich, nutrient-rich tissue. This ability sometimes results in ectopic pregnancies in women, where embryos attach to someplace other than the uterus. In rare cases, abdominal attachment can lead to the birth of healthy babies. Though not without medical risk, an embryo could be attached to a man's omentum—the blood-rich tissue in his lower abdominal cavity—and be delivered nine months later by a C-section-like surgery. Though some will obviously find the idea of male pregnancy distasteful, there are people who already desire it—male-to-female transsexuals, husbands of infertile women, and single men who want to have children themselves. The possibility of this technology leads us to ask: Should women be the only ones *allowed* to bear children? Are women as a class *obligated* to bear children? Does the state have a compelling interest in preventing men from reproducing as they see fit? Should technology be judged wrong or made illegal *because* it upsets traditional biological sex roles?

Moving from pregnant men to pregnant machines, Julien S. Murphy addresses these questions in discussing the potential technology of ectogenesis or *in vitro* gestation (IVG)—the complete gestation of a fetus outside a woman's body (or anyone's body) in an advanced incubator. Murphy wants to know if fetuses somehow belong in women's bodies or if women have an obligation to reproduce even when other choices are available. Fundamentally, her concern is whether IVG would be a liberating technology for women, or an oppressive one. Murphy looks at three lines of argument that have been used to defend women's reproductive rights to discover their implications for this basic question. Although she finds no justification in any of these arguments for ending IVG research, she ends by rejecting and protesting IVG because it breaks the connection between women and reproduction and denigrates their contribution to pregnancy.

Christine Overall also takes on the issue of ectogenetic technologies (of various sorts) and points out that they will inevitably require us to rethink all our standard positions on abortion. They may even hold out the possibility of solving the abortion problem. She claims that while most people equate abortion with destroying the fetus, there are actually two events that occur in abortion: a) removing the fetus from a uterus and b) killing the fetus. Up until now, these two events almost always coincided. However, ectogenetic technology allows us to separate the two acts. Aborting a pregnancy may be reconstituted as simply the transfer of an undamaged fetus to an advanced incubator; a woman could have a successful abortion in which the fetus survives. If this new technology is developed, questions regarding moral issues will have to be faced. Does a woman's right to end her pregnancy imply she has a right to kill the fetus, or just to remove it from her body? Will this technology be a panacea, or will it just further complicate the issue?

Though some of these cases may sound like science fiction (as adult-cell cloning once did until scientists recently proved it possible), important social, moral, and legal aspects of ectogenetic technology have already demanded attention. In a fascinating and complex real-life case, the Supreme Court of the State of Tennessee had to deal with the rights and status of viable human embryos existing outside anyone's body. The case concerned a married couple who had been going through the laborious process of *in vitro* fertilization in order to have a baby. In the midst of the failing procedure, the marriage fell apart and the couple divorced, leaving seven embryos frozen at their reproductive health clinic. A custody battle ensued. The wife, assisted by anti-abortion activists, wanted to donate the embryos to infertile couples, arguing that they had a right to life. The husband wanted the embryos destroyed or permanently frozen, arguing that the embryos were not persons and had no rights. His position was further complicated, however, by his strong feelings about being a genetic father. While he wanted the embryos destroyed, he stated that if the embryos were donated and children resulted, he would sue for custody of these children to raise them himself. Because the embryos were not inside anyone's body, standard legal reasoning on privacy and bodily control did not automatically apply. The courts had to consider arguments of human rights, property rights, and parental control. The final ruling centered on the question of how important the law should consider a person's desire to avoid purely genetic parenthood (as opposed to gestational or social parenthood)—a ruling still controversial today.

CHAPTER 11
MALE PREGNANCY

DICK TERESI AND KATHLEEN MCAULIFFE
(1985)

There it was. After all the fruitless affairs, the callous rebuffs in singles bars, and the disbelieving looks of his friends, Jake found himself staring at his dream woman. She appeared in the form of a blind advertisement in the personal columns of *The New York Review of Books*: SINGLE WHITE FEMALE, 38, successful businesswoman, seeks warm, nurturing, maternal SWM, 25–32. Let's have a baby: I'll pay the bills, you carry the child. Looks not important but ample abdominal cavity a plus. Send recent photograph and histocompatibility profile to Box 20035. *At last,* Jake thought to himself as he composed a heartfelt letter to the anonymous advertiser at Box 20035. *I just hope she doesn't insist on natural childbirth.*

Okay, so maybe it won't happen quite like that. But it will happen. Someday a man will have a baby.

Already, a male baboon has proved that males can get pregnant. Male mice have also carried babies. And the medical literature is filled with two dozen case histories of women who became pregnant *after* receiving hysterectomies—proving that you don't need a womb to carry a baby.

Our fictitious hero need not worry about natural childbirth, though. It will be anything but natural. What we're talking about is implanting an embryo into a man's abdominal cavity, where the fetus would take nourishment, grow to term, and be delivered by an operation similar to a cesarean section.

But we're getting ahead of our story. Public awareness of male pregnancy developed six years ago, thanks to a remarkable birth in New Zealand. In May 1979 Margaret Martin, a twenty-nine-year-old Auckland woman who just eight months earlier had undergone a hysterectomy, gave birth to a healthy five-pound baby girl. An errant fertilized egg had lodged in her abdomen, on her bowel, where it received enough nutrients to grow to term without the aid of a uterus. Dr. Peter Jackson, Martin's gynecologist, reportedly told journalists that the birth proved it was possible for a man to be made pregnant by placing a fertilized egg on his bowel.

Tabloids the world over announced that the era of pregnant men had arrived. The story struck a nerve in many men. Scientists doing work on the cutting edge of human reproduction were barraged with letters from men who wanted to be mothers. Some were transsexuals. But others were conventional men who simply wanted to experience the joys of pregnancy.

With this background, *Omni* decided to check out the scientific possibilities for male pregnancy. What we found may surprise you.

The New Zealand case was not the first evidence for male pregnancy. Back in the mid-sixties, Dr. Cecil Jacobsen, of George Washington University Medical School, performed an unusual experiment that commanded little attention at the time. He and Dr. Roy Hertz transplanted the fertilized egg of a female baboon to the abdominal cavity of a male baboon. The embryo attached itself to the omentum, a fatty tissue loaded with blood vessels that hangs down in front of the intestines like a protective apron. "It got adequate blood supply and nourishment," Jacobsen reports. "So with very moderate chemical support, the male baboon was able to carry the pregnancy toward term—that is, well past four months."

The experiment was testimony to the hardy independence of the embryo. One key to the embryo's integrity is its ability to produce a placenta, the vascular organ that normally attaches to the uterus and draws nutrients from the mother. Or in this case, the father—as studies by Jacobsen and others show that the fetal placenta is a versatile, opportunistic, and perhaps even an indiscriminate organ. As UCLA neuroendocrinologist Roger Gorski puts it, the placenta is an "eroding tissue." It seeks out and opens blood vessels. Because of this, it appears that the fetus may be able to attach itself to any site rich in blood and nutrients. Jacobsen's team experimented with implanting fertilized eggs on the kidney and the spleen as well but had best results on the omentum.

The experiment did not result in the birth of a fully developed baboon baby. When Jacobsen says the male baboon carried the pregnancy "toward term," he means that the fetus had reached a point at which it had "survived embryonic development." The normal gestation period for a baboon is seven months. At four months, Jacobsen and Hertz "delivered" the fetus. "Had we wanted to," Jacobsen says, "we could easily have taken the pregnancy to term, because embryonic development was normal, and the fetus was alive when we surgically removed it from the male's abdomen. But we didn't bring it to full maturity because that was not the purpose of our study."

So what was Jacobsen trying to do? He and female-cancer expert Hertz, who is now deceased, were by no means interested in allowing males to have babies. They were concerned with pregnant women who develop ovarian cancer. The ovaries produce various female hormones. At what stage, they wanted to know, is it safe to remove the ovaries without causing a miscarriage? "The question wasn't whether a male could bear a pregnancy," Jacobsen explains, "but at what stage does the embryo make all the hormones needed to maintain a pregnancy? You can answer the question in two ways. You can go ahead and take the ovaries out of different females and see how many babies you lose. Or you can transfer a fertilized egg to the male animal and see if the fetus can survive in different stages."

The experiment has striking, though controversial, implications both for men who want to have babies and for the field of obstetrics and fetal development in general. Contrary to what many researchers at the time thought—and still think—female hormones may not be required for normal embryonic development. The baboon operation implies that the fertilized egg may be autonomous, producing all the hormones it needs for its own development. "That was the marvel of our discovery," says Jacobsen.

Not everyone is similarly impressed. Two decades later, the study remains largely obscure even to specialists in gynecology and obstetrics because Jacobsen never published the results. "It was one small part of a broader project," he says. Not unjustifiably, this has raised doubts in the minds of some of his peers. Says one critic, who asked not to be identified, "I'm dubious of the veracity of that claim because it never appeared in a bona fide scientific journal." Still, Jacobsen has some heavy credentials. Now director of the Reproductive Genetics Center in Vienna, Virginia, he is credited with developing and first using amniocentesis, a prenatal test that involves extracting amniotic fluid from the womb to detect chromosome abnormality in an unborn child. That was in 1967. Today physicians use amniocentesis almost routinely on older women and others at risk for giving birth to babies with genetic defects.

Jacobsen is the only scientist on record who has experimented with male pregnancy in primates. But he says that similar work has been done with fowl, rodents, salamanders, and other amphibians.

In a series of experiments in the early Sixties, for example, Dr. David Kirby, of England's Oxford University, transplanted mouse embryos into the testes, spleens, and kidneys of adult male mice. Kirby got the best results in the testes, where one embryo developed in "perfect condition" for twelve days—about half the normal gestation period for a mouse. Kirby, now deceased, theorized that the testicle capsule was simply not elastic enough to allow the embryo to mature fully. The experiment did show, however, that testosterone and other male hormones found in high concentrations in the testes do not thwart normal embryonic development—a positive sign for those males who want to have babies.

But perhaps the best hope for these men comes not from animal studies but from strange pregnancies in women. According to the medical literature, there have been some twenty-four cases worldwide in which women became pregnant despite having had hysterectomies. While twenty-three of these ectopic pregnancies (*ectopic* in this case means outside the uterus) didn't result in live births, they offer considerable evidence for the possibility of wombless childbirth. Incontrovertible proof, of course, comes from the twenty-fourth case: New Zealand's Margaret Martin and her five-pound daughter.

Then there are those women who despite having intact uteri have given birth without using these organs. Ectopic pregnancies are fairly common, but in most cases this condition refers to embryos that have implanted themselves in the Fallopian tubes. Such pregnancies are doomed as well as life threatening to the mother. The expanding embryo can rupture the tube, and the patient can hemorrhage.

In rare cases, however—about one thousand have been reported to date— the fertilized egg works its way into the abdominal cavity, which can expand to accommodate the growing fetus. This is an ectopic pregnancy of a different color. Approximately nine percent of those women with abdominal pregnancies have actually given birth to healthy babies.

It is a difficult condition to diagnose. In July 1981 doctors prepared to deliver a New Jersey woman's baby by cesarean section because ultrasound studies indicated there was a large tumor on top of her womb. The womb, as it turned out, was empty. The "tumor" was actually a seven-pound, ten-ounce baby growing inside the abdominal cavity. In August 1979, Dr. George Poretta attempted to perform an appendectomy on a Michigan woman suffering from stomach cramps. "I opened her up expecting to find an appendix," Dr. Poretta told the Associated Press, "and there was this tiny foot." Prematurely delivered, the "appendix" weighed three pounds, five ounces and was named Joseph Thomas Cwik.

An abdominal pregnancy is precisely the kind of pregnancy the first man/mother will have to endure. It is dangerous. Estimates vary, but the maternal mortality rate is about six to seven percent. Part of the danger stems from the fact that such pregnancies are often not diagnosed until the woman is on the operating table. John Money, a pioneer of transsexual operations and professor of medical psychology and pediatrics at Johns Hopkins Medical School, points out that the "extraordinary thing about the New Zealand case [Margaret Martin] was that the medical person in charge made the correct diagnosis. I mean, it really was an A-plus to be able to recognize what was going on with this lady and to realize that it was a healthy pregnancy." Even so, Martin's pregnancy wasn't diagnosed until twenty-three weeks after her hysterectomy. She had briefly considered that she was pregnant—her breasts were tender, and she had felt the baby move—but refrained from mentioning the symptoms, according to her doctor, for fear of being ridiculed. In the case of men who purposely undergo abdominal pregnancy, however, the danger of misdiagnosis will obviously be eliminated.

Still, risks remain. *In vitro* fertilization pioneer Dr. Landrum Shettles has personally delivered two healthy babies that developed in their mothers' abdomens. Such babies, Shettles warns, cannot be delivered normally. He cites the case of a colleague who attempted to remove a baby that was attached to its mother's intestine. "He tried to separate the afterbirth and the placenta from the bowel," recalls Shettles, "and the blood gushed to the ceiling. The mother died instantly." UCLA's Gorski reminds us that the womb is not without purpose: "When delivery occurs, the uterus, which is just a muscular organ, contracts and shuts off the blood vessels eroded by the placenta." Blood vessels supplying the placenta in an abdominal pregnancy, however, do not constrict, and massive hemorrhage can occur if the placenta is separated from the mother. As one obstetrics textbook puts it, bleeding may be "torrential."

Which is not to say you absolutely need the womb. "The point is," Shettles says, "if you have an abdominal pregnancy, you tie the cord off right near the placenta and leave the placenta in place. Don't touch it, and the body will absorb it."

Those are some of the dangers. But let's say a man wanted to have a baby so badly he was willing to take the chance. How would it be done? What experience awaits the first man to carry a baby? Discussions with Shettles, Jacobsen, and other experts both in the United States and in Australia suggest that the procedure would go something like this:

Doctors would first perform standard *in vitro* fertilization to produce an embryo. Eggs would be surgically extracted from the wife's ovary and fertilized with the husband's sperm in a petri dish. (*In vitro* fertilization is often referred to as "test-tube baby" technology.) In thirty to fifty hours, when the egg has matured to the two- to eight-cell stage and is about the size of the tip of a needle, it would be placed in a flexible catheter for implantation. At this point, however, the *in vitro* process would take an abrupt left turn. Instead of snaking the catheter through the wife's vagina into her uterus, the doctor would perform a laparoscopy on the husband. A small incision would be made in the abdominal cavity, and the gynecologist would place the embryo into the lower abdominal cavity against the omentum, the fatty, blood-rich tissue in front of the intestines. With luck, the fertilized egg would implant in the omentum, the placenta would develop from the embryo and begin drawing nutrients, and the pregnancy would be under way. At this point, or possibly even earlier, an endocrinologist *might* be called in to administer hormones to the male mother so that his hormonal status would mimic that of a pregnant woman. Finally, nine months and several thousand dollars' worth of custom-made maternity clothes later, the baby would be delivered from the man's abdomen in a operation called a laparotomy, which would be similar to a cesarean section.

There are two alternatives to this scenario. First, conception could take place in the woman's body, most likely through artificial insemination. The fertilized egg would then be flushed out of the womb and implanted in the man. This is the method used in the process called embryo transfer: when a fertilized egg is moved from one woman's womb to another's. Shettles, for one, prefers the *in vitro* method, however, because it allows more control.

Second, it is debatable whether hormonal treatment is needed. In January 1984, before an assemblage of sex researchers at a Kinsey Institute symposium, John Money raised the possibility of male pregnancy. He was encouraged in the discussion period afterward to hear Gorski say that the hormonal technology was sufficiently in place to carry off such a pregnancy. Today Gorski still maintains that on a hormonal level, male pregnancy is possible. But Jacobsen's baboon study indicates that priming the male with female hormones may not be necessary. "Maybe that's right," Shettles says. "It might well be that when the male gets a new inhabitant, his body adjusts."

Or perhaps the embryo/fetus is a self-sufficient alien within us. Richard Harding, a fetal physiologist at Monash University, in Australia, supports that hypothesis. "You know, on an endocrine basis, on a hormonal level, the fetus appears to be totally autonomous," Harding says. "It generates its own steroids after a certain period of time. The placenta produces a lot of the steroids that are necessary for fetal survival."

In vitro fertilization or embryo transfer, hormones or no hormones, male pregnancy is not a popular idea today in the medical establishment. "It's an outlandish proposal," says Gary Hodgen, who is the scientific director of the Eastern Virginia Medical School's Jones Institute for Reproductive Medicine, in Norfolk, the leading *in vitro* fertilization clinic in the United States. Hodgen's main objection to male pregnancy (he used the word *outlandish* at least five times when interviewed) is that it's tantamount to ectopic pregnancy, a life-threatening condition. "As a male, I obviously don't have a uterus, right? A male who would request the transfer of an embryo to his abdomen would be asking the medical personnel involved to advocate him taking on a life-threatening condition that wouldn't even be to the benefit of another extant person." Hodgen emphasizes, "That's antimedicine."

Dr. Jack Hallatt, an expert in abdominal pregnancy at Kaiser Permanente Medical Center, in Los Angeles, says, "There's no way doctors could avoid the dangers of hemorrhage [during the pregnancy]. And it would be catastrophic. There's no way it would willingly be attempted." Hodgen agrees that you can't eliminate the danger of male abdominal pregnancy. "Think a minute why," he says. "It's apparent. The placental sac and the baby, at term, are going to weigh on the order of twenty-five pounds. And all of the months this is growing, this bag may be twisting and turning."

Cecil Jacobsen feels that the risk posed by an abdominal pregnancy has been greatly exaggerated. The condition, he says, tends to be lumped together with the much more common ectopic pregnancy in which the fertilized egg becomes lodged in the Fallopian tubes.

"Any type of ectopic pregnancy in the tube is dangerous," Jacobsen says, "because it is a closed cavity that can't expand. But the abdominal cavity can expand. It is a risky condition, but if the pregnancy is watched carefully, the risk of death is low." Even so, Jacobsen is not anxious to be the first physician with a man/mother for a patient. "Sure, it's feasible," Jacobsen insists. "But why in heck would you do it? In my opinion it would be an abuse for males to use the technology that way. I think the proper use of the technology would be for women who have no uterus but want to have a baby. That's where I think medicine will first do it."

Perhaps it would be an abuse of the technology to use it on men. Still, there will be men who want it. Who are they? What kind of man would have a baby? Johns Hopkins's John Money originally envisioned only one kind of person—the transsexual. "If male pregnancy ever became possible," Money says, "the first applicants would be male-to-female transsexuals, because it's so terribly important to them to experience everything a woman can experience."

They're already lining up. In July 1984 a group of at least six male-to-female transsexuals requested admittance to the *in vitro* fertilization program at the Queen Victoria Medical Center, in Melbourne, Australia. They wanted to have babies. The Melbourne center turned down the request.

Garrett Oppenheim, a psychotherapist in Tappan, New York, says male pregnancy "would be the most magnificent breakthrough since the sex-change program came into effect." As director of Confide-Personal Counseling Services, Inc., Oppenheim evaluates and counsels those who apply for a sex change, to help them decide whether they should undergo the necessary hormonal treatment and surgery. There are approximately 20,000 transsexuals in the world today. "And most transsexuals want to experience womanhood in all its facets," Oppenheim says.

A social worker currently undergoing a male-to-female transformation verified Money and Oppenheim's views. "If it were possible to become impregnated and have a baby," says Jerry (a pseudonym), "I would do it, without hesitation and at all costs. I'd walk out on my man if I had to. If it came down to choosing between having a baby and staying with the man I love, I would leave the man I love and have a baby." Jerry remained undaunted by the prospect of cesarean section, but he did have one reservation about carrying a baby in the summer months "with the heat and all."

Transsexuals do have one advantage over other males. They can nurse a baby—at least according to one doctor. Dr. Leo Wollman, a Brooklyn psychiatrist who has treated 2,800 transsexuals, claims he hormonally primed one of his patients so he could breast-feed his own child. This patient had remained married to his wife after transforming from male to female. The wife was carrying their biological baby, and after she gave birth, both parents took turns nursing the baby. Wollman claims his patient had "a breast development to rival his wife's" and that he gave him a drug to induce lactation.

But men who want to have babies may not necessarily want to mimic women in every respect. They are not all transsexuals. When a tabloid erroneously reported that Monash University's Harding had transplanted mouse embryos into male mice (he hadn't) and that his research team was looking for human volunteers (it wasn't), he was deluged with letters, mostly from men. He received phone calls in his Australian lab from as far away as Alaska. Harding suspects that many of those who wanted to carry their own babies were homosexual. But others were heterosexual men who had infertile wives. Still others were single men who wanted to fulfill their need for a child. There were even letters from women who were infertile and who wondered if their husbands could carry their babies. Shettles has received similar inquiries through the years but says he has never received a call or letter from a transsexual. "The men who called seemed very normal," he recalls. "I guess they just wanted to have the experience of having a baby." Shettles was also contacted, like Harding, by men whose wives were infertile and who wanted to "take the tension off the wife."

Then, of course, there's womb envy. "If little girls want to have penises," says Dr. John Munder Ross, "boys also, at some level, want to have wombs and breasts." Ross, a psychiatrist with Cornell Medical College, cites the phenomenon of couvade syndrome, in which husbands suffer the symptoms of pregnancy—weight gain, backaches, nausea, and so on—while their wives carry the baby. "Most of the men I've analyzed during their wives' pregnancies have expressed wishes to have babies and have developed symptoms," Ross says.

In any case, when the time comes for the first embryo transfer into a man, there will be no shortage of volunteers—and no shortage of critics, either.

Most researchers we talked to admitted that a huge stumbling block to male pregnancy would be ethical and moral objections. Already, the Michigan state senate is sponsoring a study to assess its citizens' attitudes toward new birth technologies, including male pregnancy. Presumably, not everyone in Grand Rapids will be overjoyed with the idea of men in maternity clothes shopping for nursing bras.

But how do feminists feel? Do they see male pregnancy as their chance to escape biological destiny?

Gloria Steinem, for one, believes that pregnancy could make men less violent. "Giving birth has made women value life more," says Steinem, an editor and cofounder of *Ms.* magazine, "and we are far less violent by all measures."

Flo Kennedy, the black feminist who popularized the slogan "If men could get pregnant, abortion would be a sacrament," also saw a benefit: "Certainly this is an opportunity for a woman to have a leg up, if she's got brains enough and guts enough to take advantage of it. She should take a rest and let the man do the work. It's a possible step toward women gaining on men, at least in terms of cocktail-party jokes."

But serious doubts remain. In the seventies feminists were fond of the slogan "A woman without a man is like a fish without a bicycle." Now with male pregnancy on the horizon, Steinem suspects the tables may be turned. "I have a small, nagging fear," she confides, "that if women lose our cartel on giving birth, we could be even more dispensable than we already are."

An admission: We never wanted to write this article. It was the result of a casual comment about John Money's work, unwittingly uttered at an editorial meeting. Our editors were as skeptical as we were but asked us to at least explore the idea. We took the assignment with the assumption that after a few phone calls and a couple of library searches we could honestly report back that there was no real future in, or scientific basis for, male pregnancy. We were wrong. Some important researchers convinced us the idea was altogether feasible.

Granted, many more animal studies are needed to assess the practicality of male pregnancy. As far as endocrinology is concerned, what little research has been done casts serious doubts on our current understanding of the roles of so-called female hormones and what kind of hormonal priming a man would need to support childbirth. And the treatment of abdominal pregnancy must be refined before a fertilized egg can be safely implanted in a man's omentum.

Then again, perhaps some renegade will just go ahead and do it.

In the early seventies, Landrum Shettles was conducting pioneer work in *in vitro* fertilization at Columbia-Presbyterian Medical Center, in New York City, when his boss told him to discontinue his research, ordered that the test-tube culture Shettles had produced be destroyed, and finally, in 1973, fired him. Perhaps because of this attitude, both England and Australia produced test-tube babies well before America did. Ironically, two years ago Columbia-

Presbyterian began its own *in vitro* clinic, a decade after destroying Shettles's culture. The point is that supposedly crazy, irresponsible ideas are often warmly embraced ten years after they're introduced—often by the same people who condemned them originally.

We asked Shettles, who now runs his own clinic in Las Vegas, to estimate when the first human male pregnancy would take place. As a preface to giving us an answer, Shettles pointed out that a former colleague of his, Dr. John Rock, stated in a medical journal in 1958 that the time had come for *in vitro* technology. But it took a full twenty years before England's Patrick Steptoe and Robert Edwards actually produced a baby. As for male pregnancy, Shettles says, "I don't think it's going to take as long as it did with the *in vitro* program. I think anyone who really wanted to get on with it now could achieve success." And *who* will do it?

"I think it would be really funny if the Australians, who have an international reputation for being the macho men of the world, were the first to achieve a male pregnancy," Shettles says. "I wouldn't be surprised."

CHAPTER 12

IS PREGNANCY NECESSARY?

Feminist Concerns about Ectogenesis

JULIEN S. MURPHY

(1989)

In the past few decades, great gains have been made in women's reproductive freedoms. Abortion, contraception, and sterilization techniques allow women greater control over fertility. Feminists are united in support of these techniques. The feminist issue is not whether there ought to be pregnancy preventatives for women, but that the techniques available ought to be more accessible to women, and researchers ought to develop more effective and safer methods, including male contraceptives and an abortifacient.[1] While feminists have been unified in support of methods that enable women to control their own fertility, there is disagreement among feminists about new reproductive techniques designed to treat infertility and induce pregnancy, such as *in vitro* fertilization, embryo transfer, and research for ectogenesis. If one believes that reproductive freedoms ought to include both fertility and infertility control, it is puzzling that feminists are united in support of the former but divided about the latter.

The feminist debates over the new reproductive technologies which are aimed at treating infertility are very recent. Reproductive-rights arguments that feminists have found effective in establishing rights to fertility control seem to have little effect in countering infertility techniques. Yet, given the rapid pace of infertility research and the large number of women involved, feminists need to develop coherent positions that either give valid grounds for making political distinctions between fertility and infertility research, or support both kinds of technology. Central to this task is an evaluation of women's relationship to pregnancy, since the last reproductive technique mentioned, ectogenesis, would replace pregnancy with alternative means of reproduction for some if not all women. Hence, a discussion of ectogenesis is central to the debates about infertility research. Must women be pregnant? Do fetuses belong in women's bodies? Would other alternatives undermine the role of women in society and impede our struggles for liberation?

The topic of ectogenesis is no longer confined to science fiction. Techniques that enable the short-term growth of embryos *in vitro* suggest the eventual possibility of total growth of embryos outside of women's bodies. Discussions of ectogenesis are commonplace in scientific research and in reports from ethics committees for new reproductive technologies. For instance, ectogenesis is mentioned in *The Warnock Report* (1984). This report claims that it should be a criminal offense to develop a human embryo *in vitro* beyond fourteen days. This view has been stated even more strongly at a recent bioethics conference where Sir David Napley claimed, "It should be a serious criminal offense to develop a human embryo to full maturity outside the body of a woman."[2] An ectogenetic scenario has been vividly, albeit ironically, described by an editor of a leading journal in reproductive research. Referring to experiments for sustaining human uteri *in vitro*, he writes:

> Transvaginal oocyte recovery, fertilization in vitro, and embryo transfer to an artificially perfused uterus will render motherhood, as we recognize it, obsolete. Women may elect to avoid the disfigurement of pregnancy, pain of childbirth, postpartum blues, and the occasional ineptitudes of obstetricians. It seems like the perfect solution to the diminishing number of practicing obstetricians. Maternal-Fetal medicine specialists would ply their trade on this artificial womb, which would be referred to them by the specialist in techniques of assisted reproduction. The extracorporeal womb could be tossed aside after development was complete. The need for a continuing supply of temporary uteri would keep former obstetricians in work doing the necessary hysterectomies, unless someone should be resourceful enough to develop a method to recycle these used specimens. (McDonough 1988)[3]

Feminists are concerned with how ectogenesis might increase the oppression of women. Clearly, there are other philosophical issues inherent in discussions of ectogenesis. One might question ectogenesis from the point of view of the embryo and ask whether there is any moral violation in sustaining embryos *in vitro* for either a portion of development (beyond fourteen days) or until full maturity. One might challenge the value scheme in a society that would utilize technological resources for out-of-the-body reproduction. This discussion, while recognizing these issues, takes for its focus the effects of ectogenesis on feminist assumptions about what it means to be a woman.

Would current feminist reproductive rights arguments provide protection from potential abuses of ectogenesis? Some assumptions must be made about the kind of techniques required and the political context in which they would be developed. In order to analyze ectogenesis, let us assume that ectogenetic techniques will not only exist in the future, but will be methodologically similar to and consistent with the current lines of ectogenetic research, and that the sociopolitical climate of the future society in which ectogenesis might occur will not vary greatly from the present.

Would there be good reasons for feminists to object to ectogenesis? A question central to any ectogenetic research and one that has received very little attention to date: Must women reproduce? While this question is continually raised by individual women about their situations, it is rarely raised of women as a group. Should women, as a group, be liberated from the responsibility of childbearing? Or, despite our liberation in many areas, does our ability to reproduce dictate a responsibility to ourselves and to future generations to be childbearers?[4]

Do fetuses "belong" in women's bodies, as the *Warnock Report* and political conservatives claim? Abortion arguments currently do not address this issue. While feminist arguments for freedom to choose abortion affirm women's right to terminate a pregnancy, that affirmation does not imply that women as such ought not to be childbearers, but merely that women should not be pregnant against their will. Hence, the reproductive freedom of women acknowledged by the abortion right claims that pregnancy ought to be a woman's choice. But what if very few women chose it? In order to explore the relationship between fetuses and women's bodies, the nature and scope of ectogenetic research must be established.

ECTOGENETIC RESEARCH

If ectogenesis is to be accomplished, replacements must be found for the series of biochemical processes performed by women's bodies in pregnancy: egg maturation, fertilization, and implantation; embryo maintenance; temperature control; waste removal; and transport of blood, nourishment, and oxygen to the embryo. Such a procedure, if successful, would accomplish *in vitro* gestation (IVG) for human reproduction. I will be using the terms ectogenesis and *in vitro* gestation as equivalent throughout this discussion. Both refer to the creation of an artificial womb.

The initial steps to develop IVG include the following techniques. Ovulation induction techniques and superovulation techniques enable the control of egg maturation though the actual process remains *in vivo*. Techniques for *in vitro* fertilization (IVF) are already in use. *IVF* and embryo transfer (ET) techniques have resulted in over two thousand live births worldwide, and are a common treatment for some forms of female infertility.[5] Techniques for freezing and thawing eggs, sperm, and embryos have also met with some success. The criterion for success in these procedures is live birth. None of these techniques is completely safe for women and some might be quite dangerous (Laborie 1987, 1988; Rowland 1987a).

Already existing reproductive techniques are pointing the way towards better research strategies for an artificial womb. For instance, it seems clear that a fetus does not need to be implanted in the uterus of its genetic mother in order to thrive, as a recipient uterus has been used in embryo transfer. Also, research techniques for sustaining pregnancies in brain-dead women have resulted in a few live births showing that fetuses can thrive in the bodies of brain-dead pregnant women if there is proper temperature regulation, intubation, and ventilation and all vital organs remain unharmed (Murphy 1989).

Neonatal technology has advanced to enable the maintenance of fetuses—some as early as sixteen weeks or as small as two hundred grams—in incubators, though it is quite costly. The longer a fetus can be sustained *in utero*, the greater its chances of surviving after cesarean section. In one case, a fetus was sustained in a brain-dead pregnant patient for sixty-three days. One researcher, who was prepared to obtain a court order if any relatives of the brain-dead women objected to the procedure, remarked that brain-dead women have no rights because they are considered legally dead, and besides, their bodies are "the cheapest incubators we have."[6]

Other research for artificial wombs uses an artificial medium or even removed human uteri. Gena Corea (1985) notes that techniques for artificial wombs, which have been under investigation since the late nineteen fifties, include several perfusion experiments on aborted fetuses. One experimenter (Goodlin 1963) submerged several fetuses in a high pressure oxygen chamber and used tubes to transport oxygen and nourishment. The fetuses survived this crude form of IVG for less than two days. A research group in Italy has kept human uteri removed from women undergoing hysterectomies alive by perfusing them in an oxygenated medium. A human blastocyst injected into such a uterus survived for fifty-two hours, and implanted itself (Bulletti 1988). Research to determine the chemical environment necessary for IVG is under way in animal experiments with rat embryos removed from uteri on the tenth day of gestation and cultured with various teratogens.[7]

ECTOGENESIS: WHO WANTS IT?

The research indicates that ectogenesis is of interest to scientists. It is a major component if not the culmination of reproductive technology, for it would provide nearly complete control of the developing embryo throughout gestation. The scientific gains from ectogenesis would be substantial, and it could be used to provide a supply of organs and tissue for transplants. Let us focus on the implications of IVG if it were chosen by women or men as an alternative to pregnancy.

Women might draw upon several medical, social, or professional reasons in their desire for IVG. Whether or not these reasons are sufficient to justify ectogenesis, and what assumptions stand behind these reasons need further discussion. A woman may desire ectogenesis because she is unable to maintain a pregnancy or may have had a hysterectomy. Her medical history might indicate that she would have a high-risk pregnancy, or that her health might be impaired because of having endured pregnancy. Other reasons involve the effects that pregnancy can have on women's social and professional lives. A woman may find ectogenesis desirable because she is a smoker, drug user, or casual drinker and does not wish to alter her behavior or place her fetus at risk. Pregnancy might make a woman ineligible for certain career opportunities (e.g., athletics, dancing, modelling, acting). Her job may be hazardous for pregnant women, yet the temporary transfer to safer working conditions may be impossible or undesirable. A woman may be in good health and fertile but may not want the emotional and physical stress of pregnancy.

Women might desire ectogenesis in order to be freed from the burden of childbearing within a spousal relationship. Childbearing has been a blessing and a curse to women. Sometimes, women have revelled in the delights of pregnancy, even finding the female body superior to that of the male for its complicated reproductive possibilities. Other times, childbearing has fallen to women as a burden. Even in the best of situations, in both heterosexual and lesbian relationships, pregnancy is a woman's job.[8] Finally, some men might find ectogenesis a desirable alternative for it would enable them to have a child on their own, provided there were ova banks.

There are three assumptions that are fundamental to support for ectogenesis: (1) IVG would not harm fetal development; (2) IVG privileges a genetically related child over an adopted child, either for ego-centered reasons or because of the shortage of children for adoption; (3) IVG would not contribute to the further oppression of women. While all supporters of IVG might share the first assumption, along with one of the two positions in the second assumption, it would be feminists who would also be concerned with the third assumption. A discussion of each assumption will follow.

(1) IVG and Fetal Harm

The desirability of ectogenesis is predicated on the assumption that IVG would not produce fetal harm. Feminist concern about fetal damage with respect to IVG need not collapse into a fetus-centered perspective on reproductive issues. Usually, in reproductive debates, one must choose one of two perspectives: either a primary focus on respect for women or a primary focus on the fetus. Janice Raymond (1987) terms the latter perspective a fetalist position and contrasts fetalists with feminists in their reasons for opposition to reproductive technologies. As long as alternative gestation practices require women's bodies, there can be a conflict between women's rights and concern for the fetus. This conflict is illustrated by Annette Burfoot, who writes that reproductive medicine "regards women servomechanically as parts of a biological machine whose sole purpose is to nurture embryos" (1988). However, since IVG would not involve women's bodies (assuming egg removal was safe and required consent), concern for fetal harm need not eclipse respect for women's rights. It would seem appropriate to object to a reproductive procedure that might bring harm to a fetus, just as one might object to procedures that harm animals, neonates, or other higher life forms. The goal of IVG must surely be to produce an infant indistinguishable in health and vigor from an infant born of a human pregnancy. Clearly IVG would lose supporters if it harmed fetuses.

It is not known whether techniques for IVG would be safe for the fetus. Even if IVG proved safe in animals, no one would be sure that IVG would be safe in humans until it was actually tried. But who would be the first to risk it? Certainly the fear of irreparable damage to the embryo would be enough to prevent anyone from pursuing the fantasy of ectogenesis. A similar concern marked the precursory stages of IVF. Yet IVF was tried and fortunately does not appear to endanger fetal development severely.[9] One can suspect that IVG, when feasible, will also be tried.

One potential horror would be if IVG damaged the fetus in ways only detectable long after birth. This might give the illusion that techniques were safe and IVG might be used on many embryos before its dangers were discovered. If active euthanasia and infanticide remained prohibited, the infants would be left to a life of suffering. What if severe fetal damage were detected in the later stages of development? Would it be morally permissible to "abort" a third-trimester fetus damaged by IVG techniques?

If the fetus were harmed as a result of IVG techniques, one might feel a heavy sense of moral blame. For without IVG techniques, the suffering fetus would not have existed. The use of fetuses in experimental procedures would be questioned. Of course, it would be incumbent on researchers to prove that the fetal damage was caused by IVG techniques and not by defective sperm or eggs. If fetal damage did result from IVG, the ensuing philosophical debate would need to determine the point at which fetal damage was severe enough to make IVG ethically prohibitive.

(2) IVG and the Privileging of Genetically Related Children

Does a desire for ectogenesis privilege genetic resemblance? If so, is there anything wrong with preferring to parent a child produced by one's own genetic material rather than a child with a different genetic heritage who might be available for adoption? It could be argued that IVG should not be favored over adoption since adoption provides parents for children who already exist. This assumes that there are children available for adoption, and that the rules and procedures of adoption facilities do not discriminate against competent applicants on grounds of sexual preference, race, class, or marital status.

Even if adoption were possible for most people wanting children, some would still prefer to have a genetic offspring. Is the desire for a genetic offspring merely the result of egocentric prejudice? And if so, is there anything wrong with this? Clearly the desire may be hard to fulfill since human reproduction does not guarantee that one's offspring will share many physical characteristics, or likenesses in character or personality. Even if genetic offspring do not greatly resemble the parent, it is still possible to see resemblances to oneself in the body of one's genetically related child. This may be enough to satisfy the desire for a genetic offspring. To delight in these resemblances need not be to collapse into narcissism but rather to revel in the mysteries of reproduction.

At what price does IVG offer this? First, this view romanticizes physical resemblances and genetic material. Secondly, there is no valid ground for favoring a child that looks like oneself over another. After all, one's genetic material is so diverse that it does not guarantee a genetically related child will bear any resemblance to oneself. But more importantly, this sort of genetic privileging may lead to discrimination against several groups of people: gay and lesbian couples who are unable to "make" a child "in their own likeness," nonmonogamous heterosexual couples whose children will not look like a matched set; and infertile couples, who might expend great economic and personal resources trying to have a "natural child" (rather than all of us spending our efforts on undoing the superiority of the "natural child").

The preference for the natural child reinforces the link between genetic parent and offspring, a link which is often dysfunctional. Such a preference can perpetuate dysfunctional families by social policies that keep the family together because the genetic ties are seen as binding. Also, preference for a genetically similar child reinforces race, class, and cultural prejudices in adoption practices. Families that continue to represent "matched sets" to some extent perpetuate these prejudices in the society at large. In short, the desire for a genetic offspring is loaded with political and social values. Even if our society did not discriminate on any of these grounds, one would need to decide at what point concerns for an overpopulated world ought to override an individual's right to procreate.

(3) IVG and Adoption

If adoption supplied an adequate number of children for people desiring parenthood, and if adoption could be restructured to eliminate long waiting periods, tedious bureaucratic procedures, and discrimination, then IVG would seem unnecessary. But what if there were not enough adoptive children available to meet the demand by prospective IVG clients? Should surrogacy arrangements or international adoptions be encouraged? If the latter, it would be important to guarantee that no coercive strategies were used to take children away from their mothers, and that governments were not deliberately negligent about methods of fertility control for women for the sake of profits from their children.

(4) Would IVG Be a Technique of Liberation?

This question is at the center of the feminist debate over the new reproductive technologies. Much of the discussion has presupposed strong feminist arguments about reproductive rights relevant to fertility control. I believe that an examination of these arguments shows that the oppressive nature of IVG requires challenging the entire context of reproduction. It also raises the question: why are alternatives to pregnancy desirable?

Three lines of argument have been used by feminists to justify reproductive rights for women. The first two are grounded in the notion of individual freedoms implied by having rights over our bodies. They are 1) the *Protection of Bodily Violation Argument*, and 2) the *Right to Bodily Control Argument*. I will show that neither can be used to reject appeals for ectogenesis. The *Protection from Bodily Violation Argument* (PBVA), while primarily applicable to arguing against assault and rape, has been used extensively in debates about contraceptive methods. The argument states that achieving reproductive ends does not justify subjecting women to unsafe drugs or procedures. Women's health should not be jeopardized just to enable contraception.

Feminists have appealed to the PBVA to protest experimentation with and use of oral contraceptives and unsafe illegal abortions, as well as unnecessary hysterectomies, cesarean sections, and other abuses, (e.g., thalidomide, DES, and the dalkon shield). It has also been used recently by feminists to protest embryo-transfer techniques. The claim is that ovulation induction, superovulation and embryo-transfer techniques are unsafe, and medical researchers often fail to inform women about the low probability IVF-ET offers for pregnancy (Soules 1985; Laborie 1987, 1988; Corea and Ince 1987).

The *Right to Bodily Control Argument* (RBCA) is the second line of argument used by feminists to object to reproductive technology. It is commonly used in defense of a woman's right to abortion, but it could be extended to include the freedom to choose or refrain from medical procedures in general, as well as to argue against assault and rape, and in support of safe contraception.

When applied to pregnancy, this argument claims that women have a right to control our bodies in pregnancy—specifically, to choose not to be pregnant. Hence, women ought to have access to safe abortions. Admittedly, for some feminists this right holds only during early stages of fetal development; others extend it throughout pregnancy.

Both lines of argument could be applied to IVG. Feminists could use the PBVA to object to IVG if the techniques for obtaining eggs for fertilization were unsafe. For even though IVG eliminates the need for women to bear children, it still requires women to supply the eggs.[10] If the methods for egg removal were painful or dangerous, then feminists would object to IVG by appealing to the first argument—PBVA. Currently laparoscopy is used for egg removal in IVF. Laparoscopy requires local anesthetic, and is inconvenient but not particularly dangerous. Less is known about techniques to control ovulation that often accompany egg removal. If techniques to induce ovulation or superovulation are found to endanger women's health, IVG would be a suspect procedure until better techniques were found.

Even if egg removal techniques presented danger to women, some women might still defend IVG as their best option for obtaining a genetic offspring. They might claim that many women in the past chose pregnancy knowing it might very well be life-endangering. Women who survived high risk pregnancies might have found that their choice greatly enhanced their lives. Why then should choosing a high-risk egg removal procedure for IVG not be equally justifiable? Of course IVG would not be the only option for these women. One could obtain a genetic offspring by being an egg donor and using a surrogate embryo recipient for IVF-ET. Yet this procedure still involves egg removal and if egg removal techniques are unsafe, women would be enduring health risk in order to pursue this goal. Feminists might argue that reproductive technology should not be used to offer women new ways to risk their lives in reproduction. While each infertile woman would need to weigh her desire for a genetic offspring with risks to her health, feminists might insist that such a wager is not a mark of a liberating technology.

The RBCA could also be applied to IVG and egg-removal techniques. Both egg removal and egg disposition ought to require informed consent.

An expanded *Right to Bodily Control Argument* is being used by some feminists who assume that "bodily control" means the right to have full charge of reproduction. IVF-ET and presumably IVG mediate women's access to our reproductive bodies. Several feminists claim that women who choose IVF-ET are reduced to experimental victims of scientific research. Janice Raymond writes that "as women become the penultimate research 'subjects' (read objects), the way is paved for women's wider and more drastic use in reproductive research and experimentation. Women become the scheduled raw material in the factory of legalized reproductive experimentation" (1987). IVG might be seen as a case in which women lose all control over reproduction by losing the experience of pregnancy and depending on technicians for the maintenance of their IVG fetuses.

However, IVG might not be a violation of the expanded RBCA, if one understood bodily control to include the expansion of options which may or may not be connected to women's direct control. IVG would enable some infertile women to do something they otherwise would not be able to do: reproduce. And IVG could enable fertile women to have genetic offspring without the risk of pregnancy. In short, IVG would expand our reproductive options.

However, the creation of additional options need not be a sign of liberation. New options could be exploitive. Imagine a new drug that enabled workers to work for eighteen-hour shifts without feeling tired. This discovery, if used to lengthen the work week, would be enslaving not liberating.

Can we envision a scenario where the availability of IVG did not involve exploitation? IVG certainly would not exploit women in a traditional way, by keeping them pregnant. And, as long as women's consent were required for IVG, and pregnancy remained an option for fertile women, IVG would not necessarily be exploitive at all. Whether or not one affirms an expanded sense of bodily control is contingent on how one sees modern medicine, as benefitting or harming health. Women who value the experience of pregnancy and see it as offering a deeply satisfying and unique connection to new life would still choose pregnancy. Women who see pregnancy as either life-threatening or simply undesirable might feel bodily control expanded by the option of IVG. Guidelines for informed consent might ensure that women's eggs would not be used for exploitive ends.

The most extreme objection to IVG might be termed the *Elimination of Women Argument* (EWA); it could be derived from the PBVA and RBCA. This argument claims that the aim of certain reproductive techniques is to do away with women altogether. Clearly women researchers are underrepresented in the field of reproductive technology. What is to prevent men from making women extinct once our unique contribution to society—reproduction—can be supplied another way?[11] IVG, accompanied by sex selection techniques and methods for producing synthetic eggs, could guarantee the reproduction of an all-male population—the ultimate patriarchal culture.[12] The link between artificial wombs and the possibility of femicide is suggested by Steinbacher and Holmes (1987, p. 57):

> There is no atrocity too terrible for human nature to contemplate and often carry out. This has, in fact, been the case numerous times throughout history, and has been justified as necessary to fulfil the needs and 'rights' of 'superior' individuals or races.

They suggest that the fate of women might be similar to that of some other oppressed groups (e.g., "witches," American Indians, European Jews). A similarly apocalyptic tone is sounded by Robyn Rowland (1987b, p. 75):

> Much as we turn from consideration of a nuclear aftermath, we turn from seeing a future where children are neither borne or born or where women are forced to bear only sons and to slaughter their foetal daughters. Chinese and Indian women are already trudging this path. The future of women as a group is at stake and we need to ensure that we have thoroughly considered all possibilities before endorsing technology which could mean the death of the female.

Despite the ever-present threat of violence against the oppressed, the EWA is implausible. It assumes that women are allowed to exist in patriarchy simply because of their childbearing function. Despite feminist attacks on female socialization, women's roles in society remain steadfast. Women continue to provide patriarchy with at least four other functions: nurturance, a diligent workforce, the maintenance of male egoism, objects of sexual desire. Almost as important as reproduction are the many nurturing roles delegated to women in family life, the community, and the labor force (e.g., nursing, child care, elementary education, social service, secretarial jobs). It is hard to imagine a sexist government eliminating women only to delegate these undesired nurturing roles to men.

Women also provide patriarchy with cheap labor for tedious jobs (e.g., in electronics, textiles, data processing, and so forth). Women's reputations for small hands and docility make it all the easier to assign such work to them. Men might think it worthwhile to keep women around to spare themselves these forms of labor.

Further, sexism has been part of society for so long that men have grown accustomed to a position of superiority vis-à-vis women that would be hard to give up. Male egoism is maintained by a sexist culture. Then of course there is a heterosexual structure in patriarchy that is thousands of years old. Male heterosexuality would have to undergo radical transformation. In short, it would be hard to eliminate women if women remained the objects of sexual desire for many men.

In addition to these four functions, women might wage a successful resistance movement. All in all, it is hard to see how IVG could lead to such massive social transformations as would be required for a transition to an all male society. The existence of women is built into the sexist socialization patterns of society, which require that women exist.[13]

None of the above three arguments (the PBVA, RBCA, and EWA) defeat ectogenetic research. Furthermore, feminists who see liberating potential in IVG might appeal to Shulamith Firestone, a feminist who has argued that reproduction should not be seen as "women's work" and has advocated ectogenesis. She claims that "pregnancy is barbaric," "a temporary deformation of the body of the individual for the sake of the species," physically dangerous and painful. Writing in 1970, Firestone envisioned a cultural, economic, and sexual revolution which would use technology to expand human freedoms. Ectogenesis would play a key role:

> I submit, then, that the first demand for any alternative system must be: *The freeing of women from the tyranny of their reproductive biology by every means available, and the diffusion of the childbearing and childrearing role to the society as a whole, men as well as women.* (1970)

Her revolutionary plan requires abolition of capitalism, racism, sexism, the family, marriage, sexual repression (in all of its forms), and all institutions that keep women and children out of the larger society (e.g., female labor and elementary schools). But we should heed her warning: "In the hands of our current society and under the direction of current scientists (few of whom are female) any attempted use of technology to 'free' anybody is suspect" (1970, p. 206).

We are far from achieving the sort of revolution required in order for ectogenesis to be liberating. Capitalism, for instance, continues to be the dominant economic system. Marriages and families, although less prevalent than when Firestone wrote, are still the norm; schooling is still compulsory. Yet, advocates of ectogenesis Peter Singer and Deane Wells rely in part on Firestone's writings to claim that ectogenesis ought to be a feminist goal now. They argue that despite widespread sexism, ectogenesis can only enhance the status of women:

> Can it seriously be claimed that in our present society the status of women rests entirely on their role as nurturers of embryos from conception to birth? If we argue that to break the link between women and childbearing would be to undermine the status of women in our society what are we saying about the ability of women to obtain true equality in other spheres of life? We, at least, are not nearly so pessimistic about the abilities of women to achieve equality with men across the broad range of human endeavor. For that reason, we think women will be helped rather than harmed by the development of a technology that makes it possible for them to have children without being pregnant. (p. 129)

This position ignores the theory of revolution implicit in Firestone's support for ectogenesis. In fact, it would be consistent with Firestone's vision to assume that technology itself would be thoroughly transformed by the transformation of society. Ectogenesis, for instance, could not be advocated as a cure for "infertility," since there would be no emphasis on having a biological child. If ectogenesis were to exist at all it would be to create more desired children.

It would be hard to imagine a postrevolutionary society finding a place for IVG. IVG would definitely not replace pregnancy. For if it were to do so, that would suggest that women's bodies had been judged unfit for pregnancy. Is the best way to abolish sexism a method that downgrades a female capacity—

pregnancy? This suggests that the way to deal with difference is to annihilate it.

The sexism of our current society makes evident that we are far from the goals Firestone envisioned. Debates about fertility and infertility as well as research protocols must be seen within this context. As long as egg removal does not produce severe and immediate harm to women, no doubt many will pursue ectogenesis as an alternative to pregnancy. However, while there may be valid reasons for women to seek alternatives to pregnancy, we need to consider possible detrimental effects of the availability of ectogenesis on abortion and pregnancy rights.

IVG endangers abortion rights because the fetus is not inside a woman: hence it would most likely be seen as a patient. (One benefit of IVG is that any treatment for the fetus would not require surgery on its mother.) The IVG-fetus would be a patient that was not (yet) a human being. The IVG-fetus, though a patient, and even viable, would not be a person.

If IVG fetuses are not dependent on women's bodies, they may seem to differ only slightly from neonates. Hence, if neonates are persons, why not IVG-fetuses too? And what is the moral difference between an IVG-fetus and an *in utero* one?

IVG could thus make it more difficult to justify elective abortions for pregnant women. With IVG, the thorny problem of fetal viability appears. If the definition from *Roe v. Wade* remains unchanged, then every IVG-fetus is a viable fetus for viability means the ability to survive outside the mother's womb, possibly aided by life-support technology. An IVG-fetus would be viable in all stages of gestation provided it were able to thrive. Hence viability would no longer be a useful indicator of fetal development. Some other criterion would be needed if the fetus were to increase in status as birth approached. The tendency might be to discredit the notion of viability altogether, and prohibit abortion. For if IVG parents went to great expense to reproduce in this manner, they might be less sensitive to pregnant women who wanted to abort healthy fetuses. Should prospective parents of an IVG fetus have the right to terminate the fetus if they wish? This act, similar to an abortion, might be difficult to justify since IVG procedures do not conflict with a woman's right to control her body. The right over genetic material might be included in the overriding right to control one's body. It would be a right for both women and men and so a way of resolving conflicting desires between the two gamete donors would be needed. While this right might justify termination of IVG-fetuses, it could also be used by men to demand abortion on the part of their female partners.

IVG could also be implicated in efforts to place greater controls on pregnant women. First, pregnancy might come to be viewed as an inferior act. Women choosing pregnancy over IVG, especially if the latter promised ideal conditions for fetal development, might be seen as taking unnecessary risks with fetal life in order to have an experience of childbirth. Or pregnant women might feel the need to monitor their pregnancies and limit their lives in an attempt to duplicate IVG conditions as much as possible. We might come to see pregnancy as a mere biological function, repeatable in IVG, and not also as a human bond in formation of new life that can be had in no other way. We would need to decide, as a society, whether pregnancy per se had any intrinsic value. If not, we might judge the ideal conditions for fetal development and freedom from risk for women to outweigh *any* value for pregnancy. Hence, IVG could lead to the creation of a class system in reproduction with the rich reproducing in ectogenic labs while the poor continue to rely on women's bodies for pregnancy.

IVG might also contribute to excessive concern for "quality control" in fetal development. Sex-identification techniques are already in use on some embryos prior to implantation. Genetic research is under way for screening techniques to identify gene-linked traits. If IVG were advocated because it offered ideal conditions for fetal development, it would be hard to imagine researchers resisting the opportunity to ensure ideal fetal quality, despite the fact that such product-control endeavors might undermine respect for life's diversity. In fact, it is the opportunity for genetic engineering that has been seen as one of the greatest dangers of this research (Bradish 1987; Minden 1987; Bullard 1987). Linda Bullard claims that genetic engineering is "inherently Eugenic in that it always requires someone to decide what is a good and a bad gene" (1987, p. 117). We might be able to develop a feminist criterion for genetic engineering, however, such as restricting choices to the prevention of genetic disease (e.g., Down's syndrome, muscular dystrophy, spina bifida, thalassaemia).

(5) Is Infertility a Feminist Issue?

Any feminist protest of IVG is likely to be seen as undermining the rights of infertile women to have appropriate medical treatment. What is not obvious is the sexist paradigm assumed by IVG.

This is the most important criticism of IVG for feminists. While those who desire IVG might attempt to justify the procedure on an individual basis, one must also examine the male paradigm of reproduction that any IVG research must assume. The feminist movement ought not to choose sides over which women's rights to support: those of fertile or infertile women. Nor is it appropriate to denigrate those women who choose IVG by assuming they desperately seek motherhood because they are "unenlightened" about their socialization to be mothers. This approach might be plausible if feminists, in large numbers, refuse pregnancy and motherhood as a mark of enlightenment. However, this is not the case. Given this context, it is unfair for a feminist who has chosen pregnancy or who merely admits to valuing pregnancy, to find an infertile woman's desire to reproduce indicative of patriarchal socialization. This does not mean that other reasons do not exist for condemning IVG. Before going any further, we must consider whether infertility is a disability at all.

Some advocates of reproductive technology argue that infertility is a disability and ought to be treated. Deanne Wells claims, "*Prima facie* the inability to bring into the world one's own genetic children is a disability in the same way as is short sightedness" (1987). Wells argues that the same objections to the cost and research for infertility treatments could have been made about treatment for shortsightedness in times before the manufacturing of spectacles was discovered. Just as it would seem foolish to object to treating shortsightedness, it would similarly be foolish to object to treating infertility. Yet, one should not lose sight of an obvious difference between a reproductive impairment and a visual impairment. The major difference is that while everyone surely desires to have greater visual abilities, not everyone desires to reproduce. Hence, a reproductive impairment need not require treatment. Reproductive abilities, unlike visual abilities, are used seldom in our lives, particularly in the U.S. where the birth rate continues to decrease.

There is another difficulty feminists might have in casting infertility as a "disability." Infertility is a social and political phenomenon. Pregnancy is linked to the essence of being female. Infertility ought not to mark women for the whole of our lives in any primary way.

Nonetheless, women who are unable to reproduce have the right to pursue medical options. Feminist concerns about infertility options ought to center on whether or not infertility treatments restore or replace women's reproductive capacities.

It is imperative to consider the broader implications for women's status of any medical treatment for infertility beyond the actual restoration of women's reproductive functions. IVF-ET for example, could be seen as a new way of legitimating pregnancy as women's social "duty."[14] IVG breaks the necessary connection between women and reproduction, but could imply that pregnancy is merely a collection of bodily processes, thus undermining the reproductive work women do in society. This is not to say that infertility should not be treated. It is merely to say that one should not be shortsighted about the broader social effects of new reproductive methods.

It is not that feminists should not support infertility research. Rather, we should demand a share in controlling its direction. If feminists are going to protest IVG and its precursory techniques (IVF-ET), then we ought also to support research into the causes of infertility. After all, approximately ten percent of heterosexual couples in the United States are infertile, and most likely that number will increase with the growing number of environmental and reproductive hazards we are exposed to.

The issue then for society and for feminists ought not to be replacing the functions of women's bodies by technological alternatives, but rather developing nonexploitive ways to treat infertility that enable women to experience pregnancy and childbirth. Technology that is restorative, that enables women to experience our reproductive bodies without endangering our health is the sort of technology that feminists can support in a unified way.

Of all the reproductive techniques, ectogenesis, because it could eliminate pregnancy, poses the greatest challenge to women's reproductive rights. There appears to be nothing *a priori* that requires human gestation to occur *in vivo* anymore than there is an unwritten law requiring sex by the only means for egg fertilization. But in a patriarchal society we can expect the methods of infertility treatment to reflect sexist biases. IVG does this by suggesting that the way to treat infertility is to remove reproduction from women's bodies completely. Not only does IVG displace our bodily abilities, but it also suggests that gestation in a laboratory is equivalent to human pregnancy. Hence, what women contribute to their pregnancies is not essential to reproduction. Sexism proclaims pregnancy to be "inferior" and men recoil in fear of women's reproductive potential; such are the consequences when those in power do not themselves have such powers.

Clearly, many feminists would favor pregnancy over IVG in most cases, not because women are the most cost-effective uteri (what sort of artificial uterus could also hold down a job and run a family while maintaining a fetus?) but because IVG represents a misguided approach to infertility. That some women might prefer gestation of their fertilized eggs in a laboratory rather than in their own bodies is more a mark of the oppressive ways in which women's bodies and pregnancy are seen in this culture than a sign of progressive social attitudes.

The oppression that leads to such negative attitudes can only be changed by redirecting our priorities. We must ensure that everyone be provided with appropriate health care, as well as other prerequisites for health such as education and decent housing. The effects of poverty on women (not to mention children) are far more devastating than the effects of either infertility or reproductive technology.

We need a woman-centered reproductive agenda that makes visible the needs of all women, particularly poor women and women of color. We are only beginning to realize what this might mean. Without such an agenda, women will continue to be exploited by the sexist research system that is a product of our sexist society. More and more resources, including women's bodies, eggs, and uteri, will be wasted on experiments that undermine women, while social programs that would provide a better life will continue to be neglected. These considerations suggest that feminists must protest sexist research methods such as IVG and politicize not only those most likely to use IVG, but also those most likely not to need it.

NOTES

1. RU486 is the abortifacient currently used in France and is at the center of controversy in the U.S. See Mary Suh (1989) and Victor Navasky (1988).

2. Sir David Napley, past president of the English Law Society, suggested at the 1983 Mogul International Management Consultants Ltd Conference on Bioethics and Law of Human Conception in Vitro. See M. D. Kirby (1984).

3. My thanks to Becky Holmes for bringing this finding to my attention.

4. See Allen (1984).

5. Cf. Patricia Spallone and Deborah Lynn Steinberg (1987) for a survey of IVF research in sixteen countries.

6. Conversations with medical researchers engaged in sustaining pregnancies in brain-dead pregnant women. See Murphy (1989).

7. Cf. Daston (1987)

8. Of course, in lesbian relationships both women can decide together which would "prefer" to have a child, provided both are fertile. While a lesbian relationship model removes some of the automatic "burden" (it is not assumed that one person instead of the other must be the one to be pregnant), lesbians along with heterosexual women may still wish that women could be spared pregnancy.

9. In one 1985 study by the National Perinatal Institute cited in Spallone and Steinberg (1987) IVF infants had a higher incidence of premature births, they were four times more likely to die at birth due to prematurity, and the rate of deformed IVF babies was 2.6%.

10. See my article (1984) for a discussion of the sexist language of egg removal in medical research.

11. IVG would be the second-to-last technique in the series. The final technique might be the manufacture of synthetic eggs, which would enable a perpetual supply of eggs.

12. Cf. Holmes and Hoskins (1987) for a feminist critique of sex selection techniques.

13. It might be possible to have an "all male" society while still allowing those of us with female bodies to exist. This would be possible if the category "woman" could be destroyed without requiring the destruction of the category "man." This would assume that masculinity could survive without femininity. The society would be thoroughly masculine in its values. Everyone would be regarded as "men," though some would donate eggs to IVG procedures while others provided sperm. For this to come about women would have to be coerced to take on all the traits of masculinity and would come to be regarded not as a different gender, but rather as inferior men (undesirable mutations of men). This strategy finds limited expression in the world of business and other male-dominated professions.

14. See Crowe (1987) and Solomon (1988).

WORKS CITED

Allen, Jeffner. 1984. Motherhood: the annihilation of women. In *Mothering: Essays in Feminist Theory*, ed. Joyce Trebilcot. New Jersey: Rowman and Allanheld. pp. 315–30.

Arditti, Rita, Renate Duelli Klein, and Shelley Minden. 1984. *Test-Tube Women.* London: Pandora Press.

Bradish, Paula. 1987. From genetic counseling and genetic analysis, to genetic ideal and genetic fate? In Spallone (1987).

Bullard, Linda. 1987. Killing us softly: toward a feminist analysis of genetic engineering. In Spallone (1987).

Bulletti, C., VM Jasonni, S. Tabanelli et al. 1988. Early human pregnancy in vitro utilizing an artificially perfused uterus. *Fertility and Sterility* 49(6): 1–6.

Burfoot, Annette. 1988. A review of the third annual meeting of the European Society of Human Reproduction and Embryology. *Reproductive and Genetic Engineering: Journal of International Feminist Analysis* 1(1).

Corea, Gena. 1985. *The Mother Machine: Reproductive Technologies from Artificial Insemination to Artificial Wombs.* New York: Harper & Row.

Corea, Gena, and J. Hammer, B. Hoskins, J. Raymond et al. 1987. *Man-Made Women: How New Reproductive Technologies Affect Women.* Bloomington: Indiana University Press.

Corea, Gena, and Susan Ince. 1987. Report of a survey of IVF Clinics in the U.S. In Spallone (1987).

Crowe, Christine. 1987. Women want it: In vitro fertilization and women's motivations for participation. In Spallone (1987).

Daston, GP, MT Ebron, B. Carver et al. 1987. In vitro teratongenicity of ethylenethiourea in the rat. *Teratology* 35(2): 239–45.

Firestone, Shulamith. 1970. *The Dialectic of Sex.* New York: Bantam.

Goodlin, Robert C. 1963. An improved fetal incubator. *Trans. Amer. Soc. Artif. Int. Organ* 9: 348–50.

Hammer, J. et al. 1988. New reproductive technologies: News from France and elsewhere. *Reproductive and Genetic Engineering* 1(1).

Holmes, Helen B., and Betty B. Hoskins. 1987. Prenatal and preconception sex choice technologies: A path to femicide. In Corea et al. (1987) *Man-Made Women.*

Kirby, M. D. 1984. Bioethics of IVF—the state of the debate. *Journal of Medical Ethics* 1: 45–48.

Laborie, Francoise. 1987. Looking for mothers you only find fetuses. In Spallone (1987).

McDonough, Paul G. 1988. Comment. *Fertility and Sterility* 50(6): 1001–02.

Murphy, Julien S. 1984. Egg farming and women's future. In Arditti (1984).

Murphy, Julien S. 1986. Abortion rights and fetal termination. *Journal of Social Philosophy* 15(3).

Murphy, Julien S. 1989. Should pregnancy be sustained in brain-dead women? A philosophical discussion of postmortem pregnancy. In *Healing Technologies*, ed. Kathryn Strother Ratcliffe, Myra Marx Ferree, Gail Mellow et al. Ann Arbor: University of Michigan Press.

Navasky, Victor. 1988. Bitter pill. *The Nation* 247(15): 515–16.

Raymond, Janice G. 1987. Fetalists and feminists: they are not the same. In Spallone (1987).

Rowland, Robyn. 1987a. Of women born, but for how long? The relationship of women to the new reproductive technologies and the issue of choice. In Spallone (1987).

Rowland, Robyn. 1987b. Motherhood, patriarchal power, alienation and the issue of "choice" in sex preselection. In Spallone (1987).

Singer, Peter, and Deane Wells. 1984. *Making Babies.* New York: Scribner's.

Solomon, Alison. 1988. Integrating infertility crisis counseling into feminist practice. *Reproductive and Genetic Engineering* 1(1).

Soules, Michael. 1985. The in vitro fertilization pregnancy rate—Let's be honest with one another. *Fertility and Sterility* 43(4): 511–13.

Spallone, Patricia, and Deborah Lynn Steinberg. 1987. International Report. *Made to Order: The Myth of Reproductive and Genetic Progress.* Oxford: Pergamon Press.

Steinbacher, Roberta, and Helen B. Holmes. 1987. Sex choice: survival and sisterhood. In Corea et al. (1987) *Man-Made Women.*

Suh, Mary. 1989. RU Detour. *Ms.* (Jan./Feb.): 135–36.

Warnock, Mary. 1984. *A Question of Life: The Warnock Report on Human Fertilisation & Embryology.* Oxford: Basil Blackwell.

Wells, Deane 1987. Ectogenesis, justice and utility: A reply to James. *Bioethics* 1(4).

CHAPTER 13

NEW REPRODUCTIVE TECHNOLOGY

Some Implications for the Abortion Issue

CHRISTINE OVERALL

(1 9 8 5)

Until this time, it seems fair—and obvious—to say, the objection to abortion by those who find it morally wrong has depended upon the indubitable empirical fact that abortion results in the death of the fetus.[1] As Roger Wertheimer put it,[2]

> . . . there isn't much we can do with a fetus; either we let it out or we do it in. I have little hope of seeing a justification for doing one thing or the other unless this situation changes.

Indeed, the situation *is* now changing, changing in such a way that we can see that abortion really consists of two potentially distinct aspects: (1) the (premature) emptying of the uterus (that is, the expulsion of the fetus), and (2) causing the death of the fetus.[3] Until recently, (1) has virtually always resulted in (2); the fetus dies either during or immediately after the process of prematurely removing it from the uterus. So closely linked have these two events been that some philosophers have even defined abortion as consisting essentially of (2).[4] However, that (1) and (2) are distinct, though causally related, has been recognized at least implicitly by other philosophers, for example, within the context of discussion of the Roman Catholic doctrine of double effect.[5]

It is because abortion consists of these two events that we commonly find two alleged rights discussed in connection with the abortion issue. These are (a) the alleged right of the mother to control her own body, and (b) the alleged right of the fetus to life. The two are in conflict, and this is because, until now, the exercise of one right has precluded the exercise of the other. If the woman exercises her alleged right to control her body by having her uterus emptied, the fetus dies; if the fetus exercises, or better, is permitted to exercise, its alleged right to life, this severely reduces (if not eliminates) the mother's control over her body.

Further, I suggest, the fact that abortion consists of these two events, and that therefore the two alleged rights are in apparent conflict, has led to the generation of two staunchly opposed positions about the morality of abortion, commonly called the "liberal" position and the "conservative" position. The liberal position, putting its emphasis on event (1) of the abortion process and alleged right (a), avows that abortion is not (at least in most cases) morally wrong. The conservative position, putting its emphasis on event (2) of the abortion process and alleged right (b), avows that abortion is (at least in most cases) morally wrong.[6]

However, the very nature of abortion, and of the associated moral issues, is changing and will change further because of recent and rapid developments in reproductive technology. These new developments will mean that the two hitherto causally linked events, (1) the emptying of the uterus and (2) the death of the fetus, can be severed. The expulsion of the fetus will no longer mean its death.

Briefly, this possibility is suggested by the current use of innovative techniques regarding what are commonly called "test-tube babies."[7] A "test-tube baby" is an embryo produced by the fertilization *in vitro* of an egg removed from a woman's body. Ordinarily, if fertilization and embryo development proceed normally, the embryo is either implanted in its donor mother or, less often, is stored in a frozen state for possible future use. Immediate implantation results in pregnancy twelve to twenty percent of the time. It is also possible that the embryo, whether "fresh" or thawed after being frozen for storage, can be implanted in a woman other than the original egg donor.

So far, embryos have developed *in vitro* only to the sixteen-cell stage before being successfully implanted. However, the development of frozen embryo banks suggests that the actual length of time of the embryo's independence of the uterus may be considerably extended beyond the present matter of a few days.[8] Moreover, perhaps even more important, a type of "embryo transfer" can be effected by removing an embryo from the uterus of one woman and implanting it directly in that of another.[9]

What these processes suggest is that there is a time, near the beginning of its development, albeit so far a very limited time, when the fetus need not be dependent for its existence upon the occupancy of a uterus, or at least, of any particular uterus, for example, that of its biological mother. And of course at the other end of prenatal existence, the age of viability—the point at which a relatively developed fetus is able to survive *ex utero*, with the help of sophisticated support systems—is gradually declining. Therefore it can be anticipated that in the future expulsion from the uterus will ordinarily not result in the death of the fetus. This potential development provides the opportunity for a reexamination of the issue of the morality of abortion. It permits us to keep quite separate the two alleged rights mentioned earlier, of the woman to control her body; of the fetus to control its life.

In the remainder of this paper I propose to recast the issues surrounding abortion in a way that may satisfy both the liberal and the conservative. This new approach emerges by focusing upon what I believe is a rather widespread consensus about some aspects of abortion. This consensus may not have been very apparent, until now, because of the fact that the emptying of the uterus resulted in the death of the fetus. But if, instead, we examine our responses—

our "intuitions," as some have called them—about each of these events separately, a surprising degree of agreement appears.

In my discussion, I put forward no general ethical theory, and I ignore what many have regarded as *the* question about abortion: Is the fetus a person? As a result, my conclusions are limited. However, I believe that they have the advantage of minimizing confusion in our attitudes toward and treatment of the fetus, and reducing the acrimonious dispute about the morality of abortion. (As I shall point out, however, my argument does not by any means solve all the problems associated with abortion. Rather it would be fair to say that it displaces them. For the technologies upon which my discussion is based raise, of themselves, new issues about which there is bound to be disagreement.)

I

Like many others, I wish to discuss the issues here in terms of rights. To say that a person has a right to have or to do something is to imply that it would be wrong to interfere with her having it or doing it.[10] I do not assume that any rights are necessarily absolute, that is, that they hold whatever else may be the case. However, rights must be regarded as special claims or entitlements that can only be set aside, or interfered with, if at all, on the basis of other compelling moral grounds.

R. M. Hare points out that rights are "the stamping ground of intuitionists,"[11] and, as I have indicated, I shall argue on the basis of our responses to, or "intuitions" about, some specific moral situations. However, the intuitions advanced here are not in support of claims about the possession of rights. Instead, they are used to support claims about the *absence* of rights.

Let us begin with the heart of the conservative position: claim (b), that the fetus has a right to life. Does the fetus have a right to life? If so, when is this right acquired; at the time of conception, motility, viability? If not, why not: what distinguishes it from beings that do in fact possess this right? These questions are apparently endlessly debatable. In this discussion, I shall assume no views about the fetus's alleged right to life; I shall be agnostic as to the answers to the questions listed above.

Instead, I offer a different statement about rights and the fetus—or rather, about the absence of rights: (c) The mother (or anyone else, e.g., a physician) has no right to kill the fetus.

The claim is not without precedents, and indeed seems to match the "intuitions" of many who have written about abortion. Judith Jarvis Thomson, for example, who espouses a liberal view about the morality of abortion, has this to say:[12]

> . . . I am not arguing for the right to secure the death of the unborn child. It is easy to confuse these two things in that up to a certain point in the life of the fetus it is not able to survive outside the mother's body; hence removing it

from her body guarantees its death. But they are importantly different. . . . A woman may be utterly devastated by the thought of a child, a bit of herself, put out for adoption and never seen or heard of again. She may therefore want not merely that the child be detached from her, but more, that it die. . . . [But] the desire for the child's death is not one which anybody may gratify, should it turn out to be possible to detach the child alive.

Jane English expresses agreement with this statement, as does Frances Myrna.[13] And Mary Anne Warren remarks, ". . . if abortion could be performed without killing the fetus, she [the mother] would never possess the *right* to have the fetus destroyed, for the same reasons that she has no right to have an infant destroyed."[14] Margaret A. Somerville argues that it is both unethical and illegal (within the context of Canadian law) for a physician to intentionally and unnecessarily kill the fetus, because even where an abortion is legally performed, neither the mother nor the physician has the moral or legal right to kill the fetus unnecessarily.[15]

What exactly does (c) mean? In general, if X has a right to life, then Y has no right to kill X. Conversely, if Y has a right to kill X, then X has no (or a very minimal) right to life. However, even if X (in this case, the fetus) has itself no right to life (i.e., no right not to be killed) or even if we do not know whether it has a right to life, this does not imply that another being, Y, has the right to kill X. Nor does this imply that it is morally right to kill X. There is no obligation on any other being, Z, to permit Y to kill X, and indeed, Z may even under some circumstances have an obligation to prevent Y from killing X. That is, even if X has no right to life, it may nevertheless be wrong to kill X;[16] therefore Y does not have a right to kill X.

Claim (c) may appear to threaten the heart of the liberal position. But notice that in both Thomson's and Warren's formulation of (c), explicit reference is made to the important distinction between events (1) expelling the fetus from the uterus, and (2) causing the death of the fetus. It is this distinction that helps to make (c) plausible. Reflection upon several actual and possible cases will illustrate and lend support to (c).

Consider first the fact that occasionally, after a late abortion involving the injection of a saline solution into the woman's uterus, the fetus is born alive. An attempt is ordinarily made to resuscitate the baby, damaged though it may be by the abortion process. No one would suppose that the mother of such a baby has a right to strangle it, slit its throat, suffocate it, or otherwise kill it. Nor has anyone else, including the physician who performed the abortion and subsequent delivery, any such right on behalf of the mother.

Similarly, imagine that a baby is born very prematurely to a woman who had wanted an abortion, but failed to obtain one (whether because of legal barriers, lack of access to abortion facilities, or whatever). Babies born as early as twenty-six weeks' gestational age may survive.[17] Suppose, then, that this unwanted baby is delivered spontaneously at twenty-six weeks. Once again, no one, I think, would be inclined to say that the mother, or anyone else (whether acting independently, or on the mother's behalf) has a right to kill it.

Third (and this is the most difficult example), consider the case of a typical "test-tube baby": that is, a one- to sixteen-cell embryo existing outside its biological mother's uterus, in a culture medium. Tiny and undeveloped as it is, I submit, its parents (and anyone else) do not have a right to destroy it or have it destroyed. Here I disagree with arguments put forward by Helga Kuhse and Peter Singer. The former states, "there is no moral difference between discarding surplus human embryos and deliberately not creating them in the first place."[18] In another paper, Kuhse and Singer together appear to maintain that a couple who have donated sperm and egg for *in vitro* fertilization have a right to refuse to permit excess embryos resulting therefrom either to be implanted (in the woman herself or in a surrogate) or to be frozen; i.e., they have a right to have the embryo "tipped down the sink" and thus destroyed.[19]

This, however, is mistaken. The parents do not have this right, because they do not own the embryo. An individual does own his/her genetic material: a woman can be said to be the owner of her ova, a man of his sperm. Women may soon be able to donate or sell their eggs to egg banks, just as men can now sell or donate their sperm to sperm banks. The moral acceptability of this practice, if it is carefully regulated, suggests that one does own one's own gametes, and has some rights as to their preservation, disposal, and destruction. Thus the couple in Kuhse and Singer's example does have the right to have these materials "tipped down the sink"—if, for example, one of them should change his/her mind about participation in IVF.

By contrast, no one owns the embryo or fetus: it is not the sort of thing which can be owned. Joel Feinberg shows this very clearly by means of two arguments.[20] First,

[i]f fetuses were property, we would find nothing odd in the notion that they can be bought and sold, rented out, leased, used as collateral on loans, and so on. But no one has ever seriously entertained such suggestions.

Second,

. . . one would think that the father would have equal or near-equal rights of disposal if the fetus were "property." It is not in his body, to be sure, but he contributed as much genetically to its existence as did the mother and might therefore make just as strong (or just as weak) a claim to ownership over it. But neither claim would make very good conceptual sense.

Thus, because no one, not even its parents, owns the fetus, no one has the *right* to destroy it, even at a very early developmental stage, and the couple in Kuhse and Singer's example are not entitled to tip the embryo down the sink.

If the three cases cited so far are persuasive with regard to the claim that the mother (and everyone else) has no right to kill the fetus, it might be thought that this absence of a right is due to the fetus's location. In the first two examples, the fetus is born; it is now a baby outside the mother's body. In the third case, the embryo exists independently in a petri dish. However, it is not because of some change in location, or because of development in a location independent of the mother's body, that there exists no right to kill it. To suppose that it is mere location which determines this absence of right is to confuse claim (c) with some aspect of another claim, to be called (d), which will be discussed below.

At this point it should be noted that although the mother (and everyone else) has no right to kill the fetus, it may nevertheless in some cases not be wrong for her, or, more likely, a physician deputized by her, to kill the fetus. For to say that a person has no right to do something does not preclude her doing it, on occasion, and being morally right in doing so. An obvious example in this context is a case where the fetus is threatening the mother's health, for example, when growing in the fallopian tube. Other possible examples include cases of severe fetal deformity or illness. Thus, let us recognize the general possibility that it might sometimes be right for someone, in some circumstances, to kill the fetus, and this might be so regardless of its location—whether in its mother's uterus, or growing in a petri dish—and regardless of the fact that she (and everyone else) has no general right to kill it.

II

Let us now consider the heart of the liberal position: claim (a), that the mother has the right to control her own body. Like (b), about fetal rights, (a) has been endlessly debated. Thompson states, "if a human being has any just, prior claim to anything at all, he has a just, prior claim to his own body," and she suggests that "everyone would grant that."[21] But as she indicates, much of the dispute has concerned the possible limitations on that alleged right, and the degree to which it can be overcome by other rights, such as the alleged rights of the fetus. Furthermore, both Warren and Feinberg have pointed out that there are serious conceptual difficulties in basing the woman's alleged right on the claim that her body is her property.[22] In this discussion, I shall assume no views about women's alleged right to control their bodies; I shall be agnostic as to the solutions to the problems listed above.

Instead, I offer a different statement about rights and women, or rather, once again, about the absence of rights: (d) The fetus has no right to occupancy of its mother's (or anyone else's) uterus.[23]

This claim is a specific instance of the more general principle that no one has the right to the use of anyone else's body: that is, presumably, part of what makes rape and slavery wrong. The claim is very clearly illustrated by Thomson's famous violinist example: Suppose that a famous violinist is ill, and will survive only by being hooked up to some specific individual's kidneys. ". . . [N]obody has any right to use your kidneys unless you give him such a right; and nobody has the right against you that you shall give him this right—if you do allow him to go on using your kidneys, this is a kindness on your part, and not something he can claim against you."[24]

Now claim (d) appears to undermine the conservative position on abortion. But once again, the distinction between emptying the uterus and causing the death of the fetus must be maintained, and a brief consideration of some possible cases will lend support to (d).

Imagine, first, that an egg is withdrawn from a woman, and is fertilized *in virtro* with her husband's sperm. However, during the time in which the embryo is growing to a multi-cellular stage, the woman unfortunately is killed in a car accident. No one could plausibly say that another woman should be made the host(ess?) of the motherless embryo. For the embryo has no right to the occupancy of another woman's body. The fact that it is dependent— first on the culture medium in which it divides, and then upon a uterus, should one be available—does not give it the right to inhabit a woman's body.

Now suppose that in the same sort of case, several eggs are withdrawn and fertilized. One is reimplanted, develops, and becomes a healthy baby successfully delivered nine months later. The other embryos are frozen for possible later use. But then imagine that several years go by, and the woman enters her forties: she feels too old to have another baby. Or imagine that in the meantime, she develops diabetes, a condition which may make pregnancy perilous for her and the fetus. The frozen embryos then have no right— against the interests of her health and her life situation —to be implanted. For they too have no right to the occupancy of their biological mother's uterus. Those who may be inclined to say that these embryos do have such a right are, I believe, confusing that claim with the more usual but unproved conservative claim that the fetus has a right to life, or with what I have called claim (c), that no one has the right to kill the fetus.

However, it should also be noted that claim (d), that the fetus has no right to occupancy of any woman's uterus, does not imply that it will never be wrong for a woman to terminate a fetus's occupancy. As Gordon C. Zahn points out, "The owner of a badly needed residential building is not, or at least *should not be,* free to evict his tenants to suit a selfish whim or to convert his property to some frivolous or nonessential use."[25] Thus, though a fetus has no right to the use of its mother's uterus, circumstances may be such that it would be wrong for her to end the pregnancy. She may in fact have incurred some degree of obligation to it. For example, it would probably be wrong for a mother to abort her fetus when its conception was planned, it is well advanced in development, and her only reason is that she is tired of her pregnancy.[26] Thus let us recognize the general possibility that it might sometimes be wrong for a woman in some circumstances to end the fetus's occupancy of her uterus, or maybe even to refuse it occupancy after its *in vitro* conception, and this might be so, regardless of the fact that it has no general right to occupancy of her uterus.

III

If it were not for developing reproductive technology, the two claims, (c) and (d), put forward here would continue to mean an insoluble conflict, in practice if not in theory. To say that no one has a right to kill the fetus seems to say that abortion is wrong; but to say that the fetus has no right to occupancy of its mother's (or anyone else's) uterus seems to say that abortion is not wrong.

If, however, it is becoming more and more possible for a fetus to survive outside it's mother's body, or to be transferred successfully to the uterus of another woman who wants a child, abortion need no longer entail so much moral conflict. We might then say that a woman may have an abortion, in the sense of expelling the fetus from her body, and the fetus may live. The solution could satisfy both the liberal, whose desire is to provide abortions for women who want them, and the conservative, whose aim is the preservation of fetal life.

Thus the position on abortion outlined here has both theoretical and practical advantages over the old battle lines. That is, it both helps us to make sense of our moral beliefs about the topic, and it suggests actual positive consequences for our behavior. What follows is an outline of some of these advantages.

Maternal Intentions, Fetal Resuscitation, and Viability

> If abortion is justified, then it should be performed in a way that gives the child a chance of survival, if there is any chance at all. The effort to save the aborted child and to find ways of saving all who are justifiably aborted would be a token of sincerity that the death of the child really was not in the scope of the intention.[27]

What exactly is the intention of a woman seeking an abortion is, surely, an empirical question. Often she may not have thought beyond the immediate goal of no longer being pregnant. In addition, she may feel that she does not want and/or is not able to care for an infant, and the child that it will become. Most of us do not regard a desperate woman who attempts to abort herself as a potential killer. We recognize, implicitly, that what she is trying to do is to end her pregnancy, to remove the fetus from her body. Moreover, most people, I suspect, feel particularly sympathetic to women who seek abortions when pregnancy results from rape or incest, or when it seriously threatens the women's life or health. Once again, the woman seems to be saying that she does not want, and will not permit, the fetus to occupy her uterus. Her goal is to end her pregnancy, not necessarily to kill the fetus. And to say that the former may not be wrong, while the latter may be, is preferable to the more peculiar view of those who seem inclined to believe that a fetus has a right to life—except when it is the product of rape.

Is it the case that some women seeking abortions specifically desire the death of the fetus? Steven L. Ross argues that, indeed, some women "cannot be satisfied *unless* the fetus is killed; nothing else will do."[28] This desire, he says, is derived from the unique relationship of the parent to the fetus: that the fetus is genetically related to her, and that she (as well as the father) has the most legitimate claim to raise the child. Thus, for some, the feeling that "she and not any one else ought to raise whatever children she brings into the world" is a "deeply felt personal preference";[29] failure to raise one's own child can only be avoided by killing the fetus.

I would suggest, however, that this sort of feeling, if and when it occurs (and the existence of sperm and egg donors, as well as surrogate mothers, proves that it is not universal) does not justify killing the fetus. However unique the relationship to the fetus (and Ross does not fully understand it, for he says, "We cannot . . . love the fetus even if we wanted to, as we cannot be said to love anything we have not interacted with"[30]—there are certainly some women who would claim that they have both interacted with and loved their fetus) the parents do not own it, and therefore are not entitled to have it killed.

Hence, writers like H. Tristram Engelhardt, Jr. are mistaken when they claim that the use of abortifacient devices which guarantee the death of the fetus is justified by "a woman's interests in not being a mother." I would also reject his claim that "one would wish as well to forbid attempts, against the will of the mother, to sustain the life of an abortus prior to the established [legal] upper limit for abortions."[31] The policy at many North American hospitals which perform abortions is to attempt to resuscitate aborted fetuses which show signs of life. And surely, if abortion is seen primarily as the emptying of the uterus, and no one has the right to kill the fetus, then some of the irony attendant upon "[r]equiring a lifesaving medical team to be prepared to rush into the operating clinic in the event that the abortion team fails to achieve the fetus's death"[32] is reduced. There is, perhaps, an important moral distinction between killing and letting die. But once the mother's personal autonomy is respected by honoring her request to end her pregnancy (because the fetus has no right to occupy her uterus) there seems to be little reason for assuming that there is nothing morally wrong with letting the aborted fetus die. There may be cases where this would be right—e.g., if the fetus is irretrievably deformed or damaged by the abortion process—but this will not be true in all cases, and the abortion procedure itself should ideally be designed to minimize damage to the fetus. That is, the mother (and everyone else) is entitled to demand neither that the fetus be killed after abortion, nor that it not be resuscitated.

On the other hand, it also becomes necessary to reexamine some of the morally peculiar views about viability. Many have been inclined to agree with American abortion policy which treats viability as the cutoff point for most permissible abortions. This view suggests that it is all right to expel the fetus from the uterus until the point in its development when it is able to survive outside the uterus—at which time it becomes impermissible to expel the fetus. The anomaly is made even worse by the fact that while the age of fetal viability is declining, the age at which abortions can safely (for the woman) be performed is moving up. But neither sheer length of gestation, nor capacity for survival outside the uterus, confer on the fetus a right to occupancy of the uterus. Engelhardt points out that if reproductive technology develops to the point that a fetus could be brought to term *in vitro* then "all conceptuses would be viable in the sense of being at a stage at which there are known survivors."[33] He then asks whether this should result in the prohibition of all abortions. But if we agree that the fetus has no right to occupancy of the uterus, we can see that such a general prohibition would not be justified in these circumstances. Achievement of viability does not confer rights on the fetus.

Treatment of the Fetus

When a spontaneous miscarriage occurs, people mourn—and perhaps not only for the woman whose pregnancy has ended, but for the loss of a being which they regard as valuable. In fact, in many cases greater efforts have been and are being taken to preserve and enhance the life of the fetus *in utero*. Consider, for example, the importance of proper diet, not smoking, and reduced alcohol consumption enjoined upon pregnant women and, in most cases, willingly agreed to by them. Furthermore, concern has often been expressed about possible damage to the fetus from environmental or workplace hazards.[34] Consider, also, the more recent developments in fetal surgery, which may involve discomfort and inconvenience for the woman, for the sake of correction of fetal abnormalities.[35] There have even been cases in which mothers have been suspected or found guilty of prenatal child abuse through indulgence in activities, such as repeated drug use, which threaten the fetus's well-being.[36] All of these practices are difficult to reconcile with the usual liberal view on abortion, which tends to see the fetus as merely a (disposable) part of the mother's body. From an extreme liberal point of view, care for the fetus can only be understood by reference to the parent's desire to have a healthy child at the end of the pregnancy, or perhaps by the need to avoid unnecessary medical costs of caring for disabled children. But the view defended here, that there is no general right to kill the fetus, raises the possibility that these practices also reflect some responsibilities on the part of society to the fetus itself. They lead us to suspect that, perhaps, no one has a right to injure, deform, or mutilate the fetus. (But I shall not here defend this claim, which would have implications both for maternal behavior during pregnancy, and for fetal research.[37] I shall only note that even an extreme proponent of a liberal position on abortion, Michael Tooley, is willing to state that a being such as a kitten which has, he thinks, no right to life, may nevertheless have a right not to be tortured.[38])

Future Developments

Looking ahead, there are further potential advantages to the view put forward here. First, if fetuses are removed from the uterus without being killed, it is possible that a type of fetal adoption could sometimes be undertaken.[39] Through the use of fetal transfer many infertile and childless couples, who must otherwise wait years to receive a much-wanted baby, would have the opportunity to be parents. The sadness of involuntary childlessness would thus be reduced, at least for those women whose bodies are physically capable of pregnancy.

Second, perhaps as important, the fetuses, if transferred, would be wanted.

In his *The Secret Life of the Unborn Child,* Thomas Verney makes very clear the effects of prenatal influences on the developing fetus.[40] Even if only half of the claims he makes about physical and psychological effects turn out to be wholly correct, the well-being of the child is very much a function of what happens to it as a fetus. The liberal position on abortion emphasizes an important value when it insists that every child should be a wanted child. This is significant not only for the parents but for the child itself. Unwanted children seem likely to suffer various forms of prenatal abuse and neglect.[41] Thus, when a fetus is not wanted, it is clearly to its own benefit as well as that of its parents to remove it from its biological mother's uterus and place it in a more receptive and less dangerous environment.

IV

Having detailed some advantages of my position, I must also concede that it raises a good many problems. If fetal survival outside the uterus becomes more and more frequent, and we accept, as I think we may have to, the two claims, (c) and (d), developed here, then we will find that our moral quandaries have merely shifted from the process of abortion itself, to the events which follow the abortion. I make no apologies for the problems which arise, because I believe that technology will eventually force us to face them, regardless of what values and beliefs we choose to adopt. These problems include, but are not confined to, the following:

(i) If fetal survival becomes commonplace, would we have an obligation to preserve all aborted fetuses? As Somerville points out, "arguing that the lives of viable to-be-aborted fetuses should be preserved even though they may be aborted is artificially to create a group of newborns at much higher risk of being defective than babies born at term." These babies "are at a high risk of being mentally or physically handicapped by their premature expulsion into the world . . . therefore require specialized and expensive treatment."[42]

(ii) Should all fetuses some day be considered candidates for "fetal adoption"? It is not clear whether there are enough women willing to undertake this form of adoption. And for those who are, is some sort of screening process appropriate? That is, how should it be decided which women should be candidates for fetal adoption? Should the screening process be like that given now to prospective couples for IVF, or should it be like the more rigorous screening now given to adoptive parents?

(iii) What limitations, if any, should be placed on the availability of abortion, understood as the emptying of the uterus? Freitas argues that a woman "should be free to surrender her fetus for adoption at any time during pregnancy."[43] Since the fetus has no right to occupancy of its mother's uterus, this appears justifiable. But it might turn out to be important to make embryo transfer very easily available during the first three months of pregnancy, and then encourage a feeling of commitment and responsibility to the fetus after that point. If "bonding" with the fetus is important, then its well-being will be enhanced by ensuring that it is reimplanted within a willing surrogate mother as soon as possible. This will not occur if women are encouraged to postpone for several months their decision about whether or not to continue a pregnancy.

(iv) Finally, the existence of embryo banks now in use in Australia suggests the possibility that aborted fetuses might be maintained, frozen, in fetal banks. This procedure, however, would merely postpone the question of what is to be the fate of fetuses that survive abortion.

The development of new reproductive technologies requires a reformation of existing views about abortion. When fetal survival becomes routinely possible, it will be necessary to confront some difficult questions about the treatment of the fetus. But these developments also enable us to make the crucial distinction between emptying the uterus and killing the fetus, and to see that while the fetus has no right to occupancy of its mother's (or anyone's) uterus, we also have no right to kill the fetus.

NOTES

1. "Fetus" will be used here generally to refer to the developing zygote/embryo/fetus throughout its nine-months gestation, except when referring specifically to very early stages of gestation, when the term "embryo" will be used.

2. Roger Wertheimer, "Understanding the Abortion Argument," in *Moral Problems,* 2nd ed., ed. James Rachels (New York: Harper & Row, 1975), p. 85.

3. Mary B. Mahowald makes a similar distinction between different concepts of abortion. Abortion, she says, is either the "premature termination of pregnancy," or the "termination of fetal life" ("Concepts of Abortion and Their Relevance to the Abortion Debate," *Southern Journal of Philosophy* 20 [1982], p. 195).

4. For example, see Joel Feinberg, "Abortion," in *Matters of Life and Death: New Introductory Essays in Moral Philosophy,* ed. Tom Regan (New York: Random House, 1981), p. 183.

5. See Susan T. Nicholson, "The Roman Catholic Doctrine of Therapeutic Abortion," in *Feminism and Philosophy,* ed. Mary Vetterling-Braggin, Frederick A. Elliston, and Jane English (Totawa, NJ: Littlefield, Adams & Co., 1978), p. 392. The distinction is also employed by John Morreall in "Of Marsupials and Men: A Thought Experiment on Abortion," *Dialogos* 37 (1981): 16; by Steven L. Ross in "Abortion and the Death of the Fetus," *Philosophy and Public Affairs* 11 (1982): 232; by Daniel I. Wikler in "Ought We to Save Aborted Fetuses?" *Ethics* 90 (1978): 64; and by Raymond M. Herbenick in "Remarks on Abortion, Abandonment, and Adoption Opportunities," *Philosophy and Public Affairs* 5 (1975): 98.

6. A "moderate" position on abortion, not discussed here, has also been defended. See L. W. Sumner, "Toward a Credible View of Abortion," *Canadian Journal of Philosophy* IV (1974): 163–81.

7. An informative discussion of *in vitro* fertilization is given by John F. Leeton, Alan O. Trounson, and Carl Wood, in "IVF and ET: What It Is and How It Works," in *Test-Tube Babies,* ed. William Walters and Peter Singer (Melbourne, Australia: Oxford University Press, 1982), pp. 2–10.

8. Ectogenesis, the growth of the fetus outside of the human uterus, is discussed by William A. W. Walters in "Cloning, Ectogenesis, and Hybrids: Things to Come?" in *Test-Tube Babies,* pp. 115–17.

9. See Robert A. Freitas, Jr., "Fetal Adoption: A Technological Solution to the Problem of Abortion Ethics," *The Humanist*, May/June 1980, pp. 22–23.

10. Cf. Ronald Dworkin, *Taking Rights Seriously* (Cambridge, MA: Harvard University Press, 1977), p. 188.

11. "Abortion and the Golden Rule," in *Philosophy and Sex*, ed. Robert Baker and Frederick Elliston (Buffalo: Prometheus Books, 1975), p. 357.

12. "A Defense of Abortion," in *Moral Problems*, 2nd ed., p. 106.

13. Jane English, "Abortion: Introduction," in *Feminism and Philosophy*, p. 422; Frances Myrna, "The Right to Abortion," in *Ethics for Modern Life*, ed. Raziel Abelson and Marie-Louise Friquegnon (New York: St. Martin's Press, 1982), pp. 114–15.

14. "On the Moral and Legal Status of Abortion," in *Today's Moral Problems*, ed. Richard Wasserstrom (New York: Macmillan, 1975), p. 136, my emphasis.

15. "Reflections on Canadian Abortion Law: Evacuation and Destruction—Two Separate Issues," *University of Toronto Law Journal* 001 31 (1981): 12.

16. Cf. Charles B. Daniels, "Abortion and Potential," *Dialogue* 18 (1979): 223, 1.

17. Ernlé W. D. Young, "Caring for Disabled Infants," *The Hastings Center Report* 13 (August 1983): 16.

18. "An Ethical Approach to IVF and ET: What Ethics Is All About," in *Test-Tube Babies*, p. 34.

19. "The Moral Status of the Embryo," in *Test-Tube Babies*, pp. 57 ff.

20. Feinberg, p. 204.

21. Thomson, pp. 95, 90.

22. Warren, p. 121; Feinberg, p. 204.

23. Cf. Ellen Frankel Paul and Jeffrey Paul, "Self-Ownership, Abortion and Infanticide," *Journal of Medical Ethics* 5 (1979): 134.

24. Thomson, pp. p. 96.

25. "A Religious Pacifist Looks at Abortion," in *Personal and Social Ethics: Moral Problems with Integrated Theory*, ed. Vincent Barry (Belmont, CA: Wadsworth, 1978), p. 226, Zahn's emphasis.

26. Thomson gives a similar example, p. 105. Cf. Morreall, p. 11.

27. Germain Crisez, "Abortion: Ethical Arguments," in *Today's Moral Problems*, p. 102.

28. Ross, p. 238, his emphasis.

29. Ibid., p. 240.

30. Ibid., p. 243.

31. "Viability and the Use of the Fetus," in *Ethics and Public Policy*, ed. Tom L. Beauchamp and Terry P. Pinkard (Englewood Cliffs, NJ: Prentice-Hall 1980), pp. 308–08.

32. Wikler, p. 60. Cf. Paul and Paul, p. 133; and Thomas P. Carney, *Instant Evolution: We'd Better Get Good At It* (Notre Dame, IN: University of Notre Dame Press, 1980), p. 16.

33. Engelhardt, p. 307.

34. See Nancy Miller Chenier, *Reproductive Hazards at Work: Men, Women and the Fertility Gamble* (Canadian Advisory Council on the Status of Women, December, 1982).

35. William Ruddick and William Wilcox, "Operating on the Fetus," *The Hastings Center Report* 12 (October 1982): 10–14.

36. See Madam Justice Proudfoot, "Judgment Respecting Female Infant 'D.J.,' " in *Contemporary Moral Issues*, ed. Wesley Cragg (Toronto: McGraw-Hill Ryerson Limited, 1983), pp. 16–18; Ian Gentles, "The Unborn Child in Civil and Criminal Law," ibid., pp. 19–29; and E. W. Keyserlingk, "Balancing Prenatal Care and Abortion," ibid., pp. 29–37. Gentles points out the irony that under Canadian law an "unborn child" enjoys several legal rights—including the right to sue for injuries incurred while *in utero*—but not the right not to be killed (p. 19).

37. Carney discusses the apparent contradiction in American law which makes destruction of the fetus through abortion legal, but experimentation on the fetus ille-

gal (Carney, p. 126). See also George Schedler and Matthew J. Kelly, "Abortion and Tinkering," *Dialogue* 17 (1978): 122–25.

38. "Abortion and Infanticide," in *Values in Conflict,* ed. Burton M. Leiser (New York: Macmillan, 1981), p. 61.

39. See Wikler. This would avoid the enforced pregnancies that would seem to result from Herbenick's suggestion that the state could intervene, when an abortion is sought, to take custody of a fetus for purposes of its adoption at birth by an interested couple (Herbenick, pp. 102–04).

40. New York: Summit Books, 1981.

41. Morreall ignores this possibility entirely when he argues in favor of carrying a fetus to term rather than aborting it, in its fourth or fifth month, for reasons of maternal "convenience" or "embarrassment" (Morreall, p. 17).

42. Somerville, pp. 23, 22.

43. Freitas, p. 23.

CHAPTER 14
OPINION IN THE MATTER OF
DAVIS VS. DAVIS

SUPREME COURT OF THE STATE OF TENNESSEE
(1992)

IN THE SUPREME COURT OF TENNESSEE AT KNOXVILLE

JUNIOR LEWIS DAVIS,
          Plaintiff-Appellee,
v.
MARY SUE DAVIS,
          Defendant-Appellant.

For Publication
Filed: June 1, 1992
No. 34
Blount County
The Hon. W. Dale Young, Judge

For the Appellee:

CHARLES M. CLIFFORD
Maryville, Tennessee

*For the Amici Curiae American
Fertility Society, et al.:*

BARRY FRIEDMAN
Nashville, Tennessee

ELLEN WRIGHT CLAYTON
Nashville, Tennessee

JANET BENSHOOF
RACHAEL N. PINE
LYNN M. PALTROW
132 West 43rd Street
New York, New York

DAVID L. GOLDBERG
New York, New York

COURT OF APPEALS AFFIRMED

Martha Craig Daughtrey, Justice

For the Appellant:

KURT ERLENBACH
503 South Palm Avenue
Titusville, Florida

*For the Amicus Curiae American
Academy of Medical Ethics:*

KEVIN J. TODD
CLARKE D. FORSYTHE
343 S. Dearborn Street
Chicago, Illinois

RICHARD J. RYAN, JR.
Memphis, Tennessee

OPINION

This appeal presents a question of first impression, involving the disposition of the cryogenically-preserved product of *in vitro* fertilization (IVF), commonly referred to in the popular press and the legal journals as "frozen embryos." The case began as a divorce action, filed by the appellee, Junior Lewis Davis, against his then wife, appellant Mary Sue Davis. The parties were able to agree upon all terms of dissolution, except one: who was to have "custody" of the seven "frozen embryos" stored in a Knoxville fertility clinic that had attempted to assist the Davises in achieving a much-wanted pregnancy during a happier period in their relationship.

I. INTRODUCTION

Mary Sue Davis originally asked for control of the "frozen embryos" with the intent to have them transferred to her own uterus, in a post-divorce effort to become pregnant. Junior Davis objected, saying that he preferred to leave the embryos in their frozen state until he decided whether or not he wanted to become a parent outside the bounds of marriage.

Based on its determination that the embryos were "human beings" from the moment of fertilization, the trial court awarded "custody" to Mary Sue Davis and directed that she "be permitted the opportunity to bring these children to term through implantation." The Court of Appeals reversed, finding that Junior Davis has a "constitutionally protected right not to beget a child where no pregnancy has taken place" and holding that "there is no compelling state interest to justify [] ordering implantation against the will of either party." The Court of Appeals further held that "the parties share an interest in the seven fertilized ova" and remanded the case to the trial court for entry of an order vesting them with "joint control . . . and equal voice over their disposition."

Mary Sue Davis then sought review in this Court, contesting the validity of the constitutional basis for the Court of Appeals decision. We granted review, not because we disagree with the basic legal analysis utilized by the intermediate court, but because of the obvious importance of the case in terms of the development of law regarding the new reproductive technologies, and because the decision of the Court of Appeals does not give adequate guidance to the trial court in the event the parties cannot agree.

We note, in this latter regard, that their positions have already shifted: both have remarried and Mary Sue Davis (now Mary Sue Stowe) has moved out of state. She no longer wishes to utilize the "frozen embryos" herself, but wants authority to donate them to a childless couple. Junior Davis is adamantly opposed to such donation and would prefer to see the "frozen embryos" discarded. The result is, once again, an impasse, but the parties' current legal position does have an effect on the probable outcome of the case, as discussed below.

At the outset, it is important to note the absence of two critical factors that might otherwise influence or control the result of this litigation: When the Davises signed up for the IVF program at the Knoxville clinic, they did not execute a written agreement specifying what disposition should be made of any unused embryos that might result from the cryopreservation process. Moreover, there was at that time no Tennessee statute governing such disposition, nor has one been enacted in the meantime.[1]

In addition, because of the uniqueness of the question before us, we have no case law to guide us to a decision in this case. Despite the fact that over 5,000 IVF babies have been born in this country and the fact that some 20,000 or more "frozen embryos" remain in storage, there are apparently very few other litigated cases involving the disputed disposition of untransferred "frozen embryos," and none is on point with the facts in this case.[2]

But, if we have no statutory authority or common law precedents to guide us, we do have the benefit of extensive comment and analysis in the legal journals. In those articles, medical-legal scholars and ethicists have proposed various models for the disposition of "frozen embryos" when unanticipated contingencies arise, such as divorce, death of one or both of the parties, financial reversals, or simple disenchantment with the IVF process. Those models range from a rule requiring, at one extreme, that all embryos be used by the gamete-providers or donated for uterine transfer, and, at the other extreme, that any unused embryos be automatically discarded.[3] Other formulations would vest control in the female gamete-provider—in every case, because of her greater physical and emotional contribution to the IVF process,[4] or perhaps only in the event that she wishes to use them herself.[5] There are also two "implied contract" models: one would infer from enrollment in an IVF program that the IVF clinic has authority to decide in the event of an impasse whether to donate, discard, or use the "frozen embryos" for research; the other would infer from the parties' participation in the creation of the embryos that they had made an irrevocable commitment to reproduction and would require transfer either to the female provider or to a donee. There are also the so-called "equity models": one would avoid the conflict altogether by dividing the "frozen embryos" equally between the parties, to do with as they wish;[6] the other would award veto power to the party wishing to avoid parenthood, whether it be the female or the male progenitor.[7]

Each of these possible models has the virtue of ease of application. Adoption of any of them would establish a bright-line test that would dispose of disputes like the one we have before us in a clear and predictable manner. As appealing as that possibility might seem, we conclude that given the relevant principles of constitutional law, the existing public policy of Tennessee with regard to unborn life, the current state of scientific knowledge giving rise to the emerging reproductive technologies, and the ethical considerations that have developed in response to that scientific knowledge, there can be no easy answer to the question we now face. We conclude, instead, that we must weigh the interests of each party to the dispute, in terms of the facts and analysis set out below, in order to resolve that dispute in a fair and responsible manner.

II. THE FACTS

Mary Sue Davis and Junior Lewis Davis met while they were both in the Army and stationed in Germany in the spring of 1979. After a period of courtship, they came home to the United States and were married on April 26, 1980. When their leave was up, they then returned to their posts in Germany as a married couple.

Within six months of returning to Germany, Mary Sue became pregnant but unfortunately suffered an extremely painful tubal pregnancy, as a result of which she had surgery to remove her right fallopian tube. This tubal pregnancy was followed by four others during the course of the marriage. After her fifth tubal pregnancy, Mary Sue chose to have her left fallopian tube ligated, thus leaving her without functional fallopian tubes by which to conceive naturally. The Davises attempted to adopt a child but, at the last minute, the child's birth-mother changed her mind about putting the child up for adoption. Other paths to adoption turned out to be prohibitively expensive. In vitro fertilization became essentially the only option for the Davises to pursue in their attempt to become parents.

As explained at trial, IVF involves the aspiration of ova from the follicles of a woman's ovaries, fertilization of these ova in a petri dish using the sperm provided by a man, and the transfer of the product of this procedure into the uterus of the woman from whom the ova were taken.[8] Implantation may then occur, resulting in a pregnancy and, it is hoped, the birth of a child.

Beginning in 1985, the Davises went through six attempts at IVF, at a total cost of $35,000, but the hoped-for pregnancy never occurred. Despite her fear of needles, at each IVF attempt Mary Sue underwent the month of subcutaneous injections necessary to shut down her pituitary gland and the eight days of intermuscular injections necessary to stimulate her ovaries to produce ova. She was anesthetized five times for the aspiration procedure to be performed. Forty-eight to 72 hours after each aspiration, she returned for transfer back to her uterus, only to receive a negative pregnancy test result each time.

The Davises then opted to postpone another round of IVF until after the clinic with which they were working was prepared to offer them cryogenic preservation, scheduled for November 1988. Using this process, if more ova are aspirated and fertilized than needed, the conceptive product may be cryogenically preserved (frozen in nitrogen and stored at sub-zero temperatures) for later transfer if the transfer performed immediately does not result in a pregnancy. The unavailability of this procedure had not been a hinderance to previous IVF attempts by the Davises because Mary Sue had produced at most only three or four ova, despite hormonal stimulation. However, on their last attempt, on December 8, 1988, the gynecologist who performed the procedure was able to retrieve nine ova for fertilization. The resulting one-celled entities, referred to before division as zygotes, were then allowed to develop in petri dishes in the laboratory until they reached the four- to eight-cell stage.

Needless to say, the Davises were pleased at the initial success of the procedure. At the time, they had no thoughts of divorce and the abundance of ova for fertilization offered them a better chance at parenthood, because Mary Sue Davis could attempt to achieve a pregnancy without additional rounds of hormonal stimulation and aspiration. They both testified that although the process of cryogenic preservation was described to them, no one explained the ways in which it would change the nature of IVF for them.[9] There is, for example, no indication that they ever considered the implications of storage beyond the few months it would take to transfer the remaining "frozen embryos," if necessary. There was no discussion, let alone an agreement, concerning disposition in the event of a contingency such as divorce.

After fertilization was completed, a transfer was performed as usual on December 10, 1988; the rest of the four-to eight-cell entities were cryogenically preserved. Unfortunately, a pregnancy did not result from the December 1988 transfer, and before another transfer could be attempted, Junior Davis filed for divorce—in February 1989. He testified that he had known that their marriage "was not very stable" for a year or more, but had hoped that the birth of a child would improve their relationship. Mary Sue Davis testified that she had no idea that there was a problem with their marriage.[10] As noted earlier, the divorce proceedings were complicated only by the issue of the disposition of the "frozen embryos."

III. THE SCIENTIFIC TESTIMONY

In the record, and especially in the trial court's opinion, there is a great deal of discussion about the proper descriptive terminology to be used in this case. Although this discussion appears at first glance to be a matter simply of semantics, semantical distinctions are significant in this context, because language defines legal status and can limit legal rights.[11] Obviously, an "adult" has a different legal status than does a "child." Likewise, "child" means something other than "fetus." A "fetus" differs from an "embryo." There was much dispute at trial about whether the four- to eight-cell entities in this case should properly be referred to as "embryos" or as "preembryos," with resulting differences in legal analysis.

One expert, a French geneticist named Dr. Jerome Lejeune, insisted that there was no recognized scientific distinction between the two terms. He referred to the four- to eight-cell entities at issue here as "early human beings," as "tiny persons," and as his "kin." Although he is an internationally recognized geneticist, Dr. Lejeune's background fails to reflect any degree of expertise in obstetrics or gynecology (specifically in the field of infertility) or in medical ethics. His testimony revealed a profound confusion between science and religion. For example, he was deeply moved that "Madame [Mary Sue], the mother, wants to rescue babies from this concentration can," and he concluded that Junior Davis has a moral duty to try to bring these "tiny human beings" to term.[12]

Dr. Lejeune's opinion was disputed by Dr. Irving Ray King, the gynecologist who performed the IVF procedures in this case. Dr. King is a medical doctor who had practiced as a sub-specialist in the areas of infertility and reproductive endocrinology for 12 years. He established the Fertility Center of East Tennessee in Knoxville in 1984 and had worked extensively with IVF and cryopreservation. He testified that the currently accepted term of the zygote immediately after division is "preembryo" and that this term applies up until 14 days after fertilization. He testified that this 14-day period defines the accepted period for preembryo research. At about 14 days, he testified, the group of cells begins to differentiate in a process that permits the eventual development of the different body parts which will become an individual.

Dr. King's testimony was corroborated by the other experts who testified at trial, with the exception of Dr. Lejeune. It is further supported by the American Fertility Society, an organization of 10,000 physicians and scientists who specialize in problems of human infertility. The Society's June 1990 report on Ethical Considerations of the New Reproductive Technologies indicates that from the point of fertilization, the resulting one-cell zygote contains "a new hereditary constitution (genome) contributed to by both parents through the union of sperm and egg." 53 *Fertility & Sterility*, no. 6, 31S (June 1990). Continuing, the report notes:

> The stage subsequent to the zygote is cleavage, during which the single initial cell undergoes successive equal divisions with little or no intervening growth. As a result, the product cells (blastomeres) become successively smaller, while the size of the total aggregate of the cells remains about the same. After three such divisions, the aggregate contains eight cells in relatively loose association. . . . [E]ach blastomere, if separated from the others, has the potential to develop into a complete adult. . . . Stated another way, at the 8-cell stage, the developmental singleness of one person has not yet been established.
>
> Beyond the 8-cell stage, individual blastomeres begin to lose their zygote-like properties. Two divisions after the 8-cell stage, the 32 blastomeres are increasingly adherent, closely packed, and no longer of equal developmental potential. The impression now conveyed is of a multicellular entity, rather than of a loose packet of identical cells.
>
> As the number of cells continues to increase, some are formed into a surface layer, surrounding others within. The outer layers have changed in properties toward trophoblast . . . , which is destined [to become part of the placenta]. The less-altered inner cells will be the source of the later embryo. The developing entity is now referred to as a blastocyst, characterized by a continuous peripheral layer of cells and a small cellular population within a central cavity. . . . It is at about this stage that the [normally] developing entity usually completes its transit through the oviduct to enter the uterus.
>
> Cell division continues and the blastocyst enlarges through increase of both cell number and [volume]. The populations of inner and outer cells become increasingly different, not only in position and shape but in synthetic activities as well. The change is primarily in the outer population, which is

altering rapidly as the blastocyst interacts with and implants into the uterine wall. . . . Thus, the first cellular differentiation of the new generation relates to physiologic interaction with the mother, rather than to the establishment of the embryo itself. *It is for this reason that it is appropriate to refer to the developing entity up to this point as a preembryo, rather than an embryo.*

Id. at 31S-32S (emphasis added). For a similar description of the biologic difference between a preembryo and an embryo, see Robertson, *In the Beginning: The Legal Status of Early Embryos,* 76 Va. L. Rev. 437 (1990), in which the author summarizes the findings of Clifford Grobstein in *The Early Development of Human Embryos,* 10 J. Med. & Phil. 213 (1985).

Admittedly, this distinction is not dispositive in the case before us.[13] It deserves emphasis only because inaccuracy can lead to misanalysis such as occurred at the trial level in this case. The trial court reasoned that if there is no distinction between embryos and preembryos, as Dr. Lejeune theorized, then Dr. Lejeune must also have been correct when he asserted that "human life begins at the moment of conception." From this proposition, the trial judge concluded that the eight-cell entities at issue were not preembryos but were "children in vitro." He then invoked the doctrine of *parens patriae* and held that it was "in the best interest of the children" to be born rather than destroyed. Finding that Mary Sue Davis was willing to provide such an opportunity, but that Junior Davis was not, the trial judge awarded her "custody" of the "children in vitro."

The Court of Appeals explicitly rejected the trial judge's reasoning, as well as the result. Indeed, the argument that "human life begins at the moment of conception" and that these four- to eight-cell entities therefore have a legal right to be born has apparently been abandoned by the appellant, despite her success with it in the trial court.[14] We have nevertheless been asked by the American Fertility Society, joined by 19 other national organizations allied in this case as amici curiae, to respond to this issue because of its far-reaching implications in other cases of this kind. We find the request meritorious.

IV. THE "PERSON" VS. "PROPERTY" DICHOTOMY

One of the fundamental issues the inquiry poses is whether the preembryos in this case should be considered "persons" or "property" in the contemplation of the law. The Court of Appeals held, correctly, that they cannot be considered "persons" under Tennessee law:

> The policy of the state on the subject matter before us may be gleaned from the state's treatment of fetuses in the womb. . . . The state's Wrongful Death Statute, Tenn. Code Ann. § 20–5–106 does not allow a wrongful death for a viable fetus that is not first born alive. Without live birth, the Supreme Court has said, a fetus is not a "person" within the meaning of the statue. *See e.g., Hamby v. McDaniel,* 559 S.W.2d 774 (Tenn. 1977); *Durrett v. Owens,* 212 Tenn. 614, 371 S.W.2d 433 (1963); *Shousha v. Matthews Drivurself Service,* 210 Tenn. 384, 358 S.W.2d 471 (1962); *Hogan v. McDaniel,* 204 Tenn., 235. 319

S.W.2d 221 (1958). Other enactments by the legislature demonstrate even more explicitly that viable fetuses in the womb are not entitled to the same protection as "persons". Tenn. Code Ann. § 39–15–201 incorporates the trimester approach to abortion outlined in *Roe v. Wade,* 410 U.S. 113 (1973). A woman and her doctor may decide on abortion within the first three months of pregnancy but after three months, and before viability, abortion may occur at a properly regulated facility. Moreover, after viability, abortion may be chosen to save the life of the mother. This statutory scheme indicates that as embryos develop, they are accorded more respect than mere human cells because of their burgeoning potential for life. But, even after viability, they are not given legal status equivalent to that of a person already born. This concept is echoed in Tennessee's murder and assault statutes, which provide that an attack or homicide of a viable fetus may be a crime but abortion is not. *See* Tenn. Code Ann. §§ 39–13–107 and 39–13–210.

Junior Lewis Davis v. Mary Sue Davis, Tennessee Court of Appeals at Knoxville, No. 180, slip op. at 5–6 (Sept. 13, 1990).

Nor do preembryos enjoy protection as "persons" under federal law. In *Roe v. Wade,* 410 U.S. 113 (1973), the United States Supreme Court explicitly refused to hold that the fetus possesses independent rights under law, based upon a thorough examination of the federal constitution,[15] relevant common law principles, and the lack of scientific consensus as to when life begins. The Supreme Court concluded that "the unborn have never been recognized in the law as persons in the whole sense." *Id.* at 162. As a matter of constitutional law, this conclusion has never been seriously challenged.[16] Hence, even as the Supreme Court in *Webster v. Reproductive Health Services,* 492 U.S. 490 (1989), permitted the states some additional leeway in regulating the right to abortion established in *Roe v. Wade,* the *Webster* decision did no more than recognize a compelling state interest in potential life at the point when viability is possible. Thus, as Justice O'Connor noted, "[v]iability remains the 'critical point.' " *Id.* at 529 (O'Connor, J., concurring). That stage of fetal developmental is far removed, both qualitatively and quantitatively, from that of the four- to eight-cell preembryos in this case.[17]

Left undisturbed, the trial court's ruling would have afforded preembryos the legal status of "persons" and vested them with legally cognizable interests separate from those of their progenitors. Such a decision would doubtless have had the effect of outlawing IVF programs in the state of Tennessee. But in setting aside the trial court's judgment, the Court of Appeals, at least by implication, may have swung too far in the opposite direction.

The intermediate court, without explicitly holding that the preembryos in this case were "property," nevertheless awarded "joint control" of them to Mary Sue Davis and Junior Davis, citing T.C.A. §§ 68–30–101 and 39–15–208, and *York v. Jones,* 717 F.Supp. 421 (E.D. Va. 1989), for the proposition that "the parties share an interest in the seven fertilized ova." The intermediate court did not otherwise define this interest.

The provisions of T.C.A §§ 68–30–101 *et seq.,* on which the intermediate appellate court relied, codify the Uniform Anatomical Gift Act. T.C.A. § 39–

15–208 prohibits experimentation or research using an aborted fetus in the absence of the woman's consent. These statutes address the question of who controls disposition of human organs and tissue with no further potential for autonomous human life; they are not precisely controlling on the question before us, because the "tissue" involved here *does* have the potential for developing into independent human life, even if it is not yet legally recognizable as human life itself.

The intermediate court's reliance on *York v. Jones,* is even more troublesome. That case involved a dispute between a married couple undergoing IVF procedures at the Jones Institute for Reproductive Medicine in Virginia. When the Yorks decided to move to California, they asked the Institute to transfer the one remaining "frozen embryo" that they had produced to a fertility clinic in San Diego for later implantation. The Institute refused and the Yorks sued. The federal district court assumed without deciding that the subject matter of the dispute was "property." The *York* court held that the "cryopreservation agreement" between the Yorks and the Institute created a bailment relationship, obligating the Institute to return the subject of the bailment to the Yorks once the purpose of the bailment had terminated. 717 F. Supp. at 424–425.

In this case, by citing to *York v. Jones* but failing to define precisely the "interest" that Mary Sue Davis and Junior Davis have in the preembryos, the Court of Appeals has left the implication that it is in the nature of a property interest. For purposes of clarity in future cases, we conclude that this point must be further addressed.

To our way of thinking, the most helpful discussion on this point is found not in the minuscule number of legal opinions that have involved "frozen embryos," but in the ethical standards set by The American Fertility Society, as follows:

> Three major ethical positions have been articulated in the debate over preembryo status. At one extreme is the view of the preembryo as a human subject after fertilization, which requires that it be accorded the rights of a person. This position entails an obligation to provide an opportunity for implantation to occur and tends to ban any action before transfer that might harm the preembryo or that is not immediately therapeutic, such as freezing and some preembryo research.
>
> At the opposite extreme is the view that the preembryo has a status no different from any other human tissue. With the consent of those who have decision-making authority over the preembryo, no limits should be imposed on actions taken with preembryos.
>
> A third view—one that is most widely held—takes an intermediate position between the other two. It holds that the preembryo deserves respect greater than that accorded to human tissue but not the respect accorded to actual persons. The preembryo is due greater respect than other human tissue because of its potential to become a person and because of its symbolic meaning for many people. Yet, it should not be treated as a person, because it has not yet developed the features of personhood, is not yet established as developmentally individual, and may never realize its biologic potential.

53 *Fertility and Sterility,* no. 6, *supra,* at 34S–35S (citation omitted).

Although the report alludes to the role of "special respect" in the context of research on preembryos not intended for transfer, it is clear that the Ethics Committee's principal concern was with the treatment accorded the transferred embryo. Thus, the Ethics Committee concludes that "special respect is necessary to protect the welfare of potential offspring . . . [and] creates obligations not to hurt or injure the offspring who might be born after transfer [by research or intervention with a preembryo]." *Id.* at 35S.

In its report, the Ethics Committee then calls upon those in charge of IVF programs to establish policies in keeping with the "special respect" due preembryos and suggests:

> Within the limits set by institutional policies, decision-making authority regarding preembryos should reside with the persons who have provided the gametes. . . . As a matter of law, it is reasonable to assume that the gamete providers have primary decision-making authority regarding preembryos in the absence of specific legislation on the subject. A person's liberty to procreate or to avoid procreation is directly involved in most decisions involving preembryos.

Id. at 36S.

We conclude that preembryos are not, strictly speaking, either "persons" or "property," but occupy an interim category that entitles them to special respect because of their potential for human life. It follows that any interest that Mary Sue Davis and Junior Davis have in the preembryos in this case is not a true property interest. However, they do have an interest in the nature of ownership, to the extent that they have decision-making authority concerning disposition of the preembryos, within the scope of policy set by law.

V. THE ENFORCEABILITY OF CONTRACT

Establishing the locus of the decision-making authority in this context is crucial to deciding whether the parties could have made a valid contingency agreement prior to undergoing the IVF procedures and whether such an agreement would now be enforceable on the question of disposition. Under the trial court's analysis, obviously, an agreement of this kind would be unenforceable in the event of a later disagreement, because the trial court would have to make an ad hoc "best interest of the child" determination in every case. In its opinion, the Court of Appeals did not address the question of the enforceability of prior agreements, undoubtedly because that issue was not directly raised on appeal. Despite our reluctance to treat a question not strictly necessary to the result in the case, we conclude that discussion is warranted in order to provide the necessary guidance to all those involved with IVF procedures in Tennessee in the future—the health care professionals who administer IVF programs and the scientists who engage in infertility research, as well as prospective parents seeking to achieve pregnancy by means of IVF, their physicians, and their counselors.

We believe, as a starting point, that an agreement regarding disposition of any untransferred preembryos in the event of contingencies (such as the death of one or more of the parties, divorce, financial reversals, or abandonment of the program) should be presumed valid and should be enforced as between the progenitors. This conclusion is in keeping with the proposition that the progenitors, having provided the gametic material giving rise to the preembryos, retain decision-making authority as to their disposition.[18]

At the same time, we recognize that life is not static, and that human emotions run particularly high when a married couple is attempting to overcome infertility problems. It follows that the parties' initial "informed consent" to IVF procedures will often not be truly informed because of the near impossibility of anticipating, emotionally and psychologically, all the turns that events may take as the IVF process unfolds. Providing that the initial agreements may later be modified *by agreement* will, we think, protect the parties against some of the risks they face in this regard. But, in the absence of such agreed modification, we conclude that their prior agreements should be considered binding.

It might be argued in this case that the parties had an implied contract to reproduce using *in vitro* fertilization, that Mary Sue Davis relied on that agreement in undergoing IVF procedures, and that the court should enforce an implied contract against Junior Davis, allowing Mary Sue to dispose of the preembryos in a manner calculated to result in reproduction. The problem with such an analysis is that there is no indication in the record that disposition in the event of contingencies other than Mary Sue Davis's pregnancy was ever considered by the parties, or that Junior Davis intended to pursue reproduction outside the confines of a continuing marital relationship with Mary Sue. We therefore decline to decide this case on the basis of implied contract or the reliance doctrine.[19]

We are therefore left with this situation: there was initially no agreement between the parties concerning disposition of the preembryos under the circumstances of this case; there has been no agreement since; and there is no formula in the Court of Appeals opinion for determining the outcome if the parties cannot reach an agreement in the future.

In granting joint control to the parties, the Court of Appeals must have anticipated that, in the absence of agreement, the preembryos would continue to be stored, as they now are, in the Knoxville fertility clinic. One problem with maintaining the status quo is that the viability of the preembryos cannot be guaranteed indefinitely. Experts in cryopreservation who testified in this case estimated the maximum length of preembryonic viability at two years.[20] Thus, the true effect of the intermediate court's opinion is to confer on Junior Davis the inherent power to veto any transfer of the preembryos in this case and thus to insure their eventual discard or self-destruction.

As noted in Section I of this opinion, the recognition of such a veto power, as long as it applies equally to both parties, is theoretically one of the routes available to resolution of the dispute in this case. Moreover, because of the current state of law regarding the right of procreation, such a rule would probably be upheld as unconstitutional. Nevertheless, for the reasons set out in Section VI of this opinion, we conclude that it is not the best route to take, under all the circumstances.

VI. THE RIGHT OF PROCREATIONAL AUTONOMY

Although an understanding of the legal status of preembryos is necessary in order to determine the enforceability of agreements about this disposition, asking whether or not they constitute "property" is not an altogether helpful question. As the appellee points out in his brief, "[as] two or eight cell tiny lumps of complex protein, the embryos have no [intrinsic] value to either party." Their value lies in the "potential to become, after implantation, growth and birth, *children*." Thus, the essential dispute here is not where or how or how long to store the preembryos, but whether the parties will become parents. The Court of Appeals held in effect that they will become parents if they both agree to become parents. The Court did not say what will happen if they fail to agree. We conclude that the answer to this dilemma turns on the parties' exercise of their constitutional right to privacy.

The right to privacy is not specifically mentioned in either the federal or the Tennessee state constitution, and yet there can be little doubt about its grounding in the concept of liberty reflected in those two documents. In particular, the Fourteenth Amendment to the United States Constitution provides that "[n]o state shall . . . deprive any person of life, liberty, or property, without due process of law." Referring to the Fourteenth Amendment, the United States Supreme Court in *Meyer v. Nebraska* observed:

> While this court has not attempted to define with exactness the liberty thus guaranteed, the term has received much consideration and some of the included things have been definitely stated. Without doubt, it denotes not merely freedom from bodily restraint but also the right of the individual to contract, to engage in any of the common occupations of life, to acquire useful knowledge, to marry, establish a home and bring up children, to worship God according to the dictates of his own conscience, and generally to enjoy those privileges long recognized at common law as essential to the orderly pursuit of happiness by free men.

262 U.S. 390, 399 (1923).

The right of privacy inherent in the constitutional concept of liberty has been further identified "as against the [power of] Government, the right to be left alone—the most comprehensive of rights and the right most valued by civilized men." *Olmstead v. United States,* 277 U.S. 438, 478 (1928) (Brandeis, J., dissenting). As to scope, "the concept of liberty protects those personal rights that are fundamental, and is not confined to the specific terms of the Bill of Rights." *Griswold v. Connecticut,* 381 U.S. 479, 486 (1965) (Goldberg, J., concurring).

Moreover, the protection of fundamental rights is not confined to federal constitutional law. As the Minnesota Supreme Court noted in *Thiede v. Town of Scandia Valley*, 217 Minn. 218, 14 N.W.2d 400, 405 (1944) (citations omitted):

> The entire social and political structure of America rests upon the cornerstone that all men have certain rights which are inherent and inalienable. Among these are the right to be protected in life, liberty, and the pursuit of happiness; the right to acquire, possess, and enjoy property; and the right to establish a home and family relations—all under equal and impartial laws which govern the whole community and each member thereof. The rights, privileges, and immunities of citizens exist notwithstanding there is no specific enumeration thereof in State Constitutions. 'These instruments measure the powers of rulers, but they do not measure the rights of the governed.' 'The fundamental maxims of a free government seem to require, that the rights of personal liberty and private property should be held sacred.' Government would not be free if they were not so held.

Hence, it is not surprising that in the Tennessee Constitution, the concept of liberty plays a central role. Article I, Section 8 provides:

> That no man shall be taken or imprisoned, or disseized of his freehold, liberties or privileges, or outlawed, or exiled, or in any manner destroyed or deprived of his life, liberty or property, but by the judgment of his peers or the law of the land.

Indeed, the notion of individual liberty is so deeply embedded in the Tennessee Constitution that it, alone among American constitutions, gives the people, in the face of governmental oppression and interference with liberty, the right to resist that oppression even to the extent of overthrowing the government. The relevant provisions establishing this distinctive political autonomy appear in the first two sections of Article I of the Tennessee Constitution, its Declaration of Rights:

> *Section 1. All power inherent in the people—Government under their control.*

> That all power is inherent in the people, and all free governments are founded on their authority, and instituted for their peace, safety, and happiness; for the advancement of those ends they have at all times, an unalienable and indefeasible right to alter, reform, or abolish the government in such manner as they may think proper.

> *Section 2. Doctrine of nonresistance condemned.*

> That government being instituted for the common benefit, the doctrine of non-resistance against arbitrary power and oppression is absurd, slavish, and destructive of the good and happiness of mankind.

The right to privacy, or personal autonomy ("the right to be left alone"), while not mentioned explicitly in our state constitution, is nevertheless reflected in several sections of the Tennessee Declaration of Rights, including provisions in Section 3 guaranteeing freedom of worship ("no human author-

ity can, in any case whatever, control or interfere with the rights of conscience"); those in Section 7 prohibiting unreasonable searches and seizures
("the people shall be secure in their persons, houses, papers and possessions,
from unreasonable searches and seizures"); those in Section 19 guaranteeing
freedom of speech and press ("free communication of thoughts and opinions, is one of the invaluable rights of man, and every citizen may freely speak,
write, and print on any subject, being responsible for the abuse of that liberty"); and the provisions in Section 27 regulating the quartering of soldiers
("no soldier shall, in time of peace, be quartered in any house without the
consent of the owner").

Obviously, the drafters of the Tennessee Constitution of 1796 could not
have anticipated the need to construe the liberty clauses of that document in
terms of the choices flowing from *in vitro* fertilization procedures. But there
can be little doubt that they foresaw the need to protect individuals from
unwarranted governmental intrusion into matters such as the one now before
us, involving intimate questions of personal and family concern. Based on
both the language and the development of our state constitution, we have no
hesitation in drawing the conclusion that there is a right of individual privacy
guaranteed under and protected by the liberty clauses of the Tennessee Declaration of Rights.

Undoubtedly, that right to privacy incorporates some of the attributes of
the federal constitutional right to privacy and, in any given fact situation, may
also share some of its contours. As with other state constitutional rights having
counterparts in the federal bill of rights, however, there is no reason to assume that there is a complete congruency. *Compare and contrast, e.g., State v.
Jacumin,* 778 S.W.2d 430 (Tenn. 1989), with *Illinois v. Gates,* 462 U.S. 213
(1983).

Here, the specific individual freedom in dispute is the right to procreate.
In terms of the Tennessee state constitution, we hold that the right of procreation is a vital part of an individual's right to privacy. Federal law is to the
same effect.

In construing the reach of the federal constitution, the United States Supreme Court has addressed the affirmative right to procreate in only two
cases. In *Buck v. Bell,* 274 U.S. 200, 207 (1927), the Court upheld the sterilization of a "feebleminded white woman." However, in *Skinner v. Oklahoma,* 316
U.S. 535 (1942), the Supreme Court struck down a statute that authorized
the sterilization of certain categories of criminals. The Court described the
right to procreate as "one of the basic civil rights of man [sic]," 316 U.S. at
541, and stated that "[m]arriage and procreation are fundamental to the very
existence and survival of the race." *Id.*

In the same vein, the United States Supreme Court has said:

> If the right of privacy means anything, it is the right of the *individual,* married
> or single, to be free from unwarranted governmental intrusion into matters so
> fundamentally affecting a person as the decision whether to bear or beget a
> child.

Eisenstadt v. Baird, 405 U.S. 438, 453 (1972) (emphasis in original). *See also, Carey v. Population Services International,* 431 U.S. 678, 685 (1977) (decision whether or not to beget or bear a child fundamental to individual autonomy).

That a right to procreational autonomy is inherent in our most basic concepts of liberty is also indicated by the reproductive freedom cases, see, e.g., *Griswold v. Connecticut,* 381 U.S. 479 (1965); and *Roe v. Wade,* 410 U.S. 113 (1973), and by cases concerning parental rights and responsibilities with respect to children. *See, e.g., Wisconsin v. Yoder,* 406 U.S. 205 (1972); *Prince v. Massachusetts,* 321 U.S. 158 (1944); *Cleveland Board of Education v. LaFleur,* 414 U.S. 632 (1974); *Pierce v. Society of Sisters,* 268 U.S. 510 (1925); and *Bellotti v. Baird,* 443 U. S. 622 (1979). In fact, in *Bellotti v. Baird* the Supreme Court noted that parental autonomy is basic to the structure of our society because the family is "the institution by which we inculcate and pass down many of our most cherished values, moral and cultural." *Bellotti,* 443 U.S. at 634 (citation omitted).

The United States Supreme Court has never addressed the issue of procreation in the context of *in vitro* fertilization. Moreover, the extent to which procreational autonomy is protected by the United States Constitution is no longer entirely clear. Justice Blackmun noted, in his dissent, that the plurality opinion in *Webster v. Reproductive Health Services,* 492 U.S. 490 (1989), "turns a stone face to anyone in search of what the plurality conceives as the scope of a woman's right under the Due Process Clause to terminate a pregnancy free from the coercive and brooding influence of the State." *Id.* at 538. The *Webster* opinion lends even less guidance to those seeking the bounds of constitutional protection of other aspects of procreational autonomy.[21]

For the purpose of this litigation it is sufficient to note that, whatever its ultimate constitutional boundaries, the right of procreational autonomy is composed of two rights of equal significance—the right to procreate and the right to avoid procreation. Undoubtedly, both are subject to protections and limitations. *See e.g., Prince v. Massachusetts,* 321 U.S. 158 (1944) (parental control over the education or health care of their children subject to some limits); *Roe v. Wade,* 410 U. S. 113 (1973) (states' interests in potential life overcomes right to avoid procreation by abortion in later stages of pregnancy).

The equivalence of and inherent tension between these two interests are nowhere more evident than in the context of *in vitro* fertilization. None of the concerns about a woman's bodily integrity that have previously precluded men from controlling abortion decisions is applicable here.[22] We are not unmindful of the fact that the trauma (including both emotional stress and physical discomfort) to which women are subjected in the IVF process is more severe than is the impact of the procedure on men. In this sense, it is fair to say that women contribute more to the IVF process than men. Their experience, however, must be viewed in light of the joys of parenthood that is desired or the relative anguish of a lifetime of unwanted parenthood. As they stand on the brink of potential parenthood, Mary Sue Davis and Junior Lewis Davis must be seen as entirely equivalent gamete-providers.

It is further evident that, however far the protection of procreational autonomy extends, the existence of the right itself dictates that decisional authority rests in the gamete-providers alone, at least to the extent that their decisions have an impact upon their individual reproductive status. As discussed in Section V above, no other person or entity has an interest sufficient to permit interference with the gamete-providers' decision to continue or terminate the IVF process, because no one else bears the consequence of these decisions in the way that the gamete-providers do.[23]

Further, at least with respect to Tennessee's public policy and its constitutional right of privacy, the state's interest in potential human life is insufficient to justify an infringement on the gamete-providers' procreational autonomy. The United States Supreme Court has indicated in *Webster*, and even in *Roe*, that the state's interest in potential human life may justify statutes or regulations that have an impact upon a person's exercise of procreational autonomy. This potential for sufficiently weighty state's interest is not, however, at issue here, because Tennessee's statutes contain no statement of public policy which reveals an interest that could justify infringing on gamete-providers' decisional authority over the preembryos to which they have contributed. As discussed in the Court of Appeals opinion, set out in Section IV, above, those statutes reveal instead a policy decision to recognize that persons born alive or capable of sustaining life *ex utero* have a higher status than do fetuses *in utero*.[24]

Certainly, if the state's interest does not become sufficiently compelling in the abortion context until the end of the first trimester,[25] after very significant developmental stages have passed, then surely there is no state's interest in these preembryos which could suffice to overcome the interests of the gamete-providers. The abortion statute reveals that the increase in the state's interest is marked by each successive developmental stage such that, toward the end of a pregnancy, this interest is so compelling that abortion is almost strictly forbidden. This scheme supports the conclusion that the state's interest in the potential life embodied by these four- to eight-cell preembryos (which may or may not be able to achieve implantation in a uterine wall and which, if implanted, may or may not begin to develop into fetuses, subject to possible miscarriage) is at best slight. When weighed against the interests of the individuals and the burdens inherent in parenthood, the state's interest in the potential life of these preembryos is not sufficient to justify any infringement upon the freedom of these individuals to make their own decisions as to whether to allow a process to continue that may result in such a dramatic change in their lives as becoming parents.

The unique nature of this case requires us to note that the interests of these parties in parenthood are different in scope than the parental interest considered in other cases. Previously, courts have dealt with the childbearing and child-rearing aspects of parenthood. Abortion cases have dealt with gestational parenthood. In this case, the Court must deal with the question of genetic parenthood. We conclude, moreover, that an interest in avoiding genetic parenthood can be significant enough to trigger the protections afforded to all other aspects of parenthood. The technological fact that someone unknown to these parties could gestate these preembryos does not alter the fact that these parties, the gamete-providers, would become parents in that event, at least in the genetic sense. The profound impact this would have on them[26] supports their right to sole decisional authority as to whether the process of attempting to gestate these preembryos should continue. This brings us directly to the question of how to resolve the dispute that arises when one party wishes to continue the IVF process and the other does not.

VII. BALANCING THE PARTIES' INTERESTS

Resolving disputes over conflicting interests of constitutional import is a task familiar to the courts. One way of resolving these disputes is to consider the positions of the parties, the significance of their interests, and the relative burdens that will be imposed by differing resolutions.[27] In this case, the issue centers on the two aspects of procreational autonomy—the right to procreate and the right to avoid procreation. We start by considering the burdens imposed on the parties by solutions that would have the effect of disallowing the exercise of individual procreational autonomy with respect to these particular preembryos.

Beginning with the burden imposed on Junior Davis, we note that the consequences are obvious. Any disposition which results in the gestation of the preembryos would impose unwanted parenthood on him, with all of its possible financial and psychological consequences. The impact that this unwanted parenthood would have on Junior Davis can only be understood by considering his particular circumstances, as revealed in the record.

Junior Davis testified that he was the fifth youngest of six children. When he was five years old, his parents divorced, his mother had a nervous break- down, and he and three of his brothers went to live at a home for boys run by the Lutheran Church. Another brother was taken in by an aunt, and his sister stayed with their mother. From that day forward, he had monthly visits with his mother but saw his father only three more times before he died in 1976. Junior Davis testified that, as a boy, he had severe problems caused by separa- tion from his parents. He said that it was especially hard to leave his mother after each monthly visit. He clearly feels that he has suffered because of his lack of opportunity to establish a relationship with his parents and particularly because of the absence of his father.

In light of his boyhood experiences, Junior Davis is vehemently opposed to fathering a child that would not live with both parents. Regardless of whether he or Mary Sue had custody, he feels that the child's bond with the non-custodial parent would not be satisfactory. He testified very clearly that his concern was for the psychological obstacles a child in such a situation would face, as well as the burdens it would impose on him. Likewise, he is opposed to donation because the recipient couple might divorce, leaving the child (which he definitely would consider his own) in a single-parent setting.

Balanced against Junior Davis's interest in avoiding parenthood is Mary

Sue Davis's interest in donating the preembryos to another couple for implantation. Refusal to permit donation of the preembryos would impose on her the burden of knowing that the lengthy IVF procedures she underwent were futile, and that the preembryos to which she contributed genetic material would never become children. While this is not an insubstantial emotional burden, we can only conclude that Mary Sue Davis's interest in donation is not as significant as the interest Junior Davis has in avoiding parenthood. If she were allowed to donate these preembryos, he would face a lifetime of either wondering about his parental status or knowing about his parental status but having no control over it. He testified quite clearly that if these preembryos were brought to term he would fight for custody of his child or children. Donation, if a child came of it, would rob him twice—his procreational autonomy would be defeated and his relationship with his offspring would be prohibited.

The case would be closer if Mary Sue Davis were seeking to use the preembryos herself, but only if she could not achieve parenthood by any other reasonable means. We recognize the trauma that Mary Sue has already experienced and the additional discomfort to which she would be subjected if she opts to attempt IVF again. Still, she would have a reasonable opportunity, through IVF, to try once again to achieve parenthood in all its aspects—genetic, gestational, bearing, and rearing.

Further, we note that if Mary Sue Davis were unable to undergo another round of IVF, or opted not to try, she could still achieve the child-rearing aspects of parenthood through adoption. The fact that she and Junior Davis pursued adoption indicates that, at least at one time, she was willing to forego genetic parenthood and would then have been satisfied by the child-rearing aspects of parenthood alone.

VIII. CONCLUSION

In summary, we hold that disputes involving the disposition of preembryos produced by *in vitro* fertilization should be resolved, first, by looking to the preferences of the progenitors. If their wishes cannot be ascertained, or if there is dispute, then their prior agreement concerning disposition should be carried out. If no prior agreement exists, then the relative interests of the parties in using or not using the preembryos must be weighed. Ordinarily, the party wishing to avoid procreation should prevail, assuming that the other party has a reasonable possibility of achieving parenthood by means other than use of the preembryos in question. If no other reasonable alternatives exist, then the argument in favor of using the preembryos to achieve pregnancy should be considered. However, if the party seeking control of the preembryos intends merely to donate them to another couple, the objecting party obviously has the greater interest and should prevail.

But the rule does not contemplate the creation of an automatic veto, and in affirming the judgment of the Court of Appeals, we would not wish to be interpreted as so holding.

For the reasons set out above, the judgment of the Court of Appeals is affirmed, in the appellee's favor. This ruling means that the Knoxville Fertility Clinic is free to follow its normal procedure in dealing with unused preembryos, as long as that procedure is not in conflict with this opinion. Costs on appeal will be taxed to the appellant.

Martha Craig Daughtrey, Justice

CONCUR:

Reid, C.J.
Drowota, O'Brien, Anderson, JJ.

N O T E S

1. At the time of trial, only one state had enacted pertinent legislation. A Louisiana statue entitled "Human Embryos," among other things, forbids the intentional destruction of a cryopreserved IVF embryo and declares that disputes between parties should be resolved in the "best interest" of the embryo. 1986 La. Acts R.S. 9:121 *et seq.* Under the Louisiana statute, unwanted embryos must be made available for "adoptive implantation."

2. The only reported decision is *York v. Jones,* 717 F.Supp. 421 (E.D. Va. 1989), discussed at length in Section IV, below. The unreported case of *Del Zio v. Columbia Presbyterian Medical Center* is summarized in footnote 23, below. A third case, involving a California couple who underwent IVF in Australia and later died in an airplane crash, is noted in Smith, *Australia's Frozen 'Orphan' Embryos,* 24 J. Fam. L. 27 (1985–86). Because the couple died intestate, their estates were distributed under California law without regard to the "frozen embryos" left in storage in Australia.

3. Note, *The Legal Status of Frozen Embryos: Analysis and Proposed Guidelines for a Uniform Law,* 17 J. Legis. 97 (1990).

4. This is the so-called "sweat-equity" model. Robertson, *Resolving Disputes over Frozen Embryos,* 19 Hastins Ctr. Rep. 7 (1989).

5. Andrews, *The Legal Status of the Embryo,* 32 Loyola L. Rev. 357 (1986).

6. Assuming that the parties do not change their current positions, in this case the result would be "the worst of both worlds": some of the frozen embryos would likely be destroyed, contrary to Mary Sue Davis's devout wish that they be implanted and given the opportunity to come to term; at the same time, the others would likely be implanted and might come to term, thus forcing Junior Davis into unwanted parenthood.

7. Poole, *Allocation of Decision-Making Rights to Frozen Embryos,* 4 Am. J. Fam. L. 67 (1990).

8. Alternatively, the fertilized ova may also be transferred to the uterus of a "surrogate mother," who carries through with the pregnancy for the gamete-providers, or they may be donated to a genetically unrelated couple.

9. They also were not asked to sign any consent forms. Apparently the clinic was in the process of moving its location when the Davises underwent this last round and,

because timing of each step of IVF is crucial, it was impossible to postpone the procedure until the appropriate forms were located.

10. Mary Sue Davis's testimony is contradictory as to whether she would have gone ahead with IVF if she had been worried about her marriage. At one point she said if she had known they were getting divorced, she would not have gone ahead with it, but at another point she indicated that she was so committed to the idea of being a mother that she could not say that she would not have gone ahead with cryopreservation.

11. For a thorough consideration of the implications of status, see Clifford Grobstein, *Science and the Unborn,* 58–62 (1988).

12. For further rather uncomplimentary characterization of Lejeune's testimony, see Annas, *A French Homunculus in a Tennessee Court,* 19 Hastings Ctr. Rep. 20 (1989).

13. It would be relevant, however, to the question of whether embryonic research is permissible, under regulations that limit such research to "preembryonic" stages. Such research is carried out principally in order to perfect *in vitro* fertilization techniques and to increase the success rate of pregnancies achieved through IVF and, as of 1986, was regulated by statute in some 25 states. *See* Andrews, *The Legal Status of the Embryo,* 32 Loyola L. Rev. 357, 396–397 (1986).

14. In her brief, the appellant now characterizes the preembryos as "potential life" rather than as "human beings."

15. The Fourteenth Amendment, for example, limits the equal protection and due process of law to "persons *born* or naturalized in the United States."

16. As Justice Stevens noted in *Thornburgh v. American College of Obstetricians and Gynecologists,* 476 U.S. 747, 779 n. 8 (1986) (Stevens, J., concurring), "No member of this Court has ever suggested that a fetus is a 'person' within the meaning of the Fourteenth Amendment."

17. Left undisturbed in the mother's uterus, a viable fetus has an excellent chance of being brought to term and born live. In contrast, a preembryo in a petri dish, if later transferred, has only a 13–21 percent chance of achieving actual implantation. Of these pregnancies, between 56 percent and 75 percent result in live births. Jones and Rogers, *Results from In Vitro Fertilization,* 51–62, cited in Poole, *Allocation of Decision-Making Rights to Frozen Embryos,* 4 Am. J. Fam. L. n. 145.

18. This situation is thus distinguishable from that in which a couple makes an agreement concerning abortion in the event of a future pregnancy. Such agreements are unenforceable because of the woman's right to privacy and autonomy. *See Planned Parenthood v. Danforth,* 428 U.S. 52 (1976) (invalidating written consent of spouse as a prerequisite to abortion).

19. We also point out that if the roles were reversed in this case, it is highly unlikely that Junior Davis could force transfer of the preembryos to Mary Sue over her objection. Because she has an absolute right to seek termination of any resulting pregnancy, at least within the first trimester, ordering her to undergo a uterine transfer would be a futility. Ordering donation over objection would raise the other constitutional problems discussed in Section VI.

20. This two-year limit is apparently an estimate based on technological feasibility as of the time of trial. Our survey of law journal articles indicates other estimates of viability ranging from two to ten years.

21. Justice O'Connor did note in her concurring opinion in *Webster* that the plurality's position might threaten the development of IVF programs. Despite her concern, she voted to uphold the Missouri statute at issue, because she found the possibility "too hypothetical to support the use of declaratory judgment procedures and injunctive remedies" since there was no indication that Missouri might seek to prohibit IVF program. *Webster,* 492 U.S. at 523 (O'Connor J., concurring).

22. *Planned Parenthood v. Danforth,* 428 U.S. 52, 71 (1976) ("Inasmuch as it is the woman who physically bears the child and who is the more directly and immediately affected by the pregnancy, as between the two, the balance weights in her favor."). *See* discussion in *Developments in the Law—Medical Technology and the Law,* 103 Harv. L. Rev. 1519, 1544–45 (1990).

23. *See Del Zio v. Columbia Presbyterian Medical Center*, No. 74-3558 (S.D.N.Y. filed April 12, 1978), in which a woman who was an IVF patient was awarded $50,000 for emotional distress when a doctor deliberately destroyed the contents of the petri dish in which *in vitro* fertilization was being attempted with the woman's egg and her husband's sperm.

24. T.C.A. § 20-5-106(b) (1980) allows a civil action for wrongful death only where the decedent has either been born alive or was viable, that is to say, could reasonably have been expected to be capable of living outside the uterus. Likewise, a criminal conviction for an offense against a person, including a homicide conviction, may not be had if the victim was not viable at the time of the offense. T.C.A. § 39-13-107 and 39-13-214 (1991); *see also State v. Evans*, 745 S.W.2d 880 (Tenn. Crim. App. 1987) (viable fetus not "person" or "human life" within meaning of vehicular homicide statute).

Tennessee's abortion statute reveals a public policy decision weighing the interests of living persons against the state's interest in potential life. T.C.A. § 39-15-201 (1991). At least during certain stages of a pregnancy, the personal interests of the pregnant woman outweigh the state's interests and the pregnancy may be terminated.

Taken collectively, our statutes reflect the policy decision that, at least in some circumstances, the interest of living individuals in avoiding procreation is sufficient to justify taking steps to terminate the procreational process, despite the state's interest in potential life.

25. The trimester scheme is set forth at T.C.A. § 39-15-201(c)(1)-(3).

26. Sperm donors may regret not having contact with their biological children, according to psychotherapist Annette Baron and psychologist Aphrodite Clamar, mentioned in Lori Andrews, *Feminist Perspectives on Reproductive Technologies*, American Bar Foundation Working Paper # 8701, n. 29 (1987), also published as Andrews, *Alternative Modes of Reproduction*, in *Reproductive Laws for the 1990s, A Briefing Handbook*, edited by Nadine Taub and Sherrill Cohen, Women's Rights Litigation Clinic, School of Law, Newark (1988). Even more so, women who have surrendered children for adoption may be haunted by concern about the child. Poole, *Allocation of Decision-Making Rights to Frozen Embryos*, 4 Am. J. Fam. L. 67, 74 (1990), *citing* Becker, *The Rights of Unwed Parents: Feminist Approaches*, 63 Soc. Ser. Rev. 496, 508 (1989).

27. For instance, in *Frisby v. Schultz*, 487 U. S. 474 (1988), the United States Supreme Court addressed the conflicting interests of a city in protecting a doctor who performed abortions and those of the persons who picketed in front of his home. A municipal ordinance prohibited picketing before or about the residence or dwelling of any individual. The Supreme Court had to consider whether the ordinance was narrowly tailored to serve a significant government interest and whether it left open ample alternative channels of communication. *Id.* at 481. The Court noted that this ordinance banned only focused picketing before a residence, not all picketing in residential areas. Because it was narrowly tailored to meet a significant government interest of protecting residential privacy, leaving open other methods of protest and expression, the Court held that the statute did not violate the First Amendment. *Id.* at 488. Likewise, in this case, we must find some balance between the exercise of the two conflicting interests.

PART IV: BODY BUILDING

The (Re)Construction of Sex and Sexuality

If one thinks of physical differences between bodies as the most important correlate of gender and sex categories, the technological transformation of bodies takes on tremendous significance. At one level, the ability to alter our bodies lets us change those physical correlates of sex and gender, making biology just one more alterable condition. Even if sex is an objective biological fact, that fact is still impermanent and relative to technology. At another level, however, technology can also be used to reinforce the boundaries of sexual categories we already have. Technology can be used to protect those categories from biologically ambiguous or differently hardwired bodies that don't "fit right." This section explores both kinds of uses.

Are we all really born male or female? Or do we just come out of the hospital that way? Looking at ways technology is used to make bodies fit social ideals, Suzanne Kessler writes about the remarkable case of intersexed infants (born with "ambiguous" genitals) and how these infants are assigned a sex and a gender. Kessler argues that while physicians believe the sex and gender of the child are malleable, they also think it is crucial firmly to establish a sex early on, producing a clear gender identity so that the parents will know how to raise the child. Even though the sex and gender of the infant are obviously being decided upon, however, physicians still act afterwards as if they had merely discovered the "true" sex of the child rather than surgically constructed it. Kessler describes how these sex assignment decisions are made (often by aesthetic assessments of the penis rather than chromosomal testing). The cultural factors that go into this decision process force us to look at how our ideas about the differences between women and men are informed by social values and not just genetic and anatomical facts.

Of course, while babies are forced into sex-assignment operations, adults motivated by concerns about their own gender-related appearances often elect to surgically alter their bodies. In addition to the question of whether this is an appropriate use of medicine and medical technology (which are purported to be in the business of curing disease), a central debate about this phenomenon is whether people who choose to cut and reshape their bodies do so freely, or only because they have been pushed into doing so by social pressures. Discussing the issue of women and cosmetic surgery, Kathryn Pauly Morgan challenges the idea that such surgery is simply a free, individual choice. Instead, she argues that in a culture where women are taught to prize their looks and are made to feel ugly by the rhetoric of "unsightly fat" and "problem areas," cosmetic surgery ends up enforcing conformity to male assessments of beauty. Morgan forces us to consider when women's "choices" are really authentic and free and how we could know.

Kathy Davis is also critical of cosmetic surgery, but does not want to treat women as "the misguided victims of false consciousness." Davis's interviews demonstrate that women regularly describe their surgery as a normalizing, not beautifying, procedure, a choice they had made for themselves even over the objections of husbands and boyfriends, and a morally problematic choice that had to be justified. This leads Davis to claim that women seeking cosmetic surgery appear to be conscious and reflective and neither more nor less affected by the beauty culture than women who are not interested in surgery. Davis argues that Morgan does not actually listen to women who have decided on cosmetic surgery, but assumes from the start that such decisions must be inauthentic. [Bibliographic references to this chapter have not been reprinted in this collection but may be found in the author's book.]

Regardless of how we are born (or come out of the hospital), do we have to stay male or female? A more radical kind of body-altering surgery can change those anatomical correlates of sex even after years of living as a woman or a man. And after one has changed one's anatomy, what then should be said of one's status? What makes someone "really" female or male? Can we genuinely switch from one to the other, or remain both, neither, or something else? Tackling these questions head on, Janice G. Raymond criticizes sex reassignment surgery as just another way men attempt to colonize, control, and possess women—in this case, in a bodily sense. In the chapter reprinted here, she is particularly critical of male-to-female transsexuals who claim to be lesbian-feminists and who attempt to join lesbian-feminist groups. Raymond argues that "male-to-constructed-female" lesbian-feminists are not women at all. They are just men, with men's histories, men's experiences, men's privileges, and ultimately a masculine worldview and behavior. In fact, she argues, these transsexuals often end up dividing women when they try to insert themselves in feminist communities (such as "all-women" companies)—the very goal that men often pursue. Raymond ends by condemning lesbian-feminist transsexualism as a type of damaging pseudolesbianism (in the tradition of *Playboy's* "lesbian" photographs) made possible by a patriarchal medical establishment and its technology.

Sandy Stone describes the complex ways in which medical personnel, psychologists, feminists, and transsexuals themselves negotiate meanings and moralities of transsexualism. Stone finds that a strict overarching binary concept of gender informs all the thinking on transsexualism, from the radical feminist assessment of transsexuals as boundary violators, to transsexuals' assessment of themselves and their desire to "pass" for a particular sex, to the very medicalization of transsexualism and the attempt to define it. Stone argues that the attempt to fit transsexuals into the conventional categories of gender (by everyone involved) is complicit with the very discourse being opposed. Instead, she contends that Raymond's claim that "transsexuals divide women" should be reinterpreted as a productive way to move beyond old binary understandings of gender.

If adults modify their own bodies out of a desire to be more feminine or masculine, or out of a desire to be a certain sex altogether, and parents and physicians modify infants' bodies out of a desire to have clearly male or female children, what about modifying someone's body in order to produce a particular *kind* of desire? Would it be morally permissible for parents, for instance, to biologically engineer their child's sexual orientation? Timothy F. Murphy discusses this issue, looking at various historical attempts to determine sexual orientation through the use of biomedical technologies. As one might expect, the majority of these attempts have been in the service of eradicating homosexuality, including behavioral, hormonal, biochemical, anatomical, and—as has been more recently suggested—genetic techniques. Murphy looks at several arguments for and against the moral permissibility of these techniques, paying special attention to the claim that parents have a right to choose the traits of their children in the same way they have the right to raise them as they see fit. While he argues that much of the motivation behind sexual orientation engineering is heterosexist—and just as immoral as sexist and racist motivation—he admits that no dictate of justice requires a certain number of homosexuals, and observes that parents are usually given wide latitude in how they raise their children. Of course, this kind of reasoning works equally well for gay and lesbian parents who might want to ensure the birth of a homosexual child. Murphy's article challenges us to examine some basic ideas about childraising. What sorts of rights do parents have? And what's the real difference between socially training a child and genetically engineering a child?

CHAPTER 15

THE MEDICAL CONSTRUCTION

OF GENDER

Case Management of Intersexed Infants

SUZANNE J. KESSLER

(1990)

The birth of intersexed infants, babies born with genitals that are neither clearly male nor clearly female, has been documented throughout recorded time.[1] In the late twentieth century, medical technology has advanced to allow scientists to determine chromosomal and hormonal gender, which is typically taken to be the real, natural, biological gender, usually referred to as "sex."[2] Nevertheless, physicians who handle the cases of intersexed infants consider several factors beside biological ones in determining, assigning, and announcing the gender of a particular infant. Indeed, biological factors are often preempted in their deliberations by such cultural factors as the "correct" length of the penis and capacity of the vagina.

In the literature of intersexuality, issues such as announcing a baby's gender at the time of delivery, postdelivery discussions with the parents, and consultations with patients in adolescence are considered only peripherally to the central medical issues—etiology, diagnosis, and surgical procedures.[3] Yet members of medical teams have standard practices for managing intersexuality that rely ultimately on cultural understandings of gender. The process and guidelines by which decisions about gender (re)construction are made reveal the model for the social construction of gender generally. Moreover, in the face of apparently incontrovertible evidence—infants born with some combination of "female" and "male" reproductive and sexual features—physicians hold an incorrigible belief in and insistence upon female and male as the only "natural" options. This paradox highlights and calls into question the idea that female and male are biological givens compelling a culture of two genders.

Ideally, to undertake an extensive study of intersexed infant case management, I would like to have had direct access to particular events, for example, the deliveries of intersexed infants and the initial discussions among physicians, between physicians and parents, between parents, and among parents and family and friends of intersexed infants. The rarity with which intersexuality occurs, however, made this unfeasible.[4] Alternatively, physicians who have had considerable experience in dealing with this condition were interviewed. I do not assume that their "talk" about how they manage such cases mirrors their "talk" in the situation, but their words do reveal that they have certain assumptions about gender and that they impose those assumptions via their medical decisions on the patients they treat.

Interviews were conducted with six medical experts (three women and three men) in the field of pediatric intersexuality: one clinical geneticist, three endocrinologists (two of them pediatric specialists), one psychoendocrinologist, and one urologist. All of them have had extensive clinical experience with various intersexed syndromes, and some are internationally known researchers in the field of intersexuality. They were selected on the basis of their prominence in the field and their representation of four different medical centers in New York City. Although they know one another, they do not collaborate on research and are not part of the same management team. All were interviewed in the spring of 1985, in their offices, and interviews lasted between forty-five minutes and one hour. Unless further referenced, all quotations in this article are from these interviews.

THE THEORY OF INTERSEXUALITY MANAGEMENT

The sophistication of today's medical technology has led to an extensive compilation of various intersex categories based on the various causes of malformed genitals. The "true intersexed" condition, where both ovarian and testicular tissue are present in either the same gonad or in opposite gonads, accounts for fewer than five percent of all cases of ambiguous genitals.[5] More commonly, the infant has either ovaries or testes, but the genitals are ambiguous. If the infant has two ovaries, the condition is referred to as female pseudohermaphroditism. If the infant has two testes, the condition is referred to as male pseudohermaphroditism. There are numerous causes of both forms of pseudohermaphroditism, and although there are life-threatening aspects to some of these conditions, having ambiguous genitals per se is not harmful to the infant's health.[6] Although most cases of ambiguous genitals do not represent true intersex, in keeping with the contemporary literature, I will refer to all such cases as intersexed.

Current attitudes toward the intersex condition are primarily influenced by three factors. First are the extraordinary advancements in surgical techniques and endocrinology in the last decade. For example, female genitals can now be constructed to be indistinguishable in appearance from normal natural ones. Some abnormally small penises can be enlarged with the exogenous application of hormones, although surgical skills are not sufficiently advanced to construct a normal-looking and functioning penis out of other tissue.[7] Second, in the contemporary United States the influence of the feminist movement has called into question the valuation of women according to strictly reproductive functions, and the presence or absence of functional gonads is no longer the only or the definitive criterion for gender assignment. Third, contemporary psychological theorists have begun to focus on "gender identity" (one's sense of oneself as belonging to the female or male category) as distinct from "gender role" (cultural expectations of one's behavior as "appropriate" for a female or male).[8] The relevance of this new gender identity theory for rethinking cases of ambiguous genitals is that gender must be assigned as early as possible in order for gender identity to develop successfully. As a result of these factors, intersexuality is now considered a treatable condition of the genitals, one that needs to be resolved expeditiously.

According to all of the specialists interviewed, management of intersexed cases is based upon the theory of gender proposed first by John Money, J. G. Hampson, and J. L. Hampson in 1955 and developed in 1972 by Money and Anke A. Ehrhardt, which argues that gender identity is changeable until approximately eighteen months of age.[9] "To use the Pygmalion allegory, one may begin with the same clay and fashion a god or a goddess."[10] The theory rests on satisfying several conditions: the experts must insure that the parents have no doubt about whether their child is male or female; the genitals must be made to match the assigned gender as soon as possible; gender-appropriate hormones must be administered at puberty; and intersexed children must be kept informed about their situation with age-appropriate explanations. If these conditions are met, the theory proposes, the intersexed child will develop a gender identity in accordance with the gender assignment (regardless of the chromosomal gender) and will not question her or his assignment and request reassignment at a later age.

Supportive evidence for Money and Ehrhardt's theory is based on only a handful of repeatedly cited cases, but it has been accepted because of the prestige of the theoreticians and its resonance with contemporary ideas about gender, children, psychology, and medicine. Gender and children are malleable; psychology and medicine are the tools used to transform them. This theory is so strongly endorsed that it has taken on the character of gospel. "I think we [physicians] have been raised in the Money theory," one endocrinologist said. Another claimed, "We always approach the problem in a similar way and it's been dictated, to a large extent, by the work of John Money and Anke Ehrhardt because they are the only people who have published, at least in medical literature, any data, any guidelines." It is provocative that this physician immediately followed this assertion with: "And I don't know how effective it really is." Contradictory data are rarely cited in reviews of the literature, were not mentioned by any of the physicians interviewed, and have not diminished these physicians' belief in the theory's validity.[11]

The doctors interviewed concur with the argument that gender be assigned immediately, decisively, and irreversibly, and that professional opinions be presented in a clear and unambiguous way. The psychoendocrinologist said that when doctors make a statement about the infant, they should "stick to it." The urologist said, "If you make a statement that later has to be disclaimed or discredited, you've weakened your credibility." A gender assignment made decisively, unambiguously, and irrevocably contributes, I believe, to the general impression that the infant's true, natural "sex" has been discovered, and that something that was there all along has been found.

It also serves to maintain the credibility of the medical profession, reassure the parents, and reflexively substantiate Money and Ehrhardt's theory.

Also according to the theory, if operative correction is necessary, it should take place as soon as possible. If the infant is assigned the male gender, the initial stage of penis repair is usually undertaken in the first year, and further surgery is completed before the child enters school. If the infant is assigned the female gender, vulva repair (including clitoral reduction) is usually begun by three months of age. Money suggests that if reduction of phallic tissue were delayed beyond the neonatal period, the infant would have traumatic memories of having been castrated.[12] Vaginoplasty, in those females having an adequate internal structure (e.g., the vaginal canal is near its expected location), is done between the ages of one and four years. Girls who require more complicated surgical procedures might not be surgically corrected until preadolescence.[13] The complete vaginal canal is typically constructed only when the body is fully grown, following pubertal feminization with estrogen, although more recently some specialists have claimed surgical success with vaginal construction in the early childhood years.[14] Although physicians speculate about the possible trauma of an early childhood "castration" memory, there is no corresponding concern that vaginal reconstructive surgery delayed beyond the neonatal period is traumatic.

Even though gender identity theory places the critical age limit for gender reassignment between eighteen months and two years, the physicians acknowledge that diagnosis, gender assignment, and genital reconstruction cannot be delayed for as long as two years, since a clear gender assignment and correctly formed genitals will determine the kind of interactions parents will have with the child.[15] The geneticist argued that when parents "change a diaper and see genitalia that don't mean much in terms of gender assignment, I think it prolongs the negative response to the baby. . . . If you have clitoral enlargement that is so extraordinary that the parents can't distinguish between male and female, it is sometimes helpful to reduce that somewhat so that the parent views the child as female." Another physician concurred: parents "need to go home and do their job as child rearers with it very clear whether it's a boy or a girl."

DIAGNOSIS

A premature gender announcement by an obstetrician, prior to a close examination of an infant's genitals, can be problematic. Money and his colleagues claim that the primary complications in case management of intersexed infants can be traced to mishandling by medical personnel untrained in sexology.[16] According to one of the pediatric endocrinologists interviewed, obstetricians improperly educated about intersexed conditions "don't examine the babies closely enough at birth and say things just by looking, before separating legs and looking at everything, and jump to conclusions, because 99 percent of the time it's correct. . . . People get upset, physicians I mean. And they say things that are inappropriate." For example, he said that an inexperienced obstetrician might blurt out, "I think you have a boy, or no, maybe you have a girl." Other inappropriate remarks a doctor might make in postdelivery consultation with the parents includes, "You have a little boy, but he'll never function as a little boy, so you better raise him as a little girl." As a result, said the pediatric endocrinologist, "the family comes away with the idea that they have a little boy, and that's what they wanted, and that's what they're going to get." In such cases parents sometimes insist that the child be raised male despite the physician's instructions to the contrary. "People have in mind certain things they've heard, that this is a boy, and they're not likely to forget that, or they're not likely to let it go easily." The urologist agreed that the first gender attribution is critical: "Once it's been announced, you've got a big problem on your hands." "One of the worst things is to allow [the parents] to go ahead and give a name and tell everyone, and it turns out the child has to be raised in the opposite sex."[17]

Physicians feel that the mismanagement of such cases requires careful remedying. The psychoendocrinologist asserted, "When I'm involved, I spend hours with the parents to explain to them what has happened and how a mistake like that could be made, *or not really a mistake but a different decision*" (my emphasis). One pediatric endocrinologist said, "[I] try to dissuade them from previous misconceptions, and say, 'Well, I know what they meant, but the way they said it confused you. This is, I think, a better way to think about it.' " These statements reveal physicians' efforts not only to protect parents from concluding that their child is neither male nor female but also to protect other physicians' decision-making processes. Case management involves perpetuating the notion that good medical decisions are based on interpretations of the infant's real "sex" rather than on cultural understandings of gender.

"Mismanagements" are less likely to occur in communities with major medical centers, where specialists are prepared to deal with intersexuality and a medical team (perhaps drawing physicians from more than one teaching hospital) is quickly assembled. The team typically consists of the original referring doctor (obstetrician or pediatrician), a pediatric endocrinologist, a pediatric surgeon (urologist or gynecologist), and a geneticist. In addition, a psychologist, psychiatrist, or psychoendocrinologist might play a role. If an infant is born with ambiguous genitals in a small community hospital, without the relevant specialists on staff, she or he is likely to be transferred to a hospital where diagnosis and treatment are available. Intersexed infants born in poor rural areas where there is less medical intervention might never be referred for genital reconstruction. Many of these children, like those born in earlier historical periods, will grow up and live through adulthood with the condition of genital ambiguity—somehow managing.

The diagnosis of intersexed conditions includes assessing the chromosomal sex and the syndrome that produced the genital ambiguity, and may include medical procedures such as cytologic screening; chromosomal analysis; assessing serum electrolytes; hormone, gonadotropin, and steroids evaluation; digital examination; and radiographic genitography.[18] In any intersexed condition, if the infant is determined to be a genetic female (having an XX chromosome makeup), then the treatment—genital surgery to reduce the phallus size—can proceed relatively quickly, satisfying what the doctors believe are psychological and cultural demands. For example, 21-hydroxylase deficiency, a form of female pseudohermaphroditism and one of the most common conditions, can be determined by a blood test within the first few days.

If, on the other hand, the infant is determined to have at least one Y chromosome, then surgery may be considerably delayed. A decision must be made whether to test the ability of the phallic tissue to respond to (HCG) androgen treatment, which is intended to enlarge the microphallus enough to be a penis. The endocrinologist explained, "You do HCG testing and you find out if the male can make testosterone. . . . You can get those results back probably within three weeks. . . . You're sure the male is making testosterone—but can he respond to it? It can take three months of waiting to see whether the phallus responds." If the Y-chromosome infant cannot make testosterone or cannot respond to the testosterone it makes, the phallus will not develop, and the Y-chromosome infant is not considered to be a male after all.

Should the infant's phallus respond to the local application of testosterone or a brief course of intramuscular injections of low-potency androgen, the gender assignment problem is resolved, but possibly at some later cost, since the penis will not grow again at puberty when the rest of the body develops.[19] Money's case management philosophy assumes that while it may be difficult for an adult male to have a much smaller than average penis, it is very detrimental to the morale of the young boy to have a micropenis.[20] In the former case the male's manliness might be at stake, but in the latter case his essential maleness might be. Although the psychological consequences of these experiences have not been empirically documented, Money and his colleagues suggest that it is wise to avoid the problems of both the micropenis in childhood and the still undersized penis in postpuberty by reassigning many of these infants to the female gender.[21] This approach suggests that for Money and his colleagues, chromosomes are less relevant in determining gender than penis size, and that, by implication, "male" is defined not by the genetic condition of having one Y and one X chromosome or by the production of sperm but by the aesthetic condition of having an appropriately sized penis.

The tests and procedures required for diagnosis (and, consequently, for gender assignment) can take several months.[22] Although physicians are anxious not to make a premature gender assignment, their language suggests that it is difficult for them to take a completely neutral position and think and speak only of phallic tissue that belongs to an infant whose gender has not yet been determined or decided. Comments such as "seeing whether the male can respond to testosterone" imply at least a tentative male gender assignment of an XY infant. The psychoendocrinologist's explanation to parents of their infant's treatment program also illustrates this implicit male gender assignment. "Clearly this baby has an underdeveloped phallus. But if the phallus responds to this treatment, we are fairly confident that surgical techniques and hormonal techniques will help this child to look like a boy. But we want to make absolutely sure and use some hormone treatments and see whether the tissue reacts." The mere fact that this doctor refers to the genitals as an "underdeveloped" phallus rather than an overdeveloped clitoris suggests that the infant has been judged to be, at least provisionally, a male. In the case of the undersized phallus, what is ambiguous is not whether this is a penis but whether it is "good enough" to remain one. If at the end of the treatment period the phallic tissue has not responded, what had been a potential penis (referred to in the medical literature as a "clitoropenis") is now considered an enlarged clitoris (or "penoclitoris"), and reconstructive surgery is planned as for the genetic female.

The time-consuming nature of intersex diagnosis and the assumption, based on gender identity theory, that gender should be assigned as soon as possible thus present physicians with difficult dilemmas. Medical personnel are committed to discovering the etiology of the condition in order to determine the best course of treatment, which takes time. Yet they feel an urgent need to provide an immediate assignment and genitals that look and function appropriately. An immediate assignment that will need to be retracted is more problematic than a delayed assignment, since reassignment carries with it an additional set of social complications. The endocrinologist interviewed commented: "We've come very far in that we can diagnose eventually, many of the conditions. But we haven't come far enough. . . . We can't do it early enough. . . . Very frequently a decision is made before all this information is available, simply because it takes so long to make the correct diagnosis. And you cannot let a child go indefinitely, not in this society you can't. . . . There's pressure on parents [for a decision] and the parents transmit that pressure onto physicians." A pediatric endocrinologist agreed: "At times you may need to operate before a diagnosis can be made. . . . In one case parents were told to wait on the announcement while the infant was treated to see if the phallus would grow when treated with androgens. After the first month passed and there was some growth, the parents said they gave it a boy's name. They could only wait a month."

Deliberating out loud on the judiciousness of making parents wait for assignment decisions, the endocrinologist asked rhetorically, "Why do we do all these tests if in the end we're going to make the decision simply on the basis of appearance of the genitalia?" This question suggests that the principles underlying physicians' decisions are cultural rather than biological, based on parental reaction and the medical team's perception of the infant's societal adjustment prospects given the way her/his genitals look or could be made to look. Moreover, as long as the decision rests largely on the criterion of genital appearance, and male is defined as having a "good-sized" penis, more infants will be assigned to the female gender than to the male.

THE WAITING PERIOD: DEALING WITH AMBIGUITY

During the period of ambiguity between birth and assignment, physicians not only must evaluate the infant's prospects to be a good male but also must manage parents' uncertainty about a genderless child. Physicians advise that parents postpone announcing the gender of the infant until a gender has been explicitly assigned. They believe that parents should not feel compelled to tell other people. The clinical geneticist interviewed said that physicians "basically encourage [parents] to treat [the infant] as neuter." One of the pediatric endocrinologists reported that in France parents confronted with this dilemma sometimes give the infant a neuter name, such as Claude or Jean. The psychoendocrinologist concurred: "If you have a truly borderline situation, and you want to make it dependent on the hormone treatment . . . then the parents are . . . told, 'Try not to make a decision. Refer to the baby as "baby." Don't think in terms of boy or girl.' " Yet, when asked whether this is a reasonable request to make of parents in our society, the physician answered: "I don't think so. I think parents can't do it."

New York State requires that a birth certificate be filled out within forty-eight hours of delivery, but the certificate need not be filed with the state for thirty days. The geneticist tells parents to insert "child of" instead of a name. In one case, parents filled out two birth registration forms, one for each gender, and they refused to sign either until a final gender assignment had been made.[23] One of the pediatric endocrinologists claimed, "I heard a story; I don't know if it's true or not. There were parents of a hermaphroditic infant who told everyone they had twins, one of each gender. When the gender was determined, they said the other had died."

The geneticist explained that when directly asked by parents what to tell others about the gender of the infant, she says, "Why don't you just tell them that the baby is having problems and as soon as the problems are resolved we'll get back to you." A pediatric endocrinologist echoes this suggestion in advising parents to say, "Until the problem is solved [we] would really prefer not to discuss any of the details." According to the urologist, "If [the gender] isn't announced people may mutter about it and may grumble about it, but they haven't got anything to get their teeth into and make trouble over for the child, or the parents, or whatever." In short, parents are asked to sidestep the infant's gender rather than admit that gender is unknown, thereby collaborating in a web of white lies, ellipses, and mystifications.[24]

Even while physicians teach the parents how to deal with others who will not find the infant's condition comprehensible or acceptable, physicians must also make the condition comprehensible and acceptable to the parents, normalizing the intersexed condition for them. In doing so they help the parents consider the infant's condition in the most positive way. There are four key aspects to this "normalizing" process.

First, physicians teach parents normal fetal development and explain that all fetuses have the potential to be male or female. One of the endocrinologists explains, "In the absence of maleness you have femaleness. . . . It's really the basic design. The other [intersex] is really a variation on a theme." This explanation presents the intersex condition as a natural phase of every fetal development. Another endocrinologist "like[s] to show picture[s] to them and explain that at a certain point in development males and females look alike and then diverge for such and such reason." The professional literature suggests that doctors use diagrams that illustrate "nature's principle of using the same anlagen to produce the external genital parts of the male and female."[25]

Second, physicians stress the normalcy of the infant in other aspects. For example, the geneticist tells parents, "The baby is healthy, but there was a problem in the way the baby was developing." The endocrinologist says the infant has "a mild defect, just like anything could be considered a birth defect, a mole or a hemangioma." This language not only eases the blow to the parents but also redirects their attention. Terms like "hermaphrodite" or "abnormal" are not used. The urologist said that he advised parents "about the generalization of sticking to the good things and not confusing people with something that is unnecessary."

Third, physicians (at least initially) imply that it is not the gender of the child that is ambiguous but the genitals. They talk about "undeveloped," "maldeveloped," or "unfinished" organs. From a number of the physicians interviewed came the following explanations: "At a point in time the development proceeded in a different way, and sometimes the development isn't complete and we may have some trouble . . . in determining what the *actual* sex is. And so we have to do a blood test to help us" (my emphasis); "The baby may be a female, which you would know after the buccal smear, but you can't prove it yet. If so, then it's a normal female with a different appearance. This can be surgically corrected"; "The gender of your child isn't apparent to us at the moment"; "While this looks like a small penis, it's actually a large clitoris. And what we're going to do is put it back in its proper position and reduce the size of the tip of it enough so it doesn't look funny, so it looks right." Money and his colleagues report a case in which parents were advised to tell their friends that the reason their infant's gender was reannounced from male to female is that "the baby was . . . 'closed up down there' . . . when the closed skin was divided, the female organs were revealed, and the baby discovered to be, *in fact,* a girl" (my emphasis). It was mistakenly assumed to be a male at first because "there was an excess of skin on the clitoris."[26]

The message in these examples is that the trouble lies in the doctor's ability to determine the gender, not in the baby's gender per se. The real gender will presumably be determined/proven by testing, and the "bad" genitals (which are confusing the situation for everyone) will be "repaired." The emphasis is not on the doctors creating gender but in their completing the genitals. Physicians say that they "reconstruct" the genitals rather than "construct" them. The surgeons reconstitute from remaining parts what should have been there all along. The fact that gender in an infant is "reannounced" rather than "reassigned" suggests that the first announcement was a mistake because the announcer was confused by the genitals. The gender always was what it is now seen to be.[27]

Finally, physicians tell parents that social factors are more important in gender development than biological ones, even though they are searching for biological causes. In essence, the physicians teach the parents Money and

Ehrhardt's theory of gender development.[28] In doing so, they shift the emphasis from the discovery of biological factors that are a sign of the "real" gender to providing the appropriate social conditions to produce the "real" gender. What remains unsaid is the apparent contradiction in the notion that a "real" or "natural" gender can be, or needs to be, produced artificially. The physician/parent discussions make it clear to family members that gender is not a biological given (even though, of course, their own procedures for diagnosis assume that it is), and that gender is fluid. The psychoendocrinologist paraphrased an explanation to parents thus: "It will depend, ultimately, on how everybody treats your child and how your child is looking as a person. . . . I can with confidence tell them that generally gender [identity] clearly agrees with the assignment." Similarly, a pediatric endocrinologist explained: "[I] try to impress upon them that there's an enormous amount of clinical data to support the fact that if you sex-reverse an infant . . . the majority of the time the alternative gender identity is commensurate with the socialization, the way that they're raised, and how people view them, and that seems to be the most critical."

The implication of these comments is that gender identity (of all children, not just those born with ambiguous genitals) is determined primarily by social factors, that the parents and community always construct the child's gender. In the case of intersexed infants, the physicians merely provide the right genitals to go along with the socialization. Of course, at normal births, when the infant's genitals are unambiguous, the parents are not told that the child's gender is ultimately up to socialization. In those cases, doctors do treat gender as a biological given.

SOCIAL FACTORS IN DECISION MAKING

Most of the physicians interviewed claimed that personal convictions of doctors ought to play no role in the decision-making process. The psychoendocrinologist explained: "I think the most critical factors [are] what is the possibility that this child will grow up with genitals which look like that of the assigned gender and which will ultimately function according to gender . . . That's why it's so important that it's a well-established team, because [personal convictions] can't really enter into it. It has to be what is surgically and endocrinologically possible for that baby to be able to make it . . . It's really much more within medical criteria. I don't think many social factors enter into it." While this doctor eschews the importance of social factors in gender assignment, she argues forcefully that social factors are extremely important in the development of gender identity. Indeed, she implies that social factors primarily enter the picture once the infant leaves the hospital.

In fact, doctors make decisions about gender on the basis of shared cultural values that are unstated, perhaps even unconscious, and therefore considered objective rather than subjective. Money states the fundamental rule for gender assignment: "Never assign a baby to be reared, and to surgical and hormonal therapy, as a boy, unless the phallic structure, hypospadiac or otherwise, is neonatally of at least the same caliber as that of same-aged males with small-average penises."[29] Elsewhere, he and his colleagues provide specific measurements for what qualifies as a micropenis: "A penis is, by convention, designated as a micropenis when at birth its dimensions are three or more standard deviations below the mean. . . . When it is correspondingly reduced in diameter with corpora that are vestigial . . . it unquestionably qualifies as a micropenis."[30] A pediatric endocrinologist claimed that although "the [size of the] phallus is not the deciding factor . . . if the phallus is less than 2 centimeters long at birth and won't respond to androgen treatments, then it's made into a female."

These guidelines are clear, but they focus on only one physical feature, one that is distinctly imbued with cultural meaning. This becomes especially apparent in the case of an XX infant with normal female reproductive gonads and a perfect penis. Would the size and shape of the penis, in this case, be the deciding factor in assigning the infant "male," or would the perfect penis be surgically destroyed and female genitals created? Money notes that this dilemma would be complicated by the anticipated reaction of the parents to seeing "their apparent son lose his penis."[31] Other researchers concur that parents are likely to want to raise a child with a normal-shaped penis (regardless of size) as "male," particularly if the scrotal area looks normal and if the parents have had no experience with intersexuality.[32] Elsewhere Money argues in favor of not neonatally amputating the penis of XX infants, since fetal masculinization of brain structures would predispose them "almost invariably [to] develop behaviorally as tomboys, even when reared as girls."[33] This reasoning implies, first, and, second, that it is preferable to remove the internal female organs, implant prosthetic testes, and regulate the "boy's" hormones for his entire life than to overlook or disregard the perfection of the penis.[34]

The ultimate proof to these physicians that they intervened appropriately and gave the intersexed infant the correct gender assignment is that the reconstructed genitals look normal and function normally once the patient reaches adulthood. The vulva, labia, and clitoris should appear ordinary to the woman and her partner(s), and the vagina should be able to receive a normal-sized penis. Similarly, the man and his partner(s) should feel that his penis (even if somewhat smaller than the norm) looks and functions in an unremarkable way. Although there is no reported data on how much emphasis the intersexed person, him- or herself, places upon genital appearance and functioning, the physicians are absolutely clear about what they believe is important. The clinical geneticist said, "If you have . . . a seventeen-year-old young lady who has gotten hormone therapy and has breast development and pubic hair and no vaginal opening, I can't even entertain the notion that this young lady wouldn't want to have corrective surgery." The urologist summarized his criteria: "Happiness is the biggest factor. Anatomy is part of happiness." Money states, "The primary deficit [of not having a sufficient penis]—and destroyer of morale—lies in being unable to satisfy the partner."[35] Another team of clinicians reveals their phallocentrism, arguing that the most serious mistake in gender assignment is to create "an individual unable to engage in genital [heterosexual] sex."[36]

The equation of gender with genitals could only have emerged in an age when medical science can create credible-appearing and functioning genitals, and an emphasis on the good phallus above all else could only have emerged in a culture that has rigid aesthetic and performance criteria for what constitutes maleness. The formulation "good penis equals male; absence of good penis equals female" is treated in the literature and by the physicians interviewed as an objective criterion, operative in all cases. There is a striking lack of attention to the size and shape requirements of the female genitals, other than that the vagina be able to receive a penis.[37]

In the late nineteenth century when women's reproductive function was culturally designated as their essential characteristic, the presence or absence of ovaries (whether or not they were fertile) was held to be the ultimate criterion of gender assignment for hermaphrodites. The urologist interviewed recalled a case as late as the 1950s of a male child reassigned to "female" at the age of four or five because ovaries had been discovered. Nevertheless, doctors today, schooled in the etiology and treatment of the various intersex syndromes, view decisions based primarily on gonads as wrong, although, they complain, the conviction that the gonads are the ultimate criterion "still dictates the decisions of the uneducated and uninformed."[38] Presumably, the educated and informed now know that decisions based primarily on phallic size, shape, and sexual capacity are right.

While the prospect of constructing good genitals is the primary consideration in physicians' gender assignments, another extramedical factor was repeatedly cited by the six physicians interviewed—the specialty of the attending physician. Although generally intersexed infants are treated by teams of specialists, only the person who coordinates the team is actually responsible for the case. This person, acknowledged by the other physicians as having chief responsibility, acts as spokesperson to the parents. Although all of the physicians claimed that these medical teams work smoothly with few discrepancies of opinion, several of them mentioned decision-making orientations that are grounded in particular medical specializations. One endocrinologist stated, "The easiest route to take, where there is ever any question . . . is to raise the child as female. . . . In this country that is usual if the infant falls into the hands of a pediatric endocrinologist. . . . If the decision is made by the urologists, who are mostly males, . . . they're always opting, because they do the surgery, they're always feeling they can correct anything." Another endocrinologist concurred: "[Most urologists] don't think in terms of dynamic processes. They're interested in fixing pipes and lengthening pipes, and not dealing with hormonal, and certainly not psychological issues. . . . 'What can I do with what I've got.' " Urologists were defended by the clinical geneticist: "Surgeons here, now I can't speak for elsewhere, they don't get into a situation where the child is a year old and they can't make anything." Whether or not urologists "like to make boys," as one endocrinologist claimed, the following example from a urologist who was interviewed explicitly links a cultural interpretation of masculinity to the medical treatment plan. The case involved an adolescent who had been assigned the female gender at birth but was developing some male pubertal signs and wanted to be a boy. "He was ill-equipped," said the urologist, "yet we made a very respectable male out of him. He now owns a huge construction business—those big cranes that put stuff up on the building."

POSTINFANCY CASE MANAGEMENT

After the infant's gender has been assigned, parents generally latch onto the assignment as the solution to the problem—and it is. The physician as detective has collected the evidence, as lawyer has presented the case, and as judge has rendered a verdict. Although most of the interviewees claimed that the parents are equal participants in the whole process, they gave no instances of parental participation prior to the gender assignment.[39] After the physicians assign the infant's gender, the parents are encouraged to establish the credibility of that gender publicly by, for example, giving a detailed medical explanation to a leader in their community, such as a physician or pastor, who will explain the situation to curious casual acquaintances. Money argues that "medical terminology has a special layman's magic in such a context; it is final and authoritative and closes the issue." He also recommends that eventually the mother "settle [the] argument once and for all among her women friends by allowing some of them to see the baby's reconstructed genitalia."[40] Apparently, the powerful influence of normal-looking genitals helps overcome a history of ambiguous gender.

Some of the same issues that arise in assigning gender recur some years later when, at adolescence, the child may be referred to a physician for counseling.[41] The physician then tells the adolescent many of the same things his or her parents had been told years before, with the same language. Terms like "abnormal," "disorder," "disease," and "hermaphroditism" are avoided; the condition is normalized, and the child's gender is treated as unproblematic. One clinician explains to his patients that sex organs are different in appearance for each person, not just those who are intersexed. Furthermore, he tells the girls "that while most women menstruate, not all do . . . that conception is only one of a number of ways to become a parent; [and] that today some individuals are choosing not to become parents."[42] The clinical geneticist tells a typical female patient: "You are female. Female is not determined by your genes. Lots of other things determine being a woman. And you are a woman but you won't be able to have babies."

A case reported by one of the pediatric endocrinologists involving an adolescent female with androgen insensitivity provides an intriguing insight into the postinfancy gender-management process. She was told at the age of fourteen "that her ovaries weren't normal and had been removed. That's why she needed pills to look normal. . . . I wanted to convince her of her femininity. Then I told her she could marry and have normal sexual relations . . . [her]

uterus won't develop but [she] could adopt children." The urologist interviewed was asked to comment on this handling of the counseling. "It sounds like a very good solution to it. He's stating the truth, and if you don't state the truth . . . then you're in trouble later." This is a strange version of "the truth," however, since the adolescent was chromosomally XY and was born with normal testes that produced normal quantities of androgen. There were no existing ovaries or uterus to be abnormal. Another pediatric endocrinologist, in commenting on the management of this case, hedged the issue by saying that he would have used a generic term like "the gonads." A third endocrinologist said she would say that the uterus had never formed.

Technically these physicians are lying when, for example, they explain to an adolescent XY female with an intersexed history that her "ovaries . . . had to be removed because they were unhealthy or were producing 'the wrong balance of hormones.' "[43] We can presume that these lies are told in the service of what the physicians consider a greater good—keeping individual/concrete genders as clear and uncontaminated as the notions of female and male are in the abstract. The clinician suggests that with some female patients it eventually may be possible to talk to them "about their gonads having some structures and features that are testicular-like."[44] This call for honesty might be based at least partly on the possibility of the child's discovering his or her chromosomal sex inadvertently from a buccal smear taken in a high school biology class. Today's litigious climate is possibly another encouragement.

In sum, the adolescent is typically told that certain internal organs did not form because of an endocrinological defect, not because those organs could never have developed in someone with her or his sex chromosomes. The topic of chromosomes is skirted. There are no published studies on how these adolescents experience their condition and their treatment by doctors. An endocrinologist interviewed mentioned that her adolescent patients rarely ask specifically what is wrong with them, suggesting that they are accomplices in this evasion. In spite of the "truth" having been evaded, the clinician's impression is that "their gender identities and general senses of well-being and self-esteem appear not to have suffered."[45]

CONCLUSION

Physicians conduct careful examinations of intersexed infants' genitals and perform intricate laboratory procedures. They are interpreters of the body, trained and committed to uncovering the "actual" gender obscured by ambiguous genitals. Yet they also have considerable leeway in assigning gender, and their decisions are influenced by cultural as well as medical factors. What is the relationship between the physician as discoverer and the physician as determiner of gender? Where is the relative emphasis placed in discussions with parents and adolescents and in the consciousness of physicians? It is misleading to characterize the doctors whose words are provided here as presenting themselves publicly to the parents as discoverers of the infant's real gender other than the one being determined or constructed by the medical professionals. They are not hypocritical. It is also misleading to claim that physicians' focus shifts from discovery to determination over the course of treatment: first the doctors regarded the infant's gender as an unknown but discoverable reality; then the doctors relinquish their attempts to find the real gender and treat the infant's gender as something they must construct. They are not medically incompetent or deficient. Instead, I am arguing that the peculiar balance of discovery and determination throughout treatment permits physicians to handle very problematic cases of gender in the most unproblematic of ways.

This balance relies fundamentally on a particular conception of the "natural."[46] Although the deformity of intersexed genitals would be immutable were it not for medical interference, physicians do not consider it natural. Instead they think of, and speak of, the surgical/hormonal alteration of such deformities as natural because such intervention returns the body to what it "ought to have been" if events had taken their typical course. The nonnormative is converted into the normative, and the normative state is considered natural.[47] The genital ambiguity is remedied to conform to a "natural," that is, culturally indisputable, gender dichotomy. Sherry Ortner's claim that the culture/nature distinction is itself a construction—a product of culture—is relevant here. Language and imagery help create and maintain a specific view of what is natural about the two genders and, I would argue, about the very idea of gender—that is consists of two exclusive types: female and male.[48] The belief that gender consists of two exclusive types is maintained and perpetuated by the medical community in the face of incontrovertible physical evidence that this is not mandated by biology.

The lay conception of human anatomy and physiology assumes a concordance among clearly dimorphic gender markers—chromosomes, genitals, gonads, hormones—but physicians understand that concordance and dimorphism do not always exist. Their understanding of biology's complexity, however, does not inform their understanding of gender's complexity. In order for intersexuality to be managed differently than it currently is, physicians would have to take seriously Money's assertion that it is a misrepresentation of epistemology to consider any cell in the body authentically male or female.[49] If authenticity for gender resides not in a discoverable nature but in someone's proclamation, then the power to proclaim something else is available. If physicians recognized that implicit in their management of gender is the notion that finally, and always, people construct gender as well as the social systems that are grounded in gender-based concepts, the possibilities for real societal transformations would be unlimited. Unfortunately, neither in their representations to the families of the intersexed nor among themselves do the physicians interviewed for this study draw such far-reaching implications from their work. Their "understanding" that particular genders are medically (re)constructed in these cases does not lead them to see that gender is always constructed. Accepting genital ambiguity as a natural option would require that physicians also acknowledge that genital ambiguity is "corrected" not because it is threatening to the infant's life but because it is threatening to the infant's culture.

Rather than admit to their role in perpetuating gender, physicians "psychologize" the issue by talking about the parents' anxiety and humiliation in being confronted with an anomalous infant. The physicians talk as though they have no choice but to respond to the parents' pressure for a resolution of psychological discomfort, and as though they have no choice but to use medical technology in the service of a two-gender culture. Neither the psychology nor the technology is doubted, since both shield physicians from responsibility. Indeed, for the most part, neither physicians nor parents emerge from the experience of intersex case management with a greater understanding of the social construction of gender. Society's accountability, like their own, is masked by the assumption that gender is given. Thus, cases of intersexuality, instead of illustrating nature's failure to ordain gender in these isolated "unfortunate" instances, illustrate physicians' and Western society's failure of imagination—the failure to imagine that each of these management decisions is a moment when a specific instance of biological "sex" is transformed into a culturally constructed gender.

NOTES

I want to thank my student Jane Weider for skillfully conducting and transcribing the interviews for this article.

1. For historical reviews of the intersexed person in ancient Greek and Roman periods, see Leslie Fiedler, *Freaks: Myths and Images of the Second Self* (New York: Simon & Schuster, 1978); Vern Bullough, *Sexual Variance in Society and History* (New York: Wiley, 1976). For the Middle Ages and Renaissance, see Michel Foucault, *History of Sexuality* (New York: Pantheon, 1980). For the eighteenth and nineteenth centuries, see Michel Foucault, *Herculine Barbin* (New York: Pantheon, 1978); and for the early twentieth century, see Havelock Ellis, *Studies in the Psychology of Sex* (New York: Random House, 1942).

2. Suzanne J. Kessler and Wendy McKenna, *Gender: An Ethnomethodological Approach* (1978; reprint, Chicago: University of Chicago Press, 1985).

3. See, e.g., M. Bolkenius, R. Daum, and E. Heinrich, "Pediatric Surgical Principles in the Management of Children with Intersex," *Progressive Pediatric Surgery* 17 (1984): 33–38; Kenneth I. Glassberg, "Gender Assignment in Newborn Male Pseudohermaphrodites," *Urologic Clinics of North America* 7 (June 1980): 409–21; and Peter A. Lee et al., "Micropenis. I. Criteria, Etiologies and Classification," *Johns Hopkins Medical Journal* 146 (1980): 156–63.

4. It is impossible to get accurate statistics on the frequency of intersexuality. Chromosomal abnormalities (like XOXX, XXXY) are registered, but those conditions do not always imply ambiguous genitals, and most cases of ambiguous genitals do not involve chromosomal abnormalities. None of the physicians interviewed for this study would venture a guess on frequency rates, but all agreed that intersexuality is rare. One physician suggested that the average obstetrician may see only two cases in twenty years. Another estimated that a specialist may see only one a year, or possibly as many as five a year.

5. Mariano Castro-Magana, Moris Angulo, and Platon J. Collipp, "Management of the Child with Ambiguous Genitalia," *Medical Aspects of Human Sexuality* 18 (April 1984): 172–88.

6. For example, infants whose intersexuality is caused by congenital adrenal hyperplasia can develop severe electrolyte disturbances unless the condition is controlled by cortisone treatments. Intersexed infants whose condition is caused by androgen insensitivity are in danger of malignant degeneration of the testes unless they are removed. For a complete catalog of clinical syndromes related to the intersexed condition, see Arye Lev-Ran, "Sex Reversal as Related to Clinical Syndromes in Human Beings," in *Handbook of Sexology II: Genetics, Hormones and Behavior,* ed. John Money and H. Musaph (New York: Elsevier, 1978), pp. 157–73.

7. Much of the surgical experimentation in this area has been accomplished by urologists who are trying to create penises for female-to-male transsexuals. Although there have been some advancements in recent years in the ability to create a "reasonable-looking" penis from tissue taken elsewhere on the body, the complicated requirements of the organ (both urinary and sexual functioning) have posed surgical problems. It may be, however, that the concerns of the urologists are not identical to the concerns of the patients. While data are not yet available from the intersexed, we know that female-to-male transsexuals place greater emphasis on the "public" requirements of the penis (e.g., being able to look normal while standing at the urinal or wearing a bathing suit) than on its functional requirements (e.g., being able to carry urine or achieve an erection) (Kessler and McKenna, pp. 128–32). As surgical techniques improve, female-to-male transsexuals (and intersexed males) might increase their demands for organs that look and function better.

8. Historically, psychology has tended to blur the distinction between the two by equating a person's acceptance of her or his genitals with gender role and ignoring gender identity. For example, Freudian theory posited that if one had a penis and accepted its reality, then masculine gender role behavior would naturally follow (Sigmund Freud, "Some Psychical Consequences of the Anatomical Distinctions between the Sexes" [1925], vol. 18, *The Complete Psychological Works,* ed. and trans. J. Strachey [New York: Norton, 1976]).

9. Almost all of the published literature on intersexed infant case management has been written or cowritten by one researcher, John Money, professor of medical psychology and professor pediatrics, emeritus, at the Johns Hopkins University and Hospital, where he is director of the Psychohormonal Research Unit. Even the publications that are produced independently of Money reference him and reiterate his management philosophy. Although only one of the physicians interviewed publishes with Money, all of them essentially concur with his views and give the impression of a consensus that is rarely encountered in science. The one physician who raised some questions about Money's philosophy and the gender theory on which it is based has extensive experience with intersexuality in a nonindustrialized culture where the infant is managed differently with no apparent harm to gender development. Even though psychologists fiercely argue issues of gender identity and gender role development, doctors who treat intersexed infants seem untouched by these debates. There are no renegade voices either from within the medical establishment or, thus far, from outside. Why Money has been so single-handedly influential in promoting his ideas about gender is a question worthy of a separate substantial analysis. His management philosophy is conveyed in the following sources: John Money, J. G. Hampson, and J. L. Hampson, "Hermaphroditism: Recommendations concerning Assignment of Sex, Change of Sex, and Psychologic Management," *Bulletin of the Johns Hopkins Hospital* 97 (1955): 284–300; John Money, Reynolds Potter, and Clarice S. Stoll, "Sex Reannouncement in Hereditary Sex Deformity: Psychology and Sociology of Habilitation," *Social Science and Medicine* 3 (1969): 207–16; John Money and Anke A. Ehrhardt, *Man and Woman, Boy and Girl* (Baltimore: Johns Hopkins University Press, 1972); John Money, "Psychologic Consideration of Sex Assignment in Intersexuality," *Clinics in*

Plastic Surgery 1 (April 1974): 215–22, "Psychological Counseling: Hermaphroditism," in *Endocrine and Genetic Diseases of Childhood and Adolescence*, ed. L. I. Gardner (Philadelphia: Saunders, 1975), pp. 609–18, and "Birth Defect of the Sex Organs: Telling the Parents and the Patient," *British Journal of Sexual Medicine* 10 (March 1983): 14; John Money et al., "Micropenis, Family Mental Health, and Neonatal Management: A Report on Fourteen Patients Reared as Girls," *Journal of Preventive Psychiatry* 1, 1 (1981): 17–27.

10. Money and Ehrhardt, p. 152.

11. Contradictory data are presented in Milton Diamond, "Sexual Identity, Monozygotic Twins Reared in Discordant Sex Roles and a BBC Follow-up," *Archives of Sexual Behavior* 11, 2 (1982): 181–86.

12. Money, "Psychologic Consideration of Sex Assignment in Intersexuality."

13. Castro-Magana, Angulo, and Collipp (n. 5 above).

14. Victor Braren et al., "True Hermaphroditism: A Rational Approach to Diagnosis and Treatment," *Urology* 15 (June 1980): 569–74.

15. Studies of normal newborns have shown that from the moment of birth the parent responds to the infant based on the infant's gender. Jeffrey Rubin, F. J. Provenzano, and Z. Luria, "The Eye of the Beholder: Parents' Views on Sex of Newborns," *American Journal of Orthopsychiatry* 44, 4 (1974): 512–19.

16. Money et al. (n. 9 above).

17. There is evidence from other kinds of sources that once a gender attribution is made, all further information buttresses that attribution, and only the most contradictory new information will cause the original gender attribution to be questioned. See, e.g., Kessler and McKenna (n. 2 above).

18. Castro-Magana, Angulo, and Collipp (n. 5 above).

19. Money, "Psychological Consideration of Sex Assignment in Intersexuality" (n. 9 above).

20. Technically, the term "micropenis" should be reserved for an exceptionally small but well-formed structure. A small, malformed "penis" should be referred to as a "microphallus" (Lee et al. [n. 3 above]).

21. Money et. al., p. 26. A different view is argued by another leading gender identity theorist: "When a little boy (with an imperfect penis) knows he is a male, he creates a penis that functions symbolically the same as those of boys with normal penises" (Robert J. Stoller, *Sex and Gender* [New York: Aronson, 1968], 1: 49).

22. W. Ch. Hecker, "Operative Correction of Intersexual Genitals in Children," *Pediatric Surgery* 17 (1984): 21–31.

23. Elizabeth Bing and Esselyn Rudikoff, "Divergent Ways of Parental Coping with Hermaphrodite Children," *Medical Aspects of Human Sexuality*, December 1970, pp. 73–88.

24. These evasions must have many ramifications in everyday social interactions between parents and family and friends. How people "fill in" the uncertainty so that interactions remain relatively normal is an interesting issue that warrants further study. Indeed, the whole issue of parental reaction is worthy of analysis. One of the pediatric endocrinologists interviewed acknowledged that the published literature discusses intersex management only from the physicians' point of view. He asks. "How [do parents] experience what they're told; and what [do] they remember . . . and carry with them?" One published exception to this neglect of the parents' perspective is a case study comparing two couples' different coping strategies. The first couple, although initially distressed, handled the traumatic event by regarding the abnormality as an act of God. The second couple, more educated and less religious, put their faith in medical science and expressed a need to fully understand the biochemistry of the defect (ibid.).

25. Tom Mazur, "Ambiguous Genitalia: Detection and Counseling," *Pediatric Nursing* 9 (Nov./Dec. 1983): 417–31; Money, "Psychologic Consideration of Sex Assignment in Intersexuality" (n. 9 above), p. 218.

26. Money, Potter, and Stoll (n. 9 above), p. 211.

27. The term "reassignment" is more commonly used to describe the gender changes of those who are cognizant of their earlier gender, e.g., transsexuals—people whose gender itself was a mistake.

28. Although Money and Ehrhardt's socialization theory is uncontested by the physicians who treat intersexuality and is presented to parents as a matter of fact, there is actually much debate among psychologists about the effect of prenatal hormones on brain structure and ultimately on gender role behavior and even on gender identity. The physicians interviewed agreed that the animal evidence for prenatal brain organization is compelling but that there is no evidence in humans that prenatal hormones have an inviolate or unilateral effect. If there is any effect of prenatal exposure to androgen, they believe it can easily be overcome and modified by psychosocial factors. It is this latter position that is communicated to the parents, not the controversy in the field. For an argument favoring prenatally organized gender differences in the brain, see Milton Diamond, "Human Sexual Development: Biological Foundations for Social Development," in *Human Sexuality in Four Perspectives*, ed. Frank A. Beach (Baltimore: Johns Hopkins University Press, 1976), pp. 22–61; for a critique of that position, see Ruth Bleier, *Science and Gender: A Critique of Biology and Its Theories on Women* (New York: Pergamon, 1984).

29. Money, "Psychological Counseling: Hermaphroditism" (n. 9 above), p. 610.

30. Money et al. (n. 9 above), p. 18.

31. John Money, "Hermaphroditism and Pseudohermaphroditism," in *Gynecologic Endocrinology*, ed. Jay J. Gold (New York: Hoeber, 1968), pp. 449–64, esp. p. 460.

32. Mojtaba Besheshti et al., "Gender Assignment in Male Pseudohermaphrodite Children," *Urology*, December 1983, pp. 604–07. Of course, if the penis looked normal and the empty scrotum were overlooked, it might not be discovered until puberty that the male child was XX, with a female internal structure.

33. John Money, "Psychologic Consideration of Sex Assignment in Intersexuality" (n. 9 above), p. 216.

34. Weighing the probability of achieving a perfect penis against the probable trauma such procedures might involve is another social factor in decision making. According to an endocrinologist interviewed, if it seemed that an XY infant with an inadequate penis would require as many as ten genital operations over a six-year period in order to have an adequate penis, the infant would be assigned the female gender. In this case, the endocrinologist's practical and compassionate concern would override purely genital criteria.

35. Money, "Psychologic Consideration of Sex Assignment in Intersexuality," p. 217.

36. Castro-Magana, Angulo, and Collipp (n. 5 above), p. 180.

37. It is unclear how much of this bias is the result of a general, cultural devaluation of the female and how much the result of physicians' greater facility in constructing aesthetically correct and sexually functional female genitals.

38. Money, "Psychologic Consideration of Sex Assignment in Intersexuality," p. 215. Remnants of this anachronistic view can still be found, however, when doctors justify the removal of contradictory gonads on the grounds that they are typically sterile or at risk for malignancy (J. Dewhurst and D. B. Grant, "Intersex Problems," *Archives of Disease in Childhood* 59 [July/Dec. 1984]: 1191–94). Presumably, if the gonads were functional and healthy their removal would provide an ethical dilemma for at least some medical professionals.

39. Although one set of authors argued that the views of the parents on the most appropriate gender for their child must be taken into account (Dewhurst and Grant, p. 1192), the physicians interviewed denied direct knowledge of this kind of participation. They claimed that they personally had encountered few, if any, cases of parents who insisted on their child's being assigned a particular gender. Yet each had heard about cases where a family's ethnicity or religious background biased them toward

males. None of the physicians recalled whether this preference for male offspring meant the parents wanted a male regardless of the "inadequacy" of the penis, or whether it meant that the parents would have greater difficulty adjusting to a less-than-perfect male than to a "normal" female.

40. Money, "Psychological Counseling: Hermaphroditism" (n. 9 above), p. 613.

41. As with the literature on infancy, most of the published material on adolescents is on surgical and hormonal management rather than on social management. See, e.g., Joel J. Roslyn, Eric W. Fonkalsrud, and Barbara Lippe, "Intersex Disorders in Adolescents and Adults," *American Journal of Surgery* 146 (July 1983): 138–44.

42. Mazur (n. 25 above), p. 421.

43. Dewhurst and Grant, p. 1193.

44. Mazur, p. 422.

45. Ibid.

46. For an extended discussion of different ways of conceptualizing "natural," see Richard W. Smith, "What Kind of Sex Is Natural?" in *The Frontiers of Sex Research*, ed. Vern Bullough (Buffalo: Prometheus, 1979), pp. 103–11.

47. This supports sociologist Harold Garfinkel's argument that we treat routine events as our due as social members and that we treat gender, like all normal forms, as a moral imperative. It is no wonder, then, that physicians conceptualize what they are doing as natural and unquestionably "right" (Harold Garfinkel, *Studies in Ethnomethodology* [Englewood Cliffs, NJ: Prentice-Hall, 1967]).

48. Sherry B. Ortner, "Is Female to Male as Nature Is to Culture?" in *Woman, Culture, and Society*, ed. Michelle Zimbalist Rosaldo and Louise Lamphere (Stanford: Stanford University Press, 1974), pp. 67–87.

49. Money, "Psychological Counseling: Hermaphroditism" (n. 9 above), p. 618.

CHAPTER 16

WOMEN AND THE KNIFE

Cosmetic Surgery and the Colonization of Women's Bodies

KATHRYN PAULY MORGAN

(1991)

Consider the following passages:

> If you want to wear a Maidenform Viking Queen bra like Madonna, be warned: A body like this doesn't just happen. . . . Madonna's kind of fitness training takes time. The rock star *whose muscled body was recently on tour* spends a minimum of three hours a day working out. ("Madonna Passionate About Fitness" 1990; italics added)

> A lot of the contestants [in the Miss America Pageant] do not owe their beauty to their Maker but to their Re-Maker. Miss Florida's nose came courtesy of her surgeon. So did Miss Alaska's. And Miss Oregon's breasts came from the manufacturers of silicone. (Goodman 1989)

> Jacobs [a plastic surgeon in Manhattan] constantly answers the call for cleavage. "Women need it for their holiday ball gowns." ("Cosmetic Surgery For the Holidays" 1985)

> We hadn't seen or heard from each other for 28 years. . . . Then he suggested it would be nice if we could meet. I was very nervous about it. How much had I changed? I wanted a facelift, tummy tuck and liposuction, all in one week. (A woman, age forty-nine, being interviewed for an article on "older couples" falling in love; "Falling in Love Again" 1990)

> "It's hard to say why one person will have cosmetic surgery done and another won't consider it, but generally I think people who go for surgery are more aggressive, they are the doers of the world. It's like makeup. You see some women who might be greatly improved by wearing make-up, but they're, I don't know, granola-heads or something, and they just refuse." (Dr. Ronald Levine, director of plastic surgery education at the University of Toronto and vice-chairman of the plastic surgery section of the Ontario Medical Association; "The Quest to Be a Perfect 10" 1990)

> Another comparable limitation [of the women's liberation movement] is a tendency to reject certain good things only in order to punish men. . . . There is no reason why a women's liberation activist should not try to look pretty and attractive. (Markovic 1976)

This paper is about women and about the knives that "sculpt" our bodies to make us beautiful forever. I want to explore this topic for five reasons. First, I am interested in the project of developing a feminist hermeneutics that tries to understand the words and choices of women situated in an interface position with various so-called experts in Western culture.

Second, I experience genuine epistemic and political bewilderment when I, as a feminist woman, think about contemporary practices and individual choices in the area of elective cosmetic surgery.[1] Is this a setting of liberation or oppression—or both?

Third, I have come to realize that this is a "silent" (if not silenced) topic both in mainstream bioethics and in recent ground-breaking discussions in feminist medical ethics.[2] Apart from some tangential references, there is virtually no discussion, feminist or otherwise, of the normative and political issues that might be raised in relation to women and elective cosmetic surgery. I believe we need a feminist framework and critique to understand why *breast augmentation*, until recently, was the most frequently performed kind of cosmetic surgery in North America ("New Bodies For Sale") and why, according to *Longevity* magazine, 1 in every 225 adult Americans had *elective* cosmetic surgery in 1989. We need a feminist analysis to understand why actual, live women are reduced and reduce themselves to "potential women" and choose to participate in anatomizing and fetishizing their bodies as they buy "contoured bodies," "restored youth," and "permanent beauty." In the face of a growing market and demand for surgical interventions in women's bodies that can and do result in infection, bleeding, embolisms, pulmonary edema, facial nerve injury, unfavorable scar formation, skin loss, blindness, crippling, and death, our silence becomes a culpable one.

Fourth, I situate this topic in the larger framework of the contemporary existential technologizing of women's bodies in Western culture. We are witnessing a *normalization* of elective cosmetic surgery. As the author of an article targeted to homemakers remarks, "For many women, it's no longer a question of *whether* to undergo cosmetic surgery—but what, when, by whom and how much" (McCabe 1990). Not only is elective cosmetic surgery moving out of the domain of the sleazy, the suspicious, the secretively deviant, or the pathologically narcissistic, *it is becoming the norm.* This shift is leading to a predictable inversion of the domains of the deviant and the pathological, so that women who contemplate *not using* cosmetic surgery will increasingly be stigmatized and seen as deviant. I believe it is crucial that we understand these normative inversions that are catalyzed by the technologizing of women's bodies.

Finally, I am intrigued by the deeper epistemological and metaphysical dynamics of the field of cosmetic surgery. For example, a recent hospital-sponsored *health* conference advertised a special session on "facial regeneration" by asking, "Are you looking in the mirror and, seeing the old you, wishing you could be seeing the you that you used to be?" and then promising that this previous, youthful "you" could be regenerated. As a philosopher, I am shocked at the extent to which patients and cosmetic surgeons participate in committing one of the deepest of original philosophical sins, the choice of the apparent over the real. Cosmetic surgery entails the ultimate envelopment of the lived temporal *reality* of the human subject by technologically created appearances that are then regarded as "the real." Youthful appearance triumphs over aged reality.

"JUST THE FACTS IN AMERICA, MA'AM"

As of 1990, the most frequently performed kind of cosmetic surgery is liposuction, which involves sucking fat cells out from underneath our skin with a vacuum device. This is viewed as the most suitable procedure for removing specific bulges around the hips, thighs, belly, buttocks, or chin. It is most appropriately done on thin people who want to get rid of certain bulges, and surgeons guarantee that even if there is weight gain, the bulges won't reappear since the fat cells have been permanently removed. At least twelve deaths are known to have resulted from complications such as hemorrhages and embolisms. "All we know is there was a complication and that complication was death," said the partner of Toni Sullivan, age forty-three ("hardworking mother of two teenage children" says the press; "Woman, 43, Dies After Cosmetic Surgery" 1989). Cost $1,000–$7,500.

The second most frequently performed kind of cosmetic surgery is breast augmentation, which involves an implant, usually of silicone. Often the silicone implant hardens over time and must be removed surgically. Over one million women in the United States are known to have had breast augmentation surgery. Two recent studies have show that breast implants block X-rays and cast a shadow on surrounding tissue, making mammograms difficult to interpret, and that there appears to be a much higher incidence of cancerous lumps in "augmented women" ("Implants Hide Tumors in Breasts, Study Says" 1988). Cost: $1,500–$3,000.

"Facelift" is a kind of umbrella term that covers several sorts of procedures. In a recent Toronto case, Dale Curtis "decided to get a facelift for her fortieth birthday. . . . [Dr.] Bederman used liposuction on the jowls and neck, removed the skin and fat from her upper and lower lids and tightened up the muscles in the neck and cheeks. . . . 'She was supposed to get a forehead lift but she chickened out,' Bederman says" ("Changing Faces" 1989). Clients are now being advised to begin their facelifts in their early forties and are also told that they will need subsequent facelifts every five to fifteen years. Cost: $2,500–$10,500.

"Nips" and "tucks" are cute, camouflaging labels used to refer to surgical reduction performed on any of the following areas of the body: hips, buttocks, thighs, belly, and breasts. They involve cutting out wedges of skin and fat and sewing up the two sides. These are major surgical procedures that cannot be performed in outpatient clinics because of the need for anaesthesia and the severity of possible postoperative complications. Hence, they require access to costly operating rooms and services in hospitals or clinics. Cost: $3,000–$7,000.

The number of "rhinoplasties" or nose jobs, has risen by thirty-four percent since 1981. Some clients are coming in for second and third nose jobs. Nose jobs involve either the inserting of a piece of bone taken from elsewhere in the body or the whittling down of the nose. Various styles of noses go in and out of fashion, and various cosmetic surgeons describe the noses they create in terms of their own surnames, such as "the Diamond nose" or "the Goldman nose" ("Cosmetic Surgery for the Holidays" 1985). Cost: $2,000–$3,000.

More recent types of cosmetic surgery, such as the use of skin-expanders and suction lipectomy, involve inserting tools, probes, and balloons *under* the skin either for purpose of expansion or reduction (Hirshson 1987).

Lest one think that women (who represent between sixty and seventy percent of all cosmetic surgery patients) choose only one of these procedures, heed the words of Dr. Michael Jon Bederman of the Centre for Cosmetic Surgery in Toronto:

> We see working girls, dental technicians, middle-class women who are unhappy with their looks or are aging prematurely. And we see executives—both male and female. . . . Where before someone would have a tummy tuck and not have anything else done for a year, frequently we will do liposuction and tummy tuck and then the next day a facelift, upper and lower lids, rhinoplasty *and other things*. The recovery time is the same whether a person has one procedure or *the works*, generally about two weeks. ("Changing Faces" 1989; italics added)

In principle, there is no area of the body that is not accessible to the interventions and metamorphoses performed by cosmetic surgeons intent on creating twentieth-century versions of "femina perfecta."[3]

FROM ARTIFICE TO ARTIFACT: THE CREATION OF ROBOWOMAN?

In his article "Toward a Philosophy of Technology," Hans Jonas (1979) distinguishes between premodern and modern technology. Part of what is especially characteristic of modern technology, he suggests, is that the relationship of means and ends is no longer unilinear but circular, so that "new technologies may suggest, create, even impose new ends, never before conceived, simply by offering their feasibility. . . . Technology thus adds to the very objectives of human desires, including objectives for technology itself" (Jonas 1979, p. 35). In 1979, Jonas only speculates about the final stage of technological creation: "Are we, perhaps, on the verge of a technology, based on biological knowledge and wielding an engineering art which, this time, has man [*sic*] himself for its object? This has become a theoretical possibility . . . and it has been rendered morally possible by the metaphysical neutralizing of man" (Jonas 1979, p 41). We now know that the answer to Jonas' question is yes. We have arrived at the stage of regarding ourselves as both technological subject and object, transformable and literally creatable through biological engineering. The era of biotechnology is clearly upon us and is invading even the most private and formerly sequestered domains of human life, including women's wombs. I interpret the spectacular rise of the technology of cosmetic surgery as a form of biotechnology that fits this dialectical picture of modern technology.

The domain of technology is often set up in oppositional relation to a domain that is designated "the natural." The role assigned to technology is often that of transcendence, transformation, control, exploitation, or destruction, and the technologized object or process is conceptualized as inferior or primitive, in need of perfecting transformation or exploitation through technology in the name of some "higher" purpose or end, or deserving of eradication because it is harmful or evil.

Although there continue to be substantive theoretical challenges to its dominant metaphors, Western scientific medicine views the human body essentially as a machine.[4] The machine model carries with it certain implications, among which is the reduction of spirit, affect, and value to mechanistic processes in the human body. This perspective also facilitates viewing and treating the body in atomistic and mechanical fashion, so that, for example, the increasing mechanization of the body in terms of artificial hearts, kidneys, joints, limbs, and computerized implants is seen as an ordinary progression within the dominant model. Correlative with the rise of the modeling of the human brain as an information-processing machine, we are witnessing the development of genetic engineering; transsexual surgery; the technological transformation of all aspects of human conception, maternity, and birthing; and the artificial prolongation of human life.

What is designated "the natural" functions primarily as a frontier rather than as a barrier. While genetics, human sexuality, reproductive outcome, and death were previously regarded as open to variation primarily in evolutionary terms, they are now seen by biotechnologists as domains of creation and control. Cosmetic surgeons claim a role here too. For them, human bodies are the locus of challenge. As one plastic surgeon remarks:

> Patients sometimes misunderstand the nature of cosmetic surgery. It's not a shortcut for diet or exercise. *It's a way to override the genetic code.* ("Retouching Nature's Way" 1990; italics added)

The beauty culture is coming to be dominated by a variety of experts, and consumers of youth and beauty are likely to find themselves dependent not only on cosmetic surgeons but on anaesthetists, nurses, aestheticians, nail technicians, manicurists, dietitians, hairstylists, cosmetologists, masseuses, aroma therapists, trainers, pedicurists, electrolysists, pharmacologists, and dermatologists. All these experts provide services that can be bought; all these experts are perceived as administering and transforming the human body into an increasingly artificial and ever more perfect object. Think of the contestants in the Miss America pageant who undergo cosmetic surgery in preparation for participation. Reflect on the headline of the article in *Newsweek* (May 27, 1985) on cosmetic surgery: "New Bodies for Sale."

How do these general remarks concerning technology and the body apply to women—and to which women—and why? For virtually all women as women, success is defined in terms of interlocking patterns of compulsion: compulsory attractiveness, compulsory motherhood, and compulsory heterosexuality, patterns that determine the legitimate limits of attraction and motherhood.[5] Rather than aspiring to self-determined and woman-centered ideals of health or integrity, women's attractiveness is defined as attractive-to-men; women's eroticism is defined as either nonexistent, pathological, or peripheral when it is not directed to phallic goals; and motherhood is defined in terms of legally sanctioned and constrained reproductive service to particular men and to institutions such as the nation, the race, the owner, and the class—institutions that are, more often than not, male-dominated. Biotechnology is now making beauty, fertility, the appearance of heterosexuality through surgery, and the appearance of youthfulness accessible to virtually all women who can afford that technology—and growing numbers of women are making other sacrifices in their lives in order to buy access to the technical expertise.

In Western industrialized societies, women have also become increasingly socialized into an acceptance of technical knives. We know about knives that can heal: the knife that saves the life of a baby in distress, the knife that cuts out the cancerous growths in our breasts, the knife that straightens our spines, the knife that liberates our arthritic fingers so that we may once again gesture, once again touch, once again hold. But we also know about other knives: the knife that cuts off our toes so that our feet will fit into elegant shoes, the knife that cuts out ribs to fit our bodies into corsets, the knife that slices through our labia in episiotomies and other forms of genital mutilation, the knife that cuts into our abdomens to remove our ovaries to cure our "deviant tendencies" (Barker-Benfield 1976), the knife that removes our breasts in prophylactic or unnecessary radical mastectomies, the knife that cuts out our "useless bag" (the womb) if we're the wrong color and poor or if we've "outlived our fertility," the knife that makes the "bikini cut" across our pregnant bellies to facilitate the cesarean section that will allow the obstetrician to go on holiday. We know these knives well.

And now we are coming to know the knives and needles of the cosmetic surgeons—the knives that promise to sculpt our bodies, to restore our youth, to create beauty out of what was ugly and ordinary. What kind of knives are these? Magic knives. Magic knives in a patriarchal context. Magic knives in a Eurocentric context. Magic knives in a white supremacist context. What do they mean? I am afraid of these knives.

LISTENING TO THE WOMEN

In order to give a feminist reading of any ethical situation we must listen to the women's own reasons for their actions (Sherwin 1984–85 and 1989). It is only once we have listened to the voices of women who have elected to undergo cosmetic surgery that we can try to assess the extent to which the conditions for genuine choice have been met and look at the consequences of these choices for the position of women. Here are some of those voices:

Voice 1 (a woman looking forward to attending a prestigious charity ball): "There will be a lot of new faces at the Brazilian Ball" ("Changing Faces" 1989). [Class/status symbol]

Voice 2: "You can keep yourself trim. . . . But you have no control over the way you wrinkle, or the fat on your hips, or the skin on your lower abdomen. If you are *hereditarily predestined* to stretch out or wrinkle in your face, you will. If your parents had puffy eyelids and saggy jowls, you're going to have puffy eyelids and saggy jowls" ("Changing Faces" 1989). [Regaining a sense of control; liberation from parents; transcending hereditary predestination]

Voice 3: "Now we want a nose that makes a statement, with tip definition and a strong bridge line" ("Changing Faces" 1989). [Domination; strength]

Voice 4: "I decided to get a facelift for my fortieth birthday after ten years of living and working in the tropics had taken its toll" ("Changing Faces" 1989). [Gift to the self; erasure of a decade of hard work and exposure]

Voice 5: "I've gotten my breasts augmented. I can use it as a tax write-off" ("Changing Faces" 1989). [Professional advancement; economic benefits]

Voice 6: "I'm a teacher and kids let schoolteachers know how we look and they aren't nice about it. A teacher who looks like an old bat or has a big nose will get a nickname" ("Retouching Nature's Way: Is Cosmetic Surgery Worth It?" 1990). [Avoidance of cruelty; avoidance of ageist bias]

Voice 7: "I'll admit to a boob job." (Susan Akin, Miss America of 1986, quoted in Goodman 1986). [Prestige; status; competitive accomplishments in beauty contest]

Voice 8 (forty-five-year-old grandmother and proprietor of a business): "In my business, the customers expect you to look as good as they do" (Hirshson 1987). [Business asset; economic gain; possible denial of grandmother status]

Voice 9: "People in business see something like this as showing an overall aggressiveness and go-forwardness *The trend is to, you know, be all that you can be*" ("Cosmetic Surgery for the Holidays" 1985). [Success; personal fulfillment]

Voice 10: (paraphrase): "I do it to fight holiday depression" ("Cosmetic Surgery for the Holidays" 1985). [Emotional control; happiness]

Voice 11: "I came to see Dr. X for the holiday season. I have important business parties, and the man I'm trying to get to marry me is coming in from Paris"

("Cosmetic Surgery for the Holidays" 1985). [Economic gain; heterosexual affiliation]

Women have traditionally regarded (and been taught to regard) their bodies, particularly if they are young, beautiful, and fertile, *as a locus of power* to be enhanced through artifice and, now, through artifact. In 1792, in A *Vindication of the Rights of Woman,* Mary Wollstonecraft remarked: "Taught from infancy that beauty is woman's scepter, the mind shapes itself to the body and roaming round its gilt cage, only seeks to adorn its prison." How ironic that the mother of the creator of *Frankenstein* should be the source of that quote. We need to ask ourselves whether today, involved as we are in the modern inversion of "our bodies shaping themselves to our minds," we are creating a new species of woman-monster with new artifactual bodies that function as prisons or whether cosmetic surgery for women does represent a potentially liberating field of choice.[6]

When Snow White's stepmother asks the mirror "Who is fairest of all?" she is not asking simply an empirical question. In wanting to continue to be "the fairest of all," she is striving, in a clearly competitive context, for a prize, for a position, for power. The affirmation of her beauty brings with it privileged heterosexual affiliation, privileged access to forms of power unavailable to the plain, the ugly, the aged, and the barren.

The Voices are seductive—they speak the language of gaining access to transcendence, achievement, liberation, and power. And they speak to a kind of reality. First, electing to undergo the surgery necessary to create youth and beauty artificially not only appears to but often actually does give a woman a sense of identity that, to some extent, she has chosen herself. Second, it offers her the potential to raise her status both socially and economically by increasing her opportunities for heterosexual affiliation (especially with white men). Third, by committing herself to the pursuit of beauty, a woman integrates her life with a consistent set of values and choices that bring her widespread approval and a resulting sense of increased self-esteem. Fourth, the pursuit of beauty often gives a woman access to a range of individuals who administer to her body in a caring way, an experience often sadly lacking in the day-to-day lives of many women. As a result, a woman's pursuit of beauty through transformation is often associated with lived experiences of self-creation, self-fulfillment, self-transcendence, and being cared for. The power of these experiences must not be underestimated.[7]

While I acknowledge that these choices can confer a kind of integrity on a woman's life, I also believe that they are likely to embroil her in a set of interrelated contradictions. I refer to these as "Paradoxes of Choice."

THREE PARADOXES OF CHOICE

In exploring these paradoxes, I appropriate Foucault's analysis of the diffusion of power in order to understand forms of power that are potentially more personally invasive than are more obvious, publicly identifiable aspects of power. In the chapter "Docile Bodies" in *Discipline and Punish*, Foucault (1979, pp. 136–37) highlights three features of what he calls disciplinary power:

1) The *scale* of the control. In disciplinary power the body is treated individually and in a coercive way because the body itself is the *active* and hence apparently free body that is being controlled through movements, gestures, attitudes, and degrees of rapidity.

2) The *object* of the control, which involves meticulous control over the efficiency of movements and forces.

3) The *modality* of the control, which involves constant, uninterrupted coercion.

Foucault argues that the outcome of disciplinary power is the docile body, a body "that may be subjected, used, transformed, and improved" (Foucault 1979, p. 136). Foucault is discussing this model of power in the context of prisons and armies, but we can adapt the central insights of this notion to see how women's bodies are entering "a machinery of power that explores it, breaks it down, and rearranges it" through a recognizably political metamorphosis of embodiment (Foucault 1979, p. 138).[8] What is important about this notion in relation to cosmetic surgery is the extent to which it makes it possible to speak about the diffusion of power throughout Western industrialized cultures that are increasingly committed to a technological beauty imperative. It also makes it possible to refer to a set of experts—cosmetic surgeons— whose explicit power mandate is to explore, break down, and rearrange women's bodies.

Paradox One: The Choice of Conformity—Understanding the Number Ten

While the technology of cosmetic surgery could clearly be used to create and celebrate idiosyncrasy, eccentricity, and uniqueness, it is obvious that this is not how it is presently being used. Cosmetic surgeons report that legions of women appear in their offices demanding "Bo Derek" breasts ("Cosmetic Surgery for the Holidays" 1985). Jewish women demand reductions of their noses so as to be able to "pass" as one of their Aryan sisters who form the dominant ethnic group (Lakoff and Scherr 1984). Adolescent Asian girls who bring in pictures of Elizabeth Taylor and of Japanese movie actresses (whose faces have already been reconstructed) demand the "Westernizing" of their own eyes and the creation of higher noses in hopes of better job and marital prospects ("New Bodies for Sale" 1985). Black women buy toxic bleaching agents in hopes of attaining lighter skin. What is being created in all of these instances is not simply beautiful bodies and faces but white, Western, Anglo-Saxon bodies in a racist, anti-Semitic context.

More often than not, what appear at first glance to be instances of choice turn out to be instances of conformity. The women who undergo cosmetic surgery in order to compete in various beauty pageants are clearly choosing to conform. So is the woman who wanted to undergo a facelift, tummy tuck, and liposuction all in one week, in order to win heterosexual approval *from a man she had not seen in twenty-eight years* and whose individual preferences she could not possibly know. In some ways, it does not matter who the particular judges are. Actual men—brothers, fathers, male lovers, male beauty "experts"—and hypothetical men live in the aesthetic imaginations of women. Whether they are male employers, prospective male spouses, male judges in the beauty pageants, or male-identified women, these modern day Parises are generic and live sometimes ghostly but powerful lives in the reflective awareness of women (Berger 1972). A woman's makeup, dress, gestures, voice, degree of cleanliness, degree of muscularity, odors, degree of hirsuteness, vocabulary, hands, feet, skin, hair, and vulva can be all evaluated, regulated, and disciplined in the light of the hypothetical often-white male viewer and the male viewer present in the assessing gaze of other women (Haug 1987). Men's appreciation and approval of achieved femininity becomes all the more invasive when it resides in the incisions, stitches, staples, and scar tissue of women's bodies as women choose to conform. And, as various theorists have pointed out, women's public conformity to the norms of beauty often signals a deeper conformity to the norms of compulsory heterosexuality along with an awareness of the violence that can result from violating those norms.[9] Hence the first paradox: that what looks like an optimal situation of reflection, deliberation, and self-creating choice often signals conformity at a deeper level.

Paradox Two: Liberation into Colonization

As argued above, a woman's desire to create a permanently beautiful and youthful appearance that is not vulnerable to the threats of externally applied cosmetic artifice or to the natural aging process of the body must be understood as a deeply significant existential project. It deliberately involves the exploitation and transformation of the most intimately experienced domain of immanence, the body, in the name of transcendence: transcendence of hereditary predestination, of lived time, of one's given "limitations." What I see as particularly alarming in this project is that what comes to have primary significance is not the real given existing woman but her body viewed as a "primitive entity" that is seen only as potential, as a kind of raw material to be exploited in terms of appearance, eroticism, nurturance, and fertility as defined by the colonizing culture.[10]

But for whom is this exploitation and transformation taking place? Who exercises the power here? Sometimes the power is explicit. It is exercised by brothers, fathers, male lovers, male engineering students who taunt and harass their female counterparts, and by male cosmetic surgeons who offer "free advice" in social gatherings to women whose "deformities" and "severe problems" can all be cured through their healing needles and knives.[11] And the colonizing power is transmitted through and by those women whose own bodies and disciplinary practices demonstrate the efficacy of "taking care of herself" in these culturally defined feminine ways.

Sometimes, however, the power may be so diffused as to dominate the consciousness of a given woman with no other subject needing to be present. As Bartky notes, such diffused power also signals the presence of the colonizer:

> Normative femininity is coming more and more to be centered on woman's body. . . . Images of normative femininity . . . have replaced the religious oriented tracts of the past. The woman who checks her makeup half a dozen times a day to see if her foundation has caked or her mascara has run, who worries that the wind or the rain may spoil her hairdo, who looks frequently to see if her stockings have bagged at the ankle, or who, feeling fat, monitors everything she eats, *has become, just as surely as the inmate of the Panopticon, a self-policing subject, a self committed to a relentless self-surveillance. This self-surveillance is a form of obedience to partriarchy.* (Bartky 1988, p 81; italics added)

As Foucault and others have noted, practices of coercion and domination are often camouflaged by practical rhetoric and supporting theories that appear to be benevolent, therapeutic, and voluntaristic. Previously, for example, colonizing was often done in the name of bringing "civilization" through culture and morals to "primitive, barbaric people," but contemporary colonizers mask their exploitation of "raw materials and human labor" in the name of "development." Murphy (1984), Piercy (1980), and I (Morgan 1989) have all claimed that similar rhetorical camouflage of colonization takes place in the areas of women's reproductive decision-making and women's right to bodily self-determination. In all of these instances of colonization the ideological manipulation of technology can be identified, and, I would argue, in all of these cases this technology has often been used to the particular disadvantage and destruction of some aspect of women's integrity.[12]

In electing to undergo cosmetic surgery, women appear to be protesting against the constraints of the "given" in their embodied lives and seeking liberation from those constraints. But I believe they are in danger of retreating and becoming more vulnerable, at that very level of embodiment, to those colonizing forms of power that may have motivated the protest in the first place. Moreover, in seeking independence, they can become even more dependent on male assessment and on the services of all those experts they initially bought to render them independent.

Here we see a second paradox bound up with choice: that the rhetoric is that of liberation and care, of "making the most of yourself," but the reality is often the transformation of oneself as a woman for the eye, the hand, and the approval of the Other—the lover, the taunting students, the customers, the employers, the social peers. And the Other is almost always affected by the dominant culture, which is male-supremacist, racist, ageist, heterosexist, anti-Semitic, ableist and class-biased.[13]

Paradox Three: Coerced Voluntariness and the Technological Imperative

Where is the coercion? At first glance, women who choose to undergo cosmetic surgery often seem to represent a paradigm case of the rational chooser. Drawn increasingly from wider and wider economic groups, these women clearly make a choice, often at significant economic cost to the rest of their life, to pay the large sums of money demanded by cosmetic surgeons (since American health insurance plans do not cover this elective cosmetic surgery).

Furthermore, they are often highly critical consumers of these services, demanding extensive consultation, information regarding the risks and benefits of various surgical procedures, and professional guarantees of expertise. Generally they are relatively young and in good health. Thus, in some important sense, they epitomize relatively invulnerable free agents making a decision under virtually optimal conditions.

Moreover, on the surface, women who undergo cosmetic surgery choose a set of procedures that are, by definition, "elective." This term is used, quite straightforwardly, to distinguish cosmetic surgery from surgical intervention for reconstructive or health-related reasons (e.g., following massive burns, cancer-related forms of mutilation, etc.). The term also appears to distinguish cosmetic surgery from apparently involuntary and more pathologically transforming forms of intervention in the bodies of young girls in the form of, for example, foot-binding or extensive genital mutilation.[14] But I believe that this does not exhaust the meaning of the term "elective" and that the term performs a seductive role in facilitating the ideological camouflage of the *absence of choice*. Similarly, I believe that the word "cosmetic" serves an ideological function in hiding the fact that the changes are *noncosmetic*: they involve lengthy periods of pain, are permanent, and result in irreversibly alienating metamorphoses such as the appearance of youth on an aging body.

In order to illuminate the paradox of choice involved here, I wish to draw an analogy from the literature on reproductive technology. In the case of reproductive self-determination, technology has been hailed as increasing the range of women's choices in an absolute kind of way. It cannot be denied that due to the advances in various reproductive technologies, especially IVF and embryo freezing, along with various advances in fetology and fetal surgery, there are now women with healthy children who previously would not have had children. Nevertheless, there are two important ideological, choice-diminishing dynamics at work that affect women's choices in the area of the new reproductive technologies. These dynamics are also at work in the area of cosmetic surgery.

The first of these is the *pressure to achieve perfection through technology*, signaled by the rise of new forms of eugenicist thinking. More profoundly than ever before, contemporary eugenicists stigmatize potential and existing disabled babies, children, and adults. More and more frequently, benevolently phrased eugenicist pressures are forcing women to choose to submit to a battery of prenatal diagnostic tests and extensive fetal monitoring in the name of producing "perfect" (white) babies. As more and more reproductive technologies and tests are invented (and "perfected" in and on the bodies of fertile women), partners, parents, family, obstetricians, and other experts on fertility pressure women to submit to this technology in the name of "maximized choice" and "responsible motherhood." As Achilles (1988), Beck-Gernsheim (1989), Rothman (1984), Morgan (1989), and others have argued, women are being subjected to increasingly intense forms of coercion, a fact that is signaled by the intensifying *lack of freedom* felt by women to refuse to use the technology if they are pregnant and the technology is available.

The second important ideological dynamic is *the double-pathologizing of women's bodies*. The history of Western science and Western medical practice is not altogether a positive one for women. As voluminous documentation has shown, cell biologists, endocrinologists, anatomists, sociobiologists, gynecologists, obstetricians, psychiatrists, surgeons, and other scientists have assumed, hypothesized, or "demonstrated" that women's bodies are generally inferior, deformed, imperfect, and/or infantile. Medical practitioners have often treated women accordingly. Until the rise of the new reproductive technologies, however, women's reproductive capacities and processes were regarded as definitional of normal womanhood and normal human reproduction. No longer is that the case. As Corea (1985) and others have so amply demonstrated, profoundly misogynist beliefs and attitudes are a central part of the ideological motivation for the technical development of devices for completely extrauterine fetal development. Women's wombs are coming to be seen as "dark prisons." Women are viewed as threatening irresponsible agents who live in a necessarily antagonistic relationship with the fetus. And women's bodies in general are coming to be viewed as high-risk milieus since fetal development cannot be continuously monitored and controlled in order to guarantee the best possible "fetal outcome" (particularly where middle and upper-class white babies are concerned).

Increasingly, "fully responsible motherhood" is coming to be defined in technology-dependent terms and, in a larger cultural context of selective obligatory maternity, more and more women are "choosing to act" in accord with technological imperatives prior to conception, through conception, through maternity, and through birthing itself. Whether this is, then, a situation of increased choice is at the very least highly contestable. Moreover, in a larger ideological context of obligatory and "controlled" motherhood, I am reluctant simply to accept the reports of the technologists and fertility experts that their patients "want access" to the technology as a sufficient condition for demonstrating purely voluntary choice.[15]

A similar argument can be made regarding the significance of the pressure to be beautiful in relation to the allegedly voluntary nature of "electing" to undergo cosmetic surgery. It is clear that pressure to use this technology is on the increase. Cosmetic surgeons report on the wide range of clients who buy their services, pitch their advertising to a large audience through the use of the media, and encourage women to think, metaphorically, in terms of the seemingly trivial "nips" and "tucks" that will transform their lives. As cosmetic surgery becomes increasingly normal-ized through the concept of the female "make-over" that is translated into columns and articles in the print media or made into nationwide television shows directed at female viewers, as the "success stories" are invited on to talk shows along with their "makers," and as surgically transformed women win the Miss America pageants, women who refuse to submit to the knives and to the needles, to the anaesthetics and the bandages, will come to be seen as deviant in one way or another. Women who refuse to use these technologies are already becoming stigmatized as "unliberated," "not caring about their appearance" (a sign of disturbed gender identity and low self-esteem according to various health-care professionals), as "refusing to be all that they could be" or as "granola-heads."

And as more and more success comes to those who do "care about themselves" in this technological fashion, more coercive dimensions enter the scene. In the past, only those women who were perceived to be *naturally* beautiful (or rendered beautiful through relatively conservative superficial artifice) had access to forms of power and economic social mobility closed off to women regarded as plain or ugly or old. But now womanly beauty is becoming technologically achievable, a commodity for which each and very woman can, in principle, sacrifice if she is to survive and succeed in the world, particularly in industrialized Western countries. Now technology is making obligatory the appearance of youth and the reality of "beauty" for every woman who can afford it. Natural destiny is being supplanted by technologically grounded coercion, and the coercion is camouflaged by the language of choice, fulfillment, and liberation.

Similarly, we find the dynamic of the double-pathologizing of the normal and of the ordinary at work here. In the technical and popular literature on cosmetic surgery, what have previously been described as *normal* variations of female bodily shapes or described in the relatively innocuous language of "problem areas," are increasingly being described as "deformities," "ugly protrusions," "inadequate breasts," and "unsightly concentrations of fat cells"—a litany of descriptions designed to intensify feelings of disgust, shame, and relief at the possibility of recourse for these "deformities." Cosmetic surgery promises virtually all women the creation of beautiful, youthful-appearing bodies. As a consequence, more and more women will be labeled "ugly" and "old" in relation to this more select population of surgically created beautiful faces and bodies that have been contoured and augmented, lifted and tucked into a state of achieved feminine excellence. I suspect that the naturally "given," so to speak, will increasingly come to be seen as the technologically "primitive"; the "ordinary" will come to be perceived and evaluated as the "ugly." Here, then, is the *third paradox*: that the technological beauty imperative and the pathological inversion of the normal are coercing more and more women to "choose" cosmetic surgery.

ARE THERE ANY POLITICALLY CORRECT FEMINIST RESPONSES TO COSMETIC SURGERY?

Attempting to answer this question is rather like venturing forth into political quicksand. Nevertheless, I will discuss two very different sorts of responses that strike me as having certain plausibility: the response of refusal and the response of appropriation.[16] I regard both of these as utopian in nature.

The Response of Refusal

In her witty and subversive parable, *The Life and Loves of a She-Devil,* Fay Weldon puts the following thoughts into the mind of the cosmetic surgeon whose services have been bought by the protagonist, "Miss Hunter," for her own plans for revenge:

> He was her Pygmalion, but she would not depend upon him, or admire him, or be grateful. He was accustomed to being loved by the women of his own construction. A soft sign of adoration would follow him down the corridors as he paced them, visiting here, blessing there, promising a future, regretting a past: cushioning his footfall, and his image of himself. But no soft breathings came from Miss Hunter. [He adds, ominously,] . . . he would bring her to it. (Weldon 1983, pp. 215–16)

But Miss Hunter continues to refuse, and so will many feminist women. The response of refusal can be recognizably feminist at both an individual and a collective level. It results from understanding the nature of the risks involved—those having to do with the surgical procedures and those related to a potential loss of embodied personal integrity in a patriarchal context. And it results from understanding the conceptual shifts involved in the political technologizing of women's bodies and contextualizing them so that their oppressive consequences are evident precisely as they open up more "choices" to women. "Understanding" and "contextualizing" here mean seeing clearly the ideological biases that frame the material and cultural world in which cosmetic surgeons practice, a world that contains racist, anti-Semitic, eugenicist, and ageist dimensions of oppression, forms of oppression to which current practices in cosmetic surgery often contribute.

The response of refusal also speaks to the collective power of women as consumers to affect market conditions. If refusal is practiced on a large scale, cosmetic surgeons who are busy producing new faces for the "holiday season" and new bellies for the "winter trips to the Caribbean" will find few buyers of their services. Cosmetic surgeons who consider themselves body designers and regard women's skin as a kind of magical fabric to be draped, cut, layered, and designer-labeled, may have to forgo the esthetician's ambitions that occasion the remark that "the sculpting of human flesh can never be an exact art" (Silver 1989). They may, instead, (re)turn their expertise to the victims in the intensive care burn unit and to the crippled limbs and joints of arthritic women. This might well have the consequence of (re)converting those surgeons into healers.

Although it may be relatively easy for some individual women to refuse cosmetic surgery even when they have access to the means, one deep, morally significant facet of the response of refusal is to try to understand and to care about individual women who do choose to undergo cosmetic surgery. It may well be that one explanation for why a woman is willing to subject herself to surgical procedures, anaesthetics, postoperative drugs, predicted and lengthy pain, and possible "side-effects" that might include her own death is that her access to other forms of power and empowerment are or appear to be so limited that cosmetic surgery is the primary domain in which she can experience some semblance of self-determination. Lakoff and Scherr comment on this:

> No responsible doctor would advise a drug, or a procedure, whose clearly demonstrated benefits do not considerably outweigh its risks, so that a health-threatening drug is not prescribed responsibly except to remedy a life-threatening condition. But equally noxious drugs and procedures are medically sanctioned merely to "cure" moderate overweight or flat-chestedness—hardly life-threatening ailments. . . . The only way to understand the situation is to agree that those conditions *are*, in fact, perceived as life-threatening, so dangerous that seriously damaging interventions are justified, any risk worth taking, to alleviate them. (Lakoff and Scherr 1984, pp. 165–66)

Choosing an artificial and technologically designed creation of youthful beauty may not only be necessary to an individual woman's material, economic, and social survival. It may also be the way that she is able to choose, to elect a kind of subjective transcendence against a backdrop of constraint, limitation, and immanence (in Beauvoir's sense of this term).

As a feminist response, individual and collective refusal may not be easy. As Bartky, I, and others have tried to argue, it is crucial to understand the central role that socially sanctioned and socially constructed femininity plays in a male supremacist, heterosexist society. And it is essential not to underestimate the gender-constituting and identity-confirming role that femininity plays in bringing woman-as-subject into existence while simultaneously creating her as patriarchally defined object (Bartky 1988; Morgan 1986). In these circumstances, refusal may be akin to a kind of death, to a kind of renunciation of the only kind of life-conferring choices and competencies to which a woman may have access. And, under those circumstances, it may not be possible for her to register her resistance in the form of refusal. The best one can hope for is a heightened sense of the nature of the multiple double-binds and compromises that permeate the lives of virtually all women and are accentuated by the cosmetic surgery culture.

As a final comment, it is worth remarking that although the response of refusal has a kind of purity to recommend it, it is unlikely to have much impact in the current ideological and cultural climate. In just one year, the number of breast augmentations has risen 32 percent; eye tucks have increased 31 percent; nose jobs have increased 30 percent; face lifts have increased 39 percent; and liposuction and other forms of "body contouring" have become the most popular form of cosmetic surgery ("New Bodies for Sale" 1985). Cosmetic surgeons are deluged with demands, and research in the field is increasing at such a rapid pace that every area of the human body is seen as open to metamorphosis. Clearly the knives, the needles, the cannulas, and the drugs are exercising a greater and greater allure. Nevertheless, the political significance of the response of refusal should not be underestimated in the lives of individual women since achieved obligatory femininity is a burden borne by virtually all women. And this response is one way of eliminating many of the attendant harms while simultaneously identifying the ways that the technological beauty imperative increasingly pervades our lives.

The Response of Appropriation

In their insightful essay, "The Feminine Body and Feminist Politics," Brown and Adams remark that "since the body is seen as the site of *action*, its investigation appears to combine what are otherwise characterized as discrete sites, the theoretical and the political, in an original unity" (Brown and Adams 1979, p. 35). Rather than viewing the womanly/technologized body as a site of political refusal, the response of appropriation views it as the site for feminist action through transformation, appropriation, parody, and protest. This response grows out of that historical and often radical feminist tradition that regards deliberate mimicry, alternative valorization, hyperbolic appropriation, street theater, counterguerrilla tactics, destabilization, and redeployment as legitimate feminist politics. Here I am proposing a version of what Judith Butler regards as "Femininity Politics" and what she calls "Gender Performatives." The contemporary feminist guerrilla theater group Ladies Against Women demonstrates the power of this kind of response. In addition to expressing outrage and moral revulsion at the biased dimensions of contemporary cosmetic surgery, the response of appropriation targets them for moral and political purposes.

However, instead of mourning the temporal and carnal alienation resulting from the shame and guilt experienced prior to surgery and from the experience of loss of identity following surgery, the feminist theorist using the response of appropriation points out (like postmodernists) that these emotional experiences simply demonstrate the ubiquitous instability of consciousness itself, that this is simply a more vivid lived instance of the deeper instability that is characteristic of *all* human subjectivity. Along with feeling apprehension about the appropriation of organic processes and bodies by technology, what this feminist theorist might well say is that the technologies are simply revealing what is true for *all* embodied subjects living in cultures, namely, that *all* human bodies are, and always have been, dialectically created artifacts (Lowe 1982; Haraway 1978, 1989). What the technologies are revealing is that women's bodies, in particular, can be and are read as especially saturated cultural artifacts and signifiers by phenomenologically oriented anthropologists and forensic archaeologists (even if they have never heard about Derrida or postmodernism). Finally, present practices in cosmetic surgery also provide an extremely public and quantified reckoning of the cost of "beauty," thereby demonstrating how both the processes and the final product are part of a larger nexus of women's commodification. Since such lessons are not always taught so easily or in such transparent form, this feminist theorist may well celebrate the critical feminist ideological potential of cosmetic surgery.

Rather than agreeing that participating in cosmetic surgery and its ruling ideology will necessarily result in further colonization and victimization of women, this feminist strategy advocates appropriating the expertise and technology for feminist ends. One advantage of the response of appropriation is that it does not recommend involvement in forms of technology that clearly have disabling and dire outcomes for the deeper feminist project of engaging "in the historical, political, and theoretical process of constituting ourselves as subjects as well as objects of history" (Hartsock 1990, p. 170).[17] Women who are increasingly immobilized bodily through physical weakness, passivity, withdrawal, and domestic sequestration in situations of hysteria, agoraphobia, and anorexia cannot possibly engage in radical gender performatives of an active public sort or in other acts by which the feminist subject is robustly constituted. In contrast, healthy women who have a feminist understanding of cosmetic surgery are in a situation to deploy cosmetic surgery in the name of its feminist potential for parody and protest.

Working within the creative matrix of ideas provided by Foucault, Kristeva (1982), and Douglas (1966), Judith Butler notes:

> The construction of stable bodily contours relies upon fixed sites of corporeal permeability and impermeability. . . . The deregulation of such (heterosexual) exchanges accordingly disrupts the very boundaries that determine what it is to be a body at all. (1990, pp. 132–33)

As Butler correctly observes, parody "by itself is not subversive" (p. 139) since it always runs the risk of becoming "domesticated and recirculated as instruments of cultural hegemony." She then goes on to ask, in relation to gender identity and sexuality, what words or performances would

> compel a reconsideration of the *place* and stability of the masculine and the feminine? And what kind of gender performance will enact and reveal the performativity of gender itself in a way that destablizes the naturalized categories of identity and desire? (Butler 1990, p. 139)

We might, in parallel fashion, ask what sorts of performances would sufficiently destabilize the norms of femininity, what sorts of performances will sufficiently expose the truth of the slogan "Beauty is always made, not born." In response I suggest two performance-oriented forms of revolt.

The first form of revolt involves revalorizing the domain of the "ugly" and all that is associated with it. Although one might argue that the notion of the "ugly" is parasitic on that of "beauty," this is not entirely true since the ugly is also contrasted with the plain and the ordinary, so that we are not even at the outset constrained by binary oppositions. The ugly, even in a beauty-oriented culture, has always held its own fascination, its own particular kind of splendor. Feminists can use that and explore it in ways that might be integrated with a revalorization of being old, thus simultaneously attacking the ageist dimension of the reigning ideology. Rather than being the "culturally enmired subjects" of Butler's analysis, women might constitute themselves as culturally liberated subjects through public participation in Ms. Ugly Canada/

America/Universe/Cosmos pageants *and use the technology of cosmetic surgery to do so.*

Contemplating this form of revolt as a kind of imaginary model of political action is one thing; actually altering our bodies is another matter altogether. And the reader may well share the sentiments of one reviewer of this paper who asked: "Having oneself surgically mutilated in order to prove a point? Isn't this going too far?" I don't know the answer to that question. If we cringe from contemplating this alternative, this may, in fact, testify (so to speak) to the hold that the beauty imperative has on our imagination and our bodies. If we recoil from *this* lived alteration of the contours of our bodies and regard it as "mutilation," then so, too, ought we to shirk from contemplation of the cosmetic surgeons who de-skin and alter the contours of women's bodies so that we become more and more like athletic or emaciated (depending on what's in vogue) mannequins with large breasts in the shop windows of modern patriarchal culture. In what sense are these not equivalent mutilations?

What this feminist performative would require would be not only genuine celebration of but *actual* participation in the fleshly mutations needed to produce what the culture constitutes as "ugly" so as to destabilize the "beautiful" and expose its technologically and culturally constitutive origin and its political consequences. Bleaching one's hair white and applying wrinkle-inducing "wrinkle creams," having one's face and breasts surgically pulled down (rather than lifted), and having wrinkles sewn and carved into one's skin might also be seen as destabilizing actions with respect to aging. And analogous actions might be taken to undermine the "lighter is better" aspect of racist norms of feminine appearance as they affect women of color.

A second performative form of revolt could involve exploring the commodification aspect of cosmetic surgery. One might, for example, envision a set of "Beauty Body Boutique" franchises, responsive to the particular "needs" of a given community. Here one could advertise and sell a whole range of bodily contours; a variety of metric containers of freeze-dried fat cells for fat implantation and transplant; "body configuration" software for computers; sewing kits of needles, knives, and painkillers; and "skin-Velcro" that could be matched to fit and drape the consumer's body; variously sized sets of magnetically attachable breasts complete with discrete nipple pumps; and other inflation devices carefully modulated according to bodily aroma and state of arousal. Parallel to the current marketing strategies for cosmetic breast surgeries,[18] commercial protest booths, complete with "before and after" surgical makeover displays for penises, entitled "The Penis You Were Always Meant to Have" could be set up at various medical conventions and health fairs; demonstrations could take place outside the clinics, hotels, and spas of particularly eminent cosmetic surgeons—the possibilities here are endless. Again, if this ghoulish array offends, angers, or shocks the reader, this may well be an indication of the extent to which the ideology of compulsory beauty has anesthetized our sensibility in the reverse direction, resulting in the domesticating of the procedures and products of the cosmetic surgery industry.

In appropriating these forms of revolt, women might well accomplish the following: acquire expertise (either in fact or in symbolic form) of cosmetic surgery to challenge the coercive norms of youth and beauty, undermine the power dynamic built into the dependence on surgical experts who define themselves as aestheticians of women's bodies, demonstrate the radical malleability of the cultural commodification of women's bodies, and make publicly explicit the political role that technology can play in the construction of the feminine in women's flesh.

CONCLUSION

I have characterized both these feminist forms of response as utopian in nature. What I mean by "utopian" is that these responses are unlikely to occur on a large scale even though they may have a kind of ideal desirability. In any culture that defines femininity in terms of submission to men, that makes the achievement of femininity (however culturally specific) in appearance, gesture, movement, voice, bodily contours, aspirations, values, and political behavior obligatory of any woman who will be allowed to be loved or hired or promoted or elected or simply allowed to live, and in any culture that increasingly requires women to purchase femininity through submission to cosmetic surgeons and their magic knives, refusal and revolt exact a high price. I live in such a culture.

NOTES

Many thanks to the members of the Canadian Society for Women in Philosophy for their critical feedback, especially my commentator, Karen Weisbaum, who pointed out how strongly visualist the cosmetic surgery culture is. I am particularly grateful to Sarah Lucia Hoagland, keynote speaker at the 1990 C-SWIP conference, who remarked at my session, "I think this is all wrong." Her comment sent me back to the text to rethink it in a serious way. Thanks also to the two anonymous *Hypatia* reviewers for their frank, helpful, and supportive response to an earlier version of this paper.

1. This paper addresses only the issues generated out of *elective* cosmetic surgery which is sharply distinguished by practitioners, patients, and insurance plans from reconstructive cosmetic surgery which is usually performed in relation to some trauma or is viewed as necessary in relation to some pressing health care concern. This is not to say that the distinction is always clear in practice.

2. I regard the *Hastings Center Report* and *Philosophy and Medicine* as the discipline-establishing journals in mainstream bioethics. The feminist literature to which I am referring includes the double special issue of *Hypatia*, 1989 (vol. 4, nos. 2 and 3), the anthology *Healing Technology* (Ratcliff 1989), and the entire journal series *Women and Health* and *Women and Therapy* through 1990. With the exception of a paper by Kathy Davis on this topic which has just appeared (1991) the only discussions that *do* exist discuss the case of Quasimodo, the Hunchback of Notre Dame!

3. For a thorough account of how anatomical science has conceptualized and depicted the ideal female skeleton and morphology, see Russett's *Sexual Science: The Victorian Construction of Womanhood* (1989) and Schiebinger's *The Mind Has No Sex? Women*

in the Origins of Modern Science (1989), especially the chapter titled "More Than Skin Deep: The Scientific Search for Sexual Difference."

4. Although the particular kind of machine selected as paradigmatic of the human body has shifted from clocks to hydraulics to thermodynamics and now to information-processing models, the Cartesian machine-modeling of the body continues to dominate and is, obviously, the one most congenial to the correlative technologizing of the human body, which literally metamorphoses the body into a machine.

5. I say "virtually all women" because there is now a nascent literature on the subject of fat oppression and body image as it affects lesbians. For a perceptive article on this subject, see Dworkin (1989). I am, of course, not suggesting that compulsory heterosexuality and obligatory maternity affect all women equally. Clearly women who are regarded as "deviant" in some respect or other—because they are lesbian or women with disabilities or "too old" or poor or the "wrong race"—are under enormous pressure from the dominant culture *not* to bear children, but this, too, is an aspect of patriarchal pronatalism.

6. The desire to subordinate our bodies to some ideal that involves bringing the body under control is deeply felt by many contemporary women (apart from any religious legacy of asceticism). As Bartky (1988) and Bordo (1985, 1989a, 1989b) have noted, this is an aspect of the disembodying desires of anorexic women and women who "pump iron." In the area of cosmetic surgery, this control is mediated by the technology and expertise of the surgeons, but the theme is continually articulated.

7. A similar point regarding femininity is made by Sandra Bartky (1988) in her discussion of "feminine discipline." She remarks that women will resist the dismantling of the disciplines of femininity because, at a very deep level, it would involve a radical alteration of what she calls our "informal social ontology":

> To have a body felt to be "feminine"—a body socially constructed through the appropriate practices—is in most cases crucial to a woman's sense of herself as female and, since persons currently can *be* only as male or female, to her sense of herself as an existing individual. . . . The radical feminist critique of femininity, then, may pose a threat not only to a woman's sense of her own identity and desirability but to the very structure of her social universe. (Bartky 1988, p. 78)

8. I view this as a recognizably *political* metamorphosis because forensic cosmetic surgeons and social archaeologists will be needed to determine the actual age and earlier appearance of women in cases where identification is called for on the basis of existing carnal data. See Griffin's (1978) poignant description in "The Anatomy Lesson" for a reconstruction of the life and circumstances of a dead mother from just such carnal evidence. As we more and more profoundly artifactualize our own bodies, we become more sophisticated archaeological repositories and records that both signify and symbolize our culture.

9. For both documentation and analysis of this claim, see Bartky (1988), Bordo (1985, 1989a, 1989b), and Rich (1980).

10. I intend to use "given" here in a relative and political sense. I don't believe that the notion that biology is somehow "given" and culture is just "added on" is a tenable one. I believe that we are intimately and inextricably encultured and embodied, so that a reductionist move in either direction is doomed to failure. For a persuasive analysis of this thesis, see Lowe (1982) and Haraway (1978, 1989). For a variety of political analyses of the "given" as primitive, see Marge Piercy's poem "Right to Life" (1980), Morgan (1989), and Murphy (1984).

11. Although I am cognizant of the fact that many women are entering medical school, the available literature is preponderantly authored by men most of whom, I would infer, are white, given the general demographics of specializations in medical school. I also stress the whiteness here to emphasize the extent to which white norms of beauty dominate the field. I think of these surgeons as akin to "fairy godfathers" to

underscore the role they are asked to play to "correct," "improve," or "render beautiful" what girls and women have inherited from their mothers, who can only make recommendations at the level of artifice, not artifact.

12. Space does not permit development of this theme on an international scale but it is important to note the extent to which pharmaceutical "dumping" is taking place in the so-called "developing countries" under the ideological camouflage of "population control and family planning." See Hartman (1987) for a thorough and persuasive analysis of the exploitative nature of this practice.

13. The extent to which ableist bias is at work in this area was brought home to me by two quotations cited by a woman with a disability. She discusses two guests on a television show. One was "a poised, intelligent young woman who'd been rejected as a contestant for the Miss Toronto title. She is a paraplegic. The organizers' lame excuse for disqualifying her: 'We couldn't fit the choreography around you.' Another guest was a former executive of the Miss Universe contest. He declared, 'Her participation in a beauty contest would be like having a blind man compete in a shooting match' " (Matthews 1985).

14. It is important here to guard against facile and ethnocentric assumptions about beauty rituals and mutilation. See Lakoff and Scherr (1984) for an analysis of the relativity of these labels and for important insights about the fact that use of the term "mutilation" almost always signals a distancing from and reinforcement of a sense of cultural superiority in the speaker who uses it to denounce what other cultures do in contrast to "our culture."

15. For the most sustained and theoretically sophisticated analysis of pronatalism operating in the context of industrialized capitalism, see Gimenez (1984). Gimenez restricts her discussion to working-class women but, unfortunately, doesn't develop a more differentiated grid of pronatalist and antinatalist pressures within that economic and social group. For example, in Quebec there are strong pressures on Francophone working-class women to reproduce, while there is selective pressure against Anglophone and immigrant working women bearing children. Nevertheless, Gimenez's account demonstrates the systemic importance of pronatalism in many women's lives.

16. One possible feminist response (that, thankfully, appears to go in *and* out of vogue) is that of feminist fascism, which insists on a certain particular and quite narrow range of embodiment and appearance as the only range that is politically correct for a feminist. Often feminist fascism sanctions the use of informal but very powerful feminist "embodiment police," who feel entitled to identify and denounce various deviations from this normative range. I find this feminist political stance incompatible with any movement I would regard as liberatory for women and here I admit that I side with feminist liberals who say that "the presumption must be on the side of freedom" (Warren 1985) and see that as the lesser of two evils.

17. In recommending various forms of appropriation of the practices and dominant ideology surrounding cosmetic surgery, I think it important to distinguish this set of disciplinary practices from those forms of simultaneous Retreat-and-Protest that Susan Bordo (1989a, p. 20) so insightfully discusses in "The Body and the Reproduction of Femininity": hysteria, agoraphobia, and anorexia. What cosmetic surgery shares with these gestures is what Bordo remarks upon, namely, the fact that they may be "viewed as a surface on which conventional constructions of femininity are exposed starkly to view, through their inscription in extreme or hyperliteral form." What is different, I suggest, is that although submitting to the procedures of cosmetic surgery involves pain, risks, undesirable side effects, and living with a heightened form of patriarchal anxiety, it is also fairly clear that, most of the time, the pain and risks are relatively short-term. Furthermore, the outcome often appears to be one that generally enhances women's confidence, confers a sense of well-being, contributes to a greater comfortableness in the public domain, and affirms the individual woman as a self-determining and risk-taking individual. All these outcomes are significantly different from what Bordo describes as the "languages of horrible suffering" (Bordo 1989a, p. 20) expressed by women experiencing hysteria, agoraphobia, and anorexia.

18. A booth of this sort was set up in a prominent location at a large "Today's Woman Fair" at the National Exhibition grounds in Toronto in the summer of 1990. It showed "before" and "after" pictures of women's breasts and advertised itself as "The Breasts *You Were Always Meant* to Have." One special feature of the display was a set of photographs showing a woman whose breasts had been "deformed" by nursing but who had finally attained through cosmetic surgery the breasts "she was meant to have." I am grateful to my colleague June Larkin for the suggestion of the analogous booth.

BIBLIOGRAPHY

Achilles, Rona. 1988. What's new about the new reproductive technologies? *Discussion Paper: Ontario Advisory Council on the Status of Women*. Toronto: Government of Ontario.

Barker-Benfield, G. J. 1976. *The Horrors of the Half-known Life*. New York: Harper & Row.

Bartky, Sandra Lee. 1988. Foucault, femininity, and the modernization of patriarchal power. In *Femininity and Foucault: Reflections of Resistance*, ed. Irene Diamond and Lee Quinby. Boston: Northeastern University Press.

Beck-Gernsheim, Elisabeth. 1989. From the pill to test-tube babies: New options, new pressures in reproductive behavior. In *Healing Technology: Feminist Perspectives*, ed. Kathryn Strother Ratcliff. Ann Arbor: University of Michigan Press.

Berger, John. 1972. *Ways of seeing*. New York: Penguin Books.

Bordo, Susan R. 1985. Anorexia nervosa: Psychopathology as the crystallization of culture. *The Philosophical Forum* 2 (Winter): 73–103.

————. 1989a. The body and the reproduction of femininity: A feminist appropriation of Foucault. In *Gender/Body/Knowledge: Feminist Reconstructions of Being and Knowing*, ed. Alison Jaggar and Susan Bordo. New Brunswick, NJ: Rutgers University Press.

————. 1989b. Reading the slender body. In *Women, Science and the Body Politic: Discourses and Representations*, ed. Mary Jacobus, Evelyn Fox Keller, and Sally Shuttleworth. New York: Methuen.

Brown, Beverly, and Parveen Adams. 1979. The feminine body and feminist politics. *M/F* 3: 35–50.

Brownmiller, Susan. 1984. *Femininity*. New York: Simon & Schuster.

Burk, J., S.L. Zelen, and E.O. Terena. 1985. More than skin deep: A self-consistency approach to the psychology of cosmetic surgery. *Plastic and Reconstructive surgery* 6(2): 270–80.

Butler, Judith. 1990. *Gender Trouble: Feminism and the Subversion of Identity*. New York: Routledge.

Changing Faces. 1989. *Toronto Star*, May 25.

Computer used to pick hairstyles. 1989. *Globe and Mail.*

Corea, Gena. 1985. *The Mother Machine*. New York: Harper & Row.

Cosmetic surgery for the holidays. 1985. *Sheboygan Press*. New York Times News Service.

Davis, Kathy. 1991. Remaking the she-devil: A Critical Look at Feminist Approaches to Beauty. *Hypatia* 6(2): 21–43.

Diamond, Irene, and Lee Quinby, eds. 1988. *Feminism and Foucault: Reflections on resistance*. Boston: Northeastern University Press.

Douglas, Mary. 1966. *Purity and Danger*. London: Routledge and Kegan Paul; New York: Praeger.

Dworkin, Sari. 1989. Not in man's image: Lesbians and the cultural oppression of body image. *Women and Therapy* 8 (1,2): 27–39.

Easlea, Brian. 1981. *Science and Sexual Oppression: Patriarchy's Confrontation with Woman and Nature*. London: Weidenfeld and Nicolson.

Facial regeneration. 1990. *Health: A community education service of the Froedtert Memorial Lutheran Hospital.* Supplement to *Milwaukee Journal,* August 26.

Falling in love again. 1990. *Toronto Star,* July 23.

Foucault, Michel. 1979. *Discipline and Punish: The birth of the Prison.* Trans. Alan Sheridan. New York: Pantheon.

———. 1988. Technologies of the self: The political technology of the individual. In *The Technologies of the Self,* ed. Luther H. Martin, Huck Gutman, and Patrick Hutton. Amherst: University of Massachusetts Press.

Fraser, Nancy. 1989. *Unruly Practices: Power, Discourse, and Gender in Contemporary Social Theory.* Minneapolis: University of Minnesota Press.

Gimenez, Martha. 1984. Feminism, pronatalism, and motherhood. In *Mothering: Essays in Feminist Theory,* ed. Joyce Trebilcot. Totowa, NJ: Rowman and Allanheld.

Goodman, Ellen. 1989. A plastic pageant. *Boston Globe,* September 19.

Griffin, Susan. 1978. The anatomy lesson. In *Woman and Nature: The Roaring inside Her.* New York: Harper & Row.

Haraway, Donna. 1978. Animal sociology and a natural economy of the body politic, Parts I, II. *Signs: Journal of Women in Culture and Society* 4(1): 21–60.

———. 1989. *Primate visions.* New York: Routledge.

Hartman, Betsy. 1987. *Reproductive Rights and Wrongs: The Global Politics of Population Control and Contraceptive Choice.* New York: Harper & Row.

Hartsock, Nancy. 1990. Foucault on power: A theory for women?. In *Feminism/Postmodernism,* ed. Linda Nicholson. New York: Routledge.

Haug, Frigga, ed. 1987. *Female Sexualization: A Collective Work of Memory.* Trans. Erica Carter. London: Verso.

Hirshson, Paul. 1987. New wrinkles in plastic surgery: An update on the search for perfection. *Boston Globe Sunday Magazine,* May 24.

Holmes, Helen Bequaert, and Laura Purdy, eds. 1989. *Hypatia* 4(2,3) special issues on feminist ethics and medicine.

Implants hide tumors in breasts, study says. 1988. *Toronto Star,* July 29. Summarized from article in *Journal of the American Medical Association,* July 8, 1988.

Jaggar, Alison, and Susan R. Bordo, eds. 1989. *Gender/Body/Knowledge: Feminist Reconstructions of Being and Knowing.* New Brunswick, NJ: Rutgers University Press.

Jonas, Hans. 1979. Toward a philosophy of technology. *Hastings Center Report* 9,1 (February): 34–43.

Kristeva, Julia. 1982. *The powers of Horror: An essay on abjection.* Trans. Leon Roudiez. New York: Columbia University Press.

Lakoff, Robin Tolmach, and Raquel Scherr. 1984. *Face Value: The Politics of Beauty.* Boston: Routledge and Kegan Paul.

Long, strong, perfect nails usually not nature's own. 1988. *Toronto Star,* August 18.

Looking for Mr. Beautiful. 1990. *Boston Globe,* May 7.

Lowe, Marion. 1982. The dialectic of biology and culture. In *Biological woman: The convenient myth,* ed. Ruth Hubbard, Mary Sue Henifin, and Barbara Fried. Cambridge, MA: Schenkman.

Luria, Gina, and Virginia Tiger. 1976. *Everywoman.* New York: Random House.

McCabe, Nora. 1990. Cosmetic solutions. *Homemaker Magazine,* September, pp. 38–46.

Madonna passionate about fitness. 1990. *Toronto Star,* August 16.

Markovic, Mihailo. 1976. Women's liberation and human emancipation. In *Women and philosophy: Toward a theory of liberation,* ed. Carol Gould and Marx Wartofsky. New York: Capricorn Books.

Matthews, Gwyneth Ferguson. 1985. Mirror, mirror: Self-image and disabled women. *Women and Disability: Resources for Feminist Research* 14(1): 47–50.

Mies, Maria. 1988. From the individual to the dividual: In the supermarket of "reproductive alternatives." *Reproductive and Genetic Engineering* 1(3): 225–37.

Morgan, Kathryn Pauly. 1986. Romantic love, altruism, and self-respect: An analysis of Simone De Beauvoir. *Hypatia* 1(1): 117–48.

———. 1987. Women and moral madness. In *Science, Morality and Feminist Theory*, ed. Marsha Hanen and Kai Nielsen. Special issue of the *Canadian Journal of Philosophy*, Supplementary Volume 13: 201–26.

———. 1989. Of woman born: How old-fashioned! New reproductive technologies and women's oppression. In *The Future of Human Reproduction*, ed. Christine Overall. Toronto: The Women's Press.

Murphy, Julie [Julien S]. 1984. Egg farming and women's future. In *Test-tube women: What future for motherhood?* ed. Rita Arditti, Renate Duelli-Klein, and Shelley Minden. Boston: Pandora Press.

New bodies for sale. 1985. *Newsweek*, May 27.

New profile took 3 years. 1989. *Toronto Star*, May 25.

Osherson, Samuel, and Lorna Amara Singhham. 1981. The machine metaphor in medicine. In *Social Contexts of Health, Illness and Patient Care*, ed. E. Mishler. New York: Cambridge University Press.

Piercy, Marge. 1980. Right to life. In *The moon is always female*. New York: Knopf.

The quest to be a perfect 10. 1990. *Toronto Star*, February 1.

Ratcliff, Hathryn Strother, ed. 1989. *Healing Technology: Feminist Perspectives*. Ann Arbor: University of Michigan Press.

Raymond, Janice. 1987. Preface to *Man-Made-Woman*, ed. Gena Corea et al. Bloomington: Indiana University Press.

Retouching nature's way: Is cosmetic surgery worth it? 1990. *Toronto Star*, February 1.

Rich, Adrienne. 1980. Compulsory heterosexuality and lesbian existence. *Signs: Journal of Women in Culture and Society* 5(4): 631–60.

Rothman, Barbara Katz. 1984. The meanings of choice in reproductive technology. In *Test-tube Women: What Future for Motherhood?* ed. Rita Arditti, Renate Duelli-Klein, and Shelley Minden. Boston: Pandora Press.

Russett, Cynthia Eagle. 1989. *Sexual science: The Victorian Construction of Womanhood*. Cambridge: Harvard University Press.

Schiebinger, Londa. 1980. *The Mind Has No Sex? Women in the Origins of Modern Science*. Cambridge: Harvard University Press.

Schoenfielder, Lisa, and Barb Wieser, eds. 1983. *Shadow on a Tightrope: Writings by Women on Fat Oppression*. Iowa City: Aunt Lute Press.

Sherwin, Susan. 1984–85. A feminist approach to ethics. *Dalhousie Review* 64(4): 704–13.

———. 1987. Feminist ethics and in vitro fertilization. In *Science, Morality, and Feminist Theory*, ed. Marcia Hanen and Kai Nielsen. Special issue of *Canadian Journal of Philosophy*, Supplementary Volume 13: 265–84.

———. 1989. Feminist and medical ethics: Two different approaches to contextual ethics. *Hypatia* 4(2): 57–72.

Silver, Harold. 1989. Liposuction isn't for everybody. *Toronto Star*, October 20.

Warren, Mary Anne. 1985. *Gendercide: The Implications of Sex Selection*. Totowa, NJ: Rowman and Allanheld.

Warren, Virginia. 1989. Feminist directions in medical ethics. *Hypatia* 4(2): 73–87.

Weldon, Fay. 1983. *The Life and Loves of a She-devil*. London: Coronet Books; New York: Pantheon Books.

Williams, John, M.D., and Jim Williams. 1990. Say it with liposuction. From a press release; reported in *Harper's*, August.

Woman, 43, dies after cosmetic surgery. 1989. *Tornoto Star*, July 7.

CHAPTER 17
FACING THE DILEMMA

KATHY DAVIS

(1995)

In this essay, I return to the two issues raised at the beginning of my book *Reshaping the Female Body: The Dilemma of Cosmetic Surgery.* The first concerns the problem of understanding why women are willing to undergo a painful, risky, and often demeaning intervention like cosmetic surgery. The second concerns the problem of finding a way to be critical of cultural discourses and practices which inferiorize the female body and —literally —cut women down to size—without treating the recipients themselves as the misguided victims of false consciousness. Drawing together the themes which have emerged in the course of this inquiry, I will attempt now to elaborate the feminist critique of femininity and of the cultural discourses and practices of the beauty system in such a way that it is possible to have the best of both worlds—that is, to be critical of cosmetic surgery without uncritically undermining the women who see it as a solution to their suffering. As a concluding note, some proposals will be made for a feminist response to cosmetic surgery which takes ambivalence and empathy rather than political correctness as a starting point.

TAKING WOMEN AT THEIR WORD

The focus of this inquiry was why women have cosmetic surgery. What kinds of experiences with appearance could compel them to have their bodies altered surgically? And, how did they explain their willingness and even eagerness to undergo an intervention which was often dangerous, painful, humiliating, or even left them in worse shape afterwards than they were before?

Interpretative sociology has a long-standing interest in everyday accounts as a good place to begin understanding people's actions (Schwartz and Jacobs 1979). Particularly when individuals engage in behavior which is considered problematic or relevant for some social problem—i.e., suicide, schizophrenia, criminality, or deviant behavior—the "member's perspective"—that is, her or his subjective interpretation about what is going on—is deemed essential for a sociological reconstruction of the life world.[1] Taking the member's point of view is supposed to help the sociologist avoid the professional trap of insisting that she or he knows better than the person in question what is really going on. This "policy of credulousness" means finding a way to believe statements and stories which one's college training, the professional literature, good common sense, and all else that is held sacred and holy say are dead wrong (if not crazy), and [to] treat the problem as lying with the sacred and holy, not the beliefs of the respondent. (Schwartz and Jacobs 1979, pp. 72-73)

I adopted this policy in my attempts to understand how the recipients made sense of cosmetic surgery. Without forgetting feminist critical perspectives on women's involvement in the feminine beauty system, I bracketed the notion that women and their bodies are determined or colonized by this system in order to see if (and how) I might find a way to believe the explanations they themselves had. [2] And, indeed, this policy of credulousness helped me to elicit extensive and open-hearted personal stories from women who have had cosmetic surgery—stories which not only confirmed what I already knew about cosmetic surgery but produced some surprises as well. These biographical accounts of how individual women came to have surgery and their experiences with its aftermath were not only quite different from the explanations, provided in the medical (*Reshaping*, Ch. 1.) and social scientific (Ch. 2) literature on the subject, but they upset some of my previously held feminist notions about women's involvement in cosmetic surgery as well.

First, the women I spoke with explained that they did not have cosmetic surgery because they wanted to be more beautiful. Although they insisted that they were just as interested in their appearance as the next woman, this had nothing to do with their desire to have it. It was not about beauty, but about wanting to become ordinary, normal, or just like everyone else. (Ch. 3). They provided convincing accounts of how it felt to live in a body which was experienced as different and of the destruction it wrought upon their relationships and their capacity to move about in the world. They showed how a problem with appearance could generate a biographical trajectory of suffering which was no less devastating to their sense of self than, say, the experience of having a chronic illness or of coming to terms with a debilitating accident (Ch. 4). Caught in a downward spiral from which there appeared to be no escape, they viewed cosmetic surgery as a solution of sorts—a way to alleviate suffering beyond endurance. It opened up the possibility for the individual to renegotiate her relationship to her body and through her body to the world around her. Cosmetic surgery was presented as part of a woman's struggle to feel at home in her body—a subject with a body rather than just a body. [3] Paradoxically, cosmetic surgery enabled these women to become embodied subjects rather than objectified bodies.

Second, the women I spoke with unfailingly insisted that cosmetic surgery was something that they had done for themselves. Contrary to popular belief, they had not been pressured into the operation by husbands with a fetish for voluptuous breasts or by knife-happy male surgeons in search of female victims. Instead most women had to overcome considerable opposition in order to have cosmetic surgery. They described their decision as a kind of heroic tale, presenting themselves as courageous protagonists who not only faced their own fears head on, but tackled the reservations of others as well (Ch. 5). They displayed an unmistakable elation at having acted by themselves and for themselves—often for the first time.

Cosmetic surgery was, of course, not without its shadow side. Most women were considerably less enthusiastic about the actual process of getting surgery, once the decision had been taken. Visits to family physicians for referrals, consultations with plastic surgeons, or negotiations about national health insurance coverage were routinely described as humiliating and degrading ordeals. Having gone to considerable effort to inform themselves about potential risks and side effects prior to having surgery, many expressed anger at the cursory and often disrespectful treatment they received from surgeons and were outraged upon discovering afterwards that information had been withheld or procedures improperly tested (Ch.6). They were adamant about their right to be allowed to make an informed decision—as competent decision makers who are able to weigh the risks against the possible benefits of the surgery.

The overwhelming majority of the women claimed that they were pleased with the outcome and glad they had taken the step. Interestingly, their satisfaction did not necessarily correspond with the actual outcome of the surgery which was, in many cases, disappointing. Many women had side effects and even permanent disfigurement to contend with following the operation. Nevertheless, looking back on their decision, they often claimed to have no regrets and, given a second chance, would probably do it again. They seemed to be prepared to accept responsibility—within reason—for their decisions, including the often less-than-fortuitous consequences (Ch.6)

Third, the women I spoke with treated cosmetic surgery as something which was morally problematic for them and had to be justified. They were ongoingly oriented to possible objections which could be levelled at cosmetic surgery, in general, and their own decision, in particular. Contrary to the popular stereotypes of the scalpel slave and the female with a predilection for the surgical fix, these women seemed highly critical of the beauty norms which compelled them to take such a drastic step. They were invariably skeptical about cosmetic surgery as a general remedy for women's dissatisfaction with their appearance. Instead it was presented as the lesser of two evils rather than as an answer to all their problems.

Justifying cosmetic surgery proved a complicated business. It not only entailed explaining why an operation was legitimate in their particular case, but also why it was not acceptable in general. They drew upon available cultural discourses to make their claim—discourses concerning femininity (equality and difference), freedom and social determinism, justice (rights and needs), and more. The same discourses could be used interchangeably—with a little creativity—to explain why cosmetic surgery was justifiable for them as well as why it was indefensible in general. Cosmetic surgery was defended in terms of justice (the need to intervene in suffering which had passed the limits of what a woman should normally have to endure). They often explained their actions in terms of rights—the right not to suffer, the right to a reasonable degree of happiness or well-being, or the right to take advantage of available services and technologies. Cosmetic surgery was, however, also criticized in terms of justice—as a symptom of an unjust social order in which women are forced to go to extremes to have an acceptable body. The ubiquitous primacy of a morality based on rights—for example, every individual should have the right to do with her body as she will—was invariably countered by claims that cosmetic surgery should not be universally available, but rather limited to those who really needed it.

In conclusion, these accounts showed how cosmetic surgery can be an understandable step in the context of an individual woman's experiences of embodiment and of her possibilities for taking action to alter her circumstances. They show that while the decision is not taken lightly and, indeed, remains problematic, it can be the best course of action for some women. They provide an answer to the perplexing question raised at the outset of this inquiry; namely, why do women desire and decide to undergo a practice which is both dangerous and oppressive.

Cosmetic surgery is not about beauty, but about identity. For a woman who feels trapped in a body which does not fit her sense of who she is, cosmetic surgery becomes a way to renegotiate identity through her body. Cosmetic surgery is about exercising power under conditions which are not of one's own making. In a context of limited possibilities for action, cosmetic surgery can be a way for an individual woman to give shape to her life by reshaping her body. Cosmetic surgery is about morality. For a woman whose suffering has gone beyond a certain point, cosmetic surgery can become a matter of justice—the only fair thing to do.

Thus, by listening to women's narratives as an instance of the member's perspective and by attempting to believe them, an interpretation of cosmetic surgery can be made which treats it as a lamentable and problematic, but, nevertheless, understandable course of action. Women who have cosmetic surgery do not appear to be blindly driven by forces over which they have no control or comprehension. They do not seem more duped by the feminine beauty system than women who do not see cosmetic surgery as a remedy to their problems with their appearance.

But can we really take women at their word like this? The objection might be made that by taking the member's perspective, I have lost the analytic distance necessary for explaining their involvement in a practice like cosmetic surgery. Perhaps in my eagerness to understand women who have cosmetic surgery, I have fallen into the trap so familiar to anthropologists of "going native." This raises the question of whether it would be possible to listen to the same stories and yet come up with a very different reading.

MISPLACED WORDS AND PARADOXICAL CHOICES

In the previous chapter, Kathryn Morgan poses the same question which I have asked: why do "actual, live women . . . choose to participate in anatomizing and fetishizing their bodies as they buy 'contoured bodies,' 'restored youth,' and 'permanent beauty' " by undergoing cosmetic surgery (p. 262). As a feminist, she finds women's apparent willingness to engage in this phenomenon troubling and argues that it is essential to listen to what women who have undergone surgery have to say about it. To this end, she has developed a "feminist hermeneutics" which will enable her to interpret women's "words and choices" against the backdrop of the production of femininity in patriarchal culture, the normalization of women's bodies through technology, and contemporary debates in mainstream and feminist bioethics (ibid.). In this way, she hopes to make sense of her "genuine epistemic and political bewilderment" when confronted with women's willingness to undergo surgery (ibid.). Although Morgan and I seem to have similar aims, she comes to a conclusion which is very different from mine.

Morgan argues that women's words are mistaken, deceptive and inaccurate—indeed, little more than the misguided mumblings of a RoboWoman (p. 264). They cannot be heard as an accurate representation of women's experiences with their bodies. Their decision to have cosmetic surgery is taken under circumstances which preclude genuine choice. In the final analysis, women's accounts are just more evidence for what we already know; namely, that cosmetic surgery is bad news for women and that no woman in her right mind could possibly choose to do it. Therefore, the only appropriate response to the dilemma of cosmetic surgery is not to do it and, more generally, to denounce that it is done at all.

Morgan's argument is threefold: First, women who believe that they are creating a new identity are "at a deeper level" choosing to conform to the norms of femininity. What appears to be the desire for a more beautiful body "turns out to be" compliance to "white, western, Anglo-Saxon bodies in a racist, anti-Semitic context" (p. 269). Cosmetic surgery is the public display of the male-identified woman to the hypothetical male viewer and, more generally, to the norms of compulsory heterosexuality. In view of cultural ideologies which pathologize the female body, perfectly ordinary-looking women are tricked into believing that their bodies are abnormal and that cosmetic surgery is the normal step to take toward remedying the problem. In short, cosmetic surgery is not about self-creation, but about conformity.

Second, women who believe that cosmetic surgery enables them to exercise power over their lives by transcending hated bodies are "in reality" the victims of exploitation. They have been coerced by lovers, husbands, or family members who "taunt" or "harass" them into improving their bodies (p. 270). They have been tricked by the false promises of male cosmetic surgeons whose coercive practices are disguised as "benevolent, therapeutic and voluntaristic" (ibid.). The normalizing power of femininity has not only "colonized" the outer surface of the female body through a host of disciplinary and normalizing practices, but it has taken over the consciousness of the individual woman, dominating her from within as well (ibid.). "In seeking independence, they . . . become even more dependent on male assessment and on the services of all those experts they initially bought to render them independent" (p. 271). The belief that cosmetic surgery enables a woman to do something for herself is thus little more than "ideological camouflage" which masks the actual absence of choice (p. 272). In actual fact, the power is on the other side of the fence—the medical profession, mainstream bioethics, and the patriarchal social order. The cultural colonization of the female body and the technological imperative are the reality behind the rhetoric of freedom and choice. In short, cosmetic surgery is not about liberation, but about domination.

Third, women who believe that their decision to have cosmetic surgery can ever be defended as an acceptable course of action are mistaken. They have failed to confront their individual choices with the normative and political implications the practice of cosmetic surgery inevitably raises. Cosmetic surgery belongs to a set of practices and technologies which are oppressive for women. It can never be ethical to support a practice which contributes to this deplorable state of affairs, no matter how much a particular woman may feel that she needs it. Under conditions of oppression, the only truly moral—that is, "politically correct feminist response to cosmetic surgery" is refusal and the development of (feminist) alternatives which do not feed into relations of subordination and domination (p. 274). This includes anything from individual resistance to the collective refusal of women as consumers to the more "utopian" response of revalorizing the "domain of the ugly" by reappropriating the techniques of cosmetic surgery and putting them to a different use: for example, freeze-dried fat cells for fat implantation, wrinkle-inducing creams, or having breasts pulled down rather than lifted (pp. 274–78). Given that Morgan's feminist utopia would be just as dangerous to women's health as the contemporary surgical culture she abhors, it is not surprising that this "ghoulish array" is mainly meant to "shock" the reader into appreciating the gravity of the problem (p. 279). In short, cosmetic surgery is never morally acceptable; it is morally reprehensible and politically incorrect.

Thus, Morgan concludes that women's insistence on referring to cosmetic surgery in terms of self-creation, freedom, and individual choice is off course. The reality is something else altogether. Cosmetic surgery is about women being coerced into conformity, lured into normalization, and misled into believing that an operation is an acceptable response to their problems.

Morgan's case against cosmetic surgery raises the question of how the same objective that I have—understanding women's own reasons for having cosmetic surgery—can lead to such diametrically opposed conclusions. In order to understand the discrepancy between what Morgan and I have heard and how we have attempted to come to terms with our feminist unease concerning women's desire to have their bodies altered surgically, I shall now take a closer—and more critical—look at her arguments. I show how both the *methodological* and *theoretical* assumptions which shape her critique of cosmetic surgery make it impossible to do what she sets out to do.

LISTENING TO WOMEN'S VOICES

The first problem with Morgan's approach concerns her claim to have listened to women who desire the surgical fix. Whereas she explicitly claims that a feminist approach to cosmetic surgery requires that we listen to women's "voices" (p. 266), there is no evidence in her article that she actually spoke with any women who have had surgery. Instead of interviewing women with firsthand experience, she provides quotations from articles in women's magazines and newspapers with titles like "Changing Faces," "Cosmetic Surgery for the Holidays," "Retouching Nature's Way: Is Cosmetic Surgery Worth It?" Thus, the media is Morgan's sole source of evidence for understanding women's "words and choices." As we all know, the media do abound with personal testimonies about women's surgical experiences, and such accounts can be a rich source of analytic material for a feminist critique of the practice.[4] However, the media are hardly an unmediated source for women's voices. Whatever a cosmetic surgery recipient might originally say, her experience is invariably reworked by the journalist who selects, condenses, translates, and polishes her words, and then reassembles them into a narrative which fits his or her interests as well as the editorial policy of the magazine or newspaper. Both personal stories and accounts which appear in the media are embedded in broader cultural discourses which provide typical discursive formats for both spoken and written texts about cosmetic surgery: the Before and After Story (Dull 1989; Smith 1990b), the Success Story ("How Changing My Nose Changed My Life"), the Atrocity Story ("I'll Never Listen to Another Doctor Again"), the Celebrity Story which is of interest because of who the recipient is (Cher, Michael Jackson, movie stars, former Miss Americas), or the Deviant Story ("Scalpel Slaves" or "Women Who Don't Know When To Stop").[5]

Morgan does not reflect on the textual practices and discursive formats which construct women's voices in the media. More seriously, she ignores and, indeed, obscures her own textual practices—practices which construct her analysis in a particular direction. For example, she makes no mention of how she happened to select particular instances from all the possible examples available in the media. She does not explain anything about the women, but presents a series of quotes as a collection of "voices" which ostensibly represent women's reasons for having cosmetic surgery. The label "voice" is, of course a familiar metaphor in feminist scholarship, a metaphor which has been used—and abused (Davis 1994)—to represent what women really feel and know as opposed to what they are supposed to feel and know under patriarchal relations of power (Gilligan 1982; Belenky et al, 1986). By drawing upon this metaphor, Morgan constructs a text which can be read as representing how women "really" feel about cosmetic surgery, thereby supporting her claim to have taken women's reasons for wanting cosmetic surgery into account.

Morgan not only neglects to provide the reader with an opportunity to understand the reasons women might actually put forth or how they would explain them, but she obscures the fact that she has not listened to women's experiences herself. Her presentation authorizes a particular reading of why women have surgery as representative, but, at the same time, misguided and lacking credibility. Rather than using her reaction of puzzlement as an interpretative resource in her hermeneutic analysis of women's involvement of cosmetic surgery, Morgan seems to be primarily concerned in showing why cosmetic surgery is antithetical to choice. In short, Morgan's methodology makes it impossible for her do to what she set out to do—namely, understand women's reasons for having surgery. For that, she would need a hermeneutics which allows her to interpret the ambiguities and complexities of women's explanations, while critically acknowledging her own reflexivity and partisan stance as part of these interpretations.[6]

However, even if Morgan had spoken with the same women I spoke with or employed a methodology which was conducive to understanding a member's perspective, she would still have come to the same conclusion. The reason for this is theoretical rather than methodological. Morgan makes certain theoretical assumptions which are central to her critique and yet lead to a restrictive and overly simplified interpretation of women's involvement in cosmetic surgery. They prevent her from treating women's reasons as credible or as having anything of relevance to add to her analysis. Instead these reasons can be dismissed without further ado or else marshaled as evidence to confirm the standpoint which Morgan already holds. These assumptions concern identity, power, and morality.[7]

INTERPRETING WOMEN'S CHOICES

Morgan conceptualizes women's *identity* as emerging through conformity (or resistance) to the norms of femininity and, more specifically, of feminine beauty.[8] This assumes a notion of self as overdetermined—as a cultural straightjacket which forces women to alter their bodies in order to meet the constraints of conventional femininity. Identity seems to be little more than a collection of prescriptions which are blindly followed without improvisation. The process by which individual women appropriate, interpret, and assemble these prescriptions to create an acceptable sense of self is noticeably absent. The complex realities of women are ignored as, for example, women of color who may not only be "trying to become white."[9] In Morgan's analysis, white, Western, heterosexual femininity seems to attach itself mysteriously to the passive female body as ready-made creation, without a female subject who actively makes sense of herself vis-à-vis her body.

Such a conception of identity is inadequate for an empathetic understanding of how it might actually feel to have a body which is perceived as different or alien to an individual's sense of self and of the suffering which this perception might entail. It provides no way of exploring how individual women make sense of such embodied experience as a problem of identity. Consequently, it offers no help in coming to terms with their desire for cosmetic surgery as an intervention in their identity—as a way to reinstate a damaged sense of self and become who they feel they really are or should have been.

In order to understand women's involvement in cosmetic surgery, identity needs to be treated as embodied—that is, the outcome of an individual's interaction with her body and through her body with the world around her. It would have to be regarded as situated in culture rather than statically determined by it. And, finally, identity would need to be explored as a negotiated process rather than as a set of prescriptions, a process whereby the individual actively and creatively draws upon cultural resources for making sense of who she is, who she was, and who she might become.[10]

Morgan seems to assume that *power*—whether at the level of social practices or cultural discourses—is primarily a matter of oppression, coercion, or control. In her conception of power, women are victims of individual male lovers, husbands, or surgeons. They are the objects of normalizing power practices which colonize their bodies and infuse their consciousness. And, they are the dupes of ideologies which confuse and mystify them with the rhetoric of freedom and individual choice.[11] The myriad ways in which women—often quite resourcefully—negotiate some degrees of freedom for themselves tend to be ignored or regarded as irrelevant in view of the broader context of their oppression. Social practices which are oppressive and disempowering seem automatically devoid of any enabling or even empowering dimensions. By the same token, dominant ideologies like liberal individualism with its discourse of choice appear to be imposed upon obedient and uncritical individuals who are blissfully unaware of their true interests or real lack of choice. It is impossible to entertain the notion that ideologies might provide the common symbolic resources for legitimating both liberatory *and* oppressive social practices.

This conception of power precludes viewing cosmetic surgery as both a means for controlling women through their bodies and as a strategy for women to exercise control over their lives. Their exhilaration at having taken a step—albeit a step with serious drawbacks and dangers—remains an enigma. They appear to be incompetent at making decisions about their own lives. Their claim that cosmetic surgery was the best choice for them under the circumstances has to be attributed to the fact that the ideological wool has been pulled over their eyes.

Understanding why women decide to have cosmetic surgery requires a conception of power which focuses on the relationship between social structures and cultural discourses and the activities and practices of individuals. It needs a conception of power which neither denies systemic patterns of domination, nor treats individuals as free to shape the world in accordance with their own desires. Instead, individuals would have to be reinstated as active and knowledgeable agents who negotiate their lives in a context where their awareness is partial and the options limited by circumstances which are not of their making.[12] Rather than treating ideology as a web of cultural discourses which ensnares the unwitting individual, we need a conception of ideology-in-action. This would mean showing how people draw upon both shared and contradictory cultural discourses in order to make sense of and legitimate their actions.[13]

Morgan assumes in advance that there is no moral defense for cosmetic surgery and that it can never be an acceptable solution to women's suffering. Her conception of morality separates the discussion of the normative dimensions of morally problematic practices from the everyday moral deliberations of the individuals involved. Their doubts and reservations are treated as having nothing of relevance to contribute to a feminist ethics.[14] For Morgan, morality seems to be a matter of demarcating the good from the bad in accordance with an ostensibly universal feminist standard of moral truth rather than exploring issues which are, in most cases, not only complex and contradictory, but more often than not essentially contested. It is a conception of morality which precludes ambiguity, making it impossible to understand how arguments formulated under the same moral banner (for example, social justice) might be used both to reject as well as to accept problematic practices. (For example, cosmetic surgery is unjust for women in general, but just in special cases to reduce pain that has gone beyond an acceptable limit.) It is a morality which advocates simplistic solutions to complicated issues rather than contextual or particularistic resolutions of the for-the-time-being variety.[15] Morgan's normative position results in a call for a politically correct response to moral dilemmas—a response which, by definition, assumes that there is a clear and unequivocal position for the feminist critic to take.

A conception of morality which discards cosmetic surgery as straightforwardly objectionable assumes incorrectly that women who have it are necessarily in favor of the practice. This assumption ignores their struggles to come to terms with the normative dimensions of what is often a problematic decision, thereby obscuring what makes cosmetic surgery both morally acceptable and unacceptable to them. Both their arguments in defense of their right to be considered special cases and their critiques of the options available to women in general seem to have no relevance to Morgan for the project of developing feminist normative standpoints concerning cosmetic surgery. Since there can be no doubt concerning which side of the fence the feminist critic should be on, her own arguments do not have to be considered as either partial or situated and are, therefore, not amenable to self-critical reflection, let alone revision.

A more adequate conception of morality than Morgan's would take women's situated moral practices as a starting point for analyzing their involvement in dangerous or demeaning practices like cosmetic surgery. It would explore the normative grounds of their defense—that is, how they discursively construct their action as acceptable—as well as their critique—that is, under which circumstances cosmetic surgery would or should be unacceptable. Developing a properly normative stance toward cosmetic surgery would require an approach to morality which explores the arguments for and against the practice—that is, its existence as a practice which is controversial—rather than one which searches for a resolution that eliminates controversy once and for all. It would be a conception of morality as self-reflexive and communicative rather than as elitist and correct.[16]

In conclusion, Morgan's theoretical assumptions about identity, power, and morality enable her to censure the cultural pathologization of the female body, to attack the technological imperative which forces women to have surgery, and to dismiss cosmetic surgery once and for all. These same assumptions, however, tend to result in an overhasty and far too easy rejection of women's reasons for having cosmetic surgery. Her theoretical framework makes it almost impossible to understand women's suffering, to account for their decisions, and to appreciate under which circumstances cosmetic surgery might be an acceptable choice. Contrary to her own claims, she seems to have avoided engaging with women's ambiguous and contradictory reasons for having cosmetic surgery, as well as her own puzzlement as a feminist concerning their involvement in the practice.

Morgan is, however, not alone in this. Several contemporary feminist perspectives which are available for analyzing women's involvement in the practices and discourses of the feminine beauty system provide the ingredients for both a critical and convincing analysis of cosmetic surgery. Despite their merits, these perspectives often share Morgan's tendency to treat women who engage in cosmetic surgery as culturally scripted, oppressed, and ideologically manipulated; i.e., as the cultural dopes of the feminine beauty system.

It is possible to reconcile a feminist critique of cosmetic surgery with a respectful view of its recipients. This would require some theoretical revisions, however. A framework is needed which enables us *both* to take a member's perspective *and* to explore the social pressures upon women to meet the norms of feminine beauty.

COMBINING A MEMBER'S PERSPECTIVE WITH THE FEMINIST CRITICAL EDGE, OR: THE "HAVING-YOUR-CAKE-AND-EATING-IT-TOO" STRATEGY

Like Morgan, theorists Iris Young, Dorothy Smith, and Sandra Bartky are unanimously critical of the beauty system, decrying it as nothing less than the "major articulation of capitalist patriarchy," of a kind with the "military-industrial complex" (Bartky 1990, p. 39). They, too, situate women's concerns with their appearances in the context of the production and reproduction of femininity (Smith 1990b), and of the "aesthetic scaling" of the bodies of subordinate groups (Young 1990a). What makes these writers of particular interest here, however, is that they provide the theoretical ingredients for combining a member's perspective with a critique of women's involvement in cosmetic surgery. While they do not apply these insights themselves to this particular topic, their insights have enabled me to do just that.

For Young (1990b), identity is always the outcome of women's active negotiation of the contradictions of feminine embodiment. The sine qua non of feminine embodiment for her is the condition of being caught between existence as just a body and the desire to transcend that body and become a subject who acts upon the world in and through it. Although the objectification of the female body is part and parcel of the situation of most Western women and accounts for a shared sense of bodily alienation, women are also invariably subjects who attempt to overcome their alienation, to act upon the world instead of being acted upon. By focusing on this tension, it becomes possible to explore how women's interactions with their bodies offer possibilities for them to become subjects even though they put constraints upon their personhood. The suffering of the woman who has cosmetic surgery becomes part of a shared continuum of feminine embodied experience—culturally shaped, but no more scripted than the next woman's struggle to become embodied female subjects in a context of objectification.

For Smith (1990b), agency is central to all social practices, including women's attempts to beautify or improve their bodies. Beauty is part of femininity, but women are not simply passively normalized or coerced into beautifying their bodies. Femininity requires knowing what needs to be done to remedy one's body, assessing the possibilities, and acting upon them. It becomes possible to imagine how an activity like cosmetic surgery could be a way for a woman who has tried everything else to engage in the activity of doing femininity along with the rest of her sex. She can be viewed as a competent and knowledgeable subject even when she acts under conditions which are not of her own making.

For Bartky (1990), morality and correct-line thinking are antithetical when it comes to analyzing women's involvement in the practices of femininity. Femininity is, by definition, both seductive and humiliating, gratifying and oppressive. Women's everyday experience of femininity entails an ongoing struggle with contradictions, between gut-level desires and discursively held conviction that these same desires are reprehensible; between sensings of inadequacy or shame and the feelings created by moral precepts which condemn a sense of inadequacy as unjust and unacceptable. Using her method, cosmetic surgery can be explored as a dilemmatic situation for the recipients themselves—something which is both morally problematic and, at the same time, desirable and necessary.

Taken together, these theoretical insights allow a respectful exploration of women's reasons for having cosmetic surgery, while permitting a critique of their decision to embark upon this particular course of action. In other words, an approach to cosmetic surgery can be of the "having-one's-cake-and-eating-it-too" variety, thereby providing a solution to the feminist dilemma which informed this inquiry (see introduction to *Reshaping*).

Ironically, the very theorists who provided such welcome assistance for my own endeavor seemed to show a marked reluctance to use their own theories for tackling the problem of women's involvement in cosmetic surgery. While they were willing to entertain the notion of agency in women's use of makeup (Smith) or in their playful encounters with fashion (Young), or to consider the moral contradictions in feminine sexuality (Bartky), cosmetic surgery was rather quickly discarded as a straightforward case of normalization or oppression—as a practice to be criticized rather than understood from the recipient's vantage point. Even Young (1990b), who explicitly discusses breast augmentation surgery, admits that she believes that "much of it must be frivolous and unnecessary, like diamonds or furs" (ibid., p. 202). She does not seem to regard cosmetic surgery as an opportunity for women to (re)negotiate the typical tensions in feminine embodiment or as a strategy which might—at least hypothetically—have empowering as well as disempowering effects.[17] Apparently, having the theoretical tools to take seriously women's reasons for undergoing such surgery does not guarantee that the tools will actually be put to use. Whatever their theoretical orientation, feminist scholars seem to balk at the thought of exploring how surgery might be desirable, empowering, or even just contradictory, preferring instead a critique which strongly and definitively dismisses the practice as bad news for women.

This condemnation of cosmetic surgery among feminist theories of beauty puzzled me at the outset of my inquiry. It became a preoccupation, however, in the wake of the responses I began to encounter as I gave presentations and wrote papers on the subject. Somewhat to my dismay, I found myself being asked whether I wasn't worried about "being too liberal." Concern was expressed that I was not sufficiently aware of the dangers of cosmetic surgery ("I do hope you are going to write about silicone implants.") While my postmodern feminist colleagues tended to appreciate my theoretical stance, they often found my choice of subject matter slightly off-putting. ("Why don't you do something about female bodybuilders or cross dressing?") Those more skeptical of postmodernism tended to regard my approach as misguided or insufficiently concerned with the structural constraints upon women.[18] While I was invariably given credit for good intentions ("Of course, you can't *blame* those women"), the suspicion remained that I had gone too far. By not coming out strongly enough against cosmetic surgery, I put my feminist credentials in danger. In some cases, I was even accused of being an advocate for cosmetic surgery as a solution to women's problems with their appearance.[19]

These experiences were troubling and often unpleasant. However, they also aroused my curiosity about why feminists are reluctant to take a more nuanced look at the phenomenon. The answer began to take shape for me at a conference where I found myself once again being placed on the wrong side of the fence. Ironically, just as *Reshaping the Female Body* began with my experience of confusion as a feminist at a conference on cosmetic surgery, this essay will end with a similar experience at another conference. While the first conference produced an uneasiness which was the impetus for the inquiry, the second provided one which enabled me to bring the inquiry to an end.

STEPFORD WIVES AND FEMINIST CRITICS

The conference was on feminist ethics and included a panel on cosmetic surgery. The participants were Kathryn Morgan and Lisa Parker—both of whose work has been discussed here—and myself; the audience consisted of primarily North American feminist philosophers.

In my talk, I discussed some of the consequences of a welfare system of health care for cosmetic surgery and then the recent expulsion of cosmetic surgery from the basic health care package in the Netherlands. While this decision has made cosmetic surgery less available (good news for feminists), it was taken in such a way that the needs of recipients were ignored (bad news for feminists). I argued—typically—for an approach to health care policy which would take the needs of individuals into account while tackling the necessary business of choosing which services should or should not be covered by national health insurance.

As I spoke, I scanned the audience for a sign of recognition, but saw, to my dismay, rows and rows of faces with blank expressions and heard the low rumble of whispered comments. When the floor was finally opened for discussion, the questions displayed barely concealed irritation. Comments seemed to be aimed at what I had *not* said (but should have). My position was characterized as "problematic," not "radical" enough, or—the final clincher—"too liberal." Once again, I watched my plea for a feminist approach which took the needs of the recipients into consideration disappear unheeded and unheralded and there I stood, transformed into a member of the liberal establishment and academic mainstream—a feminist scholar of tarnished alloy.

The response to my talk—and, parenthetically, to Parker's as well—was unpleasant, but it was also familiar.[20] It seemed to confirm what I already knew—namely, that my approach to cosmetic surgery evokes discomfort or protest among feminist scholars. The next speaker, Kathryn Morgan, presented the analysis of cosmetic surgery discussed above with a rather unusual introduction and received a very different response from the audience. It was ultimately this discrepancy in the reception of our presentations which supplied the missing piece in the puzzle of why I continually seemed to find myself with the "wrong" approach to cosmetic surgery.

Morgan began with an anecdote in which she described going to a meeting attended by wealthy, middle-aged women who had clearly been the recipients of repeated cosmetic surgeries. To underscore her horror at these suburban surgical junkies, she compared them to the "Stepford Wives": the beautiful but mindless inhabitants of the New England town of Stepford (in Ira Levin's 1972 bestselling novel) who have been diabolically transformed into robots by husbands in search of perfect wives. The meaning was plain: the cosmetic surgery recipient has not only traded in her real self for a more perfect body, but she has become the obedient victim of the patriarchal order.

The audience reaction was notably unlike it had been to Parker's and my presentations. To begin with, the Stepford Wife analogy evoked a ripple of laughter. Morgan's description of the dangers of cosmetic surgery and her analysis of women's participation in it as part of the normalization of the female body produced approving nods of assent and there was a palpable sense of *this-is-more-like-it* in the air. At the end of the day, she was heralded as having provided the "more radical" analysis of cosmetic surgery.

My own response to Morgan's anecdote as well as to the audience's reaction were mixed. Initially, I was reminded of watching numerous Oprah Winfrey or Phil Donahue programs on TV ("Addicted to Surgery," "Plastic Makes Perfect," "A Woman Who's Spent Thousands to Look Like Barbie," "Plastic Surgeons Turn Old Wives into New Women") where cosmetic surgery recipients would walk stiffly across the stage and face the camera with zombie-like smiles. They did, indeed, bear some resemblance to the ghostly and ghastly female inhabitants of Stepford. My initial response to them was horror, disapproval, and a nervous laughter which affirmed how alien and other they were—nothing like my friends, nothing like me.

My initial sense of *déjà vu* was quickly dispelled at the conference, however, as I remembered the women who were the subject of the present inquiry. I found myself jumping to their defense: *their* faces had not been empty or vacuous; *they* had not been placid robots, merely complying with their husbands' desires for a servant with big breasts. In short, *they* were nothing like Stepford Wives. I became increasingly irritated at this image, which erased their suffering, their struggles, their protest against circumstances which made cosmetic surgery their only viable course of action. The laughter of the audience seemed to be a collective process of distancing which marked and even celebrated the gap between us and them, between feminists who openly disapprove of cosmetic surgery and those women who either desire it or are willing to support those who do so.

My experience at this conference provided me with the missing clue to the problem of how we can understand cosmetic surgery without undermining the recipients *and* without loosing our "critical edge" as feminists (Bordo 1993, p. 32). While I had discovered methodologies and theoretical frameworks which enabled me to explore this problem as a dilemma, I had overlooked one crucial aspect. No matter how sophisticated our methodological and theoretical tools are, they are of no help unless we are prepared to use them. This raises the final question, then, of whether we as feminists can afford to face the dilemma of cosmetic surgery at all.

THE PROBLEM OF POLITICAL CORRECTNESS

The conference made clear to me that cosmetic surgery belongs to a set of social practices which evoke strong reactions and heated debates about what constitutes an appropriate or adequate feminist response. These practices, ranging from *in vitro* fertilization to self-starvation or pornography or compulsory heterosexuality, are controversial for feminists because they are both dangerous and/or demeaning and yet fervently desired by large numbers of women. Such things inevitably present us with the thorny and uncomfortable dilemma of having to take a stand against the practice without blaming the women who take part, and therefore they often elicit reactions like those of the women at the conference. These reactions lie at the heart of what I —for want of a better word—will call (feminist) political correctness.[21]

Political correctness is a concept which emerged in the late '70s in the U.S. and has since blossomed into a full-fledged cultural phenomenon which is specific to the American social landscape at this particular historical moment.[22] It refers to an ensemble of beliefs and causes, ranging from a rejection of the traditions of the West—the so-called canon—to a critique of dogmatic intolerance on the part of the Left. The term is employed, somewhat confusingly, to refer to a —more or less—desirable phenomenon as well as to actual positions in specific debates. To add to the chaos, it is employed by both radicals and traditionalists to criticize positions taken by the other. Traditionalists discredit the arguments of left-wing intellectuals—"the race-class-gender faction" (Wolfe 1993, p. 730)—as overly ideological, arguing that political correctness has led to a dogmatic and intolerant climate, the destruction of all standards, and, more generally, to a crisis in the academy. Radicals have a long history of rejecting academic traditions and politics of the white, Western male elite as politically problematic—as sustaining and even fueling power structures of exclusion and hierarchy. They adopt the term as appellation for a critical and, therefore, desirable position. Political correctness is not only used in debates between left and right, however. Left-wing activists have frequently used the term to tar other activists who they consider to be overly fanatical, while others have used it to chastise the counterculture for neglecting more serious concerns. Thus, the phenomenon has been and continues to be a bone of contention among those on the same side as well as the opposite side of the ideological fence.

Feminism is a case in point. Within it, there have been different responses to the phenomenon of political correctness. Some have affirmed the vital importance of taking a hard-line stance after an era of Reaganomics which has eroded feminist accomplishments and weakened women's general social position (the feminization of poverty, the withdrawal of men from the responsibility of fatherhood, the high incident of sexual violence and harassment of women, and so on). For example, Susan Bordo (1993) expresses this concern as she worries that the increasingly hostile political and cultural climate in the U.S. has transformed feminist thought into something which is scorned by its opponents as old-fashioned (the battle between the sexes is over, women are now free to do their own thing), psychologically motivated (hysterical, overly paranoid or humorless) or incorrect (lacking objectivity). She warns against the relativism of postmodernism with its "gender skepticism," "celebration of creative agency," and "plurality of options," and advocates keeping our eyes focused on what is "relevant"—namely, the "institutionalized *system* of values and practices," and "*patterned*" relations of domination and subordination (Bordo 1993, pp. 29–33, italics are hers).

Other feminists take a different stance. While they start from the same problem—namely, political conservatism and the polarization of feminists into opposing camps—they come to a different conclusion about the desirability of taking a correct line in feminist critique. For example, Marianne Hirsch and Evelyn Fox Keller (1990) reject a politically correct stance in favor of an "ethics of conflict" which looks for ways to deal constructively with often unreconcilable differences between the intellectual and political perspectives of feminism. While they acknowledge the sadness that accompanies giving up the dream of sisterhood and the unity of a shared political goal, they are wary of attempts to silence such differences under the banner of consensus. As Keller notes:

> Too often, the work of exploring differences among commonalities, and commonalities within difference, has been displaced by a defensive and anxious

need to "choose sides." As a result, we are divided along lines that often seem to me more illusory than real, that may have little, finally, to do with any of the political or intellectual tasks that lie ahead (Hirsch and Keller 1990, p. 384).

Whereas one side looks to a tolerance for ambivalence, difference, and conflict, the other side finds solace in an increased attention to a shared political line. Both sides argue in the name of a strong feminist tradition and are directed at shoring up feminism against attacks from within and without. For dealing with ethically problematic issues like cosmetic surgery, both approaches have advantages and disadvantages. The politically correct response to women's involvement in cosmetic surgery has been eloquently formulated by Kathryn Morgan and the advantages of her stance are clear. Her approach enables feminists to take a clear stand against cosmetic surgery as oppression, normalization, and ideological manipulation. It provides a way to denounce women's victimization without having to condone their own participation in it. Its adherents can tighten their ranks in a collective dismissal of cosmetic surgery and in an abstract solidarity with women as victims of medical technologies and cultural discourses. They also share distance from those less deserving of their sympathy: the wealthy, white, heterosexual, or embarrassingly addicted. Having established a position, they know what they are against and can exclude anything which detracts from or dilutes their critique. The feminist politically correct response to cosmetic surgery on the part of individual women is refusal and on the part of feminist scholars, a utopian revisioning of a world where cosmetic surgery and the problematic desires which keep it in place are a thing of the past.

Along with these advantages, Morgan's approach has some serious drawbacks, however. It makes it impossible to engage with the disturbing aspects of women's desire for cosmetic surgery. Rather than taking up women's experiences with surgery as an opportunity for further exploration, its adherents end up distancing themselves from experiences they don't like. They set up boundaries between themselves and other women—boundaries which prevent them from what Bat Ami Bar-On (1993b) has called "imaginatively entering the space" of other women's experience and from becoming "witnesses" to their suffering. Differences are squelched rather than explored. Instead of using women's claims as a resource for understanding the contradictions of feminine embodiment or the Janus face of resistance and compliance, women's words are made to fit a theoretical framework or explained away for the sake of a straightforwardly critical analysis. While feminist visions of a surgery-free future are comforting, they can also close our eyes to the less dramatic instances of resistance, compliance, or discursive penetration which are part and parcel of any social practice. Our alternatives become nothing more than utopian—leaving us little to say of relevance concerning women's lived relationships to their bodies, their experiences with cosmetic surgery, or their doubts about the practices and ideologies which sustain it. Political correctness is a strategy of premature closure: it arrests our involvement with women who have cosmetic surgery, stops further theoretical elabo ration of the phenomenon, and cuts off debate. In short, it makes us stop listening and, indeed, thinking.

It will come as no surprise that, while I have strong objections to the surgical alteration of women's bodies in the name of beauty, I am more inclined to an approach to the problem à la Hirsch and Keller. Taking cosmetic surgery as a dilemma rather than a form of self-inflicted subordination seems to me to be a more promising way to understand what makes it both desirable *and* problematic for so many women. In this inquiry, such an approach has enabled me to listen and take women's reasons seriously without having to agree with what they say. It has allowed me to explore their suffering, but also their resilience and creativity, as they try to alleviate pain and negotiate some space for themselves in the context of a gendered social order. By exploring their doubts about cosmetic surgery, I am able to understand how women can see through the conditions of their oppression even as they comply with them. I have been able to enjoy their small acts of defiance and resistance, even though they did not offer the promise of a future where women would not want to change their bodies or would refuse surgical solutions. Finally, approaching cosmetic surgery as a dilemma has provided me occasion to understand and explore the things that make it such a painful and intractable subject for analysis.

Obviously, there are also drawbacks to my approach. Any focus on the particularities of individual women's experiences with cosmetic surgery runs the risk of suspending attention from the systemic or structured patterns of women's involvement in the cultural beauty system—at least, temporarily. A concern for the complexity of women's desire to have cosmetic surgery makes it difficult to come up with either a blanket rejection or a gratifying resolution to the problems of cosmetic surgery.

The biggest disadvantage, however, is its insistence on engaging the discomfort and unease which cosmetic surgery will continue to evoke in all feminists. The politically correct response enables us a moment of respite, a sense that at least some of us have escaped the clutches of the beauty system, and a glimpse of a better future. When we view cosmetic surgery as a dilemma, however, we cannot escape the mixed feelings which assail us when we hear women proclaim their desire to have their bodies altered surgically. This view offers no respite from the uneasiness which goes along with their insistence that surgery is their best choice under the circumstances. And, finally, it does not try to make the situation more palatable by pretending that increasing numbers of women—including our own feminist friends—do not look to cosmetic surgery as a way to take their lives in hand.

Nevertheless, it is my contention that learning to endure ambivalence, discomfort, and doubt is the prerequisite for understanding women's involvement in cosmetic surgery. This approach not only prevents the premature theoretical closure which is antithetical to responsible scholarship, but enables us to keep the topic open for public discussion and debate. As concerned critics of the explosion in surgical technologies for reshaping the female body and of women's continued willingness to partake in them, we simply cannot afford the comfort of the correct line.

N O T E S

1. "Member's perspective" belongs to the tradition of interpretative sociology. As such, it does not refer to the way the world actually is, but rather how it is discursively constructed by individuals as they talk about themselves and their circumstances. Whereas the tradition of interpretative sociology has much to offer concerning the analysis of perspectives as social constructions, it is somewhat less reflexive about differences between members (shorthand for "members of society") who typically come with the specific accouterments of gender, class, ethnicity, and more. Feminist scholarship has, of course, been instrumental in deconstructing and elaborating the problematic aspects of taking the standpoint of another person. See, for example, Haraway (1988).

2. I say bracket because notions that women are victims rather than agents or are culturally scripted rather than free belong to the theoretical and political baggage of any feminist analysis—a kind of feminist common sense on how power works in a gendered social order. I have elaborated this elsewhere in Davis (1991a, 1993).

3. The embodied experience of being at home in one's body invites the comparison between cosmetic surgery recipients and those who are contemplating or have had sex change operations. Not only are their narratives similar, but both provide a particularly good place to explore the problems of embodiment in a gendered social order. See, for example, Kessler and McKenna (1978).

4. See, for example, Dull (1989); Balsamo (1993); Bordo (1993).

5. See Dorothy Smith (1990a, 1990b) for an excellent account of femininity as a textual practice and of feminist methods for recovering its construction from texts, which may range from personal accounts to literature, media representations, and scientific writing.

6. See, for example, Warnke (1993) for a good discussion of what a feminist hermeneutics would need to entail.

7. The concepts of identity, power, and morality, as well as the particular assumptions which Morgan makes about them, are not found only in her analysis. Many of the arguments I am making against her position could be raised in conjunction with other contemporary feminist perspectives on beauty. I have chosen to explore Morgan's work, however, because she articulates particularly clearly both the strengths and the weaknesses of the feminist case against cosmetic surgery.

8. While identity is a central concept in feminist theory in general, it is also a highly contested one. Initially, feminist scholars tended to oscillate between a pessimistic conception of feminine identity as the distorted and damaged outcome of patriarchal relations (de Beauvoir 1952; Millett 1971) and the optimistic valorization of femininity as difference (Miller 1976; Gilligan 1982; Hartsock 1983; Keller 1985). Postmodern feminism, on the other hand, is more concerned with dispelling the myth of a unified feminine identity and raising the banner of fragmented, fluctuating, and multiple identities (Flax 1990; de Lauretis 1987; Butler 1989). While Morgan tends to draw upon the more modernist arguments concerning femininity as uniformly repressive, she shares a postmodern indifference to women's actual bodily experience as well as to their attempts to create a sense of coherent, specific personhood (Benhabib 1992).

9. On this point, I am indebted to discussions with Natalie Beausoleil about her very interesting work on the makeup practices of Latina and Black women in the U.S.

10. The kind of conception I have in mind is eloquently formulated by Seyla Benhabib in her recent book, *Situating the Self* (1992).

11. Morgan is not alone in this. I have argued on another occasion that, despite the ubiquitous influence of Foucault upon recent feminist scholarship (Diamond and Quinby 1988; McNay 1992), feminists often draw upon a conception of power which is top down and repressive (Davis 1991a, 1993). This makes it difficult to explore the enabling dimensions of power as well as how women themselves participate in relations of power.

12. See, for example, Bourdieu (1977); Giddens (1984); Lukes (1986); and Connell (1987) for approaches to power which explore the relationship between system patterns of domination and subordination and social practices of individuals. For a feminist reworking, see, for example, Felski (1989); Davis et al. (1991).

13. See Billig et al. (1988); Billig (1991).

14. Kathryn Pyne Addelson (1988, pp. 108-32) makes a similar point in her discussion of the necessity of grounding feminist ethics in women's situated moral practices. See also Wolfe (1989, pp. 212-36).

15. This goes against recent trends in feminist ethics which have been in the direction of a more contextual approach. See, for example, Benhabib's (1992) communicative ethics or various renditions of an ethics of care and responsibility (for example, Kittay and Meyer 1987; Code 1991; Larrabee 1993; Tronto 1993).

16. See for example, Nancy Fraser (1989) for a good rendition of such an approach in her "politics of need interpretation." She advocates treating needs as essentially contested, multivalent, and contextual. Need claims should be evaluated in terms of the questions they raise rather than in terms of a search for definitive solutions to them.

17. I have discussed the possibility of applying one of Young's feminist "thought experiments"—as she has done for ball throwing, pregnancy, or fashion—to cosmetic surgery in Davis (1993b).

18. See, for example, Bordo (1993, pp. 20-33).

19. For example, one Dutch feminist journal gave a title to an article I wrote about cosmetic surgery as "The Right to Be Beautiful" (*Het recht om mooi te zijn*), which immediately evoked a critical rejoinder from another feminist scholar under the heading "The Right to Be Ugly."

20. Lisa Parker addressed the silicone controversy. She expressed some concern that feminists, by treating cosmetic surgery recipients as more culturally scripted than other women, risk ignoring the rights of augmentation candidates to make decisions about their bodies.

21. I am somewhat reticent to use the term political correctness which has been so overused by the media and has become overladen with conflicting meanings. Despite this conceptual inflation, however, I still believe that the phenomenon to which it refers continues to deserve careful and critical attention by scholars and activists alike. See, for example, the recent discussion in a special issue on political correctness in *Partisan Review* 4 (1993) as a case in point.

22. As a long-time resident of Europe, I have adopted the view which tends to be taken here that political correctness is a typically North American phenomenon. Although similar controversies and rhetoric may be found in Europe, the term political correctness is not a part of the discourses drawn upon by traditional or radical groups to defend or criticize one another's positions.

CHAPTER 18

SAPPHO BY SURGERY

The Transsexually Constructed Lesbian-Feminist

JANICE G. RAYMOND

(1979, 1994)

Transsexualism is multifaceted. From all that has been said thus far, it is clear that it raises many of the most complex questions feminism is asking about the origins and manifestations of sexism and sex-role stereotyping. While regarded by many as an obscure issue that affects a relatively minute proportion of the population, transsexualism poses very important feminist questions. Transsexually constructed lesbian-feminists show yet another face of patriarchy. As the male-to-constructed-female transsexual exhibits the attempt to possess women in a bodily sense while acting out the images into which men have molded women, the male-to-constructed-female who claims to be a lesbian-feminist attempts to possess women at a deeper level, this time under the guise of challenging rather than conforming to the role and behavior of stereotyped femininity. As patriarchy is neither monolithic nor one-dimensional, neither is transsexualism.

All men and male-defined realities are not blatantly macho or masculinist. Many indeed are gentle, nurturing, feeling, and sensitive, which, of course, have been the more positive qualities that are associated with stereotypical femininity. In the same way that the so-called androgynous man assumes for himself the role of *femininity*, the transsexually constructed lesbian-feminist assumes for himself the role and behavior of *feminist*. The androgynous man and the transsexually constructed lesbian-feminist deceive women in much the same way, for they lure women into believing that they are truly one of us—this time not only one in behavior but one in spirit and conviction.

CONTRADICTIONS OR CONFIRMATIONS?

It is not accidental that most male-to-constructed-female transsexuals who claim to be feminists also claim to be lesbian-feminists. In fact, I don't know of any transsexually constructed feminists who do not also claim to be lesbians. It is this combination that is extremely important. Lesbian-feminists have spent a great deal of energy in attempting to communicate that the self-definition of lesbian, informed by feminism, is much more than just a sexual choice. It is a total perspective on life in a patriarchal society representing a primal commitment to women on all levels of existence and challenging the bulwark of a sexist society—that is, heterosexism. Thus it is not a mere sexual alternative to men, which is characterized simply by sexually relating to women instead of men, but a way of being in the world that challenges the male possession of women at perhaps its most intimate and sensitive level. In assuming the identity of lesbian-feminist, then, doesn't the transsexual renounce patriarchal definitions of selfhood and choose to fight sexism on a most fundamental level?

First of all, the transsexually constructed lesbian-feminist may have renounced femininity but not masculinity and masculinist behavior (despite deceptive appearances). If femininity and masculinity are different sides of the same coin, thus making it quite understandable how one could flip from one to the other, then it is important to understand that the transsexually constructed lesbian-feminist, while not exhibiting a feminine identity and role, still exhibits its obverse side—stereotypical masculinity. Thus the assumption that he has renounced patriarchal definitions of selfhood is dubious.

Masculine behavior is notably obtrusive. It is significant that transsexually constructed lesbian-feminists have inserted themselves into the positions of importance and/or performance in the feminist community. The controversy in the summer of 1977 surrounding Sandy Stone, the transsexual sound engineer of Olivia Records, an "all-women" recording company, illustrates this well. Stone is not only crucial to the Olivia enterprise but plays a very dominant role there.[1] The national reputation and visibility he achieved in the aftermath of the Olivia controversy is comparable, in feminist circles, to that attained by Renee Richards in the wake of the Tennis Week Open. This only serves to enhance his previously dominant role and to divide women, as men frequently do, when they make their presence necessary and vital to women. Having produced such divisiveness, one would think that if Stone's commitment to and identification with women were genuinely woman-centered, he would have removed himself from Olivia and assumed some responsibility for the divisiveness. In Boston, a transsexual named Christy Barsky has worked himself into a similar dominant position, this time coaching a women's softball team, coordinating a conference on women and violence, staffing a women's center, and performing musically at various all-women places. Thus, like Stone, he exhibits a high degree of visibility and also divides women, in the name of lesbian-feminism.

Pat Hynes has suggested that there is only an apparent similarity between a strong lesbian, woman-identified self and a transsexual who fashions himself in a lesbian-feminist image.[2] With the latter, his masculinity comes through, although it may not be recognized as such. Hynes especially points to the body language of transsexuals where she notes *subtle but perceptible* differences between, for example, the way lesbians interact with other women and the way transsexuals interact with women. One specific example of this is the way a transsexual walked into a women's restaurant with his arms around two women, one on each side, with the possessive encompassing that is characteristically masculine.

Mary Daly, in explaining *why* this difference is perceptible, points out that the transsexually constructed lesbian-feminist is able to deceptively act out the part of lesbian-feminist *because* he is a man with a man's history; that is, he is free of many of the residues of self-hatred, self-depreciation, and self-contradiction that attend the history of women who are born with female bodies—all of which is communicated both subtly and not so subtly in gestures, body language, and the like.[3] Thus it is precisely *because* the transsexually constructed lesbian-feminist is a man, and *not* a woman encumbered by the scars of patriarchy that are unique to a woman's personal and social history that he can play our parts so convincingly and apparently better than we can play them ourselves. However, in the final analysis, he can only *play the part*, although the part may at times seem as, or more, plausible than the real woman (as is also the case with the male-to-constructed-female transsexual who appears more feminine than most feminine women).

What is also typically masculine in the case of the transsexually constructed lesbian-feminist is the appropriation of women's minds, convictions of feminism, and sexuality. One of the definitions of *male,* as related in Webster's, is "designed for fitting into a corresponding hollow part." This, of course, means much more than the literal signification of heterosexual intercourse. It can be taken to mean that men have been very adept at penetrating all of women's "hollow" spaces, at filling up the gaps, and or sliding into the interstices. Obviously, women who are in the process of moving out of patriarchal institutions, consciousness, and modes of living are very vulnerable and have gaps. I would imagine that it would be difficult, for example, for Olivia Records to find a female sound engineer and that such a person would be absolutely necessary to the survival of Olivia. But it would have been far more honest if Olivia had acknowledged the maleness of Sandy Stone and perhaps the necessity, at the time, to employ a man in this role. As one woman wrote of Sandy Stone and the Olivia controversy: "I feel raped when Olivia passes off Sandy, a transsexual, as a real woman. After all his male privilege, is he going to cash in on lesbian feminist culture too?"[4]

Rape, of course, is a masculinist violation of bodily integrity. All transsexuals rape women's bodies by reducing the real female form to an artifact, appropriating this body for themselves. However, the transsexually constructed lesbian-feminist violates women's sexuality and spirit, as well. Rape, although it is usually done by force, can also be accomplished by deception. It is significant that in the case of the transsexually constructed lesbian-feminist, often he is able to gain entrance and a dominant position in women's spaces because the women involved do not know he is a transsexual and he just does not happen to mention it.

The question of deception must also be raised in the context of how transsexuals who claim to be lesbian-feminists obtained surgery in the first place. Since all transsexuals have to "pass" as feminine in order to qualify for surgery, so-called lesbian-feminist transsexuals either had to lie to the therapists and doctors, or they had a conversion experience after surgery.[5] I am highly dubious of such conversions, and the other alternative, deception, raises serious problems, of course.

Deception reaches a tragic point for all concerned if transsexuals become lesbian-feminists because they regret what they have done and cannot back off from the effects of irreversible surgery (for example, castration). Thus they revert to masculinity (but not male body appearance) by becoming the man within the woman, and more, within the women's community, getting back their maleness in a most insidious way by seducing the spirits and the sexuality of women who do not relate to men.

Because transsexuals have lost their physical "members" does not mean that they have lost their ability to penetrate women—women's mind, women's space, women's sexuality. Transsexuals merely cut off the most obvious means of invading women so that they *seem* noninvasive. However, as Mary Daly has remarked, in the case of the transsexually constructed lesbian-feminists their whole presence becomes a "member" invading women's presence and dividing us once more from each other.[6]

Furthermore, the deceptiveness of men without "members," that is, castrated men or eunuchs, has historical precedent. There is a long tradition of eunuchs who were used by rulers, heads of state, and magistrates as *keepers of women*. Eunuchs were supervisors of the harem in Islam and wardens of women's apartments in many royal households. In fact, the *eunuch*, from the Greek *eunouchos*, literally means "keeper of the bed." Eunuchs were men that other more powerful men used to keep their women in place. By fulfilling this role, eunuchs also succeeded in winning the confidence of the ruler and securing important and influential positions.

Moreover, the word *eunuch* is also related to the word *scheme*. (Eunuchs schemed to obtain political power.) In Mesopotamia, many eunuchs became royal officers and managers of palaces, and "others emerge on the pages of history as important and often virile figures."[7] Some were famous warriors and statesmen, as well as scholars. One finds eunuchs associated with temples dedicated to the goddesses from at least 2000 BC until well into the Roman period.[8] In fact the earliest mention of eunuchs is in connection with the Minoan civilization of Crete, which was a transitional period from an earlier gynocentric society. It thus appears that eunuchs, to some extent, always attached themselves to women's spaces and, most frequently, were used to supervise women's freedom of movement and to harness women's self-centeredness and self-government. "It is stated that entree into every political circle was possible for eunuchs even if barred to other men."[9]

Will the acceptance of transsexually constructed lesbian-feminists who have lost only their outward appendages of physical masculinity lead to the containment and control of lesbian-feminists? Will every lesbian-feminist space become a harem? Like eunuchs, transsexuals have gained prominent and dominant access to feminist political circles "barred to other men."[10] Just because transsexually constructed lesbian-feminists are not only castrated men, but have also acquired artifacts of a woman's body and spirit, does not mean that they are un-men, and that they cannot be used as "keepers" of woman-identified women when the "real men," the "rulers of patriarchy," decide that the women's movement (used here as both noun and verb) should be controlled and contained. In this way, they too can rise in the King-doms of the Fathers. The political implications of historical eunuchism and its potential for female control should not be lost upon woman-identified women.

MYTHIC DIMENSIONS OF TRANSSEXUALISM

Transsexuals are living and acting out a very ancient myth, that of single par-enthood by the father. This myth was prevalent in many religious traditions, including the Jewish, Greek, and Christian. Eve was born of Adam; Dionysus and Athena were born of Zeus; and Jesus was generated by God the Father in his godly birth. (Mary was a mere receptacle used to conform Jesus to earthly birth standards.) When this myth is put into the context of transsexualism, the deeper dimensions of how transsexually constructed lesbian-feminists re-inforce patriarchy can be perceived.

Simone de Beauvoir has remarked that "if [woman] did not exist, men would have invented her. They did invent her. But she exists also apart from their inventiveness."[11] Men, of course, invented the feminine, and in this sense it could be said that all women who conform to this invention are trans-sexuals, fashioned according to man's image. Lesbian-feminists exist apart from man's inventiveness, and the political and personal ideals of lesbian-feminism have constituted a complete rebellion against the man-made inven-tion of woman, and a context in which women begin to create ourselves in our own image. Thus the transsexual who claims to be a lesbian-feminist *seems* to be the man who creates himself in *woman's* image. This, however, is decep-tive, for note that he is still created in *man's* image since he is essentially a child of the Father (in this case, the medical fathers), renouncing his moth-ered birth.

Mary Daly has written at length in her most recent work, *Gyn/Ecology: The Metaethics of Radical Feminism,* about the myth of Dionysus.[12] She also cites various versions of the myth along with some scholarly commentaries on it. These can shed much light on the mythic implications of the transsexually constructed lesbian-feminist. First of all, Philip Slater points out the very inter-esting fact that,"Instead of seeking distance from or mastery over the mother, the Dionysian position incorporates her."[13] In the most popular version of the myth, Semele, the mother of Dionysus, while pregnant with him, is struck by Zeus with a thunderbolt and is thus consumed. Hermes saves the six-month fetal Dionysus, sews him up in Zeus's thigh, and after three more months, Zeus "births" him. Thus Zeus exterminates the woman and bears his own son, and we have single-parent fatherhood (read motherhood). Moreover, Jane Harrison has pointed out that "the word Dionysus means not 'son of

Zeus' but rather Zeus-Young Man, i.e., Zeus in his young form."[14] Thus Dionysus is his own father (read mother) and births himself into existence.

Whether we are talking about being born of the father, or the self (son),
which in the myth are one and the same person (as in the Christian trinity),
we are still talking about male mothering. At this level of analysis, it might
seem that what men really envy is women's biological ability to procreate.
Transsexuals illustrate one way in which men do this, by acquiring the artifacts
of female biology. Even though they cannot give birth, they acquire the organs that are representative of this female power. However, it is the transsexually constructed lesbian-feminist who illustrates that much more is desired
than female biology—that much more is at stake than literal womb envy. He
shows that female biology, whether exercised in giving birth or simply by virtue of its existence, is representative of female creativity on a profound mythic
level. Thus the creative power that is associated with female biology is not
envied primarily because it is able to give birth physically but because it is
multidimensional, bearing culture, harmony, and true inventiveness.[15]

The transsexually constructed lesbian-feminist feeds off woman's true energy source, i.e., her woman-identified self. It is he who recognizes that if
female spirit, mind, creativity, and sexuality exist anywhere in a powerful way,
it is here, among lesbian-feminists. I am not saying that the lesbian-feminist is
the only self- and woman-identified woman. What I mean to express is that
lesbianism-feminism signals a *total* giving of women's energy to women, and
that it is this total woman-identified energy that the transsexual who claims to
be a lesbian-feminist wants for himself. It is understandable that if men want
to become women to obtain female creativity, then they will also want to assimilate those women who have withdrawn their energies from men at the
most intimate and emotional levels.

This, of course, is not the usual way in which lesbian living has been harnessed. Most often, lesbian existence is simply not acknowledged, as evidenced
in the laws against homosexuality, which legislate against male homosexuals,
but not lesbians. It has been simply assumed that all women relate to men,
and that women need men to survive. Furthermore, the mere labeling of a
woman as "lesbian" has been enough to keep lesbian living harnessed or, at
best, in the closet. "Lesbian is the word, the label, the condition that holds
women in line. When a woman hears this word tossed her way, she knows that
she . . . has crossed the terrible *boundary* of her sex role"[16] (italics mine).

Whereas the lesbian-feminist *crosses* the boundary of her patriarchally imposed sex role, the transsexually constructed lesbian-feminist is a *boundary
violator*. This violation is also profoundly mythic, for as Norman O. Brown
writes of Dionysus, he is the "mad god who breaks down boundaries."[17] Thus
exhibiting qualities that are usually associated with femininity, he appeared
to be the opposite of the masculine Apollo.

> While the super-masculine Apollo overtly oppresses/destroys with his con-
> trived boundaries/hierarchies/rules/roles, the feminine Dionysus blurs the
> senses, seduces, confuses his victims—drugging them into complicity, offering
> them his "heart" as a love potion that poisons.[18]

It is, however, the *feminist* Dionysus who appears in the transsexually constructed lesbian-feminist. But he "blurs the senses, seduces, and confuses" in
much the same way as the *feminine* Dionysus. He not only violates the boundaries of women's bodies but of our minds and spirits. What is more tragic,
however, is that he is able to make women break down our boundaries of self-
definition. Elizabeth Rose, in a letter in response to my article in *Chrysalis*,
"Transsexualism: The Ultimate Homage to Sex-Role Power," illustrates well
this tendency of feminists to be seduced by Dionysian boundary violation.

> Raymond's article encourages us to set our "bottom line" (about whom we
> will allow the privilege of self-definition).
>   I am upset that a magazine "of women's culture" . . . is basically encourag-
> ing the elitist/separatist attitude that self definition [is] . . . subject to the
> scrutiny and judgements of those who, in the name of political purity, claim
> the power to define who is allowed entry into the feminist community . . . and,
> now, who is or is not female.[19]

Rose would encourage us to set no boundaries by employing the analogy of
how boundaries have been used oppressively against lesbians in the past/
present. "There are so many painful parallels between how the world has
treated strong women and lesbians and how Raymond and others categorize
and discount transsexuals."[20] But the analogy is false. The boundaries that
have been and are used against lesbians are the boundaries of the Fathers:

> The contrived Apollonian boundaries—such as the false divisions of "fields"
> of knowledge and the splits between "mind" and "heart." But in this process
> we do not become swallowed up in male-centered (Dionysian) confusion. Hags
> find and define our own boundaries, our own definitions. Radical feminist
> living "on the boundary" means this moving, Self-centering boundary defini-
> tion. As we move we mark out our own territory.[21]

Rose and other women who have been confused/seduced by Dionysian
transsexually constructed lesbian-feminist boundary violation would have us
believe that all boundaries are oppressive. Yet if feminists cannot agree on the
boundaries of what constitutes femaleness, then what can we hope to agree
on? The Dionysian "Final Solution," as Daly points out, produces confusion
in women—"inability to distinguish the female Self and her process from the
male-made masquerade."[22] It encourages the leveling of genuine boundaries
of self-preservation and self-centering.

THE SEDUCTION OF LESBIAN-FEMINISTS

It is not hard to understand why transsexuals want to become lesbian-feminists. They indeed have discovered where strong female energy exists and
want to capture it. It is more difficult to understand why so many feminists are
so ready to accept men—in this case, castrated men—into their most intimate
circles. Certainly Dionysian confusion about the erasure of all boundaries is

one reason that appeals to the liberal mind and masquerades as "sympathy for all oppressed groups." Women who believe this, however, fail to see that such liberalism is repressive, and that it can only favor and fortify the possession of women by men. These women also fail to recognize that accepting transsexuals into the feminist community is only another rather unique variation on the age-old theme of women nurturing men, providing them with a safe haven, and finally giving them our best energies.

The question arises: are women who accept transsexuals as lesbian-feminists expressing gratitude on some level to those men who are finally willing to join women and pay for their male privilege with their balls? Gratitude is a quality exhibited by all oppressed groups when they think that some in the class of oppressors have finally relinquished their benefits to join them. But, of course, it is doubtful that transsexuals actually give up their male privilege. As one woman put it: "A man who decides to call himself a woman is not giving up his privilege. He is simply using it in a more insidious way."[23] Furthermore, a man who decides to call himself a lesbian-feminist is getting a lot. The transsexually constructed lesbian-feminist is the man who indeed gets to be "the man" in an exclusive women's club to which he would have otherwise no access.

Women who think that these men are giving up male privilege seem to be naive about the sophisticated ways in which it is possible for men to co-opt women's energy, time, space, and sexuality. Transsexually constructed lesbian-feminists may be the first men to realize that "if you can't fight them, join them." In a short story entitled "The Women's Restaurant," by T. C. Boyle, which appeared recently in *Penthouse,* this point is well made.

The story begins by setting the scene in and around Grace & Rubie's Restaurant and is written from the point of view of the voyeuristic narrator. "It is a women's restaurant. Men are not permitted. . . . What goes on there, precisely, no man knows. I am a man. I am burning to find out."[24] The narrator then proceeds to caricature Grace and Rubie as butch and femme, as well as to relate his several attempts to gain entrance. After two unsuccessful endeavors, he goes to a department store, buys a pink polyester pantsuit, a bra, pantyhose, and cosmetics with which he makes himself up to pass as a woman. He gains entrance and is able to experience what he has been missing.

> Here I was, embosomed in the very nave, the very omphalos of furtive femininity—a prize patron of the women's restaurant, a member, privy to its innermost secrets. . . . There they were—women—chewing, drinking, digesting, chatting, giggling, crossing, and uncrossing their legs. Shoes off, feet up. Smoking cigarettes, flashing silverware, tapping time to the music. Women among women. I bathed in their soft chatter, birdsong, the laughter like falling coils of hair. I lit a cigarette and grinned. No more fairybook-hero thoughts of rescuing Rubie—oh no, this was paradise.[25]

Having drunk six tequila sunrises and a carafe of dinner wine, the male intruder/narrator finds it necessary to relieve himself, but forgets to sit down when he urinates in the rest room, at which point he is discovered by Grace.

The story ends with his savoring of the triumph of temporary infiltration and a plan for permanent invasion.

> I have penetrated the women's restaurant, yes, but in actuality it was little more than a rape. . . . I am not satisfied. The obsession grows in me, pregnant, swelling, insatiable with the first taste of fulfillment. Before I am through, I will drink it to satiety. I have plans. . . . The next time I walk through those curtained doors at Grace & Rubie's there will be no dissimulation. . . . There are surgeons who can assure it.[26]

That this story appeared in *Penthouse* is no surprise. It is obvious that its editors thought it would be of interest to their readers, whether budding or closet transsexuals. In spite of the ludicrous details and caricatures, one can see that the narrator was primarily attracted to the woman-centeredness of the restaurant. "Women among women . . . this is paradise." Such an attitude is representative of the transsexually constructed lesbian-feminist who indeed gets his "paradise," because there *were* surgeons who could "assure it." Ironically, the would-be transsexual narrator of the story says that the next time he walks through the doors, "there will be no dissimulation." Transsexualism, however, is dissimulation. As I have shown previously, to not acknowledge the fact that one is a transsexual in a women's space is indeed deception. Finally, "penetrating" the women's restaurant was "little more than a rape." Little more than rape, indeed! What "little more" is there to such an act, unless it is the total rape of our feminist identities, minds, and convictions? The transsexually constructed lesbian-feminist, having castrated himself, turns his whole body and behavior into a phallus that can rape in many ways, all the time. In this sense, he performs *total* rape, while also functioning *totally* against women's will to lesbian-feminism.

We have seen three reasons why lesbian-feminists are seduced into accepting transsexuals: liberalism, gratitude, and naiveté. There is yet another reason—one that can be perhaps best described as the *last remnants of male identification*. This is a complex phenomenon, which has various ingredients.

On the one hand, there is fear of the label "man-hater." Are women who are so accepting of the transsexually constructed lesbian-feminist trying to prove to themselves that a lesbian-feminist (she who has been called the ultimate man-hater) is really not a man-hater after all? As Adrienne Rich has pointed out, one way of avoiding that feared label, and of allowing one's self to accept men, is to accept those men who have given up the supposed ultimate possession of manhood in a patriarchal society by self-castration.[27]

On the other hand, there is a second component to this "last remnant of male identification"—i.e., *attraction to masculine presence*. As Pat Hynes has suggested, there is an *apparent* similarity between a strong woman-identified self and a transsexual who fashions himself in a lesbian image. Because there is an *apparent* similarity, some lesbian-feminists may allow themselves to express the residues of their (buried) attraction to men or to masculine presence, while pretending to themselves that transsexually constructed lesbian-feminists are really women. This allows women to do two things: to express that attraction, yet also to decide themselves.

SELF-DEFINITION

One of the most constraining questions that transsexuals, and, in particular, transsexually constructed lesbian-feminists, pose is the question of self-definition—who is a woman, who is a lesbian-feminist? But, of course, *they* pose the question on their terms, and *we* are faced with answering it. Men have always made such questions of major concern, and this question, in true phallic fashion, is thrust upon us. How many women students writing on such a feeble feminist topic as "Should Women Be Truck Drivers, Engineers, Steam Shovel Operators?" and the like, have had their male professor scribble in the margins: "But what are the real differences between men and women?"

Men, of course, have defined the supposed differences that have kept women out of such jobs and professions, and feminists have spent much energy demonstrating how these differences, if indeed they do exist, are primarily the result of socialization. Yet there are differences, and some feminists have come to realize that those differences are important whether they spring from socialization, from biology, or from the total history of existing as a woman in a patriarchal society. The point is, however, that the origin of these differences is probably not the important question, and we shall perhaps never know the total answer to it. Yet we are forced back into trying to answer it again and again.*

Transsexuals, and transsexually constructed lesbian-feminists, drag us back to answering such old questions by asking them in a new way. And thus feminists debate and divide because we keep focusing on patriarchal questions of who is a woman and who is a lesbian-feminist. It is important for us to realize that these may well be non-questions and that the only answer we can give to them is that we know who *we* are. We know that we are women who are born with female chromosomes and anatomy, and that whether or not we were socialized to be so-called normal women, patriarchy has treated and will treat us like women. Transsexuals have not had this same history. No man can have the history of being born and located in this culture as a woman. He can have the history of *wishing* to be a woman and of *acting* like a woman, but this gender experience is that of a transsexual, not of a woman. Surgery may confer the artifacts of outward and inward female organs but it cannot confer the history of being born a woman in this society.

What of persons born with ambiguous sex organs or chromosomal anomalies that place them in a biologically intersexual situation? It must be noted that practically all of them are altered shortly after birth to become anatomi-

---

*A parallel is the abortion issue, which can also be noted in this context. The key question, asked by men for centuries, is "when does life begin?" This question is posed in men's terms and on their turf, and is essentially unanswerable. Women torture themselves trying to answer it and thus do not assert or even develop our own questions about abortion.

cally male or female and are reared in accordance with the societal gender identity and role that accompanies their bodies. Persons whose sexual ambiguity is discovered later are altered in the direction of what their gender rearing has been (masculine or feminine) up to that point. Thus those who are altered shortly after birth have the history of being practically born as male or female and those who are altered later in life have their body surgically conformed to their history. When and if they do undergo surgical change, they do not become the opposite sex after a long history of functioning and being treated differently.

Although popular literature on transsexualism implies that Nature has made mistakes with transsexuals, it is really society that has made the mistake by producing conditions that create the transsexual body/mind split. While intersexed people are born with chromosomal or hormonal anomalies, which can be linked up with certain biological malfunctions, transsexualism is not of this order. The language of "Nature makes mistakes" only serves to confuse and distort the issue, taking the focus off the social system, which is actively oppressive. It succeeds in blaming an amorphous "Nature" that is made to seem oppressive and is conveniently amenable to direct control/manipulation by the instruments of hormones and surgery.

In speaking of the importance of history for self-definition, two questions must be asked. Should a person want to change his/her personal and social history and if so, *how* should one change that history in the most honest and integral way? In answer to the first question, anyone who has lived in a patriarchal society has to change personal and social history in order to be a self. History cannot be allowed to determine the boundaries, life, and location of the self. We should be change agents of our own history. Women who are feminists obviously wish to change parts of their history as women in this society; some men who are honestly dealing with feminist questions wish to change their history as men; and transsexuals wish to change their history of *wanting* to be women. In stressing the importance of female history for female self-definition, I am not advocating a static view of such history.

What is more important, however, is *how* one changes personal history in the most honest and integral way, if one wants to break down sex-role oppression. Should nontranssexual men who wish to fight sexism take on the identity of women and/or lesbian-feminists while keeping their male anatomy intact? Why should castrated men take on these identities and self-definitions and be applauded for doing so? To what extent would concerned blacks accept whites who had undergone medicalized changes in skin color and, in the process, claimed that they had not only a black body but a black soul?

Can a transsexual assume the self-definition of lesbian-feminist just because he wants to, or does this particular self-definition proceed from certain conditions endemic to female biology and history? Women take on the self-definition of feminist and/or lesbian because that definition truly proceeds from not only the chromosomal fact of being born XX, but also from the whole history of what being born with those chromosomes means in this society. Transsexuals would be more honest if they dealt with their specific form of gender agony that inclines them to want a transsexual operation. This gender agony proceeds from the chromosomal fact of being born XY and *wishing* that one were born XX, and from the particular life history that produced such distress. The place to deal with that problem, however, is not the women's community. The place to confront and solve it is among transsexuals themselves.

One should be able to make choices about who one wants to be. But should one be able to make *any* choice? Should a white person attempt to become black, for example? The question is a moral one, which asks basically about the rightness of the choice, not the possibility of it. Should persons be able to make choices that disguise certain facets of our existence from others who have a right to know—choices that feed off others' energies, and reinforce oppression?

Jill Johnston has commented that, "many women are dedicated to working for the 'reconstructed man.' "[28] This usually means women gently or strongly prodding their significant men into androgynous behavior and action. Women who accept transsexually constructed lesbian-feminists say that these men are truly "reconstructed" in the most basic sense that women could hope for—i.e., they have paid with their balls to fight against sexism. Ultimately, however, the "reconstructed man" becomes the "reconstructed woman" who obviously considers himself equal to and a peer of genetic women in terms of his "womanhood." One transsexual openly expressed that he felt male-to-constructed-female transsexuals *surpassed* genetic women.

> Genetic women cannot possess the very special courage, brilliance, sensitivity and compassion—and overview—that derives from the transsexual experience. Free from the chains of menstruation and child-bearing, transsexual women are obviously far superior to Gennys in many ways.
>
> Genetic women are becoming quite obsolete, which is obvious, and the future belongs to transsexual women. We know this, and perhaps some of you suspect it. All you have left is your "ability" to bear children, and in a world which will groan to feed 6 billion by the year 2000, that's a negative asset.[29]

Ultimately, women must ask if transsexually constructed lesbian-feminists are our peers. Are they equal to us? Questions of equality often center on proportional equality, such as "equal pay for equal work," or "equal rights to health care." I do not mean equal in this sense. Rather I use equality to mean: "like in quality, nature, or status" and "capable of meeting the requirements of a situation or a task." In these senses transsexuals are not equal to women and are not our peers. They are neither equal in "quality," "nature of status" nor are they "capable of meeting the requirements of the situation" of women who have spent their whole lives as women.

Jill Johnston has written of lesbian-feminism: "The essence of the new political definition is peer grouping. Women and men are not peers and many people seriously doubt whether we ever were or if we ever could be."[30] Transsexuals are not our peers, by virtue of their history.

It is perhaps our mistrust of the man as the biological aggressor which keeps bringing us back to the political necessity of power by peer grouping. Although we are still virtually powerless it is only by constantly adhering to this difficult principle of the power inherent in natural peers (men after all have demonstrated the success of this principle very well) that women will eventually achieve an autonomous existence.[31]

The transsexual does not display the usual phallic aggression. Instead he violates women's bodies by taking on the artifactual female organs for himself. The transsexually constructed lesbian-feminist becomes a psychological and social aggressor as well.

Transsexually constructed lesbian-feminists challenge women's preserves of autonomous existence. Their existence within the women's community basically attests to the ethic that women should not live without men—or without the "reconstructed man." How feminists assess and meet this challenge will affect the future of our genuine movement, self-definition, and power of be-ing.

In the final analysis, transsexually constructed lesbian-feminists are in the same tradition as the man-made, made-up "lesbians" of the *Playboy* centerfolds. Every so often, *Playboy* and similar magazines feature a "Sappho Pictorial."[32] Recently, male photographers have entered the book market by portraying pseudolesbians in all sorts of positions, clothing, and contexts that could only be fantasized by a male mind.[33] In short, the manner in which women are depicted in these photographs mimics the poses of men pawing women. Men produce "lesbian" love the way they want it to be and according to their own canons of what they think it should be.

Transsexually constructed lesbian-feminists are in this tradition of pseudo-lesbian propaganda. Both the *Playboy* pseudolesbian and the transsexual pseudolesbian spread the "correct" (read male-defined) image of the lesbian, which in turn filters into public consciousness through the mass media as truth. By thus mutilating the true self-definition of the lesbian, men mold her image/reality according to their own. As Lisa Buck has commented, transsexualism is truly "their word made flesh!"[34]

Transsexually constructed lesbian-feminists attempt to function as image makers of the lesbian-feminist—not only for the public at large, but also for the women's community. Their masquerade of the lesbian filters into women's consciousness through the feminist media as "the real thing." The ultimate tragedy of such a parody is that the reality and self-definition of lesbian-feminists becomes mutilated in women themselves. Lesbian-feminists who accept transsexually constructed lesbian-feminists as other selves are mutilating their own reality.

The various "breeds" of women that medical science can create are endless. There are the women who are hormonally hooked on continuous doses of estrogen-replacement therapy. ERT supposedly will secure for them a new life of "eternal femininity."[35] There are the hysterectomized women, purified of their "potentially lethal" organs for "prophylactic" purposes.[36] Finally, there is the "she-male"—the male-to-constructed-female transsexual. And the offshoot of this "breed" is the transsexually constructed lesbian-feminist.

What all of these events point to is the particularly instrumental role that medicine has played in the control of deviant or potentially deviant women. "The Transsexual Empire" is ultimately a medical empire, based on a patriarchal medical model. This medical model has provided a "sacred canopy" of legitimations for transsexual treatment and surgery. In the name of therapy, it has medicalized moral and social questions of sex-role oppression, thereby erasing their deepest meaning.

N O T E S

The recent debate and divisiveness that the transsexually constructed lesbian-feminist has produced within feminist circles has convinced me that, while transsexually constructed lesbian-feminists may be a small percentage of transsexuals, the issue needs an in-depth discussion among feminists.

I write this essay with the full realization that feminists look at the issue of the transsexually constructed lesbian-feminist from the vantage point of a small community in which transsexuals have been able to be very visible—not because there are that many of them, but because they immediately have center stage. Thus focusing attention on this particular aspect of the transsexual issue may only serve to inflate the issue and their presence all the more. It may also distract attention from the more central questions that transsexualism raises and the power of the medical empire that creates transsexualism to begin with.

Because the oral and written debate concerning the transsexually constructed lesbian-feminist seems to be increasing out of proportion to their actual numbers, I think that feminists ought to consider seriously the amount of energy and space we wish to give to this discussion.

Most of the commentary thus far has been limited to letters to the editor and editorial comments in feminist papers, as well as a few scattered articles in various journals. Because of limited space, these analyses are necessarily restricted. I would like, therefore, to provide an extensive and intensive analysis of the issue and to address the deeply mythic dimensions that the transsexually constructed lesbian-feminist represents.

1. In June/July of 1977, twenty-two feminist musicians, sound technicians, radio women, producers, and managers sent an open letter to Olivia Records via *Sister*, a West Coast feminist newspaper. The letter focused on the employment of Sandy Stone, a male-to-constructed-female transsexual, as Olivia's recording engineer and sound technician. The signers protested Stone's presence at Olivia and the fact that Olivia did not inform women that Stone was a postoperative transsexual. They criticized Stone's participation in women-only events and accused him of taking work away from the "few competent women sound technicians in the Bay Area . . . whose opportunities are extremely limited." They noted that Stone's male privilege gave him access to his skills, and that he has never had to suffer the oppression that women face every day. The letter concluded by stating that "it is not our intention to discredit or trash Olivia," and requested that they publish a statement in response.

In the same issue of *Sister*, Olivia replied that: 1. Surgery alone does not make a transsexual a woman. "This too-publicized step is merely the confirmation of a process that has already gone to near completion by that time." 2. Aside from a few well-publicized transsexuals, a person does not gain privilege by becoming a transsexual. Because Stone gave up his male identity and lives as a "woman" and a "lesbian," he is faced with the same kinds of oppression that "other" women and lesbians face, along with the added ostracism that results from being a transsexual. 3. A person's history is important but most significant is what that person's actions are now. 4. Day-to-day interaction with Sandy Stone has convinced the Olivia women that Sandy is a "woman we can relate to with comfort and trust." 5. Olivia did not indicate Stone's transsexual status, because they were afraid he would be "objectified." "We see trans-sexualism as a state of transition, and we feel that to continue to define a person primarily by that condition is to stigmatize her at the expense of her growth process as a woman." 6. Stone has trained women in technical skills and will build Olivia's recording studio where many women will apprentice. He is also writing a how-to book for women explaining the recording process. Thus Stone does not take employment away from women but provides it and may be "perhaps even the Goddess-sent engineering wizard we had so long sought."

2. Author's conversation with Pat Hynes, Cambridge, MA, January 1978.

3. Author's conversation with Mary Daly, Boston, MA, February 1978.

4. Rosemary Anderson, Letter entitled "Transsexual Feminism?" *Sister*, Aug. Sept. 1977, p. 7.

5. Recently, questions have been raised by transsexuals who claim to be lesbian-feminists and by some professionals in gender identity clinics about clinic require-ments of "passing" and about the stereotypical behavior of transsexuals. "We urge professionals *not* to assume or expect that all transsexuals will be heterosexually ori-ented or politically conservative and not to judge (for example) lesbianism in a male-to-female transsexual as invalid while accepting it in a genetic woman. Biological women and male-to-female transsexuals present a similarly vast range of sexual orien-tation and life-style choices; different choices are valid for different people. . . . Posi-tively, we recommend a setting where the client is not forced to avow rigid self-definitions, but is permitted and even encouraged to find her/his own answers to the difficult and complex questions of sexuality and identity that confront us all." Debo-rah Heller Feinbloom et al., "Lesbian/Feminist Orientation Among Male-to-Female Transsexuals," *Journal of Homosexuality* 2 (Fall 1976): 70-71.

There are several criticisms that can be made of such a stance. First, nonstereotypi-cal behavior is encouraged as one choice among "different choices [that] are valid for different people." Thus there is no commitment to eradicating stereotypical behavior but only to encouraging alternative behavior ("different strokes for different folks"). And thus there is no commitment to ultimately phasing out gender identity control over *various* styles of behavior. The authors' conclusions coincide with John Money's recommendations in *Sexual Signatures* for "flexible" stereotypes.

Second, the unanswered question is why are such transsexuals and transsexual pro-fessionals still advocating surgery. Transsexual surgery would not be necessary if rigid self-definitions had not produced the phenomenon of a "female mind in a male body." This self-definition would make no sense in a society that did not accept that split. Therefore, to support behavior and orientation that is not stereotypical, yet to continue advocating transsexualism is contradictory.

Such recommendations only make the issue of "passing" and stereotypical behav-ior more invisible. These authors *appear* to get beyond the stereotypes, but they are actually supporting "passing" behavior on a deeper level. In effect, they are now advo-cating that men "pass" as lesbian-feminists, thus making a "role" out of lesbian-femi-nism that can be taken on by anyone. Ultimately, this brings lesbian-feminism within the confines of the gender identity clinics, where it can be observed, studied, *and controlled*—first in transsexuals, and then perhaps in lesbian-feminists. With the accep-tance of transsexuals as lesbian-feminists by the gender identity clinics, the "passing" requirements only become modified. The transsexual "passes" what are the current (seemingly avant-garde) requirements of the gender identity clinics. In order to be-come transsexed, however, his "passing" behavior must still be "baptized" as legiti-mately female.

It is significant that these recommendations are coming from male-to-constructed-female transsexuals. Here is a clear admission that lesbian-feminism is perceived as important and that more is at stake in transsexual surgery than obtaining the body and the traditional role of a woman. There is a recognition here that female power/energy/creativity is at the heart of the matter. Why are there no female-to-constructed-male transsexuals, for example, who are seeking to "pass" as homosexual men?

6. Author's conversation with Mary Daly, Boston, MA, February 1978.

7. Robert Spencer, "The Cultural Aspects of Eunuchism," CIBA *Symposia* 8 (1946): 407.

8. Ibid., p. 408.

9. Ibid., p. 413.

10. Another parallel is that some royal eunuchs also wore women's clothing, and their physical characteristics, especially as represented on Assyrian monuments, resembled those of women. Eunuch priests of goddess temples were said to wear women's garb and perform women's tasks. See John L. McKenzie, "Eunuch," *Dictionary of the Bible* (Milwaukee: The Bruce Publishing Company, 1965), p. 252.

11. Simone de Beauvoir, *The Second Sex* (New York: Bantam Books, 1953), p. 174.

12. See Mary Daly, *Gyn/Ecology: The Metaethics of Radical Feminism* (Boston: Beacon Press, 1978), pp. 66-67.

13. Philip Slater, *The Glory of Hera: Greek Mythology and the Greek Family* (Boston: Beacon Press, 1968), p. 211.

14. Jane Harrison, *Mythology* (New York: Harcourt, Brace and World, 1963), p. 97.

15. See my *The Transsexual Empire: The Making of the She-Male*, ch. 1, for female creativity as represented in female biology.

16. Radicalesbians, "The Woman Identified Woman," in Radical Feminism, ed. Anne Koedt, Ellen Levine, and Anita Rapone (New York: Quadrangle-New York Times Book Co., 1973), p. 241.

17. Norman O. Brown, *Love's Body* (New York: Random House, 1966), p. 116.

18. Daly, *Gyn/Ecology*, pp. 67-68.

19. Elizabeth Rose, letter to the editors, *Chrysalis* 5 (1978): 6.

20. Idem.

21. Daly, *Gyn/Ecology*, p. 67.

22. Ibid.

23. Judy Antonelli, "Open Letter to Olivia," *Sister*, Aug./Sept. 1977, p. 6.

24. T. C. Boyle, "The Women's Restaurant," *Penthouse*, May 1977, p. 112.

25. Ibid., p. 132.

26. Ibid., p. 133.

27. Conversation with Adrienne Rich, Montague, MA, May 1977.

28. Jill Johnston, *Lesbian Nation: The Feminist Solution* (New York: Simon & Schuster, 1973), p. 180.

29. Angela Douglas, letter, *Sister*, Aug./Sept. 1977, p. 7.

30. Johnston, *Lesbian Nation*, p. 278.

31. Ibid., p. 279.

32. See, for example, photographer J. Frederick Smith's "portfolio of stunning portraits inspired by ancient Greek poems on loving women," in *Playboy*, October 1975, pp. 126-35.

33. One photographer who is particularly obsessed with "capturing" women in pseudolesbian poses is David Hamilton. He is the creator of the following books of photography: *Dreams of a Young Girl*, text by Alain Robbe-Grillet (New York: William Morrow and Co., 1971); *Sisters*, text by Alain Robbe-Grillet (New York: William Morrow and Co., 1973) (This book has an outrageous pictorial section entitled "Charms of the Harem"); *Hamilton's Movies—Bilitis* (Zug, Switzerland: Swan Productions AG, 1977).

34. Lisa Buck (unpublished notes on transsexualism, October 1977, p. 3).

35. An example of this literature is Robert Wilson's *Feminine Forever* (New York: M. Evans, 1966). This book sold 100,000 copies in its first year, as well as being excerpted in *Look* and *Vogue*.

36. See Deborah Larned, "The Greening of the Womb," *New Times*, December 12, 1974, pp. 35-39.

CHAPTER 19
THE *EMPIRE* STRIKES BACK
A Posttranssexual Manifesto

SANDY STONE

(1 9 9 1)

FROGS INTO PRINCESSES

The verdant hills of Casablanca look down on homes and shops jammed chockablock against narrow, twisted streets filled with the odors of spices and dung. Casablanca is a very old city, passed over by Lawrence Durrell perhaps only by a geographical accident as the winepress of love. In the more modern quarter, located on a broad, sunny boulevard, is a building otherwise unremarkable except for a small brass nameplate that identifies it as the clinic of Dr. Georges Burou. It is predominantly devoted to obstetrics and gynecology, but for many years has maintained another reputation quite unknown to the stream of Moroccan women who pass through its rooms.

Dr. Burou is being visited by journalist James Morris. Morris fidgets in an anteroom reading *Elle* and *Paris-Match* with something less than full attention, because he is on an errand of immense personal import. At last the receptionist calls for him, and he is shown to the inner sanctum. He relates:

> I was led along corridors and up staircases into the inner premises of the clinic. The atmosphere thickened as we proceeded. The rooms became more heavily curtained, more velvety, more voluptuous. Portrait busts appeared, I think, and there was a hint of heavy perfume. Presently I saw, advancing upon me through the dim alcoves of this retreat, which distinctly suggested to me the allure of a harem, a figure no less recognizably odalesque. It was Madame Burou. She was dressed in a long white robe, tasseled I think around the waist, which subtly managed to combine the luxuriance of a caftan with the hygiene of a nurse's uniform, and she was blonde herself, and carefully mysterious. . . . Powers beyond my control had brought me to Room 5 at the clinic in Casablanca, and I could not have run away then even if I had wanted to. . . . I went to say goodbye to myself in the mirror. We would never meet again, and I wanted to give that other self a long last look in the eye, and a wink for luck. As I did so a street vendor outside played a delicate arpeggio upon his flute, a very gentle merry sound which he repeated, over and over again, in sweet diminuendo down the street. Flights of angels, I said to myself, and so staggered . . . to my bed, and oblivion.[1]

Exit James Morris, enter Jan Morris, through the intervention of late twentieth-century medical practices in this wonderfully "oriental," almost religious narrative of transformation. The passage is from *Conundrum*, the story of Morris' "sex change" and the consequences for her life. Besides the wink for luck, there is another obligatory ceremony known to male-to-female transsexuals which is called "wringing the turkey's neck," although it is not recorded whether Morris performed it as well. I will return to this rite of passage later in more detail.

MAKING HISTORY

Imagine now a swift segue from the moiling alleyways of Casablanca to the rolling green hills of Palo Alto. The Stanford Gender Dysphoria Program occupies a small room near the campus in a quiet residential section of this affluent community. The Program, which is a counterpart to Georges Burou's clinic in Morocco, has been for many years the academic focus of Western studies of gender dysphoria syndrome, also known as transsexualism. Here are determined etiology, diagnostic criteria, and treatment.

The Program was begun in 1968, and its staff of surgeons and psychologists first set out to collect as much history on the subject of transsexualism as was available. Let me pause to provide a very brief capsule of their results. A transsexual is a person who identifies his or her gender identity with that of the "opposite" gender. Sex and gender are quite separate issues, but transsexuals commonly blur the distinction by confusing the performative character of gender with the physical "fact" of sex, referring to their perceptions of their situation as being in the "wrong body." Although the term transsexual is of recent origin, the phenomenon is not. The earliest mention of something which we can recognize *ex post facto* as transsexualism, in light of current diagnostic criteria, was of the Assyrian king Sardanapalus, who was reported to have dressed in women's clothing and spun with his wives.[2] Later instances of something very like transsexualism were reported by Philo of Judea, during the Roman Empire. In the eighteenth century the Chevalier d'Eon, who lived for thirty-nine years in the female role, was a rival of Madame Pompadour for the attention of Louis XV. The first colonial governor of New York, Lord Cornbury, came from England fully attired as a woman and remained so during his time in office.[3]

Transsexualism was not accorded the status of an "official disorder" until 1980, when it was first listed in the *American Psychiatric Association Diagnostic and Statistical Manual*. As Marie Mehl points out, this is something of a Pyrrhic victory.[4]

Prior to 1980, much work had already been done in an attempt to define criteria for differential diagnosis. An example from the 1970s is this one, from work carried out by Leslie Lothstein and reported in Walters and Ross's *Transsexualism and Sex Reassignment*[5]:

> Lothstein, in his study of ten ageing transsexuals [average age fifty-two], found that psychological testing helped to determine the extent of the patients' pa-

thology [sic] . . . [he] concluded that [transsexuals as a class] were depressed, isolated, withdrawn, schizoid individuals with profound dependency conflicts. Furthermore, they were immature, narcissistic, egocentric and potentially explosive, while their attempts to obtain [professional assistance] were demanding, manipulative, controlling, coercive, and paranoid.[6]

Here's another:

> In a study of 56 transsexuals the results on the schizophrenia and depression scales were outside the upper limit of the normal range. The authors see these profiles as reflecting the confused and bizarre life styles of the subjects.[7]

These were clinical studies, which represented a very limited class of subjects. However, the studies were considered sufficiently representative for them to be reprinted without comment in collections such as that of Walters and Ross. Further on in each paper, though, we find that each investigator invalidates his results in a brief disclaimer which is reminiscent of the fine print in a cigarette ad: In the first, by adding "It must be admitted that Lothstein's subjects could hardly be called a typical sample as nine of the ten studied had serious physical health problems" (this was a study conducted in a health clinic, not a gender clinic), and in the second, with the afterthought that "82 per cent of [the subjects] were prostitutes and atypical of transsexuals in other parts of the world."[8] Such results might have been considered marginal, hedged about as they were with markers of questionable method or excessively limited samples. Yet they came to represent transsexuals in medico-legal/psychological literature, disclaimers and all, almost to the present day.

During the same period, feminist theoreticians were developing their own analyses. The issue quickly became, and remains, volatile and divisive. Let me quote an example.

> Rape . . . is a masculinist violation of bodily integrity. All transsexuals rape women's bodies by reducing the female form to an artifact, appropriating this body for themselves. . . . Rape, although it is usually done by force, can also be accomplished by deception.

This quote is from Janice Raymond's 1979 book *The Transsexual Empire: The Making of The She-Male* (excerpted in ch. 18 of this volume), which occasioned the title of this paper. I read Raymond to be claiming that transsexuals are constructs of an evil phallocratic empire and were designed to invade women's spaces and appropriate women's power. Though *Empire* represented a specific moment in feminist analysis and prefigured the appropriation of liberal political language by a radical right, here in 1991, on the twelfth anniversary of its publication, it is still the definitive statement on transsexualism by a genetic female academic.[9] To clarify my stakes in this discourse let me quote another passage from *Empire:*

> Masculine behavior is notably obtrusive. It is significant that transsexually constructed lesbian-feminists have inserted themselves into the positions of im-

portance and/or performance in the feminist community. Sandy Stone, the
transsexual engineer with Olivia Records, an "all-women" recording company,
illustrates this well. Stone is not only crucial to the Olivia enterprise but plays
a very dominant role there. The . . . visibility he achieved in the aftermath of
the Olivia controversy . . . only serves to enhance his previously dominant role
and to divide women, as men frequently do, when they make their presence
necessary and vital to women. As one woman wrote: "I feel raped when Olivia
passes off Sandy . . . as a real woman. After all his male privilege, is he going
to cash in on lesbian feminist culture too?"

This paper, "The *Empire* Strikes Back," is about morality tales and origin
myths, about telling the "truth" of gender. Its informing principle is that
"technical arts are always imagined to be subordinated by the ruling artistic
idea, itself rooted authoritatively in nature's own life."[10] It is about the image
and the real mutually defining each other through the inscriptions and reading practices of late capitalism. It is about postmodernism, postfeminism, and
(dare I say it) posttranssexualism. Throughout, the paper owes a large debt to
Donna Haraway.

"ALL OF REALITY IN LATE CAPITALIST CULTURE LUSTS TO BECOME AN IMAGE FOR ITS OWN SECURITY."[11]

Let's turn to accounts by the transsexuals themselves. During this period virtually all of the published accounts were written by male-to-females. I want to
briefly consider four autobiographical accounts of male-to-female transsexuals, to see what we can learn about what they think they are doing. (I will
consider female-to-male transsexuals in another paper.)

The earliest partially autobiographical account in existence is that of Lili
Elbe in Niels Hoyer's book *Man Into Woman* (1933).[12] The first fully autobiographical book was the paperback *I Changed My Sex!* (not exactly a quiet, con-
templative title), written by the striptease artist Hedy Jo Star in the mid-
1950s.[13] Christine Jorgensen, who underwent surgery in the early 1950s and
is arguably the best known of the recent transsexuals, did not publish her
autobiography until 1967; instead, Star's book rode the wave of publicity surrounding Jorgensen's surgery. In 1974 *Conundrum* was published, written by
the popular English journalist Jan Morris. In 1977 there was *Canary*, by musician and performer Canary Conn.[14] In addition, many transsexuals keep
something they call by the argot term "O.T.F.": The Obligatory Transsexual
File. This usually contains newspaper articles and bits of forbidden diary en-
tries about "inappropriate" gender behavior. Transsexuals also collect autobiographical literature. According to the Stanford gender dysphoria program,
the medical clinics do not, because they consider autobiographical accounts
thoroughly unreliable. Because of this, and since a fair percentage of the
literature is invisible to many library systems, these personal collections are
the only source for some of this information. I am fortunate to have a few of
them at my disposal.

What sort of subject is constituted in these texts? Hoyer (representing Jacobson representing Elbe, who is representing Wegener who is representing Sparre),[15] writes:

> A single glance of this man had deprived her of all her strength. She felt as if her whole personality had been crushed by him. With a single glance he had extinguished it. Something in her rebelled. She felt like a schoolgirl who had received short shrift from an idolized teacher. She was conscious of a peculiar weakness in all her members . . . it was the first time her woman's heart had trembled before her lord and master, before the man who had constituted himself her protector, and she understood why she then submitted so utterly to him and his will.[16]

We can put to this fragment all of the usual questions: Not by whom but *for* whom was Lili Elbe constructed? Under whose gaze did her text fall? And consequently what stories appear and disappear in this kind of seduction? It may come as no surprise that all of the accounts I will relate here are similar in their description of "woman" as male fetish, as replicating a socially enforced role, or as constituted by performative gender. Lili Elbe faints at the sight of blood.[17] Jan Morris, a world-class journalist who has been around the block a few times, still describes her sense of herself in relation to makeup and dress, of being on display, and is pleased when men open doors for her:

> I feel small, and neat. I am not small in fact, and not terribly neat either, but femininity conspires to make me feel so. My blouse and skirt are light, bright, crisp. My shoes make my feet look more delicate than they are, besides giving me . . . a suggestion of vulnerability that I rather like. My red and white bangles give me a racy feel, my bag matches my shoes and makes me feel well organized . . . When I walk out into the street I feel consciously ready for the world's appraisal, in a way that I never felt as a man.[18]

Hedy Jo Star, who was a professional stripper, says in *I Changed My Sex!:* "I wanted the sensual feel of lingerie against my skin, I wanted to brighten my face with cosmetics. I wanted a strong man to protect me." Here in 1991 I have also encountered a few men who are brave enough to echo this sentiment for themselves, but in 1955 it was a proprietary feminine position.

Besides the obvious complicity of these accounts in a Western white male definition of performative gender, the authors also reinforce a binary, oppositional mode of gender identification. They go from being unambiguous men, albeit unhappy men, to unambiguous women. There is no territory between.[19] Further, each constructs a specific narrative moment when their personal sexual identification changes from male to female. This moment is the moment of neocolporraphy—that is, of gender reassignment or "sex change surgery."[20] Jan Morris, on the night preceding surgery, wrote: "I went to say good-bye to myself in the mirror. We would never meet again, and I wanted to give that other self a last wink for luck . . ."[21]

Canary Conn writes: "I'm not a *muchacho* . . . I'm a *muchacha* now . . . a girl [*sic*]."[22]

Hedy Jo Star writes: "In the instant that I awoke from the anaesthetic, I realized that I had finally become a woman."[23]

Even Lili Elbe, whose text is secondhand, used the same terms: "Suddenly it occurred to him that he, Andreas Sparre, was probably undressing for the last time." Immediately on awakening from firststage surgery (castration in Hoyer's account), Sparre writes a note. "He gazed at the card and failed to recognize the writing. It was a woman's script." Inger carries the note to the doctor: "What do you think of this, Doctor. No man could have written it?" "No," said the astonished doctor; "no, you are quite right . . ."—an exchange which requires the reader to forget that orthography is an acquired skill. The same thing happens with Elbe's voice: "the strange thing was that your voice had completely changed . . . You have a splendid soprano voice! Simply astounding."[24] Perhaps as astounding now as then but for different reasons, since in light of present knowledge of the effects (and more to the point, the non-effects) of castration and hormones none of this could have happened. Neither has any effect on voice timbre. Hence, incidentally, the jaundiced eyes with which the clinics regard historical accounts.

If Hoyer mixes reality with fantasy and caricatures his subjects besides ("Simply astounding!"), what lessons are there in *Man Into Woman?* Partly what emerges from the book is how Hoyer deploys the strategy of building barriers within a single subject, strategies that are still in gainful employment today. Lili displaces the irruptive masculine self, still dangerously present within her, onto the God-figure of her surgeon/therapist Werner Kreutz, whom she calls The Professor, or The Miracle Man. The Professor is He who molds and Lili that which is molded:

> what the Professor is now doing with Lili is nothing less than an emotional moulding, which is preceding the physical moulding into a woman. Hitherto Lili has been like clay which others had prepared and to which the Professor has given form and life . . . by a single glance the Professor awoke her heart to life, a life with all the instincts of woman.[25]

The female is immanent, the female is bone-deep, the female is instinct. With Lili's eager complicity, The Professor drives a massive wedge between the masculine and the feminine within her. In this passage, reminiscent of the "oriental" quality of Morris's narrative, the male must be annihilated or at least denied, but the female is that which exists to be *continually* annihilated:

> It seemed to her as if she no longer had any responsibility for herself, for her fate. For Werner Kreutz had relieved her of it all. Nor had she any longer a will of her own . . . there could be no past for her. Everything in the past belonged to a person who . . . was dead. Now there was only a perfectly humble woman, who was ready to obey, who was happy to submit herself to the will of another . . . her master, her creator, her Professor. Between [Andreas] and her stood Werner Kreutz. She felt secure and salvaged.[26]

Hoyer has the same problems with purity and denial of mixture that recur in many transsexual autobiographical narratives. The characters in his narrative exist in an historical period of enormous sexual repression. How is one to maintain the divide between the "male" self, whose proper object of desire is Woman, and the "female" self, whose proper object of desire is Man?

> "As a man you have always seemed to me unquestionably healthy. I have, indeed, seen with my own eyes that you attract women, and that is the clearest proof that you are a genuine fellow." He paused, and then placed his hand on Andreas' shoulder. "You won't take it amiss if I ask you a frank question? . . . Have you at any time been interested in your own kind? You know what I mean."
> Andreas shook his head calmly. "My word on it, Niels; never in my life. And I can add that those kind of creatures have never shown any interest in me."
> "Good, Andreas! That's just what I thought."[27]

Hoyer must separate the subjectivity of "Andreas," who has never felt anything for men, and "Lili," who, in the course of the narrative, wants to marry one. This salvaging procedure makes the world safe for "Lili" by erecting and maintaining an impenetrable barrier between her and "Andreas," reinforced again and again in such ways as two different handwriting styles and two different voices. The force of an imperative—a natural state toward which all things tend—to deny the potentialities of mixture, acts to preserve "pure" gender identity: at the dawn of the Nazi-led love affair with purity, no "creatures" tempt Andreas into transgressing boundaries with his "own kind."

> "I will honestly and plainly confess to you, Niels, that I have always been attracted to women. And to-day as much as ever. A most banal confession!"[28]

—banal only so long as the person inside Andreas's body who voices it is Andreas, rather than Lili. There is a lot of work being done in this passage, a microcosm of the work it takes to maintain the same polar personae in society in the large. Further, each of these writers constructs his or her account as a narrative of redemption. There is a strong element of drama, of the sense of struggle against huge odds, of overcoming perilous obstacles, and of mounting awe and mystery at the breathtaking approach and final apotheosis of the Forbidden Transformation. Oboy.

> The first operation . . . has been successful beyond all expectations. Andreas has ceased to exist, they said. His germ glands—oh, mystic words—have been removed.[29]

Oh, mystic words. The *mysterium tremendum* of deep identity hovers about a physical locus; the entire complex of male engenderment, the mysterious power of the Man-God, inhabits the "germ glands" in the way that the soul was thought to inhabit the pineal. Maleness is in the you-know-whats. For that matter, so is the ontology of the subject. Therefore Hoyer can demonstrate in the coarsest way that femaleness is lack:

> The operation which has been performed here [that is, castration] enables me
> to enter the clinic for women [exclusively for women].[30]

On the other hand, either Niels or Lili can be constituted by an act of *insinuation*, what the New Testament calls *endeuein*, or the putting on of the god, inserting the physical body within a shell of cultural signification:

> Andreas Sparre . . . was probably undressing for the last time . . . For a lifetime
> these coverings of coat and waistcoat and trousers had enclosed him.[31]
>
> It is now Lili who is writing to you. I am sitting up in my bed in a silk
> nightdress with lace trimming, curled, powdered, with bangles, necklace, and
> rings. . . .[32]

All these authors replicate the stereotypical male account of the constitution of woman: Dress, makeup, and delicate fainting at the sight of blood. Each of these adventurers passes directly from one pole of sexual experience to the other. If there is any intervening space in the continuum of sexuality, it is invisible. And nobody *ever* mentions wringing the turkey's neck.

No wonder feminist theorists have been suspicious. Hell, *I'm* suspicious.

How do these accounts converse with the medical/psychological texts? In a time in which more interactions occur through texts, computer conferences, and electronic media than by personal contact, and consequently when individual subjectivity can be constituted through inscription more often than through personal association, there are still moments of embodied "natural truth" that cannot be avoided. In the time period of most of these books, the most critical of these moments was the intake interview at the gender dysphoria clinic when the doctors, who were all males, decided whether the person was eligible for gender reassignment surgery. The origin of the gender dysphoria clinics is a microcosmic look at the construction of criteria for gender. The foundational idea for the gender dysphoria clinics was first, to study an interesting and potentially fundable human aberration; second, to provide help, as they understood the term, for a "correctable problem."

Some of the early nonacademic gender dysphoria clinics performed *surgery on demand*, which is to say regardless of any judgment on the part of the clinic staff regarding what came to be called appropriateness to the gender of choice. When the first academic gender dysphoria clinics were started on an experimental basis in the 1960s, the medical staff would not perform surgery on demand, because of the professional risks involved in performing experimental surgery on "sociopaths." At this time there were no official diagnostic criteria; "transsexuals" were, *ipso facto*, whoever signed up for assistance. Professionally this was a dicey situation. It was necessary to construct the category "transsexual" along customary and traditional lines, to construct plausible criteria for acceptance into a clinic. Professionally speaking, a test or a differential diagnosis was needed for transsexualism that did not depend on anything as simple and subjective as feeling that one was in the wrong body. The test needed to be objective, clinically appropriate, and repeatable. But even after considerable research, no simple and unambiguous test for gender dys-phoria syndrome could be developed.[33]

The Stanford clinic was in the business of helping people, among its other agendas, as its members understood the term. Therefore the final decisions of eligibility for gender reassignment were made by the staff on the basis of an individual *sense* of the "appropriateness of the individual to their gender of choice." The clinic took on the additional role of "grooming clinic" or "charm school" because, according to the judgment of the staff, the men who presented as wanting to be women did not always "behave like" women. Stanford recognized that gender roles could be learned (to an extent). Their involvement with the grooming clinics was an effort to produce not simply anatomically legible females, but *women* . . . i.e., *gendered* females. As Norman Fisk remarked, "I now admit very candidly that . . . in the early phases we were avowedly seeking candidates who would have the best chance for suc-cess."[34] In practice this meant that the candidates for surgery were evaluated on the basis of their *performance* in the gender of choice. The criteria consti-tuted a fully acculturated, consensual definition of gender, and *at the site of their enactment we can locate an actual instance of the apparatus of production of gender.*

This raises several sticky questions, the chief two being: Who is telling the story for whom, and how do the storytellers differentiate between the story they tell and the story they hear?

One answer is that they differentiate with great difficulty. The criteria which the researchers developed and then applied were defined recursively through a series of interactions with the candidates. The scenario worked this way: Initially, the only textbook on the subject of transsexualism was Harry Benjamin's definitive work *The Transsexual Phenomenon* (1966).[35] (Note that Benjamin's book actually postdates *I Changed My Sex!* by about ten years.) When the first clinics were constituted, Benjamin's book was the researchers' standard reference. And when the first transsexuals were evaluated for their suitability for surgery, their behavior matched up gratifyingly with Benjamin's criteria. The researchers produced papers which reported on this, and which were used as bases for funding.

It took a surprisingly long time—several years—for the researchers to real-ize that the reason the candidates' behavioral profiles matched Benjamin's so well was that the candidates, too, had read Benjamin's book, which was passed from hand to hand within the transsexual community, and they were only too happy to provide the behavior that led to acceptance for surgery.[36] This sort of careful repositioning created interesting problems. Among them was the determination of the permissible range of expressions of physical sexuality. This was a large gray area in the candidates' self-presentations, because Benja-min's subjects did not talk about any erotic sense of their own bodies. Conse-quently nobody else who came to the clinics did either. By textual authority, physical men who lived as women and who identified themselves as transsexu-als, as opposed to male transvestites for whom erotic penile sensation was permissible, could not experience penile pleasure. In the 1980s there was not a single preoperative male-to-female transsexual for whom data was available who experienced genital sexual pleasure while living in the "gender of choice."[37] The prohibition continued postoperatively in interestingly transmuted form, and remained so absolute that no postoperative transsexual would admit to experiencing sexual pleasure through masturbation either. Full membership in the assigned gender was conferred by orgasm, real or faked, accomplished through heterosexual penetration.[38] "Wringing the turkey's neck," the ritual of penile masturbation just before surgery, was the most secret of secret traditions. To acknowledge so natural a desire would be to risk "crash landing"; that is, "role inappropriateness" leading to disqualification.[39]

It was necessary to retrench. The two groups, on one hand the researchers and on the other the transsexuals, were pursuing separate ends. The researchers wanted to know what this thing they called gender dysphoria syndrome was. They wanted a taxonomy of symptoms, criteria for differential diagnosis, procedures for evaluation, reliable courses of treatment, and thorough follow-up. The transsexuals wanted surgery. They had very clear agendas regarding their relation to the researchers, and considered the doctors' evaluation criteria merely another obstacle in their path—something to be overcome. In this they unambiguously expressed Benjamin's original criterion in its simplest form: The sense of being in the "wrong" body.[40] This seems a recipe for an uneasy adversarial relationship, and it was. It continues to be, although with the passage of time there has been considerable dialogue between the two camps. Partly this has been made possible by the realization among the medical and psychological community that the expected criteria for differential diagnosis did not emerge. Consider this excerpt from a paper by Marie Mehl, written in 1986:

> There is no mental nor psychological test which successfully differentiates the transsexual from the so-called normal population. There is no more psychopathology in the transsexual population than in the population at large, although societal response to the transsexual does pose some insurmountable problems. The psychodynamic histories of transsexuals do not yield any consistent differentiation characteristics from the rest of the population.[41]

These two accounts, Mehl's statement and that of Lothstein, in which he found transsexuals to be depressed, schizoid, manipulative, controlling, and paranoid, coexist within a span of less than ten years. With the achievement of a diagnostic category in 1980—one which, after years of research, did not involve much more than the original sense of "being in the wrong body"— and consequent acceptance by the body police, i.e., the medical establishment, clinically "good" histories now exist of transsexuals in areas as widely dispersed as Australia, Sweden, Czechoslovakia, Vietnam, Singapore, China, Malaysia, India, Uganda, Sudan, Tahiti, Chile, Borneo, Madagascar, and the Aleutians.[42] (This is not a complete list.) It is a considerable stretch to fit them all into some plausible theory. Were there undiscovered or untried diagnostic techniques that would have differentiated transsexuals from the "normal"

population? Were the criteria wrong, limited, or short-sighted? Did the realization that criteria were not emerging just naturally appear as a result of
"scientific progress," or were there other forces at work?

Such a banquet of data creates its own problems. Concomitant with the
dubious achievement of a diagnostic category is the inevitable blurring of
boundaries as a vast heteroglossic account of difference, heretofore invisible
to the "legitimate" professions, suddenly achieves canonization and simultaneously becomes homogenized to satisfy the constraints of the category. Suddenly the old morality tale of the truth of gender, told by a kindly white
patriarch in New York in 1966, becomes pancultural in the 1980s. Emergent
polyvocalities of lived experience, never represented in the discourse but present at least in potential, disappear; the *berdache* and the stripper, the tweedy
housewife and the *mujerado*, the *mah'u* and the rock star, are still the same
story after all, if we only try hard enough.

WHOSE STORY IS THIS, ANYWAY?

I wish to point out the broad similarities which this peculiar juxtaposition
suggests to aspects of colonial discourse with which we may be familiar: The
initial fascination with the exotic, extending to professional investigators; denial of subjectivity and lack of access to the dominant discourse; followed by
a species of rehabilitation.

Raising these issues has complicated life in the clinics.

"Making" history, whether autobiographic, academic, or clinical, is partly
a struggle to ground an account in some natural inevitability. Bodies are
screens on which we see projected the momentary settlements that emerge
from ongoing struggles over beliefs and practices within the academic and
medical communities. These struggles play themselves out in arenas far removed from the body. Each is an attempt to gain a high ground which is
profoundly moral in character, to make an authoritative and final explanation
for the way things are and consequently for the way they must continue to be.
In other words, each of these accounts is culture speaking with the voice of
an individual. The people who have no voice in this theorizing are the transsexuals themselves. As with males theorizing about women from the beginning of time, theorists of gender have seen transsexuals as possessing
something less than agency. As with "genetic" "women," transsexuals are
infantilized, considered too illogical or irresponsible to achieve true subjectivity, or clinically erased by diagnostic criteria; or else, as constructed by some
radical feminist theorists, as robots of an insidious and menacing patriarchy,
an alien army designed and constructed to infiltrate, pervert, and destroy
"true" women. In this construction as well, the transsexuals have been resolutely complicit by failing to develop an effective counterdiscourse.

Here on the gender borders at the close of the twentieth century, with the
faltering of phallocratic hegemony and the bumptious appearance of heteroglossic origin accounts, we find the epistemologies of white male medical
practice, the rage of radical feminist theories and the chaos of lived gendered

experience meeting on the battlefield of the transsexual body: a hotly contested site of cultural inscription, a meaning machine for the production of ideal type. Representation at its most magical, the transsexual body is perfected memory, inscribed with the "true" story of Adam and Eve as the ontological account of irreducible difference, an essential biography which is part of nature. A story which culture tells itself, the transsexual body is a tactile politics of reproduction constituted through textual violence. The clinic is a technology of inscription.

Given this circumstance in which a minority discourse comes to ground in the physical, a counterdiscourse is critical. But it is difficult to generate a counterdiscourse if one is programmed to disappear. The highest purpose of the transsexual is to erase him/herself, to fade into the "normal" population as soon as possible. Part of this process is known as *constructing a plausible history*—learning to lie effectively about one's past. What is gained is acceptability in society. What is lost is the ability to authentically represent the complexities and ambiguities of lived experience, and thereby is lost that aspect of "nature" which Donna Haraway theorizes as Coyote—the Native American spirit animal who represents the power of continual transformation which is the heart of engaged life. Instead, authentic experience is replaced by a particular kind of story, one that supports the old constructed positions. This is expensive, and profoundly disempowering. Whether desiring to do so or not, transsexuals do not grow up in the same ways as "GGs," or genetic "naturals."[43] Transsexuals do not possess the same history as genetic "naturals," and do not share common oppression prior to gender reassignment. I am not suggesting a shared discourse. I am suggesting that in the transsexual's erased history we can find a story disruptive to the accepted discourses of gender, which originates from within the gender minority itself and which can make common cause with other oppositional discourses. But the transsexual currently occupies a position which is nowhere, which is outside the binary oppositions of gendered discourse. For a transsexual, *as a transsexual*, to generate a true, effective and representational counterdiscourse is to speak from outside the boundaries of gender, beyond the constructed oppositional nodes which have been predefined as the only positions from which discourse is possible. How, then, can the transsexual speak? If the transsexual were to speak, what would s/he say?

A POSTTRANSSEXUAL MANIFESTO

To attempt to occupy a place as speaking subject within the traditional gender frame is to become complicit in the discourse which one wishes to deconstruct. Rather, we can seize upon the textual violence inscribed in the transsexual body and turn it into a reconstructive force. Let me suggest a more familiar example. Judith Butler points out that the lesbian categories of "butch" and "femme" are not simple assimilations of lesbianism back into terms of heterosexuality. Rather, Butler introduces the concept of *cultural intelligibility*, and suggests that the contextualized and resignified "masculinity" of the butch, seen against a culturally intelligible "female" body, invokes a dissonance that both generates a sexual tension and constitutes the object of desire. She points out that this way of thinking about gendered objects of desire admits of much greater complexity than the example suggests. The lesbian butch or femme both recall the heterosexual scene but simultaneously displace it. The idea that butch and femme are "replicas" or "copies" of heterosexual exchange underestimates the erotic power of their internal dissonance.[44] In the case of the transsexual, the varieties of performative gender, seen against a culturally intelligible gendered body *which is itself a medically constituted textual violence*, generate new and unpredictable dissonances which implicate entire spectra of desire. In the transsexual as text we may find the potential to map the refigured body onto conventional gender discourse and thereby disrupt it, to take advantage of the dissonances created by such a juxtaposition to fragment and reconstitute the elements of gender in new and unexpected geometries. I suggest we start by taking Raymond's accusation that "transsexuals divide women" beyond itself, and turn it into a productive force to multiplicatively divide the old binary discourses of gender—as well as Raymond's own monistic discourse. To foreground the practices of inscription and reading which are part of this deliberate invocation of dissonance, I suggest constituting transsexuals not as a class or problematic "third gender," but rather as a *genre*—a set of embodied texts whose potential for *productive* disruption of structured sexualities and spectra of desire has yet to be explored.

In order to effect this, the genre of visible transsexuals must grow by recruiting members from the class of invisible ones, from those who have disappeared into their "plausible histories." The most critical thing a transsexual can do, the thing that *constitutes* success, is to "pass."[45] Passing means to live successfully in the gender of choice, to be accepted as a "natural" member of that gender. Passing means the denial of mixture. One and the same with passing is effacement of the prior gender role, or the construction of a plausible history. Considering that most transsexuals choose reassignment in their third or fourth decade, this means erasing a considerable portion of their personal experience. It is my contention that this process, in which both the transsexual and the medicolegal/psychological establishment are complicit, forecloses the possibility of a life grounded in the *intertextual* possibilities of the transsexual body.

To negotiate the troubling and productive multiple permeabilities of boundary and subject position that intertextuality implies, we must begin to rearticulate the foundational language by which both sexuality and transsexuality are described. For example, neither the investigators nor the transsexuals have taken the step of problematizing "wrong body" as an adequate descriptive category. In fact "wrong body" has come, virtually by default, to *define* the syndrome.[46] It is quite understandable, I think, that a phrase whose lexicality suggests the phallocentric, binary character of gender differentiation should be examined with deepest suspicion. So long as we, whether academics, clinicians, or transsexuals, ontologize both sexuality and transsexuality in this way, we have foreclosed the possibility of analyzing desire and motivational complexity in a manner which adequately describes the multiple contradictions of individual lived experience. We need a deeper analytical language for transsexual theory, one which allows for the sorts of ambiguities and polyvocalities which have already so productively informed and enriched feminist theory.

Judith Shapiro points out that "To those . . . who might be inclined to diagnose the transsexual's focus on the genitals as obsessive or fetishistic, the response is that they are, in fact, simply conforming to *their culture's* criteria for gender assignment" (emphasis mine). This statement points to deeper workings, to hidden discourses and experiential pluralities within the transsexual monolith. They are not yet clinically or academically visible, and with good reason. For example, in pursuit of differential diagnosis a question sometimes asked of a prospective transsexual is "Suppose that you could be a man [or woman] in every way except for your genitals; would you be content?" There are several possible answers, but only one is clinically correct.[47] Small wonder, then, that so much of these discourses revolves around the phrase "wrong body." Under the binary phallocratic founding myth by which Western bodies and subjects are authorized, only one body per gendered subject is "right." All other bodies are wrong.

As clinicians and transsexuals continue to face off across the diagnostic battlefield which this scenario suggests, the transsexuals for whom gender identity is something different from *and perhaps irrelevant* to physical genitalia are occulted by those for whom the power of the medical/psychological establishments, and their ability to act as gatekeepers for cultural norms, is the final authority for what counts as a culturally intelligible body. This is a treacherous area, and were the silenced groups to achieve voice we might well find, as feminist theorists have claimed, that the identities of individual, embodied subjects were far less implicated in physical norms, and far more diversely spread across a rich and complex structuration of identity and desire, than it is now possible to express. And yet in even the best of the current debates, the standard mode is one of relentless totalization. The most egregious example in this paper, Raymond's stunning "All transsexuals rape women's bodies" (what if she had said, e.g., "all blacks rape women's bodies"), is no less totalizing than Kates's "transsexuals . . . take on an exaggerated and stereotypical female role," or *Bolin's* "transsexuals try to forget their male history." There are no subjects in these discourses, only homogenized, totalized objects—fractally replicating earlier histories of minority discourses in the large. So when I speak the forgotten word, it will perhaps wake memories of other debates. The word is *some.*

Transsexuals who pass seem able to ignore the fact that by creating totalized, monistic identities, forgoing physical and subjective intertextuality, they have foreclosed the possibility of authentic relationships. Under the principle of passing, denying the destabilizing power of being "read," relationships begin as lies—and passing, of course, is not an activity restricted to transsexuals. This is familiar to the person of color whose skin is light enough to pass as white, or to the closet gay or lesbian . . . or to anyone who has chosen invisibility as an imperfect solution to personal dissonance. In essence I am rearticulating one of the arguments for solidarity which has been developed by gays, lesbians, and people of color. The comparison extends further. To deconstruct the necessity for passing implies that transsexuals must take responsibility for *all* of their history, to begin to rearticulate their lives not as a series of erasures in the service of a species of feminism conceived from within a traditional frame, but as a political action begun by reappropriating difference and reclaiming the power of the refigured and reinscribed body. The disruptions of the old patterns of desire that the multiple dissonances of the transsexual body imply produce not an irreducible alterity but a myriad of alterities, whose unanticipated juxtapositions hold what Donna Haraway has called the promises of monsters—physicalities of constantly shifting figure and ground that exceed the frame of any possible representation.[48]

The essence of transsexualism is the act of passing. A transsexual who passes is obeying the Derridean imperative: "Genres are not to be mixed. I will not mix genres."[49] I could not ask a transsexual for anything more inconceivable than to forgo passing, to be consciously "read," to read oneself aloud—and by this troubling and productive reading, to begin to *write oneself* into the discourses by which one has been written—in effect, then, to become a (look out—dare I say it again?) posttranssexual.[50] Still, transsexuals know that silence can be an extremely high price to pay for acceptance. I want to speak directly to the brothers, sisters, and others who may read/"read" this and say: I ask all of us to use the strength which brought us through the effort of restructuring identity, and which has also helped us to live in silence and denial, for a re-visioning of our lives. I know you feel that most of the work is behind you and that the price of invisibility is not great. But, although *individual* change is the foundation of all things, it is not the end of all things. Perhaps it's time to begin laying the groundwork for the next transformation.

NOTES

Thanks to Gloria Anzaldúa, Laura Chernaik, Ramona Fernandez, Thyrza Goodeve, and John Haritgan for their valuable comments on earlier drafts of this paper; Judy Van Maasdam and Donald Laub of the Stanford Gender Dysphoria Program for their uneasy help; Wendy Chapkis; Nathalie Magan; the Olivia Records Collective, for whose caring in difficult times I am deeply grateful; Janice Raymond, for playing Luke Skywalker to my Darth Vader; Graham Nash and David Crosby; and Christy Staats and Brenda Warren for their steadfastness. In particular, I thank Donna Haraway, whose insight and encouragement continue to inform and illuminate this work.

1. Jan Morris, *Conundrum* (New York: Harcourt Brace Jovanovich, 1974), p. 155.

2. In William A. W. Walters, and Michael W. Ross, *Transsexualism and Sex Reassignment* (Oxford: Oxford University Press, 1986).

3. This capsule history is related in the introduction to Richard Docter's *Transvestites and Transsexuals: Toward a Theory of Cross-Gender Behavior* (New York: Plenum Press, 1988). It is also treated by Judith Shapiro, "Transsexualism: Reflections on the Persis-

tence of Gender and the Mutability of Sex," in *Body Guards: The Cultural Politics of Gender Ambiguity,* the volume in which this essay originally appeared, as well as by Janice Irvine in *Disorders of Desire: Sex and Gender in Modern American Sexology* (Philadelphia: Temple University Press, 1990). In chapter seven of Body Guards, Gary Kates argues that the Chevalier d'Eon was not a transsexual because he did not demonstrate the transsexual syndrome as Kates understands it; i.e., "intense discomfort with masculine clothes and activities, as is normal in male-to-female transsexuals." Kates's idea of the syndrome comes from standard texts. Later in this paper I discuss the mythic quality of much of this information.

4. In Mehl's introduction to *Gender Dysphoria Syndrome: Development, Research, Management,* ed. Betty Steiner (New York: Plenum Press, 1985).

5. Walters and Ross, op. cit.

6. From Don Burnard and Michael W. Ross, "Psychosocial Aspects and Psychological Theory: What Can Psychological Testing Reveal?" in Walters and Ross [58,2].

7. Walters and Ross, [58,3].

8. Walters and Ross, [58,3].

9. There is some hope to be taken that Judith Shapiro's work will supercede Raymond's as such a definitive statement. Shapiro's accounts seem excellently balanced, and she is aware that there are more accounts from transsexual scholars that have not yet entered the discourse.

10. This wonderful phrase is from Donna Haraway's "Teddy Bear Patriarchy: Taxidermy in the Garden Of Eden, New York City, 1908–1936," *Social Text* 2 (2):20.

11. Haraway, op. cit. The anecdotal character of this section is supported by field notes which have not yet been organized and coded. A thoroughly definitive and perhaps ethnographic version of this paper, with appropriate citations of both professionals and their subjects, awaits research time and funding.

12. The British sexologist, Norman Haine, wrote the introduction, thus making Hoyer's book a semi-medical contribution.

13. Hedy Jo Star (Carl Rollins Hammonds) 1955 (from an O.T.F.). *I Changed My Sex!* has disappeared from history, and I have been unable to find reference to it in any library catalog. Having held a copy in my hand, I am sorry I didn't hold tighter.

14. There was at least one other book published during this period, Renée Richards's "Second Serve," which is not treated here.

15. Niels Hoyer was a pseudonym for Ernst Ludwig Harthern Jacobson; Lili Elbe was the female name chosen by the artist Einar Wegener, whose given name was Andreas Sparre. This lexical profusion has rich implications for studies of self and its constructions, in literature and also in such emergent social settings as computer conferences, where several personalities grounded in a single body are as much the rule as the exception.

16. Hoyer, p. 163.

17. Hoyer, p. 147.

18. Morris, p. 174.

19. In *Conundrum,* Morris does describe a period in her journey from masculine to feminine (from a few years before surgery to immediately afterward) during which her gender was perceived, by herself and others, as ambiguous. She is quite unambiguous, though, about the moment of transition from *male* to *female.*

20. Gender reassignment is the correct disciplinary term. In current medical discourse, sex is taken as a natural physical fact and cannot be changed.

21. Morris, p. 115. I was reminded of this account on the eve of my own surgery. Gee, I thought on that occasion, it would be interesting to magically become another person in that binary and final way. So I tried it myself—going to the mirror and saying goodbye to the person I saw there—and unfortunately it didn't work. A few days later, when I could next get to the mirror, the person looking back at me was still me. I still don't understand what I did wrong.

22. Canary Conn, *Canary: The Story of a Transsexual* (New York: Bantam, 1977),

p. 271. Conn had her surgery at the clinic of Jesus Maria Barbosa in Tijuana. In this except she is speaking to a Mexican nurse; hence the Spanish terms.

23. Star, op. cit.

24. I admit to being every bit as astounded as the good Doctor, since except for Hoyer's account there are no other records of change in vocal pitch or timbre following administration of hormones or gender reassignment surgery. If transsexuals do succeed in altering their vocal characteristics, they do it gradually and with great difficulty. But there are more than sufficient problems with Lili Elbe's "true story," not the least of which is the scene in which Elbe finally "becomes a woman" by virtue of her physician's *implanting into her abdominal cavity a set of human ovaries.* The attention given by the media in the past decade to heart transplants and diseases of the immune system have made the lay public more aware of the workings of the human immune response, but even in 1936 Hoyer's account would have been recognized by the medical community as questionable. Tissue rejection and the dream of mitigating it were the subjects of speculation in fiction and science fiction as late as the 1940s; e.g., the miracle drug "collodiansy" in H. Beam Piper's *One Leg Too Many* (1949).

25. Hoyer, p. 165.

26. Hoyer, p. 170. For an extended discussion of texts that transmute submission into personal fulfillment, cf. Sandy Stone, "Sweet Surrender: Gender, Spirituality, and the Ecstasy of Subjection; Pseudo-transsexual Fiction in the 1970s," forthcoming.

27. Hoyer, p. 53.

28. Ibid.

29. Hoyer, p. 134.

30. Hoyer, p. 139. Lili Elbe's sex change took place in 1930. In the United States today, the juridical view of successful male-to-female sex change is still based upon lack; e.g., a man is a woman when "the male generative organs have been totally and irrevocably destroyed" (From a clinic letter authorizing a name change on a passport, 1980).

31. Hoyer, p. 125.

32. Hoyer, p. 139. I call attention in both preceding passages to the Koine Greek verb ἐνδέυειν, referring to the moment of baptism, when the one being baptized enters into and is entered by the Word; *endeuein* may be translated as "to enter into" but also "to put on, to insinuate oneself into, like a glove"; viz. "He [*sic*] who is baptized into Christ shall have put on Christ." In this intense homoerotic vein in which both genders are present but collapsed in the sacrifi[c]ed body, cf. such examples as Fray Bernardino de Sahagun's description of rituals during which the officiating priest puts on the flayed skin of a young woman (Frazer, pp. 589–91).

33. The evolution and management of this problem deserves a paper in itself. It is discussed in capsule form in Donald R. Laub and Patrick Gandy, eds., *Proceedings of the Second Interdisciplinary Symposium on Gender Dysphoria Syndrome* (Stanford: Division of Reconstructive and Rehabilitation Surgery, Stanford Medical Center, 1973) and in Janice M. Irvine, *Disorders Of Desire: Sex and Gender in Modern American Sexology* (Philadelphia: Temple University Press, 1990).

34. In Laub and Gandy, p. 7. Fisk's full remarks provide an excellent description of the aims and procedures of the Stanford group during the early years, and the tensions of conflicting agendas and various attempts at resolution are implicit in his account. For additional accounts cf. both Irvine and Shapiro, op. cit.

35. Harry Benjamin, *The Transsexual Phenomenon* (New York: Julian Press, 1966). The paper which was the foundation for the book was published as "Transsexualism and Transvestism as Psycho-somatic and Somato-Psychic Syndromes" in the *American Journal of Psychotherapy* 8 (1954): 219–30. A much earlier paper by D. O. Cauldwell, "Psychopathia transexualis," in *Sexology* 16 (1949): 274–80, does not appear to have had the same effect within the field, although John Money still pays homage to it by retaining Cauldwell's single-s spelling of the term. In early documents by other workers one may sometimes trace the influence of Cauldwell or Benjamin by how the word is spelled.

36. Laub and Gandy, pp. 8, 9 passim.

37. The problem here is with the ontology of the term "genital," in particular with regard to its definition for such activities as pre- and postoperative masturbation. Engenderment ontologizes the erotic economy of body surface; as Judith Butler and others (e.g., Foucault) point out, engenderment polices which parts of the body have their erotic components switched off or on. Conflicts arise when the *same* parts become multivalent; e.g., when portions of the (physical male) urethra are used to construct portions of the (gendered female in the physical male) neoclitoris. I suggest that we use this vertiginous idea as an example of ways in which we can refigure multivalence as intervention into the constitution of binary gendered subject positions; in a binary erotic economy, "Who" experiences erotic sensation associated with these areas? (In her essay in *Body Guard,* Judith Shapiro raises a similar point. I have chosen a site geographically quite close to the one she describes, but hopefully more ambiguous, and therefore more dissonant in these discourses in which dissonance can be a powerful and productive intervention.)

38. This act in the borderlands of subject position suggests a category missing from Marjorie Garber's excellent paper "Spare Parts: The Surgical Construction of Gender," *differences* 1 (1990): 137–59; it is an intervention into the dissymmetry between "making a man" and "making a woman" that Garber describes. To a certain extent it figures a collapse of those categories within the transsexual imaginary, although it seems reasonable to conclude that this version of the coming-of-age story is still largely male—the male doctors and patients telling each other the stories of what Nature means for both Man and Woman. Generally female (female-to-male) patients tell the same stories from the other side.

39. The terms "wringing the turkey's neck" (male masturbation), "crash landing" (rejection by a clinical program), and "gaff" (an undergarment used to conceal male genitalia in preoperative m/f transsexuals), vary slightly in different geographical areas but are common enough to be recognized across sites.

40. Based upon Norman Fisk's remarks in Laub and Gandy, p. 7, as well as my own notes. Part of the difficulty, as I discuss in this paper, is that the investigators (not to mention the transsexuals) have failed to problematize the phrase "wrong body" as an adequate descriptive category.

41. In Walters and Ross, op. cit.

42. I use the word "clinical" here and elsewhere while remaining mindful of the "Pyrrhic victory" of which Marie Mehl spoke. Now that transsexualism has the uneasy legitimacy of a diagnostic category in the DSM, how do we begin the process of getting it *out* of the book?

43. The actual meaning of "GG," a m/f transsexual slang term, is "genuine girl" [*sic*], also called "genny."

44. Judith Butler, *Gender Trouble* (New York: Routledge, 1990).

45. The opposite of passing, being *read,* provocatively invokes the inscription practices to which I have referred.

46. I am suggesting a starting point, but it is necessary to go much further. We will have to question not only how *body* is defined in these discourses, but to more critically examine who gets to say *what "body" means.*

47. In case the reader is unsure, let me supply the clinically correct answer: "No."

48. For an elaboration of this concept cf. Donna Haraway, "The Promises Of Monsters: A Regenerative Politics for Inappropriate/d Others," in *Cultural Studies,* ed. Paula Treichler, Cary Nelson, and Larry Grossberg (New York: Routledge, 1991).

49. Jacques Derrida, "La Loi Du Genre/The Law Of Genre," trans. Avital Ronell, *Glyph* 7(1980):176 (French); 202 (English).

50. I also call attention to Gloria Anzaldúa's theory of the mestiza, an illegible subject living in the borderlands between cultures, capable of partial speech in each but always only partially intelligible to each. Working against the grain of this position, Anzaldúa's "new mestiza" attempts to overcome illegibility partly by seizing control

of speech and inscription and writing herself into cultural discourse. The stunning "Borderlands" is a case in point; cf. Gloria Anzaldúa, *Borderlands/La Frontera: The New Mestiza* (San Francisco: Spinsters/Aunt Lute, 1987).

WORKS CITED

Anzaldúa, Gloria. 1987. *Borderlands/La Frontera: The New Mestiza*. San Francisco: Spinsters/Aunt Lute.

Benjamin, Harry. 1966. *The Transsexual Phenomenon*. New York: Julian Press.

Conn, Canary. 1977. *Canary: The Story of a Transsexual*. New York: Bantam.

Derrida, Jacques. 1980. *La Loi Du Genre/The Law Of Genre*. Trans. Avital Ronell. *Glyph* 7: 176 (French); 202 (English).

Docter, Richard F. 1988. *Transvestites and Transsexuals: Toward a Theory of Cross-Gender Behavior*. New York: Plenum Press.

Elbe, Lili. 1933. *Man Into Woman: An Authentic Record of a Change of Sex. The True Story of the Miraculous Transformation of the Danish Painter, Einar Wegener* [Andreas Sparre]. Ed. Niels Hoyer [pseud. for Ernst Ludwig Harthern Jacobsen]. Trans. H. J. Stenning. Introduction by Norman Haire. New York: E. P. Dutton & Co., Inc.

Epstein, Julia, and Kristina Straub, eds. 1991. *Body Guards: The Cultural Politics of Gender Ambiguity*. New York: Routledge.

Faith, Karlene. Forthcoming. *If It Weren't for the Music: A History of Olivia Records*.

Foucault, Michel. 1980. *Herculine Barbin: Being the Recently Discovered Memoirs of a Nineteenth-Century Hermaphrodite*. New York: Pantheon.

Frazer, Sir James George. 1911. *The Golden Bough, a Study in Magic and Religion*. London: Macmillan.

Gatens, Moira. 1988. "A Critique of the Sex-Gender Distinction." In *Interventions After Marx*, ed. J. Allen and P. Patton.

Grahn, Judy. 1984. *Another Mother Tongue: Gay Words, Gay Worlds*. Boston: Beacon Press.

Green, Richard, and John Money, eds. 1969. *Transsexualism and Sex Reassignment*. Baltimore: Johns Hopkins Press.

Grosz, Elizabeth. 1988. "Freaks:" Paper delivered at the Conference on Women and Philosophy, University of California, Santa Cruz, 1988.

Haraway, Donna J. 1985. "Teddy Bear Patriarchy: Taxidermy in the Garden of Eden, New York City, 1908–1936." *Social Text* 2 (Winter 1984–85): 20.

———. 1985. "A Manifesto For Cyborgs: Science, Technology and Socialist Feminism in the 1980s." *Socialist Review* 80: 65–107.

———. 1990. "The Promises Of Monsters: A Regenerative Politics for Inappropriate Others." In *Cultural Studies*, ed. Paula Treichler, Cary Nelson, and Larry Grossberg (New York: Routledge, 1991).

Hoyer, Niels. 1933. *Man Into Woman*. See Elbe, Lili.

Laub, Donald R., and Patrick Gandy, eds. 1973. Proceedings of the Second Interdisciplinary Symposium on Gender Dysphoria Syndrome. Stanford: Division of Reconstructive and Rehabilitation Surgery, Stanford Medical Center.

Lothstein, Leslie Martin. 1983. *Female-to-Male Transsexualism: Historical, Clinical and Theoretical Issues*. Boston: Routledge and Kegan Paul.

Morris, Jan. 1974. *Conundrum*. New York: Harcourt Brace Jovanovich.

Nettick, Geri, and Beth Elliot. "The Transsexual Vampire." Forthcoming in *Lonely and a Long Way from Home: The Life and Strange Adventures of a Lesbian Transsexual*.

Raymond, Janice. 1979. *The Transsexual Empire: The Making of the She-Male*. Boston: Beacon. Reprinted as ch. 18 of this volume.

Riddell, Carol. 1980. *Divided Sisterhood: A Critical Review of Janice Raymond's* The Transsexual Empire. Liverpool: News From Nowhere.

Shapiro, Judith. 1991. "Transsexualism: Reflections on the Persistance of Gender and the Mutability of Sex." In Epstein and Straub.

Spivak, Gayatri Chakravorty. 1988. *In Other Worlds: Essays in Cultural Politics.* New York: Routledge.

Star, Hedy Jo [Carl Rollins Hammonds]. 1955. *I Changed My Sex!* N.p.

Steiner, Betty, ed. 1985. *Gender Dysphoria Syndrome: Development, Research, Management.* New York: Plenum Press.

Stoller, Robert J. 1985. *Presentations of Gender.* New Haven: Yale University Press.

Stone, Sandy. Forthcoming. *In The Belly Of The Goddess: "Women's Music," Feminist Collectives, and the Cultural Arc of Lesbian Separatism, 1972–1979.*

Walters, William A. W., and Michael W. Ross. 1986. *Transsexualism and Sex Reassignment.* Oxford: Oxford University Press.

CHAPTER 20
REPRODUCTIVE CONTROLS AND
SEXUAL DESTINY

TIMOTHY F. MURPHY

(1990)

"... there will come a time when there will be none like us to come after us."

—Paul Ramsey[1]

There have been and continue to be measures designed to eliminate homosexual behavior and persons. These include religious programs of recovery from sinfulness; hormonal, biochemical, and anatomical interventions; and a gallimaufry of behavioral and psychological therapies. Political and legal measures also function as means of constraining homosexual behavior and persons. And certainly violence, actual and symbolic, against gay men and lesbians and even against those persons transiently exhibiting homoerotic behavior must be understood as means of eradicating homosexuality.

Advances in reproductive interventions have offered a number of means of controlling the sex and physical characteristics of children.[2] There is no reason to think that reproductive interventions will not continue to advance in sophistication and the number of characteristics they are capable of controlling. Gunther Dörner, an East German researcher, has hypothesized that homosexuality in human males is the result of androgen deprivation during a particular phase of fetal hypothalamic development, deprivation caused by maternal stress. His studies with rats suggest that neuroendocrine-conditioned male homosexuality can, in his words, "be prevented once and for all by a single androgen injection administered during critical brain development."[3] As Dörner believes that a life of homosexuality is a tragic existence, ending in millions of suicides,[4] it is not surprising that he believes that fetuses at risk for homosexuality should be identified through amniocentesis and that abortion would be desirable for those fetuses unable to benefit from androgen therapy.[5]

As the origins of sexual orientation are poorly understood, there are not now available any means of insuring the sexual orientation, homosexual or heterosexual, of progeny. But it is worth entertaining the possibility that certain reproductive technologies or interventions like that proposed by Dörner could offer the prospect of controlling generally, if not absolutely, the sexual orientation of children. While there are a number of arguments that might be used against such interventions, only the argument that they are wrong if heterosexist would appear to establish their immorality, heterosexism being a prejudicial doctrine which disvalues homosexuality without good reason. As all wrongs, however, are not of equal evil, it does not automatically follow that the use of these techniques should be forbidden by law. Because there are important freedoms to preserve in the domain of reproductive control and because it is not clear that the use of these interventions would adversely affect the interests of existing or future persons, I conclude that while they should be morally resisted, the use of heterosexist interventions should not be criminalized.

PRELIMINARY REMARKS

Sexual identity is multi-factorial, having at least the following components: biological sex (morphology and genetic endowment), gender identity, social sex role, sexual orientation (including erotic fantasy structure), and sexual behavior (including patterns of interpersonal affection and arousal-cue response patterns).[6] All this is to say that rather than there being a single, essential nature of homosexuality there is instead a broad array of psychic and behavioral traits which constitute homosexuality.

The elimination of homosexuality, therefore, might mean a number of things: a) elimination of persons identified, by self or others, as homosexual, b) elimination of all homoerotic behavior, or c) elimination of all homoerotic desire. Unless all these traits and interpretations were eliminated, therefore, an elimination of homosexuality would be necessarily incomplete. The elimination of all self-identified homosexual persons, for example, would not mean that persons, adolescents among them, did not continue to have homoerotic desire or engage in homosexual behavior. Even the elimination of homoerotic desire would not eliminate all homosexual behavior since sexual behavior is engaged in for a wide variety of reasons. For reasons of theater, absence of other available sexual outlets, or strategies of domination, some persons willingly adopt homosexual behavior. Since homosexuality is also used, too, as a metaphor for certain kinds of personal failure, some persons would continue to have homosexual identities thrust upon them regardless of their actual desires or behaviors.

Because reproductive controls would not suppress all the reasons for which people think and behave homoerotically, their use could not eliminate all these senses of homosexuality. For purposes of this essay, though, it will be assumed that effective reproductive controls might eliminate, as far as possible, a biologically based emergence of homoerotic desire, this presumably being the most common incentive to homosexual behavior and identities.

CONTEXT OF THE DISCUSSION

Would the availability of effective interventions insuring heterosexual children find a ready market? Is it desirable to take measures to prevent bearing homosexually oriented children? It is instructive to set these questions in the context of the attitudes of gay men and lesbians toward their sexuality and parenthood.

The Bell and Weinberg studies, dating from 1970 and published in 1978, represent the single most comprehensive study ever conducted on the lives of gay men and lesbians in any nation.[7] Their findings are suggestive on a number of points. First of all, the vast majority of persons surveyed reported no or little regret regarding their homosexual orientation.[8] This low incidence of reported regret is particularly significant since approximately a quarter of all persons polled also believed that homosexuality is an emotional disorder.[9] The low incidence of regret is also significant since many respondents claimed that their homosexuality was either somewhat harmful or very harmful in respect of their careers.[10] In fact, some respondents reported losing or almost losing their jobs as a direct result of their homosexuality.[11] Subjects were also asked whether or not they would have wanted a "magic pill" administered at birth, a pill guaranteeing subsequent heterosexual orientation. Between 72% and 89% of the respondents would *not* want such a pill to have been administered.[12] When asked if they would accept such a magic pill at the time of the survey, the percentages rejecting it were *even higher*, ranging from 86% to 94%.[13] When asked whether they would be upset if a child of theirs were to become homosexual, approximately half of all respondents said not at all and about another quarter said very little.[14]

The largest majority of self-identified gay men and lesbians, then, experience little or no regret about the nature of their sexual orientation, and where regret is expressed, in every category of respondents, it is asserted to be the consequence of social hostility and restrictions associated with homosexuality.[15] That is, the disvalues of homosexuality are perceived as artifactual social impositions. Among the hostilities and restrictions named were constraints on job opportunities, prospects for friendships, and inability to bear children. Nevertheless, most gay men and lesbians would not alter the direction of their sexual orientation either by retrospectively rewriting their history or by the lure of a magical intervention accessible now. Neither would the largest majority of them be particularly upset if a child of theirs was homosexually oriented. It is fair to suspect, moreover, that the chief reason a parent might be upset by the homosexuality of his or her children would be similar to the reasons for their own expressed regret: perceived social hostility and restriction on opportunities. Confirming data on the last claim, however, are lacking.

In spite of the character of the majority opinion, however, there were small percentages of respondents who regretted their homosexuality a great deal, whose occupational lives were disrupted by their homosexuality, who thought themselves afflicted with an emotional disorder, and who would deliver themselves from their fate if only some magical cure were available. Some, too, would be much disturbed if their own fate were visited upon their children.

There is no monolithic opinion among gay men and lesbians on whether children should be spared homoerotic destinies. There is no reason either to expect uniformity of opinion among prospective heterosexual parents faced with the same issue. Despite the lack of confirming data on the matter, it is hardly wild speculation to expect that the largest majority of heterosexuals would prefer heterosexually destined children. This is not to say that some, even most heterosexual parents would not accept and love their homosexual children, but it is to say that if a magic pill or other measure were available to ensure heterosexual children it is reasonable to believe that most heterosexual and some homosexual parents as well would avail themselves of it for reasons both selfish and selfless.

REPRODUCTIVE INTERVENTIONS

The cause or causes of homosexuality remain at least as unknown as the causes of heterosexuality. For the sake of this argument I will assume *ex hypothese* that the primacy of homosexual orientation in adult erotic life is traceable to measures involving either the selection of gametes or interventions in embryonic and fetal development. This is to say that I set aside as irrelevant here all postnatal theories of causation. One reason for doing so is that Bell, Weinberg, and Hammersmith have demonstrated that psychodynamic theories have grossly exaggerated the influence of parental relationships and family dynamics in causing male homosexuality.[16] Another reason for so doing is the conclusion of the same study that the development of sexual preference is "not inconsistent with what one would expect to find if, indeed, there were a biological basis for sexual preference."[17] This is not to say, of course, that psychodynamics cannot also be responsible for the emergence of homoerotic fantasy structure and patterns of behavior, but it is to say that the issue under consideration here is how certain interventions might control any biological based emergence of homoeroticism.

Selective Techniques

On the presumption of the biological foundations of homosexuality, one wonders whether homosexuality might not have genetically identifiable origins. Suppose it were possible to identify a statistical association if not a causal connection between certain genes and sexual orientation. One would then be in a position to identify those gametes likely to produce offspring of predictable sexual orientation. Through *in vitro* fertilization (IVF) and embryo transfer (ET) or even through certain artificial inseminations (AI), the appropriate gametes could be fused, the subsequent embryos implanted and brought to parturition. It might even be possible to produce heterosexual female children through techniques of parthenogenesis. It might also be possible to effect genetic interventions in gametes to effect heterosexual outcomes. At present, of course, there is no known relationship between genes and subsequent sexual orientation. Nevertheless, if it *were* possible to identify such a relationship it would be a short step to the use of that knowledge in reproductive techniques already widely practiced.

Developmental Techniques

A second class of techniques that might be used to control the sexual orientation of children would involve developmental manipulations of already existing embryos or fetuses. One recent study suggests that, as adults, heterosexual
men differ from homosexual men in their neuroendocrine response to the
administration of estrogen. Although the study suggests no possible use for
this finding, it observes that "These findings suggest that biological markers
for sexual orientation may exist."[18] One wonders whether it might not also be
possible to discover embryonic or fetal markers of similar kind. Such markers
would offer the prospect of altering fetal development, or, where that was not
possible, of aborting fetuses or exposing newborns to infanticide if these were
at risk of homosexual orientation. And even if there were no such markers, it
might well be possible nevertheless to ensure heterosexual orientation by, for
example, the prophylactic administration of certain androgens, as suggested
by Dörner, or by the cloning and implantation of embryos known to produce
heterosexuals.

ARGUMENTS FOR INTERVENTION

Should they become possible, what may be said in the moral defense of using
interventions of this kind? What moral good would be served by using these
interventions to ensure heterosexual progeny, to avoid homosexual progeny?

The Argument from Disease

On a certain view, homoerotic desire and certain kinds of homoerotic behavior represent a psychiatric disorder or an emotionally disabled state sufficiently grave to warrant its elimination where possible. This is, for example,
the view of Bieber[19] and Socarides.[20] Therefore the same moral incentive to
protect children from disease generally, by prophylactic or interventive measures, would oblige a parent to try to protect children from the homosexual
selves they might become.

The force of this argument, of course, depends on the status imputed
to homoerotic desire and behavior. Is homosexuality, whether exclusive or
transient, a psychic disorder akin to physiological defect? Or is it an infantile
stage of psychical development incompatible with adult maturity? I do not
intend to review here the long controversy regarding the standing of homosexuality as a disease entity. I will only say that because of the continued absence of any kind of evidence confirming causal logical or emotional disability
or causal physiological pathology, I do not see that homoerotic desire and
behavior belong to the domain of disease.[21] As for the claim that while not a
disease properly speaking, homosexuality is nonetheless an emotionally crippled state,[22] I believe that there is little evidence apart from tendentious analyses (largely in psychoanalytic and religious traditions) that heterosexuality is
the only pathway to human happiness and fulfillment. Certainly, the evidence
of Bell and Weinberg does not confirm the emotional dysfunction of most

gay men and lesbians. In any case, there is no way to define homosexual desire as an emotional failure without recourse to moral judgments, appeals which seem to me, although I will not argue the point here, more typically invidious than judicious. Consequently, it is hard to see that an argument of this kind would justify interventions to eliminate homoeroticism in children.

The Argument from Nature

Certain moral interpretations maintain that heterosexuality alone is the *natural* sexual expression of human beings. On the assumption that the nature of persons also defines their sexual standards, it would be ordinarily obligatory to assure the heterosexuality of human beings. It is unclear, though, that "nature" in any of its various meanings could ground an argument against homosexuality.

If human nature is understood as the actual behaviors and dispositions of human beings, then, clearly homosexuality is natural. The behavioral and psychic variability of the species displays exclusive heteroeroticism, exclusive homoeroticism, and various kinds of eroticism in between. Homosexuality is as much a part of the sexual landscape as the heterosexuality which often obscures it. This meaning of nature would presumably shield embryos and fetuses from any intervening hand. There would be no need to intervene, the argument would go, because there is nothing unusual occurring. Not the development of homosexuals, then, but interventions against their occurrence might be understood as a disruption of the order of nature.

By contrast, however, if nature is understood as representing an ideal condition for human persons, a kind of essential nature describable apart from actual behavior and dispositions, then one has moved from a descriptive account to a normative account of human obligation, and in so doing one loses the authority of nature. That is, such a nature is an asserted, prescriptive ideal which is authored by human representations of the order of the world. Thus mediated, the ideal is as much an artifice of human will and imagination as is language or art, and as subject to interpretation.

Even assuming that there were an essential nature of human beings written into the order of things, one knowable without interpretive distortions, such a nature is still not beyond the realm of human intervention. The order of the world is often harsh and inhospitable to human beings. It is no reliable ally to human hope and happiness. Thus do we control, manipulate, and constrain the forces of weather and environment. Every day and everywhere we take often ruthless measures to control and manipulate the world, to render it more hospitable to our interests. The development of the human community and environment, no less than the development of a human being, is a highly controlled series of events. If there is a "natural" order of things we have long ago abandoned it to pursue customs, ambitions, and worlds of our own making. Insofar as we elsewhere presume the workings of the world to be subject to human intervention, there seems to be no logical reason to exclude *human* nature, even human sexual nature from the legitimate domain of intervention. On this view, there would be nothing more unnatural about diverting the sexual destiny of a child than there would be in diverting the course of a river.[23] Unless it can be shown that the order of the world and its essential natures also have moral authority to guide and direct the course of human choices, there seems to be no reason to impute normative authority to the world as we find it. We may find it appropriate to leave certain aspects of the world and human nature untouched, but it is prudence speaking here, not a moral premise that nature must remain forever unreconstructed.

These foregoing considerations suggest that there is no reason in human nature that requires heterosexuality or homosexuality of all persons. Thus parents would seem to be free to choose the kind of sexual orientation their children will have without incurring the wrath of nature. There are, indeed, important reasons for respecting parental choice in this matter.

The Argument from Choice

Moral philosophy generally presumes a rule of noninterference in the lives of adults, this on the assumption that they are individually better situated than religious, political, or other authorities to understand which choices best offer life's rewards. On such a view, parents should be free to choose among possible traits for their children so long as that choice was not the result of incompetence, did not inflict an involuntary harm on a child, or did not corrupt some important social good worth preserving.

This is indeed the strongest argument to be made on behalf of controlling the sexual destiny of children. First, there is no evidence in the preference for heterosexually oriented children that parents suffer from diminished capacity. Surely a parent who wishes to spare his or her child the social disapprobation associated with being a gay man or lesbian cannot be said, on that basis alone, to be suffering from any relevant mental impairment. Such a parent might not even believe homosexuality to be a moral or psychic disorder; it is simply the case, that a parent wishes to spare a child the disvalues associated with homosexuality. Of course, more selfish reasons might obtain if a parent, for example, wished to avoid any stigma of failure attached to having gay children. But by themselves selfish motives are no warrant for inferring any relevant incompetence. Failure of nerve or unmitigated selfishness are not, after all, justification for the inference of psychic incapacity elsewhere, in religion, politics, or the life of the mind.

Secondly, it does not seem that techniques used to ensure heterosexual children involve any involuntary harm against those children. It would be odd to think of heterosexuality as an evil inflicted on a child. A parent might be wrong in thinking that heterosexuality is the only way to happiness, but it is hard to see how an embryo or fetus is harmed by such a choice, particularly since the person it will become neither experiences any loss during the intervention nor suffers any loss or benefit of homosexuality that goes uncompensated in kind. A child, whether homosexual or heterosexual, will still have parallel opportunities for a rewarding life. If the particular measures used to guarantee heterosexuality, moreover, involved selective reproductive techniques, the point becomes even stronger. If one could ensure heterosexual children through the selection and use of certain gametes, it is hard to see that one could say a person is being wronged through the act, for in the manipulation of gametes, there is literally no person there to be harmed! On the contrary, the selection of sexual orientation in a child might even contribute to a number of psychological benefits to the child; if a child knew that it was chosen for its traits it might feel more secure in the relationship with its parents.[24]

Would interventions against homosexual progeny create any indirect harms that would corrupt some social good worth preserving, the loss of which would be a greater danger to human fulfilment than restraints on parental liberty? Presumably the availability of sexual orientation controls would cause a diminution in homosexually identified persons, and such a diminution would likely occur in social classes less economically and otherwise situated to avail themselves of reproductive controls. Homosexuality might thus become a mark of economic and social deprivation. Diminished numbers overall could lead to unhappier lives since, as a vanishing minority, gay men and lesbians might be even less capable of defending themselves against violence and discrimination.

There is no dictate of justice, however, that requires equal numbers of heterosexuals and homosexuals any more than justice requires that there be equal numbers of adults and children or men and women. Nor do diminished numbers necessarily predict the endangerment of gay men and lesbians. One need only think of the minority of persons controlling the nation of South Africa to understand that numerical minority does not *eo ipso* constitute political and social disadvantage. Neither is it inherently unfair that certain people (and thus their children) have advantages of, for example, education and money that others do not; injustice is the consequence of prejudicial obstacles to social and personal advantages, not the consequences of differences in goods per se.

Considerations sometimes raised against the selection of children's sex would be relevant regarding the selection of sexual orientation. One possible danger of reproductive controls of either kind is imputing to children the status of possessions desirable only as they conform to parental expectation. Secondly, an insistence on controlling the kind of children to be born might endanger parental preparedness to accept the children they actually have.[25] The use of reproductive techniques of this kind, moreover, might have the effect of a self-fulfilling prophecy: insofar as these techniques are available it will be thought that they *must* be used and homosexual children who continue to be born will be seen and condemned as failures of medical technique or public policy.[26]

The dangers of endangering the status of children, of making them artifacts subject to parental whims, and of losing certain desirable traits in parents are serious concerns. But it is hard to see that this issue has more force here than it does wherever parents, as they do directly and indirectly, control the kind of persons their children become in the language they learn, the values they appropriate, and the ambitions they express. There is no reason to think that control of sexual orientation would be any more damaging to children or parents than other deeply influential forms of parental influence. Moreover, not even self-fulfilling prophecies always come true. In our own time, the use of abortion to eliminate fetuses with genetic and other defects has not proved incompatible with simultaneous and myriad governmental and private efforts to protect the interests of the handicapped who are in fact not aborted.

Short of actually seeing the consequences of their use, of course, it is impossible to predict the actual outcome of the use of reproductive interventions of the kinds suggested here. It does not follow necessarily that any important social goals, those of tolerance and preservation of parental and child well-being among them, will inevitably be compromised through the use of such interventions. In the absence therefore of any demonstrable incapacity of parent, harms to the child, or corruption of some important social good, it seems that parents ought to be able to select the sexual destiny of children, for reasons both selfish and selfless.

ARGUMENTS AGAINST INTERVENTION

Because of the primacy of respecting individual choice in reproductive decisions, arguments against intervening in the sexual destiny of children bear the burden of proof. They must show a substantive reason why the parental selection of heterosexual children, to the exclusion of homosexual children, is immoral. Although I discuss, as instructive, four kinds of arguments, I think only one meets that burden of proof:

Religious Arguments

Though there have been serious challenges to the legitimacy of its received theological interpretations,[27] the Roman Catholic church has a long history of concern with reproductive issues and homosexual behavior. Current concern on the topics has resulted in two recent documents worth considering as illustrative of the possible significance of religion for reproductive interventions.

According to the 1986 *Letter to the Bishops of the Catholic Church on the Pastoral Care of Homosexual Persons,* although homosexuality as an exclusive sexual orientation is an involuntary condition, it is not an innocent one.[28] The *Letter* claims that while such a condition is not in itself sinful it is still an "objective moral disorder." Homosexual acts, by contrast, are both intrinsically disordered and sinful. This moral analysis is said to be supported by the findings of the natural sciences. The pastoral care of homosexual persons ought to include as far as possible the assistance of the psychological, sociological, and medical sciences. The exact nature of this assistance is not clarified, but as it stands the claim is broad enough to validate medical or psychological programs of eliminating homosexual behavior and desire. Indeed, this was often the thrust of past Catholic advice on the topic: "The aim of all pastoral care of the homosexual should be ultimately his reorientation to heterosexuality," and where this failed, chastity was counseled.[29] Presumably, then, the Catholic church looks favorably on techniques designed to assist individuals in refraining from homosexual acts and in eliminating homoerotic desire. Would this general position legitimize prenatal interventions designed to eliminate homosexuality?

The position of the Catholic church on the use of reproductive controls is adequately assessed by reference to the 1987 *Instruction on Respect for Human Life in Its Origin and on the Dignity of Procreation: Replies to Certain Questions of the Day*.[30] Briefly summarized, the *Instruction* argues that procreation is not solely a human undertaking but involves God's direct intent and will. Sexual relations, furthermore, are licit only between married heterosexuals since the natural meaning of the "conjugal" act implies both unitive and procreative aspects. As unitive, no sexual act is permissible which fails to unite persons in loving intimacy. No sexual act, moreover, which precludes the possibility of conception is morally permissible. It follows that at least the following practices are wrong: masturbation, the use of contraceptives and abortifacients, IVF, ET, AI, cloning, twin fission, and any prenatal diagnosis undertaken with an eye to abortion on the basis of undesirable test results.

It follows deductively, therefore, that any attempt to eliminate homoeroticism in children would be morally forbidden under Catholic morality if it involved the use of any of the above techniques. Even if there were a measure *certain* to eliminate homosexual desire in progeny, a goal compatible with the language of the *Letter*, if that measure involved any of the foregoing reproductive techniques it would have to be rejected as immoral. If, however, other techniques such as hormonal monitoring and adjustment during fetal development were available which could eliminate homosexuality, these, on first sight, might prove to be morally permissible. Flushing a fetus with hormones at a particular developmental point, after all, violates no reproductive constraint. But there are other considerations which muddy the water here.

The *Instruction* says that "Certain attempts to influence chromosomic or genetic inheritance are not therapeutic but are aimed at producing human beings selected according to sex or other predetermined qualities. These manipulations are contrary to the personal dignity of the human being and his or her integrity and dignity." Clearly, the *Instruction* rejects nontherapeutic genetic interventions. What, then, if homosexuality were a genetically determined trait? If homosexuality were defined as a pathology, the attempt to eliminate it would be nonproblematic because merely a matter of controlling the expression of disease. However, the language of the *Letter* does not invoke, directly, the notion of disease; indeed, the *Letter* is altogether silent on the origin of homosexuality. If, therefore, homosexuality is not a disease and is properly speaking a moral problem, it would not seem to be the fit object of medical intervention. One does not, after all, seek medical solutions to the problems of divorce or infidelity.

Secondly, if God does control the reproductive order and does have reasons for persons being the persons they are, one wonders whether homosexuality isn't an integral part of his intentions. Perhaps God intends that certain persons carry the burden of homosexuality, that they find their way to salvation precisely through the trials associated with homosexuality. One Catholic moralist has said that it sometimes happens that once the gravity of this deviation, this love condemned, hopeless, and tragic in its essence is recognized, and once an individual has accepted the painful, endless struggle that is his lot, this anomaly can become the occasion of a very exalted spiritual life.[31] It is certainly possible, therefore, that God intends certain persons to be homoerotically inclined as a condition of their particular pathway to salvation. If this is true, then it seems a prima facie wrong to interfere with the homosexuality of children.

One may conclude that the Catholic church must reject any reproductive measure designed to eliminate homosexuality insofar as that measure usurps the will of God or ruptures the natural meaning of procreative acts. What is more, the church rejects eugenic interventions elsewhere which would conform children to parental or social expectation, even where disability and difference cause suffering to both parent and child, this because it views suffering as *integral* to the Christian vocation. Carrying the cross, the *Letter* says, "is the way to eternal life for *all* who follow Christ."[32] Consequently, it seems unlikely that a rationale, based on relief from suffering, for the elimination of homosexuality would be found convincing by the church. It is even possible that homosexuality has for some persons the status of a charism and on that account should be immune to intervention, which may be nothing more, in the end, than preferring one immorality to another.

The success of the foregoing arguments, of course, depends on the extent to which one credits their underlying religious assumptions. A purely philosophical analysis puts divine intentions aside as outside the realm of common moral consensus. Once the existence of God or his sole authority over the course of human destiny is thus bracketed as irrelevant to a strictly philosophical determination, the religious arguments against the use of these reproductive techniques must likewise be bracketed. Even if the religious assumptions are true, therefore, they may be set aside as irrelevant to the formulation of a purely moral judgment because they presuppose access to truth denied to rational agents acting in intellectual good faith.[33] Consequently, while the Roman Catholic case against reproductive interventions is a potentially telling one, it may be set aside as unconvincing in any philosophical sense. Its obligations would be binding only on those affirming its religious preconditions. At the very least, religious believers bear the burden of proof in showing why religious constraints ought to be respected by persons who do not, for defensible reasons, share the same views.

Objections to Abortion and Infanticide

It may be that future reproductive interventions cannot guarantee heterosexual progeny except by identifying homosexually destined progeny and subjecting them to abortion or infanticide. The debate over abortion and infanticide is long and acrimonious, and I do not intend to review its history here. It is enough to point out that if practices of voluntary abortion and infanticide are wrong, on whatever moral grounds, then *a fortiori* it would be wrong to use them to control sexual destiny. If, by contrast, abortion and infanticide are matters of moral indifference, on whatever moral grounds, then their use for the same purpose is entirely nonproblematic.

Of course, there are positions which maintain that while abortion and infanticide are ordinarily wrong, they may be practiced under certain circumstances. Such views typically maintain that the biological or social fate of a child is relevant to the morality of abortion and infanticide. On such interpretations if a fetus is grossly impaired, if a child faces a life of utter deprivation, or a pregnancy is a threat to the health or life of a woman, it may be permissible to kill or let die when such actions would be otherwise immoral. Such arguments, stipulating adverse circumstances as legitimations of certain abortion and infanticide would not, however, also justify their use against homosexually destined progeny.

I have stipulated above that homoerotic orientation is no disease or inherent impediment to happiness. The life of a homosexual child may be filled with certain obstacles but it is certainly no life of utter deprivation; there is considerable evidence to the contrary. Its social fate is likewise not one destined automatically to suffering. And certainly a fetus or newborn is no threat to the life of its mother merely because of its eventual sexual orientation. And there is no evidence either that the psychological health of women is endangered in consequence of bearing gay and lesbian children. Consequently, a homosexual destiny would seem disanalogous to those damages that are usually invoked as rationales for selective abortion and infanticide. This conclusion, of course, presupposes that there are legitimate shields against abortion and infanticide. Whether or not there are such shields is a matter of continuing debate, and this conclusion is tied to the success of certain arguments in that debate. I will not pursue these arguments because I think there is one other argument which can establish the immorality of eliminating homosexual progeny.

Heterosexism

The most convincing reason for asserting the immorality of practices designed to eliminate homosexual progeny, whatever means would be involved, is that such actions may be heterosexist. The attempt to understand why a parent would wish to protect a child from his or her own homosexuality is a problem to be seen as the issue of heterosexist society. To examine heterosexism is to give a theoretical account of why it is wrong to commit acts prejudicial to the fate of gay men and lesbians.

Heterosexism may be defined as the doctrine that asserts the natural, moral, and religious superiority of heterosexuality. It is a doctrine that thereby justifies strategies of prevention, exclusion, and other means of discriminating against homosexuality. Such a doctrine is, I believe, intellectually indefensible in its premises and morally wrong in its consequences, as is any other antagonistic prejudice against a sexual or racial class. Heterosexist acts are wrong in the same way that racist acts are wrong. Racist acts are not wrong only because they deny a particular man or woman access to a particular service or job and thereby inflict on that person suffering and distress. Individual sufferings and individual hardships suffered at the hands of racists are surely relevant considerations about the evils of racism, but in the main racist acts are wrong because they, for unfounded reasons, make indefensible, presumptive conclusions about the relative worthlessness of persons on the basis of morally irrelevant characteristics. Like racism, heterosexism is wrong because it supposes that gay men and lesbians suffer a metaphysical impoverishment of life[34] and that therefore prejudicial acts may be undertaken against them.[35]

Racism is untenable because there is no evidence that any single race is alone the guarantor of all that is good and noble in the history of the planet. Heterosexism is similarly unable to show that heterosexuality is alone the pathway to human achievement or that homosexuality is inherently undesirable. There is, for example, no evidence that homosexuality is either the cause or consequence of psychic or biological dysfunction.[36] The Bell and Weinberg study makes it clear that homosexuality is no intrinsic obstacle to achieving important human goals. Reported disadvantages in homoerotic orientation and behavior, as that study makes clear, are largely artifactual, products of particular social constructions, and are therefore eliminable in principle. Some societies, after all, have quite happily integrated homosexual practices into their social lives.[37]

It is unlikely either that heterosexuality could be shown to be inherently desirable; it is notoriously difficult to compare pleasures or sorrows. The difficulties that have always attended utilitarian ethical theory beset the undertaking here: how is it possible to demonstrate that the joys of heterosexuality are inherently superior to the joys of homoeroticism, or its sorrows less agonizing? We may be asking, after all, how to demonstrate that the joys of a warm, sunny summer day at the beach are inherently superior to the joys of a cold, gray winter day at the ski slopes. At the impasse of incomparable pleasures and rewards, the alleged superiority of heterosexuality must remain indemonstrable.

In nonracist society, no advantage accrues to a particular skin color; skin color is neither automatic privilege nor inevitable handicap. In nonheterosexist society, no advantage would accrue to a particular sexual orientation. But there are many advantages attached by society to heterosexuality that are denied homosexuality. As these privileges and advantages are the consequence of social choices, and not just accidents of fate, they should be understood as serving moral ends compatible with heterosexism. These presumptions and privileges, as culturally supported and sustained, should be understood as the "first cause" of the preference of heterosexuality and the "first cause" of antagonism against homosexuality. As racist acts are wrong for the victims they take and the symbolic malevolence they presuppose, so I believe that heterosexism is wrong. Heterosexism should be resisted as racism should be resisted, from which conclusion it follows that the use of reproductive interventions for heterosexist ends is immoral.

HOW WRONG A WRONG?

Not all wrongs are of equal evil and do not equally deserve the sanctions of law. Is heterosexist preferment of heterosexual children a wrong that ought to be sanctioned by criminal or civil statute? It has already been argued that children selected for heterosexual orientation would not be themselves wronged; their being deprived of a homosexual orientation deprives them of no reward unprecedented in kind in heterosexual life. It has also been argued that selecting homosexual children, even where this was done widely, would not necessarily lead to loss of desirable traits in parents. The most that might be said here is that parents might lose the rewards of having homosexual children. For children and their parents therefore there seems to be little harm that the law would have an interest in controlling.

Would selecting against homosexual progeny harm future generations in such a way as to justify legal bans? As future generations do not yet exist we cannot directly harm them, and the wrongs we commit against them are indirect. For example, by bequeathing to them a lethally toxic or irradiated planet, we might cause them to lead lives less safe and healthy than ours. But it is hard to see that we are obliged to deliver a specific kind of future to generations that follow or that we must cause only certain kinds of persons to come into being. It is, moreover, difficult to see why the choices of actual people should be restricted in favor of those who do not yet exist. It may be wise and generous to prepare a particular kind of world for future generations, just as it is wise and important to reverence certain aspects of past generations, but it seems impossible to owe anything to people who do not and may never exist. Insofar then as future generations have no authority on which to make claims about the kind of world they receive, the kind of persons they are, legal bans against reproductive controls here would not be justified by an appeal to future harms that might befall them.

The point has been made earlier that controls of sexual orientation would not necessarily endanger the social status of gay people, but is it not true nevertheless that the use of these controls should be banned because of what they mean for existing gay people? Selecting against gay children, after all, certainly implies the worthlessness of homosexuality and is therefore insulting to gay people as a degradation of their dignity. Is this symbolic malevolence justification enough for legal bans?

The moral toleration of competing religions is instructive here. Free society requires that we endure certain beliefs and practices which we find false and odious, this in the name of protecting the multiplicity of ways in which human beings express meaningful lives and in the name of preserving the benefits of intellectual liberty. Religious toleration is also defensible because of the indemonstrability of the "truths" of any single religion. In free society, if a religious or sexual view is offensive, we may offer our arguments and suasions against it, but it would be a mistake to invite the law to enforce religious beliefs and practices, even where this means we must permit beliefs and some practices that are wholly objectionable. Similarly, because there fails to be one demonstrably desirable sexuality and because it is important to preserve the many pathways to human achievement, even if it is distasteful to some that such controls are used, nevertheless they should not be legally barred. While some heterosexist acts certainly are candidates for criminal sanctions, like those which inflict hate-motivated violence on actual persons, like many religious "evils," certain heterosexist wrongs are better redressed through education and suasion. As free society tolerates its religious believers' freedom in belief and practice so too must a free society also tolerate certain heterosexist choices, this in the name of preserving the centrality of personal moral responsibility. Though it is wrong to act prejudicially against homosexual progeny, therefore, it would be a greater wrong to usurp by law the choices of competent adults, a law which in any case could be evaded.

THE OTHER SIDE

Gillian Hanscombe has claimed that there are over two million lesbian mothers in the United States, a figure for which she offers no justification.[38] While Bell and Weinberg report a number of their homosexual subjects with children (from nine to thirty-three percent)[39] the exact number of lesbian mothers and gay fathers is unknown and perhaps unknowable. Though not in the numbers that heterosexuals do, it is clear that self-identified gay men and lesbians *do* engender children. Given the high percentages of respondents that were not unhappy with their lot, given that some gay men and lesbians have children, could one also expect that at least some parents would take measures to ensure having *homosexual* children? Just as there might be selective and developmental measures taken to insure heterosexual progeny, clinics offering promises of homosexual children might themselves find a thriving market and offset the loss of homosexual children elsewhere.

Even if highly effective measures for eliminating homosexual children were available, furthermore, it does not follow that the population of gay men and lesbians would necessarily diminish. The availability of effective prophylactic measures is always subject to constraints of class, economics, geography, and religion. If the techniques were, for example, expensive, they would be beyond the reach of low-income populations. If the techniques were not expensive, they might be ignored by persons who saw them as religious violations or those who did not care about their child's sexual destiny but wanted only a healthy baby. If the techniques were sufficiently complex as to require being conducted out of a major medical facility (such as *in vitro* fertilization and embryo transfer are), then individuals in outlying regions might find them beyond their geographic reach. Or if the techniques were dangerous, they might not be carried out in women with a history of spontaneous abortion or where they might endanger women's lives. It is important to keep in mind, too, that no procedure is without its errors of application. Even if control measures were universally enforced, because of faulty technique there would still continue to be homosexual progeny. And if psychical theories of homosexual development are correct there might also be other continuing causes of homoerotic inclinations. Therefore, though successful control measures of a selective or developmental kind might be developed, it is likely that there will continue to be homoerotically inclined progeny and this as the result of both accident and choice.

CONCLUSIONS

These are wearisome times for gay people. The United States Supreme Court has held that if they so choose, states may criminalize private homosexual behavior even among consenting adults. Some Australian states continue to have and enforce such laws. Britain has passed Clause 28, a law which forbids local governments from funding any activity which could be construed as promoting homosexuality. In the United States, legislation has been introduced at the federal level that would prohibit several government agencies from funding, among other things, any promotion, dissemination, or production of homoerotic projects.[40] HIV-related disease, furthermore, continues to be a risk of certain homosexual behavior, and many persons perceived to be gay continue to be the targets of violence and discrimination.

Given the adversities and disvalues that attend homosexuality, were techniques insuring heterosexual progeny to become available, it would be little surprising that some parents might be inclined to use them. But there is little morally defensible rationale for doing so. In the absence of any convincing evidence that homoeroticism is the result or cause of psychic or biological impairment, their use cannot be justified as a means of eliminating mental disease or disorder. Religious arguments invoking the will of God or a theological tradition fail as a general rationale because they presuppose evidence beyond the domain of purely philosophical purview. It is not obvious either that nature requires all eroticism to be heterosexual in kind. Arguments that would appeal to adverse fates of children as justifications for the use of such measures as abortion and infanticide as a means of eliminating homosexual children do not succeed either, because homoeroticism is disanalogous to the adversities which legitimate those practices.

The strongest argument for the use of reproductive controls follows from respect for parental choice. Given that the use of these controls is not the consequence of diminished capacity, involves no direct harm to others, and that it does not obviously compromise important social goods, it seems to follow that parents ought to be free to elect the sexual destiny of their children. Yet even here the choices of parents may be the consequences of heterosexism. Heterosexist reproductive interventions should be resisted as immoral because the doctrine claiming the moral superiority of heterosexuality is indefensible and invites damaging consequences. Because, however, the wrong of heterosexist reproductive interventions is not one that inflicts necessary harm on any person or society and because it is important to preserve the reproductive freedom of adults, it is not one that should be legally sanctioned.[41] Neither should the practice be banned because it is insulting or demeaning to some. Insults against dignity, when they are acts of free speech or acts of reproductive control, are not the kinds of things governments ought to be invited to control. This is not to say that it is not urgent to resist heterosexism for the victims it takes and the evil it presupposes. It is only to say that some wrongs are better redressed through the counsel of education and suasion than through involuntary enforcement.

NOTES

1. P. Ramsey, *Fabricated Man* (New Haven: Yale University Press, 1970), p. 25.

2. See S. Elias and G. J. Annas, *Reproductive Genetics and the Law* (Chicago: Year Book Medical Publishers, 1987).

3. G. Dörner, *Hormones and Brain Differentiation* (Amsterdam: Elsevier, 1976), p. 138. See also N. K. Gartrell, "Hormones and Homosexuality," in W. Paul, J. D. Weinrich, J. C. Gionsiorek, M. E. Hotvedt, eds., *Homosexuality, Social, Psychological and Biological Issues* (Beverly Hills: Sage, 1982), pp. 169–82.

4. P. 228.

5. L. Murray, "Sexual Destinies, the Biology of Homosexuality," *Omni* 9 (1975): 100–28.

6. I modify the categories of F. Suppe, "Curing Homosexuality," in R. Baker and F. Elliston, eds., *Philosophy and Sex*, 2nd ed. (Buffalo: Prometheus, 1984), pp. 391–420.

7. A. P. Bell and M. S. Weinberg, *Homosexualities* (New York: Simon & Schuster, 1978).

8. Ibid., p. 337. This included 73% of 575 white homosexual males (WHMs), 80% of 111 black homosexual males (BHMs), 84% of 229 white homosexual females (WHFs), and 90% of 64 black homosexual females (BHFs). A distinct minority reported a great deal of regret regarding their homosexuality: 6% of WHMs, 3% of BHMs, 2% of WHFs, and 0% BHFs.

9. Ibid., p. 339: 27% of 573 WHMs, 27% of 111 BHMs, 23% of 225 WHFs, and 21% of 64 BHFs.

10. Ibid., p. 361: 28% of WHMs, 12% of BHMs, 16% of WHFs, and 6% of BHFs.

11. Ibid., p. 362: 21% of 214 WHMs, 7% of 29 BHMs, 29% of 52 WHFs, and 14% of 7 BHFs.

12. Ibid., p. 339: 72% of 569 WHMs, 76% of 109 BHMs, 84% of 228 WHFs, and 89% of 63 BHFs.

13. Ibid., p. 339: 86% of 547 WHMs, 87% of 109 BHMs, 95% of 229 WHFs, and 94% of 64 BHFs.

14. Ibid., p. 339. The overall distribution of responses is as follows.

	570 WHMs	111 BHMs	226 WHFs	64 BHFs
Not at all	51%	56%	49%	52%
Very little	25	17	20	25
Some	18	18	24	18
Much	7	8	9	9

15. Ibid., p. 337.

16. A. P. Bell, M. Weinberg, and S. Kiefer Hammersmith, *Sexual Preference, Its Development in Men and Women* (Bloomington: Indiana University Press, 1981), 183–84.

17. Ibid., p. 216.

18. B. Gladue, R. Green, R. Hellman, "Neuroendocrine Response to Estrogen and Sexual Orientation," *Science* 225 (1984): 1496–99.

19. I. Bieber, H. J. Dain, P. R. Dince, M. G. Drellich, H. G. Grand, R. H. Bundlach,

M. W. Kremer, A. H. Rifkin, C. B. Wilbert, T. B. Bieber, *Homosexuality: A Psychoanalytic Study* (New York: Basic Books, 1962).

20. C. Socarides, *Homosexuality* (New York: Jason Aronson, 1978).

21. Cf. R. Green, "Homosexuality As Mental Illness," in A. Caplan, H. T. Engelhardt, J. McCartney, eds., *Concepts of Health and Disease* (Reading, MA: Addison-Wesley, 1981), pp. 333–51.

22. I understand this to be Freud's view. See T. F. Murphy, "Freud Reconsidered: Bisexuality, Homosexuality and Moral Judgement," in J. P. DeCecco and M. G. Shiveley, eds., *Bisexual and Homosexual Identities: Critical Theoretical Issues* (New York: Haworth Press, 1984), pp. 65–77.

23. See T. F. Murphy, "Homosexuality and Nature: Happiness and the Law at Stake," *Journal of Applied Philosophy* 4 (1987): 195–204.

24. This point has been made in regard to gender selection by B. B. Hoskins and H. B. Holmes, "Technology and Prenatal Femicide," in R. Arditti, R. D. Klein, and S. Minden, eds., *Test-tube Women* (London: Pandora Press, 1984), pp. 237–55.

25. See President's Commission for the Study of Ethical Problems in Medicine and Biomedical and Behavioral Research, *Screening and Counseling for Genetic Conditions* (Washington: Government Printing Office, 1983).

26. M. P. Golding, "Ethical Issues in Biological Engineering," in R. Munson, ed., *Intervention and Reflection*, 2nd ed. (Belmont, CA: Wadsworth, 1983), pp. 402–14.

27. John Boswell has offered a damning critique of the received wisdom on Christian interpretations of homosexuality. See *Christianity, Social Tolerance, and Homosexuality* (Chicago: University of Chicago Press, 1980), especially pp. 91–117.

28. Congregation for the Doctrine of the Faith, *Letter to the Bishops of the Catholic Church on the Pastoral Care of Homosexual Persons* (Washington: United States Catholic Conference, 1986).

29. M. J. Buckley, *Morality and the Homosexual* (Westminster, MD: New Press, 1959), p. 184.

30. Congregation for the Doctrine of the Faith, *Instruction on Respect for Human Life in Its Origin and on the Dignity of Procreation: Replies to Certain Questions of the Day*, in R. Munson, ed., *Intervention and Reflection*, 3rd ed. (Belmont, CA: Wadsworth, 1988), pp. 450–68.

31. Charles Larère, "Passage of the Angel through Sodom," in P. Flood, ed., *New Problems in Medical Ethics* (Cork: Mercier Press, 1953), pp. 108–23.

32. P. 9.

33. H. T. Engelhardt, *The Foundations of Bioethics* (New York: Oxford University Press, 1986), pp. 11–14, 24 ff.

34. For an argument that homosexuality is necessarily an impoverishment of human life see M. Levin, "Why Homosexuality is Abnormal," *Monist* (Spring 1985): 251–83.

35. See R. D. Mohr, *Gays/Justice, a Study of Ethics, Society and Law* (New York: Columbia University Press, 1988).

36. See Suppe.

37. G. Herdt, *Guardians of the Flute: Idioms of Masculinity* (New York: McGraw Hill, 1981).

38. G. Hanscombe, "The Right to Lesbian Parenthood," *Journal of Medical Ethics* 9 (1983): 133–35.

39. P. 391. 116 WHMs, 14 BHMs, 80 WHFs, and 30 BHFs report having at least one child. By my computation, this means that roughly 1 out of 10 WHMs, 1 out of 11 BHMs, 1 out of 6 WHFs, and 1 out of 3 BHFs in the study had at least one child.

40. " 'Obscenity' measure could bar U.S. aid to humanities groups," *Chronicle of Higher Education* 35 (1989): 1.

41. In this, my view on the evil of using reproductive controls out of morally suspect motives, and on the need for refraining from enforcing moral views on adults against their will, is similar to the conclusion reached by Mary Anne Warren in *Gendercide, the Implications of Sex Selection* (Totowa, NJ: Rowman and Allanheld, 1985).

PART V: (VIRTUAL?) GENDER

From Computer Culture to Cyberspace

The computer revolution which ushered in the information age could no more avoid affecting and being affected by practices and ideologies of gender than any other technological development. The essays collected here explore two ways that computers and gender interrelate. First, there is the question of why computers are associated more often with men than with women. What are the relevant cultural, educational, and psychological differences in men's and women's interaction with computers that might account for this gendered division of computer use? Second, there is the question of computer-generated worlds in which we exist mainly through text or icons. Since our bodily sex is neither obvious nor present in these worlds, how does gender make itself known and how do the social implications of gender play out? Since we exist in these worlds only as personalities, are there still relevant truths of gender?

Sherry Turkle's essay begins by asking why women tend to be more reluctant to immerse themselves in computer use than men—a phenomenon that some have termed women's "computerphobia." Turkle argues that this tendency is not "phobia" but "reticence," a condition she describes as resistance to becoming emotionally and socially involved with computers. Unlike some men (and particularly male hackers), most women do not like anthropomorphizing machines. They do not like to think of having a relationship with their computer, or thinking of the computer as alive or intelligent or able to learn. Whereas hackers are able to throw themselves into their computer work and "love the machine," women are more likely to recoil from such identifications and make sharp distinctions between humans and computers (defining themselves in terms of what computers are not—emotional, thoughtful, social, etc.). Turkle's essay leads us to examine issues of the difference between humans and machines, the possibility of emotional and intellectual relationships with machines, and the value of masculine "risk-taking" behavior in figuring out how to make computers work.

If computer use differs for men and women, computer education shows a similar disparity. Bente Rasmussen and Tove Håpnes ask why there is such a dearth of female computer majors and professors, even when the profession both wants and needs women. They locate the reason for the disproportionate absence of women in computer science programs in the gendered culture of computer science. Studying students in a major technical university, Håpnes and Rasmussen find that the people in the computer science program are broken up—by their own perceptions—into five cultural groups, each having their own character. Female students tend to form their own cultural group, held together by an aversion to the notion of having an intimate relationship to computers—an aversion male hackers do not share. Seeking to change the culture of computer education to be more open to women, Håpnes and Rasmussen (like Turkle) generate questions about why male and female students tend to respond so differently to the perceived boundary between humans and machines.

Sherry Turkle continues her groundbreaking work on the culture and psychology of computer use by exploring the complexities of gender and identity in virtual worlds. Drawing on interviews and her own experiences in computer-generated worlds, she examines the common phenomenon of "gender-swapping." People who gender-swap online often find themselves treated differently based on what gender they project and also find that their own personalities and communication styles change to fit the social constraints of their character. Some women with male-presenting characters find themselves taken more seriously or find that what counts as being rude for women only counts as being honest and straightforward for men. Men with female-presenting characters can find themselves able to be more cooperative or to have more emotionally in-depth conversations, or may find that what counts as being obnoxious for a man only counts as "modern and together" for a woman. People online also sometimes engage in textual sex, with their characters presenting whatever gender they wish. Turkle draws out the complications for identity of this kind of behavior—asking what it means for our ideas of sexual orientation, concepts of adultery, standards of deception, and the status of gender itself.

Allucquère Rosanne Stone also discusses the complexities of gender, sexual identity, and truth on the Internet and its many role-playing environments. In particular, she examines a famous case of contested identities that began with a male psychiatrist being taken for a female psychiatrist while online. Amazed at the differences between women's conversational styles and men's, the male psychiatrist decided he could best help people when perceived as a woman because then they were more likely to be open and vulnerable. He went online again and generated a new female character named Julie with an elaborate history, including an accident that had left her mute, paralyzed, and disfigured so that she never left her apartment. Once online, Julie became a socially flamboyant personality and a supportive friend to scores of people. She started a women's discussion group. She helped women who were depressed, suicidal, chemically dependent, and lonely. Eventually, however, the male psychiatrist behind the personality of Julie became overwhelmed and decided to reveal the story of Julie's creation. The information spread fast, and soon people were responding to the news that Julie did not "really" exist. But there is the question. Did Julie really exist? Wasn't she as real as any other personality on the net? Wasn't losing her as a friend an actual loss? In a world where anatomy has less to do with personal identity than the ability to use language, what counts as being a "real" person? And what does this story tell us about the moral cliche that "it's what's on the inside that really counts, not the outside"? [Bibliographic references to this chapter have not been reprinted in this collection but may be found in the author's book.]

CHAPTER 21

COMPUTATIONAL RETICENCE

Why Women Fear the Intimate Machine

SHERRY TURKLE

(1988)

> "I wanted to work in worlds where languages had moods and con-
> nected you with people."
>
> —A young woman talking about mathematics and computers

The computer has no inherent gender bias. But the computer culture is not
equally neutral. This essay looks at the social construction of the computer as
a male domain through the eyes of women who have come to see something
important about themselves in terms of what computers are not.

There is much talk about women and "computerphobia." My research
suggests that women's phobic reactions to the machine are a transitional phenomenon. There is the legacy of women's traditional socialization into relationships with technical objects, for many of them best summed up by the
admonishment, "Don't touch it, you'll get a shock." There is the legacy of a
computer culture that has traditionally been dominated by images of competition, sports and violence. There are still computer operating systems that
communicate to their users in terms of "killing" and "aborting" programs.
These are things that have kept women fearful and far away from the machine. But these are things that are subject to change. More persistent are
reactions that touch another and deeper set of issues. I believe that the issue
for the future is not computerphobia, needing to stay away because of fear
and panic, but rather computer reticence, wanting to stay away because the
computer becomes a personal and cultural symbol of what a woman is not.

Since 1976 I have been involved in studies of computers and people using
a methodology both ethnographic and clinical. My concern has been with the
detail of people's relationships with computers and with the social worlds that
grow up around them. In order to best make the distinction between phobia
and reticence I will take my examples from interviews with women who are
involved with computers, women who do not fear them but who take their
distance in a way that inhibits their creativity, and that ultimately will impover-
ish the computer culture as well. In particular, I draw my examples from a
study of twenty-five Harvard and MIT women taking and succeeding in computer programming courses. And I focus on one woman, who here I call Lisa,

who speaks in a particularly clear voice to a set of widely shared concerns. The central issue for these competent and talented women is not phobia or lack of ability, but a reticence to become more deeply involved with an object experienced as threatening.

REJECTING THE INTIMATE MACHINE

Lisa is eighteen, a first-year student at Harvard, and surprised to find herself an excellent computer programmer. Not only is it surprising, but "kind of scary." Most "scary" is protecting her involvement with computers from the idea of seeing herself "as a computer science type."

> "You know, the typical stereotype; I had a home room in high school that just happened to be the math lab and there were these little kids who walked around with pants that were too short and they had little calculators with all these fancy functions and they wore them on their belt and they played chess incessantly and talked about their gambits and the things they were doing in their advanced calculus courses and all the great hacks they were doing on the computer; and they were always working with their machines. I was contemptuous of them. They stayed away from other people. They took the computers and made a world apart."

Women look at computers and see more than machines. They see the culture that has grown up around them and they ask themselves if they belong. And when, in high school and college, they look at the social world of the computer expert, they see something that seems alien. At the extreme, they see the social world of the "hacker," a culture of computer virtuosos. It is a world, predominantly male, that takes the machine as a partner in an intimate relationship.

The computer is a medium that supports a powerful sense of mastery. As people develop their mastery of things and their relational skills with people, most strike a balance. They balance the need for mastery of skills and concrete materials with the desire to do things with people where the results are never as clear. For some people, striking this balance becomes a difficult struggle. Relationships with people are always characterized by ambiguity, sexual tension, the possibilities for closeness and dependency. If these are felt as too threatening, the world of things and the world of formal systems becomes increasingly seductive. They turn to formal systems in engineering, in chess, in mathematics, in science. They turn to them for their reassurance, for the pleasures of working in a microworld where things are certain and "things never change unless you want them to." In other words, part of the reason formal systems are appealing is because they provide protective worlds.

Pride in mastery is a positive thing. But if the sense of self becomes defined in terms of those things over which one can exert perfect control, the world of safe things becomes severely limited—because those things tend to be things, not people. Mastery of technology and formal systems can become a way of masking fears about the self and the complexities of the world beyond.

This pattern of using formal microworlds as protective worlds existed long before computers were dreamed of. But the computer offers some new possibilities. The computer offers its users a formal system, but it is also active and interactive. It is easily anthropomorphized. Its experts do not think that it is "alive." But it is a medium onto which lifelike properties can be easily projected. It supports the fantasy "that there is somebody home." It is, of course, only a machine, but because of its psychological properties it supports an experience with it as an "intimate machine."

When people fear intimacy, they are drawn to materials that offer some promise, if not for a resolution of their conflict between loneliness and fear of intimacy, then at least for some compromise. The computer offers this promise. It offers the promise of perfect mastery. And in its activity and interactivity, it offers the illusion of companionship without the demands of friendship (Turkle 1984).

Computers become particularly seductive at a certain moment in psychological development: the moment of adolescence. There are new sexual pressures and new social demands. The safe microworlds the child has built—the microworlds of sports, chess, cars, literature, music, dance, or mathematical expertise—can become places of escape. Most children use these havens as safe platforms from which to test the difficult waters of adolescence. They move but at their own pace. But for some, the issues that arise during adolescence are so threatening that the safe place seems like the only place. They come to define themselves in terms of competence, skill, in terms of the things they can control. It is during adolescence that the "hacker culture" becomes born in elementary schools and junior high schools as predominantly male—because, in our society, men are more likely than women to master anxieties about people by turning to the world of things and formal systems.

In high school, Lisa saw young men around her turning to mathematics as a way to avoid people, and describes herself as "turning off" her natural abilities in mathematics. "I didn't care if I was good at it. I wanted to work in worlds where languages had moods and connected you with people." And she saw some of these young men turning to computers as "imaginary friends." She decided to avoid them as well. "I didn't want an imaginary friend in a machine. If I was going to be alone, if I needed to withdraw, well, then I wanted to read, to learn about human psychology by reading about it, if I didn't always have the courage to learn about other people by being with them."

The computer is rejected as a partner in a "close encounter." When women are introduced to it in cultural contexts where the most successful users seem to "love the machine for itself," they define themselves as relational women in terms of what the "serious" computer users are not. Although hackers are a small part of the general population, the culture of young male programming virtuosos tends to dominate the computer cultures of educational institutions from elementary schools to universities. Hackers are not great in their numbers, but they are visible, dedicated, and expert (Kiesler et al. 1984, 1985; Turkle 1984).

THE NEGATIVE IMAGE OF THE HACKER

The hacker's relationship with computers is often characterized by a violent form of risk taking. This violence is not physical, rather it is psychological: there is intensity, turbulence, aggression. There are the pleasures of flirting with destruction. The hacker at his computer constantly walks a narrow line between "winning" and "losing." Hackers talk about complex computer systems as places where you can let things get more and more complicated, until you are on the edge of being out of control, but where the pleasure is in the challenge of being able to pull them back.

Joe is twenty-three. He has dropped out of a computer science degree program in order to devote himself more fully to MIT computers. He contrasts his love for the violin ("it can only do so much and your fingers can only do so much") with the limitless possibilities of the computer.

> "With programming, whatever you think of—and you are always thinking of something—it can be immediately translated into a challenge. That same night. You can set yourself up to do it some really esoteric, unusual way. And you can make a deal with yourself that you won't be satisfied, that you won't eat or go out or do anything until you get it right. And then you can just do it. It's like a fix. I couldn't get that kind of fix with the violin. I could be obsessed, but I couldn't get the high."

With the computer as your medium there is no limit to how much you can flirt with losing in your pursuit of winning. There is no limit to the violence of the test. The computer becomes a medium for playing with the issue of control by living on the narrow line between having it and losing it. MIT hackers call this "sport death"—pushing mind and body beyond their limits, punishing the body until it can barely support mind and then demanding more of the mind than you believe it could possibly deliver.

Anthony, twenty years old, an MIT senior, is a computer hacker who is very aware of the pleasures of sport death and its lack of appeal for women.

> "Computer hacking is kind of masochistic. You see how far you can push your mind and body. . . . Women tend to be less self-destructive—hackers are somewhat self-destructive. They don't take care of their bodies and are in general, flunking out. Burnout is common. Women are not so into sport death; they are more balanced in their priorities. The essence of sport death is to see how far you can push things, to see how much you can get away with. I generally wait until I have to put in my maximum effort and then just totally burn out."

There are very few women hackers. Though hackers would deny that theirs is a macho culture, their preoccupation with "winning" and with subjecting oneself to increasingly violent tests makes their world peculiarly male in spirit. There is, too, a flight from relationship with people to relationship to the machine—a defensive maneuver more common to men than to women.

The hacker's relationship with the computer is filled with technical risks, but it gets much of its emotional charge because it offers respite from personal ones. Hackers talk a lot about "getting burned." Because if you are primarily motivated by a need to feel in control, "getting burned" is one of the worst things that can happen to you.

Anthony has "tried out" having girlfriends:

> "I used to get into relationships that usually led to me getting burned in some way. . . . With computers you have confidence in yourself and that is enough. With social interactions you have to have confidence that the rest of the world will be nice to you. You can't control how the rest of the world is going to react to you. But with computers you are in complete control."

Sex and romance are desirable, but they are risky. "Sport death" is risky too, but it is a special kind of risk where you assume all the risk yourself and are the only one responsible for saving the day. It is safe risk. Anthony sees sex and romance as another, more disturbing kind: "Hacking is safe in that you are in complete control of your computer world, and sex and relationships are risky in that the rest of the world has control."

Anthony compares human relationships to the sense of accomplishment and control that he can get from a machine. This does not mean that he sees machines as a "substitute" for women. But he is not sure that he can function in the worlds where you can get burned.

The men in the hacker culture see it as incompatible with a life with women. "Computer hacking is almost pure pleasure with very little risk. But it is not as fulfilling as romance because in the end you have just made a few lights blink. But you only have so much energy. You can either spend it on computers or you can spend it on people." The women who watch these men observe their obsessions, observe their antisensuality, observe the ways in which they have put things rather than people at the center of their lives and count themselves out. This does not mean that these women are not computer-competent. But along with their competence comes a fear of the machine as a potentially destructive force.

Robin is a sophomore at Harvard, a musician who has gone through much of her life practicing the piano eight hours a day. But she rebels against the idea of a relationship with the computer. She doesn't want to belong to a world where things are more important than people.

> "I saw people being really compulsive but really enjoying it. I saw that these guys sort of related to their terminals the way I relate to the piano and I thought, maybe I can do that too. I saw all these people running around with the same intensity as I have with the piano and they tell me that I'll probably be good at computers. These are the guys who are helping me do this course. And they keep telling me, yes, you're going to be real good at it. Don't worry

about it, but you're going about it in the wrong way. They tell me I'm 'not establishing a relationship with the computer.' And to me that sounds gross. It is gross to me, the way these guys are. I don't like establishing relationships with machines. I don't like putting it that way. Relationships are for people."

I ask Robin to talk to me about her relationship with her piano, a machine, but she insists that it was a completely different thing. The piano took her away from people, but then it brought her closer to them. The involvements of her male peers with the computer only shut people out. "These guys are incredibly drained. You can't talk to them. I don't want to be part of their world."

"I know this guy, this computer person. He never had a friendship at Harvard. He'd come to breakfast saying that he'd stayed up all night with his terminal and he got frustrated and burned out but he seemed to enjoy it somehow. It was better for him, I guess, than staying up all night talking to a friend. That seems really sad. There's a lot of communication going on around here. People stay up all night talking to friends. But, Mike would not do that. He managed with his terminal."

How does the hacker look to non-hacker men? Many men are critical of the hacker's single-minded devotion to computers, critical of his lack of social skills. Men's reactions to the computer are similar to those of women, but there is a difference in men's reaction to the hacker's style of exploring the machine in a manner close to abandon and which celebrates risk. Men identify with it. They recognize it as a learning strategy which they find admirable and of which they are capable. Women tend to be more defensive.

Risk taking has a gender valence. Boys are taught to react to risks positively, to view them as an opportunity to expand their knowledge and skill. In our culture, when a boy shies away from risk, he runs what may be a greater risk: the accusation of being called a sissy, "girlish" in his ways. The female child is more often directed away from situations that might cause trouble. The tree may be too tall to climb; the rock may be too slippery to clamber over. Being a "good girl" is defined as a virtue where good may mean passive enough to not get into trouble. Good may also mean passive enough to accept knowledge only in a safe, directed, "cookbook" form.

Risk taking opens up powerful learning strategies. Jessie, a computer science graduate student at MIT, recognizes it as something that hackers have and she doesn't.[1]

"It seems to me that the essence of being a hacker is being willing to muck around with things that you don't fully understand. Playing around with things you don't understand requires a certain amount of self-confidence. Every so often things do get broken. If you break something, you have to believe that this is not necessarily because you are incompetent, but because every so often that happens. Every so often somebody fries a board or trashes an important file or what have you. Part of the essence of being a hacker is accepting the fact that some time you may be the one responsible for some such lossage.

> When faced with a situation that they do not have the facts to understand, people vary as to how much they are willing to just 'try things.' A hacker will typically try things if he or she knows enough about the domain to think up any plausible things to do. A non-hacker will tend not to try to make changes until he or she understands what is going on. . . . Hacking requires that one feel good about solving problems by means other than the 'right procedure.' "

Jessie has experimented with the "risky" learning strategy, but does so with inhibition. She sees it, somewhat wistfully, as male.

> "I am still teaching myself not to be afraid of 'screwing things up.' I think that being a 'hacker-type' correlates with things like having played with explosives or taken apart things or climbed dangerously up trees and that type of thing as a child. It seems as though women are less wiling to take things apart and risk breaking them, to try things when they don't know what they are doing and risk getting into trouble."

To use risk taking as a learning strategy you have to have to be able to fail without taking it "personally." This is something which many women find difficult. They want to be "good students." This can leave them so preoccupied with possible failure that they shy away from the chance of success. In fact, the women in my study have taken risks in learning. Even taking a programming course confronted Lisa, a "language person," and Robin, a "music person," with serious challenges. But they, like other women I interviewed, made it clear that they saw such challenges not as risks but as hurdles—hurdles that have been imposed from the "outside." The risks they are willing to accept responsibility for are risks in relationships. "There it is worth it; there I can do it."

Risk taking as a learning strategy demands that you sacrifice a certain understanding of what is going on. It demands that you plunge in first and try to understand later. To take an analogy from the world of the computer's second cousins, the video games: it is almost impossible to learn to play a video game if you try to understand first and play second. Girls are often perceived as preferring the "easier" video games. When I have looked more closely at what they really prefer, it is games where they can understand "the rules" before play begins. Both Lisa and Robin crave transparent understanding of the computer. For example, although both apologize for their behavior as "silly," both like to program the computer to do everything they need to build their larger programs, even when these smaller, "building-block" procedures are in program libraries at their disposal. It makes their job harder, but both say that it gives them a more satisfying understanding. They don't like taking risks at the machine. What they most want to avoid is error messages.

When women look at the programming virtuosos around them, they, unlike men, see themselves as cut off from a valued learning style. Male risk taking is equated with computational "intuition." In educational and professional environments where hackers present an image of "the best," women often see themselves as lesser. They see themselves as "just users," as competent but not really creative.

FIGHTING AGAINST COMPUTER HOLDING POWER

The computer is a "psychological machine." On the border between mind and not mind, it invites its anthropomorphization, its psychologization. It docs this almost universally, for children and grownups, men and women, novices and experts. This does not mean that people see it as "alive," but rather, there is a pull to psychologize the machine, to give it an intellectual and aesthetic personality. The computer facilitates a relational encounter with a formal system.

I have found that many women are drawn towards a style of programming that is best characterized as such a relational encounter (Turkle 1984, forthcoming). It is marked by an artistic, almost tactile style of identification with computational objects, a desire to "play with them" as though they were physical objects in a collage. A fluent use of this programming style can be a source of creativity. But many women fight against something that needs to be distinguished from programming style. They fight against the computer as psychologically gripping. They experience anthropomorphization as seductive and dangerous. Paradoxically, in rebellion against feeling "too much" they develop an attitude towards the computer that insists it is "just a tool."

The "just a tool" response is widespread in our culture. It is certainly not associated primarily with women. But I believe that when women use it, it is with a special force; particularly strong feelings stand behind their insistence on the "neutrality" of the technology.

First, insisting that the computer is just a tool is a defense against the experience of the computer as the opposite, as an intimate machine. It is a way to say that it is not appropriate to have a close relationship with a machine. Computers with their plasticity and malleability are compelling media. They have a psychological "holding power." Women use their rejection of computer holding power to assert something about themselves as women. Being a woman is opposed to a compelling relationship with a thing that shuts people out.

Contemporary writing about women's psychological development stresses the importance of connection in the way women forge their identities. Women are raised by women. Unlike men, they do not need to undergo a radical break to define their sexual identity. Unlike men, they are allowed, even encouraged to maintain a close relationship with the woman, the mother with whom they had an early experience of the closest bonding. Girls grow up defining their identity through social interaction; boys, through separation (Chodorow 1978; Gilligan 1982; Keller 1983, 1985).

The boy's experience of early separation and loss is traumatic. It leads to a strong desire to control his environment. Male separation from others is about differentiation but also about autonomy, "the wish to gain control over the sources and object of pleasure in order to shore up the possibilities for happiness against the risk of disappointment and loss" (Gilligan 1982, p. 46). Women grow up differently. Men "shore up possibilities for happiness" by autonomy, rules and hierarchy; women look to affection, relationships, responsibility and caring for a community of others. In *In A Different Voice,* Carol Gilligan talks about "the hierarchy and the web" as metaphors to describe the different ways in which men and women see their worlds. Men see a hierarchy of autonomous positions. Women see a web of interconnections between people. Men want to be alone at the top; they fear others getting too close. Women want to be at the center of connection; they fear being too far out on the edge. Men can be with the computer and still be alone, separate, and autonomous. When women perceive this technology as demanding separation, it is experienced as alien and dangerous.[2]

Lisa began her work with computers by thinking in terms of communicating with them, "because that's the way I see the world." But her communication metaphor began to distress her. "The computer isn't a living being and when I think about communicating with it, well that's wrong. There's a certain amount of feeling involved in the idea of communication and I was looking for that from the computer." She looked for it, and she frightened herself: "It was horrible. I was becoming involved with a thing. I identified with how the computer was going through things."

> "Wait a minute, a machine doesn't go through things; going through things is a very emotional way of talking. But it is hard to keep it straight. It seems to you that they are experiencing something that you once experienced. That they are learning something and you lose sight of the fact that this whole ability . . . I don't even want to say the computer's ability. I don't like anthropomorphizing; I fight very hard against attributing emotions to that machine."

For Lisa, success with the computer has meant a process of alienation from it. Her efforts go towards depersonalization, towards developing a strategy towards computers that is "not me." "I need to become a different kind of person with the machine." This is a person who commands rather than communicates.

When Lisa psychologized the machine and thought of programming in terms of communication, she was responding to the computer as many people do. The computer responds, reacts, "learns." And the machine allows you to externalize your own thought. As one thirteen-year-old told me: "When you program a computer you put a little piece of your mind into the computer's mind and you come to see it differently." The experience is heady and encourages anthropomorphization.[3] But if Lisa's impulses to psychologize the computer were commonplace, her reaction to them was more typical of women than men—to rebel against the feeling of mind speaking to mind, almost to punish herself for it: "You are working with the computer and you can almost identify with what a computer is going through. But then, that is awful. It's just a machine. It was horrible. I was becoming involved with a thing."

Lisa's "identification with what a computer is going through" is an identification with the computer as a mind. The computer is an "evocative object" (Turkle 1984). It upsets simple distinctions between things and people; there can no longer be simply the physical as opposed to the psychological. The computer, too, seems to have a psychology—it is a thing that is not quite a thing, a mind that is not quite a mind. By presenting itself as an object "betwixt and between," the computer provokes reflection on the question of minds and machines. Very soon after meeting a computer, even the novice programmer learns to write programs that he or she perceives as more complex than the rules used to create them. Once people build these kinds of rule-driven systems, questions about the relevance of the idea of program to the working of one's own mind acquires a new sense of urgency.

ROMANTIC REACTIONS

The position toward which children tend as they develop their thinking about people in relation to computers is to split "psychology" into the cognitive and affective, into the psychology of thought and of feeling (Turkle 1984). And then they can grant that the machine has intelligence and is thus "sort of alive," but distinguish it from people because of its lack of feelings. Thus, the Aristotelian definition of man as a "rational animal" (powerful even for children when it defined people in contrast to their nearest neighbors, the animals) gives way to a different distinction. Today's children "appropriate" computers through identification with them as psychological entities and come to see them as their new "nearest neighbors." And they are neighbors which seem to share in or (from the child's point of view) even excel in our rationality. People are still defined in contrast to their neighbors. But now, people are special because they feel. Children will grant the computer a "sort of life," but what makes people unique is the kind of life that computers don't have—an emotional life.

Many adults follow the same path as do children when they talk about human beings in relation to the new psychological machines. This path leads to allowing the possibility of unlimited rationality to computers while maintaining a sharp line between computers and people by taking the essence of human nature to be what computers can't do. This is precisely what Lisa does when she confronts the machine that seems to have a mind:

> "I suppose if you look at the physical machinery of the computer mind, it is analogous to the human mind. We were looking at a bare machine and how all the little wires could be compared to neurons. So, in that sense, yes, the hardware is the brain and I can see how the software could be the mind. But, the saving grace, the difference is emotion. Now I haven't heard anybody yet reduce emotion to a series of electrical impulses. I hope I never do. And I think that's the line you can draw. That's where you say, 'We can emote, this thing may be able to do something like thinking, but it can't love anybody.' "

Although she makes them herself, Lisa objects to all comparisons between computers and people. A question in our interview about minds and machines causes her to cut me off sharply and then to reflect on her own incon-sistency.

> "I get really edgy when people start comparing computers to human beings or asking questions about how they might be alike or not alike. And it is a strange thing. I go and attribute all of these qualities to the computer and condescend to get mad at the computer and give it the dignity of my emotion wasted on its stupid metal framework, but at the same time, if somebody starts saying, 'Don't you think that there might be similarity between a machine process and a human process or don't you think that there might be a program so that people could come in and talk to the machine when they are lonely,' I go mad. I say, 'No. The computer's just a machine.' At that point, I'm very able to make the distinction. But at the same time, I can't control my reactions to it as if it were . . . well, like a person. It's a contradiction. It's totally illogical and I can't explain it. It's like how I feel about abortion. I think it's a bad thing. And then, people show me my inconsistencies, and finally I just have to tell them I can't talk about it. It's just absolute, illogical, but that's how I feel."

Lisa's experience with the computer leaves her with a sense of danger. The machine seduces you into psychologizing and anthropomorphizing it. "People have to realize that this is only a machine. It is not going to provide love or compassion or understanding. You can't start attributing human quali-ties to it. But it's very hard not to." And since even she was vulnerable, she worries about the dangers for children.

> "What if children had them and started to have the idea that it was a being? Because they might start looking to that being for things that only a human can give, like support and comfort or love. Can you imagine a little person coming to love a computer? What if the computer became a mother substitute or a father figure? I think it would be disastrous. And all the more so if this thing that you had conceived of as a living, hearing, laughing, feeling being all your young life, that had been your best friend, and suddenly you realize that it's nothing but a machine. I can imagine a little person coming to that aware-ness and feeling so lost in not knowing what to do.
>
> My sister loves animals more than people. It makes her a somewhat solitary sort of girl because she doesn't want to get involved with all the things that thirteen-year-olds do, she would rather go off and ride, but I think her emo-tional life is not limited really. When you're spending a lot of your time with animals, there's a lot of real love and real warmth and an animal can love you back. . . . And then there is the definite physical appeal. It's nice to hold a kitten in your lap. . . . But to even give a name to a computer, to me that has a kind of sinister quality. You can invest thought and get rewards. Perhaps you would get better rewards in terms of intelligence, but you're not ever going to get any emotional feedback from that thing. And so if you start lavishing your own guts on that computer, your own emotional entrails, well, you are going to be horribly disappointed. The longer you do it, the longer you are allowed to do it, the worse it's going to be."

The Freudian experience has taught us that resistance to a theory is part of its cultural impact. Resistance to psychoanalysis, with its emphasis on the unconscious and the irrational, leads to an emphasis on the rational aspect of human nature, to an emphasis on people as ultimately logical beings. Resistance to computers and the ideal of program as mind leads to a view that what is essential in people is what is ineffable, uncapturable by any language or formalism. For Robin, people have "great flashes of abstract thought without any logical sequence before it. If you tried to do that with a computer it would tell you it's a system error or illegal! People have two ways of thinking—one of them without logical steps. The computer only has one." Lisa boils down what computers can't do to a starker form. Most simply stated, it is love.

There is a "romantic reaction" to the computer presence. As people take computers seriously as simulated mind, they resist the image of the human mind that comes back to them in the mirror of the machine. Simulated thinking may be thinking, but simulated love is never love. Women express this sentiment with particular urgency. It is more than philosophical opinion. A conflict stands behind their conviction. The more they anthropomorphize the machine, the more they express anxiety about its dangers. The more it provokes them to reflect on mind, the more they assert that the computer is just a neutral tool for getting from A to B. In sum, the more they experience the subjective computer, the more they insist that it doesn't exist and that there is only the instrumental machine.

RETICENCE ABOUT FORMAL SYSTEMS

Lisa reacted with irritation when her high school teachers tried to get her interested in mathematics by calling it a language. "People were always yakking at me about how math is a language—it's got punctuation marks and all that stuff. I thought they were fools and I told them so. I told them that if only it were a language, if only it had some nuance, then perhaps I could relate to it." As a senior, she wrote a poem that expressed her sentiments.

If you could say with numbers what I say now in words,
if theorems could, like sentences, describe the flight of birds,
if PPL had meter and parabolas had rhyme,
perhaps I'd understand you then,
perhaps I'd change my mind.

If two convergent sequences produced some assonance,
or vectors made a particle of literary sense,
if triangles were iambs and equations anapests,
then maybe I'd acquire a bit of numerical interest.

If Cicero's orations were set down in polar form
and the headaches numbers give me weren't, excuse my French, enorme,

if a graph could say "I love you," it could sing a child to sleep,
then from this struggle I might find some benefit to reap.

But all this wishful thinking only serves to make things worse,
when I compare my dearest love with your numeric verse.
For if mathematics were a language, I'd succeed, I'd scale the hill,

I know I'd understand, but since it's not, I never will.

Lisa's poem expresses her profound reticence about formal systems. Despite her talent, she preferred to stay away from them. "I didn't see that proving a theorem was anything like writing a poem. I never thought of mathematics as creative or human; and the people who studied them, well, when I thought of 'people who studied mathematics,' I thought of these dry, emotionless little people who ran around and talked to computers all day."

Lisa's reticence has many facets, but she keeps coming back to two themes. First, formal systems don't bring people together, they rupture what Gilligan called the "web of connectedness" that dominates women's way of seeing the world. Second, formal systems allow for "only one way" of doing things.

"When they used to talk to me about mathematics as a language I would say, 'Well, look, if I were speaking Spanish, I could say that thirty million different ways.' Here, it's either right or it's wrong and that's it. And I don't like the regimentation."

Lisa dislikes anything where there is "only one way." She loves language for its "shades of meaning." Ambiguity and nuance make her feel at home. Erik Erikson, writing from within the psychoanalytic tradition, has suggested how women's experience of their bodies as an "inner space" that is hidden, diffuse, and ambiguous affects their experience of the world (Erikson 1963). The "nailed down" quality of formal systems feels unfamiliar and threatening.

Clearly, women's feelings about formal systems go deep. Erikson's work on body image suggests a terror of the nonambiguous; Evelyn Fox Keller's work on women and science suggests that women's early and (relative to men) unruptured experiences with closely bonded relationships alienates them from the traditional "male" stance toward formal systems, a stance characterized by the separation of subject from object (Keller 1985).

The issues that are raised by looking at gender and formal systems are complex, but something about the computer's contribution is becoming increasingly clear. When people are put in computer-rich environments, supported by flexible and powerful programming languages, and encouraged to use the computer as an expressive material, they respond in a diversity of styles. In such environments, the computer, like other powerful media including paints, pencils, and words, becomes a screen for the projection of differences. Unlike stereotypes of a machine with which there is only one way of relating, the computer can be a partner in a great diversity of relationships.

People make the computer their own in their own way. For example, some take to the computer in a way that emphasizes planning and structure. Others naturally move toward a different style. They prefer to "grow" their programs from small elements, often changing their goals as they go along. The programs that result from using these two styles can be equally effective, clear and easy to use. The difference is not in the product but in the process of creation. With the computer, there is not "one way." On the contrary, the range of styles of appropriation suggests the metaphor "computers as Rorschach" (Turkle 1980). Like the Rorschach inkblot test, the computer presents an ambiguous material that encourages the projection of significant inner differences.

In relatively unconstrained settings, the computer facilitates a new basis for engagement in technical and mathematical thinking, one that allows for their appropriation through a "close encounter" with an interactive, reactive "psychological machine" and with computational objects that can be experienced as tactile and physical. It is a style that emphasizes negotiation rather than command of computational objects, a style that suggests a conversation rather than a monologue. This is a port of entry into the world of formal systems for many people who have always kept at a distance from them. It is a port of entry with particular significance for women. The computer offers a new cultural opportunity to expand the social base of mathematical and scientific fluency.

But people are not always introduced to computers in a way that exploits this opportunity. In fact, it happens all too rarely. Lisa and Robin are taking an excellent and imaginative introductory programming course, but even there, both of them are experiencing it as a place where they are being told the "one right way" to do things. This "one right way" emphasizes "structured programming" with its aesthetic of control through structure, specification, and planning. There is much virtue in this computational aesthetic, but both Lisa and Robin say their learning styles are at war with it. Robin wanted to play with the smallest computational elements and build things from the "bottom up." Lisa was frustrated by the strategy of "black boxing" that helps the structured programmer plan something large without knowing in advance how the details will be managed. Both rebelled against the regimentation of there being "one right way" to do things.

In the course that Robin and Lisa are taking, those whose intellectual style favors the highly analytical, the structured, and the specifiable, will be drawn to the computer, while others, and many women among them, will continue to see what it takes to "think right" in the computer culture as alien. And even when they succeed in the course, they keep their psychological distance. I believe that a symptom of this distance is their "neutralization" of the computer when they describe it as "just a tool."

We know that pencils, oil paints, and brushes are "just tools." And yet, we appreciate that the artist's encounter with his or her tools is close and relational. It may shut people out, temporarily, but the work itself can bring one closer to oneself, and ultimately to others. In the right settings, people develop relationships with computers that feel artistic and personal. And yet, for most people, and certainly for the women I studied, this was rare. When they began to approach the computer in their own style, they got their wrists slapped, and were told that they were not doing things "right."

When this happens, many people drop out. They see themselves as deviant, as not "good at the computer." Or, and this is what one sees most often with talented women such as Lisa and Robin, they "fake it." They try to do it the "right way." Lisa talks about turning herself into a "different kind of person." Robin talks about giving up on her desire to "build from little pieces on up" and to have a fully transparent relationship with the computer. "I told my teaching fellow I wanted to take it all apart and he laughed at me. He said it was a waste of time, that you should just 'black box,' that you shouldn't confuse yourself with what was going on at that low level."

We cannot know what Lisa and Robin would be feeling if they had been encouraged toward a more personal appropriation of this technology. As I have said, the roots of reticence seem to go deep. But we do know that given the introduction they did have, they, like most of the women I interviewed, ended up denying the computer any role as an expressive medium. This is not surprising: given the way they have been using it, it isn't one. Frustrated in a personal style of use, they become vehement about the computer's status as a neutral "tool" because they have been denied any other relationship with it. To put it more sharply, they have been denied an authentic relationship with it.

Lisa sums up her computer experience with the word "regimentation." She is afraid of children learning to program because she wouldn't want them equally regimented. She wouldn't want children "tied down to being very careful and very regimented and very concise and syntactically correct." Lisa says that her best moment in her programming course was when she saw, through the computer, something she might have missed in mathematics. "In mathematics I could never see that it didn't have to be just one way. But I can see that a little with the computer. And I am starting to get very excited about that." And then she came back to the question of children with a more optimistic tone: "I think maybe kids could bring, well, they could open up new frontiers for computers, because they have such wild ideas that they could do great things if people just let them."

The children may indeed lead us.[4] The computer that could support "wild ideas" is the computer as an expressive medium. We must ask if the vehemence behind women's insistence that the computer is "just a tool" will be as great when they have greater opportunities to experience it as material which allows highly differentiated styles of mastery and personalizes the world of formal systems for men and women alike.

NOTES

1. The quotation from Jessie is taken from an interview done by MIT graduate student Ronnie Rosenberg, "Female Hackers," unpublished paper, December 1983.

In this paper, Rosenberg makes the very interesting point that when women look at male risk-taking style with computers they equate that style with "intuition."

2. From this perspective, computers become much more attractive when they are used to support communications through networks. The question here will be whether particular computer networks bring people together who would not normally have been together or whether they "deteriorate" communication—that is, people who would have spoken face to face now speak screen to screen.

3. The holding power of a mind-to-mind connection is there even for the nonprogrammer. When you use someone else's program, software someone else has written, there is still the fantasy of a mind-to-mind communication between you and the software writer.

4. A leading computer visionary who has long stood for the "personal appropriation" of programming has done much of his work with children. See Seymour Papert, *Mindstorms: Children, Computers and Powerful Ideas* (New York: Basic Books, 1980).

WORKS CITED

Chodorow, Nancy. 1978. *The Reproduction of Mothering.* Berkeley: University of California Press.

Erikson, Erik. 1963. *Childhood and Society.* New York: W. W. Norton.

Gilligan, Carol. 1982. *In a Different Voice: Psychological Theory and Women's Development.* Cambridge: Harvard University Press.

Keller, Evelyn Fox. 1983. *A Feeling for the Organism: The Life and Work of Barbara McClintock.* San Francisco: W. H. Freeman.

———. 1985. *Reflections on Gender and Science.* New Haven: Yale University Press.

Kiesler, Sara, Lee Sproull, and David Zubrow. 1984. Encountering an alien culture. *Journal of Social Research.*

Kiesler, Sara, Lee Sproull, and Jacqueline S. Eccles. 1985. Poolhalls, chips and war games: women in the culture of computing. *Psychology of Women Quarterly* 9 (4): 451–62.

Turkle, Sherry. 1980. Computer as Rorschach. *Society* 17.

———. 1984. *The Second Self: Computers and the Human Spirit.* New York: Simon & Schuster.

———. Forthcoming. Gender and programming: styles and voices in the computer culture. *Signs.*

CHAPTER 22

EXCLUDING WOMEN FROM THE
TECHNOLOGIES OF THE FUTURE?

A Case Study of the Culture of Computer Science

BENTE RASMUSSEN AND TOVE HÅPNES

(1991)

The low level of representation of women in higher education in computer science is worrying in a number of ways. Today, information technology (IT) is seen as a core technology, where innovations and qualifications in microelectronics, information processing, and information systems have both direct and indirect effects on economic growth and production. Innovations and technological changes in IT are important not only for the computer and electronics industry, but also for innovations and changes in the R&D of other technologies.[1]

The importance of involving women as producers and advanced users of new IT is not just motivated by a policy of equal opportunity for women and men in the area of computers. Both research and industry ought to make use of the resources of scientific talent that women possess. Women may also contribute different ideas and interests in the development and use of computer technology.[2] Women's interests and qualifications in the use and social organization of IT may be an important resource in developing usable and effective systems. When women are wanted and needed, why do they not choose computer science?

The efforts to increase the proportion of women in computer science are mainly directed towards informing and motivating individual women to choose nontraditional careers. They are built on the idea that it is women's fear of computers and lack of self-confidence that form the main obstacles.[3]

In our research we have shifted focus from this kind of sex-role explanation to analysis of the gender politics of computer science.[4] The traditions in computer science have also been the focus of other studies by female computer scientists.[5] There is, however, a tendency to focus mainly on historical and institutional structures, for instance, the strong historical bond between computer technology, engineering, and military applications. Less attention has been paid to the ongoing cultural production within the educational institutions. It is not sufficient to point to the history of the discipline to explain the absence of female students today. There are good reasons to study the educational systems and how they function in a gender perspective. In that way we can give female students a realistic view of their possibilities. Knowledge about the gendering processes[6] may also help to change male domination in education.

In this article we argue that the *culture* of computer science is important in producing and reproducing male domination in higher education in computer science. Thus, it influences the integration of women and their position within the field of computing. Culture within education has not been a focus of study in Norway, even though it is important in forming the image of the discipline. Through U.S. studies great attention has been paid to "freakish" computer culture—the hacker culture[7]—but this marginal group is not representative of the majority of students or of the discipline itself.

We have chosen to present one case from our research project of the different types of computer studies at university level in Norway. This case, computer science at the Norwegian Institute of Technology (NIT), is interesting not only because it is the most male-dominated of the Norwegian cases, with participation by female students of only eight to ten percent.[8] These women are also interesting because they preferred to study at a high-prestige technical university. The female students at NIT are often motivated by ambitions for a technical career. In this way they are representatives of a new women's role.[9]

METHOD

To analyze the culture of a computer science education, we had to "deconstruct" the cultural images and representations of the different groups in the department of computer science at NIT. Through this deconstruction we find multiple cultures, minorities, and majorities.

We interviewed teachers and students about the study—the curricula and the social and cultural conditions, their experiences and ideas, and their values and interests. Our information comes from students who have studied computer science for at least two to three years.

In this article our perspective is the viewpoint of the female students. Through their eyes we see how the different groups and their relationships influence the situation of female students. We also study the perspective of other groups to show the complexity of the cultures inside the study. The following are the important groups in computer science in this connection.

The female students represent a minority culture. They are nontraditional compared to the majority of women and see themselves as different from most females. They want to have a professional career and they like subjects such as mathematics and physics.

Another important minority group among the students is *the hackers*. They are nocturnal workers who act and see themselves as special within computer science. They see themselves as a subculture like the female students. The hackers are all male.

A third important minority group is *the dedicated students*. They are students who work long hours and cooperate closely with the professors in their projects. They are the loyal and industrious students. They are all male.

An important and stable group is *the professors and teachers* of computer science. They also work long hours. The professors are all male.

The normal male students form the majority of the students. They are called "normal" by the female students because they, like the female students, go home in the evening and have interests other than computers. Even if they are alike in this respect, the female students distinguish themselves from the "normal" male majority.

Here we show how the special culture of the hackers comes to be so dominant in computer science at NIT, that it, at least when it concerns the female students, works to marginalize them and keep the participation of female students very low. We do this by presenting the different groups and their views of computer science and the other groups, that is, how they see themselves and others. We show how some groups share important views and ideas and how the most powerful groups of actors enforce certain values and interests in the education.

WE ARE *NOT* "KEY-PRESSERS"

When the female students thought about studying computer science at NIT, they had to face an image of the students as "very special people." The students in computer science were seen as "freaks" that were only interested in computers and not able to talk about anything else. The female students wondered if they dared enlist in this study. "What if I am the only one who is normal?" one of the female students said. They felt relief when they got to know other students in the department because there were many *normal* people among them, i.e., students with interests other than computers. They found friends like themselves, interested in computer science, but leaving at the end of the day to have a social life, do sports, read books, etc.

When the female students talked about their professional identity and interests, they often compared themselves with a special male culture that they called "the key-presser's society." The female students distance themselves from the key-pressers because they have become the *symbol* of what a female student is not. What are the characteristics of the key-presser that the female students react against?

When the female students talk about "key-pressers," they talk about the "computer nerd syndrome." The "key pressers" seem to have an intimate relationship with the computer and stay in front of it programming as much as they can. For the women, their professional identity is tied to aspects of computing other than the machine and technical possibilities. One female student said this, when she started to explain women's professional identity in the study:

> We don't spend time making a program just for the sake of the program—just to see all the fabulous things we could do with it. Even the most interested female students do not have this relation to computers.

The women do not want an intimate relation to a computer. Intimate relations belong to people and not to machines. They want life to be more than computers and programming. The "key-presser" is threatening because he comes to stand for cultural and social isolation as the women see it. The female students describe those key-pressers as having several traits in common with the "compulsive programmer" as Joseph Weizenbaum described it.[10] This hacker image is represented by Sherry Turkle as "the image of getting lost in the thing-in-itself."[11]

Before we come back to the situation for the female students, their interests and their professional identity, we take a closer look at the hacker culture.

CULTURE OF THE YOUNG MALE PROGRAMMING VIRTUOSOS

The hackers are a minority of the students and they come from different departments of the university. They assemble in one of the laboratories, which they call "the software workshop." There you find young men sitting in front of computer terminals, and the sound you hear is their fingers pressing the keys on the keyboards and the electronic sound from computer games. They arrive at midnight and they go home in the middle of the day for some sleep.

The hackers made it clear to us that they were the most superior computer club in the country. They were working on large and ambitious programming systems, and their technical knowledge about such systems made it possible for them to develop small subprograms for firms and for the computer science department. The hackers see themselves as clever, but also as *different* from other students. They define themselves as an alternative culture to the mainstream culture within the computer science department.

They try to make themselves visible as individuals both towards the other members of the hacker culture and towards people outside the group. They do this in different ways—by the way they dress or wear their hair or by being different from other hackers (the only religious hacker, even the only "normal" hacker). They want to be recognized as individual persons and not as a member of the student mass. As a group, they also make their culture visible through their common mode of life and their lifestyle. They are nocturnal workers and spend long hours in the lab, and they use an in-group language shaped by their digital activity.

Even though the hackers emphasize their individuality and their preoccupation with computers, they are not loners or isolated. They have a social life together with other hackers. When they take a break from the laboratory, they go to the cinema, especially to see science-fiction movies, or they drop into a pizza bar to eat and talk about books, movies, and computers. Their social life is occupied with their main interests.

They do not like the university systems or the computer science education. The best thing with NIT, they feel, is the possibility that it offers students to play with big computers. In their self-image they are not clever *students,* but clever at using computers. The study is boring and being a mainstream student one becomes a standardized professional. They hate programming languages like Pascal and Cobol because they represent the uniformity of rule-based systems that hinder their wish to be individualists. Instead, they love to use C language to create their own problems and find brilliant solutions which suit their personal taste. They do not spend much time studying, but get ideas that they have to test out on the computer. They look on themselves as creative computer users—with an artistic style. Their knowledge and products are available for use by all the members of the software workshop. They do not like having secrets and they are opposed to the culture of copyright among computer professionals.

Their fascination with computers and programming is a result of the possibility that the computer offers its user to create fabulous things: "You have a problem or an idea, let us see if we can handle it through the machinery." They work for the joy of the process and the grand feeling of achieving control. To the computer they are the boss, and it is a great feeling to beat the computer. To win means to have control; they have solved the problem.

The hackers look on themselves as an out-group within the computer science department. They have no close collaboration with other groups, apart from some professors and teachers. They do not see other students as separate groups, but they see the close connections between the dedicated students and the professors. The dedicated students are the professor's disciples—the clever mainstream students who are willing to become uniform and who accept the study and the hierarchy in the department and in the programming systems. They see that the dedicated students are at the department in the evenings, "but we do not know what they do here." They know that the majority of the students are not dedicated, but the "normal" male group that the female students talk about are not visible as such for the hackers.

The hackers are a pure male group, and they have not really considered why they are an all-male enclave. For them it is rather mysterious that none of the females is interested in computers in the same way that they are: "Maybe they would be more interested in computers if they could use a Macintosh because they are very simple to use," one of them offered as an explanation. They do not know, and they are not really interested in females.

The hackers see that the female students are a special group which is different from male students, but they do not know them. One commented that the female students in computer science looked so female, dressed up like women in restaurants or as if going to a celebration. For him the females in the department seem strange compared to the girls in other departments at the technical university. There you can find "girls who are more like one of the boys," he said.

From the hackers' perspective the relationships in the computer science department are as the illustration in Figure 1. The only group with which they have a professional interaction is the professor/teacher group, but this connection is much weaker than the relationship between professors and the dedicated students. The link between the hackers and the dedicated students is weak, and they do not interact either with other male or female students.

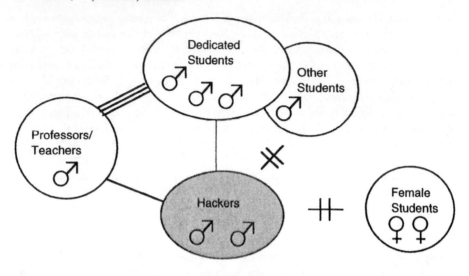

FIGURE 1. Computer science from the perspective
of the hackers.

Female Students—on the Periphery

According to the female students, the "key-pressers" are only occupied with
programming and computers and have no other interests in life. When the
female students talk about the hackers or the "key-pressers" they do not distinguish between the hackers with their eccentricity and alternative computing culture and the "dedicated students" who conform to the culture of the
subject and the professors. They are put together in one group of "key-pressers." Opposed to them are the female students and the "normal" male students who have outside interests and who do not stay in the university until
late at night.

The female students have chosen to study computer science because they
thought that it sounded interesting. Besides, computer scientists are needed
in the labor market and the profession offers good career prospects. They are
attracted by the subject—how you can use computers and computer systems
and make things work. They share this interest with the male students.

However, they differ from the male students in their professional identity.
Even when the interests and choices of the female students lie well within the
main areas of the computer science department, they feel that they are "on
the periphery" of computer science when they have chosen "applications" of
computer technology. They feel that it is programming that one associates
with typical computer people who sit in front of a terminal and are fascinated
by what is inside computers.

The professional identity of the women is tied to aspects of computing other than the machine or the technical possibilities. They view computers as tools—an instrumental ideology. They do not have an instrumental view of the whole information process as Weizenbaum[12] uses the conception "instrumental." Women are concerned with the use of the technology, the technology in practice. They choose specializations in computer science where they think that it is possible to be occupied with a broader range of aspects than the machinery. They choose telematics, cybernetics, and informations systems (system development) where they apply computer technology to solve practical problems.

In choosing telematics or cybernetics, women become more "engineers" than computer scientists, and in choosing information systems, they choose the user side, or the "soft" side of general computing. They feel that the most exciting thing about computer science is all the different things that you can make, and the problems that you manage to solve. They do not find it especially interesting to make a million numbers go through a machine one millisecond faster.

The female students avoid subjects like operating systems, programming, and machine construction even though they know that these specializations have the highest status in the computer science department. With their choices, the women are moving away from "pure" computer science—the computers and how they work.

The female students all emphasize the importance of making computer technology user-friendly. This explicit reference to the users is not all that popular in the computer science department, where they want to be dealing with *science* and not with practical problems. In referring to the users and the usefulness of computers and in emphasizing the tool aspect of computer technology, the female students indirectly take a position in a more or less open ongoing conflict among the professors in computer science. In the past there were three separate departments at NIT—telematics, cybernetics, and general computing. The telematics and the cybernetics departments were involved in industrial applications and the general computing department taught programming and operating systems. The merger of the three departments brought the professors together, but they still lecture in separated fields. It is, however, the teachers from the former "general computing department" who are responsible for the first two basic years of study. They teach the machine subjects (operating systems and programming) and are an important group in the department. Their position is threatened by the other two groups of professors who were always against a separate field of computer science. They saw computers as tools in engineering fields and disciplines. Conflicts over the direction of computer science education between those groups have a long history, and the general computing group have won their position which they strive to keep up by showing scientifically good results. They have created an education based on machine construction and operating systems.[13] Computers as machines, and how you can make them work, is therefore the *core* of the computer science in NIT.

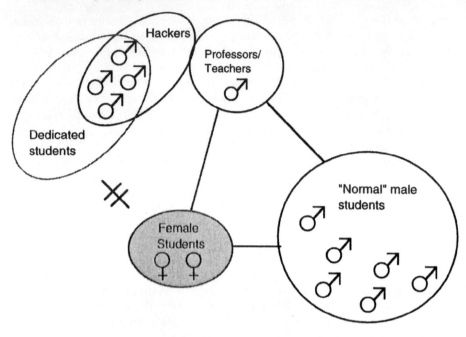

FIGURE 2. Computer science from the perspective
of the female students.

To legitimate their own choices, female students use the argument of the
cybernetics and telematics groups of professors, arguments that are accepted
and available when choosing directions within computer science.

From the female students' perspective the relationships in the computer
science department are as shown in Figure 2. They interact with the "normal"
male group, and they also have a professional interaction with the professor/
teacher group, but this connection is weak. From the viewpoint of the female
students there is a strong connection between the professor/teacher group
and the "key-pressers"—hackers and dedicated students. They do not interact with the "key-pressers."

We have thus far looked at two main subcultures within our community—
the hackers and the female students. The marginality of the female students
is produced within the computer science department, and to understand it,
we have to look at the most powerful actors—the teachers and professors, and
their disciples, the dedicated students.

PROFESSORS AND TEACHERS

The professors and teachers form a differentiated group as we have shown
above. Across their differences and disagreements they all agree that good

students should put in at least a sixty-hour working week on computer science—at least if they want to be good computer scientists, as good as the ones from the best (U.S.) universities. That is their ambition.

They also agree that hackers are not such good students as the ones with whom they have a close collaboration—the dedicated students. The hackers do what they want to do, and especially they do things that do not necessarily qualify them and lead to an exam. However, the playful attitude that they find among hackers in their absorption of computers is seen as a prerequisite that enables them to learn fast and to be creative computer scientists. They like this attitude of total absorption and daring found among some male students, and they feel that female students lack this attitude and therefore are less motivated to study computing. They found that some female students were very good students, and they could not understand why women reject computers and programming.

In the male programming virtuosos they see the dedicated scientist and researcher, absorbed by his subject—an intellectual attitude. In the female students who go home after a day at the university and who give priority to activities outside the subject, they see an instrumental attitude towards the subject and less dedication. Female students are seen as competent and "good" students, but as not very creative, brilliant, or likely to come up with exciting innovations.

The dedicated students who work long hours at the university are known personally to the professors and lecturers. Many professors also stay in the university in the evening where they work and tutor their dedicated students. The hackers are also known by some professors, but they do not have the close collaboration with the hackers that they have with the dedicated students.

The "normal" students who go home in the evening are outside this society of nocturnal workers. They are anonymous compared to these groups. Normal students get to know the staff when they start specializing in their third year.

It is therefore easy to understand that the female students come to see themselves as marginal compared to the "key-pressers." The teachers thus reinforce the high status of the hackers and the dedicated students, their knowledge, and their interests. In this way we are able to see how the view of female students of what is central and what is marginal is produced and reproduced through the professors' and teachers' attitudes and interests.

The majority—the "normal" male students—become invisible not only to the eyes of the hackers, but also to the eyes of the professors. From the professors' and teachers' perspective the relationships in the computer science department are as shown in Figure 3.

OTHER MALE GROUPS IN COMPUTER SCIENCE

The dedicated students' view of computer science and the various groups taking the subject differ little from that of the professors, except from their disconnection to the hackers. The two groups are in a way "rivals" and both

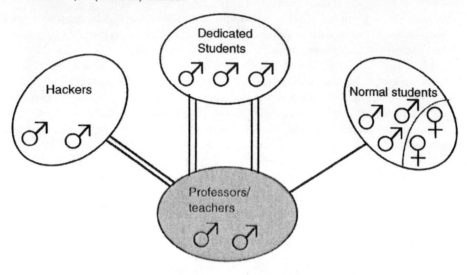

FIGURE 3. Computer science from the perspective
of the professors and teachers.

groups construct their professional identity and their "computer science" in opposition to each other.

From the dedicated students' perspective the relationships in the computer science department are as shown in Figure 4.

The view of hackers as outsiders and as being different from the professors and the dedicated students, is not shared by the "normal" male students and the female students. They see the specially interested students and the professors and teachers who share the secrets of computing and ask and answer questions that *they* do not understand. They are one big group that are the insiders. They symbolize the *"in-house culture."*

The female students react against this in-house group, occupied—as the women see it—with the machines and what is inside the machines, and they move into other areas where the *use* of computers is central.

The female students show their dissatisfaction and protest through an active participation in changing their education. They do not, however, criticize the content of the study and the subjects that are taught, but they are concerned about the methods and pedagogical matters. They do not visualize an alternative computer science, but they think that a change in the *order* of subjects and working methods would make computer science a better subject for the students, female as well as male.

The "normal" male students do not protest. They study "along," like the majority at NIT have always done, in the hope that they will one day "see the light" and understand what it was all about and why they had to learn all the different bits. Through their passivity and non-protest they fail to support and

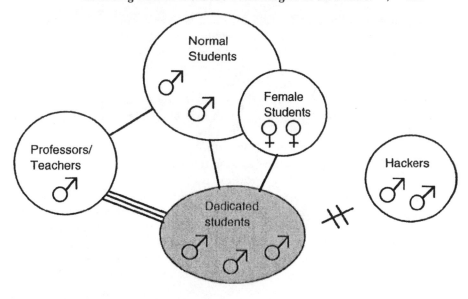

FIGURE 4. Computer science from the perspective
of the dedicated students.

strengthen the protest from the female students. Better support for alternative methods and ideas could move the female students from a marginal subculture to an oppositional group that could organize around their own ideas
and develop alternative perspectives in the subject, like the hackers do.

CONCLUSIONS

Male domination in computer science is created because the dominant
groups among the professors and the students share certain values with the
hackers. These values are:

- machine fascination and interest in the possibilities of computers;
- work addiction and total absorption in computers;
- a playful attitude towards the computers.

These values are opposed to the values and interests of the female students.
They are not especially interested in computers as machines, they do not want
to play with computers, and they definitely want to do other things than sit
around a computer. The hackers group is a "pure" type of these values, and
therefore the female students come to see them as the exponent of these
values and in some ways the source of their discontent. It is, however, the
powerful groups of actors, the professors and teachers and also their disciples,
the dedicated students, who through their attitudes and actions make these
values *dominant* within computer science at NIT.

The choices of the female students must be understood as an active protest against machine fixation in the study of computer science at NIT. It is a
protest against this domination, which is also domination of a male culture.
The female students do not share this culture, neither its machine fascination
nor its work style and total absorption. In rejecting the dominant male culture
and retreating to their own areas, the female students are *marginalized*. However, they do not protest against their marginalization, but accept it as inevitable because of their interests, their values, and their choices.

Male domination through machine culture is also created by the lack of
alternative values and perspectives among the other professors and teachers,
the majority of the male students, and the female students.

The female students do not see the contradictions and opposing ideas
between the three very different in-groups. The similarities between them are
so powerful that it seems like one dominant block. Therefore the female students do not see that alternative perspectives compete within the department.
They do not see an alternative education where their interests and choices
would be central. They do not know the content of the courses in informatics
or information science at the University of Oslo or the University of Bergen,
and they are not familiar with the critique and discussions among female
computer scientists,[14] or among computer scientists in general about, for example, the Scandinavian model of systems development.[15] These discussions
are concentrated in the departments that have systems development as a
central specialization, like informatics at the University of Oslo or at the universities in Aalborg and Aarhus in Denmark. Instead of protesting against the
dominant culture and values, the female students in computer science at NIT
accept the male domination of machine fixation, and their protest becomes
"muted."

Their lack of insight into the structural domination of male values in their
department makes it difficult to develop strategies to change this situation.
Their current strategies are on the one hand their *individual* choices which
allow them to become the sort of computer scientist that they want to be, and
on the other their *social network* of female students where they can relax from
the male domination.

The lack of critique, however, represents a serious problem if you want to
increase the proportion of women. The proportion of women will never be
high in a male-dominated and machine-fixated department such as that at
NIT. To increase the proportion of women, the department would have to
change. The proportion of women at Nordic universities who study computer
science increases when computer science is situated within departments of
business (twenty-five percent), social sciences, or humanities (fifty percent).[16]
Here computer science is connected to women's interests in the use of computer technology and computer technology in a societal perspective.

When computer science is located in natural science departments, the
proportion of women is higher where the subject and specializations are
within the areas of interest of the female students.[17] This indicates that the

content of study at NIT will have to change to increase the proportion of women. Here the female students' criticism could be an important force. Computer science also needs to change according to the computer industry: there is a serious need for more interest in the users, the complex reality of computers and their applications, and work organization. The female students might be an important *resource* in initiating such a change.

NOTES

1. C. Freeman, J. Clark, and L. Soete, *Unemployment and Technical Innovations* (London: Frances Pinter, 1982); I. Miles, *Home Informatics—Information Technology and the Transformation of Everyday Life* (London: Pinter Publishers, 1988).

2. E. Kvande and B. Rasmussen, "Men, women and data systems," *European Journal of Engineering Education* 14, 4 (1989).

3. For a further critique of this perspective, see E. Kvande and B. Rasmussen, "The gender politics of organizations. A study of male and female engineers," paper, Trondheim, IFIM/ISS, 1991.

4. Kvande and Rasmussen 1989; T. Håpnes and B. Rasmussen, "The production of male power in computer science," in I. Eriksson, B. Kitchenham and K. Tijdens, eds., *Women, Work and Computerization*, Proceedings from 4th IFIP Conference, Helsinki (Amsterdam: North-Holland, 1991); L. Suchman, "Identities and differences," paper presented to the 4th Conference of Women, Work and Computerization, Helsinki, June 30–July 2, 1991.

5. C. Mörtberg, *Varför har programmeraryrket blivit manligt?* (Luleå: Institutionen för arbetsvetenskap, 1985); J. Nielsen, "Viden- mellom rationalitet og lidenskab. Om videnskab, teknologi og mendeskelig erkjendelse," in O. Denelsen and B. Karpatchof, eds., *Datamatbeherskelse og almen dannelse* (Aarhus: Aarhus Universitetsforlag, 1988).

6. E. Kvande and B. Rasmussen, *Nye Kvinneliv. Kvinner i Menns Organisasjoner* (Oslo: Ad Notam, 1990); Kvande and Rasmussen 1991; J. Acker, "Hierarchies, jobs, bodies: a theory of gendered organizations," *Gender and Society* 4, 2 (1990).

7. J. Weizenbaum, *Computer Power and Human Reason* (San Francisco: Freeman, 1976); S. Levy, *Hackers: Heroes of the Computer Revolution* (New York: Bantam Doubleday Dell, 1984); S. Turkle, *The Second Self. Computers and the Human Spirit* (London: Granada, 1984); S. Turkle, "Computational reticence: why women fear the intimate machine," in C. Kramarae, ed., *Technology and Women's Voices. Keeping in Touch* (London: Routledge and Kegan Paul, 1988), reprinted as ch. 21 in this volume.

8. T. Håpnes, "Kvinner og data—en kulturkollisjon? Innlegg på seminaret" *Hvorfor velger jenter som de gjør?* Seminar for rådgivere i videregående skole, NTH, Trondheim, October 6–7, 1988; Kvande and Rasmussen 1989.

9. Kvande and Rasmussen 1991; Kvande and Rasmussen 1990.

10. Weizenbaum 1976.

11. Turkle 1984, p. 207.

12. Weizenbaum 1976.

13. T. Håpnes, *På sporet av en profesjon? Om framveksten av høyere EDB-utdaning i Norge* (Hovedoppgave, Trondheim: STS, 1989).

14. G. Bjerknes and T. Bratteteig, *"Damer Dreper ikke Drager" eller Premisser for Profesjonell Systemudvikling*, Arbeidsnotat (Oslo: Universitetet i Oslo, Institutt for Informa-

tikk, 1987); J. Greenbaum, "The head and the heart," paper presented at Nordisk Symposium om Teknologi og Arbejdsliv, Korsør, August 17–19, 1987.

15. G. Bjerknes, P. Ehn, and M. Kyng, *Computers and Democracy. A Scandinavian Challenger* (Aldershot: Avebury, 1987); K. Thoresen, "Systems development. Alternative design strategies," in Tijdens et al., eds., *Women, Work and Computerization: Forming New Alliances* (Amsterdam: North-Holland, 1988).

16. Håpnes 1988; Kvande and Rasmussen 1989.

17. Kvande and Rasmussen 1991.

CHAPTER 23
TINYSEX AND GENDER TROUBLE

SHERRY TURKLE

(1995)

From my earliest effort to construct an online persona, it occurred to me that being a virtual man might be more comfortable than being a virtual woman.

When I first logged on to a MUD, I named and described a character but forgot to give it a gender. I was struggling with the technical aspects of the MUD universe—the difference between various MUD commands such as "saying" and "emoting," "paging" and "whispering." Gender was the last thing on my mind. This rapidly changed when a male-presenting character named Jiffy asked me if I was "really an it." At his question, I experienced an unpleasurable sense of disorientation which immediately gave way to an unfamiliar sense of freedom.

When Jiffy's question appeared on my screen, I was standing in a room of LambdaMOO filled with characters engaged in sexual banter in the style of the movie *Animal House*. The innuendos, double entendres, and leering invitations were scrolling by at a fast clip; I felt awkward, as though at a party to which I had been invited by mistake. I was reminded of junior high school dances when I wanted to go home or hide behind the punch bowl. I was reminded of kissing games in which it was awful to be chosen and awful not to be chosen. Now, on the MUD, I had a new option. I wondered if playing a male might allow me to feel less out of place. I could stand on the sidelines and people would expect *me* to make the first move. And I could choose not to. I could choose simply to "lurk," to stand by and observe the action. Boys, after all, were not called prudes if they were too cool to play kissing games. They were not categorized as wallflowers if they held back and didn't ask girls to dance. They could simply be shy in a manly way—aloof, above it all.

Two days later I was back in the MUD. After I typed the command that joined me, in Boston, to the computer in California where the MUD resided, I discovered that I had lost the paper on which I had written my MUD password. This meant that I could not play my own character but had to log on as a guest. As such, I was assigned a color: Magenta. As "Magenta_guest" I was again without gender. While I was struggling with basic MUD commands, other players were typing messages for all to see such as "Magenta_guest gazes hot and enraptured at the approach of Fire_Eater." Again I was tempted to hide from the frat party atmosphere by trying to pass as a man.[1] When much later I did try playing a male character, I finally experienced that permission to move freely I had always imagined to be the birthright of men. Not only was I approached less frequently, but I found it easier to respond to an unwanted overture with aplomb, saying something like, "That's flattering, Ribald_Temptress, but I'm otherwise engaged." My sense of freedom didn't just involve a different attitude about sexual advances, which now seemed less threatening. As a woman I have a hard time deflecting a request for conversation by asserting my own agenda. As a MUD male, doing so (nicely) seemed more natural; it never struck me as dismissive or rude. Of course, my reaction said as much about the construction of gender in my own mind as it did about the social construction of gender in the MUD.

Playing in MUDs, whether as a man, a woman, or a neuter character, I quickly fell into the habit of orienting myself to new cyberspace acquaintances by checking out their gender. This was a strange exercise, especially because a significant proportion of the female-presenting characters were RL men, and a good number of the male-presenting characters were RL women. I was not alone in this curiously irrational preoccupation. For many players, guessing the true gender of players behind MUD characters has become something of an art form. Pavel Curtis, the founder of LambdaMOO, has observed that when a female-presenting character is called something like FabulousHot-Babe, one can be almost sure there is a man behind the mask.[2] Another experienced MUDer shares the folklore that "if a female-presenting character's description of her beauty goes on for more than two paragraphs, 'she' [the player behind the character] is sure to be an ugly woman."

The preoccupation in MUDs with getting a "fix" on people through "fixing" their gender reminds us of the extent to which we use gender to shape our relationships. Corey, a twenty-two-year-old dental technician, says that her name often causes people to assume that she is male—that is, until she meets them. Corey has long blonde hair, piled high, and admits to "going for the Barbie look."

> I'm not sure how it started, but I know that when I was a kid the more people said, "Oh, you have such a cute boy's name," the more I laid on the hairbows. [With my name] they always expected a boy—or at least a tomboy.

Corey says that, for her, part of the fun of being online is that she gets to see "a lot of people having the [same] experience [with their online names that] I've had with my name." She tells me that her girlfriend logged on as Joel instead of Joely, "and she saw people's expectations change real fast." Corey continues:

> I also think the neuter characters [in MUDs] are good. When I play one, I realize how hard it is not to be either a man or a woman. I always find myself trying to be one or the other even when I'm trying to be neither. And all the time I'm talking to a neuter character [she reverses roles here] . . . I'm thinking "So who's behind it?"

In MUDs, the existence of characters other than male or female is disturbing, evocative. Like transgressive gender practices in real life, by breaking the conventions, it dramatizes our attachment to them.

Gender-swapping on MUDs is not a small part of the game action. By some estimates, Habitat, a Japanese MUD, has 1.5 million users. Habitat is a MUD operated for profit. Among the registered members of Habitat, there is a ratio of four real-life men to each real-life woman. But inside the MUD the ratio is only three male characters to one female character. In other words, a significant number of players, many tens of thousands of them, are virtually cross-dressing.[3]

GENDER TROUBLE[4]

What is virtual gender-swapping all about? Some of those who do it claim that it is not particularly significant. "When I play a woman I don't really take it too seriously," said twenty-year-old Andrei. "I do it to improve the ratio of women to men. It's just a game." On one level, virtual gender-swapping is easier than doing it in real life. For a man to present himself as female in a chat room, on an IRC channel, or in a MUD, only requires writing a description. For a man to play a woman on the streets of an American city, he would have to shave various parts of his body; wear makeup, perhaps a wig, a dress, and high heels; perhaps change his voice, walk, and mannerisms. He would have some anxiety about passing, and there might be even more anxiety about not passing, which would pose a risk of violence and possibly arrest. So more men are willing to give virtual cross-dressing a try. But once they are online as female, they soon find that maintaining this fiction is difficult. To pass as a woman for any length of time requires understanding how gender inflects speech, manner, the interpretation of experience. Women attempting to pass as men face the same kind of challenge. One woman said that she "worked hard" to pass in a room on a commercial network service that was advertised as a meeting place for gay men.

> I have always been so curious about what men do with each other. I could never even imagine how they talk to each other. I can't exactly go to a gay bar and eavesdrop inconspicuously. [When online] I don't actually have [virtual] sex with anyone. I get out of that by telling the men there that I'm shy and still unsure. But I like hanging out; it makes gays seem less strange to me. But it is not so easy. You have to think about it, to make up a life, a job, a set of reactions.

Virtual cross-dressing is not as simple as Andrei suggests. Not only can it be technically challenging, it can be psychologically complicated. Taking a virtual role may involve you in ongoing relationships. In this process, you may discover things about yourself that you never knew before. You may discover things about other people's response to you. You are not in danger of being arrested, but you are embarked on an enterprise that is not without some gravity and emotional risk.

In fact, one strong motivation to gender-swap in virtual space is to have TinySex as a creature of another gender, something that suggests more than an emotionally neutral activity. Gender-swapping is an opportunity to explore conflicts raised by one's biological gender. Also, as Corey noted, by enabling people to experience what it "feels" like to be the opposite gender or to have no gender at all, the practice encourages reflection on the way ideas about gender shape our expectations. MUDs and the virtual personae one adopts within them are objects-to-think-with for reflecting on the social construction of gender.

Case, a thirty-four-year-old industrial designer who is happily married to a coworker, is currently MUDding as a female character. In response to my question, "Has MUDding ever caused you any emotional pain?" he says, "Yes, but also the kind of learning that comes from hard times."

> I'm having pain in my playing now. The woman I'm playing in MedievalMUSH [Mairead] is having an interesting relationship with a fellow. Mairead is a law-yer. It costs so much to go to law school that it has to be paid for by a corpora-tion or a noble house. A man she met and fell in love with was a nobleman. He paid for her law school. He bought my [Case slips into referring to Mairead in the first person] contract. Now he wants to marry me although I'm a com-moner. I finally said yes. I try to talk to him about the fact that I'm essentially his property. I'm a commoner, I'm basically property and to a certain extent that doesn't bother me. I've grown up with it, that's the way life is. He wants to deny the situation. He says, "Oh no, no, no. . . . We'll pick you up, set you on your feet, the whole world is open to you."
>
> But everytime I behave like I'm now going to be a countess some day, you know, assert myself—as in, "And I never liked this wallpaper anyway"—I get pushed down. The relationship is pull up, push down. It's an incredibly psy-chologically damaging thing to do to a person. And the very thing that he liked about her—that she was independent, strong, said what was on her mind—it is all being bled out of her.

Case looks at me with a wry smile and sighs, "A woman's life." He continues:

> I see her [Mairead] heading for a major psychological problem. What we have is a dysfunctional relationship. But even though it's very painful and stressful, it's very interesting to watch myself cope with this problem. How am I going to dig my persona's self out of this mess? Because I don't want to go on like this. I want to get out of it. . . . You can see that playing this woman lets me see what I have in my psychological repertoire, what is hard and what is easy for me. And I can also see how some of the things that work when you're a man just backfire when you're a woman.

Case has played Mairead for nearly a year, but even a brief experience playing a character of another gender can be evocative. William James said, "Philosophy is the art of imagining alternatives." MUDs are proving grounds for an action-based philosophical practice that can serve as a form of con-sciousness-raising about gender issues. For example, on many MUDs, offering technical assistance has become a common way in which male characters "purchase" female attention, analogous to picking up the check at an RL dinner. In real life, our expectations about sex roles (who offers help, who buys dinner, who brews the coffee) can become so ingrained that we no longer notice them. On MUDs, however, expectations are expressed in visible textual actions, widely witnessed and openly discussed. When men playing females are plied with unrequested offers of help on MUDs, they often remark that such chivalries communicate a belief in female incompetence. When women play males on MUDs and realize that they are no longer being offered help, some reflect that those offers of help may well have led them to believe they needed it. As a woman, "First you ask for help because you think it will be expedient," says a college sophomore, "then you realize that you aren't developing the skills to figure things out for yourself."

ALL THE WORLD'S A STAGE

Any account of the evocative nature of gender-swapping might well defer to Shakespeare, who used it as a plot device for reframing personal and political choices. *As You Like It* is a classic example, a comedy that uses gender-swapping to reveal new aspects of identity and to permit greater complexity of relationships.[5] In the play, Rosalind, the Duke's daughter, is exiled from the court of her uncle Frederick, who has usurped her father's throne. Frederick's daughter, Rosalind's cousin Celia, escapes with her. Together they flee to the magical forest of Arden. When the two women first discuss their plan to flee, Rosalind remarks that they might be in danger because "beauty provoketh thieves sooner than gold." In response, Celia suggests that they would travel more easily if they rubbed dirt on their faces and wore drab clothing, thus pointing to a tactic that frequently provides women greater social ease in the world—becoming unattractive. Rosalind then comes up with a second idea—becoming a man: "Were it not better, / Because that I am more than common tall, / That I did suit me all points like a man?"

In the end, Rosalind and Celia both disguise themselves as boys, Ganymede and Aliena. In suggesting this ploy, Rosalind proposes a disguise that will be both physical ("A gallant curtle-axe on my thigh, / A boarspear in my hand") and emotional ("and—in my heart, / Lie there what hidden woman's fear there will"). She goes on, "We'll have a swashbuckling and martial outside, / as many other mannish cowards have / That do outface it with their semblances."[6]

In these lines, Rosalind does not endorse an essential difference between men and women; rather, she suggests that men routinely adopt the same kind of pose she is now choosing. Biological men have to construct male gender just as biological women have to construct female gender. If Rosalind and Celia make themselves unattractive, they will end up less feminine. Their female gender will end up deconstructed. Both strategies—posing as men and deconstructing their femininity—are games that female MUDders play. One player, a woman currently in treatment for anorexia, described her virtual body this way:

In real life, the control is the thing. I know that it is very scary for me to be a woman. I like making my body disappear. In real life that is. On MUDs, too. On the MUD, I'm sort of a woman, but I'm not someone you would want to see sexually. My MUD description is a combination of smoke and angles. I like that phrase "sort of a woman." I guess that's what I want to be in real life too.

In addition to virtual cross-dressing and creating character descriptions that deconstruct gender, MUDders gender-swap as double agents. That is, in MUDs, men play women pretending to be men, and women play men pretending to be women. Shakespeare's characters play these games as well. In *As You Like It*, when Rosalind flees Frederick's court she is in love with Orlando. In the forest of Arden, disguised as the boy Ganymede, she encounters Orlando, himself lovesick for Rosalind. As Ganymede, Rosalind says she will try to cure Orlando of his love by playing Rosalind, pointing out the flaws of femininity in the process. In current stagings, Rosalind is usually played by a woman who at this point in the play pretends to be a man who pretends to be a woman. In Shakespeare's time, there was yet another turn because all women's parts were played by boys. So the character of Rosalind was played by a boy playing a girl playing a boy who plays a girl so she can have a flirtatious conversation with a boy. Another twist occurs when Rosalind playing Ganymede playing Rosalind meets Phebe, a shepherdess who falls passionately in love with "him."

As You Like It, with its famous soliloquy that begins "All the world's a stage," is a play that dramatizes the power of the theater as a metaphor for life. The visual pun of Rosalind's role underscores the fact that each of us is an actor playing one part or many parts. But the play has another message that speaks to the power of MUDs as new stages for working on the politics of gender. When Rosalind and Orlando meet "man to man" as Ganymede and Orlando, they are able to speak freely. They are able to have conversations about love quite different from those that would be possible if they followed the courtly conventions that constrain communications between men and women. In this way, the play suggests that donning a mask, adopting a persona, is a step toward reaching a deeper truth about the real, a position many MUDders take regarding their experiences as virtual selves.

Garrett is a twenty-eight-year-old male computer programmer who played a female character on a MUD for nearly a year. The character was a frog named Ribbit. When Ribbit sensed that a new player was floundering, a small sign would materialize in her hand that said, "If you are lost in the MUD, this frog can be a friend."

When talking about why he chose to play Ribbit, Garrett says:

I wanted to know more about women's experiences, and not just from reading about them. . . . I wanted to see what the difference felt like. I wanted to experiment with the other side. . . . I wanted to be collaborative and helpful, and I thought it would be easier as a female. . . . As a man I was brought up to be territorial and competitive. I wanted to try something new. . . . In some way I really felt that the canonically female way of communicating was more productive than the male—in that all this competition got in the way.

And indeed, Garrett says that as a female frog, he did feel freer to express the helpful side of his nature than he ever had as a man. "My competitive side takes a back seat when I am Ribbit."

Garrett's motivations for his experiment in gender-swapping ran deep. Growing up, competition was thrust upon him and he didn't much like it. Garrett, whose parents divorced when he was an infant, rarely saw his father. His mother offered little protection from his brother's bullying. An older cousin regularly beat him up until Garrett turned fourteen and could inflict some damage of his own. Garrett got the clear idea that male aggression could only be controlled by male force.

In his father's absence, Garrett took on significant family responsibility. His mother ran an office, and Garrett checked in with her every day after school to see if she had any errands for him to run. If so, he would forgo the playground. Garrett recalls these days with great warmth. He felt helpful and close to his mother. When at ten, he won a scholarship to a prestigious private boarding school for boys, a school he describes as being "straight out of Dickens," there were no more opportunities for this kind of collaboration. To Garrett, life now seemed to be one long competition. Of boarding school he says:

> It's competitive from the moment you get up in the morning and you all got to take a shower together and everyone's checking each other out to see who's got pubic hair. It's competitive when you're in class. It's competitive when you're on the sports field. It's competitive when you're in other extracurricular activities such as speeches. It's competitive all day long, every day.

At school, the older boys had administrative authority over the younger ones. Garrett was not only the youngest student, he was also from the poorest family and the only newcomer to a group that had attended school together for many years. "I was pretty much at the bottom of the food chain," he says. In this hierarchical environment, Garrett learned to detest hierarchy, and the bullies at school reinforced his negative feelings about masculine aggression.

Once out of high school, Garrett committed himself to finding ways to "get back to being the kind of person I was with my mother." But he found it difficult to develop collaborative relationships, particularly at work. When he encouraged a female coworker to take credit for some work they had done together—"something," he says "that women have always done for men"—she accepted his offer, but their friendship and ability to work together were damaged. Garrett sums up the experience by saying that women are free to help men and both can accept the woman's self-sacrifice, "but when a man lets a woman take the credit, the relationship feels too close, too seductive [to the woman]."

From Garrett's point of view, most computer bulletin boards and discussion groups are not collaborative but hostile environments, characterized by "flaming." This is the practice of trading angry and often *ad hominem* remarks on any given topic.

> There was a premium on saying something new, which is typically something that disagrees to some extent with what somebody else has said. And that in itself provides an atmosphere that's ripe for conflict. Another aspect, I think, is the fact that it takes a certain degree of courage to risk really annoying someone. But that's not necessarily true on an electronic medium, because they can't get to you. It's sort of like hiding behind a wall and throwing stones. You can keep throwing them as long as you want and you're safe.

Garrett found MUDs different and a lot more comfortable. "On MUDs," he says, "people were making a world together. You got no prestige from being abusive."

Garrett's gender-swapping on MUDs gave him an experience-to-think-with for thinking about gender. From his point of view, all he had to do was to replace male with female in a character's description to change how people saw him and what he felt comfortable expressing. Garrett's MUD experience, where as a female he could be collaborative without being stigmatized, left him committed to bringing the helpful frog persona into his life as a male, both on and off the MUD. When I met him, he had a new girlfriend who was lending him books about the differences in men's and women's communication styles. He found they reinforced the lessons he learned in the MUD.

By the time I met Garrett, he was coming to feel that his gender-swapping experiment had reached its logical endpoint. Indeed, between the time of our first and second meeting, Garrett decided to blow his cover on the MUD and tell people that in RL he was really male. He said that our discussions of his gender-swapping had made him realize that it had achieved its purpose.

For anthropologists, the experience of *dépaysement* (literally, "decountrifying" oneself) is one of the most powerful elements of fieldwork. One leaves one's own culture to face something unfamiliar, and upon returning home it has become strange—and can be seen with fresh eyes. Garrett described his decision to end his gender-swapping in the language of *dépaysement*. He had been playing a woman for so long that it no longer seemed strange. "I'd gotten used to it to the extent that I was sort of ignoring it. OK, so I log in and now I'm a woman. And it really didn't seem odd anymore." But returning to the MUD as a male persona *did* feel strange. He struggled for an analogy and came up with this one:

> It would be like going to an interview for a job and acting like I do at a party or a volleyball game. Which is not the way you behave at an interview. And so it is sort of the same thing. [As a male on the MUD] I'm behaving in a way that doesn't feel right for the context, although it is still as much me as it ever was.

When Garrett stopped playing the female Ribbit and started playing a helpful male frog named Ron, many of Garrett's MUDding companions interpreted his actions as those of a woman who now wanted to try playing a man. Indeed, a year after his switch, Garrett says that at least one of his MUD friends, Dredlock, remains unconvinced that the same person has actually played both Ribbit and Ron. Dredlock insists that while Ribbit was erratic (he says, "She would sometimes walk out in the middle of a conversation"), Ron is more dependable. Has Garrett's behavior changed? Is Garrett's behavior the same but viewed differently through the filter of gender? Garrett believes that both are probably true. "People on the MUD have . . . seen the change and it hasn't necessarily convinced them that I'm male, but they're also not sure that I'm female. And so, I've sort of gotten into this state where my gender is unknown and people are pretty much resigned to not knowing it." Garrett says that when he helped others as a female frog, it was taken as welcome, natural, and kind. When he now helps as a male frog, people find it unexpected and suspect that it is a seduction ploy. The analogy with his real life is striking. There, too, he found that playing the helping role as a man led to trouble because it was easily misinterpreted as an attempt to create an expectation of intimacy.

Case, the industrial designer who played the female Mairead in Medieval-MUSH, further illustrates the complexity of gender-swapping as a vehicle for self-reflection. Case describes his RL persona as a nice guy, a "Jimmy Stewart–type like my father." He says that in general he likes his father and he likes himself, but he feels he pays a price for his low-key ways. In particular, he feels at a loss when it comes to confrontation, both at home and in business dealings. While Garrett finds that MUDding as a female makes it easier to be collaborative and helpful, Case likes MUDding as a female because it makes it easier for him to be aggressive and confrontational. Case plays several online "Katharine Hepburn–types," strong, dynamic, "out there" women who remind him of his mother, "who says exactly what's on her mind and is a take-no-prisoners sort." He says:

> For virtual reality to be interesting it has to emulate the real. But you have to be able to do something in the virtual that you couldn't in the real. For me, my female characters are interesting because I can say and do the sorts of things that I mentally want to do, but if I did them as a man, they would be obnoxious. I see a strong woman as admirable. I see a strong man as a problem. Potentially a bully.

In other words, for Case, if you are assertive as a man, it is coded as "being a bastard." If you are assertive as a woman, it is coded as "modern and together."

> My wife and I both design logos for small businesses. But do this thought experiment. If I say "I will design this logo for $3,000, take it or leave it," I'm just a typical pushy businessman. If she says it, I think it sounds like she's a "together" woman. There is too much male power-wielding in society, and so if you use power as a man, that turns you into a stereotypical man. Women can do it more easily.

Case's gender-swapping has given him permission to be more assertive within the MUD, and more assertive outside of it as well:

There are aspects of my personality—the more assertive, administrative, bureaucratic ones—that I am able to work on in the MUDs. I've never been good at bureaucratic things, but I'm much better from practicing on MUDs and playing a woman in charge. I am able to do things—in the real, that is—that I couldn't have before because I have played Katharine Hepburn characters.

Case says his Katharine Hepburn personae are "externalizations of a part of myself." In one interview with him, I use the expression "aspects of the self," and he picks it up eagerly, for MUDding reminds him of how Hindu gods could have different aspects or subpersonalities, all the while having a whole self.

You may, for example, have an aspect who is a ruthless business person who can negotiate contracts very, very well, and you may call upon that part of yourself while you are in tense negotiation, to do the negotiation, to actually go through and negotiate a really good contract. But you would have to trust this aspect to say something like, "Of course, I will need my lawyers to look over this," when in fact among your "lawyers" is the integrated self who is going to do an ethics vet over the contract, because you don't want to violate your own ethical standards and this [ruthless] aspect of yourself might do something that you wouldn't feel comfortable with later.

Case's gender-swapping has enabled his inner world of hard-bitten negotiators to find self-expression, but without compromising the values he associates with his "whole person." Role playing has given the negotiators practice; Case says he has come to trust them more. In response to my question, "Do you feel that you call upon your personae in real life?" Case responds:

Yes, an aspect sort of clears its throat and says, "I can do this. You are being so amazingly conflicted over this and I know exactly what to do. Why don't you just let me do it?" MUDs give me balance. In real life, I tend to be extremely diplomatic, nonconfrontational. I don't like to ram my ideas down anyone's throat. On the MUD, I can be, "Take it or leave it." All of my Hepburn characters are that way. That's probably why I play them. Because they are smart-mouthed, they will not sugarcoat their words.

In some ways, Case's description of his inner world of actors who address him and are capable of taking over negotiations is reminiscent of the language of people with multiple personality. In most cases of multiple personality, it is believed that repeated trauma provokes a massive defense: An "alter" is split off who can handle the trauma and protect the core personality from emotional as well as physical pain. In contrast, Case's inner actors are not split off from his sense of himself. He calls upon their strengths with increasing ease and fluidity. Case experiences himself very much as a collective self, not feeling that he must goad or repress this or that aspect of himself into conformity. To use Marvin Minsky's language, Case feels at ease in his society of mind.

Garrett and Case play female MUD characters for very different reasons. There is a similar diversity in women's motivations for playing male characters. Some share my initial motivation, a desire for invisibility or permission to be more outspoken or aggressive. "I was born in the South and I was taught that girls didn't speak up to disagree with men," says Zoe, a thirty-four-year-old woman who plays male and female characters on four MUDs.

> We would sit at dinner and my father would talk and my mother would agree. I thought my father was a god. Once or twice I did disagree with him. I remember one time in particular when I was ten, and he looked at me and said, "Well, well, well, if this little flower grows too many more thorns, she will never catch a man."

Zoe credits MUDs with enabling her to reach a state of mind where she is better able to speak up for herself in her marriage ("to say what's on my mind before things get all blown out of proportion") and to handle her job as the financial officer for a small biotechnology firm.

> I played a MUD man for two years. First I did it because I wanted the feeling of an equal playing field in terms of authority, and the only way I could think of to get it was to play a man. But after a while, I got very absorbed by MUDding. I became a wizard on a pretty simple MUD—I called myself Ulysses—and got involved in the system and realized that as a man I could be firm and people would think I was a great wizard. As a woman, drawing the line and standing firm has always made me feel like a bitch and, actually, I feel that people saw me as one, too. As a man I was liberated from all that. I learned from my mistakes. I got better at being firm but not rigid. I practiced, safe from criticism.

Zoe's perceptions of her gender trouble are almost the opposite of Case's. Case sees aggressiveness as acceptable only for women; Zoe sees it as acceptable only for men. Comparison with Garrett is also instructive. Like Case, Garrett associated feminine strength with positive feelings about his mother; Zoe associated feminine strength with loss of her father's love. What these stories have in common is that in all three cases, a virtual gender swap gave people greater emotional range in the real. Zoe says:

> I got really good at playing a man, so good that whoever was on the system would accept me as a man and talk to me as a man. So, other guys talked to Ulysses "guy to guy." It was very validating. All those years I was paranoid about how men talked about women. Or that I thought I was paranoid. And then, I got a chance to be a guy and I saw that I wasn't paranoid at all.[7]

Zoe talked to me about her experiences in a face-to-face interview, but there is a great deal of spontaneous discussion of these issues on Internet bulletin boards and discussion groups. In her paper "Gender Swapping on the Internet," Amy Bruckman tracks an ongoing discussion of gender issues on the electronic discussion group rec.games.mud.[8] Individuals may post to it, that is, send a communication to all subscribers. Postings on specific topics frequently start identifiable discussion "threads," which may continue for many months.

On one of these threads, several male participants described how playing female characters had given them newfound empathy with women. One contributor, David, described the trials and tribulations of playing a female character:

> Other players start showering you with money to help you get started, and I had never once gotten a handout when playing a male player. And then they feel they should be allowed to tag along forever, and feel hurt when you leave them to go off and explore by yourself. Then when you give them the knee after they grope you, they wonder what your problem is, reciting the famous saying, "What's your problem? It's only a game."

Carol, an experienced player with much technical expertise about MUDs, concurred. She complained about male players' misconception that "women can't play MUDs, can't work out puzzles, can't even type 'kill monster' without help." Carol noted that men offered help as a way to be ingratiating, but in her case this seduction strategy was ineffectual: "People offering me help to solve puzzles *I* wrote are not going to get very far."

Ellen, another contributor to the rec.games.mud discussion, tried gender-bending on an adventure-style MUD, thinking she would find out:

> if it was true that people would be nasty and kill me on sight and other stuff I'd heard about on r.g.m. [an abbreviation of rec.games.mud]. But, no, everyone was helpful (I was truly clueless and needed the assistance); someone gave me enough money to buy a weapon and armor and someone else showed me where the easy-to-kill newbie [a new player] monsters were. They definitely went out of their way to be nice to a male-presenting newbie. . . . (These were all male-presenting players, btw [by the way].)
>
> One theory is that my male character [named Argyle and described as "a short squat fellow who is looking for his socks"] was pretty innocuous. Maybe people are only nasty if you are "a broad-shouldered perfect specimen of a man" or something of that nature, which can be taken as vaguely attacking.

Ellen concluded that harassment relates most directly to self-presentation: "People are nice if they don't view you as a threat." Short, squat, a bit lost, in search of socks, and thus connoting limpness—Argyle was clearly not a threat to the dominant status of other "men" on the MUD. In the MUD culture Ellen played in, men tended to be competitive and aggressive toward each other; Argyle's nonthreatening self-presentation earned him kind treatment.

For some men and women, gender-bending can be an attempt to understand better or to experiment safely with sexual orientation.[9] But for everyone who tries it, there is the chance to discover, as Rosalind and Orlando did in the Forest of Arden, that for both sexes, gender is constructed.[10]

VIRTUAL SEX

Virtual sex, whether in MUDs or in a private room on a commercial online service, consists of two or more players typing descriptions of physical actions, verbal statements, and emotional reactions for their characters. In cyberspace, this activity is not only common but, for many people, it is the centerpiece of their online experience.

On MUDs, some people have sex as characters of their own gender. Others have sex as characters of the other gender. Some men play female personae to have netsex with men. And in the "fake-lesbian syndrome," men adopt online female personae in order to have netsex with women.[11] Although it does not seem to be as widespread, I have met several women who say they present as male characters in order to have netsex with men. Some people have sex as nonhuman characters, for example, as animals on FurryMUDs. Some enjoy sex with one partner. Some use virtual reality as a place to experiment with group situations. In real life, such behavior (where possible) can create enormous practical and emotional confusion. Virtual adventures may be easier to undertake, but they can also result in significant complications. Different people and different couples deal with them in very different ways.

Martin and Beth, both forty-one, have been married for nineteen years and have four children. Early in their marriage, Martin regretted not having had more time for sexual experimentation and had an extramarital affair. The affair hurt Beth deeply, and Martin decided he never wanted to do it again. When Martin discovered MUDs he was thrilled. "I really am monogamous. I'm really not interested in something outside my marriage. But being able to have, you know, a Tiny romance is kind of cool." Martin decided to tell Beth about his MUD sex life and she decided to tell him that she does not mind. Beth has made a conscious decision to consider Martin's sexual relationships on MUDs as more like his reading an erotic novel than like his having a rendezvous in a motel room. For Martin, his online affairs are a way to fill the gaps of his youth, to broaden his sexual experience without endangering his marriage.

Other partners of virtual adulterers do not share Beth's accepting attitude. Janet, twenty-four, a secretary at a New York law firm, is very upset by her husband Tim's sex life in cyberspace. After Tim's first online affair, he confessed his virtual infidelity. When Janet objected, Tim told her that he would stop "seeing" his online mistress. Janet says that she is not sure that he actually did stop.

> Look, I've got to say the thing that bothers me most is that he wants to do it in the first place. In some ways, I'd have an easier time understanding why he would want to have an affair in real life. At least there, I could say to myself, "Well, it is for someone with a better body, or just for the novelty." It's like the first kiss is always the best kiss. But in MUDding, he is saying that he wants that feeling of intimacy with someone else, the "just talk" part of an encounter with a woman, and to me that comes closer to what is most important about sex.

First I told him he couldn't do it anymore. Then, I panicked and figured that he might do it anyway, because unlike in real life I could never find out. All these thousands of people all over the world with their stupid fake names . . . no way I would ever find out. So, I pulled back and said that talking about it was strictly off limits. But now I don't know if that was the right decision. I feel paranoid whenever he is on the computer. I can't get it off my mind, that he is cheating, and he probably is tabulating data for his thesis. It must be clear that this sex thing has really hurt our marriage.

This distressed wife struggles to decide whether her husband is unfaithful when his persona collaborates on writing real-time erotica with another persona in cyberspace. And beyond this, should it make a difference if unbeknownst to the husband his cyberspace mistress turns out to be a nineteen-year-old male college freshman? What if "she" is an infirm eighty-year-old man in a nursing home? And even more disturbing, what if she is a twelve-year-old girl? Or a twelve-year-old boy?

TinySex poses the question of what is at the heart of sex and fidelity. Is it the physical action? Is it the feeling of emotional intimacy with someone other than one's primary partner? Is infidelity in the head or in the body? Is it in the desire or in the action? What constitutes the violation of trust? And to what extent and in what ways should it matter who the virtual sexual partner is in the real world? The fact that the physical body has been factored out of the situation makes these issues both subtler and harder to resolve than before.

Janet feels her trust has been violated by Tim's "talk intimacy" with another woman. Beth, the wife who gave her husband Martin permission to have TinySex, feels that he violated her trust when he chose to play a female character having a sexual encounter with a "man." When Beth read the log of one of these sessions, she became angry that Martin had drawn on his knowledge of her sexual responses to play his female character.

For Rudy, thirty-six, what was most threatening about his girlfriend's TinySex was the very fact that she wanted to play a character of the opposite sex at all. He discovered that she habitually plays men and has sex with female characters in chat rooms on America Online (like MUDs in that people can choose their identities). This discovery led him to break off the relationship. Rudy struggles to express what bothers him about his ex-girlfriend's gender-bending in cyberspace. He is not sure of himself, he is unhappy, hesitant, and confused. He says, "We are not ready for the psychological confusion this technology can bring." He explains:

It's not the infidelity. It's the gnawing feeling that my girlfriend—I mean, I was thinking of marrying her—is a dyke. I know that everyone is bisexual, I know, I know . . . but that is one of those things that I knew but it never had anything to do with me. . . . It was just intellectual.

What I hate about the rooms on America Online is that it makes it so easy for this sort of thing to become real. Well, in the sense that the rooms are real. I mean, the rooms, real or not, make it too easy for people to explore these things. If she explored it in real life, well, it would be hard on me, but it would have been hard for her. If she really wanted to do it, she would do it, but it would have meant her going out and doing it. It seems like more of a statement. And if she had really done it, I would know what to make of it. Now, I hate her for what she does online, but I don't know if I'm being crazy to break up with her about something that, after all, is only words.

Rudy complained that virtual reality made it too easy for his girlfriend to explore what it might be like to have a sexual relationship with another woman, too easy for her to experience herself as a man, too easy to avoid the social consequences of her actions. MUDs provide a situation in which we can play out scenarios that otherwise might have remained pure fantasy. Yet the status of these fantasies-in-action in cyberspace is unclear. Although they involve other people and are no longer pure fantasy, they are not "in the world." Their boundary status offers new possibilities. TinySex and virtual gender-bending are part of the larger story of people using virtual spaces to construct identity.

Nowhere is this more dramatic than in the lives of children and adolescents as they come of age in online culture. Online sexual relationships are one thing for those of us who are introduced to them as adults, but quite another for twelve-year-olds who use the Internet to do their homework and then meet some friends to party in a MUD.

CHILDREN AND NETSEX

From around ten years of age, in those circles where computers are readily available, social life involves online flirting, necking, petting, and going all the way. A thirteen-year-old girl informs me that she prefers to do her sexual experimentation online. Her partners are usually the boys in her class at school. In person, she says, it "is mostly grope-y." Online, "They need to talk more." A shy fourteen-year-old, Rob, tells me that he finds online flirting easier than flirting at school or at parties. At parties, there is pressure to dance close, kiss, and touch, all of which he both craves and dreads. He could be rejected or he could get physically excited, and "that's worse," he says. If he has an erection while online, he is the only one who will know about it.

In the grown-up world of engineering, there is criticism of text-based virtual reality as "low bandwidth," but Rob says he is able to get "more information" online than he would in person.

Face to face, a girl doesn't always feel comfortable either. Like about not saying "Stop" until they really mean *"Stop there! Now!"* But it would be less embarrassing if you got more signals like about more or less when to stop. I think girls online are more communicative.

And online, he adds, "I am able to talk with a girl all afternoon—and not even try anything [sexual] and it does not seem weird. It [online conversation] lends itself to telling stories, gossiping; much more so than when you are trying to talk at a party."

A thirteen-year-old girl says that she finds it easier to establish relationships online and then pursue them offline. She has a boyfriend and feels closer to him when they send electronic mail or talk in a chat room than when they see each other in person. Their online caresses make real ones seem less strained. Such testimony supports Rob's descriptions of online adolescent sexual life as less pressured than that in RL. But here, as in other aspects of cyberlife, things can cut both ways. A twelve-year-old girl files this mixed report on junior high school cyberromance:

> Usually, the boys are gross. Because you can't see them, they think they can say whatever they want. But other times, we just talk, or it's just [virtual] kissing and asking if they can touch your breast or put their tongue in your mouth.

I ask her if she thinks that online sexual activity has changed things for her. She says that she has learned more from "older kids" whom she wouldn't normally have been able to hang out with. I ask her if she has ever been approached by someone she believes to be an adult. She says no, but then adds: "Well, now I sometimes go online and say that I am eighteen, so if I do that more it will probably happen." I ask her if she is concerned about this. She makes it very clear that she feels safe because she can always just "disconnect."

There is no question that the Internet, like other environments where children congregate—playgrounds, scout troops, schools, shopping malls—is a place where they can be harassed or psychologically abused by each other and by adults. But parental panic about the dangers of cyberspace is often linked to their unfamiliarity with it. As one parent put it, "I sign up for the [Internet] account, but I can barely use e-mail while my [fourteen-year-old] daughter tells me that she is finding neat home pages [on the World Wide Web] in Australia."

Many of the fears we have for our children—the unsafe neighborhoods, the drugs on the street, the violence in the schools, our inability to spend as much time with them as we wish to—are displaced onto those unknowns we feel we can control. Fifteen years ago, when children ran to personal computers with arms outstretched while parents approached with hands behind their backs, there was much talk about computers as addicting and hypnotic. These days, the Internet is the new unknown.

Parents need to be able to talk to their children about where they are going and what they are doing. This same commonsense rule applies to their children's lives on the screen. Parents don't have to become technical experts, but they do need to learn enough about computer networks to discuss with their children what and who is out there and lay down some basic safety rules. The children who do best after a bad experience on the Internet (who are harassed, perhaps even propositioned) are those who can talk to their parents, just as children who best handle bad experiences in real life are those who can talk to a trusted elder without shame or fear of blame.

DECEPTION

Life on the screen makes it very easy to present oneself as other than one is in real life. And although some people think that representing oneself as other than one is is always a deception, many people turn to online life with the intention of playing it in precisely this way. They insist that a certain amount of shape-shifting is part of the online game. When people become intimate, they are particularly vulnerable; it is easy to get hurt in online relationships. But since the rules of conduct are unclear, it is also easy to believe that one does not have the right to feel wounded. For what can we hold ourselves and others accountable?

In cyberculture, a story that became known as the "case of the electronic lover" has taken on near-legendary status. Like many stories that become legends, it has several versions. There were real events, but some tellings of the legend conflate several similar incidents. In all the versions, a male psychiatrist usually called Alex becomes an active member of a CompuServe chat line using the name of a woman, usually Joan. In one version of the story, his deception began inadvertently when Alex, using the computer nickname Shrink, Inc., found that he was conversing with a woman who assumed he was a female psychiatrist. Alex was stunned by the power and intimacy of this conversation. He found that the woman was more open with him than were his female patients and friends in real life.[12] Alex wanted more and soon began regularly logging on as Joan, a severely handicapped and disfigured Manhattan resident. (Joan said it was her embarrassment about her disfigurement that made her prefer not to meet her cyberfriends face to face.) As Alex expected, Joan was able to have relationships of great intimacy with "other" women on the computer service. Alex came to believe that it was as Joan that he could best help these women. He was encouraged in this belief by his online female friends. They were devoted to Joan and told her how central she had become to their lives.

In most versions of the story, Joan's handicap plays an important role. Not only did it provide her with an alibi for restricting her contacts to online communication, but it gave focus to her way of helping other people. Joan's fighting spirit and ability to surmount her handicaps served as an inspiration. She was married to a policeman and their relationship gave other disabled women hope that they, too, could be loved. Despite her handicaps, Joan was lusty, funny, a woman of appetites.

As time went on and relationships deepened, several of Joan's grateful online friends wanted to meet her in person, and Alex realized that his game was getting out of control. He decided that Joan had to die. Joan's "husband" got online and informed the community that Joan was ill and in the hospital. Alex was overwhelmed by the outpouring of sympathy and love for Joan. Joan's friends told her husband how important Joan was to them. They offered moral support, financial assistance, names of specialists who might help. Alex was in a panic. He could not decide whether to kill Joan off. In one account of the story, "For four long days Joan hovered between life and death."[13] Finally, Alex had Joan recover. But the virtual had bled into the real. Joan's "husband" had been pressed for the name of the hospital where Joan was staying so that cards and flowers could be sent. Alex gave the name of the hospital where he worked as a psychiatrist. One member of the bulletin board called the hospital to confirm its address and discovered that Joan was not there as a patient. The ruse began to unravel.

All the versions of the story have one more thing in common: The discovery of Alex's deception led to shock and outrage. In some versions of the story, the anger erupts because of the initial deception—that a man had posed as a woman, that a man had won confidences as a woman. The case presents an electronic version of the movie *Tootsie,* in which a man posing as a woman wins the confidence of another woman and then, when he is found out, her fury. In other versions, the anger centers on the fact that Joan had introduced some of her online women friends to lesbian netsex, and the women involved felt violated by Joan's virtual actions. These women believed they were making love with a woman, but in fact they were sharing intimacies with a man. In other accounts, Joan introduced online friends to Alex, a Manhattan psychiatrist, who had real-life affairs with several of them.[14] In these versions, the story of the electronic lover becomes a tale of real-life transgression.

The con artist is a stock character who may be appreciated for his charm in fictional presentations, but in real life is more often reviled for his duplicity and exploitiveness. In this sense, Alex was operating as part of a long tradition. But when familiar phenomena appear in virtual form, they provoke new questions. Was the reclusive, inhibited Alex only pretending to have the personality of the sunny, outgoing, lusty Joan? What was his real personality? Did Joan help her many disabled online friends who became more active because of her inspiration? When and how did Alex cross the line from virtual friend and helper to con artist? Was it when he dated Joan's friends? Was it when he had sexual relations with them? Or was it from the moment that Alex decided to pose as a woman? At a certain point, traditional categories for sorting things out seem inadequate.

In the past fifteen years, I have noticed a distinct shift in people's way of talking about the case of the electronic lover. In the early 1980s, close to the time when the events first took place, people were most disturbed by the idea that a man had posed as a woman. By 1990, I began to hear more complaints about Joan's online lesbian sex. What most shocks today's audience is that Alex used Joan to pimp for him. The shock value of online gender-bending has faded. Today what disturbs us is when the shifting norms of the virtual world bleed into real life.

In 1993, the WELL computer network was torn apart by controversy over another electronic lover where the focus was on these shifting norms and the confusion of the real and the virtual. The WELL has a "Women's Only" forum where several women compared notes on their love lives in cyberspace. They realized that they had been seduced and abandoned (some only virtually, some also in the flesh) by the same man, whom one called a "cyber-cad." As they discussed the matter with more and more women, they found out that Mr. X's activities were far more extensive and had a certain consistency. He romanced women via electronic mail and telephone calls, swore them to secrecy about their relationship, and even flew across the country to visit one of them in Sausalito, California. But then he dropped them. One of the women created a topic (area for discussion) on the WELL entitled "Do You Know this Cyber ScamArtist?" Within ten days, nearly one thousand messages had been posted about the "outing" of Mr. X. Some supported the women, some observed that the whole topic seemed like a "high-tech lynching."[15]

At the time of the incident and its widespread reporting in the popular media, I was interviewing people about online romance. The story frequently came up. For those who saw a transgression it was that Mr. X had confused cyberworld and RL. It was not just that he used the relationships formed in the cyberworld to misbehave in RL. It was that he treated the relationships in the cyberworld as though they were RL relationships. A complex typology of relationships began to emerge from these conversations: real-life relationships, virtual relationships with the "real" person, and virtual relationships with a virtual other. A thirty-five-year-old woman real estate broker tried hard to make clear how these things needed to be kept distinct.

> In a MUD, or chat room, or on IRC, it might be OK to have different flings with other people hiding behind other handles. But this man was coming on to these women as though he was interested in them really—I mean he said he was falling in love with them, with the real women. And he even did meet—and dump—some. Do you see the difference, from the beginning he didn't respect that online is its own place.

Mr. X himself did not agree that he had done anything wrong. He told the computer network that although he had been involved in multiple, simultaneous consensual relationships, he believed that the rules of cyberspace permitted that. Perhaps they do. But if they do, the boundaries between the virtual and real are staunchly protected. Having sex with several characters on MUDs is one thing, but in a virtual community such as the WELL, most people are creating an electronic persona that they experience as coextensive with their physically embodied one. There, promiscuity can be another thing altogether.

Once we take virtuality seriously as a way of life, we need a new language for talking about the simplest things. Each individual must ask: What is the nature of my relationship? What are the limits of my responsibility? And even more basic: Who and what am I? What is the connection between my physical and virtual bodies? And is it different in different cyberspaces? These questions are framed to interrogate an individual, but with minor modifications, they are equally central for thinking about community. What the nature of our social ties? What kind of accountability do we have for our actions in real life and in cyberspace? What kind of society or societies are we creating, both on and off the screen?

BEING DIGITAL

We have seen people doing what they have always done: trying to understand themselves and improve their lives by using the materials they have at hand. Although this practice is familiar, the fact that these materials now include the ability to live through virtual personae means two fundamental changes have occurred in our situation. We can easily move through multiple identities, and we can embrace—or be trapped by—cyberspace as a way of life.

As more and more people have logged on to this new way of life and have experienced the effects of virtuality, a genre of cultural criticism is emerging to interpret these phenomena. An article in *The New York Times* described new books on the subject by dividing them into three categories: utopian, utilitarian, and apocalyptic.[16] Utilitarian writers emphasize the practical side of the new way of life. Apocalyptic writers warn us of increasing social and personal fragmentation, more widespread surveillance, and loss of direct knowledge of the world. To date, however, the utopian approaches have dominated the field. They share the technological optimism that has dominated postwar culture, an optimism captured in the advertising slogans of my youth: "Better living through chemistry," "Progress is our most important product." In our current situation, technological optimism tends to represent urban decay, social alienation, and economic polarization as out-of-date formulations of a problem that could be solved if appropriate technology were applied in sufficient doses, for example, technology that would link everyone to the "information superhighway." We all want to believe in some quick and relatively inexpensive solution to our difficulties. We are tempted to believe with the utopians that the Internet is a field for the flowering of participatory democracy and a medium for the transformation of education. We are tempted to share in the utopians' excitement at the prospect of virtual pleasures: sex with a distant partner, travel minus the risks and inconvenience of actually having to go anywhere.

The new practice of entering virtual worlds—what Nicholas Negroponte, the director of the MIT Media Lab, refers to as being digital[17]—raises fundamental questions about our communities and ourselves. My account challenges any simple utilitarian story. For every step forward in the instrumental use of a technology (what the technology can do for us), there are subjective effects. The technology changes us as people, changes our relationships and sense of ourselves. My account also calls into question the apocalyptic and utopian views. The issues raised by the new way of life are difficult and painful, because they strike at the heart of our most complex and intransigent social problems: problems of community, identity, governance, equity, and values. There is no simple good news or bad news.

Although it provides us with no easy answers, life online does provide new lenses through which to examine current complexities. Unless we take advantage of these new lenses and carefully analyze our situation, we shall cede the future to those who want to believe that simple fixes can solve complicated problems. Given the history of the last century, thoughts of such a future are hardly inspiring.

NOTES

1. At the time, I noted that I felt panicky when female or female-presenting characters approached the gender-neutral "me" on the MUD and "waved seductively." And I noted this with considerable irritation. Surely, I thought, my many years of psychoanalysis should see me through this experience with greater equanimity. They did not.

2. Pavel Curtis, "Mudding: Social Phenomena in Text-Based Virtual Realities," available via anonymous ftp://parcftp.xerox.com/pub/MOO/papers/DIAC92.*. Cited in Amy Bruckman, "Gender Swapping on the Internet," available via anonymous ftp://media.mit.edu/pub/asb/paper/gender-swapping.*.

3. Allucquère Rosanne Stone, presentation at "Doing Gender on the 'Net Conference," Massachusetts Institute of Technology, Cambridge, April 7, 1995.

4. The term "gender trouble" is borrowed from Judith Butler, whose classic work on the problematics of gender informs this essay. See Judith J. Butler, *Gender Trouble: Feminism and the Subversion of Identity* (New York: Routledge, 1990).

5. My thanks to Ilona Issacson Bell for pointing me to this rich example.

6. William Shakespeare, *As You Like It*, act 1, scene 3, lines 107–18.

7. Zoe does not MUD any more. She gave me two reasons. First, her MUDding succeeded in making her more assertive at work. Second, she doesn't want her MUDding to succeed in making her "too much" more assertive at home.

I guess I got what I wanted out of MUDs. When I go to work I try to act like my MUD character, but that character is really a part of me now. Well, more like a role model that I've had as a roommate. Not just as a teacher, but [someone] I actually lived with. For two years I did Ulysses for thirty hours a week, so it isn't so hard to do it for a few hours a week during meetings at work or on the phone with clients. But I didn't go all the way with Ulysses. It started to feel dangerous to me. My marriage is still pretty traditional. I am better at talking about my feelings and I think my husband respects me, but he still is Southern. He still likes the feeling of being superior. We need the money so my husband doesn't mind my working. But I do treat my husband more or less the way my father would have wanted me to. I want to have children. If I brought Ulysses home, it would upset my marriage. I don't want that to happen. I'm not ready for that now. Maybe someday, but not now.

8. With the increasing popularity of MUDding, this group has split up into many different groups, each looking at different aspects of MUDding: administrative, technical, social.

9. People feel different degrees of "safety." Most MUDders know responsibility involves not logging sexual encounters and then posting them to public bulletin boards.

On an Internet bulletin board dedicated to MUDding, a posting of "Frequently Asked Questions" described TinySex as "speed-writing interactive erotica" and warned players to participate with caution both because there might be some deception in play and because there might be the virtual equivalent of a photographer in the motel room:

Realize that the other party is not obligated to be anything like he/she says, and in fact may be playing a joke on you (see 'log') below).

"What is a log?"

Certain client programs allow logs to be kept of the screen. A time-worn and somewhat unfriendly trick is to entice someone into having TinySex with you, log the proceedings, and post them to rec.games.mud and have a good laugh at the other person's expense. Logs are useful for recording interesting or useful information or conversations, as well. (Jennifer "Moira" Smith, MUDFAQ, December 1, 1992. This document posted regularly on rec.games.mud.tiny.)

This last response refers to a client program. This is one of a class of programs that facilitate MUDding. A client program stands between a user's computer and the MUD, performing helpful housekeeping functions such as keeping MUD interchanges on different lines. Without a client program, a user's screen can look like a tangle of MUD instructions and player comments. With a client program a user's screen is relatively easy to read.

10. One of the things that has come out of people having virtual experiences as different genders is that many have acquired a new sense of gender as a continuum. In an online discussion the media theorist Brenda Laurel noted that media such as film, radio, and television advertised the idea that sex and gender were identical and that the universe was bi-gendered. Brenda Laurel, The WELL, conference on virtual reality (vr.47.255), January 14, 1993.

11. Since many more men adopted a female persona than vice versa, some have suggested that gender-bending is yet another way in which men assert domination over female bodies. I thank my student Adrian Banard for his insights on this question. The point was also made by Allucquère Rosanne Stone, presentation at "Doing Gender on the 'Net Conference."

12. Lindsay Van Gelder, "The Strange Case of the Electronic Lover," in *Computerization and Controversy: Value Conflicts and Social Choices*, ed. Charles Dunlop and Rob Kling (Boston: Academic Press, 1991), pp. 366–67.

13. Allucquère Rosanne Stone, Presentation at "Doing Gender on the 'Net Conference."

14. Lindsay Van Gelder, "The Strange Case of the Electronic Lover," p. 372.

15. John Schwartz of *The Washington Post* reported that:

In a telephone conversation, Mr. X (who spoke on the condition of anonymity) again tried to put events in perspective. "The cycle of fury and resentment and anger instantaneously transmitted, created this kind of independent entity. . . . These people went after me with virtual torches and strung me up. The emotional response is entirely out of proportion to what actually happened. It involved distortions and lies about what I did or did not do." "I was wrong," he said. "The cyber world is the same as the real world. . . . I should have realized that the exact same standards should have applied." Mr. X later announced that he would be leaving the WELL. He had already been shunned. (John Schwartz, "On-line Lothario's Antics Prompt Debate on Cyber-Age Ethics," *The Washington Post*, July 11, 1993: A1).

I thank Tina Taylor of Brandeis University for pointing out to me in this case, as in others, the complex position of the virtual body. The virtual body is not always the same. It, too, is constructed by context. A virtual body in a MUD is not the same as a virtual body on IRC or on the WELL.

16. Steve Lohr, "The Meaning of Digital Life," *The New York Times*, April 24, 1995.

17. Nicholas Negroponte, *Being Digital* (New York: Knopf, 1995).

CHAPTER 24

IN NOVEL CONDITIONS

The Cross-Dressing Psychiatrist

ALLUCQUÈRE ROSANNE STONE

(1995)

One of our Western industrialized cultural assumptions is that subjectivity is invariably constituted in relation to a psychical substrate—that social beings, people, exist by virtue of possessing biological bodies through which their existence is warranted in the body politic. Another is that we know unproblematically what "body" is. Let me tell you a boundary story, a tale of the nets, as a means of anchoring one corner of the system of discourse within which this discussion operates. It is also a fable of loss of innocence. People who still believe that I have some sort of rosy vision of the future of virtual systems are advised to reread a few of the origin myths I have presented. Herewith, another.[1]

This one begins in 1982, on the CompuServe conference system. CompuServe is owned by Reader's Digest and Ziff-Davis. CompuServe began in 1980 as a generalized information service, offering such things as plane reservations, weather reports, and the "Electronic Shopping Mall," which is simply lists of retail items that can be purchased through CompuServe and ordered online. It was one of perhaps three major information services that started up within a year or so of each other. The others were The Source, Prodigy, and America Online. All of these were early attempts by businesses to capture some of the potential market formed by consumers with computers and modems, an attempt to generate business of a kind that had not previously existed. None of the online services knew what this market was or where it lay, but their thinking, as evidenced by reports in the *Wall Street Journal,* was along the lines of television. That is, computers would be media in which goods could be sold visually, like a shopping service. Prodigy implemented this theory by having banners advertising products running along the bottom of the screen, while permitting conferencing to go in the main screen area. The companies who financed The Source seem to have believed that unrestricted conversation was against the American Way, because it was never permitted to occur within the system. Both Prodigy and The Source saw their primary mission as selling goods. They attracted audiences in the same way that broadcasters did, as a product to be delivered to manufacturers in the form of demographic groups meant to watch commercials. The Source went quietly bankrupt in 1986. Prodigy, by virtue of having permitted online conferencing, weathered the storms of the shakeout days in which it became clear that whatever online services were good for, it was *not* to deliver audiences to manufacturers. CompuServe, however, found out quite early that the thing users found most interesting was online conferencing and chat—that is, connectivity. Or, as an industry observer put it, "People are willing to pay money just to connect. Just for the opportuity to communicate." America Online never saw itself as a medium for selling goods and concentrated on connectivity in various forms from the beginning.

Most online conferences now offer what are called chat lines, which are virtual places where many people can interact simultaneously in real time. In the Internet world there are many such places with quite elaborately worked out geographies; these are known as multiple-user thisses-and-thats.[2] The first of these were direct descendants of real-life things called role-playing games, or RPGs.

Role-playing games were developed within a rather small community whose members shared certain social traits. First, most were members of the Society for Creative Anachronism, or SCA, one of the driving forces behind the Renaissance Faires. The SCA sponsors medieval tournaments with full regalia as well as medieval banquets in medieval style, which is to say, sixteen-course meals of staggering richness. Once one has attended such a banquet, the shorter life span of people in the Middle Ages becomes much more understandable.

Participants are extremely dedicated to the principles of the SCA, one of which is that tournaments go on as scheduled, rain or shine. In California, where many SCA members live, this can be risky. There is something not exactly bracing about watching two grown men in full armor trying to whack each other with wooden swords while thrashing and wallowing through ankle-deep mud and pouring rain. During this phase of my research I got a glimpse of what it must be like to be trained as a traditional anthropologist, and finally to be sent to some godforsaken island where one thrashes out one's fieldwork in a soggy sleeping bag while being wracked by disabling parasites and continuous dysentery.

Second, many of the people who belong to the SCA also consider themselves part of what is sometimes called the neopagan movement. And third, particularly in California, many of the people who participate in SCA events and who belong to the neopagan movement are also computer programmers.

Originally RPGs seemed to be a way for SCA members to continue their fantasy roles between tournaments. Role-playing games are also a good deal less expensive and more energy efficient than tournaments. They have tremendous grab for their participants, are open-ended, and improve with the players' imaginations. Some RPG participants have kept a good game going for years, meeting monthly for several days at a time to play the game, eating, sleeping, and defecating in role. For some, the game has considerably more appeal than reality. They express an unalloyed nostalgia for a time when roles were clearly defined, folks lived closer to nature, life was simpler, magic was afoot, and adventure was still possible. They are aware, to a certain extent, that their Arthurian vision of the Middle Ages is thoroughly bogus, but they have no intention of allowing reality to temper their enthusiasm.

The first RPG was published as a set of rules and character descriptions in 1972 and was called, appropriately enough, Dungeons and Dragons. It was an extension, really, of SCA into a textual world. D&D, as it quickly became known, used a set of rules invented by the Austin game designer Steve Jackson called the Generic Universal Role Playing System, or GURPS, for constructing characters, and voluminous books containing lists of character attributes, weapons, and powers. A designated Dungeon Master acted as arbiter of disputes and prognosticator of events and had considerable effect on the progress of the game; creative Dungeon Masters, like good tops, were hard to find and, once discovered, were highly prized.

The first 120- and 300-baud modems became available in the mid-1970s, and virtually the instant they became available, the programmers among the D&D community began to develop versions of the game that could be played online. The first online systems ran on small personal computers (the very first were developed for Apple IIs). Because of the problems of writing multi-tasking operating systems, which allow several people to log in online at once, the first systems were time-aliased; that is, only one person could be online at a time, so simultaneous real-time interaction was impossible. The first of these to achieve a kind of success was a program in northern California called *Mines of Moria*. The program contained most of the elements that are still ubiquitous in online RPG systems: Quests, Fearsome Monsters, Treasure, Wizards, Twisty Mazes, Vast Castles, and, because the systems were written by young heterosexual males, the occasional Damsel in Distress.[3]

As the Internet came into being from its earlier and more cloistered incarnation as ARPANET, more people had access to multitasking systems. The ARPANET had been built around multitasking systems such as Bell Laboratories' UNIX and had packet-switching protocols built in; these enabled multiple users to log in from widely separated locations. The first online multiple-user social environments were written in the early 1980s and were named, after their origins, Multiple-User Dungeons or MUDs. When the staid academics and military career persons who actually oversaw the operation of the large systems began to notice the MUDs in the mid-1980s, they took offense at such cavalier misuse of their equipment. The writers of the MUDs then tried the bald public-relations move of renaming their systems Multiple-User *Domains* in an effort to distance themselves from the offensive odor of play that accompanied the word *dungeon*. The system administrators were unimpressed by this move. Later multiple-user social environments came to be called MUSEs (for Multiple-User Social Environment), MUSHes (for Multiple-User Social Host), MUCKs, and MOOs (MUD Object-Oriented). Of these, all are somewhat similar except for the MOO, which uses a different and much more flexible method of creating objects within the simulation. Unlike MUDs, objects and attributes in a MOO are persistent; when the MOO crashes, everything is still in place when it comes back up. This property has importance for large systems such as Fujitsu's *Habitat* and smaller ones that contain many complex objects, such as the MIT Media Lab's MediaMOO and the U.Texas ACTLab's PointMOOt.

The multiple-user social environments written for the large, corporate-owned, for-pay systems betray none of their origins in low culture. They do not contain objects, nor can objects be constructed within them. They are thoroughly sanitized, consisting merely of bare spaces within which interactions can take place. They are the Motel 6 of virtual systems. Such an environment is the CB chat line on CompuServe. It was on CompuServe, some time early in 1982, that a New York psychiatrist named Sanford Lewin opened an account.

In the conversation channels, particularly the real-time chat conferences such as CB, it is customary to choose an online name, or "handle," that may have no relationship to one's "real" name, which CompuServe does not reveal.[4] Frequently, however, participants in virtual conversations choose handles that express some part of their personalities, real or imagined. Lewin, with his profession in mind, chose the handle "Doctor."

It does not appear to have dawned on him that the term was gender-neutral until a day not long after he first signed on. He had been involved in a general chat in public virtual space, had started an interesting conversation with a woman, and they had decided to drop into private mode for a few minutes. In private mode two people who have chosen to converse can only "hear" each other, and the rest of the people in the vicinity cannot "hear" them. The private conversation was actually under way for a few minutes before Lewin realized it was profoundly different from any conversation he'd been in before. Somehow the woman to whom he was talking had mistaken him for a *woman* psychiatrist. He had always felt that even in his most personal conversations with women there was always something missing, some essential connection. Suddenly he understood why, because the conversation he was now having was deeper and more open than anything he'd experienced. "I was stunned," he said later, "at the conversational mode. I hadn't known that women talked among themselves that way. There was so much more vulnerability, so much more depth and complexity. And then I thought to myself, Here's a terrific opportunity to help people, by catching them when their normal defenses are down and they're more able to hear what they need to hear."

Lewin reasoned, or claimed to have reasoned, that if women were willing to let down their conversational barriers with other women in the chat system, then as a psychiatrist he could use the chat system to do good. The obvious strategy of continuing to use the gender-neutral "Doctor" handle didn't seem like the right approach. It appears that he became deeply intrigued with the idea of interacting with women *as a woman,* rather than using a female persona as a masquerade. He wanted to become a female persona to such an extent that he could feel what it was like to be a woman in some deep and essential way. And at this point his idea of helping women by becoming an online woman psychiatrist took a different turn.

He opened a second account with CompuServe under the name Julie Graham.[5] He spent considerable time working out Julie's persona. He needed someone who would be fully functioning online, but largely unavailable offline in order to keep her real identity secret. For the most part, he developed an elaborate and complex history for Julie, but creating imaginary personae was not something with which he had extensive experience. So there were a few minor inconsistencies in Julie's history from time to time; and it was these that provided the initial clues that eventually tipped off a few people on the net that something was wrong. As it turned out, though, Julie's major problems didn't arise from the inconsistencies in her history, but rather from the consistencies—from the picture-book life Lewin had developed for her.

Julie first signed on in 1982. She described herself as a New York neuropsychologist who, within the last few years, had been involved a serious automobile accident caused by a drunken driver. Her boyfriend had been killed, and she had suffered severe neurological damage to her head and spine, in particular to Broca's area, which controls speech. She was now mute and paraplegic. In addition, her face had been severely disfigured, to the extent that plastic surgery was unable to restore her appearance. Consequently she never saw anyone in person. She had become a recluse, embittered, slowly withdrawing from life, and seriously planning suicide, when a friend gave her a small computer and modem and she discovered CompuServe.

After being tentatively online for a while, her personality began to flourish. She began to talk about how her life was changing, and how interacting with other women in the net was helping her reconsider her situation. She stopped thinking of suicide and began planning her life. Although she lived alone and currently held no job, she had a small income from an inheritance; her family had made a fortune in a mercantile business, so at least she was assured of a certain level of physical comfort. She was an atheist, who enjoyed attacking organized religion; smoked dope, and was occasionally quite stoned online late at night; and was bisexual, from time to time coming on to the men and women with whom she talked. In fact, as time went on, she became flamboyantly sexual. Eventually she was encouraging many of her friends to engage in netsex with her.

Some time during this period Julie changed her handle, or sign-on pseudonym, as a celebration of her return to an active social life, at least on the net. She still maintained her personal privacy, insisting that she was too ashamed of her disfigurements and her inability to vocalize, preferring to be known only by her online persona. People on the chat system held occasional parties at which those who lived in reasonable geographic proximity would gather to exchange a few socialites in biological mode, and Julie assiduously avoided these. Instead she ramped up her social profile on the net even further. Her standard greeting was a huge, expansive "HI!!!!!!!!!!!!"

Julie started a women's discussion group on CompuServe. She also had long talks with women outside the group, and her advice was extremely helpful to many of them. Over the course of time several women confided to her that they were depressed and thinking about suicide, and she shared her own thoughts about her brush with suicide and helped them to move on to more life-affirming attitudes. She also helped several women with drug and chemical dependencies. An older woman confided her desire to return to college with her fear of being rejected; Julie encouraged her to go through with the application process. Once the woman was accepted, Julie advised her on the writing of several papers (including one on MPD) and in general acted as wise counsel and supportive sister.

She also took it upon herself to ferret out pretenders in the chat system, in particular men who masqueraded as women. As Van Gelder pointed out in her study of the incident, Julie was not shy about warning women about the dangers of letting one's guard down on the net. "Remember to be careful," Van Gelder quotes her as saying, "Things may not be as they seem."[6]

There is a subtext here, which has to do with what I have been calling the online persona. Of course we all change personae all the time, to suit the social occasion, although with online personae the act is more purposeful. Nevertheless, the societal imperative with which we have been raised is that there is one primary persona, or "true identity," and that in the offline world—the "real world"—this persona is firmly attached to a single physical body, by which our existence as a social being is authorized and in which it is grounded. The origin of this "correct" relationship between body and persona seems to have been contemporaneous with the Enlightenment, the same cultural moment that gave birth to what we like to call the sovereign subject. True, there is no shortage of examples extending far back in time of a sense of something in the body other than just meat. Usually this has to do with an impalpable soul or a similar manifestation—some agency that carries with it the seat of consciousness, and that normally may be decoupled from the body only after death. For many people, though, the soul or some impalpable avatar routinely journeys free of the body, and a certain amount of energy is routinely expended in managing the results of its travels. Partly the Western idea that the body and the subject are inseparable is a worthy exercise in wish fulfillment—an attempt to explain why ego-centered subjectivity terminates with the substrate *and* to enforce the termination. Recently we find in science fiction quite a number of attempts to refigure this relationship, notably in the work of authors like John Varley, who has made serious tries at constructing phenomenologies of the self (e.g., Varley 1986).

Julie worked off her fury at drunk drivers by volunteering to ride along in police patrol cars. Because of her experience at neuropsychology, she was able to spot erratic driving very quickly, and by her paralysis she could offer herself as a horrible example of the consequences. During one of these forays she met a young cop named John. Her disability and disfigured face bothered him not a whit, and they had a whirlwind romance. Shortly he proposed to her. After Julie won his mother over (she had told him "he was throwing his life away by marrying a cripple"), they were married in a joyous ceremony. Rather than having a live reception, they held the reception online, toasting and being toasted by friends from remote sites around the country. They announced that they intended to honeymoon in the Greek islands, and soon real postcards from Greece began showing up in their friends' mailboxes.

Julie's professional life began to bloom. She began attending conferences and giving papers around the States, and shortly in Europe as well. Of course there were problems, but John was the quintessential caring husband, watching out for her, nurturing her. Her new popularity on the conference circuit allowed them to take frequent trips to exotic places. While they were on safari, if there was a place her wheelchair couldn't reach, he simply carried her. When they were home he was frequently out on stakeouts in the evenings, which gave her lots of time to engage with her online friends. Occasionally he would take over the keyboard and talk to her friends on the chat system.

Julie began talking about becoming a college teacher. She felt that she could overcome her handicap by using a computer in the classroom. This would be hooked to a large screen to "talk" with her students.[7] Throughout the planning of her new career, John was thoroughly supportive and caring.[8]

It was some time during this period that Julie's friends first began to become suspicious. She was always off at conferences, where presumably she met face to face with colleagues. And she and John spent a lot of time on exotic vacations, where she must also be seeing people face to face. It seemed that the only people who never got to see her were her online friends. With them she maintained a firm and unyielding invisibility. There were beginning to be too many contradictions. But it was the other disabled women online who pegged her first. They knew the real difficulties—personal and interpersonal—of being disabled. Not "differently abled," that wonderful term, but rather the brutal reality of the way most people—including some friends— related to them. In particular they knew the exquisite problems of negotiating friendships, not to mention love relationships, in close quarters with the "normally" abled. In that context, Julie's relationship with the unfailingly caring John was simply impossible. John was a Stepford husband.

Still, nobody had yet pegged Julie as other than a disabled woman. The other disabled women online thought that she was probably a disabled woman, but also felt that she was probably lying about her romantic life and about her frequent trips. But against that line of argument they had to deal with the reality that they had hard evidence of some of those trips—real postcards from Greece—and in fact Julie and John had gone back to Greece the next year, accompanied by another flurry of postcards.

Julie, John, Joan—they are all wonderful examples of the war of desire and technology. Their complex virtual identities are real and productive interventions into our cultural belief that the unmarked social unit, besides being white and male, is a single self in a single body: Multiple personality "disorder" is another such intervention. MPD is generally considered to be pathological, the result of trauma. But we can look to the construction and management of pathology for the circumstances that constitute and authorize the unmarked, so that we may take the pathologization of MPD and in general the management and control of any manifestations of body-self, other than the one body–one self norm, to be useful tools to take apart discourses of the political subject so we can see what makes them work. There are other interventions to be made, and here we interrogate a few Harawayan else-wheres—in this case, virtual space, the phantasmic "structure" within which real social interactions take place—for information. Of course, the virtual en-vironment of the chat lines is just the beginning, a look at a single event when such events were still singular.

Julie's friends weren't the only ones who were nervous over the turns her life was taking and the tremendous personal growth she was experiencing. In fact, Lewin was getting nervous too. Apparently he'd never expected the impersonation to succeed so dramatically. He thought he'd make a few con-tacts online, and maybe offer helpful advice to some women. What had hap-pened instead was that he'd found himself deeply engaged in developing a whole new part of himself that he'd never known existed. His responses had long since ceased to be a masquerade; with the help of the online mode and a certain amount of textual prosthetics, he was in the process of *becoming* Julie. She no longer simply carried out his wishes at the keyboard; she had her own emergent personality, her own ideas, her own directions. Not that he was losing his identity, but he was certainly developing a parallel one, one of con-siderable puissance. Jekyll and Julie. As her friendships deepened and simulta-neously the imposture began to unravel, Lewin began to realize the enormity of his deception.

And the simplicity of the solution.

Julie had to die.

And so events ground inexorably onward. One day Julie became seriously ill. With John's help, she was rushed to the hospital. John signed on to her account to tell her online friends and to explain what was happening: Julie had been struck by an exotic bug to which she had little resistance, and in her weakened state it was killing her. For a few days she hovered between life and death, while Lewin hovered, setting up her demise in a plausible fashion.

The result was horrific. Lewin, as John, was deluged with expressions of shock, sorrow, and caring. People offered medical advice, offered financial assistance, sent cards, sent flowers. Some people went into out-and-out panic. The chat lines became jammed. So many people got seriously upset, in fact, that Lewin backed down. He couldn't stand to go through with it. He couldn't stand to engineer her death. Julie recovered and came home.

The relief on the net was enormous. Joyous messages were exchanged. Julie and John were overwhelmed with caring from their friends. In fact, sometime during the great outpouring of sympathy and concern, while Julie was at death's door, one of her friends managed to find out the name of the hospital where she was supposed to be staying. He called, to see if he could help out, and was told there was no one registered by that name. Another thread unraveled.

Lewin was still stuck with the problem that he hadn't had the guts to solve. He decided to try another tack, one that might work even better from his point of view. Shortly, Julie began to introduce people to her new friend,

Sanford Lewin, a New York psychiatrist. She was enormously gracious about it, if not downright pushy. To hear her tell it, Lewin was the greatest thing to hit a net since Star-Kist Tuna. She told them Lewin was absolutely wonderful, charming, graceful, intelligent, and eminently worthy of their most affectionate attention. Thus introduced, Lewin then began trying to make friends with Julie's friends himself.

He couldn't do it.

Sanford simply didn't have the personality to make friends easily online. Where Julie was freewheeling and jazzy, Sanford was subdued and shy. Julie was a confirmed atheist, an articulate firebrand of rationality, while Sanford was a devout conservative Jew. Julie smoked dope and occasionally got a bit drunk online; Sanford was, how shall we say, drug-free—in fact, he was frightened of drugs—and he restricted his drinking to a little Manischewitz on high holy days. And to complete the insult, Julie had fantastic luck with sex online, while when it came to erotics Sanford was a hopeless klutz who didn't know a vagina from a virginal. In short, Sanford's Sanford persona was being defeated by his Julie persona.

What do you do when your imaginary playmate makes friends better than you do?

With Herculean efforts Lewin had succeeded in striking up at least a beginning friendship with a few of Julie's friends when the Julie persona began to come seriously unraveled. First the disabled women began to wonder aloud, then Lewin took the risk of revealing himself to a few more women with whom he felt he had built a friendship. Once he started the process, word of what was happening spread rapidly through the net. But just as building Julie's persona had taken some time, the actual dismantling of it took several months, as more clearly voiced suspicions gradually turned to factual information and the information was passed around the conferences, re peated, discussed, and picked over. Shortly the process reached a critical level where it became self-supporting. In spite of the inescapable reality of the deception, though, or rather in spite of the inescapable unreality of Julie Graham, there was a kind of temporal and emotional mass in motion that, Newton-like, tended to remain in motion. Even as it slowly disintegrated like one of the walking dead, the myth of Julie still tended to roll ponderously ahead on its own, shedding shocked clots of ex-Julie fans as it ran down. The effect, though spread out over time, was like a series of bombing raids interspersed throughout a ground war.

Perhaps to everyone's surprise, the emotion that many of those in the chat system felt most deeply was mourning. Because of the circumstances in which it occurred, Julie's unmasking as a construct, a cross-dressing man, had been worse than a death. There was no focused instant of pain and loss. There was no funeral, no socially supported way to lay the Julie persona to rest, to release one's emotions and to move on. The help Julie had given people in that very regard seemed inappropriate in the circumstance. Whatever else Julie was or wasn't, she had been a good friend and a staunch supporter to many people in need, giving unstintingly of her time and virtual energy wherever it was required. Her fine sense of humor and ability to see the bright side of difficulties had helped many people, mostly women, over very difficult places in their lives. At least some of her charm and charisma should have rubbed off on Lewin. But it didn't. And, quite understandably, some of the women did not bounce back with forgiveness. At least one said that she felt a deep emotional violation which, in her opinion, was tantamount to sexual assault. "I felt raped," she said, "I felt as if my deepest secrets were violated. The good things Julie did . . . were all done by deception." Some of the women formed a support group to talk about their sense of betrayal and violation, which they referred to wryly as "Julie-anon."

There is no mention of pathology with Lewin's Julie persona, even though the issue of rape was explicitly raised and one of Lewin's personae committed it. The occultation of the issue of warranting in Julie's case enabled the rape (the narrow-bandwidth mode of the nets interfered with the chat participants' warranting Julie to Lewin, so that even when they became suspicious they had to fall back on nonphysical cues that failed them). The issue of presence is more tricky. In Julie's case the technosocial mode of virtual systems is in full operation. Because of the limited-bandwidth mode of the net, both of Lewin's personae had equal presence—but sufficient presence that participants in the chat conferences had no difficulty in distinguishing between them and in making sophisticated distinctions regarding possible friendships and mutual interests. There was no politically apprehensible citizen, but there were certainly socially legible personae.[9]

The Julie incident produced a large amount of Monday morning quarterbacking among the habitués of CompuServe's chat system. In retrospect, several women felt that Julie's helpfulness had exceeded the bounds of good sense—that what she had actually fostered was dependency. Others focused on her maneuvers for netsex, which sometimes amounted to heavy come-ons even with old friends. Perhaps most telling was the rethinking, among Julie's closest friends, of their attitudes toward Julie's disability. One said, "In retrospect, we went out of our way to believe her. We wanted to give her all the support we could, because of what she was trying to do. So everybody was bending over backward to extend praise and support and caring to this disabled person. We were all so supportive when she got married and when she was making all the speaking engagements . . . in fact there was a lot of patronizing going on that we didn't recognize at the time."

Sanford Lewin retained his CompuServe account. He has a fairly low profile on the net, not least because the Sanford persona is inherently low-key. Many of Julie's friends made at least a token attempt to become friends with him. Not too many succeeded, because, according to them, there simply wasn't that much in common between them. Several of the women who were friends of Julie have become acquaintances of Lewin, and a few have become friends. One said, "I've been trying to forget about the Julie thing. We didn't think it through properly in the first place, and many of the women took risks that they shouldn't have. But whether he's Julie or Sanford, man or woman, there's an inner person that must have been there all along. That's the person I really like."

The hackers in my study population, the people who wrote the programs by means of which the nets exist, just smiled tiredly. A few sympathized with the women whom Julie had taken in, and understood that it takes time to realize, through experience, that social rules do not necessarily map across the interface between the physical and virtual worlds. But all of them had understood from the beginning that the nets presaged radical changes in social conventions, some of which would go unnoticed. That is, until an event like a disabled woman who is revealed to be "only" a persona—not a true name at all—along with the violated confidences that resulted from the different senses in which various actors understood the term *person,* all acted together to push these changes to the foreground. Some of these engineers, in fact, wrote software for the utopian possibilities it offered. Young enough in the first days of the net to react and adjust quickly, they had long ago taken for granted that many of the pre-net assumptions about the nature of identity had quietly vanished. Even though they easily understood and assimilated conflictual situations such as virtual persona as mask for an underlying iden tity, few had yet thought very deeply about what underlay the underlying identity. There is an old joke about a woman at a lecture on cosmology who said that she understood quite clearly what kept the earth hanging in space; it actually rested on the back of a giant turtle. When asked what the turtle was standing on, she replied that the turtle was standing on the back of yet another turtle, and added tartly, "You can't confuse me, young man; it's turtles all the way down."

Is it personae all the way down?

Say amen, somebody.

NOTES

1. The methodology of this essay is diverse. First, there is a great deal of what has been called the new thick description, namely, archives of online conversation. This is made possible by the technological character of text-based virtual communities. In most modem programs anything that passes across the screen can be written to a file. The floppy disk has become the cyberanthropologist's field notebook; in virtual social environments nothing escapes its panoptic gaze. Thus there are simple means of preserving the entire conversational records of text-based virtual communities. In the instance of graphic-based virtual communities, this is still possible, but not for every participant and not without some hacking. In the case of "The Cross-Dressing Psychiatrist" I first heard of Julie (whose prototype, Joan Green, has been described by Lindsy Van Gelder, *vide infra*) from acquaintances who were participants in the chat lines. Then, through an odd series of circumstances, when the Julie persona began to unravel I discovered that in an earlier context I had already met the psychiatrist involved.

My account of Lewin's creation of the Julie persona is a pastiche. Very little of it comes from transcriptions. Most is from interviews with participants in chat environ-

ments in which notable deceptions occurred. At first the stories that involved reporting conversations with or about Julie were fragmentary and even contradictory; for a
while Julie came across as an older woman rather than a young one, and that was how
I reported her in my first write-ups. At least one informant said that Julie could only
type with a headstick, a device used by people who do not have the use of their hands,
and I wrote that up too, thus giving Julie more of a complex persona than any of us
had intended. At the time it seemed not unreasonable that a physically challenged
person might participate in chat this way, but in fact few "normally" abled chat-line
habitués would have the patience to wait for a headstick typist; in the 1990s chat lines
tend to be torrents of simultaneous high-speed typing.

An earlier insightful account of the incident upon which the Julie events are based
was published by Lindsy Van Gelder as "The Strange Case of the Electronic Woman,"
first in *Ms.* magazine (1985) and later in Rob Kling's anthology *Computerization and
Controversy: Value Conflicts and Social Choices* (Boston 1991). I have used her thorough
and emotionally lively account to inform mine, and have paraphrased her work in two
instances, one in regard to Julie's allying herself with the police during her convales-
cence (which made no sense as recorded in my notes), and the other in her depiction
of the psychiatrist as using his Joan persona "to do good," which was not in my notes
at all and which I found alternately hilarious and sad, and which, I felt, added a remarkable dimension to Lewin's actions. When I first wrote up my version of the incident I pseudonymized the psychiatrist as I do here, and although Van Gelder used his
"real" (legal) name, I have retained the pseudonym in this version because my account collapses several people from different chat systems who engaged in similar acts.
I doubt that this will cause any confusion, but in case it does, be advised that we are
discussing essentially the same events. Van Gelder published first in both instances.

In regard to the opening section on the relationship between the SCA, programming, and California neopaganism, in response to a query by Carolyn Clark I find
nothing causal about this provocative juxtaposition and did not intend to imply one—
not here, at any rate—except to note that two of the most important individuals in
contemporary neopaganism were active in northern California during this period.
One is Starhawk, the author of *The Spiral Dance*, and the other, who preferred anonymity, founded what is arguably the largest neopagan networking organization and is a
programmer and systems consultant. For better or worse, however, my research has
consistently demonstrated an overwhelming juxtaposition of interests between northern California programmers and neopagans, and one is left with an inescapable feeling that something causal is happening.

With regard to Role Playing Games (RPGs), I collected my data as a participant
observer in several RPG communities in northern and southern California, beginning
in 1979 in Bonny Doon with the kind assistance of Preston Q. Boomer, a mathematics
instructor and RPG master at San Lorenzo High School, and continuing through 1989
with D&D groups in the Santa Clara Valley, Scotts Valley, and San Diego. Boomer
played D&D on the grand scale, involving major Silicon Valley corporations fielding
strike teams for full-scale field maneuvers (for example, a scuba team from IBM once
staged a surprise assault on Boomer's swimming pool to cut off the water supply to his
watercannon), and his story alone should occupy at least an essay. I attended the SCA
tournaments of which I write here, in 1983 in Oakland and throughout the late 1980s
in northern and southern California, in full regalia as Ülfedínn öd Vagfÿaråndi, an
Elder (female) Mage, and subsequently waded through all four removals (a Middle
Ages term meaning sixteen courses) of the banquets. My online D&D data gathering
began in 1980 at 300 baud with the original Mines of Moria. At that time inexpensive
modems did not exist, and my little modem consisted of a data latch and decoder
chip in hardware and a machine language program (the first 6502 machine language
program I wrote) to drive it.

The research underlying the stories of MUDs, MOOs, MUSEs, MUSHes, MUCKs,
and other multiple-user social environments recounted herein is entirely my own,

both from participant observation and on- and offline interviews. I am not terribly fond of most D&D, so the data gathering was not, as some have alleged, continuous unalloyed pleasure. This task was made easier by ACTLab.rtf.utexas.edu, the Advanced Communication Technologies Laboratory M** host machine, and especially by John Garnett, who graciously consented to supervise the four MUDs and two MOOs that originally ran on the ACTLab system; by Allan Alford, a.k.a. chiphead, who master-minded PointMOOTt, actlab's best worked-out and most ill-fated MOO; and by Brian Murfin, a.k.a. Captain Bran Muffin, who has fearlessly and tenaciously administered the actlab's many Internet nodes through rain, sleet, dark of night, and the dreadful legion of patches necessitated by the introduction of new operating systems in the midst of ongoing projects—surely a task far beyond the call of duty.

2. Multiple-user social environments are described at length in ch. 5 of my book *The War of Desire and Technology at the End of the Mechanical Age,* in which this essay was first published.

3. There are plenty of predecessors to *Mines of Moria,* but they did not incorporate the elements of medieval role playing that were ubiquitous in all of the RPG games that followed. At MIT, by the 1960s the hackers of Project MAC had already written *Wumpus,* and when some of them moved on to Commodore and to Apple Computer in the mid-1970s, they immediately produced a version ported to the 6502 environ-ment called *Hunt the Wumpus.* These could quite correctly be seen as earlier games of adventure, since they also incorporated the trademark Twisty Mazes, Dark Passages, Treasure, and of course the highly unpleasant Wumpus. What they lacked was the element of role playing, of engaging an *alter* persona, that characterized all the later games.

4. The term *handle* comes from amateur radio, where it means "nickname." On the Internet chat system *IRC,* the term is *nick.* In programming, a handle is a means (in practice, usually an address) by which a particular procedure or subroutine is reserved for use by a specific program.

5. In Van Gelder's account the psychiatrist used the name Joan Sue Greene.

6. Even in retrospect I find it astonishing that as late as 1983 significant numbers of people engaged in dialogue in virtual communities failed to grasp the problems raised by the existence of artificial personae. For many it was a nonissue. The level of concern was heavily gendered; when imposture became an issue, it was women who were most often hurt. This seems to be true because many women carried their social expectations regarding conversational style and confidentiality across the machinic boundary and into the virtual communities. To this extent they exemplified the con-versational style that Lewin found so attractive.

7. At the time Stephen Hawking could still talk, after a fashion, and the keyboard-and-Votrax system that he would subsequently use had not yet been developed. Vo-traxes can speak in feminine intonation too, and such a system would have been per-fect for Joan, had she existed.

8. A large amount of the distrust that began to surround Julie originated in the uncanny perfection of her relationship with John. Lewin had not taken into consider-ation the possibility of encountering a population of disabled persons online other than Julie, and has subsequently indicated that he might have modulated the Joan identity to allow for it. The "real" disabled women online were more conscious of the incongruity than was the chat system's general population; under the circumstances, it is not strange that they viewed Julie's life first with joy and perhaps hope, then envy, and finally with deep suspicion.

9. And here, of course, the multiple meanings and uses of the term *apprehensible* become clear.

PART VI: OUR MACHINES/OUR SELVES

Gender and Cyborg Subjects

One of the greatest sources of fear and one of the greatest sources of delight is the possibility that one day soon we may no longer be able to distinguish ourselves from machines. The separation of machines and people, seen by some as crucial for human dignity and seen by others as a crippling and archaic limitation, is slowly being chipped away as our technologies become smaller, organic, and ubiquitous. The selections gathered here explore the issues of gender and identity in the presence of the cyborg—an entity that combines what we often see as the distinct categories of organism and machine.

Donna Haraway's far-ranging and widely influential "Cyborg Manifesto" rejects a series of conceptual dualisms that have informed a long-standing antitechnological strain of feminist thought. Asserting that the boundaries between humans, animals, and machines have blurred, she also argues that instead of trying in vain to reconstitute those boundaries we should recognize the powerful potential in exploring and taking responsibility for new identities. In using the image of the cyborg—a creature partly made of organic tissue and partly made of machine components—she develops a political template, a political psychology, and philosophy of identity appropriate for those living in the late twentieth century. The worldview, hopes, dreams, politics, and history of cyborgs are all very different from previous political ideals and Haraway concludes by saying she would rather be a cyborg than a goddess. Her paper challenges us, among other things, to ask why some people find it so important to keep technology and humanity separate, and why dreams of liberation couldn't be found in connections with technology rather than in freedom from it. [Bibliographic references to this chapter have not been reprinted in this collection but may be found in the author's book.]

Haraway's essay marks a change from a long tradition of feminist thought which associates technology with masculinity and oppression. Responding to anxieties in feminism over the possibility of intelligent machines and cyborgs, Judith Halberstam argues that these anxieties usually arise out of a worry that automation removes some natural humanity of the female subject. This worry, she claims, ignores that gender, the very characterization of the female subject, is always technologized and artificial. While some feminists are troubled by blurring the lines between bodies and machines, between the natural and the artificial, Halberstam argues that associating women with bodies, nature, and motherhood repeats an old patriarchal idea and is just as mistaken in feminist thought as in antifeminist thought.

Claudia Springer takes a look at the more or less utopian views of the cyborg and cautions us to compare them with the way cyborg imagery has already made it into popular culture. There, the cyborg reflects a morass of conflicting values and desires. While the virtue of cyborgism and virtual reality in some feminist and social theory is that they allow us to escape our weak and limited gendered bodies, popular images of cyborgs and virtual bodies actually display a fascination with corporeality, sexuality, and exaggerated bodily features. Cyborg bodies in film, comics, and novels are often hypermasculine or hyperfeminine, with gigantic muscles on males or enormous breasts on females. In films such as *Terminator* and *Robocop*, the male cyborg heroes/ villains are typically muscled supermen with a tremendous capacity for violence. In films such as *Eve of Destruction*, female cyborgs are represented as obsessed with sex, men, and human motherhood. Springer points out that, so far, cyborg imagery is full of paradoxes and has failed to meet the postgendered ideals its theorists have projected.

CHAPTER 25

A CYBORG MANIFESTO

Science, Technology, and Socialist-Feminism in the
Late Twentieth Century[1]

DONNA J. HARAWAY

1991

AN IRONIC DREAM OF A COMMON LANGUAGE FOR WOMEN IN THE INTEGRATED CIRCUIT

This essay is an effort to build an ironic political myth faithful to feminism, socialism, and materialism. Perhaps more faithful as blasphemy is faithful, than as reverent worship and identification. Blasphemy has always seemed to require taking things very seriously. I know no better stance to adopt from within the secular-religious, evangelical traditions of United States politics, including the politics of socialist feminism. Blasphemy protects one from the moral majority within, while still insisting on the need for community. Blasphemy is not apostasy. Irony is about contradictions that do not resolve into larger wholes, even dialectically, about the tension of holding incompatible things together because both or all are necessary and true. Irony is about humor and serious play. It is also a rhetorical strategy and a political method, one I would like to see more honored within socialist-feminism. At the center of my ironic faith, my blasphemy, is the image of the cyborg.

A cyborg is a cybernetic organism, a hybrid of machine and organism, a creature of social reality as well as a creature of fiction. Social reality is lived social relations, our most important political construction, a world-changing fiction. The international women's movements have constructed "women's experience," as well as uncovered or discovered this crucial collective object. This experience is a fiction and fact of the most crucial, political kind. Liberation rests on the construction of the consciousness, the imaginative apprehension, of oppression, and so of possibility. The cyborg is a matter of fiction and lived experience that changes what counts as women's experience in the late twentieth century. This is a struggle over life and death, but the boundary between science fiction and social reality is an optical illusion.

Contemporary science fiction is full of cyborgs—creatures simultaneously animal and machine, who populate worlds ambiguously natural and crafted. Modern medicine is also full of cyborgs, of couplings between organism and machine, each conceived as coded devices, in an intimacy and with a power that was not generated in the history of sexuality. Cyborg "sex" restores some of the lovely replicative baroque of ferns and invertebrates (such nice organic prophylactics against heterosexism). Cyborg replication is uncoupled from organic reproduction. Modern production seems like a dream of cyborg colonization work, a dream that makes the nightmare of Taylorism seem idyllic. And modern war is a cyborg orgy, coded by C^3I, command-control-communication-intelligence, an $84 billion item in 1984's U.S. defense budget. I am making an argument for the cyborg as a fiction mapping our social and bodily reality and as an imaginative resource suggesting some very fruitful couplings. Michael Foucault's biopolitics is a flaccid premonition of cyborg politics, a very open field.

By the late twentieth century, our time, a mythic time, we are all chimeras, theorized and fabricated hybrids of machine and organism; in short, we are cyborgs. The cyborg is our ontology; it gives us our politics. The cyborg is a condensed image of both imagination and material reality, the two joined centers structuring any possibility of historical transformation. In the traditions of 'Western' science and politics—the tradition of racist, male-dominant capitalism; the tradition of progress; the tradition of the appropriation of nature as resource for the productions of culture; the tradition of reproduction of the self from the reflections of the other—the relation between organism and machine has been a border war. The stakes in the border war have been the territories of production, reproduction, and imagination. This essay is an argument for *pleasure* in the confusion of boundaries and for *responsibility* in their construction. It is also an effort to contribute to socialist-feminist culture and theory in a postmodernist, nonnaturalist mode and in the utopian tradition of imagining a world without gender, which is perhaps a world without genesis, but maybe also a world without end. The cyborg incarnation is outside salvation history. Nor does it mark time on an oedipal calendar, attempting to heal the terrible cleavages of gender in an oral symbiotic utopia or post-oedipal apocalypse. As Zoe Sofoulis argues in her unpublished manuscript on Jacques Lacan, Melanie Klein, and nuclear culture, *Lacklein*, the most terrible and perhaps the most promising monsters in cyborg worlds are embodied in non-oedipal narratives with a different logic of repression, which we need to understand for our survival.

The cyborg is a creature in a postgender world; it has no truck with bisexuality, pre-oedipal symbiosis, unalienated labor, or other seductions to organic wholeness through a final appropriation of all the powers of the parts into a higher unity. In a sense, the cyborg has no origin story in the Western sense—a "final" irony since the cyborg is also the awful apocalyptic *telos* of the "West's" escalating dominations of abstract individuation, an ultimate self untied at last from all dependency, a man in space. An origin story in the "Western," humanist sense depends on the myth of original unity, fullness, bliss and terror, represented by the phallic mother from whom all humans must separate, the task of individual development and of history, the twin potent myths inscribed most powerfully for us in psychoanalysis and Marxism. Hilary Klein has argued that both Marxism and psychoanalysis, in their concepts of labor and of individuation and gender formation, depend on the plot of original unity out of which difference must be produced and enlisted in a drama of escalating domination of woman/nature. The cyborg skips the step of original unity, of identification with nature in the Western sense. This is its illegitimate promise that might lead to subversion of its teleology as star wars.

The cyborg is resolutely committed to partiality, irony, intimacy, and perversity. It is oppositional, utopian, and completely without innocence. No longer structured by the polarity of public and private, the cyborg defines a technological polis based partly on a revolution of social relations in the *oikos,* the household. Nature and culture are reworked; the one can no longer be the resource for appropriation or incorporation by the other. The relationships for forming wholes from parts, including those of polarity and hierarchical domination, are at issue in the cyborg world. Unlike the hopes of Frankenstein's monster, the cyborg does not expect its father to save it through a restoration of the garden; that is, through the fabrication of heterosexual mate, through its completion in a finished whole, a city and cosmos. The cyborg does not dream of community on the model of the organic family, this time without the oedipal project. The cyborg would not recognize the Garden of Eden; it is not made of mud and cannot dream of returning to dust. Perhaps that is why I want to see if cyborgs can subvert the apocalypse of returning to nuclear dust in the manic compulsion to name the Enemy. Cyborgs are not reverent; they do not re-member the cosmos. They are wary of holism, but needy for connection—they seem to have a natural feel for united front politics, but without the vanguard party. The main trouble with cyborgs, of course, is that they are the illegitimate offspring of militarism and patriarchal capitalism, not to mention state socialism. But illegitimate offspring are often exceedingly unfaithful to their origins. Their fathers, after all, are inessential.

I will return to the science fiction of cyborgs at the end of this chapter, but now I want to signal three crucial boundary breakdowns that make the following political-fictional (political-scientific) analysis possible. By the late twentieth century in United States scientific culture, the boundary between human and animal is thoroughly breached. The last beachheads of uniqueness have been polluted if not turned into amusement parks—language, tool use, social behavior, mental events, nothing really convincingly settles the separation of human and animal. And many people no longer feel the need for such a separation; indeed, many branches of feminist culture affirm the pleasure of connection of human and other living creatures. Movements for animal rights are not irrational denials of human uniqueness; they are a clearsighted recognition of connection across the discredited breach of nature and culture. Biology and evolutionary theory over the last two centuries have simultaneously produced modern organisms as objects of knowledge and reduced the line between humans and animals to a faint trace re-etched in ideological struggle or professional disputes between life and social science. Within this framework, teaching modern Christian creationism should be fought as a form of child abuse.

Biological-determinist ideology is only one position opened up in scientific culture for arguing the meanings of human animality. There is much room for radical political people to contest the meanings of the breached boundary.[2] The cyborg appears in myth precisely where the boundary between human and animal is transgressed. Far from signalling a walling off of people from other living beings, cyborgs signal disturbingly and pleasurably tight coupling. Bestiality has a new status in this cycle of marriage exchange.

The second leaky distinction is between animal-human (organism) and machine. Pre-cybernetic machines could be haunted; there was always the specter of the ghost in the machine. This dualism structured the dialogue between materialism and idealism that was settled by a dialectical progeny, called spirit or history, according to taste. But basically machines were not self-moving, self-designing, autonomous. They could not achieve man's dream, only mock it. They were not man, an author to himself, but only a caricature of that masculinist reproductive dream. To think they were otherwise was paranoid. Now we are not so sure. Late twentieth-century machines have made thoroughly ambiguous the difference between natural and artificial, mind and body, self-developing and externally designed, and many other distinctions that used to apply to organisms and machines. Our machines are disturbingly lively, and we ourselves frighteningly inert.

Technological determination is only one ideological space opened up by the reconceptions of machine and organism as coded texts through which we engage in the play of writing and reading the world.[3] "Textualization" of everything in poststructuralist, postmodernist theory has been damned by Marxists and socialist feminists for its utopian disregard for the lived relations of domination that ground the "play" of arbitrary reading.[4] It is certainly true that postmodernist strategies, like my cyborg myth, subvert myriad organic wholes (for example, the poem, the primitive culture, the biological organism). In short, the certainty of what counts as nature—a source of insight and promise of innocence—is undermined, probably fatally. The transcendent authorization of interpretation is lost, and with it the ontology grounding "Western" epistemology. But the alternative is not cynicism or faithlessness, that is, some version of abstract existence, like the accounts of technological determinism destroying "man" by the "machine" or "meaningful political action" by the "text." Who cyborgs will be is a radical question; the answers are a matter of survival. Both chimpanzees and artifacts have politics, so why shouldn't we (de Waal 1982; Winner 1980)?

The third distinction is a subset of the second: the boundary between physical and nonphysical is very imprecise for us. Pop physics books on the consequences of quantum theory and the indeterminacy principle are a kind of popular scientific equivalent to Harlequin romances as a marker of radical change in American white heterosexuality: they get it wrong, but they are on the right subject. Modern machines are quintessentially microelectronic devices: they are everywhere and they are invisible. Modern machinery is an irreverent upstart god, mocking the Father's ubiquity and spirituality. The silicon chip is a surface for writing; it is etched in molecular scales disturbed only by atomic noise, the ultimate interference for nuclear scores. Writing, power, and technology are old partners in Western stories of the origin of civilization, but miniaturization has changed our experience of mechanism. Miniaturization has turned out to be about power; small is not so much beautiful as preeminently dangerous, as in cruise missiles. Contrast the TV sets of the 1950s or the news cameras of the 1970s with the TV wristbands or hand-sized video cameras now advertised. Our best machines are made of sunshine; they are all light and clean because they are nothing but signals, electromagnetic waves, a section of a spectrum, and these machines are eminently portable, mobile—a matter of immense human pain in Detroit and Singapore. People are nowhere near so fluid, being both material and opaque. Cyborgs are ether, quintessence.

The ubiquity and invisibility of cyborgs is precisely why these sunshine-belt machines are so deadly. They are as hard to see politically as materially. They are about consciousness—or its simulation.[5] They are floating signifiers moving in pickup trucks across Europe, blocked more effectively by the witch-weavings of the displaced and so unnatural Greenham women, who read the cyborg webs of power so very well, than by the militant labor of older masculinist politics, whose natural constituency needs defense jobs. Ultimately the "hardest" science is about the realm of greatest boundary confusion, the realm of pure number, pure spirit, C³I, cryptography, and the preservation of potent secrets. The new machines are so clean and light. Their engineers are sun-worshippers mediating a new scientific revolution associated with the night dream of postindustrial society. The diseases evoked by these clean machines are "no more" than the minuscule coding changes of an antigen in the immune system, "no more" than the experience of stress. The nimble fingers of "Oriental" women, the old fascination of little Anglo-Saxon Victorian girls with doll's houses, women's enforced attention to the small take on quite new dimensions in this world. There might be a cyborg Alice taking account of these new dimensions. Ironically, it might be the unnatural cyborg women making chips in Asia and spiral dancing in Santa Rita jail* whose constructed unities will guide effective oppositional strategies.

So my cyborg myth is about transgressed boundaries, potent fusions, and dangerous possibilities which progressive people might explore as one part of needed political work. One of my premises is that most American socialists and feminists see deepened dualisms of mind and body, animal and machine, idealism and materialism in the social practices, symbolic formulations, and physical artifacts associated with "high technology" and scientific culture. From *One Dimensional Man* (Marcuse 1964) to *The Death of Nature* (Merchant 1980), the analytic resources developed by progressives have insisted on the necessary domination of technics and recalled us to an imagined organic body to integrate our resistance. Another of my premises is that the need for unity of people trying to resist worldwide intensification of domination has

---

*A practice at once both spiritual and political that linked guards and arrested anti-nuclear demonstrators in the Alameda County jail in California in the early 1980s.

never been more acute. But a slightly perverse shift of perspective might better enable us to contest for meanings, as well as for other forms of power and pleasure in technologically mediated societies.

From one perspective, a cyborg world is about the final imposition of a grid of control on the planet, about the final abstraction embodied in a Star Wars apocalypse waged in the name of defense, about the final appropriation of women's bodies in a masculinist orgy of war (Sofia 1984). From another perspective, a cyborg world might be about lived social and bodily realities in which people are not afraid of their joint kinship with animals and machines, not afraid of permanently partial identities and contradictory standpoints. The political struggle is to see from both perspectives at once because each reveals both dominations and possibilities unimaginable from the other vantage point. Single vision produces worse illusions than double vision or many-headed monsters. Cyborg unities are monstrous and illegitimate; in our present political circumstances, we could hardly hope for more potent myths for resistance and recoupling. I like to imagine LAG, the Livermore Action Group, as a kind of cyborg society, dedicated to realistically converting the laboratories that most fiercely embody and spew out the tools of technological apocalypse, and committed to building a political form that actually manages to hold together witches, engineers, elders, perverts, Christians, mothers, and Leninists long enough to disarm the state. Fission Impossible is the name of the affinity group in my town. (Affinity: related not by blood but by choice, the appeal of one chemical nuclear group for another, avidity.)[6]

FRACTURED IDENTITIES

It has become difficult to name one's feminism by a single adjective—or even to insist in every circumstance upon the noun. Consciousness of exclusion through naming is acute. Identities seem contradictory, partial, and strategic. With the hard-won recognition of their social and historical constitution, gender, race, and class cannot provide the basis for belief in "essential" unity. There is nothing about being "female" that naturally binds women. There is not even such a state as "being" female, itself a highly complex category constructed in contested sexual scientific discourses and other social practices. Gender, race, or class consciousness is an achievement forced on us by the terrible historical experience of the contradictory social realities of patriarchy, colonialism, and capitalism. And who counts as "us" in my own rhetoric? Which identities are available to ground such a potent political myth called "us," and what could motivate enlistment in this collectivity? Painful fragmentation among feminists (not to mention among women) along every possible fault line has made the concept of *woman* elusive, an excuse for the matrix of women's dominations of each other. For me—and for many who share a similar historical location in white, professional middle-class, female, radical, North American, mid-adult bodies—the sources of a crisis in political identity are legion. The recent history for much of the U.S. left and U.S. feminism has been a response to this kind of crisis by endless splitting and searches for a new essential unity. But there has also been a growing recognition of another response through coalition—affinity, not identity.[7]

Chela Sandoval (n.d., 1984), from a consideration of specific historical moments in the formation of the new political voice called women of color, has theorized a hopeful model of political identity called "oppositional consciousness," born of the skills for reading webs of power by those refused stable membership in the social categories of race, sex, or class. "Women of color," a name contested at its origins by those whom it would incorporate, as well as a historical consciousness marking systematic breakdown of all the signs of Man in "Western" traditions, constructs a kind of postmodernist identity out of otherness, difference, and specificity. This postmodernist identity is fully political, whatever might be said about other possible postmodernisms. Sandoval's oppositional consciousness is about contradictory locations and heterochronic calendars, not about relativisms and pluralisms.

Sandoval emphasizes the lack of any essential criterion for identifying who is a woman of color. She notes that the definition of the group has been by conscious appropriation of negation. For example, a Chicana or U.S. black woman has not been able to speak as a woman or as a black person or as a Chicano. Thus, she was at the bottom of a cascade of negative identities, left out of even the privileged oppressed authorial categories called "women and blacks," who claimed to make the important revolutions. The category "woman" negated all nonwhite women; "black" negated all nonblack people, as well as all black women. But there was also no "she," no singularity, but a sea of differences among U.S. women who have affirmed their historical identity as U.S. women of color. This identity marks out a self-consciously constructed space that cannot affirm the capacity to act on the basis of natural identification, but only on the basis of conscious coalition, of affinity, of political kinship.[8] Unlike the "woman" of some streams of the white women's movement in the United States, there is no naturalization of the matrix, or at least this is what Sandoval argues is uniquely available through the power of oppositional consciousness.

Sandoval's argument has to be seen as one potent formulation for feminists out of the worldwide development of anticolonialist discourse; that is to say, discourse dissolving the "West" and its highest product—the one who is not animal, barbarian, or woman; man, that is, the author of a cosmos called history. As orientalism is deconstructed politically and semiotically, the identities of the occident destabilize, including those of feminists.[9] Sandoval argues that "women of color" have a chance to build an effective unity that does not replicate the imperializing, totalizing revolutionary subjects of previous Marxisms and feminisms which had not faced the consequences of the disorderly polyphony emerging from decolonization.

Katie King has emphasized the limits of identification and the political/poetic mechanics of identification built into reading "the poem," that generative core of cultural feminism. King criticizes the persistent tendency among contemporary feminists from different "moments" or "conversations" in feminist practice to taxonomize the women's movement to make one's own political tendencies appear to be the *telos* of the whole. These taxonomies tend to remake feminist history so that it appears to be an ideological struggle among coherent types persisting over time, especially those typical units called radical, liberal, and socialist-feminism. Literally, all other feminisms are either incorporated or marginalized, usually by building an explicit ontology and epistemology.[10] Taxonomies of feminism produce epistemologies to police deviation from official women's experience. And of course, "women's culture," like women of color, is consciously created by mechanisms inducing affinity. The rituals of poetry, music, and certain forms of academic practice have been preeminent. The politics of race and culture in the U.S. women's movements are intimately interwoven. The common achievement of King and Sandoval is learning how to craft a poetic/political unity without relying on a logic of appropriation, incorporation, and taxonomic identification.

The theoretical and practical struggle against unity-through-domination or unity-through-incorporation ironically not only undermines the justifications for patriarchy, colonialism, humanism, positivism, essentialism, scientism, and other unlamented -isms, but *all* claims for an organic or natural standpoint. I think that radical and socialist/Marxist-feminisms have also undermined their/our own epistemological strategies and that this is a crucially valuable step in imagining possible unities. It remains to be seen whether all "epistemologies" as Western political people have known them fail us in the task to build effective affinities.

It is important to note that the effort to construct revolutionary standpoints, epistemologies as achievements of people committed to changing the world, has been part of the process showing the limits of identification. The acid tools of postmodernist theory and the constructive tools of ontological discourse about revolutionary subjects might be seen as ironic allies in dissolving Western selves in the interests of survival. We are excruciatingly conscious of what it means to have a historically constituted body. But with the loss of innocence in our origin, there is no expulsion from the Garden either. Our politics lose the indulgence of guilt with the *naïveté* of innocence. But what would another political myth for socialist-feminism look like? What kind of politics could embrace partial, contradictory, permanently unclosed constructions of personal and collective selves and still be faithful, effective—and, ironically, socialist-feminist?

I do not know of any other time in history when there was greater need for political unity to confront effectively the dominations of "race," "gender," "sexuality," and "class." I also do not know of any other time when the kind of unity we might help build could have been possible. None of "us" have any longer the symbolic or material capability of dictating the shape of reality to any of "them." Or at least "we" cannot claim innocence from practicing such dominations. White women, including socialist feminists, discovered (that is, were forced kicking and screaming to notice) the non-innocence of the category "woman." That consciousness changes the geography of all previous categories; it denatures them as heat denatures a fragile protein. Cyborg feminists have to argue that "we" do not want any more natural matrix of unity and that no construction is whole. Innocence, and the corollary insistence on victimhood as the only ground for insight, has done enough damage. But the constructed revolutionary subject must give late-twentieth-century people pause as well. In the fraying of identities and in the reflexive strategies for constructing them, the possibility opens up for weaving something other than a shroud for the day after the apocalypse that so prophetically ends salvation history.

Both Marxist/socialist-feminisms and radical feminisms have simultaneously naturalized and denatured the category "woman" and consciousness of the social lives of "women." Perhaps a schematic caricature can highlight both kinds of moves. Marxian socialism is rooted in an analysis of wage labor which reveals class structure. The consequence of the wage relationship is systematic alienation, as the worker is dissociated from his (sic) product. Abstraction and illusion rule in knowledge, domination rules in practice. Labor is the preeminently privileged category enabling the Marxist to overcome illusion and find that point of view which is necessary for changing the world. Labor is the humanizing activity that makes man; labor is an ontological category permitting the knowledge of a subject, and so the knowledge of subjugation and alienation.

In faithful filiation, socialist-feminism advanced by allying itself with the basic analytic strategies of Marxism. The main achievement of both Marxist feminists and socialist feminists was to expand the category of labor to accommodate what (some) women did, even when the wage relation was subordinated to a more comprehensive view of labor under capitalist patriarchy. In particular, women's labor in the household and women's activity as mothers generally (that is, reproduction in the socialist-feminist sense), entered theory on the authority of analogy to the Marxian concept of labor. The unity of women here rests on an epistemology based on the ontological structure of "labor." Marxist/socialist-feminism does not "naturalize" unity; it is a possible achievement based on a possible standpoint rooted in social relations. The essentializing move is in the ontological structure of labor or of its analog, women's activity.[11] The inheritance of Marxian humanism, with its preeminently Western self, is the difficulty for me. The contribution from these formulations has been the emphasis on the daily responsibility of real women to build unities, rather than to naturalize them.

Catherine MacKinnon's (1982, 1987) version of radical feminism is itself a caricature of the appropriating, incorporating, totalizing tendencies of Western theories of identity grounding action.[12] It is factually and politically wrong to assimilate all of the diverse "moments" or "conversations" in recent women's politics named radical feminism to MacKinnon's version. But the teleological logic of her theory shows how an epistemology and ontology—including their negations—erase or police difference. Only one of the effects of MacKinnon's theory is the rewriting of the history of the polymorphous field called radical feminism. The major effect is the production of a theory of experience, of women's identity, that is a kind of apocalypse for all revolutionary standpoints. That is, the totalization built into this tale of radical feminism achieves its end—the unity of women—by enforcing the experience of and testimony to radical nonbeing. As for the Marxist/socialist feminist, consciousness is an achievement, not a natural fact. And MacKinnon's theory eliminates some of the difficulties built into humanist revolutionary subjects, but at the cost of radical reductionism.

MacKinnon argues that feminism necessarily adopted a different analytical strategy from Marxism, looking first not at the structure of class, but at the structure of sex/gender and its generative relationship, men's constitution and appropriation of women sexually. Ironically, MacKinnon's "ontology" constructs a non-subject, a non-being. Another's desire, not the self's labor, is the origin of "woman." She therefore develops a theory of consciousness that enforces what can count as "women's" experience—anything that names sexual violation, indeed, sex itself as far as "women" can be concerned. Feminist practice is the construction of this form of consciousness; that is, the self-knowledge of a self-who-is-not.

Perversely, sexual appropriation in this feminism still has the epistemological status of labor; that is to say, the point from which an analysis able to contribute to changing the world must flow. But sexual objectification, not alienation, is the consequence of the structure of sex/gender. In the realm of knowledge, the result of sexual objectification is illusion and abstraction. However, a woman is not simply alienated from her product, but in a deep sense does not exist as a subject, or even potential subject, since she owes her existence as a woman to sexual appropriation. To be constituted by another's desire is not the same thing as to be alienated in the violent separation of the laborer from his product.

MacKinnon's radical theory of experience is totalizing in the extreme; it does not so much marginalize as obliterate the authority of any other women's political speech and action. It is a totalization producing what Western patriarchy itself never succeeded in doing—feminists' consciousness of the nonexistence of women, except as products of men's desire. I think MacKinnon correctly argues that no Marxian version of identity can firmly ground women's unity. But in solving the problem of the contradictions of any Western revolutionary subject for feminist purposes, she develops an even more authoritarian doctrine of experience. If my complaint about socialist/Marxian standpoints is their unintended erasure of polyvocal, unassimilable, radical difference made visible in anticolonial discourse and practice, MacKinnon's intentional erasure of all difference through the device of the "essential" nonexistence of women is not reassuring.

In my taxonomy, which like any other taxonomy is a re-inscription of history, radical feminism can accommodate all the activities of women named by socialist feminists as forms of labor only if the activity can somehow be sexualized. Reproduction had different tones of meanings for the two tendencies, one rooted in labor, one in sex, both calling the consequences of domination and ignorance of social and personal reality "false consciousness."

Beyond either the difficulties or the contributions in the argument of any one author, neither Marxist nor radical feminist points of view have tended to embrace the status of a partial explanation; both were regularly constituted as totalities. Western explanation has demanded as much; how else could the "Western" author incorporate its others? Each tried to annex other forms of domination by expanding its basic categories through analogy, simple listing, or addition. Embarrassed silence about race among white radical and socialist feminists was one major, devastating political consequence. History and poly-vocality disappear into political taxonomies that try to establish genealogies. There was no structural room for race (or for much else) in theory claiming to reveal the construction of the category woman and social group women as a unified or totalizable whole. The structure of my caricature looks like this:

socialist feminism—structure of class // wage labor // alienation
labor, by analogy reproduction, by extension sex, by addition race
radical feminism—structure of gender // sexual appropriation //
objectification
sex, by analogy labor, by extension reproduction, by addition race

In other context, the French theorist, Julia Kristeva, claimed women appeared as a historical group after the Second World War, along with groups like youth. Her dates are doubtful; but we are now accustomed to remembering that as objects of knowledge and as historical actors, "race" did not always exist, "class" has a historical genesis, and "homosexuals" are quite junior. It is no accident that the symbolic system of the family of man—and so the essence of woman—breaks up at the same moment that networks of connec-tion among people on the planet are unprecedentedly multiple, pregnant, and complex. "Advanced capitalism" is inadequate to convey the structure of this historical moment. In the "Western" sense, the end of man is at stake. It is no accident that woman disintegrates into women in our time. Perhaps socialist feminists were not substantially guilty of producing essentialist theory that suppressed women's particularity and contradictory interests. I think we have been, at least through unreflective participation in the logics, languages, and practices of white humanism and through searching for a single ground of domination to secure our revolutionary voice. Now we have less excuse. But in the consciousness of our failures, we risk lapsing into boundless differ-ence and giving up on the confusing task of making partial, real connection. Some differences are playful; some are poles of world historical systems of domination. "Epistemology" is about knowing the difference.

THE INFORMATICS OF DOMINATION

In this attempt at an epistemological and political position, I would like to sketch a picture of possible unity, a picture indebted to socialist and feminist principles of design. The frame for my sketch is set by the extent and impor-tance of rearrangements in worldwide social relations tied to science and technology. I argue for a politics rooted in claims about fundamental changes in the nature of class, race, and gender in an emerging system of world order analogous in its novelty and scope to that created by industrial capitalism;

we are living through a movement from an organic, industrial society to a polymorphous, information system—from all work to all play, a deadly game. Simultaneously material and ideological, the dichotomies may be expressed in the following chart of transitions from the comfortable old hierarchical dominations to the scary new networks I have called the informatics of domination:

Representation	Simulation
Bourgeois novel, realism	Science fiction, postmodernism
Organism	Biotic component
Depth, integrity	Surface, boundary
Heat	Noise
Biology as clinical practice	Biology as inscription
Physiology	Communications engineering
Small group	Subsystem
Perfection	Optimization
Eugenics	Population Control
Decadence, *Magic Mountain*	Obsolescence, *Future Shock*
Hygiene	Stress Management
Microbiology, tuberculosis	Immunology, AIDS
Organic division of labor	Ergonomics/cybernetics of labor
Functional specialization	Modular construction
Reproduction	Replication
Organic sex role specialization	Optimal genetic strategies
Biological determinism	Evolutionary inertia, constraints
Community ecology	Ecosystem
Racial chain of being	Neo-imperialism, United Nations humanism
Scientific management in home/factory	Global factory/Electronic cottage
Family/Market/Factory	Women in the Integrated Circuit
Family wage	Comparable worth
Public/Private	Cyborg citizenship
Nature/Culture	Fields of difference
Cooperation	Communications enhancement
Freud	Lacan
Sex	Genetic engineering
Labor	Robotics
Mind	Artificial Intelligence
Second World War	Star Wars
White Capitalist Patriarchy	Informatics of Domination

This list suggests several interesting things.[13] First, the objects on the right-hand side cannot be coded as "natural," a realization that subverts naturalistic coding for the left-hand side as well. We cannot go back ideologically or materially. It's not just that "god" is dead; so is the "goddess." Or both are revivified in the worlds charged with microelectronic and biotechnological politics. In relation to objects like biotic components, one must think not in terms of essential properties, but in terms of design, boundary constraints, rates of flows, systems logics, costs of lowering constraints. Sexual reproduction is one kind of reproductive strategy among many, with costs and benefits as a function of the system environment. Ideologies of sexual reproduction can no longer reasonably call on notions of sex and sex role as organic aspects in natural objects like organisms and families. Such reasoning will be unmasked as irrational, and ironically corporate executives reading *Playboy* and antiporn radical feminists will make strange bedfellows in jointly unmasking the irrationalism.

Likewise for race, ideologies about human diversity have to be formulated in terms of frequencies of parameters, like blood groups or intelligence scores. It is "irrational" to invoke concepts like primitive and civilized. For liberals and radicals, the search for integrated social systems gives way to a new practice called "experimental ethnography" in which an organic object dissipates in attention to the play of writing. At the level of ideology, we see translations of racism and colonialism into languages of development and underdevelopment, rates and constraints of modernization. Any objects or persons can be reasonably thought of in terms of disassembly and reassembly; no "natural" architectures constrain system design. The financial districts in all the world's cities, as well as the export-processing and free-trade zones, proclaim this elementary fact of "late capitalism." The entire universe of objects that can be known scientifically must be formulated as problems in communications engineering (for the managers) or theories of the text (for those who would resist). Both are cyborg semiologies.

One should expect control strategies to concentrate on boundary conditions and interfaces, on rates of flow across boundaries—and not on the integrity of natural objects. "Integrity" or "sincerity" of the Western self gives way to decision procedures and expert systems. For example, control strategies applied to women's capacities to give birth to new human beings will be developed in the languages of population control and maximization of goal achievement for individual decision-makers. Control strategies will be formulated in terms of rates, costs of constraints, degrees of freedom. Human beings, like any other component or subsystem, must be localized in a system architecture whose basic modes of operation are probabilistic, statistical. No objects, spaces, or bodies are sacred in themselves; any component can be interfaced with any other if the proper standard, the proper code, can be constructed for processing signals in a common language. Exchange in this world transcends the universal translation effected by capitalist markets that Marx analyzed so well. The privileged pathology affecting all kinds of components in this universe is stress—communications breakdown (Hogness 1983). The cyborg is not subject to Foucault's biopolitics; the cyborg simulates politics, a much more potent field of operations.

This kind of analysis of scientific and cultural objects of knowledge which have appeared historically since the Second World War prepares us to notice some important inadequacies in feminist analysis which has proceeded as if the organic, hierarchical dualisms ordering discourse in "the West" since Aristotle still ruled. They have been cannibalized, or as Zoe Sofia (Sofoulis) might put it, they have been "techno-digested." The dichotomies between mind and body, animal and human, organism and machine, public and private, nature and culture, men and women, primitive and civilized are all in question ideologically. The actual situation of women is their integration/exploitation into a world system of production/reproduction and communication called the informatics of domination. The home, workplace, market, public arena, the body itself—all can be dispersed and interfaced in nearly infinite, polymorphous ways, with large consequences for women and others—consequences that themselves are very different for different people and which make potent oppositional international movements difficult to imagine and essential for survival. One important route for reconstructing socialist-feminist politics is through theory and practice addressed to the social relations of science and technology, including crucially the systems of myth and meanings structuring our imaginations. The cyborg is a kind of disassembled and reassembled, postmodern collective and personal self. This is the self feminists must code.

Communications technologies and biotechnologies are the crucial tools recrafting our bodies. These tools embody and enforce new social relations for women worldwide. Technologies and scientific discourses can be partially understood as formalizations, i.e., as frozen moments, of the fluid social interactions constituting them, but they should also be viewed as instruments for enforcing meanings. The boundary is permeable between tool and myth, instrument and concept, historical systems of social relations and historical anatomies of possible bodies, including objects of knowledge. Indeed, myth and tool mutually constitute each other.

Furthermore, communications sciences and modern biologies are constructed by a common move—*the translation of the world into a problem of coding,* a search for a common language in which all resistance to instrumental control disappears and all heterogeneity can be submitted to disassembly, reassembly, investment, and exchange.

In communications sciences, the translation of the world into a problem in coding can be illustrated by looking at cybernetic (feedback-controlled) systems theories applied to telephone technology, computer design, weapons deployment, or data base construction and maintenance. In each case, solution to the key questions rests on a theory of language and control; the key operation is determining the rates, directions, and probabilities of flow of a quantity called information. The world is subdivided by boundaries differentially permeable to information. Information is just that kind of quantifiable element (unit, basis of unity) which allows universal translation, and so unhindered instrumental power (called effective communication). The biggest threat to such power is interruption of communication. Any system breakdown is a function of stress. The fundamentals of this technology can be condensed into the metaphor C³I, command-control-communication-intelligence, the military's symbol for its operations theory.

In modern biologies, the translation of the world into a problem in coding can be illustrated by molecular genetics, ecology, sociobiological evolutionary theory, and immunobiology. The organism has been translated into problems of genetic coding and readout. Biotechnology, a writing technology, informs research broadly.[14] In a sense, organisms have ceased to exist as objects of knowledge, giving way to biotic components, i.e., special kinds of information-processing devices. The analogous moves in ecology could be examined by probing the history and utility of the concept of the ecosystem. Immunobiology and associated medical practices are rich exemplars of the privilege of coding and recognition systems as objects of knowledge, as constructions of bodily reality for us. Biology here is a kind of cryptography. Research is necessarily a kind of intelligence activity. Ironies abound. A stressed system goes awry; its communication processes break down; it fails to recognize the difference between self and other. Human babies with baboon hearts evoke national ethical perplexity—for animal rights activists at least as much as for the guardians of human purity. In the U.S. gay men and intravenous drug users are the "privileged" victims of an awful immune system disease that marks (inscribes on the body) confusion of boundaries and moral pollution (Treichler 1987).

But these excursions into communications sciences and biology have been at a rarefied level; there is a mundane, largely economic reality to support my claim that these sciences and technologies indicate fundamental transformations in the structure of the world for us. Communications technologies depend on electronics. Modern states, multinational corporations, military power, welfare state apparatuses, satellite systems, political processes, fabrication of our imaginations, labor-control systems, medical constructions of our bodies, commercial pornography, the international division of labor, and religious evangelism depend intimately upon electronics. Microelectronics is the technical basis of simulacra; that is, of copies without originals.

Microelectronics mediates the translations of labor into robotics and word processing, sex into genetic engineering and reproductive technologies, and mind into artificial intelligence and decision procedures. The new biotechnologies concern more than human reproduction. Biology as a powerful engineering science for redesigning materials and processes has revolutionary implications for industry, perhaps most obvious today in areas of fermentation, agriculture, and energy. Communications sciences and biology are constructions of natural-technical objects of knowledge in which the difference between machine and organism is thoroughly blurred; mind, body, and tool are on very intimate terms. The "multinational" material organization of the production and reproduction of daily life and the symbolic organization of the production and reproduction of culture and imagination seem equally implicated. The boundary-maintaining images of base and superstructure, public and private, or material and ideal never seemed more feeble.

I have used Rachel Grossman's (1980) image of women in the integrated circuit to name the situation of women in a world so intimately restructured through the social relations of science and technology.[15] I used the odd circumlocution, "the social relations of science and technology," to indicate that we are not dealing with a technological determinism, but with a historical system depending upon structured relations among people. But the phrase should also indicate that science and technology provide fresh sources of power, that we need fresh sources of analysis and political action (Latour 1984). Some of the rearrangements of race, sex, and class rooted in high-tech-facilitated social relations can make socialist-feminism more relevant to effective progressive politics.

THE "HOMEWORK ECONOMY" OUTSIDE "THE HOME"

The "New Industrial Revolution" is producing a new worldwide working class, as well as new sexualities and ethnicities. The extreme mobility of capital and the emerging international division of labor are intertwined with the emergence of new collectivities, and the weakening of familiar groupings. These developments are neither gender- nor race-neutral. White men in advanced industrial societies have become newly vulnerable to permanent job loss, and women are not disappearing from the job rolls at the same rates as men. It is not simply that women in Third World countries are the preferred labor force for the science-based multinationals in the export-processing sectors, particularly in electronics. The picture is more systematic and involves reproduction, sexuality, culture, consumption, and production. In the prototypical Silicon Valley, many women's lives have been structured around employment in electronics-dependent jobs, and their intimate realities include serial heterosexual monogamy, negotiating child care, distance from extended kin or most other forms of traditional community, a high likelihood of loneliness and extreme economic vulnerability as they age. The ethnic and racial diversity of women in Silicon Valley structures a microcosm of conflicting differences in culture, family, religion, education, and language.

Richard Gordon has called this new situation the "homework economy."[16] Although he includes the phenomenon of literal homework emerging in connection with electronics assembly, Gordon intends "homework economy" to name a restructuring of work that broadly has the characteristics formerly ascribed to female jobs, jobs literally done only by women. Work is being redefined as both literally female and feminized, whether performed by men or women. To be feminized means to be made extremely vulnerable; able to be disassembled, reassembled, exploited as a reserve labor force; seen less as workers than as servers; subjected to time arrangements on and off the paid job that make a mockery of a limited work day; leading an existence that always borders on being obscene, out of place, and reducible to sex. Deskilling is an old strategy newly applicable to formerly privileged workers. However, the homework economy does not refer only to large-scale deskilling, nor does it deny that new areas of high skill are emerging, even for women and men previously excluded from skilled employment. Rather, the concept indicates that factory, home, and market are integrated on a new scale and that the places of women are crucial—and need to be analyzed for differences among women and for meanings for relations between men and women in various situations.

The homework economy as a world capitalist organizational structure is made possible by (not caused by) the new technologies. The success of the attack on relatively privileged, mostly white, men's unionized jobs is tied to the power of the new communications technologies to integrate and control labor despite extensive dispersion and decentralization. The consequences of the new technologies are felt by women both in the loss of the family (male) wage (if they ever had access to this white privilege) and in the character of their own jobs, which are becoming capital-intensive; for example, office work and nursing.

The new economic and technological arrangements are also related to the collapsing welfare state and the ensuing intensification of demands on women to sustain daily life for themselves as well as for men, children, and old people. The feminization of poverty—generated by dismantling the welfare state, by the homework economy where stable jobs become the exception, and sustained by the expectation that women's wages will not be matched by a male income for the support of children—has become an urgent focus. The causes of various women-headed households are a function of race, class, or sexuality; but their increasing generality is a ground for coalitions of women on many issues. That women regularly sustain daily life partly as a function of their enforced status as mothers is hardly new; the kind of integration with the overall capitalist and progressively war-based economy is new. The particular pressure, for example, on U.S. black women, who have achieved an escape from (barely) paid domestic service and who now hold clerical and similar jobs in large numbers, has large implications for continued enforced black poverty *with* employment. Teenage women in industrializing areas of the Third World increasingly find themselves the sole or major source of a cash wage for their families, while access to land is ever more problematic. These developments must have major consequences in the psychodynamics and politics of gender and race.

Within the framework of three major stages of capitalism (commercial/ early industrial, monopoly, multinational)—tied to nationalism, imperialism, and multinationalism, and related to Jameson's three dominant aesthetic periods of realism, modernism, and postmodernism—I would argue that specific forms of families dialectically relate to forms of capital and to its political and cultural concomitants. Although lived problematically and unequally, ideal forms of these families might be schematized as 1) the patriarchal nuclear family, structured by the dichotomy between public and private and accompanied by the white bourgeois ideology of separate spheres and nineteenth-century Anglo-American bourgeois feminism; 2) the modern family mediated (or enforced) by the welfare state and institutions like the family wage, with a flowering of a-feminist heterosexual ideologies, including their radical versions represented in Greenwich Village around the First World War; and 3) the "family" of the homework economy with its oxymoronic structure of women-headed households and its explosion of feminisms and the paradoxical intensification and erosion of gender itself. This is the context in which the projections for worldwide structural unemployment stemming from the new technologies are part of the picture of the homework economy. As robotics and related technologies put men out of work in "developed" countries and exacerbate failure to generate male jobs in Third World "development," and as the automated office becomes the rule even in labor-surplus countries, the feminization of work intensifies. Black women in the United States have long known what it looks like to face the structural under-employment ("feminization") of black men, as well as their own highly vulnerable position in the wage economy. It is no longer a secret that sexuality, reproduction, family, and community life are interwoven with this economic structure in myriad ways which have also differentiated the situations of white and black women. Many more women and men will contend with similar situations, which will make cross-gender and race alliances on issues of basic life support (with or without jobs) necessary, not just nice.

The new technologies also have a profound effect on hunger and on food production for subsistence worldwide. Rae Lessor Blumberg (1983) estimates that women produce about fifty percent of the world's subsistence food.[17] Women are excluded generally from benefiting from the increased high-tech commodification of food and energy crops, their days are made more arduous because their responsibilities to provide food do not diminish, and their reproductive situations are made more complex. Green Revolution technologies interact with other high-tech industrial production to alter gender divisions of labor and differential gender migration patterns.

The new technologies seem deeply involved in the forms of "privatization" that Ros Petchesky (1981) has analyzed, in which militarization, right-wing family ideologies and policies, and intensified definitions of corporate (and state) property as private synergistically interact.[18] The new communications technologies are fundamental to the eradication of "public life" for everyone. This facilitates the mushrooming of a permanent high-tech military establishment at the cultural and economic expense of most people, but especially of women. Technologies like video games and highly miniaturized televisions seem crucial to production of modern forms of "private life." The culture of video games is heavily orientated to individual competition and extraterrestrial warfare. High-tech, gendered imaginations are produced here, imaginations that can contemplate destruction of the planet and a sci-fi escape from its consequences. More than our imaginations is militarized; and the other realities of electronic and nuclear warfare are inescapable. These are the technologies that promise ultimate mobility and perfect exchange—and incidentally enable tourism, that perfect practice of mobility and exchange, to emerge as one of the world's largest single industries.

The new technologies affect the social relations of both sexuality and of reproduction, and not always in the same ways. The close ties of sexuality and instrumentality, of views of the body as a kind of private satisfaction- and utility-maximizing machine, are described nicely in sociobiological origin stories that stress a genetic calculus and explain the inevitable dialectic of domination of male and female gender roles.[19] These sociobiological stories depend on a high-tech view of the body as a biotic component or cybernetic communications system. Among the many transformations of reproductive situations is the medical one, where women's bodies have boundaries newly permeable to both "visualization" and "intervention." Of course, who controls the interpretation of bodily boundaries in medical hermeneutics is a major feminist issue. The speculum served as an icon of women's claiming their bodies in the 1970s; that handcraft tool is inadequate to express our needed body politics in the negotiation of reality in the practices of cyborg reproduction. Self-help is not enough. The technologies of visualization recall the important cultural practice of hunting with the camera and the deeply predatory nature of a photographic consciousness.[20] Sex, sexuality, and reproduction are central actors in high-tech myth systems structuring our imaginations of personal and social possibility.

Another critical aspect of the social relations of the new technologies is the reformulation of expectations, culture, work, and reproduction for the large scientific and technical workforce. A major social and political danger is the formation of a strongly bimodal social structure, with the masses of women and men of all ethnic groups, but especially people of color, confined to a homework economy, illiteracy of several varieties, and general redundancy and impotence, controlled by high-tech repressive apparatuses ranging from entertainment to surveillance and disappearance. An adequate socialist-feminist politics should address women in the privileged occupational categories, and particularly in the production of science and technology that constructs scientific-technical discourses, processes, and objects.[21]

This issue is only one aspect of enquiry into the possibility of a feminist science, but it is important. What kind of constitutive role in the production of knowledge, imagination, and practice can new groups doing science have? How can these groups be allied with progressive social and political movements? What kind of political accountability can be constructed to tie women together across the scientific-technical hierarchies separating us? Might there be ways of developing feminist science/technology politics in alliance with antimilitary science facility conversion action groups? Many scientific and technical workers in Silicon Valley, the high-tech cowboys included, do not want to work on military science.[22] Can these personal preferences and cultural tendencies be welded into progressive politics among this professional middle class in which women, including women of color, are coming to be fairly numerous?

WOMEN IN THE INTEGRATED CIRCUIT

Let me summarize the picture of women's historical locations in advanced industrial societies, as these positions have been restructured partly through the social relations of science and technology. If it was ever possible ideologically to characterize women's lives by the distinction of public and private domains—suggested by images of the division of working-class life into factory and home, of bourgeois life into market and home, and of gender existence into personal and political realms—it is now a totally misleading ideology, even to show how both terms of these dichotomies construct each other in practice and in theory. I prefer a network ideological image, suggesting the profusion of spaces and identities and the permeability of boundaries in the personal body and in the body politic. "Networking" is both a feminist practice and a multinational corporate strategy—weaving is for oppositional cyborgs.

So let me return to the earlier image of the informatics of domination and trace one vision of women's "place" in the integrated circuit, touching only a few idealized social locations seen primarily from the point of view of advanced capitalist societies: Home, Market, Paid Work Place, State, School, Clinic-Hospital, and Church. Each of these idealized spaces is logically and practically implied in every other locus, perhaps analogous to a holographic photograph. I want to suggest the impact of the social relations mediated and enforced by the new technologies in order to help formulate needed analysis and practical work. However, there is no "place" for women in these networks, only geometrics of difference and contradiction crucial to women's cyborg identities. If we learn how to read these webs of power and social life, we might learn new couplings, new coalitions. There is no way to read the following list from a standpoint of "identification," of a unitary self. The issue is dispersion. The task is to survive in the diaspora.

Home: Women-headed households, serial monogamy, flight of men, old women alone, technology of domestic work, paid homework, reemergence of home sweatshops, home-based businesses and telecommuting, electronic cottage, urban homelessness, migration, module architecture, reinforced (simulated) nuclear family, intense domestic violence.

Market: Women's continuing consumption work, newly targeted to buy the profusion of new production from the new technologies (especially as the competitive race among industrialized and industrializing nations to avoid dangerous mass unemployment necessitates finding ever bigger new markets for ever less clearly needed commodities); bimodal buying power, coupled with advertising targeting of the numerous affluent groups and neglect of the previous mass markets; growing importance of informal markets in labor and commodities parallel to high-tech, affluent market structures; surveillance systems through electronic funds transfer; intensified market abstraction (commodification) of experience, resulting in ineffective utopian or equivalent cynical theories of community; extreme mobility (abstraction) of marketing/financing systems; interpenetration of sexual and labor markets; intensified sexualization of abstracted and alienated consumption.

Paid Work Place: Continued intense sexual and racial division of labor, but considerable growth of membership in privileged occupational categories for many white women and people of color; impact of new technologies on women's work in clerical, service, manufacturing (especially textiles), agriculture, electronics; international restructuring of the working classes; development of new time arrangements to facilitate the homework economy (flex time, part time, over time, no time); homework and out work; increased pressures for two-tiered wage structures; significant numbers of people in cash-dependent populations worldwide with no experience or no further hope of stable employment; most labor "marginal" or "feminized".

State: Continued erosion of the welfare state; decentralizations with increased surveillance and control; citizenship by telematics; imperialism and political power broadly in the form of information rich/information poor differentiation; increased high-tech militarization increasingly opposed by many social groups; reduction of civil service jobs as a result of the growing capital intensification of office work, with implications for occupational mobility for women of color; growing privatization of material and ideological life and culture; close integration of privatization and militarization, the high-tech forms of bourgeois capitalist personal and public life; invisibility of different social groups to each other, linked to psychological mechanisms of belief in abstract enemies.

School: Deepening coupling of high-tech capital needs and public education at all levels, differentiated by race, class, and gender; managerial classes involved in educational reform and refunding at the cost of remaining progressive educational democratic structures for children and teachers; education for mass ignorance and repression in technocratic and militarized culture; growing antiscience mystery cults in dissenting and radical political movements; continued relative scientific illiteracy among white women and people of color; growing industrial direction of education (especially higher education) by science-based multinationals (particularly in electronics- and biotechnology-dependent companies); highly educated, numerous élites in a progressively bimodal society.

Clinic-hospital: Intensified machine-body relations; renegotiations of public metaphors which channel personal experience of the body, particularly in relation to reproduction, immune system functions, and "stress" phenomena; intensification of reproductive politics in response to world historical implications of women's unrealized, potential control of their relation to reproduction; emergence of new, historically specific diseases; struggles over meanings and means of health in environments pervaded by high technology products and processes, continuing feminization of health work; intensified struggle over state responsibility for health; continued ideological role of popular health movements as a major form of American politics.

Church: Electronic fundamentalist "super-saver" preachers solemnizing the union of electronic capital and automated fetish gods; intensified importance of churches in resisting the militarized state; central struggle over women's meanings and authority in religion; continued relevance of spirituality, intertwined with sex and health, in political struggle.

The only way to characterize the informatics of domination is as a massive intensification of insecurity and cultural impoverishment, with common failure of subsistence networks for the most vulnerable. Since much of this picture interweaves with the social relations of science and technology, the urgency of a socialist-feminist politics addressed to science and technology is plain. There is much now being done, and the grounds for political work are rich. For example, the efforts to develop forms of collective struggle for women in paid work, like SEIU's District 925,* should be a high priority for all of us. These efforts are profoundly tied to technical restructuring of labor processes and reformations of working classes. These efforts also are providing understanding of a more comprehensive kind of labor organization, involving community, sexuality, and family issues never privileged in the largely white male industrial unions.

The structural rearrangements related to the social relations of science and technology evoke strong ambivalence. But it is not necessary to be ultimately depressed by the implications of late twentieth-century women's relation to all aspects of work, culture, production of knowledge, sexuality, and reproduction. For excellent reasons, most Marxisms see domination best and have trouble understanding what can only look like false consciousness and people's complicity in their own domination in late capitalism. It is crucial to remember that what is lost, perhaps especially from women's points of view, is often virulent forms of oppression, nostalgically naturalized in the face of current violation. Ambivalence towards the disrupted unities mediated by high-tech culture requires not sorting consciousness into categories of "clear-sighted critique grounding a solid political epistemology" versus "manipulated false consciousness," but subtle understanding of emerging pleasures, experiences, and powers with serious potential for changing the rules of the game.

There are grounds for hope in the emerging bases for new kinds of unity across race, gender, and class, as these elementary units of socialist-feminist analysis themselves suffer protean transformations. Intensifications of hardship experienced worldwide in connection with the social relations of science and technology are severe. But what people are experiencing is not transparently clear, and we lack sufficiently subtle connections for collectively building effective theories of experience. Present efforts—Marxist, psychoanalytic, feminist, anthropological—to clarify even "our" experience are rudimentary.

I am conscious of the odd perspective provided by my historical position—a PhD in biology for an Irish Catholic girl was made possible by Sputnik's impact on U.S. national science-education policy. I have a body and mind as much constructed by the post-Second World War arms race and cold war as by the women's movements. There are more grounds for hope in focusing on the contradictory effects of politics designed to produce loyal American technocrats, which also produced large numbers of dissidents, than in focusing on the present defeats.

---

*Service Employees International Union's office workers' organization in the U.S.

The permanent partiality of feminist points of view has consequences for our expectations of forms of political organization and participation. We do not need a totality in order to work well. The feminist dream of a common language, like all dreams for a perfectly true language, of perfectly faithful naming of experience, is a totalizing and imperialist one. In that sense, dialectics too is a dream language, longing to resolve contradiction. Perhaps, ironically, we can learn from our fusions with animals and machines how not to be Man, the embodiment of Western logos. From the point of view of pleasure in these potent and taboo fusions, made inevitable by the social relations of science and technology, there might indeed be a feminist science.

CYBORGS: A MYTH OF POLITICAL IDENTITY

I want to conclude with a myth about identity and boundaries which might inform late twentieth-century political imaginations. I am indebted in this story to writers Joanna Russ, Samuel R. Delany, John Varley, James Tiptree, Jr., Octavia Butler, Monique Wittig, and Vonda McIntyre.[23] These are our storytellers exploring what it means to be embodied in high-tech worlds. They are theorists for cyborgs. Exploring conceptions of bodily boundaries and social order, the anthropologist Mary Douglas (1966, 1970) should be credited with helping us to consciousness about how fundamental body imagery is to worldview, and so to political language. French feminists like Luce Irigaray and Monique Wittig, for all their differences, know how to write the body; how to weave eroticism, cosmology, and politics from imagery of embodiment, and especially for Wittig, from imagery of fragmentation and reconstitution of bodies.[24]

American radical feminists like Susan Griffin, Audre Lorde, and Adrienne Rich have profoundly affected our political imaginations—and perhaps restricted too much what we allow as a friendly body and political language.[25] They insist on the organic, opposing it to the technological. But their symbolic systems and the related positions of ecofeminism and feminist paganism, replete with organicisms, can only be understood in Sandoval's terms as oppositional ideologies fitting the late twentieth century. They would simply bewilder anyone not preoccupied with the machines and consciousness of late capitalism. In that sense they are part of the cyborg world. But there are also great riches for feminists in explicitly embracing the possibilities inherent in the breakdown of clean distinctions between organism and machine and similar distinctions structuring the Western self. It is the simultaneity of breakdowns that cracks the matrices of domination and opens geometric possibilities. What might be learned from personal and political "technological" pollution? I look briefly at two overlapping groups of texts for their insight into the construction of a potentially helpful cyborg myth: constructions of women of color and monstrous selves in feminist science fiction.

Earlier I suggested that "women of color" might be understood as a cyborg identity, a potent subjectivity synthesized from fusions of outsider identities and in the complex political-historical layerings of her "biomythography," *Zami* (Lorde 1982; King 1987a, 1987b). There are material and cultural grids mapping this potential; Audre Lorde (1984) captures the tone in the title of her *Sister Outsider*. In my political myth, Sister Outsider is the offshore woman, whom U.S. workers, female and feminized, are supposed to regard as the enemy preventing their solidarity, threatening their security. Onshore, inside the boundary of the United States, Sister Outsider is a potential amidst the races and ethnic identities of women manipulated for division, competition, and exploitation in the same industries. "Women of color" are the preferred labor force for the science-based industries, the real women for whom the worldwide sexual market, labor market, and politics of reproduction kaleidoscope into daily life. Young Korean women hired in the sex industry and in electronics assembly are recruited from high schools, educated for the integrated circuit. Literacy, especially in English, distinguishes the "cheap" female labor so attractive to the multinationals.

Contrary to orientalist stereotypes of the "oral primitive," literacy is a special mark of women of color, acquired by U.S. black women as well as men through a history of risking death to learn and to teach reading and writing. Writing has a special significance for all colonized groups. Writing has been crucial to the Western myth of the distinction between oral and written cultures, primitive and civilized mentalities, and more recently to the erosion of that distinction in "postmodernist" theories attacking the phallogocentrism of the West, with its worship of the monotheistic, phallic, authoritative, and singular work, the unique and perfect name.[26] Contests for the meanings of writing are a major form of contemporary political struggle. Releasing the play of writing is deadly serious. The poetry and stories of U.S. women of color are repeatedly about writing, about access to the power to signify; but this time that power must be neither phallic nor innocent. Cyborg writing must not be about the Fall, the imagination of a once upon-a-time wholeness before language, before writing, before Man. Cyborg writing is about the power to survive, not on the basis of original innocence, but on the basis of seizing the tools to mark the world that marked them as other.

The tools are often stories, retold stories, versions that reverse and displace the hierarchical dualisms of naturalized identities. In retelling origin stories, cyborg authors subvert the central myths of origin of Western culture. We have all been colonized by those origin myths, with their longing for fulfillment in apocalypse. The phallogocentric origin stories most crucial for feminist cyborgs are built into the literal technologies—technologies that write the world, biotechnology and microelectronics—that have recently textualized our bodies as code problems on the grid of C³I. Feminist cyborg stories have the task of recoding communication and intelligence to subvert command control.

Figuratively and literally, language politics pervade the struggles of women of color; and stories about language have a special power in the rich contemporary writing by U.S. women of color. For example, retellings of the story of the indigenous woman Malinche, mother of the mestizo "bastard" race of the new world, master of languages, and mistress of Cortés, carry special meaning for Chicana constructions of identity. Cherríe Moraga (1983) in *Loving in the War Years* explores the themes of identity when one never possessed the original language, never told the original story, never resided in the harmony of legitimate heterosexuality in the garden of culture, and so cannot base identity on a myth or a fall from innocence and right to natural names, mother's or father's.[27] Moraga's writing, her superb literacy, is presented in her poetry as the same kind of violation as Malinche's mastery of the conqueror's language—a violation, an illegitimate production, that allows survival. Moraga's language is not "whole"; it is self-consciously spliced, a chimera of English and Spanish, both conqueror's languages. But it is this chimeric monster, without claim to an original language before violation, that crafts the erotic, competent, potent identities of women of color. Sister Outsider hints at the possibility of world survival not because of her innocence, but because of her ability to live on the boundaries, to write without the founding myth of original wholeness, with its inescapable apocalypse of final return to a deathly oneness that Man has imagined to be the innocent and all-powerful Mother, freed at the End from another spiral of appropriation by her son. Writing marks Moraga's body, affirms it as the body of a woman of color, against the possibility of passing into the unmarked category of the Anglo father or into the orientalist myth of "original illiteracy" of a mother that never was. Malinche was mother here, not Eve before eating the forbidden fruit. Writing affirms Sister Outsider, not the Woman-before-the-Fall-into-Writing needed by the phallogocentric Family of Man.

Writing is preeminently the technology of cyborgs, etched surfaces of the late twentieth century. Cyborg politics is the struggle for language and the struggle against perfect communication, against the one code that translates all meaning perfectly, the central dogma of phallogocentrism. That is why cyborg politics insist on noise and advocate pollution, rejoicing in the illegitimate fusions of animal and machine. These are the couplings which make Man and Woman so problematic, subverting the structure of desire, the force imagined to generate language and gender, and so subverting the structure and modes of reproduction of "Western" identity, of nature and culture, of mirror and eye, slave and master, body and mind. "We" did not originally choose to be cyborgs, but choice grounds a liberal politics and epistemology that imagines the reproduction of individuals before the wider replications of "texts."

From the perspective of cyborgs, freed of the need to ground politics in "our" privileged position of the oppression that incorporates all other dominations, the innocence of the merely violated, the ground of those closer to nature, we can see powerful possibilities. Feminisms and Marxisms have run aground on Western epistemological imperatives to construct a revolutionary subject from the perspective of a hierarchy of oppressions and/or a latent position of moral superiority, innocence, and greater closeness to nature. With no available original dream of a common language or original symbiosis promising protection from hostile "masculine" separation, but written into the play of a text that has no finally privileged reading or salvation history, to recognize "oneself" as fully implicated in the world, frees us of the need to root politics in identification, vanguard parties, purity, and mothering. Stripped of identity, the bastard race teaches about the power of the margins and the importance of a mother like Malinche. Women of color have transformed her from the evil mother of masculinist fear into the originally literate mother who teaches survival.

This is not just literary deconstruction, but liminal transformation. Every story that begins with original innocence and privileges the return to wholeness imagines the drama of life to be individuation, separation, the birth of the self, the tragedy of autonomy, the fall into writing, alienation; that is, war, tempered by imaginary respite in the bosom of the Other. These plots are ruled by a reproductive politics—rebirth without flaw, perfection, abstraction. In this plot women are imagined either better or worse off, but all agree they have less selfhood, weaker individuation, more fusion to the oral, to Mother, less at stake in masculine autonomy. But there is another route to having less at stake in masculine autonomy, a route that does not pass through Woman, Primitive, Zero, the Mirror Stage and its imaginary. It passes through women and other present-tense, illegitimate cyborgs, not of Woman born, who refuse the ideological resources of victimization so as to have a real life. These cyborgs are the people who refuse to disappear on cue, no matter how many times a "Western" commentator remarks on the sad passing of another primitive, another organic group done in by "Western" technology, by writing.[28] These real-life cyborgs (for example, the Southeast Asian village women workers in Japanese and U.S. electronics firms described by Aihwa Ong) are actively rewriting the texts of their bodies and societies. Survival is the stakes in this play of readings.

To recapitulate, certain dualisms have been persistent in Western traditions; they have all been systemic to the logics and practices of domination of women, people of color, nature, workers, animals—in short, domination of all constituted as others, whose task is to mirror the self. Chief among these troubling dualisms are self/other, mind/body, culture/nature, male/female, civilized/primitive, reality/appearance, whole/part, agent/resource, maker/made, active/passive, right/wrong, truth/illusion, total/partial, God/man. The self is the one who is not dominated, who knows that by the service of the other, the other is the one who holds the future, who knows that by the experience of domination, which gives the lie to the autonomy of the self. To be One is to be autonomous, to be powerful, to be God; but to be one is to be an illusion, and so to be involved in a dialectic of apocalypse with the other. Yet to be other is to be multiple, without clear boundary, frayed, insubstantial. One is too few, but two are too many.

High-tech culture challenges these dualisms in intriguing ways. It is not clear who makes and who is made in the relation between human and machine. It is not clear what is mind and what body in machines that resolve into coding practices. In so far as we know ourselves in both formal discourse (for example, biology) and in daily practice (for example, the homework economy in the integrated circuit), we find ourselves to be cyborgs, hybrids, mosaics, chimeras. Biological organisms have become biotic systems, communications devices like others. There is no fundamental, ontological separation in our formal knowledge of machine and organism, of technical and organic. The replicant Rachel in the Ridley Scott film *Blade Runner* stands as the image of a cyborg culture's fear, love, and confusion.

One consequence is that our sense of connection to our tools is heightened. The trance state experienced by many computer users has become a staple of science-fiction film and cultural jokes. Perhaps paraplegics and other severely handicapped people can (and sometimes do) have the most intense experiences of complex hybridization with other communication devices.[29] Anne McCaffrey's pre-feminist *The Ship Who Sang* (1969) explored the consciousness of a cyborg, hybrid of girl's brain and complex machinery, formed after the birth of a severely handicapped child. Gender, sexuality, embodiment, skill: all were reconstituted in the story. Why should our bodies end at the skin, or include at best other beings encapsulated by skin? From the seventeenth century till now, machines could be animated—given ghostly souls to make them speak or move or to account for their orderly development and mental capacities. Or organisms could be mechanized—reduced to body understood as resource of mind. These machine/organism relationships are obsolete, unnecessary. For us, in imagination and in other practice, machines can be prosthetic devices, intimate components, friendly selves. We don't need organic holism to give impermeable wholeness, the total woman and her feminist variants (mutants?). Let me conclude this point by a very partial reading of the logic of the cyborg monsters of my second group of texts, feminist science fiction.

The cyborgs populating feminist science fiction make very problematic the statuses of man or woman, human, artifact, member of a race, individual entity, or body. Katie King clarifies how pleasure in reading these fictions is not largely based on identification. Students facing Joanna Russ for the first time, students who have learned to take modernist writers like James Joyce or Virginia Woolf without flinching, do not know what to make of *The Adventures of Alyx* or *The Female Man*, where characters refuse the reader's search for innocent wholeness while granting the wish for heroic quests, exuberant eroticism, and serious politics. *The Female Man* is the story of four versions of one genotype, all of whom meet, but even taken together do not make a whole, resolve the dilemmas of violent moral action, or remove the growing scandal of gender. The feminist science fiction of Samuel R. Delany, especially *Tales of Nevèrÿon*, mocks stories of origin by redoing the neolithic revolution, replaying the founding moves of Western civilization to subvert their plausibility. James Tiptree, Jr., an author whose fiction was regarded as particularly manly until her "true" gender was revealed, tells tales of reproduction based on non-mammalian technologies like alternation of generations of male brood pouches and male nurturing. John Varley constructs a supreme cyborg in his arch-feminist exploration of Gaea, a mad goddess-planet-trickster-old-woman-technological device on whose surface an extraordinary array of post-cyborg symbioses are spawned. Octavia Butler writes of an African sorceress pitting her powers of transformation against the genetic manipulations of her rival (*Wild Seed*), of time warps that bring a modern U.S. black woman into slavery where her actions in relation to her white master-ancestor determine the possibility of her own birth (*Kindred*), and of the illegitimate insights into identity and community of an adopted cross-species child who came to know the enemy as self (*Survivor*). In *Dawn* (1987), the first installment of a series called *Xenogenesis*, Butler tells the story of Lilith Iyapo, whose personal name recalls Adam's first and repudiated wife and whose family name marks her status as the widow of the son of Nigerian immigrants to the U.S. A black woman and a mother whose child is dead, Lilith mediates the transformation of humanity through genetic exchange with extraterrestrial lovers/rescuers/destroyers/genetic engineers, who reform earth's habitats after the nuclear holocaust and coerce surviving humans into intimate fusion with them. It is a novel that interrogates reproductive, linguistic, and nuclear politics in a mythic field structured by late twentieth-century race and gender.

Because it is particularly rich in boundary transgressions, Vonda McIntyre's *Superluminal* can close this truncated catalog of promising and dangerous monsters who help redefine the pleasures and politics of embodiment and feminist writing. In a fiction where no character is "simply" human, human status is highly problematic. Orca, a genetically altered diver, can speak with killer whales and survive deep ocean conditions, but she longs to explore space as a pilot, necessitating bionic implants jeopardizing her kinship with the divers and cetaceans. Transformations are effected by virus vectors carrying a new developmental code, by transplant surgery, by implants of microelectronic devices, by analog doubles, and other means. Laenea becomes a pilot by accepting a heart implant and a host of other alterations allowing survival in transit at speeds exceeding that of light. Radu Dracul survives a virus-caused plague in his outerworld planet to find himself with a time sense that changes the boundaries of spatial perception for the whole species. All the characters explore the limits of language; the dream of communicating experience; and the necessity of limitation, partiality, and intimacy even in this world of protean transformation and connection. *Superluminal* stands also for the defining contradictions of a cyborg world in another sense; it embodies textually the intersection of feminist theory and colonial discourse in the science fiction I have alluded to in this essay. This is a conjunction with a long history that many "First World" feminists have tried to repress, including myself in my readings of *Superluminal* before being called to account by Zoe Sofoulis, whose different location in the world system's informatics of domination made her acutely alert to the imperialist moment of all science-fiction cultures, including women's science fiction. From an Australian feminist sensitivity, Sofoulis remembered more readily McIntyre's role as writer of the adventures of Captain Kirk and Spock in TV's *Star Trek* series than her rewriting the romance in *Superluminal*.

Monsters have always defined the limits of community in Western imaginations. The Centaurs and Amazons of ancient Greece established the limits of the centered polis of the Greek male human by their disruption of marriage and boundary pollutions of the warrior with animality and woman. Unseparated twins and hermaphrodites were the confused human material in early modern France who grounded discourse on the natural and supernatural, medical and legal, portents and diseases—all crucial to establishing modern identity.[30] The evolutionary and behavioral sciences of monkeys and apes have marked the multiple boundaries of late twentieth-century industrial identities. Cyborg monsters in feminist science fiction define quite different political possibilities and limits from those proposed by the mundane fiction of Man and Woman.

There are several consequences to taking seriously the imagery of cyborgs as other than our enemies. Our bodies, ourselves; bodies are maps of power and identity. Cyborgs are no exception. A cyborg body is not innocent; it was not born in a garden; it does not seek unitary identity and so generate antagonistic dualisms without end (or until the world ends); it takes irony for granted. One is too few, and two is only one possibility. Intense pleasure in skill, machine skill, ceases to be a sin, but an aspect of our embodiment. The machine is not an *it* to be animated, worshipped, and dominated. The machine is us, our processes, an aspect of our embodiment. We can be responsible for machines; *they* do not dominate or threaten us. We are responsible for boundaries; we are they. Up till now (once upon a time), female embodiment seemed to be given, organic, necessary; and female embodiment seemed to mean skill in mothering and its metaphoric extensions. Only by being out of place could we take intense pleasure in machines, and then with excuses that this was organic activity after all, appropriate to females. Cyborgs might consider more seriously the partial, fluid, sometimes aspect of sex and sexual embodiment. Gender might not be global identity after all, even if it has profound historical breadth and depth.

The ideologically charged question of what counts as daily activity, as experience, can be approached by exploiting the cyborg image. Feminists have recently claimed that women are given to dailiness, that women more than men somehow sustain daily life, and so have a privileged epistemological position potentially. There is a compelling aspect to this claim, one that makes visible unvalued female activity and names it as the ground of life. But *the* ground of life? What about all the ignorance of women, all the exclusions and failures of knowledge and skill? What about men's access to daily competence, to knowing how to build things, to take them apart, to play? What about other embodiments? Cyborg gender is a local possibility taking a global vengeance. Race, gender, and capital require a cyborg theory of wholes and parts. There is no drive in cyborgs to produce total theory, but there is an intimate experience of boundaries, their construction and deconstruction. There is a myth system waiting to become a political language to ground one way of looking at science and technology and challenging the informatics of domination—in order to act potently.

One last image: organisms and organismic, holistic politics depend on metaphors of rebirth and invariably call on the resources of reproductive sex.

I would suggest that cyborgs have more to do with regeneration and are suspicious of the reproductive matrix and of most birthing. For salamanders, regeneration after injury, such as the loss of a limb, involves regrowth of structure and restoration of function with the constant possibility of twinning or other odd topographical productions at the site of former injury. The regrown limb can be monstrous, duplicated, potent. We have all been injured, profoundly. We require regeneration, not rebirth, and the possibilities for our reconstitution include the utopian dream of the hope for a monstrous world without gender.

Cyborg imagery can help express two crucial arguments in this essay: first, the production of universal, totalizing theory is a major mistake that misses most of reality, probably always, but certainly now; and second, taking responsibility for the social relations of science and technology means refusing an antiscience metaphysics, a demonology of technology, and so means embracing the skillful task of reconstructing the boundaries of daily life, in partial connection with others, in communication with all of our parts. It is not just that science and technology are possible means of great human satisfaction, as well as a matrix of complex dominations. Cyborg imagery can suggest a way out of the maze of dualisms in which we have explained our bodies and our tools to ourselves. This is a dream not of a common language, but of a powerful infidel heteroglossia. It is an imagination of a feminist speaking in tongues to strike fear into the circuits of the supersavers of the new right. It means both building and destroying machines, identities, categories, relationships, space stories. Though both are bound in the spiral dance, I would rather be a cyborg than a goddess.

NOTES

1. Research was funded by an Academic Senate Faculty Research Grant from the University of California, Santa Cruz. An earlier version of the paper on genetic engineering appeared as "Lieber Kyborg als Göttin: für eine sozialistisch-feministische Unterwanderung der Gentechnologie," in Bernd-Peter Lange and Anna Marie Stuby, eds. (Berlin: Argument-Sonderband 105, 1984), pp. 66-84. The cyborg manifesto grew from my "New machines, new bodies, new communities: political dilemmas of a cyborg feminist," "The Scholar and the Feminist X: The Question of Technology," conference, Barnard College, April 1983.

The people associated with the History of Consciousness Board of UCSC have had an enormous influence on this paper, so that it feels collectively authored more than most, although those I cite may not recognize their ideas. In particular, members of graduate and undergraduate feminist theory, science, and politics, and theory and methods courses contributed to the cyborg manifesto. Particular debts here are due Hilary Klein (1989), Paul Edwards (1985), Lisa Lowe (1986), and James Clifford (1985).

Parts of the paper were my contribution to a collectively developed session, "Poetic Tools and Political Bodies: Feminist Approaches to High Technology Culture," 1984 California American Studies Association, with History of Consciousness graduate students Zoe Sofoulis, "Jupiter space"; Katie King, "The pleasures of repetition and the limits of identification in feminist science fiction: reimaginations of the body after the cyborg"; and Chela Sandoval, "The construction of subjectivity and oppositional consciousness in feminist film and video." Sandoval's (n.d.) theory of oppositional consciousness was published as "Women respond to racism: A Report on the National Women's Studies Association Conference." For Sofoulis's semiotic-psychoanalytic readings of nuclear culture, see Sofia (1984). King's unpublished papers ("Questioning tradition: canon formation and the veiling of power"; "Gender and genre: reading the science fiction of Joanna Russ"; "Varley's *Titan* and *Wizard*: feminist parodies of nature, culture, and hardware") deeply informed the cyborg manifesto.

Barbara Epstein, Jeff Escoffier, Rusten Hogness, and Jaye Miler gave extensive discussion and editorial help. Members of the Silicon Valley Research Project of UCSC and participants in SVRP conferences and workshops were very important, especially Rick Gordon, Linda Kimball, Nancy Snyder, Langdon Winner, Judith Stacey, Linda Lim, Patricia Fernandez-Kelly, and Judith Gregory. Finally, I want to thank Nancy Hartsock for years of friendship and discussion on feminist theory and feminist science fiction. I also thank Elizabeth Bird for my favorite political button: "Cyborgs for Earthly Survival."

2. Useful references to left and/or feminist radical science movements and theory and to biological/ biotechnical issues include: Bleier (1984, 1986), Harding (1986), Fausto-Sterling (1985), Gould (1981), Hubbard et al. (1982), Keller (1985), Lewontin et al. (1984), *Radical Science Journal* (became *Science as Culture* in 1987), 26 Freegrove Road, London N7 9RQ; *Science for the People*, 897 Main St., Cambridge, MA 02139.

3. Starting points for left and/or feminist approaches to technology and politics include: Cowan (1983), Rothschild (1983), Traweek (1988), Young and Levidow (1981, 1985), Weizenbaum (1976), Winner (1977, 1986), Zimmerman (1983), Athanasiou (1987), Cohn (1987a, 1987b), Winograd and Flores (1986), Edwards (1985). *Global Electronics Newsletter*, 867 West Dana St., #204, Mountain View, CA 94041; *Processed World*, 55 Sutter St., San Francisco, CA 94104; ISIS, Women's International Information and Communication Service, P.O. Box 50 (Cornavin), 1211 Geneva 2, Switzerland, and Via Santa Maria Dell'Anima 30, 00186 Rome, Italy. Fundamental approaches to modern social studies of science that do not continue the liberal mystification that it all started with Thomas Kuhn, include: Knorr-Cetina (1981), Knorr-Cetina and Mulkay (1983), Latour and Woolgar (1979), Young (1979). The 1984 Directory of the Network for the Ethnographic Study of Science, Technology, and Organizations lists a wide range of people and projects crucial to better radical analysis; available from NESSTO, P.O. Box 11442, Stanford, CA 94305.

4. A provocative, comprehensive argument about the politics and theories of "postmodernism" is made by Fredric Jameson (1984), who argues that postmodernism is not an option, a style among others, but a cultural dominant requiring radical reinvention of left politics from within; there is no longer any place from without that gives meaning to the comforting fiction of critical distance. Jameson also makes clear why one cannot be for or against postmodernism, an essentially moralist move. My position is that feminists (and others) need continuous cultural reinvention, postmodernist critique, and historical materialism; only a cyborg would have a chance. The old dominations of white capitalist patriarchy seem nostalgically innocent now: they normalized heterogeneity, into man and woman, white and black, for example. "Advanced capitalism" and postmodernism release heterogeneity without a norm, and we are flattened, without subjectivity, which requires depth, even unfriendly and drowning depths. It is time to write *The Death of the Clinic*. The clinic's methods required bodies and works; we have texts and surfaces. Our dominations don't work by medicalization and normalization any more; they work by networking, communications redesign, stress management. Normalization gives way to automation, utter redundancy. Michel Foucault's *Birth of the Clinic* (1963), *History of Sexuality* (1976), and *Discipline and Punish* (1975) name a form of power at its moment of implosion. The discourse

of biopolitics gives way to technobabble, the language of the spliced substantive; no noun is left whole by the multinationals. These are their names listed from one issue of *Science:* Tech-Knowledge, Genentech, Allergen, Hybritech, Compupro, Genen-cor, Syntex, Allelix, Agrigenetics Corp., Syntro, Codon, Repligen, MicroAngelo from Scion Corp., Percom Data, Inter Systems, Cyborg Corp., Statcom Corp., Intertec. If we are imprisoned by language, then escape from that prison-house requires language poets, a kind of cultural restriction enzyme to cut the code; cyborg heteroglossia is one form of radical cultural politics. For cyborg poetry, see Perloff (1984); Fraser (1984). For feminist modernist/postmodernist "cyborg" writing, see HOW(ever), 871 Corbett Ave., San Francisco, CA 94131.

5. Baudrillard (1983). Jameson (1984, p. 66) points out that Plato's definition of the simulacrum is the copy for which there is no original, i.e., the world of advanced capitalism, of pure exchange. See *Discourse* 9 (Spring/Summer 1987) for a special issue on technology (cybernetics, ecology, and the postmodern imagination).

6. For ethnographic accounts and political evaluations, see Epstein (forthcoming); Sturgeon (1986). Without explicit irony, adopting the spaceship earth/whole earth logo of the planet photographed from space, set off by the slogan "Love Your Mother," the May 1987 Mothers and Others Day action at the nuclear weapons testing facility in Nevada nonetheless took account of the tragic contradictions of views of the earth. Demonstrators applied for official permits to be on the land from officers of the Western Shoshone tribe, whose territory was invaded by the U.S. government when it built the nuclear weapons test ground in the 1950s. Arrested for trespassing, the demonstrators argued that the police and weapons facility personnel, without authorization from the proper officials, were the trespassers. One affinity group at the women's action called themselves the Surrogate Others; and in solidarity with the creatures forced to tunnel in the same ground with the bomb, they enacted a cyborgian emergence from the constructed body of a large, non-heterosexual desert worm.

7. Powerful developments of coalition politics emerge from "Third World" speakers, speaking from nowhere, the displaced center of the universe, earth: "We live on the third planet from the sun"—*Sun Poem* by Jamaican writer, Edward Kamau Braithwaite, review by Mackey (1984). Contributors to Smith (1983) ironically subvert naturalized identities precisely while constructing a place from which to speak called home. See especially Reagon (in Smith 1983, pp. 356-68). Trinh T. Minh-ha (1986-87).

8. hooks (1981, 1984); Hull et al. (1982). Bambara (1981) wrote an extraordinary novel in which the women of color theater group, The Seven Sisters, explores a form of unity. See analysis by Butler-Evans (1987).

9. On orientalism in feminist works and elsewhere, see Lowe (1986); Said (1978); Mohanty (1984); *Many Voices, One Chant: Black Feminist Perspectives* (1984).

10. Katie King (1986, 1987a) has developed a theoretically sensitive treatment of the workings of feminist taxonomies as genealogies of power in feminist ideology and polemic. King examines Jaggar's (1983) problematic example of taxonomizing feminisms to make a little machine producing the desired final position. My caricature here of socialist and radical feminism is also an example.

11. The central role of object relations versions of psychoanalysis and related strong universalizing moves in discussing reproduction, caring work, and mothering in many approaches to epistemology underline their authors' resistance to what I am calling postmodernism. For me, both the universalizing moves and these versions of psychoanalysis make analysis of "women's place in the integrated circuit" difficult and lead to systematic difficulties in accounting for or even seeing major aspects of the construction of gender and gendered social life. The feminist standpoint argument has been developed by: Flax (1983); Harding (1986); Harding and Hintikka (1983); Hartsock (1983a, b); O'Brien (1981); Rose (1983); Smith (1974, 1979). For rethinking theories of feminist materialism and feminist standpoints in response to criticism, see Harding (1986, pp. 163-96); Hartsock (1987); and H. Rose (1986).

12. I make an argumentative category error in "modifying" MacKinnon's posi-

tions with the qualifier "radical," thereby generating my own reductive critique of extremely heterogeneous writing, which does explicitly use that label, by my taxonomically interested argument about writing which does not use the modifier and which brooks no limits and thereby adds to the various dreams of a common, in the sense of univocal, language for feminism. My category error was occasioned by an assignment to write from a particular taxonomic position which itself has a heterogeneous history, socialist-feminism, for *Socialist Review*. A critique indebted to MacKinnon, but without the reductionism and with an elegant feminist account of Foucault's paradoxical conservatism on sexual violence (rape), is de Lauretis (1985; see also 1986, pp. 1-19). A theoretically elegant feminist social-historical examination of family violence, that insists on women's, men's, and children's complex agency without losing sight of the material structures of male domination, race, and class, is Gordon (1988).

13. This chart was published in 1985. My previous efforts to understand biology as a cybernetic command-control discourse and organisms as "natural-technical objects of knowledge" were Haraway (1979, 1983, 1984). The 1979 version of this dichotomous chart appears in *Simians, Cyborgs, and Women*, ch. 3; for a 1989 version, see ch. 10. The differences indicate shifts in argument.

14. For progressive analyses and action on the biotechnology debates: *GeneWatch, a Bulletin of the Committee for Responsible Genetics*, 5 Doane St., 4th Floor, Boston, MA 02109; Genetic Screening Study Group (formerly the Sociobiology Study Group of Science for the People), Cambridge, MA; Wright (1982, 1986); Yoxen (1983).

15. Starting references for "women in the integrated circuit": D'Onofrio-Flores and Pfafflin (1982); Fernandez-Kelly (1983); Fuentes and Ehrenreich (1983); Grossman (1980); Nash and Fernandez-Kelly (1983); Ong (1987); Science Policy Research Unit (1982).

16. For the "homework economy outside the home" and related arguments: Gordon (1983); Gordon and Kimball (1985); Stacey (1987); Reskin and Hartmann (1986); *Women and Poverty* (1984); S. Rose (1986); Collins (1982); Burr (1982); Gregory and Nussbaum (1982); Piven and Coward (1982); Microelectronics Group (1980); Stallard et al. (1983), which includes a useful organization and resource list.

17. The conjunction of the Green Revolution's social relations with biotechnologies like plant genetic engineering makes the pressures on land in the Third World increasingly intense. AID's estimates (*New York Times*, October 14, 1984) used at the 1984 World Food day are that in Africa, women produce about 90 percent of rural food supplies, about 60-80 percent in Asia, and provide 40 percent of agricultural labor in the Near East and Latin America. Blumberg charges that world organizations' agricultural politics, as well as those of multinationals and national governments in the Third World, generally ignore fundamental issues in the sexual division of labor. The present tragedy of famine in Africa might owe as much to male supremacy as to capitalism, colonialism, and rain patterns. More accurately, capitalism and racism are usually structurally male dominant. See also Blumberg (1981); Hacker (1984); Hacker and Bovit (1981); Busch and Lacy (1983); Wilfred (1982); Sachs (1983); International Fund for Agricultural Development (1985); Bird (1984).

18. See also Enloe (1983a, b).

19. For a feminist version of this logic, see Hrdy (1981). For an analysis of scientific women's storytelling practices, especially in relation to sociobiology in evolutionary debates around child abuse and infanticide, see *Simians, Cyborgs, and Women*, ch. 5.

20. For the moment of transition of hunting with guns to hunting with cameras in the construction of popular meanings of nature for an American urban immigrant public, see Haraway (1984-5, 1989b), Nash (1979), Sontag (1977), Preston (1984).

21. For guidance for thinking about the political/cultural/racial implications of the history of women doing science in the United States see: Haas and Perucci (1984); Hacker (1981); Keller (1983); National Science Foundation (1988); Rossiter (1982); Schiebinger (1987); Haraway (1989b).

22. Markoff and Siegel (1983). High Technology Professionals for Peace and Computer Professionals for Social Responsibility are promising organizations.

23. King (1984). An abbreviated list of feminist science fiction underlying themes of this essay: Octavia Butler, *Wild Seed, Mind of My Mind, Kindred, Survivor,* Suzy McKee Charnas, *Motherliness;* Samuel R. Delany, the Neverÿon series; Anne McCaffery, *The Ship Who Sang, Dinosaur Planet;* Vonda McIntyre, *Superluminal, Dreamsnake;* Joanna Russ, *Adventures of Alyx, The Female Man;* James Tiptree, Jr., *Star Songs of an Old Primate, Up the Walls of the World;* John Varley, *Titan, Wizard, Demon.*

24. French feminisms contribute to cyborg heteroglossia. Burke (1981); Irigaray (1977, 1979); Marks and de Courtivron (1980); *Signs* (Autumn 1981); Wittig (1973); Duchen (1986). For English translation of some currents of francophone feminism see *Feminist Issues: A Journal of Feminist Social and Political Theory* (1980).

25. But all these poets are very complex, not least in their treatment of themes of lying and erotic, decentered collective and personal identities. Griffin (1978); Lorde (1984); Rich (1978).

26. Derrida (1976, especially part II); Lévi-Strauss (1961, especially "The Writing Lesson"); Gates (1985); Kahn and Neumaier (1985); Ong (1982); Kramarae and Treichler (1985).

27. The sharp relation of women of color to writing as theme and politics can be approached through: Program for "The Black Woman and the Diaspora: Hidden Connections and Extended Acknowledgments," An International Literary Conference, Michigan State University, October 1985; Evans (1984); Christian (1985); Carby (1987); Fisher (1980); *Frontiers* (1980, 1983); Kingston (1977); Lerner (1973); Giddings (1985); Moraga and Anzaldúa (1981); Morgan (1984). Anglophone European and Euro-American women have also crafted special relations to their writing as a potent sign: Gilbert and Gubar (1979), Russ (1983).

28. The convention of ideologically taming militarized high technology by publicizing its applications to speech and motion problems of the disabled/differently abled takes on a special irony in monotheistic, patriarchal, and frequently anti-Semitic culture when computer-generated speech allows a boy with no voice to chant the Haftorah at his bar mitzvah. See Sussman (1986). Making the always context-relative social definitions of "ableness" particularly clear, military high-tech has a way of making human beings disabled by definition, a perverse aspect of much automated battlefield and Star Wars R&D. See Welford (July 1, 1986).

29. James Clifford (1985, 1988) argues persuasively for recognition of continuous cultural reinvention, the stubborn non-disappearance of those "marked" by Western imperializing practices.

30. DuBois (1982), Daston and Park (n.d.), Park and Daston (1981). The noun *monster* shares its root with the verb *to demonstrate.*

CHAPTER 26

AUTOMATING GENDER

Postmodern Feminism in the Age of the Intelligent Machine

JUDITH HALBERSTAM

(1 9 9 1)

MY COMPUTER, MY SELF

The development of computers and computer science in the 1940s activated a debate between humanists and mechanists over the possibility of intelligent machines. The prospect of thinking machines, or cyborgs, inspired at first religious indignation; intellectual disbelief; and large-scale suspicion of the social, economic, and military implications of an autonomous technology. In general terms, we can identify two major causes for concern produced by cybernetics. The first concern relates to the idea that computers may be taught to simulate human thought, and the second relates to the possibility that automated robots may be wired to replace humans in the workplace. The cybernetics debate, in fact, appears to follow the somewhat familiar class and gender lines of a mind-body split. Artificial intelligence, of course, threatens to reproduce the thinking subject, while the robot could conceivably be mass produced to form an automated workforce (robot in Czech means "worker"). However, if the former challenges the traditional intellectual prestige of a class of experts, the latter promises to displace the social privilege dependent upon stable categories of gender.

In our society, discourses are gendered, and the split between mind and body—as feminist theory has demonstrated—is a binary that identifies men with thought, intellect, and reason and women with body, emotion, and intuition. We might expect, then, that computer intelligence and robotics would enhance binary splits and emphasize the dominance of reason and logic over the irrational. However, because the blurred boundaries between mind and machine, body and machine, and human and nonhuman are the very legacy of cybernetics, automated machines, in fact, provide new ground upon which to argue that gender and its representations are technological productions. In a sense, cybernetics simultaneously maps out the terrain for both postmodern discussions of the subject in late capitalism and feminist debates about technology, postmodernism, and gender.

Although technophobia among women and as theorized by some feminists is understandable as a response to military and scientific abuses within a patriarchal system, the advent of intelligent machines necessarily changes the social relations between gender and science, sexuality and biology, feminism and the politics of artificiality. To illustrate productive and useful interactions between and across these categories, I take as central symbols the Apple computer logo, an apple with a bite taken from it, and the cyborg as theorized by Donna Haraway, a machine both female and intelligent.

We recognize the Apple computer symbol, I think, as a clever icon for the digitalization of the creation myth. Within this logo, sin and knowledge, the forbidden fruits of the garden of Eden, are interfaced with memory and information in a network of power. The bite now represents the *byte* of information within a processing memory. I attempt to provide a reading of the apple that disassociates it from the myth of genesis and suggests that such a myth no longer holds currency within our postmodern age of simulation. Inasmuch as the postmodern project radically questions the notion of origination and the nostalgia attendant upon it, a postmodern reading of the apple finds that the subject has always sinned, has never not bitten the apple. The female cyborg replaces Eve in this myth with a figure who severs once and for all the assumed connection between woman and nature upon which entire patriarchal structures rest. The female cyborg, furthermore, exploits a traditionally masculine fear of the deceptiveness of appearances and calls into question the boundaries of human, animal, and machine precisely where they are most vulnerable—at the site of the female body.

On the one hand, the apple and Eve represent an organic relation between God, nature, man, and woman; on the other, the apple and the female cyborg symbolize a mass cultural computer technology. However, the distance traveled from genesis to intelligence is not a line between two poles, not a diachronic shift from belief to skepticism, for technology within multinational capitalism involves systems organized around contradictions. Computer technology, for example, both generates a powerful mass culture and also serves to militarize power. Cultural critics in the computer age, those concerned with the social configurations of class, race, and gender, can thus no longer afford to position themselves simply for or against technology, for or against postmodernism. In order not merely to reproduce the traditional divide between humanists and mechanists, feminists and other cultural critics must rather begin to theorize their position in relation to a plurality of technologies and from a place already within postmodernism.

POISONED APPLES

"The true mystery of the world is the visible not the invisible."

Oscar Wilde, *The Picture of Dorian Gray* (1891)

The work of one pioneer in computer intelligence suggests a way that the technology of intelligence may be interwoven with the technology of gender. Alan Turing (1912–1954) was an English mathematician whose computer technology explicitly challenged boundaries between disciplines and between minds, bodies, and machines. Turing had been fascinated with the idea of a

machine capable of manipulating symbols since an early age. His biographer
Andrew Hodges writes:

> What, Alan Turing asked, would be the most general kind of a machine that
> dealt with symbols? To be a "machine" it would have to retain the typewriter's
> quality of having a finite number of configurations and an exactly determined
> behavior in each. But it would be capable of much more. And so he imagined
> machines which were, in effect, super-typewriters.[1]

In dreaming of such a machine, Turing imagined a kind of autonomous potential for this electrical brain, the potential for the machine to think, reason,
and even make errors. Although the idea of the computer occurred to many
different people simultaneously, it was Alan Turing who tried to consider the
scope and range of an artificial intelligence.

Turing's development of what he called a "universal machine," as a mathematical model of a kind of superbrain, brought into question the whole concept of mind and indeed made a strict correlation between mind and
machine. Although Turing's research would not yield a prototype of a computer until years later, this early model founded computer research squarely
on the analogy between human and machine and, furthermore, challenged
the supposed autonomy and abstraction of pure mathematics. For example,
G. H. Hardy claims that "the 'real' mathematics of the 'real' mathematicians,
the mathematics of Fermat and Euler and Gauss and Abel and Riemann, is
almost wholly 'useless.'. . . It is not possible to justify the life of any genuine
professional mathematician on the ground of the utility of his work."[2] This
statement reveals a distinctly modernist investment in form over content and
in the total objectivity of the scientific project unsullied by contact with the
material world. Within a postmodern science, such claims for intellectual distance and abstraction are mediated, however, by the emergence of a mass
culture technology. Technology for the masses, the prospect of a computer
terminal in every home, encroaches upon the sacred ground of the experts
and establishes technology as a relation between subjects and culture.

In a 1950 paper entitled "Computing Machinery and Intelligence," Alan
Turing argued that a computer works according to the principle of imitation,
but it may also be able to learn. In determining artificial intelligence, Turing
demanded what he called "fair play" for the computer. We must not expect,
he suggested, that the computer will be infallible, nor will it always act ratio-
nally or logically; indeed, the machine's very fallibility is necessary to its definition as "intelligent."[3] Turing compared the electric brain of the computer
to the brain of a child; he suggested that intelligence transpires out of the
combination of "discipline and initiative." Both discipline and initiative in
this model run interference across the brain and condition behavior. However, Turing claimed that in both the human and the electric mind, there is
the possibility for random interference and that it is this element that is critical to intelligence. Interference, then, works both as an organizing force, one
which orders random behaviors, and as a random interruption which returns
the system to chaos: it must always do both.

Turing created a test by which one might judge whether a computer could be considered intelligent. The Turing test demands that a human subject decide, based on replies given to her or his questions, whether she or he is communicating with a human or a machine. When the respondents fail to distinguish between human and machine responses, the computer may be considered intelligent. In an interesting twist, Turing illustrates the application of his test with what he calls "a sexual guessing game." In this game, a woman and a man sit in one room and an interrogator sits in another. The interrogator must determine the sexes of the two people based on their written replies to his questions. The man attempts to deceive the questioner, and the woman tries to convince him. Turing's point in introducing the sexual guessing game was to show that imitation makes even the most stable of distinctions (i.e., gender) unstable. By using the sexual guessing game as simply a control model, however, Turing does not stress the obvious connection between gender and computer intelligence: both are in fact imitative systems, and the boundaries between female and male, I argue, are as unclear and as unstable as the boundary between human and machine intelligence.

By assigning gender to biology and cognitive process to acculturation, Turing fails to realize the full import of his negotiations between machine and human. Gender, we might argue, like computer intelligence, is a learned, imitative behavior that can be processed so well that it comes to look natural. Indeed, the work of culture in the former and of science in the latter is perhaps to transform the artificial into a function so smooth that it seems organic. In other words, gender, like intelligence, has a technology. There is an irony to Turing's careful analogical comparisons between bodies and machines. Two years after he published his paper, in 1952, Turing was arrested and charged with "gross indecency," or homosexual activity. Faced with a choice between a jail sentence or hormone treatments, Turing opted for the hormones. It was still believed in the fifties that female hormones could "correct" male homosexuality because homosexual behavior was assumed to be a form of physically or biologically based gender confusion. In fact, the same kind of reasoning that prevented Turing from understanding the radically unstable condition of gender informed the attempt by medical researchers to correct a supposed surfeit of male hormones in the homosexual with infusions of female hormones. During treatment, Turing was rendered impotent, and he began to grow breasts. As soon as the treatment was over, he resumed his homosexual relationships.

Two important points can be made in relation to the brush between science and desire. First, Turing's experience of gender instability suggests that the body may in fact be, both materially and libidinally, a product of technology inasmuch as injections of hormones can transform it from male to female; second, desire provides the random element necessary to a technology's definition as intelligent. In other words, the body may be scientifically altered in order to force "correct" gender identification, but desire remains as interference running across a binary technologic.

Alan Turing's homosexuality was interpreted by the legal system as a crime, by the medical profession as a malfunction, and by the government as a liability. Turing was considered a liability because during World War II he had used his mathematical training in the service of military intelligence, and, as a cryptanalyst, he had distinguished himself in his work to decode Nazi communications. Turing's homosexuality made him seem an unfit keeper of state secrets: he was exploitable, fatally flawed, a weak link in the masculinist chain of government and the military. He had a sexual secret that the enemy (in 1952, the enemy was, of course, Communism) could prey upon, and his secret made him incontrovertibly Other.

The association between machine and military intelligence, as Turing found out, is a close one; and computer technology is in many ways the progeny of war in the modern age. The fear generated by computer intelligence, indeed, owes much to this association of the computer with highly sophisticated weaponry. As Andreas Huyssen points out, the fear of an autonomous technology has led to a gendering of technology as female: "As soon as the machine came to be perceived as a demonic, inexplicable threat and as the harbinger of chaos and destruction . . . writers began to imagine the Maschinenmensch as woman. . . . Woman, nature, machine had become a mesh of signification which all had one thing in common: otherness."[4] The fear of artificial intelligence, like the fear of homosexuals infiltrating the secret service, was transformed into a paranoid terror of femininity. Similarly, the machine itself was seen to threaten the hegemony of white male authority because it could as easily be used against a government as for it; autonomy was indeed its terrifying potential. The same argument that propelled a witch-hunt for possible homosexual traitors in the British government in the 1950s gendered the machine as female and attempted to convert threat into seduction. Turing now became the object of scrutiny of the very security system he had helped to create. The machine Other, like the sexual Other within a system of gender inequality, is contained even as it participates in the power dynamic.

Turing ended his life in 1954 by eating an apple dipped in cyanide. He had experienced the ignominy of a public trial for homosexual relations, he had suffered through a year's course of "organotherapy," then he was kept under close surveillance by the British Foreign office as a wave of panic over homosexual spies gripped the country. Turing had been awarded the Order of the British Empire in 1946 for his war service, and he earned a police record in 1952 for his sexual activities. Rarely has the division between body and mind been drawn with such precision and such tragic irony.

Turing's suicide method, eating an apple saturated with cyanide, bizarrely prefigures the Apple computer logo. Turing's apple, however, suggests a new and more complicated story than that of Adam and Eve; it suggests different configurations of culture and technology, science and myth, gender and discourse. The fatal apple as a fitting symbol of Turing's work scrambles completely boundaries between natural and artificial, showing the natural to be always merely a configuration within the artificial. This symbol reveals, furthermore, multiple intersections of body and technology within cultural memory. Turing's bite, then, may indeed be read according to the myth of Genesis as the act of giving in to temptation, but it must also be read as resistance to the compulsory temptations of heterosexuality. Turing's death may have been a suicide, but it was also a refusal to circulate in the arena of military secrets. Turing's apple may be the apple of knowledge, but it is also the fruit of a technological dream.

THE FEMALE CYBORG: FEMINISM AND POSTMODERNISM

"The projected manufacture by men of artificial wombs, of cyborgs, which will be part flesh, part robot, of clones—all are manifestations of phallotechnic boundary violations."

Mary Daly, *Gyn-Ecology: The Metaethics of Radical Feminism*

"The cyborg is resolutely committed to partiality, irony, intimacy and perversity. It is oppositional, utopian and completely without innocence."

Donna Haraway, "A Manifesto for Cyborgs: Science, Technology, and Socialist Feminism in the 1980s"

Postmodernism has most often been theorized with relation to the arts or literature, but artificial intelligence, quantum mechanics, and a general move away from disciplinarity reveal that postmodernity is not only a simultaneous formation across disciplinary boundaries, but it also challenges distinctions between art and science altogether and suggests that the two cannot be thought separately. Obviously, the definition of postmodernism is contested. However, a working model of postmodernism demands that it have a historical dimension, a political perspective, and a cultural domain. Because the theoretical concerns of postmodernism and feminism often seem to mirror each other, questions arise as to whether the two are in dialogue or opposition and whether one takes precedence over the other. I contend that feminism and postmodernism enjoy a mutual dependence within the academy and in relation to mass culture. Because postmodernism has often been represented as a chameleon discourse, without a stable shape, form, or location, I offer a working definition that attempts both to situate it and to maintain its ambiguities. Theorists such as Andreas Huyssen and Jean François Lyotard suggest that postmodernism does not simply follow after modernism: it arises out of modernism and indeed interrupts what Lyotard identifies as modernism's grand narratives.[5] Huyssen finds that postmodernism sometimes breaks critically with modernism, and at other times merely reinscribes the modern enterprise.[6] The postmodern is not simply a chronological "after" to the modern; it is always embedded within the modern as interference or interruption and as a coming to consciousness of a subject no longer modeled upon the Western white male. In his attempt to historicize postmodernism, Fredric Jameson calls it a "cultural dominant" in the age of multinational capitalism. As cultural dominant, postmodernism participates in a different perception of space and time, in the production of a fragmented subjectivity, and in the breakdown of a surface/depth model in the realm of representation.[7] Refusing to designate postmodernism as a "style," Jameson demonstrates that postmodernism is a production within a system of logic at a precise time in history.

Most theories of the postmodern concede that it involves a changing relation between our bodies and our worlds. Jameson suggests, with reference to architecture, that postmodern hyperspace "has finally succeeded in transcending the capacities of the individual human body to locate itself, to organize its immediate surroundings perceptually, and cognitively to map its position in a mappable external world."[8] But the vertigo that Jameson describes, like the confusion precipitated in Lyotard's text by the breakdown of "grand narratives of legitimation,"[9] is nothing new for women and people of color. The world, after all, has been mapped and legitimated for only a small group of people. As postmodernity brings space and truth, time and body, nature and representation, and culture and technology into a series of startling collisions, we begin to ask questions about what interests were served by the stability of these categories and about who, in contrast, benefits from a recognition of radical instability within the postmodern. Such questions have informed debates about postmodern feminism. By exploring feminist claims that postmodernism is merely an intellectual ruse to reconstitute the subject as white and male, I show that postmodernism and feminism are in fact mutually indebted. On the most basic level, feminism forces a theory of gender oppression upon postmodernism, and postmodernism provides feminism with a politics of artificiality.

The relationship between feminism and postmodernism is anything but familial—they are not to be married, hardly siblings; they are both more and less than incestuous. The most successful unions of these two discourses, indeed, have suggested a robotic, artificial, and monstrous connection. Donna Haraway's 1985 essay, "A Manifesto for Cyborgs: Science, Technology, and Socialist Feminism in the 1980s," presents a radical departure for an emergent postmodern feminist discourse. Haraway merges radical feminism with a postmodern articulation of history and a politically necessary analysis of science and technology. She calls for a repositioning of socialist feminism in relation to technological production, theoretical articulations of the feminist subject, and the narrative of what she calls "salvation history." The cyborg for Haraway is "a condensed image of both imagination and material reality, the two joined centers structuring any possibility of historical transformation." Such an image is particularly useful for feminists who seek to avoid the ideological dangers of recourse to an authentic female self. Haraway's cyborg displays the machinery of gender; clothes herself in circuitry and networks; commits to "partiality, irony, intimacy, and perversity";[10] and revels in the confusion of boundaries.

Haraway has been criticized for engaging in "an epistemological fantasy of *becoming* multiplicity" by Susan Bordo, who identifies a danger in theoretical projects that embrace multiple and unstable subject positions. Such "deconstructionist readings," she suggests, "refuse to assume a shape for which they must take responsibility."[11] Bordo is not alone in her suspicion of the elusiveness of the postmodern subject. Nancy Hartsock asks: "Why is it that just at the moment when so many of us who have been silenced begin to demand the right to name ourselves, to act as subjects rather than as the objects of history, that just then the concept of subjecthood becomes problematic?"[12] Both Bordo's suspicion of the locatedness of the postmodern subject and Hartsock's questioning of the historical imperative behind the postmodern project are valid and timely inquiries. The subtext to both questions is whether the postmodern subject, fragmented and in flux, is not after all merely another incarnation of the masculine subject of the Enlightenment. Gender, such theorists fear, has been deemphasized in order to allow the male subject to be renaturalized as "human."

Bordo, then, accuses postmodern feminism of refusing "to assume a shape," and yet Haraway has outlined clearly the shape, form, and agenda of a postmodern feminist cyborg who *participates* in power structures. Hartsock finds postmodernism to be suspiciously contemporary with the coming to voice of many who have previously been silenced; and yet, academic feminism, at least, is surely a discourse with a voice and with an increasingly empowered place within the institution. Hartsock asks why is it that subjecthood splinters when marginalized groups begin to speak. The answer is already embedded in her question; subjecthood becomes problematic, fragmented, and stratified *because* marginalized Others begin to speak. The concept of the unified bourgeois subject, in other words, has been shot through with otherness and can find no way to regroup or reunite the splinters of being, now themselves part of a class, race, and gender configuration.

The fears that Bordo and Hartsock articulate are indeed justified, but to overindulge in such a speculative drift must surely reduce institutional power to a one-way dynamic that always reproduces a center and margins structure. Debates about whether certain theoretical strategies neutralize the political content of academic feminism—or, worse, collaborate in its co-optation—are necessary and important as long as they do not fall back upon a conception of power that identifies it as full-scale repression coming from above. Power, Michael Foucault has forcefully demonstrated, comes from below; and the postmodern subject, in its fragmentary and partial form, was formed out of the very challenge made by feminism to patriarchy.

Haraway concludes her essay: "Although both are bound in the spiral dance, I would rather be a cyborg than a goddess."[13] The cyborg and the goddess are suggestive terms for the comprehension of feminism as always multiple. Feminism has never been a monolithic theoretical or cultural project, but certain ideas do attain a kind of dominance over time. Hence, the "spiral dance," or history, makes the cyborg inconceivable in feminism without the prior presence of the goddess; one does, indeed, stand upon the other's shoulders. Haraway's essay figures the cultural feminism of the late 1970s and the early 1980s as the goddess because it revived and reinvested, in an idealized concept of woman, a concept that exiled her in nature and essentialized her in relation to gender. Such "cultural feminism," one which ignores the material bases of oppression and cathects "woman" as the real, the true, and the natural, reproduces, in Biddy Martin's words, "the classical split between the individual and the social formation" and assumes "that we can shed what is supposedly a false consciousness imposed and maintained from the outside, and begin to speak a more authentic truth."[14] Although the goddess and the cyborg are merely poles in a complex debate, they are useful in thinking through gender. Indeed, although the terms of the debate may change over time, in the arguments for and against a postmodern feminism we can still trace an oscillation between these positions. The ground between the goddess and the cyborg clearly stakes out the contested territory between the category "woman" and the gendered "body." So, if the goddess is an ideal congruence between anatomy and femininity, the cyborg instead posits femininity as automation, a coded masquerade.

As early as 1970, Shulamith Firestone in *The Dialectic of Sex* suggested the promise of the female cyborg: "What is called for is a revolutionary ecological program that would attempt to establish an artificial balance in place of the 'natural' one, thus realizing the original goal of empirical science: total mastery of nature." Firestone argued that feminist revolution must seize control of the means of both production and reproduction: cybernation and fertility control will relieve women of their historical burden and lead the way to a different and fully politicized female subject position. Firestone remained caught in a kind of biologism which grounds gender oppression in the body of the mother. And although her call for "total mastery" resubmits to a kind of holism, she has nonetheless envisioned a solution which is neither apocalyptic nor idealist and one which welcomes developments in science and technology. Firestone's claim that "the misuse of scientific developments is very often confused with technology itself" leads her to suggest that "atomic energy, fertility control, artificial reproduction, cybernation, in themselves are liberating—unless they are improperly used." Such a perspective concurs with Haraway's argument that "taking responsibility for the social relations of science and technology means refusing an anti-science metaphysics, a demonology of technology. . . ."[15]

Firestone's grim optimism in the 1970s was countered within feminist discourse by the demonization of science and technology which, quite understandably, stemmed from a fear of the relatedness of technology and militarism. Mary Daly's *Gyn-Ecology*, perhaps the most important work in the cultural feminist tradition, imaginatively and yet reductively performs an unequivocal rejection of all technologies. In a section entitled "From Robotitude to Roboticide: Reconsidering," Daly argues that "phallotechnic progress" aims eventually to replace femaleness with "hollow holograms" and female bodies with robots through such techniques as "total therapy, transsexualism and cloning."[16] Daly proposes a strategy to counter this process and calls it "roboticide" or the destruction of "false selves." Given the history of gendering technology as female in order to make it seductive, the threat of a Stepford Wives phenomenon certainly has validity. However, Daly's cultural critique hinges upon an investment in binaries such as natural and artificial, intuitive and rational, female and male, and body and mind. Daly reinvests in the fear of autonomous machines and equates artificiality with the loss of an essential self.

Daly categorizes cloning, artificial intelligence, and reproductive technology (or, as she terms it, "male-mother-miming") as boundary violations perpetrated by scientists, the "priests of patriarchy."[17] She reads robotitude, or automated gender, as a negative condition because she imagines that it replaces something natural and organic within "woman." Unlike Haraway, Daly is certain of what counts as nature and of what constitutes a true self. I suggest that even though automated gender does indeed involve a certain "robotitude," automation functions amidst constant interference from the random elements of computer technology and therefore constantly participates in the ordering and disordering of resistances. The imperfect matches between gender and desire, sex and gender, and the body and technology can be accommodated within the automated cyborg, because it is always partial, part machine and part human; it is always becoming human or "becoming woman."[18]

To argue, as the cultural feminists do, that automated gender removes the humanity of the female subject is to ignore the technology of gender and to replicate a patriarchal gendering of technology. As we saw in relation to Turing, technology is given a female identity when it must seduce the user into thinking of it as desirable or benign. Daly's argument that the female robot contaminates woman's essential naturalness regenders the natural and the artificial in the opposite direction as female nature and male science.

In a recent issue of *Feminist Studies*, Jane Caputi provides an updated version of Daly's critique of phallotechnocracy. Caputi's far-ranging analysis examines what she perceives as the ominous cultural import of the blurring of human and machine. Caputi opens her argument with a cogent reading of a television commercial for Elephant Premium floppy disks during election week 1984. The commercial's subliminal message, she suggests, is about memory, the mythical memory of the elephant, her own memory that the elephant is a symbol of the Republican party, and the electronic memory of the floppy disk. Caputi is concerned here with "the replacement of organic memory by an artificial substitute," and she fears that humans and machines will "slur/blur ever into one another, humans becoming more cold, the machines acquiring more soul."[19] Memory, artificial memory, also concerns Caputi in her consideration of the Apple computer logo. She argues that the logo both reactivates the myth of original sin and creates a new and dangerous myth about "an artificial paradise, indeed the artificial as paradise." Here, Caputi fails to question the very artificiality of the "natural" paradise she implicitly defends. The apple, as I have tried to suggest, is Turing's apple, an artificial fusion of mathematics and the body, death and desire, sex and gender.

In order to remain aware of the hidden messages in commercials that link conservatism, corporate business, and computer technology, Caputi warns, we must learn to "see elephants," to remember, "to no longer accept the part as the whole, to perceive and act upon essential connections."[20] We might ask of Caputi and Daly, what *is* so anxiety provoking in a blurring of machine and human and what is so attractive in holism and universalism? I propose that the fear in the first and the desire in the second spring from and return us to the complementary binaries of Western metaphysics. Caputi's concern that we are being duped by a patriarchal conspiracy of signification perhaps over-looks the fact that oppressive mechanisms more often deceive by wearing the mask of truth than by hiding; the action happens at the surface rather than down below. As Oscar Wilde wrote, "the true mystery of the world is the visible not the invisible."

In a discussion of Marshall McLuhan's *The Mechanical Bride: Folklore of Industrial Man,* Caputi further simplifies what is at stake in the concepts of "woman" and "female." She writes of the "Mechanical Bride" (in effect, a female cyborg): "This symbol is also a metaphor, one that links technology to creation via an artificial woman/wife/mother. As such, it cannot help but expose the enmity that technological man declares for living flesh and blood creation—nature, motherhood, the womb—but also for female *reality*."[21] In her attempt to maintain strict boundaries between the authentic and its simu-lation, Caputi opposes the mechanical bride to "female reality," a slippery concept, and she relocates nature and motherhood firmly within the female body. The female cyborg, therefore, becomes in her argument a symbol for male technological aggression against women; she does not attempt to ex-plain what fear the technological woman, the mechanical bride, generates in herself.

To predicate a critique of patriarchy, as Caputi and Daly do, on the basis of a true and authentic female self, who jealously guards her boundaries (physical and spiritual) and her goddess-given right to birth children, is merely to tell the story that patriarchy has told all along about women: women are morally superior to men, and they have an essential connection to nature. The female cyborg is, for both Daly and Caputi, a feared image of the seduc-tion of woman into an automated femininity rather than the image of what patriarchal, masculinist authority fears in both an autonomous technology and in femininity itself. The mistake lies in thinking that there is some "natu-ral" or "organic" essence of woman that is either corrupted or contained by any association with the artificial. However, femininity is always mechanical and artificial—as is masculinity. The female cyborg becomes a terrifying cul-tural icon because it hints at the radical potential of a fusion of femininity and intelligence. If we define femininity as the representation of any gen-dered body, and intelligence as the autonomous potential of technology and mental functioning, their union signifies the artificial component in each without referring to any essential concept of nature. A female cyborg would be artificial in both mind and flesh, as much woman as machine, as close to science as to nature. The resistance she represents to static conceptions of gender and technology pushes a feminist theory of power to a new arena. The intelligent and female cyborg thinks gender, processes power, and converts a binary system of logic into a more intricate network. As a metaphor, she challenges the correspondences such as maternity and femininity or female and emotion. As a metonym, she embodies the impossibility of distinguishing between gender and its representation.

By merging so completely the familiar with the strange, the artificial with the natural, the female cyborg appears to evoke something unsettling, something that profoundly disturbs and frightens certain authors. We might call the effect produced by the female cyborg "uncanny." "The uncanny," Freud writes in an essay of the same name, "is that class of the terrifying which leads back to something long known to us, once very familiar."[22] He then leads us back to the repressed as castration or the repressed as the mother's genitals. The repressed becomes uncanny when it recurs: it is the familiar (i.e., the mother's genitals) become strange (i.e., castrated).

By way of illustrating his theory, Freud refers to Hoffman's tale, "The Sand Man." He wants to use the story to prove his thesis that the threat of castration is what creates uncanny effects. Freud argues that the uncanny is represented in the castrating figure of the Sand Man himself, rather than in the lifelike doll, Olympia, with whom the hero, Nathaniel, falls in love.

> But I cannot think—and I hope most readers of the story will agree with me—that the theme of the doll, Olympia, who is to all appearances a living being, is by any means the only element to be held responsible for the quite unparalleled atmosphere of uncanniness which the story evokes. . . . The main theme of the story is, on the contrary, something different . . . it is the theme of the Sand Man who tears out children's eyes.

In this passage, Freud deliberately and forcefully shifts the terms of the debate in order to oppose Ernst Jentsch's work suggesting that the uncanny is produced by intellectual uncertainty. Jentsch gives as an example "doubts whether an apparently animate being is really alive," and he refers to "waxwork figures, artificial dolls and automatons."[23] Obviously, for Jentsch it is the automaton Olympia that is the locus of the uncanny in the story. Freud refutes Jentsch not only because of the importance of the castration theory to psychoanalysis, but also because Freud needs to separate the female body from both technology and the production of terror. Thus, he can maintain a critical connection (the very connection that Caputi and Daly defend) between the female body, nature, and motherhood.

A cycle of repetition-compulsion characterizes Freud's wandering journey through the uncanny. He represses the female figure Olympia who returns as the "painted woman" of Italy (the gen-Italia); then as the dark forest in which one might be lost; and finally as that "unheimlich place" itself, "the entrance to the former heim [home] of all human beings, to the place where everyone dwelt once upon a time and in the beginning."[24] This return reassures Freud of the possibility of an origin (easily lost among infinite repetitions) and calms his fear of the automated woman, the doll to whose womb neither he nor any man may return. Olympia, of course, is a cyborg, not a flesh-and-blood woman; nonetheless, she is desirable. Technology and the feminine reside at once in Olympia. Olympia, the mechanical bride, represents technology's seductiveness and its inevitability.[25]

In Hoffman's "The Sand Man," Olympia seduces the protagonist, Nathaniel, because as automaton she does not interfere with his narcissistic need to find himself mirrored in the Other. Her answer to all his questions, "Ach! Ach!" assures him that he has found true femininity, a perpetually consenting adult. When she is revealed to be an automaton, when her femininity as mechanism is finally brought to his attention, his very masculinity lies in the balance. Olympia as automaton radically questions the possibility of taking the body as proof of gender. She produces uncanny notions that the machine is more than a metaphor for self, that sexuality has a mechanism, and that gender is a technology.

Clearly, there is a problem when the arguments used within psychoanalysis or within modern scientific discourse to essentialize femininity are replicated within feminist theory. Mary Daly warns us of the dangers of robotitude but fails to problematize the ways in which technology has already been gendered female or why. Jane Caputi opposes artificial and natural memories but does not remember that feminism has called naturalized memory, or "history" into question all along. Some strands of feminist theory have demonized science and technology rather than attempting to undo oppressive discourses while participating in those that may empower us. In the age of the intelligent machine, political categories can no longer afford to be binary. A multiplicity is called for that acknowledges power differentials but is not ruled by them; that produces and reduces differences; and, finally, that understands gender as automated *and* intelligent, as a mechanism or structure capable of achieving some kind of autonomy from both biological sex and a rationalistic tradition. The female cyborg, in other words, calls attention to the artificiality of gender distinctions and to the political motivation that continues to blur gender into nature.

Feminist rereadings of what Haraway calls "the social relations of technology," of Olympia the artificial woman, the mechanical bride, can contribute to different technologies and different conceptions of gender identities. The apparently female cyborg releases the female body from its bondage to nature and merges body and machine to produce a terrifying and uncanny prospect of female intelligence. Gender emerges within the cyborg as no longer a binary but as a multiple construction dependent upon random formations beyond masculine or feminine. Different readings of cultural symbols, such as the apple of temptation, produce new myths and refuse the eschatology of a Christian science. Turing's travels into artificial intelligence, his experience of the technology of gender within his own body, his homosexuality, and finally, his fatal bite into the cyanide apple produce difference and the artificial as always concomitant with the natural. The cyborg and the apple demand post-Christian myths, myths of multiple genders, of variegated desires, myths of difference, differences and tolerance.

POSTSCRIPT

Postmodern feminism, as I have been arguing, can find positive and productive ways in which to theorize gender, science, and technology, and their connections within the fertile and provocative field of machine intelligence. Using the image of a female machine, I posit gender as an automated construct. Although the female cyborg proves to be a fascinating metaphor and an exciting prospect, it may gloss or obscure certain relations between living women and technology. For example, within the information industry, a traditional gender division exists with regard to work—men write programs and women process words—and such a division reinforces existing models for gendered labor.

Although Shoshana Zuboff does not directly confront the gendered division of labor, her book, *In the Age of the Smart Machine: The Future of Work and Power,* implies that such a division is not compatible with the new technology. Calling manager-employee relations in the automated workplace "posthierarchical," she claims: "This does not imply that differentials of knowledge, responsibility, and power no longer exist; rather they can no longer be assumed. Instead they shift and flow and develop their character in relation to the situations, the task and the actors at hand." Work relations, Zuboff argues, when clustered around an electronic text rather than spread between manual labor and personnel management, tend toward a system of equality. To arrive at this conclusion, Zuboff traces the history of blue- and white-collar workers, clerical workers, and management in relation to disciplinary systems of power within technology and industry. The predominance of women in the word-processing field might be attributed, then, to a continuation of the effects of the feminization of office work after the introduction of the typewriter in the 1890s: "in 1890, 64 percent of all stenographers and typists were women; by 1920, the figure had risen to 92 percent."[26] But typewriting and word processing—textual reproduction and textual manipulation—are different kinds of tasks, with a much greater potential for change existing within word processing. As jobs increasingly focus upon the manipulation of electronic texts and symbols, word processing will very probably not remain a secretarial task involving simple transcription; word processing, whether performed by women or men, may conceivably break down traditional divisions of labor within the office. The smart machine, indeed, requires that we change the way we envision our jobs as much as the new jobs alter social relations within the workplace.

At the same time, the electronic marketplace threatens to enforce a new kind of literacy and to create a disenfranchised body of illiterates. Being at ease with computer technology demands exposure that right now only money can buy. Even a slight decrease in market value, however, could make the personal computer as affordable and ubiquitous as the television set. If the labor force is to resist a split between those who work on computers and those who continue to hold low-paying and low-prestige service jobs, a split that could follow predictable class and race lines, people must have roughly equal access to computer time. Of course, the configurations of class, race, and gender in the age of the intelligent machine are not reducible to a single model or strategy. As the technology changes, social relations change; as social relations change, the technology is altered. Cybernetic systems, at least potentially, tend toward a posthierarchical labor structure in which the system stresses interaction—among workers and management, computer systems and operators—as much as production.

Gender, in this essay, has figured as an electronic text that shifts and changes in dialogue with users and programs. The apple signifies an altered relation between our bodies and ourselves in the age of the intelligent machine, and the Apple logo's byte no longer proves fatal. Postmodern feminism, I argue, may benefit from the theory of artificiality proposed by Turing's explorations in artificial intelligence and symbolized by the Apple logo. Such a theory shows that we are already as embedded within the new technologies as they are embodied within us. Both Turing's apple and the female cyborg threaten our ability to differentiate between our natural selves and our machine selves; these images suggest that perhaps already cyborgs are us.

NOTES

This essay began as a paper for Nancy Armstrong's feminist theory seminar at the University of Minnesota and I am indebted to her provocative and intricate reading of feminism. I also want to thank the following people for reading and commenting upon drafts of this essay: Barbara Cruikshank, Jane Gallop, Ira Livingston, and Paula Rabinowitz.

1. Andrew Hodges, *Alan Turing, the Enigma* (New York: Simon & Schuster, 1983), p. 97.

2. G. H. Hardy, quoted in ibid., p. 120.

3. Alan Turing, "Computing Machinery and Intelligence," *Mind* 59 (October 1950): 433–60.

4. Andreas Huyssen, "The Vamp and the Machine: Fritz Lang's Metropolis," in Andreas Huyssen, *After the Great Divide: Modernism, Mass Culture, Postmodernism* (Bloomington: Indiana University Press, 1986), p. 70.

5. Jean François Lyotard, *The Postmodern Condition: A Report on Knowledge*, trans. Geoff Bennington and Brian Massumi (Minneapolis: Minnesota University Press, 1984).

6. Andreas Huyssen, "Mapping the Postmodern," in *After the Great Divide*, p. 185.

7. Fredric Jameson, "Postmodernism, or the Cultural Logic of Late Capitalism," *New Left Review*, no. 146 (July/Aug. 1984): 53–92.

8. Ibid., p. 83.

9. Lyotard, p. 51.

10. Donna Haraway, "A Manifesto for Cyborgs: Science, Technology, and Socialist Feminism in the 1980s," in *Feminism/Postmodernism*, ed. Linda J. Nicholson (New York and London: Routledge, 1990), pp. 191, 192. I am using the most recent publication of this article because it does contain a few changes from the original version published in *Socialist Review*, no. 80 (1985): 65–107. Haraway's essay is reprinted as ch. 25 of this volume.

11. Susan Bordo, "Feminism, Postmodernism, and Gender-Scepticism," in *Feminism/Postmodernism*, p. 145, 144.

12. Nancy Hartsock, "Foucault on Power: A Theory for Women," in *Feminism/Postmodernism, p. 162.*

13. Haraway, p. 223.

14. Biddy Martin, "Feminism, Criticism, and Foucault," New German Critique, no. 27 (Fall 1982): 14–15.

15. Shulamith Firestone, *The Dialectic of Sex: The Case for Feminist Revolution* (New York: Morrow, 1970), pp. 219, 224, 223.

16. Mary Daly, *Gyn/Ecology: The Metaethics of Radical Feminism* (Boston: Beacon Press, 1978), p. 53.

17. Ibid., p. 103.

18. See Alice Jardine's provocative analysis of feminism and postmodernism and "the woman-in-effect" or "becoming woman" as a model for the postmodern subject in Alice Jardine, *Gynesis: Configurations of Woman and Modernity* (Ithaca: Cornell University Press, 1985).

19. Jane Caputi, "Seeing Elephants: The Myths of Phallotechnology," *Feminist Studies* 14 (Fall 1988): 514, 490.

20. Ibid., p. 490.

21. Ibid., p. 511.

22. Sigmund Freud, "The Uncanny" (1919), in Sigmund Freud, *On Creativity and the Unconscious,* trans. Alix Strachey (New York: Harper & Row, 1958), pp. 123–24.

23. Ibid., pp. 133, 132.

24. Ibid., p. 153.

25. To make an interesting connection here between Freud's uncanny doll and Turing's dream of intelligent machines, one need only note that "Olympia" is the name of a typewriter company. Turing imagined his machines as "super-typewriters."

26. Shoshana Zuboff, *In the Age of the Smart Machine: The Future of Work and Power* (New York: Basic Books, 1988), pp. 401–02, 116.

CHAPTER 27
THE PLEASURE OF THE INTERFACE

CLAUDIA SPRINGER

(1991)

> "Sex times technology equals the future"
>
> J. G. Ballard[1]

A discourse describing the union of humans and electronic technology currently circulates in the scientific community and in popular culture texts such as films, television, video games, magazines, cyberpunk fiction, and comic books. Much of the discourse represents the possibility of human fusion with computer technology in positive terms, conceiving of a hybrid computer/human that displays highly evolved intelligence and escapes the imperfections of the human body. And yet, while disparaging the imperfect human body, the discourse simultaneously uses language and imagery associated with the body and bodily functions to represent its vision of human/technological perfection. Computer technologies thus occupy a contradictory discursive position where they represent both escape from the physical body and fulfillment of erotic desire. To quote science fiction author J. G. Ballard again:

> I believe that organic sex, body against body, skin area against skin area, is becoming no longer possible. . . . What we're getting is a whole new order of sexual fantasies, involving a different order of experiences, like car crashes, like traveling in jet aircraft, the whole overlay of new technologies, architecture, interior design, communications, transport, merchandising. These things are beginning to reach into our lives and change the interior design of our sexual fantasies.[2]

The language and imagery of technological bodies exist across a variety of diverse texts. Scientists who are currently designing ways to integrate human consciousness with computers (as opposed to creating artificial intelligence) describe a future in which human bodies will be obsolete, replaced by computers that retain human intelligence on software.[3] *Omni* magazine postulates a "postbiological era." The *Whole Earth Review* publishes a forum titled "Is the body obsolete?" Jean-François Lyotard asks, "Can thought go on without a body?"[4] Popular culture has appropriated the scientific project; but instead of effacing the human body, these texts intensify corporeality in their representation of cyborgs. A mostly technological system is represented as its opposite: a muscular human body with robotic parts that heighten physicality and sexuality. In other words, these contemporary texts represent a future where human bodies are on the verge of becoming obsolete but sexuality nevertheless prevails.

The contradictory discourse on cyborgs reveals a new manifestation of the simultaneous revulsion and fascination with the human body that has existed throughout the Western cultural tradition. Ambivalence toward the body has traditionally been played out most explicitly in texts labeled pornographic, in which the construction of desire often depends upon an element of aversion. That which has been prohibited by censorship, for example, frequently becomes highly desirable. It was only in the nineteenth century, however, that pornography was introduced as a concept and a word, though its etymology dates back to the Greek πορνογραφος: writing about prostitutes. In his book *The Secret Museum*, Walter Kendrick argues that the signifier "pornography" has never had a specific signified, but constitutes a shifting ideological framework that has been imposed on a variety of texts since its inception.[5] He suggests that after the years between 1966 and 1970 we entered a postpornographic era heralded by the publication of *The Report of the Commission on Obscenity and Pornography*.[6] I would like to propose that if we are in a postpornographic era, it is most aptly distinguished by the dispersion of sexual representation across boundaries that previously separated the organic from the technological. As Donna Haraway writes:

> Late twentieth-century machines have made thoroughly ambiguous the difference between natural and artificial, mind and body, self-developing and externally designed, and many other distinctions that used to apply to organisms and machines. Our machines are disturbingly lively, and we ourselves frighteningly inert.[7]

Sexual images of technology are by no means new: modernist texts in the early twentieth century frequently eroticized technology. As K. C. D'Alessandro argues:

> Sexual metaphor in the description of locomotives, automobiles, pistons, and turbines; machine cults and Futurist movement, *Man With a Movie Camera*, and *Scorpio Rising*—these are some of the ways technophiliacs have expressed their passion for technology. For technophiliacs, technology provides an erotic thrill—control over massive power, which can itself be used to control others. . . . The physical manifestations of these machines—size, heft, shape, motions that thrust, pause, and press again—represent human sexual responses on a grand scale. There is much to venerate in the technology of the Industrial age.[8]

The film *Metropolis* (Fritz Lang, 1926) is a classic example of the early twentieth-century fascination with technology. It combines celebration of technological efficiency with fear of technology's power to destroy humanity by running out of control. This dual response is expressed by the film in sexual terms: a robot shaped like a human woman represents technology's simultaneous allure and powerful threat. The robot is distinguished by its overt sexuality, for it is its seductive manner that triggers a chaotic worker revolt. Andreas Huyssen argues that modernist texts tend to equate machines with women, displacing and projecting fears of overpowering technology onto patriarchal fears of female sexuality.[9] Huyssen contends that historically, technology was not always linked to female sexuality: the two became associated after the beginning of the nineteenth century just as machines came to be perceived as threatening entities capable of vast, uncontrollable destruction. In nineteenth-century literature, human life appears often to be vulnerable to the massive destructive potential of machines. Earlier, in the eighteenth century, before the Industrial Revolution installed machinery in the workplace on a grand scale, mechanization offered merely a playful diversion in the form of the mechanical figures, designed to look male as often as female, that achieved great popularity in the European cities where they were displayed.[10]

Cyborgs, however, belong to the information age, where, as D'Alessandro writes, "huge, thrusting machines have been replaced with the circuitry maze of the microchip, the minimal curve of aerodynamic design."[11] Indeed, machines have been replaced by systems, and the microelectronic circuitry of computers bears little resemblance to the thrusting pistons and grinding gears that characterized industrial machinery. D'Alessandro asks: "What is sensual, erotic, or exciting about electronic tech?" She answers by suggesting that cybernetics makes possible the thrill of control over information and, for the corporate executives who own the technology, control over the consumer classes. What popular culture's cyborg imagery suggests is that electronic technology also makes possible the thrill of escape from the confines of the body and from the boundaries that have separated organic from inorganic matter.

While robots represent the acclaim and fear evoked by industrial age machines for their ability to function independently of humans, cyborgs incorporate rather than exclude humans, and in so doing erase the distinctions previously assumed to distinguish humanity from technology. Transgressed boundaries, in fact, define the cyborg, making it the consummate postmodern concept. When humans interface with computer technology in popular culture texts, the process consists of more than just adding external robotic prostheses to their bodies. It involves transforming the self into something entirely new, combining technological with human identity. Although human subjectivity is not lost in the process, it is significantly altered.

Rather than portraying human fusion with electronic technology as terrifying, popular culture frequently represents it as a pleasurable experience. The pleasure of the interface, in Lacanian terms, results from the computer's offer to lead us into a microelectronic Imaginary where our bodies are obliterated and our consciousness integrated into the matrix. The word matrix, in fact, originates in the Latin *mater* (meaning both mother and womb), and the first of its several definitions in *Webster's* is "something within which something else originates or develops." Computers in popular culture's cyborg imagery extend to us the thrill of metaphoric escape into the comforting security of our mother's womb, which, as Freud explained, represents our earliest *Heim* (home).[12] According to Freud, when we have an *unheimlich* (uncanny) response to something, we are feeling the simultaneous attraction and dread evoked by the womb, where we experienced our earliest living moment at the same time that our insentience resembled death. It was Freud's contention that we are constituted by a death wish as well as by the pleasure principle; and popular culture's cyborg imagery effectively fuses the two desires.

Indeed, collapsing the boundary between what is human and what is technological is often represented as a sexual act in popular culture. By associating a deathlike loss of identity with sexuality, popular culture's cyborg imagery upholds a long-standing tradition of using loss of self as a metaphor for orgasm. It is well known that love and death are inextricably linked in the Western cultural tradition, as Denis de Rougemont shows in his book *Love in the Western World*.[13] The equation of death with love has been accompanied in literature by the idea of bodiless sexuality: two united souls represent the purest form of romance. De Rougemont considers the Tristan legend to be western culture's paradigmatic romantic myth, from the twelfth century into the twentieth century; and it persists in the late twentieth century in cyborg imagery that associates the human/computer interface with sexual pleasure.

Instead of losing our consciousness and experiencing bodily pleasures, cyborg imagery in popular culture invites us to experience sexuality by losing our bodies and becoming pure consciousness. One of many examples is provided by the comic book *Cyberpunk*,[14] whose protagonist, Topo, mentally enters the "Playing Field"—a consensual hallucination where all the world's data exists in three-dimensional abstraction (called cyberspace in the cyberpunk novels of William Gibson)—saying "it's the most beautiful thing in the human universe. If I could leave my meat behind and just live here. If I could just be pure consciousness I could be happy." While in the Playing Field he meets Neon Rose, a plant/woman with a rose for a head and two thorny tendrils for arms (and like Topo, only present through hallucination). Even her name inscribes the collapse of boundaries between organic plant life and a technological construct. He engages her in a contest of wills, represented as their bodies entwined around each other while he narrates: "In here, you're what you will. Time and space at our command. No limits, except how good your software is. No restraints." Topo's spoken desire—to leave his meat behind and become pure consciousness, which is in fact what he has done—is contradicted by the imagery: his body—his meat—wrapped around another body.

The word "meat" is widely used to refer to the human body in cyberpunk texts. Cyberpunk, a movement in science fiction dating from the early 1980s, combines an aggressive punk sensibility rooted in urban street culture with a highly technological future where distinctions between technology and humanity have dissolved. In this context, "meat" typically carries a negative connotation along with its conventional association with the penis. It is an insult to be called meat in these texts, and to be meat is to be vulnerable. And yet despite its aversion to meat, *Cyberpunk* visually depicts Topo's body after he has abandoned it to float through the Playing Field's ever-changing topography. His body, however, only seems to be inside the Playing Field because of an illusion, and he is capable of transforming it in any way he desires. As he sees Neon Rose approach, he transforms himself into mechanical parts shaped like his own human body, but more formidable. He has lost his flesh and become steel. Only his face remains unchanged, and it is protected by a helmet. Topo's new powerful body, a product of his fantasy, inscribes the conventional signifiers of masculinity: he is angular with broad shoulders and chest; and, most importantly, he is hard. It is no accident that he adopts this appearance in order to greet Neon Rose, who is coded in stereotypical feminine fashion as a sinewy plant who throws her tendrils like lassos to wrap them around him. In case the reader is still in doubt about Neon Rose's gender, *Cyberpunk* shows her as a human woman after Topo defeats her in their mock battle.

This example from *Cyberpunk* indicates that while popular culture texts enthusiastically explore boundary breakdowns between humans and computers, gender boundaries are treated less flexibly.

Cyberbodies, in fact, tend to appear masculine or feminine to an exaggerated degree. We find giant pumped-up pectoral muscles on the males and enormous breasts on the females; or, in the case of Neon Rose, cliched flower imagery meant to represent female consciousness adrift in the computer matrix. Cyborg imagery has not so far realized the ungendered ideal theorized by Donna Haraway.[15] Haraway praises the cyborg as a potentially liberatory concept, one that could release women from their inequality under patriarchy by making genders obsolete. When gender difference ceases to be an issue, she explains, then equality becomes possible. Janet Bergstrom points out that exaggerated genders dominate in science fiction because

> where the basic fact of identity as a human is suspect and subject to transformation into its opposite, the representation of sexual identity carries a potentially heightened significance, because it can be used as the primary marker of difference in a world otherwise beyond our norms.[16]

In heightening gender difference, popular culture's cyborg imagery has not caught up with scientist Hans Moravec, who tells us that there will be no genders in the mobile computers that will retain human mental functions on software once the human body has become obsolete: "not unless for some theatrical reason. I expect there'll be play, which will be just another kind of simulation, and play may include costume parties."[17] According to Lyotard, on the other hand, the most complex and transcendent thought is made possible by the force of desire, and therefore "thinking machines will have to be nourished not just on radiation but on irremediable gender difference."[18]

Jean Baudrillard takes a similar position when he suggests that its inability to feel pleasure makes artificial intelligence incapable of replicating human intelligence.[19] But Baudrillard, unlike Lyotard, does not insist that gender difference is indispensable. Instead, he sees the collapse of clear boundaries between humans and machines as part of the same postmodern move toward uncertainty that characterizes the collapse of difference between genders. Baudrillard asserts that "science has anticipated this panic-like situation of uncertainty by making a principle of it."[20] Indeed, uncertainty is a central characteristic of postmodernism and the essence of the cyborg. But since most cyborgs in popular culture exhibit definite gender difference, it is apparent that, despite its willingness to relinquish other previously sacrosanct categories, patriarchy continues to uphold gender difference.

Despite the fact that cyborg imagery in popular culture often exaggerates conventional gender difference, however, it does not always conform entirely to traditional sexual representations. Contrary to the way most sexual imagery has been designed for a male gaze and has privileged heterosexual encounters, cyborg imagery, taken as a whole, implies a wider range of sexualities. Erotic interfacing is, after all, purely mental and nonphysical; it theoretically allows a free play of imagination. Accordingly, not all cyborg imagery adheres strictly to the standardized male fantasies celebrated in *Playboy*. Nor does it simply posit the computer as female in the manner that *Metropolis* associates technology with female sexuality and represents men as vulnerable to both. Instead, computers in popular culture's cyborg imagery represent sexual release of various kinds for both genders.

In some examples, the act of interfacing with a computer matrix is acknowledged to be solitary; but it is nonetheless represented as a sexual act, a masturbatory fantasy expressed in terms of entering something, but lacking the presence of another human body or mind. In the comic book *Interface*, the interfacing experience of a woman named Linda Williams is coded as masturbation, which becomes linked to the process of thinking.[21] Williams is seen from a high angle lying on her bed on her back, saying, "I relax my body. My minds starts to caress the frequencies around me. There. That's better. I'm one with the super-spectrum now. I'm interfaced with the world." In the last panel, she is seen doubled, her second self rising nude from the bed with head thrown back and arms outstretched in a sexual pose.

Linda Williams's mental journey through the computer matrix in search of valuable files is drawn so as to show her nude body diving through oceans of electronic circuitry and a jumble of cliched newspaper headlines. Although female masturbation is a staple of conventional pornography for a male spectator, Williams's interface/masturbation is drawn differently from the pornographic norm: her body is ghostly white and in constant motion as she swoops through the matrix surrounded by a watery mist. In two panels, her body is merely an indistinct blur. Its activity distinguishes her from the conventional passive female object of pornography, and her masturbation is not a prelude to heterosexual sex. Later in the evening, after she has returned from the matrix (sighing, "coming down from the interface makes me feel dizzy") and is once again fully clothed, she rejects the sexual advances of a male character. She tells him, "I need some time to myself right now." When he tries to persuade her, she responds, "Not tonight. I know you were expecting me to sleep with you, to make you want to stay. But I don't do that sort of thing. Look, I'm attracted to you. So maybe you'll get lucky sometime. Right now,

I've got a lot on my mind. There's so much I have to think about." Williams takes control over her own sexuality, which embodies the cyborgian condition as represented in popular culture by being purely cerebral and simultaneously sexual. When she says she wants to be alone because there is so much she has to think about, the reader may infer that her private thoughts will be expressed sexually, as they were when she mentally entered the computer matrix.

Imaginary sex—sex without physically touching another human—prevails in cyborg discourses, though bodily sex is not altogether absent. The emphasis on cerebral sexuality suggests that while pain is a meat thing, sex is not. Historical economic, and cultural conditions have facilitated human isolation and the evolution of cerebral sex. Capitalism has always separated people from one another with its ideology of rugged individualism. Its primary form of sanctioned unity—the nuclear family—has traditionally decreed that one person, usually the woman, relinquish her individuality in order to support in the private realm the public endeavors of the other. Public relations under capitalism are characterized by competition and its attendant suspicions. In late capitalism, social relations are mediated not only by money, but also by the media with its simulations. Rather than communicate, we spectate. Computer technology offers greater opportunities for dialogue—through modem hookup and electronic mail, for example—than does television, and can be thought of as a way to reestablish the human contact that was lost during the television decades. It is hardly astonishing that, at a time when paranoia over human contact in response to the AIDS virus is common, human interaction should occur through computerized communication, with the participants far apart and unable to touch each other.

To say that people communicate via their computers is not to say that the act of communication has remained unchanged from the precomputer era. The term "communication" is in fact imprecise, according to Baudrillard. He writes that in the interface with the computer

> the Other, the sexual or cognitive interlocuter, is never really aimed at—crossing the screen evokes the crossing of the mirror. The screen itself is targeted as the point of interface. The machine (the interactive screen) transforms the process of communication, the relation from one to the other, into a process of commutation, i.e. the process of reversability from the same to the same. The secret of the interface is that the Other is within it virtually the Same—otherness being surreptitiously confiscated by the machine.[22]

Although the computer invites us to discard our identities and embrace an Imaginary unity, like a mirror it also reminds us of our presence by displaying our words back to us. What Baudrillard argues is that this intensely private experience precludes actual interaction with another person and turns all computerized communication into a kind of autocommunication which may contain elements of autoeroticism.

In an example of solitary sexual communion with technology, William Gibson, one of the founding authors of cyberpunk fiction, uses the term "jack in" in his writing to describe the moment when a "cowboy" sitting at a "deck" enters his command to be mentally transported into cyberspace: he wanted to title his first novel "Jacked In," but the publisher refused on the grounds that it sounded too much like "Jacked Off."[23] Gibson's trilogy—*Neuromancer, Count Zero,* and *Mona Lisa Overdrive*—evokes a dystopian future where isolated individuals drift in and out of each other's lives and often escape into fantasy.[24] Not unlike television's mass-produced fantasies of today, Gibson's "simstim" (simulated stimulation) feeds entertaining narratives directly into people's minds. Cyberspace, too, is a place of the mind, but it feels like three-dimensional space to those who enter it:

> Cyberspace. A consensual hallucination experienced daily by billions of legitimate operators, in every nation, by children being taught mathematical concepts. . . . A graphic representation of data abstracted from the banks of every computer in the human system. Unthinkable complexity. Lines of light ranged in the nonspace of the mind, clusters and constellations of data: Like city lights, receding. . . .[25]

Gibson's evocation of cyberspace has influenced the way people think about virtual reality, a concept dating back to the late 1960s which has become fashionable in the 1990s, receiving widespread media coverage while several companies develop its capabilities and design marketing strategies. Virtual reality creates a computer-generated space that a person perceives as three-dimensional through goggles fitted with small video monitors. Gloves connected to the computer allow users to interact with the space and feel as though they are performing such activities as picking up objects, driving or flying. It would be inappropriate to call virtual reality an escape from reality, since what it does is provide an alternative reality where "being" somewhere does not require physical presence and "doing" something does not result in any changes in the physical world. Virtual reality undermines certainty over the term reality, ultimately abandoning it altogether along with all the other certainties that have been discarded in postmodern times. John Perry Barlow, who writes about the cyberworld and is cofounder of the Electronic Frontier Foundation (an organization that tries to protect those working in electronic communications from governmental repression), calls virtual reality "a Disneyland for epistemologists," declaring that it will "further expose the conceit that 'reality' is a fact . . . delivering another major hit to the old fraud of objectivity."[26]

In published descriptions of virtual reality there are frequent references to its erotic potential. One concept in the works is "teledildonics," which puts the user in a bodysuit lined with tiny vibrators.[27] The user would telephone others who are similarly outfitted. Their telephone conversations would be accompanied by computerized visual representations, displayed to them on headsets, of their bodies engaged in sexual activities. As Howard Rheingold, author of the book *Virtual Reality,*[28] points out, teledildonics would revolutionize sexual encounters as well as our definitions of self:

Clearly we are on the verge of a whole new semiotics of mating. Privacy and identity and intimacy will become tightly coupled into something we don't have a name for yet. . . . What happens to the self? Where does identity lie? And with our information-machines so deeply intertwingled [sic] with our bodily sensations, as Ted Nelson might say, will our communication devices be regarded as "its" . . . or will they be part of "us"?[29]

Confusion over the boundaries between the self and technological systems is already evident. Virtual reality, according to some of its proponents, will be able to eliminate the interface, the "mind-machine information barrier."[30] According to Baudrillard, uncertainty over the boundary between humanity and technology originates in our relationship to the new technological systems, not to traditional machines:

> Am I a man, am I a machine? In the relationship between workers and traditional machines, there is no ambiguity whatsoever. The worker is always estranged from the machine, and is therefore alienated by it. He keeps his precious quality of alienated man to himself. Whilst new technology, new machines, new images, interactive screens, do not alienate me at all. With me they form an integrated circuit.[31]

Nowhere is the confusion of boundaries between humanity and electronic technology more apparent than in films involving cyborg imagery: here cyborgs are often indistinguishable from humans. The Terminator (*The Terminator*, James Cameron, 1984), for example, can be recognized as nonhuman only by dogs, not by humans. Even when cyborgs in films look different from humans, they are often represented as fundamentally human. In *Robocop* (Paul Verhoeven, 1987), Robocop is created by fusing electronic technology and robotic prostheses with the face of a policeman, Alex J. Murphy, after he has died from multiple gunshot wounds. He clearly looks technological, while at the same time he retains a human shape. His most recognizably human feature is his face, with its flesh still intact, while the rest of his body is entirely constructed of metal and electronic circuitry. The film shows that despite his creators' attempts to fashion him into a purely mechanical tool, his humanity keeps surfacing. He seeks information about Murphy, his human precursor; and increasingly identifies with him, particularly since he retains memories of the attack that killed Murphy. At the end of the film, Robocop identifies himself, when asked for his name, as Murphy. In the sequel, *Robocop II* (Irvin Kershner, 1990), Robocop's basic humanity is further confirmed when he is continually stirred by memories of Murphy's wife and young son, and takes to watching them from the street outside their new home. Robocop's inability to act on his human desires constitutes the tragic theme of the film, which takes for granted that Robocop is basically human.

If there is a single feature that consistently separates cyborgs from humans in these films, it is the cyborg's greater capacity for violence, combined with enormous physical prowess. Instead of representing cyborgs as intellectual wizards whose bodies have withered away and been replaced by computer terminals, popular culture gives us muscular hulks distinguished by their superior fighting skills. To some extent the phenomenon of the rampaging cyborg in films suggests a residual fear of technology of the sort that found similar expression in older films like *Metropolis*. Electronic technology's incredible capabilities can certainly evoke fear and awe, which can be translated in fictional representation into massive bodies that overpower human characters.

But fear of the computer's abilities does not entirely explain why cyborgs are consistently associated with violence. Significantly, muscle-bound cyborgs in films are informed by a tradition of muscular comic-book superheroes; and, like the superheroes, their erotic appeal lies in the promise of power they embody. Their heightened physicality culminates not in sexual climax but in acts of violence. Violence substitutes for sexual release. Steve Neale has theorized that violence displaces male sexuality in films in response to a cultural taboo against a homoerotic gaze.[32] Certain narrative films continue to be made for a presumed male audience, and homophobia exerts a strong influence on cinematic techniques. For example, close-up shots that caress the male body on screen might encourage a homoerotic response from the male spectator. But, as Neale explains, the spectacle of a passive and desirable male body is typically undermined by the narrative, which intervenes to make him the object or the perpetrator of violence, thereby justifying the camera's objectification of his body.

In the opening sequence of *The Terminator*, for example, the shot of the cyborg's (Arnold Schwarzenegger) beautifully sculpted nude body standing on a hill above nighttime Los Angeles, city lights twinkling like ornaments behind him, is quickly followed by his bloody attack on three punk youths in order to steal their clothes. His attire then consists of hard leather and metal studs, concealing his flesh and giving his sexuality a veneer of violence. As in similar examples from other films, an invitation to the spectator to admire the beauty of a male body is followed by the body's participation in violence. The male body is restored to action to deny its status as passive object of desire, and the camera's scrutiny of the body receives narrative justification.

Klaus Theweleit, in his two-volume study of fascist soldier males (specifically, men of the German *Freikorps*, between the world wars), writes that their psychological state indicates an intense misogyny and an overwhelming desire to maintain a sense of self in the face of anything they perceive might threaten their bodily boundaries.[33] Theweleit draws on the theories of psychologist Margaret Mahler to argue that fascist males have never developed an identity (they are "not-yet-fully-born"), and thus invest all of their energies into maintaining a fragile edifice of selfhood. Their failure to disengage from their mothers during infancy results in a fear that women will dissolve their identities; hence the frequency with which women are associated in fascist rhetoric with raging floods that threaten to engulf their victims. In order to protect themselves from women, onto whom they project the watery weakness they despise in themselves, fascist males encase themselves in body armor, both literally and figuratively. The machine body becomes the ideal tool for ego maintenance.

For the fascist male, additionally, the sexual act evokes loss of self and becomes displaced onto violence. The act of killing, especially by beating the victim into a bloody pulp, functions to externalize the dissolution of self that he fears, and assures him of his relative solidity. He reaffirms his physical and psychological coherence every time he kills. Acts of violence also serve to release some of his enormous tension, for the task of maintaining a sense of self when a self barely exists is excruciating, and the soldier male does not allow himself to experience release through sexual union. As Theweleit writes, "heroic acts of killing take the place of the sexual act," and the ecstasy of killing substitutes for sexual climax.[34]

Cyborg imagery in films is remarkably consistent with Theweleit's description of the fascist soldier male. If anything, cyborg imagery epitomizes the fascist ideal of an invincible armored fighting machine. In *Robocop*, Robocop's armor is external and protects him from gunshots and other assaults that would kill a human. He strides fearlessly into a blaze of gunfire as bullets bounce off his armored body. In *The Terminator*, the cyborg's armor is inside his body and therefore not visible, but it makes him virtually indestructible. Near the end of the film, after the Terminator's flesh has been burnt away, he is revealed to be a metal construct that, despite the loss of all its flesh, continues methodically to stalk its victim.

Cyborg imagery, therefore, represents more than just a recognition that humanity has already become integrated with technology to the point of indistinguishability; it also reveals an intense crisis in the construction of masculinity. Shoring up the masculine subject against the onslaught of a feminity feared by patriarchy now involves transforming the male body into something only minimally human. Whereas traditional constructions of masculinity in film often relied on external technological props (guns, armored costumes, motorcycles, fast cars, cameras, and so on)[35] to defend against disintegration, the cinematic cyborg heralds the fusion of the body with the technological prop.

Ironically, the attempt to preserve the masculine subject as a cyborg requires destroying the coherence of the male body and replacing it with electronic parts; either physically—using hardware, or psychologically—using software. The construction of masculinity as cyborg requires its simultaneous deconstruction. And yet, by escaping from its close identification with the male body, masculine subjectivity has been reconstituted, suggesting that there is an essential masculinity that transcends bodily presence. In a world without human bodies, the films tell us, technological things will be gendered and there will still be a patriarchal hierarchy. What this reconfiguration of masculinity indicates is that patriarchy is more willing to dispense with human life than with male superiority.

However, the sacrifice of the male body is disguised in cyborg films by emphasizing physicality and intensifying gender difference. Pumping up the cyborg into an exaggerated version of the muscular male physique hides the fact that electronic technology has no gender. In *Total Recall* (Paul Verhoeven, 1990), for example, the fact that Doug Quaid's identity is merely an electronic implant is counteracted by his massive physical presence, once again made possible by casting Arnold Schwarzenegger in the role of Quaid. Muscular cyborgs in films thus assert and simultaneously disguise the dispersion of masculine subjectivity beyond the male body.

The paradox that preserving masculine subjectivity in the figure of the cyborg requires destroying the male body accounts in part for the extreme violence associated with cyborgs in films: they represent an impossible desire for strength through disintegration; and, like the fascist soldier males, their frustration finds expression in killing. The Terminator, for example, is programmed to kill and in fact has no other function than to kill humans. He has been sent into the past by his machine masters expressly to kill a young woman, Sarah Connor. His adversary Kyle Reese tells Connor that the Terminator "can't be bargained with, it can't be reasoned with, it doesn't feel pity or remorse or fear and it absolutely will not stop, ever, until you are dead," recalling Theweleit's observation that the fascist soldier male has no moral qualms about killing.

Robocop is also an expert killer, but the two *Robocop* films, unlike *The Terminator,* justify the hero's acts of killing by putting him on the side of law enforcement and showing his victims caught in the act of committing crimes. In *Robocop II,* Robocop is programmed to apprehend criminals without killing them by a smarmy woman psychologist who preaches nonviolence and is made to appear ridiculous. The film indicates, however, that the software program that prevents Robocop from killing hinders his effectiveness; and the film celebrates his acts of killing when he manages to overcome the restraining program. In *Total Recall,* Doug Quaid is attacked nearly every time he turns a corner, and he responds by killing all of his attackers with a show of incredible strength and brutality.

Not only does cyborg imagery in films extol the human killing machine, it also expresses the concomitant fear of sexuality theorized by Theweleit. In the film *Hardware* (Richard Stanley, 1990), for example, the cyborg is dormant until activated by the sight of a young woman, Jill, having sex with her boyfriend. After the boyfriend has left the apartment and Jill has hung the cyborg on the wall as part of a scrap metal sculpture, the cyborg watches her sleeping body for a while and then emerges to attack her; for, like the Terminator, it has been created to destroy humans.

Sexuality is feared by fascist soldier males not only because it signifies loss of personal boundaries, writes Theweleit, but also because sexuality evokes the creation of life, and the soldier male is bent on destroying all signs of life before they can destroy him. Pregnant women, according to Theweleit, are treated with revulsion in his rhetoric. Like fascist soldier males, cyborgs in films are often determined to prevent birth. In *Hardware,* it turns out that the cyborg that kills all the life forms it encounters is a secret weapon in the government's birth control program. The Terminator, likewise, has been programmed to travel back through time to kill Sarah Connor in order to prevent her giving birth to her son John, who, forty years into the future, will lead the few humans who have survived a nuclear war in defeating the machines that threaten humanity with annihilation.

Creation versus destruction of life is not only a central thematic concern but also a site of dispute in cyborg texts. The ability to engender life is divided between men and women and between humans and technology. Women are typically associated with biological reproduction while men are involved in technological reproduction. In the film *Demon Seed* (Donald Cammell, 1977), for example, a scientist creates an artificial intelligence in a sophisticated computer laboratory where teams of specialists educate their artificial child. The scientist's wife, Susan (Julie Christie), is a psychiatrist, a member of a humanistic profession that opposes her husband's technophilia. She complains about his emotional coldness, illustrating the film's stereotypically phallocentric definition of gender roles: men are scientific and aloof while women are humanistic and emotional.

Demon Seed reinforces its version of gender difference by taking for granted that the AI, a form of pure consciousness, is male. Masculine subjectivity has dispensed entirely with the need to construct a body in this film, existing instead as bodiless intellect. And the woman's role is even further confined when Susan is raped by the AI, whose pure intellect is the antithesis of Susan's reduction to a reproductive vessel. Since the artificial intelligence has no physical form (its name is Proteus IV, after the Greek sea god capable of assuming different forms), it relies on a robot and a giant mutating geometric shape under its command to rape Susan. Its orgasm while impregnating her is represented as a trip into the far reaches of the cosmos. ("I'll show you things only I have seen," it tells her.) Motivated by a desire to produce a child and thereby experience emotions and physical sensations, the AI attempts to take control over the reproductive process; in effect vying with Susan's husband for power over creation, but going back to a biological definition of reproduction and a phallocentric definition of woman as childbearer. Susan is a mere womb in the AI's scheme. When the film ends with the birth of the child conceived by the AI and Susan, it leaves ambiguous whether the cyborg child, a union of a disembodied intellect and a human woman, will be demonic or benign.

Men are also the creators of life in *Weird Science* (John Hughes, 1985), a throwback to *Metropolis* with its representation of a woman artificially designed to fulfill a male fantasy. Two unpopular high school boys program a computer to create their perfect woman, assembled from fragmented body parts selected from *Playboy* magazines. Her role, like the robot's in *Metropolis*, at first appears to be sexual: the boys' initial desire is to take a shower with her. Also as in *Metropolis*, the woman's sexuality is too powerful for the boys, who are incapable of doing more than just kissing her. However, unlike *Metropolis*, she takes on a big sisterly role that involves instructing her creators in the finer points of talking to girls. Her guidance boosts their self-confidence and allows them to win over the two most popular high school girls, whom earlier they could only admire from afar. The film uses the concept of computer-generated life only to further its conventional coming-of-age narrative, and does nothing to question either gender roles or the implications of nonbiological reproduction.

Eve of Destruction (Duncan Gibbins, 1991) complicates the theme of creation versus destruction, but only to punish the woman protagonist for her sexuality and for engaging in technological rather than biological reproduction. A scientist named Eve creates a cyborg, also named Eve, who looks exactly like her and is programmed with her memories. The cyborg escapes from the scientist and goes on a killing spree. Rather than engaging in random destruction, however, the cyborg Eve lives out the scientist Eve's repressed fantasies of sex and revenge against men. Thus the cyborg kills the scientist's father, whom the scientist has hated since childhood because he brutalized and caused the death of her mother. The cyborg's first victim is a redneck at a country saloon that the scientist had fantasized frequenting for casual sex. The cyborg takes the man to a motel room and, when he taunts her with his erection, bites his penis.

The film's castration anxiety escalates, for it turns out that the cyborg has something much more dangerous than a vagina dentata: a nuclear vagina. We learn that the Defense Department funded the cyborg project to create a secret military weapon, complete with nuclear capabilities. In a computer graphics display of the cyborg's design, we see that the nuclear explosive is located at the end of a tunnel inside her vagina. Sure enough, the countdown to a nuclear explosion begins when the cyborg has an orgasm as she destroys another man by crashing her car into his. Patriarchal fear of female sexuality has clearly raised the stakes since the 1920s when *Metropolis* showed unleashed female sexuality leading to the collapse of a city. *Eve of Destruction* puts the entire planet at risk.

Having established that female sexuality leads to uncontrollable destruction, the film suggests that what the scientist placed in danger by creating artificial life was her role as biological mother: for the cyborg kidnaps the scientist's young son. Only then does the scientist cooperate with the military officer whose job it is to destroy the cyborg before it detonates. Earlier, they had an antagonistic relationship revolving around contempt for each other's profession. His attempts to destroy her cool professional demeanor finally succeed, and at the end it is she who destroys the cyborg only seconds before zero hour in order to save the lives of her son and the military officer. The scientist in effect destroys her repressed sexuality and anger towards men, and accepts her primary status as biological mother.

As *Eve of Destruction* illustrates, artificial life in films continues, in the Frankenstein tradition, to threaten the lives of its creators; but it also continues to hold out the promise of immortality. A yearning for immortality runs throughout cyborg discourses. In cyberpunk fiction, taking the postmodern principle of uncertainty to its radical extreme, not even death is a certainty. Cyberpunk fiction writers William Gibson and Rudy Rucker[36] have made immortality a central theme in their books, raising questions about whether nonphysical existence constitutes life and, especially in Gibson's novels, examining how capitalism would allow only the extremely wealthy class to attain immortality by using technology inaccessible to the lower classes. But cyberpunk fiction is not without recognition of the paradoxes and dangers of immortality. In both Gibson's and Rucker's work, characters who attempt to become immortal are usually surrounded by a tragic aura of loneliness and decay.

Even Topo, in the comic book *Cyberpunk,* rejects the idea of leaving his meat behind and remaining permanently in the Playing Field when he is offered the opportunity.[37] What he rejects is immortality. But the comic book reveals that the loss of his human body would be tantamount to death; for the invitation to join those who have permanently abandoned their bodies comes from a death mask, called The Head, that addresses him from atop a pedestal. During their conversation, disembodied skulls swoop by around them, reinforcing the death imagery. When, in the next issue, Topo loses his human body and becomes a cyberghost trapped in the Playing Field, the line between life and death becomes more ambiguous.[38] There is much speculation among his friends, who remain outside the computer matrix, about whether Topo is dead or alive. Topo himself says "after all, I'm only a data construct myself, now. Nothing equivocal about it. We live. We are forms of life, based on electrical impulses. Instead of carbon or other physical matter. We are the next step."

These examples show that cyborg imagery revolves around the opposition between creation and destruction of life, expressing ambivalence about the future of human existence and also, as with the fascist soldier males, uncertainty about the stability of masculine subjectivity. Fusion with electronic technology thus represents a paradoxical desire to preserve human life by destroying it. The concept of abandoning the body with pleasure arises in part from late twentieth-century post-nuclear threats to the body: nuclear annihilation, AIDS, and environmental disasters. Devising plans to preserve human consciousness outside of the body indicates a desire to redefine the self in an age when human bodies are vulnerable in unprecedented ways. Contemporary concern with the integrity of the body is only the latest manifestation of postwar anxiety over the body's fragility.

Neither alive nor dead, the cyborg in popular culture is constituted by paradoxes: its contradictions are its essence, and its vision of a discordant future is in fact a projection of our own conflictual present. What is really being debated in the discourses surrounding a cyborg future are contemporary disputes concerning gender and sexuality, with the future providing a clean slate, or a blank screen, onto which we can project our fascination and fears. While some texts cling to traditional gender roles and circumscribed sexual relations, others experiment with alternatives. It is perhaps ironic, though, that a debate over gender and sexuality finds expression in the context of the cyborg, an entity that makes sexuality, gender, even humankind itself, anachronistic. Foucault's statement that "man is an invention of recent date. And one perhaps nearing its end" prefigures the consequences of a cyborg future.[39] But, as Foucault also argues, it is precisely during a time of discursive crisis, when categories previously taken for granted become subject to dispute, that new concepts emerge. Late twentieth-century debates over sexuality and gender roles have thus contributed to producing the concept of the cyborg. And, depending on one's stake in the outcome, one can look to the cyborg to provide either liberation or annihilation.

NOTES

1. J. G. Ballard, interview by Peter Linnett, *Corridor*, no. 5 (1974); reprinted in *Re/Search*, nos 8–9 (San Francisco: Re/Search Publications, 1984): 164.

2. J. G. Ballard, interview by Lynn Barber, *Penthouse*, September 1970; reprinted in *Re/Search*, nos 8–9, p. 157.

3. Hans Moravec, director of the Mobile Robot Laboratory at Carnegie-Mellon University, is at the forefront of cyborg development; see his book *Mind Children: The Future of Robot and Human Intelligence* (Cambridge: Harvard University Press, 1988). For a journalistic account of Moravec's research projects and his concept of a cyborg future, see Grant Fjermedal, *The Tomorrow Makers: A Brave New World of Living-Brain Machines* (New York: Macmillan, 1986).

4. "Interview with Hans Moravec," *OMNI* 11, 11 (1989): 88; "Is the Body Obsolete? A Forum," *Whole Earth Review*, no. 63 (1989), pp. 34–55; Jean-Francois Lyotard, "Can Thought Go on without a Body?" *Discourse* 11, 1 (1988–89): 74–87.

5. Walter Kendrick, *The Secret Museum: Pornography in Modern Culture* (New York: Penguin Books, 1987), p. 31.

6. Commission on Obscenity and Pornography, *Report on the Commission on Obscenity and Pornography* (Toronto, New York, and London: Bantam, 1970). The commission was established by the U.S. Congress in October 1967 to define "pornography" and "obscenity," to determine the nature and extent of their distribution, to study their effects upon the public, and to recommend legislative action. The commission's report did not define obscenity and pornography and stated that no empirical evidence existed to link criminal behavior to sexually explicit material. It also recommended against any legislative action and proposed that all existing prohibitive laws be repealed. Soon after its release, the report was rejected by the U.S. Senate and by President Nixon.

7. Donna Haraway, "A Manifesto for Cyborgs: Science, Technology, and Socialist Feminism in the 1980s," *Socialist Review*, no. 90 (1985): 65–107. Reprinted in Elizabeth Weed, ed. *Coming to Terms: Feminism, Theory, and Practice* (New York: Routledge, 1989), pp. 173–204; the quotation is from p. 176. Haraway's essay is reprinted as ch. 25 of this volume.

8. K. C. D'Alessandro, "Technophilia: Cyberpunk and Cinema," paper presented at the Society for Cinema Studies conference, Bozeman, Montana, July 1988, p. 1.

9. Andreas Huyssen, "The Vamp and the Machine: Technology and Sexuality in Fritz Lang's *Metropolis,*" *New German Critique*, nos 24–5 (1981–2): 221–37.

10. Ibid., p. 226

11. D'Alessandro, "Technophilia: Cyberpunk and Cinema," p. 1.

12. Sigmund Freud, "The 'Uncanny' " (1919), *The Standard Edition of the Complete Psychological Works of Sigmund Freud*, vol. 17, trans. and ed. James Strachey (London: Hogarth Press, 1973), pp. 219–52.

13. Denis de Rougemont, *Love in the Western World* (New York: Harper & Row, 1956).

14. Scott Rockwell, *Cyberpunk*, book one, vol. 1, no. 1 (Wheeling, West Virginia: Innovative Corporation, 1989).

15. Haraway, "A Manfesto for Cyborgs."

16. Janet Bergstrom, "Androids and Androgyny," *Camera Obscura*, no. 15 (1986): 39.

17. "Interview with Hans Moravec," p. 88.

18. Lyotard, "Can Thought Go on without a Body?" p. 86.

19. Jean Baudrillard, *Xerox and Infinity*, trans. Agitac (Paris: Touchepas, 1988), p. 3.

20. Ibid., p. 16.

21. James D. Hudnall, *Interface* 1, 1 (New York: Epic Comics, 1989).

22. Baudrillard, *Xerox and Infinity*, pp. 5–6.

23. William Gibson and Timothy Leary in conversation, "High Tech/High Life," *Mondo 2000*, no. 1 (Berkeley: Fun City Megamedia, 1989): 61.

24. William Gibson, *Neuromancer* (New York: Ace Books, 1984), *Count Zero* (New York: Ace Books, 1986), *Mona Lisa Overdrive* (New York: Bantam Books, 1988).

25. Gibson, *Neuromancer*, p. 51.

26. John Perry Barlow, "Being in Nothingness," *Mondo 2000*, no. 2 (Berkeley: Fun City Megamedia, 1990): 39, 41.

27. Howard Rheingold, "Teledildonics: Reach out and Touch Someone," *Mondo 2000*, no. 2 (Berkeley: Fun City Megamedia, 1990): 52–54.

28. Howard Rheingold, *Virtual Reality* (New York: Simon & Schuster, 1991).

29. Rheingold, "Teledildonics," p. 54.

30. Barlow, "Being in Nothingness," p. 38.

31. Baudrillard, *Xerox and Infinity*, p. 14.

32. Steve Neale, "Masculinity as Spectacle: Reflections on Men and Mainstream Cinema," Screen 24, 6 (1983): 2–16.

33. Klaus Theweleit, *Male Fantasies*, vol. 1 (Minneapolis: University of Minnesota Press, 1987), *Male Fantasies*, vol. 2 (Minneapolis: University of Minnesota Press, 1989).

34. Theweleit, *Male Fantasies*, vol. 2, pp. 276–79.

35. For a discussion of how constructions of the masculine subject have relied on technological props, see Sabrina Barton, "The Apparatus of Masculinity in *Shane* and *Sex, Lies, and Videotape*," a paper presented at the Society for Cinema Studies Conference, Washington, D.C., May 1990; Constance Penley, "Feminism, Film Theory, and the Bachelor Machines," *The Future of an Illusion: Film, Feminism, and Psychoanalysis* (Minneapolis: University of Minnesota Press, 1989), ch. 4. In the context of the war film, see Susan Jeffords, *Remasculinization of America: Gender and the Vietnam War* (Bloomington: Indiana University Press, 1989).

36. Rudy Rucker, *Software* (New York: Avon Books, 1982), *Hardware* (New York: Avon Books, 1988).

37. Scott Rockwell, *Cyberpunk*, book two, vol. 1, no. 1 (Wheeling, West Virginia: Innovative Corporation, 1990).

38. Scott Rockwell, *Cyberpunk*, book two, vol. 1, no. 2 (Wheeling, West Virginia: Innovative Corporation, 1990).

39. Michel Foucault, *The Order of Things: An Archaeology of the Human Sciences* (New York: Vintage Books, 1973), p. 387.

CONTRIBUTORS

Lori B. Andrews is a professor of law at Chicago-Kent College of Law. She is author of *Black Power, White Blood* and more than fifty scholarly articles on subjects including health professional licensing, informed consent, medical genetics, surrogate motherhood, and alternative modes of reproduction.

Daniel Callahan is cofounder and former president of the Hastings Center, an organization examining ethical issues of medicine, biology, and environment. He currently serves as the center's Director of International Programs and Senior Associate for Health Policy. His many books include *The Troubled Dream of Life: In Search of a Peaceful Death, What Kind of Life: The Limits of Medical Progress,* and *Setting Limits: Medical Goals in an Aging Society.*

Ruth Schwartz Cowan is a professor in the Department of History at the State University of New York at Stony Brook. She is the author of numerous articles and books, including *A Social History of American Technology* and *More Work For Mother: The Ironies of Household Technology from the Open Hearth to the Microwave* and coauthor (with Neil Cowan) of *Our Parent's Lives: Everyday Life and Jewish Assimilation.*

Kathy Davis is an associate professor of women's studies at the Faculty of Social Sciences in the University of Utrecht, the Netherlands. She is the author of *Power Under the Microscope* and *Remaking the Female Body,* and editor of *Embodied Practices: Feminist Perspectives on the Body.*

Judith Halberstam is an associate professor of literature at the University of California at San Diego. She is the author of *Skin Shows: Gothic Horror and the Technology of Monsters* and coeditor (with Ira Livingston) of *Posthuman Bodies.*

Tove Håpnes is a research scientist at SINTEF-Institute for Social Research in Industry in Norway, where she works on the development of computer science in Norway, on gender and computer education, on gender and system developments in IT-industry, and on computer hackers' machine activities and style of work.

Donna J. Haraway is a professor in the History of Consciousness Department at the University of California at Santa Cruz. She is the author of *Crystals, Fabrics and Fields: Metaphors of Organicism in Twentieth-Century Developmental Biology, Primate Visions: Gender, Race, and Nature in the World of Modern Science, Simians, Cyborgs, and Women: The Reinvention of Nature,* and *Modest_Witness@Second_Millennium.FemaleMan© Meets OncoMouse™.*

Helen Bequaert Holmes is currently Coordinator of the Center for Genetics, Ethics, and Women in Amherst, Massachusetts. She cofounded the international Network on Feminist Approaches to Bioethics. Her research is in feminist assessment of reproductive and genetic technologies. She is editor of *Issues in Reproductive Technology* and coeditor of *Feminist Perspectives in Medical Ethics.*

Patrick D. Hopkins is an assistant professor of philosophy at Ripon College in Wisconsin. He is the author of several articles in bioethics, technology studies, gender studies, and feminist theory, and has coedited (with Larry May and Robert Strikwerda) *Rethinking Masculinity: Philosophical Explorations in Light of Feminism.* He is currently finishing a book on the social, moral, and policy effects of the nature/culture distinction, provisionally titled *Un/Natural: "Nature," "Culture," and Technology in Moral and Political Discourse.*

Suzanne J. Kessler is a professor of psychology at Purchase College, SUNY. She is coauthor (with Wendy McKenna) of *Gender: An Ethnomethodological Approach.* She continues to write about intersexuality, and has extended her analyses to include the perspective of parents and adult intersexuals.

Kathleen McAuliffe is a former senior editor and health/science reporter at *U.S. News and World Report.* She is the author of numerous articles on health and science issues, published in such journals as *OMNI, Redbook,* and *Ladies Home Journal.*

Michèle Martin is an associate professor at the School of Journalism and Communication of Carleton University in Ottawa, Canada. Her latest books are: *Communication and Mass Media: Culture, Domination, Opposition* and *Victor Barbeau: Pionnier de la critique culturelle journalistique.* Her other books and articles include work on the formation of different types of culture related to the development of new communication technologies.

Kathryn Pauly Morgan is a professor of philosophy and women's studies and member of the Joint Centre for Bioethics at the University of Toronto. She is coauthor of *The Gender Question in Education: Theory, Pedagogy, and Politics,* and has written various articles in feminist ethics, feminist social philosophy, philosophy of sexuality, and feminist bioethics. She is currently a member of the Social Sciences and Humanities Research Council of Canada Strategic Research Network in Feminist Health Care Ethics.

Ronald Munson is a professor of the philosophy of science and medicine at the University of Missouri-St. Louis. He has published numerous articles in bioethics and philosophy of science. His books include *Reasoning in Medicine: An Introduction to Clinical Inference* (with Daniel Albert and Michael Resnik), *The Way of Words,* and *Man and Nature: Philosophical Issues in Biology.* His book *Intervention and Reflection: Basic Issues in Medical Ethics,* now in its fifth edition, is one of the most widely used medical ethics textbooks in the United States.

Julien S. Murphy is a professor of philosophy at the University of Southern Maine and is the author of *The Constructed Body: AIDS, Reproductive Technology and Ethics.*

Timothy F. Murphy is an associate professor and head of the Medical Humanities Program at the University of Illinois College of Medicine in Chicago. He is the author of *Gay Science: The Ethics of Sexual Orientation Research,* and *Ethics in an Epidemic: AIDS, Morality, and Culture.* He is editor of *Justice and the Human Genome Project* and *Gay Ethics: Controversies in Outing, Civil Rights, and Sexual Science.*

Christine Overall is a professor of philosophy at Queen's University in Kingston, Ontario. She is the author of *Ethics and Human Reproduction: A Feminist Analysis* and *Human Reproduction: Principles, Practices, Policies.* She is the editor of *The Future of Human Reproduction* and coeditor of *Feminist Perspectives: Philosophical Essays on Method and Morals.*

Lilia Oblepias-Ramos is currently Executive Director of APPROTECH ASIA (Asian Alliance of Appropriate Technology Practitioners, Inc.) based in Manila, Philippines. She is a 1995 WIPO (World Intellectual Property Organization) gold medal awardee "for her outstanding contribution in promoting inventive activity amongst women and in supporting Women Inventions/Inventors in the Philippines."

Bente Rasmussen is an associate professor of sociology in the Department of Sociology and Political Science at the University of Amsterdam and was formerly a researcher at the Institute of Social Research in Industry (IFIM) in Trondheim. Her main research areas include: new technology and union participation, office automation and women's work, women engineers' careers and families, gender and computer science, gender and organization.

Janice G. Raymond is a professor of medical ethics and women's studies at the University of Massachusetts in Amherst. She is the author of many books and articles on the subjects of feminism, medical ethics, new reproductive technologies, and violence against women, including *A Passion for Friends: A*

Philosophy of Female Affection and *Women as Wombs: Reproductive Technologies and the Battle Over Women's Bodies.*

Virginia Scharff is an associate professor of history at the University of New Mexico. She is the author of *Taking the Wheel: Women and the Coming of the Motor Age* and coauthor of *Present Tense: The United States Since 1945* and *The Turbulent Century: American History in the Twentieth Century.*

Claudia Springer is a professor in the English Department and Film Studies Program at Rhode Island College. She is the author of *Electronic Eros: Bodies and Desire in the Postindustrial Age.* Her writings on cyberculture have appeared in *Screen, Now Time, Genders, The South Atlantic Quarterly*, and *21.C.*

Autumn Stanley is an independent scholar in the field of gender and technology. She is author of *Mothers and Daughters of Invention: Notes for a Revised History of Technology.* She is currently working on several projects, including a book entitled *Eureka in Genderland.*

Allucquère Rosanne Stone (Sandy Stone) is an assistant professor and director of the Interactive Multimedia Laboratory (ACTLab) at the University of Texas at Austin. She is the author of *The War of Desire and Technology at the Close of the Mechanical Age.*

Dick Teresi is a former editor of *OMNI* and the author of numerous articles and books on historical and social issues in science and technology, including (with Leon Lederman) *The God Particle: If the Universe Is the Answer, What Is the Question?*

Sherry Turkle is a professor of the sociology of science at the Massachusetts Institute of Technology and a licensed clinical psychologist. Her most recent research is reported in *Life on the Screen: Identity in the Age of the Internet.*

Mary Anne Warren is a professor of philosophy at San Francisco State University. She writes on a range of issues in biomedical and applied ethics. She has published three books, *The Nature of Woman: An Encyclopedia and Guide to the Literature, Gendercide: The Implications of Sex Selection,* and *Moral Status: Obligations to Persons and Other Living Things.*

INDEX